EDUCATIONAL PSYCHOLOGY 91/92

Sixth Edition

Editor

Kathleen M. Cauley
Virginia Commonwealth University

Kathleen M. Cauley received her Ph.D. in educational studies/human development from the University of Delaware in 1985. Her research interests center on applying cognitive developmental research to school learning. Currently, she is studying children's construction of the logic of the borrowing algorithm in multidigit subtraction.

Editor

Fredric Linder
Virginia Commonwealth University

Fredric Linder received an A.B. in American civilization from the University of Miami, Fla.; an M.A. in psychology from the New School for Social Research; and a Ph.D. in educational psychology from the State University of New York at Buffalo. His research and publications focus on the value, locus of control, and cognitive learning styles of students in higher education.

Editor

James H. McMillan
Virginia Commonwealth University

James H. McMillan received his bachelor's degree from Albion College in 1970, his M.A. from Michigan State University in 1972, and his Ph.D. from Northwestern University in 1976. He has reviewed and written extensively on many topics in educational psychology. Currently, he is researching critical thinking, values, and student outcomes assessment.

Cover illustration by Mike Eagle

Annual Editions
A Library of Information from the Public Press

The Dushkin Publishing Group, Inc.
Sluice Dock, Guilford, Connecticut 06437

The Annual Editions Series

Annual Editions is a series of over fifty volumes designed to provide the reader with convenient, low-cost access to a wide range of current, carefully selected articles from some of the most important magazines, newspapers, and journals published today. Annual Editions are updated on an annual basis through a continuous monitoring of over 200 periodical sources. All Annual Editions have a number of features designed to make them particularly useful, including topic guides, annotated tables of contents, unit overviews, and indexes. For the teacher using Annual Editions in the classroom, an Instructor's Resource Guide with test questions is available for each volume.

VOLUMES AVAILABLE

Africa
Aging
American Government
American History, Pre-Civil War
American History, Post-Civil War
Anthropology
Biology
Business and Management
Business Ethics
Canadian Politics
China
Comparative Politics
Computers in Education
Computers in Business
Computers in Society
Criminal Justice
Drugs, Society, and Behavior
Early Childhood Education
Economics
Educating Exceptional Children
Education
Educational Psychology
Environment
Geography
Global Issues
Health
Human Development
Human Resources
Human Sexuality

Latin America
Macroeconomics
Management
Marketing
Marriage and Family
Microeconomics
Middle East and the Islamic World
Money and Banking
Nutrition
Personal Growth and Behavior
Psychology
Public Administration
Race and Ethnic Relations
Social Problems
Sociology
Soviet Union and Eastern Europe
State and Local Government
Third World
Urban Society
Violence and Terrorism
Western Civilization,
   Pre-Reformation
Western Civilization,
   Post-Reformation
Western Europe
World History, Pre-Modern
World History, Modern
World Politics

Library of Congress Cataloging in Publication Data
Main entry under title: Annual Editions: Educational Psychology 1991/92.
1. Educational psychology—Periodicals. 2. Teaching—Periodicals.
I. Cauley, Kathleen M., *comp.*; Linder, Fredric, *comp.*; McMillan, James H., *comp.*
II. Title: Educational psychology.
ISBN 1–56134–020–0   370.15′05   82–640517

Sixth Edition

Manufactured by The Banta Company, Harrisonburg, Virginia 22801

Editors/ Advisory Board

To the Reader

In publishing ANNUAL EDITIONS we recognize the enormous role played by the magazines, newspapers, and journals of the *public press* in providing current, first-rate educational information in a broad spectrum of interest areas. Within the articles, the best scientists, practitioners, researchers, and commentators draw issues into new perspective as accepted theories and viewpoints are called into account by new events, recent discoveries change old facts, and fresh debate breaks out over important controversies.

Many of the articles resulting from this enormous editorial effort are appropriate for students, researchers, and professionals seeking accurate, current material to help bridge the gap between principles and theories and the real world. These articles, however, become more useful for study when those of lasting value are carefully *collected, organized, indexed,* and *reproduced* in a *low-cost format,* which provides easy and permanent access when the material is needed. That is the role played by *Annual Editions.* Under the direction of each volume's *Editor,* who is an expert in the subject area, and with the guidance of an *Advisory Board,* we seek each year to provide in each *ANNUAL EDITION* a current, well-balanced, carefully selected collection of the best of the public press for your study and enjoyment. We think you'll find this volume useful, and we hope you'll take a moment to let us know what you think.

Educational psychology is an interdisciplinary subject that includes human development, learning strategies, intelligence, motivation, measurement, and classroom management. It also gives special attention to the application of this knowledge to teaching.

Annual Editions: Educational Psychology 91/92 is presented in six units. An overview precedes each unit and explains how the articles in the unit are related to the broader issues within educational psychology. The first unit presents issues central to the teaching role. It discusses the challenges of responding to calls for educational reform and the role of educational research in meeting those challenges.

The second unit is concerned with human development and covers the cognitive, social, and moral development of children and adolescents. The articles in this unit discuss the developmental implications of early childhood thinking for teachers, the social forces affecting children and adolescents, and the personal and social skills they need in order to cope with developmental phases and school learning tasks.

The third unit includes articles about theories of learning and instructional strategies. The different views of learning, such as information processing, behaviorism, and humanistic learning, represent the accumulation of years of research on the way humans change in thinking or behavior due to experience. The principles generated from each approach have important implications for teaching. These implications are addressed in a subsection on instructional strategies, covering such topics as instructional methods, grouping students, using controversy, questioning, and creativity.

The topic of motivation is perhaps one of the most important aspects of school learning. Effective teachers need to motivate their students both to learn and to behave responsibly. How to manage children and what forms of discipline to use are issues that concern parents as well as teachers and administrators. The articles in the fourth unit present a variety of perspectives on motivating students, and approaches to managing student behavior are discussed.

The fifth unit, concerning exceptional children, focuses on the learning disabled, the culturally different, and the gifted. All of these children are different in some way and require an individualized approach to education. The articles in this unit discuss the characteristics of such children and suggest programs and strategies to meet their needs.

The articles in unit six review assessment approaches that can be used to diagnose learning and improve instruction. The focus is on grading practices and appropriate uses of standardized tests. Performance-based assessment is introduced as a promising new approach to classroom measurement.

This sixth edition of *Educational Psychology* has been revised to present articles that are current and useful. Your responses to the selection and organization of materials are appreciated. Please fill out and return the article rating form on the last page of the book.

Kathleen M. Cauley

Fredric Linder

James H. McMillan
Editors

Contents

Unit 1

Overview: Psychology Applied to Education and Teaching

Four selections discuss the importance of research and the value of scientific inquiry to the teaching process. The effects of teaching behaviors on classroom performance are also discussed.

Unit 2

Development

Ten articles examine how social interaction in the classroom influences a child's development.

To the Reader   iv
Topic Guide   2
Overview   4

1. **Of Robins' Eggs, Teachers, and Education Reform,** Richard C. Nelson, *Phi Delta Kappan,* April 1989.   6
   Teachers need to respond carefully to *educational reform* to ensure that they promote exciting, meaningful, and joyful learning.

2. **Does the "Art of Teaching" Have a Future?** David J. Flinders, *Educational Leadership,* May 1989.   12
   How can the status of teaching as a profession be enhanced? The author argues that as we debate this *professional issue,* the extent to which the *teaching role* includes the "arts" of communication, cooperation, and appreciation needs to be considered.

3. **Tap Into Teacher Research,** Linda Shalaway, *Instructor,* August 1990.   15
   Should research become part of the *teaching role*? The author suggests that all teachers who experiment with ways to solve classroom problems are doing *classroom research.* This article describes the experiences of four different teacher researchers, providing insight into this *professional issue.*

4. **Creating Conditions for Learning: From Research to Practice,** Carolyn M. Evertson, *Theory Into Practice,* 1987.   18
   The author explains that *educational research* identifies effective teaching practices for teachers to reflect on and use in making informed decisions about their teaching.

Overview   24

A. *CHILDHOOD*

5. **Formal Education and Early Childhood Education: An Essential Difference,** David Elkind, *Phi Delta Kappan,* May 1986.   26
   Dr. Elkind contends that we are ignoring the facts about how young children learn. He discusses the history of *early childhood education* and describes the damage caused by early formal instruction.

6. **Developmentally Appropriate Education for 4-Year-Olds,** David Elkind, *Theory Into Practice,* Winter 1989.   32
   Dr. Elkind describes three major principles regarding the *education of 4-year-old children* in the public schools with respect to their *intellectual, social, and emotional development.*

The concepts in bold italics are developed in the article. For further expansion please refer to the Topic Guide and the Index.

7. **Societal Influences on Children,** Joan Isenberg, *Childhood Education,* June 1987.   38

    This article identifies children's **social needs**, describes **social pressures** that affect those needs, and provides suggestions for balancing the social priorities of children.

8. **The Development of Self-Concept,** Hermine H. Marshall, *Young Children,* July 1989.   45

    The author discusses research regarding **self-concept** and the factors that influence the development of a positive **self-esteem** as well as a sense of competence in children.

9. **Encouraging Prosocial Behavior in Young Children,** Susan M. Doescher and Alan I. Sugawara, *Childhood Education,* Summer 1989.   52

    This article describes several strategies teachers may use in developing a more **prosocial classroom** environment for **pre-school children**.

10. **Four Strategies for Fostering Character Development in Children,** Thomas Lickona, *Phi Delta Kappan,* February 1988.   56

    The author maintains that teachers can create classroom settings that promote positive **social growth** by building self-esteem, a sense of community, cooperation, moral reflection, and participatory decision-making.

11. **Prosocial Influences in the Classroom,** W. Dean McCafferty, *The Clearing House,* April 1990.   61

    The author describes **prosocial behaviors** and the cognitive and affective processes that encourage responsible cooperative behavior.

B.   ADOLESCENCE

12. **Changing Conditions for Young Adolescents: Reminiscences and Realities,** Judith A. Brough, *Educational Horizons,* Winter 1990.   65

    The author discusses the many societal and personal problems **adolescents** face and how the **middle schools** can assist with these problems.

13. **Meeting the Needs of Young Adolescents: Advisory Groups, Interdisciplinary Teaching Teams, and School Transition Programs,** Douglas J. Mac Iver, *Phi Delta Kappan,* February 1990.   68

    The author discusses how advisory groups, interdisciplinary teaching teams, and school transition programs can meet the **needs of young adolescents**.

14. **Respectful, Dutiful Teenagers,** Robert Atkinson, *Psychology Today,* October 1988.   74

    Robert Atkinson describes how **teenagers** in different countries view their families and their friends. A portrait of today's youth emerges that is very different from the popular image of adolescent alienation.

The concepts in bold italics are developed in the article. For further expansion please refer to the Topic Guide and the Index.

Unit
3

Learning

Twelve selections explore the important types of
student/teacher interaction.

Overview   **76**

A.   INFORMATION PROCESSING/COGNITIVE LEARNING

15. The Celebration of Thinking, Elliot W. Eisner, *National*   **78**
    Forum, Spring 1988.
    The author suggests that the multiple forms of ***mental represen-***
    tation that comprise ***thinking*** should be a tool for educating
    students.

16. Putting Learning Strategies to Work, Sharon J. Derry,   **82**
    Educational Leadership, December 1988/January 1989.
    Learning strategies are defined that involve the use of tactics to
    acquire knowledge and procedural skills and to use appropriate
    self-motivation. The processes of ***attention***, ***schema*** building,
    and ***self-monitoring*** are discussed in the context of ***problem***
    solving.

17. Rediscovering Discovery Learning, Ray T. Wilcox, *The*   **88**
    Clearing House, October 1987.
    This article presents 10 approaches to discovery learning that are
    effective in helping students integrate new insights with existing
    knowledge.

18. Linking Metacognition to Classroom Success, Martin   **92**
    N. Ganz and Barbara C. Ganz, *The High School Journal,*
    February/March 1990.
    Research has shown that when students apply ***metacognitive***
    skills ***learning*** and ***retention*** are improved. This article summa-
    rizes implications of metacognition for teaching.

B.   BEHAVIORISTIC LEARNING

19. Practicing Positive Reinforcement, Thomas R. McDaniel,   **97**
    The Clearing House, May 1987.
    The author presents 10 practical classroom techniques based on
    principles of ***behaviorism***. Effective use of ***positive reinforce-***
    ment can enhance student self-esteem, improve attitudes, and
    increase motivation.

C.   HUMANISTIC/SOCIAL PSYCHOLOGICAL LEARNING

20. Teacher Expectations: A Model for School Improve-   **101**
    ment, C. Patrick Proctor, *The Elementary School Journal,*
    March 1984.
    The expectations of teachers have been shown to have important
    influences on student ***learning***. This article summarizes studies
    of expectation effects, proposes a model for how the expectations
    work, and shows how to use expectations to improve student
    learning.

The concepts in bold italics are developed in the article. For further expansion please refer to the Topic Guide and the Index.

21. **Cooperative Learning and the Cooperative School,** 111
Robert E. Slavin, *Educational Leadership,* November 1987.
Research has demonstrated that **cooperative learning**, in which
students work in small, mixed-ability groups, effectively enhances
achievement, motivation, and **interpersonal skills**. The author
suggests techniques for implementing cooperative learning at
both the classroom and school levels.

D. *INSTRUCTIONAL STRATEGIES*

22. **Productive Teaching and Instruction: Assessing the** 117
Knowledge Base, Herbert J. Walberg, *Phi Delta Kappan,*
February 1990.
In the past two decades there have been thousands of studies on
effective teaching. Herbert Walberg summarizes this research to
show how psychological principles, **instructional methods and
systems**, **computer-assisted instruction**, **student grouping**,
and other factors affect student learning.

23. **Critical Thinking Through Structured Controversy,** 126
David W. Johnson and Roger T. Johnson, *Educational Leadership,* May 1988.
The authors show how teachers can use **controversy** and argumentation in the classroom to involve students in **learning**,
increase **retention**, improve **decision-making**, enhance **critical
thinking**, and broaden students' perspectives of other people
and ideas.

24. **Questioning: An Effective Teaching Method,** Imogene 131
Ramsey, Carol Gabbard, Kenneth Clawson, Lynda Lee, and
Kenneth T. Henson, *The Clearing House,* May 1990.
This article summarizes **questioning** in the classroom. Sugges-
tions are presented to effectively use four types of questioning to
enhance student learning.

25. **Survey of Research on Learning Styles,** Rita Dunn, 134
Jeffrey S. Beaudry, and Angela Klavas, *Educational Leadership,* March 1989.
Research is summarized which shows how important it is to
match student **learning styles** with instructional factors, such as
the senses students use to learn, grouping, time of instruction,
and length of instruction.

26. **Fostering Creativity: The Innovative Classroom Envi-** 142
ronment, Randall P. Pruitt, *Educational Horizons,* Fall
1989.
Teaching methods are suggested to enhance student **creativity**.
The emphasis is on a classroom environment characterized by
flexibility, variety, careful use of time, and assessment with delayed judgment.

The concepts in bold italics are developed in the article. For further expansion please refer to the Topic Guide and the Index.

Unit 4

Motivation and Classroom Management

Eight selections discuss student control and motivation in the classroom.

Overview   146

A.   APPROACHES TO MOTIVATION

27. Synthesis of Research on Strategies for Motivating   148
Students to Learn, Jere Brophy, *Educational Leadership,*
October 1987.
Jere Brophy distinguishes **motivation to learn** from motivation to
perform and intrinsic motivation. The author lists numerous strategies for motivating students by fulfilling the preconditions for
motivation, maintaining expectations for success in the classroom, and enhancing the value of educational tasks for students.

28. Motivation for At-Risk Students, M. Kay Alderman,   155
Educational Leadership, September 1990.
This framework for applying attribution theory and learning strategies to goal setting is the key to helping **at-risk students** take
responsibility for their learning. Student **self-efficacy** and **motivation** for learning are improved.

29. Teetering . . . on the Edge of Failure, Richard Sagor,   159
Learning, April 1988.
Richard Sagor examines the problems of potential **dropouts**.
Why are they unmotivated? What **teaching techniques** will help
them feel more successful?

30. Students Need Challenge, Not Easy Success, Margaret   164
M. Clifford, *Educational Leadership,* September 1990.
To control the **drop-out** rate, contradictions between principles of
motivation and widespread school practices must be eliminated.
The author argues that error tolerance needs to replace error-free
learning, error correction needs to be rewarded, not error avoidance, and challenge needs to replace easy success.

B.   CLASSROOM MANAGEMENT AND DISCIPLINE

31. Good Teachers Don't Worry About Discipline, T. R. Ellis,   169
Principal, March 1989.
T. R. Ellis describes **effective teaching** strategies that should
eliminate most **discipline** problems.

32. Assertive Discipline—More Than Names on the Board   173
and Marbles in a Jar, Lee Canter, *Phi Delta Kappan,*
September 1989.
Lee Canter reviews the key components of assertive **discipline**
and addresses common errors in using this approach.

The concepts in bold italics are developed in the article. For further expansion please refer to the Topic Guide and the Index.

33. Order in the Classroom, David Hill, *Teacher Magazine,* April 1990.   177

Providing a counterpoint to the above article, the author suggests that Lee Canter's assertive *discipline* approach may be harmful to students. Some of the criticisms apply to *behaviorism* in general.

34. Non-verbal Language Techniques for Better Classroom Management and Discipline, Steven Grubaugh, *The High School Journal,* October/November 1989.   182

Steven Grubaugh explains how to strengthen *classroom management* techniques and improve *discipline* by combining body language, proxemics, and silence with established *teaching strategies*.

Unit 5

Exceptional Children

Eight articles look at the problems and positive effects of educational programs for exceptional children.

Overview   188

A.   EDUCATIONALLY DISADVANTAGED

35. The Masks Students Wear, Sally L. Smith, *Instructor,* April 1989.   190

The author discusses the characteristics of *learning disabled* students and the many ways they attempt to hide their disabilities.

36. Educating the Handicapped in the Regular Classroom, Gary Adkins, *The Education Digest,* September 1990.   194

The author discusses the hazards in *labeling* students and the benefits that *integrated programs* may bring with careful planning and staff training.

37. Facilitating Mainstreaming Through Cooperative Learning, Howard Margolis and Elliot Schwartz, *The High School Journal,* December 1988/January 1989.   197

Cooperative learning activities are presented and strategies are suggested for *mainstreaming* mildly handicapped students into the regular classroom.

B.   GIFTED AND TALENTED

38. Synthesis of Research on Gifted Youth, John F. Feldhusen, *Educational Leadership,* March 1989.   201

The author presents research that helps to identify *gifted youth*, and he recommends the use of accelerated instruction and ability grouping in order to meet their needs.

39. Gifted Child Education, Myrliss Hershey, *The Clearing House,* February 1988.   206

The author recommends that we identify *gifted students* and provide them with an appropriate *individualized educational program*. The results of *labeling* and its implications for gifted child education are also discussed.

The concepts in bold italics are developed in the article. For further expansion please refer to the Topic Guide and the Index.

40. **Learning Strategies Can Help,** Mary E. Scott, *Teaching Exceptional Children,* Spring 1988.   **209**
This article explores **learning strategies** for gifted students and asserts that teachers can instruct all students to be more effective learners.

C. CULTURALLY DIFFERENT

41. **Educating Language-Minority Children: Challenges and Opportunities,** Barbara T. Bowman, *Phi Delta Kappan,* October 1989.   **213**
Barbara Bowman identifies some developmental principles for teaching **culturally different children**.

42. **Teaching to the Distinctive Traits of Minority Students,** James A. Vasquez, *The Clearing House,* March 1990.   **216**
In this article James A. Vasquez identifies several traits in three **minority student** groups and suggests teaching strategies to fit the distinctive traits of **ethnic minority students**.

Unit
6

Measurement and Evaluation

Four articles discuss the implications of educational measurement for the classroom decision-making process and for the teaching profession.

Overview   **222**

43. **It's a Good Score! Just a Bad Grade,** Robert Lynn Canady and Phyllis Riley Hotchkiss, *Phi Delta Kappan,* September 1989.   **224**
This article highlights several common but inappropriate **grading** practices, such as varying grading scales, worshipping averages, using zeros indiscriminately, and failing to recognize **measurement error**.

44. **Classroom Standard Setting and Grading Practices,** James S. Terwilliger, *Educational Measurement: Issues and Practice,* Summer 1989.   **228**
The author presents a **grading** system based on the use of different types of **objectives** that differentiate between **minimum competency** and the use of **norms** to maximize student achievement.

45. **Teaching to the (Authentic) Test,** Grant Wiggins, *Educational Leadership,* April 1989.   **233**
Performance-based, **authentic** testing is a new form of assessment that requires students to demonstrate complex tasks in contexts that more closely approximate applied, real-life settings. Such assessments demand a synthesis of questioning, inquiry, problem solving, creation of a product or performance, and public demonstration of mastery.

46. **The Tyranny of Testing,** Robert J. Sternberg, *Learning,* March 1989.   **238**
The author, a noted researcher of **intelligence**, shows that current **standardized aptitude tests** do not measure important traits such as creativity and practical abilities.

Index   **241**
Article Review Form   **244**
Article Rating Form   **245**

The concepts in bold italics are developed in the article. For further expansion please refer to the Topic Guide and the Index.

Topic Guide

This topic guide suggests how the selections in this book relate to topics of traditional concern to educational psychology students and professionals. It is useful for locating articles that relate to each other for reading and research. The guide is arranged alphabetically according to topic. Articles may, of course, treat topics that do not appear in the topic guide. In turn, entries in the topic guide do not necessarily constitute a comprehensive listing of all the contents of each selection.

TOPIC AREA	TREATED IN:	TOPIC AREA	TREATED IN:
At-Risk Students	28. Motivation for At-Risk Students	Discipline	31. Good Teachers Don't Worry About Discipline 32. Assertive Discipline 33. Order in the Classroom 34. Non-verbal Language Techniques
Authentic Testing	45. Teaching to the (Authentic) Test		
Behaviorism	19. Practicing Positive Reinforcement 32. Assertive Discipline 33. Order in the Classroom	Discovery Learning	17. Rediscovering Discovery Learning
		Dropout	29. Teetering . . . On the Edge of Failure
Character Development	10. Fostering Character Development in Children	Early Childhood Education	5. Formal Education 6. Developmentally Appropriate Education for 4-Year-Olds 9. Encouraging Prosocial Behavior
Child/Adolescent Development	5. Formal Education 6. Developmentally Appropriate Education for 4-Year-Olds 7. Societal Influences on Children 8. Development of Self-Concept 12. Changing Conditions for Young Adolescents 13. Meeting the Needs of Young Adolescents 14. Respectful, Dutiful Teenagers	Educational Reform	1. Of Robins' Eggs
		Gifted Children and Youth	38. Synthesis of Research on Gifted Youth 39. Gifted Child Education 40. Learning Strategies Can Help
		Grading	43. It's a Good Score! Just a Bad Grade 44. Classroom Standard Setting and Grading Practices
Classroom Management	34. Non-verbal Language Techniques	Grouping Students	22. Productive Teaching and Instruction
Classroom Research	3. Tap Into Teacher Research	Individual Differences	25. Research on Learning Styles 39. Gifted Child Education
Cognitive Development	6. Developmentally Appropriate Education for 4-Year-Olds	Information Processing	15. Celebration of Thinking 16. Putting Learning Strategies to Work
Cognitive Learning	16. Putting Learning Strategies to Work 17. Rediscovering Discovery Learning 18. Linking Metacognition to Classroom Success	Intelligence	15. Celebration of Thinking 46. Tyranny of Testing
Computer-Assisted Instruction	22. Productive Teaching and Instruction	Labeling	36. Educating the Handicapped
Cooperative Learning	21. Cooperative Learning and the Cooperative School 29. Teetering . . . On the Edge of Failure	Learning Styles/ Strategies	16. Putting Learning Strategies to Work 25. Research on Learning Styles 40. Learning Strategies Can Help 42. Teaching to the Distinctive Traits of Minority Students
Creativity	26. Fostering Creativity	Mainstreaming	36. Educating the Handicapped
Criterion-Referenced Tests	44. Classroom Standard Setting and Grading Practices 45. Teaching to the (Authentic) Test	Mastery Learning	44. Classroom Standard Setting and Grading Practices
Critical Thinking	23. Critical Thinking Through Structured Controversy	Memory	18. Linking Metacognition to Classroom Success 22. Productive Teaching and Instruction
Disabilities	35. Masks Students Wear 37. Facilitating Mainstreaming Through Cooperative Learning	Metacognition	16. Putting Learning Strategies to Work 18. Linking Metacognition to Classroom Success

TOPIC AREA	TREATED IN:	TOPIC AREA	TREATED IN:
Minority Students	41. Educating Language-Minority Children 42. Teaching to the Distinctive Traits of Minority Students	**Research on Teaching and Learning**	4. Creating Conditions for Learning 22. Productive Teaching and Instruction
Motivation	21. Cooperative Learning and the Cooperative School 23. Critical Thinking Through Structured Controversy 27. Motivating Students to Learn 28. Motivation for At-Risk Students 29. Teetering . . . On the Edge of Failure 30. Students Need Challenge, Not Easy Success	**Self-Concept/Self-Esteem**	7. Societal Influences on Children 10. Fostering Character Development in Children 20. Teacher Expectations
		Self-Efficacy/Self-Reliance	7. Societal Influences on Children 28. Motivation for At-Risk Students
Multicultural Education	41. Educating Language-Minority Children 42. Teaching to the Distinctive Traits of Minority Students	**Social Competence**	7. Societal Influences on Children 10. Fostering Character Development in Children
Norms	44. Classroom Standard Setting and Grading Practices	**Social Development**	6. Developmentally Appropriate Education for 4-Year-Olds 9. Encouraging Prosocial Behavior 11. Prosocial Influences in the Classroom
Objectives	44. Classroom Standard Setting and Grading Practices 45. Teaching to the (Authentic) Test	**Standardized Tests**	46. Tyranny of Testing
Positive Reinforcement/ Praise	19. Practicing Positive Reinforcement 22. Productive Teaching and Instruction	**Teacher Effectiveness**	22. Productive Teaching and Instruction 25. Research on Learning Styles
Problem Solving	17. Rediscovering Discovery Learning 23. Critical Thinking Through Structured Controversy 45. Teaching to the (Authentic) Test	**Teacher Expectations**	20. Teacher Expectations
Professional Issues	2. Does the "Art of Teaching" Have a Future? 3. Tap Into Teacher Research 4. Creating Conditions for Learning	**Teaching Role**	2. Does the "Art of Teaching" Have a Future? 3. Tap Into Teacher Research
		Teaching Strategies	25. Research on Learning Styles
Questioning	24. Questioning: An Effective Teaching Method 43. It's a Good Score! Just a Bad Grade	**Time-on-Task**	20. Teacher Expectations

Overview: Psychology Applied to Education and Teaching

The teaching-learning process in schools is enormously complex. Many factors influence pupil learning—such as family background, developmental level, prior knowledge, motivation, and of course, effective teachers. Educational psychology investigates these factors to better understand and explain student learning. We begin our exploration of the teaching-learning process by considering the teaching role, particularly as it is being defined in the educational reform movement.

Educators face new challenges as they rise to meet the call for educational reform. Teachers are under renewed pressure to raise standards and improve standardized test scores. Some reports argue for more homework and longer school days. As Richard Nelson argues in the first selection, these reforms will succeed only if teachers are empowered with the flexibility and responsibility to create truly meaningful learning activities. That empowerment requires teachers to have a solid understanding not only of the subject that they will teach, but also of how to teach that content.

In the second article, David Flinders argues that technical expertise and subject-matter knowledge are insufficient to characterize the professionalism of teachers. He believes that the artistry of teaching is being overlooked in the reform movements. Flinders suggests that the artistry of teaching is evident in the complexity of interpersonal interactions as teachers are perceptive of and sensitive to students, and as they negotiate their student's cooperation in learning.

Another perspective in the reform of education is that teachers need to engage in more systematic inquiry—or research. As the professional development schools envisioned by the Holmes Group and others are established, teacher research will become more widespread. As the third selection illustrates, teacher researchers not only improve their teaching, but contribute in significant ways to the growing body of research on effective teaching.

In the final article, Carolyn Evertson argues that teaching research can provide only general principles of teaching, not prescriptive rules or algorithms. She depicts teachers as decisionmakers who use research as a source of solutions to problems that they find in their classrooms. Although written from a staff development perspective, the article gives beginning teachers a useful framework for interpreting and using educational research.

Educational psychology is a resource for teachers that emphasizes disciplined inquiry, a systematic and objective analysis of information, and a scientific attitude toward decision-making. The field provides information for decisions that is based on quantitative and qualitative studies of learning and teaching, rather than intuition, tradition, authority, or subjective feelings. It is our hope that this aspect of educational psychology is communicated throughout these readings, and that as a student you will adopt the analytic, probing attitude that is a part of the discipline.

While educational psychologists have helped to establish a knowledge base about teaching and learning, the unpredictable, spontaneous, evolving nature of teaching suggests that the best they will ever do is provide concepts and skills that teachers can adapt for use in their classrooms. The issues raised in these articles about the impact of the reform movement on teachers help us understand the teaching role and its demands. As you read articles in other chapters, consider the demands they place on the teaching role as well.

Looking Ahead: Challenge Questions

Can teachers effectively perform all the roles expected of them?

Do you agree that educational reform is not addressing the right issues?

If educational reform succeeds, what new demands do you think it will place on teachers?

Of Robins' Eggs, Teachers, And Education Reform

LITTLE EGG UPON THE GROUND, USED TO BE SO SAFE AND ROUND...

Illustration by Randy Glasbergen

RICHARD C. NELSON

RICHARD C. NELSON is a professor in the Department of Education at Purdue University, West Lafayette, Ind.

Joy in teaching and learning — not testing, not more and longer school days — is the key to true education reform, Mr. Nelson reminds us.

ON THE SAME day in two different locations, two fourth-graders — we'll call them Paul and Jean — each find a piece of the shell of a robin's egg. Each takes the piece of eggshell to school and shows it to the teacher.

Paul's teacher invites him to take his piece around and show it to the other students. Then the teacher says, "Thank you for sharing that with us, Paul. I love that color." Paul smiles. "All right, everybody," the teacher says, "now turn to page 78 in your science books."

Jean's teacher, too, invites her to show her piece to the other children. But then the teacher asks a challenging question, "What does Jean's piece of eggshell *mean*?" One child wonders, "Maybe it means a cat got into the nest?" Jean, a quiet child, says in a throaty whisper, "I think it just hatched." A discussion follows, and one topic leads to another:

baby birds, spring, survival, where robins spend the winters, how they find mates, the messages in birdcalls, whether or not robins migrate, what migration means, and so on.

One child tells of visiting the Jasper-Pulaski Wildlife Preserve and seeing sandhill cranes on their spring migration. Another mentions the whooping crane, and attention shifts to the topic of protecting endangered species. Children wonder aloud whether eagles and other birds migrate.

Jean's teacher sees the opportunity to make science real — to connect the classroom to the world outside — and decides to seize the moment. A process begins that changes the classroom schedule for nearly an hour a day for the next several days. The teacher writes the children's ideas and questions on the chalkboard, and a plan ultimately emerges.

Children choose to join one of five groups, and they scurry off happily to reference books and to the library to begin seeking answers to their questions. In their eagerness to learn, many of the children struggle through references that are "above their reading level." They do so because they are challenged and have a desire to know. When each day's time for research is up, they leave the books reluctantly, making notes about the sources they wish to return to on the following day.

Later, during art time, the teacher picks up the piece of eggshell and says, "Wonderful color. Maybe some of you would like to try to mix paint to match." The drawings sparked by this remark range from a simple blue oval to a handsome primitive rendering of a whooping crane in flight. As the children work, they chatter about birds and about their

From *Phi Delta Kappan*, April 1989, pp. 632-638. Reprinted by permission of *Phi Delta Kappan* and the author.

drawings, and they smile at their accomplishments.

A week passes, and the children's level of enthusiasm is still high. "Could we have a program and give it for the other fourth-grade rooms?" one asks. Another quickly adds, "We could run it like a TV talk show and have different people tell what they know. Other kids could ask questions." A third chimes in, "What about moms and dads? Could we invite them?"

Opportunities abound for capitalizing on everyday events, on news reports related to science and health, and on issues raised by television programs. Nor are such opportunities restricted to elementary school settings; many are complex enough for secondary students to explore at deeper levels.

If today's education reforms result in greater numbers of eager children and adolescents exploring topics about which they've become excited, learning things that they wish to share with others, and finding intrinsic rewards in learning, then the reforms will have succeeded. If instead today's education reforms discourage teachers from taking time to "seize the moment," encourage them to devote more time to drilling for standardized tests, and lead students to work more diligently for grades and test scores, then the reforms will have failed.

A CHALLENGE TO TEACHERS

Teachers should take the current climate of reform as a challenge to use their creative abilities in more effective and challenging ways. They should accept this challenge despite the obvious difficulties that hinder their best efforts: young people who come from homes in which there is little support for education; young people who come to school with emotional needs that prevent them from giving attention to educational tasks; pressures — including threats of litigation — from parents; mounting curricular requirements; administrators who discourage even well-thought-out, creative ideas; mountains of paperwork; and on and on.

Moreover, teachers must let others know when they succeed despite the odds. Many are teaching in wonderfully creative ways. But they are not telling their stories. The stories need to be told, so that these fine teachers can receive the recognition they deserve and so that their efforts may inspire those who are not living up to the challenge that the profession offers them.

It is time for teachers to have courage and conviction about the good things they do. Teachers need to construe criticism as support for positive action. They need to look on demands for change as a mandate to create more meaningful learning opportunities. They need to be convinced that the changes they make that create excitement in their students and in themselves will result in better-motivated and higher-achieving students. And they must insist that measures of success go beyond standardized testing.

If teachers don't view today's reform movement as an opportunity and a challenge, they are likely to feel discouraged and to teach less and less creatively. Many of the best will even leave the profession. We can't afford to allow that to happen.

Teachers must avoid using administrators, the curriculum, and the recent education reforms as excuses. More often than necessary, teachers blame their failure to explore new content and new ways of teaching on an administration that "won't let me," on a tightly scheduled curriculum, or on the need to teach the material covered in a standardized test. Effective teachers have the courage to take the time to do what they believe must be done; ineffective teachers should seek employment elsewhere.

Teachers must understand that the members of blue-ribbon commissions and citizens at large who are calling for education reform are sincerely concerned about the well-being of young people. They are adults, and adults know something about schools because they've all spent time in them. They believe that they know what's wrong with schools and how to make them better. However, when they begin to attack educational problems seriously, they turn their attention to structural and organizational matters that can be changed without really making the kinds of differences that are required. They don't see that increasing the time students spend at their desks completing repetitious tasks will not improve education. They don't understand that such changes may result in schools that meet the needs of young people *less* well than today's schools.

Education reformers must support teacher empowerment. Albert Shanker, president of the American Federation of Teachers, has suggested that, wherever six or more teachers can find a considered and creative direction to pursue in their teaching, they ought to develop the concept, seek the support of the principal, commit themselves to the change, work out the details, and create a school-within-a-school.[1] Such creative, participatory leadership offers far more potential for improving the lot of children in our schools than any of the structural changes that have been offered for consideration. To Shanker's suggestion I would add another. Each school might well develop a number of leadership teams, involving all staff members who wish to participate and organized by administrators or teachers. These teams should focus their efforts on one primary objective: to make the school better for the children.

Dedicated, concerned, and creative teachers must take charge of their destinies and help those who are responsible for designing education reforms to see that many teachers are willing to take the lead in working toward better schools. Teachers should seek greater empowerment by asserting their desire to assume some measure of the responsibility for improving schools.

SEVEN QUESTIONS FOR REFORMERS

Those charged with designing and implementing school reform should answer the following seven questions about each proposed reform that they consider.

1. *How will this reform contribute positively to the emotional atmosphere of schools for young people and teachers?* In a presentation to a seminar on schools for the 21st century, Donald Brown, a vice president of Purdue University, suggested that neither schools nor their reformers pay sufficient attention to the emotional impact of the changes they make.[2] Brown's point is well-taken. All too frequently we design curricula and institute changes without considering the emotional impact of our efforts on children and youth. The prevailing attitude seems to be that it doesn't matter whether or not children *like* the curriculum or whether or not proposed changes will engage them and help them become excited about learning. The message is "We know what's best for them." The scores of today's children on achievement tests are lower than those of their counterparts in past years. Therefore, we conclude that children must spend more time-on-task, so we extend the school day and year, add summer school, increase requirements, and expect the scores to rise.

From the point of view of children and young people, however, schools have long been seen as joyless, puritanical, nose-to-the-grindstone places from which they want to escape as quickly as possible. We need to take seriously the comment of Mihaly Csikszentmihalyi and Jane McCormack that, "of all the places teenagers hang out, the school is the one place they least wish to be. Moreover, when they are in school, the classroom is the one place they most strongly wish to avoid."[3] We must ask whether the changes being implemented are likely to increase this pattern of negativism among young people, cause more young people to fail, add to the dropout rate, and inadvertently increase the number of young people involved in the street culture of drugs and crime.

We must seek to create schools of a different kind.

Schools . . . must be more than places to develop intellectual skills and acquire information, or young people will not develop well personally. The often ignored developmental needs of these young people require that schools be places where trust, warmth, comfort, support, and affection flourish.[4]

In earlier times, when the alternative to participating effectively in school was harsh physical work under strong home discipline, young people tended to be somewhat willing participants in school. Now the world of young people is filled with gadgets and activities that may absorb their attention endlessly, if not well. And there is no way to turn back the clock. Curricular activities compete with superbly designed gadgets, with television, with instant transportation, and with a youth culture that is often beyond the reach of the schools.

Exciting and joy-producing experiences in school don't have to be continuous; indeed, they probably can't be. But somewhere in the school day of each child and adolescent, there needs to be a place for challenge, growth, joy, and excitement. While individual teachers in individual classrooms cannot and should not attempt to compete with Madison Avenue all day long, they must recognize the need for students to experience excitement and joy in the process of learning. The reforms that are designed for today's students will fail unless they actively encourage teachers to create joyful, positive learning experiences for young people.

It seems to me that we have two basic options. One, we relegate about half of our students to a second-class education and focus on an elite. We institute a U.S. version of the screening examinations in England or Japan, we shunt the chaff into lower-level tracks with fewer educational opportunities, and we let the teachers of the stronger students get on with their tasks. Or two, we accept with enthusiasm the challenge of educating *all* the youth of our country. As recently as 1930 U.S. schools *enrolled* less than half of the

> **R**eforms will fail unless they actively encourage teachers to create joyful, positive learning experiences for young people.

young people of high school age; today three-fourths of the same population *graduate* from high school.[5] The task of educating everyone in one system is more difficult than operating a two-tiered system, and it is bound to fail with some individuals. But if we're going to accept the mission, we must design a greater number of positive learning experiences for young people, and we must free teachers and encourage them to function creatively in ways that contribute positively to the emotional climate of the school.

How might emotional climate be assessed? Administrators should be able to ask teachers what actions they took, within the past two days, that were designed to improve the emotional climate in the classroom — and they should have a reasonable chance of hearing positive responses. Administrators might also ask themselves what they might do to help teachers create more positive school or classroom climates.

2. *How will a given reform contribute positively to the attitudes that young people develop toward learning and toward school?* Young people are not machines that mindlessly stamp out the work they are given according to a programmed set of instructions. They are lively and energetic. They develop attitudes toward everything they learn.

> In one of Kipling's tales there is recounted the struggles of a little boy learning to read. He and his tutor wrestle with the problem long and valiantly, but progress is slow and halting. The process is an unhappy one for both participants. At last the day comes when the tutor says, "You have learned to read." The boy throws down his book, saying, "Now I can read — I shall never read again!"[6]

Reform efforts must avoid creating schools that are even more joyless and puritanical than they have been in the past. Young people will willingly, if not gladly, sit at their desks — as they must — and commit the multiplication tables to memory. They will endure — as they must — the slow process of learning to spell almost as many irregular as regular words, because that is the way the English language is. They will do these things because they are told that they must and because they've heard — as some of us used to hear about cod-liver oil — that it's good for them. But no reform movement will succeed with real children and adolescents until it gives attention to the attitudes that it fosters.

Once again, the key is that each student should experience at least one genuinely positive learning experience at some time during nearly every day at school — something that he or she can share excitedly with others at home or, at the very least, feel deep pleasure about. Administrators should be able to ask students what really interesting learning activities they have been involved in, within the past two days, and have a reasonable chance of hearing positive responses.

3. *How will a given reform contribute positively to the feelings that young people have about themselves?* The emotional climate of the school affects young people's attitudes and self-concepts. Children and adolescents carry their self-concepts with them, like baggage, wherever they go. For various students, the baggage may be labeled "I'm a good person" and "I'm OK" or "I ain't gonna amount to nothin' " and "I can't do all that stuff."

When children begin school, their self-concepts tend to be highly flexible, and the ways in which teachers and other children receive them have strong effects on their feelings about themselves. As children continue through the grades, their self-concepts become more fixed. That means that all teachers at all levels of education — but especially those who work with young children — have considerable influence on how their students feel about themselves. And teachers can exercise that influence either positively or negatively. Theirs is an awesome responsibility.

The variation in self-concepts is great. If Marie, an eighth-grader, has a strong, positive self-concept, she is likely to meet all manner of learning experiences with a positive attitude, though certainly she will respond more positively to activities that offer a reasonable level of excitement and challenge and the potential for success. Her classmate, Tim, may respond apathetically to nearly everything. His defense is "If I don't try, I can't fail." It will take much more effort to design educational experiences that will intrigue and involve Tim.

All teachers need to pay close attention to the contributions they make to the self-concepts of those in their charge. Such offhand comments as "Do you want to grow up to be a ditch digger, Tim?" can undo in an instant years of efforts to contribute positively to the feelings of a young person. Derisive comments, even those that are intended to jolt students into action, should be avoided. Teachers should strive to build the self-concepts of all students in their charge by frequent positive statements and actions — whether or not those students are *academically* capable.

Administrators have an awesome responsibility to enhance the self-concepts of teachers and other staff members, to promote educational experiences that contribute positively to the feelings that students have about themselves, and to support teachers in their efforts to help young people feel good about themselves — as opposed to simply accomplishing the tasks assigned.

Administrators should be able to ask teachers what they did, within the past two days, that contributed positively to the self-concepts of students — with special emphasis on those whose feelings about themselves need to be enhanced — and have a reasonable chance of hearing positive responses. Equally important, at least once a week administrators should ask themselves what they have done to enhance the self-concepts of teachers.

4. *How will this reform help teachers to work with young people in more creative ways?* It is essential that teachers be vigorously encouraged to be flexible and creative in their approaches to teaching, so that they can develop challenging, exciting, and joyful classroom environments. In the absence of such encouragement, additional requirements placed on students (and therefore on teachers) are likely to contribute to the

mounting evidence that many of this country's teachers act as educational functionaries, faithfully but mindlessly following prescriptions about what and how to teach. Conducting classes in routine, undemanding ways, far too many teachers give out directions, busywork, and fact-fact-fact lectures in ways that keep students intellectually passive, if not actually deepening their disregard for learning and schooling.[7]

> **A**ll teachers need to pay close attention to the contributions they make to the self-concepts of those in their charge.

The Indiana Department of Education and the Indiana Curriculum Advisory Council of the State Board of Education supported that view and chastised the schools for being "remarkably rigid and uncreative with regard to the use of time."[8] However, extensions of the school day and year and additional graduation requirements almost guarantee that the rigidity of schools and the uncreative uses of school time will *increase*, unless teachers are challenged to teach — and are recognized for their teaching — in ways that generate and seize exciting opportunities for student learning.

In an article titled "The Having of Wonderful Ideas," Eleanor Duckworth made a strong case that teachers need to catch the interests of young people, to encourage them to raise and answer their own questions, and to help them see that what they can do is significant — thus enhancing their interests and developing

> **E**ducational efforts must be designed to have intrinsic rewards if young people are to have their needs met.

the confidence that enables them to continue learning on their own. She argued that teachers, too, must feel confidence in their own ideas. "If teachers feel that their class must do things just as the book says, and that their excellence as a teacher depends upon that, they cannot possibly accept children's divergence and children's creations."[9]

If teachers are going to accept the mandate to be creative, they must see themselves as professionals. And they must be treated as professionals, as the report of the Carnegie Forum on Education and the Economy makes clear.

Professionals are presumed to know what they are doing and are paid to exercise their judgment. Schools, on the other hand, operate as if consultants, school district experts, textbook authors, trainers, and distant officials possess more relevant expertise than the teachers in the schools. . . . Properly staffed schools can only succeed if they operate on the principle that the essential resource is already inside the school: determined, intelligent, and capable teachers.[10]

The Carnegie Forum also made it clear that teachers must be the implementers of any reforms.

Textbooks cannot do it. Principals cannot do it. Directives from state authorities cannot do it. Only the people with whom the students come in contact every day can do it. Though many people have vital roles to play, only teachers can finally accomplish the reform agenda.[11]

To that point, I would add that only teachers can implement the reform agenda *in creative ways* and that they will be more likely to do so if they are treated as professionals whose expertise regarding both teaching and reform is needed.

How might the creativity of teaching be assessed? Administrators should be able to ask teachers what joyful, creative experience they have provided for young people in the classroom, within the past two days, and have a reasonable chance of hearing positive responses. Administrators might ask as well what they might do to assist the efforts of teachers to teach creatively.

5. *How will a given reform contribute toward enabling young people to meet their own immediate and long-term needs?* Altogether too many students see little in school that meets the needs that they have today or expect to have in the future. Current reform efforts seem destined to contribute most to enabling the

more capable young people to meet their future needs; at the same time, these reforms may be increasing the educational risk for those students who are unable to take a long-term view. The Indiana Department of Education and the Indiana Curriculum Advisory Council of the State Board of Education expressed concern for at-risk students.

> That group, the potential serfs of the information age, will define the social overhead costs of the twenty-first century if we do not take a more realistic view toward student motivation and plan accordingly. Many students view themselves as the unwilling conscripts of the war against ignorance.[12]

Educational efforts must be designed to have intrinsic rewards — they must be interesting and motivating in and of themselves — if young people are to have their immediate needs met.

Student needs will be better met in the future if we recognize and put to use more effectively the most abundant human resource we have in schools: the students. Reluctant students — if they want to be in school at all — most often want to be there to be with friends. Efforts to foster cooperative learning would seem to be an obvious strategy to achieve both social and educational benefits.

Robert Slavin examined more than 30 studies of student team learning and noted that 82% found that students using the team-learning approach gained more in achievement than did students in traditionally taught classes working on the same objectives.[13] These findings held true in urban, rural, and suburban schools across the U.S. and across a range of subjects. Students liked the team-learning classes better, and their self-esteem, attendance, and behavior also improved. Furthermore, mainstreamed students with academic handicaps who took part in team learning improved in achievement and behavior, and they were better accepted by their classmates.

Teaching meets significant social needs when it allows for interaction among students. Currently, I know of an arithmetic project under way in a local elementary school in which students work in pairs with membership rotating frequently. When they are given assignments, they complete a single paper. Preliminary data strongly suggest that students learn more effectively in this way and that they learn social skills at the same time. A comparable project in a senior high school is demonstrating similar benefits.

Administrators should be able to ask students what learning activities they

> *Multiple-choice tests that focus on traditional content tend to encourage highly structured, information-based teaching.*

were involved in, within the past two days, for which they can see a clear need either today or in the future, and administrators should have a reasonable chance of hearing positive responses.

6. *How will a given reform enable teachers to work more effectively with children who come from outside the mainstream culture?* Dean Corrigan, in his reaction paper to *The Purposes of American Education Today*, put the matter in perspective.

> America's schools at present are set up to produce "winners and losers." Many children are doomed to fail before they start. None of us, as adults, would continue to play a game we had no chance of winning, yet we expect some children to do this every day in school. Because of the relationship between poverty and access to equal educational opportunity, usually it is the children from poor families who find themselves at the bottom of the heap. Outdated organizational structures and school policies continue to lock the poor into their poverty.[14]

Corrigan went on to say that success in rebuilding the education system means teaching knowledge, skills, and values in new ways — "ways that creatively engage students of all backgrounds and all ability levels."[15]

Demographic trends indicate that minority children, mostly Hispanics and blacks, will constitute an ever-larger share of the public school population, and those are the young people with whom standard educational approaches have been least successful. If only for that reason, we must break away from traditional educational programming. Otherwise, the gap

between the haves and the have-nots will widen, as school organizations become more rigid and test structures fail to respond effectively to minority youths.

Frequent, absorbing, and involving educational experiences are essential if we are to reach those who have been reached ineffectively in the past, and those experiences must include opportunities for minority students to share elements of their cultures with others. All students will benefit if teaching responds to the needs of minority youths by creating more deeply engaging and involving educational experiences.

How might the effectiveness of teaching be assessed for those who do not come from the mainstream culture? Administrators should be able to ask teachers what recent classroom experiences they have provided for young people that were particularly effective in engaging those who are outside the mainstream culture. Administrators might also ask what they might do to help teachers work effectively with all the various populations that are represented within the school.

7. *How will a given reform enable children to demonstrate their learning beyond the traditional approach of classroom tests or standardized achievement tests?* Emphasis on tests that use multiple-choice questions that focus on traditional content tends to encourage highly structured, information-based teaching, rather than expansive, opportunistic, creative teaching. If education reform is not to inhibit, but to promote, creativity in teaching, it must creatively assess the effects of that teaching.

Corrigan criticized the use of test scores as the primary indicators of excellence. He suggested that we broaden the focus of assessment and "consider the skills successful adults need in America today: negotiating ability, making good judgments about people and situations, having the courage and ability to know when to persist in risk-taking situations, demonstrating a sense of loyalty and a concern for the human rights of others as well as one's own rights."[16]

We may well ask how the significant skills Corrigan cited, as well as those of speaking and writing effectively and persuasively, are to be measured in light of the increased emphasis on testing. Bruce Wilson and Thomas Corcoran summarized the successful efforts of 212 diverse elementary schools.[17] They concluded that outstanding schools are places in which creativity and cooperation characterize the setting and learning is not confined within the walls of the building. In many of these schools a galvanizing motto, such as "Learning Is Fun," drives the efforts of students, teachers, and administrators alike and gives young people a sense of *identity with*, as opposed to *alienation from*, the school.

How might the effectiveness of teaching be assessed when student learning has expanded beyond the traditional confines of classroom tests or standardized achievement tests? Creatively — with the support and encouragement of the school administration.

I recently visited an elementary school on the day when groups of sixth-graders demonstrated devices worthy of Rube Goldberg. The students had been assigned the task of breaking an ice cube using at least 10 steps. Each student had contributed something to the device, and each described his or her contribution. I was impressed by the creativity of the children's efforts and the poise with which they described their innovations. The inventers and the audience in the gymnasium were excited, and a local television station covered the story. The sixth-graders are unlikely to forget that day; they all benefited by having cooperated and contributed and by having stood before a gathering of students and adults and spoken for themselves. Such an experience suggests that group presentations may be among the better means for young people to demonstrate what they have learned. Creative teaching must be assessed creatively.

Nelson's first law of education reform follows. *Make schools more exciting, meaningful, and joyful places for young people, and education will improve more than through any alternative approach.* We concern ourselves with achievement test scores, with Scholastic Aptitude Test scores, with world competitiveness, and with illiteracy. Yet we do not sufficiently acknowledge that we have a free soci-

> **L**ike it or not, we *must* create experiences that draw students in, and the world of young people will be better if we do.

ety and that people will *choose* on their own to participate fully or not. We cannot, as some other countries can, impose requirements and expect young people automatically to follow them — unless we want to create a two-tiered school system. Like it or not, we *must* create educational experiences that draw students in, and the world of young people will be better if we do.

If I could address education reformers, I would ask them, What excites *you*? What kinds of activities engage you so thoroughly that you can hardly pull yourself away? What might you do late into the night, resisting the rational impulse to stop? Today's young people can be — and want to be — similarly engaged, and education reforms must fit the needs of these young people. If there are activities that absorb you thoroughly, chances are that they are not stereotypical, repetitious tasks involving rote learning. Probably, they are quite the opposite. We need to engage young people in similar absorbing ways. Our future depends on it. As Duckworth suggested, "The more

we can help children to have their own wonderful ideas, and feel good about themselves for having them, the more likely it is that they will some day happen upon ideas that nobody also has happened upon before."[18]

Joy in teaching and learning — not testing, not more and longer school days — is the key to true education reform.

1. Albert Shanker, "Address to the National Press Club," Washington, D.C., 31 March 1988.
2. Donald R. Brown, "Address to a Seminar on Schools for the 21st Century," Purdue University, West Lafayette, Ind., 11 January 1988.
3. Mihaly Csikszentmihalyi and Jane McCormack, cited in *Indiana Schooling for the Twenty-First Century* (Indianapolis: Indiana Department of Education and Indiana Curriculum Advisory Council of the State Board of Education, 1987), p. 29.
4. *The Purposes of American Education Today* (College Station, Tex.: Association of Colleges and Schools of Education in State Universities and Land-Grant Colleges, 1988), p. 11.
5. Ernest L. Boyer, *High School* (New York: Harper & Row, 1983), pp. 52-55.
6. William H. Burton, *The Guidance of Learning Activities* (New York: Appleton-Century-Crofts, 1962), p. 116.
7. *Tomorrow's Teachers: A Report of the Holmes Group* (East Lansing, Mich.: Holmes Group, 1986), pp. 29-30.
8. *Indiana Schooling . . . ,* p. 41.
9. Eleanor Duckworth, "The Having of Wonderful Ideas," *Harvard Educational Review*, vol. 42, 1972, p. 225.
10. *A Nation Prepared: Teachers for the 21st Century* (New York: Carnegie Forum on Education and the Economy, 1986), pp. 57-58.
11. Ibid., p. 26.
12. *Indiana Schooling . . . ,* p. 29.
13. Robert Slavin, "Cooperative Learning," *Instructor*, vol. 96, 1987, pp. 74-76, 78.
14. Dean Corrigan, "Creating the American School: Reaction Paper No. 2," *The Purposes . . . ,* p. 33.
15. Ibid., p. 42.
16. Ibid., pp. 34-35.
17. Bruce L. Wilson and Thomas B. Corcoran, *Places Where Children Succeed: A Profile of Outstanding Elementary Schools* (Philadelphia: Research for Better Schools, 1987).
18. Duckworth, p. 231.

Does the "Art of Teaching" Have a Future?

We need to broaden our image of professionalism to include the artistic dimensions teachers consider central to their work.

DAVID J. FLINDERS

David J. Flinders is Assistant Professor, University of Oregon, Division of Teacher Education, Eugene, OR 97403-1215.

Penelope Harper quickly takes roll, steps out from behind her desk, and glances around the classroom. Her eyes meet those of her students. Standing with her back to the chalkboard, she clasps her hands close in front of her, a ballpoint pen intertwined between her fingers. She holds her arms close to her sides and shifts her weight onto the heels of her shoes. This posture signals the beginning of class.

The students quiet down. Harper shakes back her dark hair and then addresses the class: "OK, today we need to discuss chapter two. Who would like to share something from your reading notes?" Silence. Harper breathes out, assuming a more casual and relaxed attitude. She is smiling softly now, confident that her students have read the assignment and that the silent classroom alone will motivate someone to risk putting forth an idea. Someone does. Harper listens intently and nods her head. "Good," she replies. "I really hadn't thought of it that way, but it tells us something, doesn't it? What's the author getting at here?" Harper steps forward, closer to her students, as their discussion begins to unfold.

Artistry in Professional Life

Penelope Harper (the name is a pseudonym) is good at what she does. She's a professional. But in Harper's line of work, what exactly does it mean to be a professional? Does it mean simply possessing a body of expert knowledge and a repertoire of techni-

cal skills? Climbing a career ladder toward greater autonomy and increased occupational rewards? Or, for classroom teachers, does professionalism mean something more?

These questions were the focus of a qualitative study I conducted on the nature of professional life in schools (Flinders 1987). Penelope Harper was one of six high school English teachers I observed and interviewed as part of this study. My purpose was to identify what Harper and her colleagues regard as the salient concerns of their day-to-day work experience. I hoped to view professional life through the eyes of classroom teachers.

I began my research with an understanding of professional life strongly influenced by the "new reform"

> **Effective communication begins with the processes of learning to see and to hear: the art of perception.**

(Shulman 1987). Two prominent examples of this reform are the reports by the Carnegie Task Force (1986) and the Holmes Group (1986). These reports share a common theme: the need to increase the professional status of teaching. In particular, they call for strengthening the career advancement opportunities, the subject-matter knowledge, and the technical expertise of all classroom teachers.

This focus on career development and expert knowledge reflects a widely shared and commonsense image of professionalism (Schon 1983). However, in listening to teachers talk about their work and in observing their teaching day after day, I soon realized that this image did not match their daily routines and their concerns. This image of professionalism failed to capture the artistry that these teachers often spoke of and demonstrated as central to their work.

Perhaps I can clarify this point by referring to my description of Penelope Harper. Consider, for example, her ability to signal the beginning of class through body language or her use of silence to motivate student participation. These skills reveal something of the grace, subtlety, and drama of Harper's day-to-day teaching. Granted, these deft moves cannot be evaluated solely by conventional testing procedures or through the use of systematic rating scales. Yet

David J. Flinders, "Does the 'Art of Teaching' Have a Future?" *Educational Leadership*, Vol. 46, No. 8, May 1989, pp. 16-20.

they are no less important than Harper's technical expertise or subject-matter knowledge. As my study progressed, the challenge became to understand this other side of teaching—the artistic side.

The Arts of Teaching

Elliot Eisner (1983) has examined at a theoretical level various ways in which teaching can be regarded as art and craft. He calls attention, for example, to the dynamic and emergent qualities of classroom life, as well as to the intricate skill and grace that can characterize the teacher's classroom performance. In this context, Eisner uses the term *art* in its broad sense to signify engaging, complex, and expressive human activity. It is this sense that allows us to speak of a beautiful lesson or of a well-orchestrated class discussion.

If we want to observe artistry in teaching, where might we look in order to find it? My research suggests several possible locations. The first I have already touched on in my brief description of Harper's work: the art of communication.

Communication. On a day-to-day basis, classroom teachers rely heavily on interpersonal forms of communication. Philip Jackson's (1965) early research, for example, suggests that teachers engage in as many as a thousand interpersonal interactions each day. This is an impressive number, particularly if we consider the intricate nature of even the most routine instances of face-to-face communication. Such communication, as Harper's teaching reveals, goes far beyond the spoken and written word—it also encompasses the use of space (what sociolinguists call *proxemics*), body language, and paralinguistics (voice tone and rhythm). One teacher I observed, for example, consistently demonstrated uncanny responsiveness toward her students. When a student asked a question or made a comment, that student could feel the teacher's undivided attention. In talking with students, the teacher would face them directly, lean or step in their direction, and maintain eye contact. At appropriate moments she would raise her eyebrows, nod her head, smile, and bring the index finger of her right hand up to her lips in a gesture of serious concentration. All of these

> **The teachers I observed displayed various strategies for negotiating a cooperative relationship with their students, including using humor and providing opportunities for individual recognition.**

nonverbal cues were coordinated to signal a coherent message: *I care about what you have to say*. This unspoken message was often as important to the students as the substantive meaning of her verbal responses.

Nonverbal cues serve primarily as a form of metalanguage (Tannen 1986). That is, they help teachers establish a context for communication. Consider yet another, somewhat different example. During a literature class, one teacher I observed lighted a kerosene lamp, asked his students to sit in a circle, turned on a recording of the sound effects of a storm, and read passages from Dickens' *Bleak House*, just as a Victorian father might have read the novel to his family. This teacher's well-calculated nonverbal cues provided a context for his students to gain insight into the novel that could not be "explained to them" using words alone. Creating a setting—this too is part of communication.

Perception. It would be difficult to imagine good teachers who could not communicate well with their students. Yet effective communication does not begin with formulating a message or selecting a medium, but rather with the processes of learning to see and to hear. This notion suggests another, perhaps more fundamental art relevant to classroom teaching: the art of perception.

The teachers in my study often alluded to this art in describing their work. During an interview, for example, one teacher casually mentioned that she adapts her daily lesson plans depending on "how the group comes in at the beginning of the period." Such a comment underscores her ability to read those subtle cues in student behavior that signal the changing mood and tone of a class. Another teacher, when I asked how he evaluates his work, replied: "The real test in teaching is how the kids feel about you, and it's the vibrations that you pick up from them that tell you the most." Again, this comment suggests that perceptiveness—the ability to pick up on student attitudes, motives, beliefs, and so forth—lies at the heart of this teacher's professional expertise.

The type of perceptiveness and sensitivity to which these examples refer is a largely tacit dimension of social life. It depends on the ability to make complex and fine-grained distinctions between, for example, a wink and a blink, or between a sigh of relief and a sigh of frustration. All of us learn to make such discernments, at varying levels of sophistication, through social interaction. The point, however, is that this learning reflects an intuitive receptivity that Noddings (1984) has identified as critical to sound pedagogy. At a practical level, learning to operate in a receptive mode is basic to getting to know the students, and I was not surprised to find that all of the teachers in my study mentioned this process as central to their work.

Cooperation. Knowledge of students, of "what they are like as people," as one teacher described perception, serves as the foundation for a third art that is salient in the professional lives of teachers: cooperation. For classroom teachers this means negotiating an alliance with their students. As one teacher commented, "You have to get the students on your side with honesty and a certain amount of candor, so they understand you, and you understand them." This teacher continued, "I'm here to work *with* the kids; I'm not here just to shovel out stuff and let them grab it." The other teachers were also quick to stress the practical value of student-teacher cooperation. One teacher summed it up simply: "You can't force students to do what you want them to do, but if they know you're working hard and care about 'em, from there on it's gravy."

The teachers I observed displayed various strategies for negotiating a cooperative relationship with their students. Some of these strategies include: (1) using humor and self-disclosure to promote teacher-student solidarity, (2) allowing students to choose activities, (3) occasionally bending school and classroom rules in the students' interest, (4) providing opportunities for individual recognition, and (5) creating pockets of time that allow teachers to interact one-to-one with students.

An example of this last strategy, creating pockets of time, is illustrated by a teacher who set aside every Thursday for mini-conferences. On this day, while his students worked independently, he went around the classroom to speak individually with as many students as possible. He justified this routine by insisting that "it helps break the mannequin-like image of me standing up in front of the room. It pays tremendous dividends. It allows the students to ask questions, and I find out a lot."

Appreciation. The final art of teaching is appreciation. Unlike communication, perception, and cooperation, the art of appreciation is not primarily something that teachers *do*. Instead, it is a product of their artistry and, thus, cannot always be directly observed. Nevertheless, I found it readily apparent in how teachers describe the types of satisfaction they derive from their teaching. As Harper explained: "In almost any job you do, if you do it well, you get a certain ego-satisfaction from it. It's really a good feeling—when I run a discussion—to know that I did it well." Eisner (1983) describes the same idea in another way: "The aesthetic in teaching is the experience secured from being able to put your own signature on your own work—to look at it and say it was good (p. 13)." Both the classroom teacher and the scholar are describing the intrinsic sense of worth that comes from having

done a difficult job well. This idea is central to the daily work of classroom teachers.

A Challenge to Educational Leaders

The artistic dimensions that teachers recognize as basic to their profession stand in sharp contrast to the priorities of the new reform movement. Of course, professionalism is about opportunities for career advancement, the expert knowledge teachers possess, and the types of learning that can be easily tested. Yet the day-to-day experience of teachers reminds us that teaching is also about much more. It is about subtle interpersonal skills, discernment, caring, and "ego-satisfaction." These artistic aspects reflect highly complex forms of human expression that may well influence teacher effectiveness more than career ladders and fifth-year preparation programs.

If the art of teaching is to have a future, we must enlarge our understanding of professionalism to include the artistic skills and judgment that good teaching demands. This task presents a challenge to educational leaders for at least two reasons. First, artistry cannot be mandated by the central office. Neither can it be fostered by an afternoon of inservice training once or twice a year. Therefore, we have to think more deeply about the conditions under which teachers work, their opportunities for interacting with each other, the amount of discretionary time in their daily schedules, the number of students they see each day, and the resources with which they have to work. Second, the art of teaching is simply less well understood than technical aspects of instruction. We know more, for example, about the mechanics of lesson planning, test construction, and curriculum development than we do about how Penelope Harper is able to gracefully orchestrate a class discussion.

The profession can learn much about the complexity and artistry of teaching from colleagues like Penelope

Harper. We might begin by cultivating our own abilities to engage teachers in genuine dialogue. Basic to this dialogue is our perceptiveness—learning to see and hear teachers in ways that take us beyond stereotypical images. Like teachers, we must operate in a receptive mode. We might also promote a cooperative alliance both with and between classroom teachers, for example, by occasionally bending rules for their professional well-being and by involving them in decision making. Finally, we might strive to fully appreciate the multifaceted nature of this collaborative effort as an art and craft in its own right.

References

Carnegie Task Force on Teaching as a Profession. (1986). *A Nation Prepared: Teachers for the 21st Century*. Washington, D.C.: Carnegie Forum on Education and the Economy.

Eisner, E. W. (January 1983). "The Art and Craft of Teaching." *Educational Leadership* 40: 4-13.

Flinders, D. J. (June 1987). "What Teachers Learn from Teaching: Educational Criticisms of Instructional Adaptation." Doctoral dissertation submitted to the Graduate School of Education, Stanford University.

The Holmes Group. (1986). "Tomorrow's Teachers, A Report of the Holmes Group." East Lansing, Mich.: The Holmes Group, Inc.

Jackson, P. W. (1965). "Teacher-Pupil Communication in the Elementary Classroom: An Observational Study." Paper presented at the American Educational Research Association Annual Meeting, Chicago.

Noddings, N. (1984). *Caring: A Feminine Approach to Ethics and Moral Education*. Berkeley: University of California Press.

Schon, D. A. (1983) *The Reflective Practitioner*. New York: Basic Books.

Shulman, L. S. (February 1987). "Knowledge and Teaching: Foundations of the New Reform." *Harvard Educational Review* 57, 1: 1-22.

Tannen, D. (1986). *That's Not What I Meant!* New York: Ballantine Books.

Tap into
TEACHER RESEARCH

Whether you're aware of it or not, you conduct research in your classroom every day. This year, why not put those informal observations and reflections to work for you and your students?

LINDA SHALAWAY

LINDA SHALAWAY *is an education writer based in West Virginia and is the author of* Learning to Teach.

Jay Sugarman of Massachusetts recently took a year's leave from his classroom to join a national research team. Laura Fendel of Oregon and Jean Medick of Michigan conduct research right in their own classrooms. At the Professional Development Center in Palo Alto, California, teachers design and conduct a variety of research projects.

For these teachers, and many like them, *research* is more often a verb than a noun. They are active producers of knowledge about teaching, and they represent a rapidly growing segment of professionals who call themselves teacher researchers.

Some teacher researchers participate in formal projects. Others work on their own. But no matter how or where they work, teacher researchers all engage in the same basic process—systematic inquiry. They ask questions and look for answers. In the process, they improve practice, grow intellectually and professionally, establish rewarding relationships with school and university colleagues, increase self-esteem, and create new career opportunities for themselves.

In this article, you'll learn how four different teachers have put research to work in their classrooms.

FIGHTING LEARNING PROBLEMS WITH RESEARCH

Some teachers, in seeking help for a specific classroom problem, wind up creating research of their own. For example, teacher Laura Fendel uses research to help students with behavioral and learning problems.

"I had a bizarre class of second graders one year," says the Portland, Oregon teacher. She explains that testing and observations by specialists revealed that 16 of her 26 students were only as socially mature as three or four year olds.

"I wanted the knowledge to do the best job I could do for these students, and I'm not intimidated by asking for help," says the veteran teacher. So Fendel attended a workshop on behavior problems and positive reinforcement, then experimented in her own classroom.

But she didn't stop there. She developed original materials and aids that would help her implement her research findings. "I used the theory, but I also got into the kids' world," she explains.

It all began with a stuffed animal named Bubba. Realizing how interested her students were in this toy, she started using it to motivate the children to work harder and pay attention. By staying on task, students earned the opportunity to see Bubba in the various outfits Fendel made for him.

That was six years ago. Since then Fendel has developed materials and activities around another character she calls Koala-Roo-Can-Do. She asked colleagues outside her district to field-test the activities, searched the research literature on self-esteem, wrote a book, and found a publisher for it (*Building Self-Esteem with Koala-Roo Can-Do,* Scott Foresman, 1989).

Now her second book is about to be published, she conducts workshops and in-services for her district, and she reviews manuscripts for an educational publisher.

"I feel very empowered by the whole experience," Fendel asserts. "Teachers make excellent researchers because they have tremendous organizational skills. We don't realize our capabilities."

RESEARCHING A WAY OUT OF DISCIPLINE PROBLEMS

By Thanksgiving break in Jean Medick's third year of teaching fourth and fifth graders in East Lansing, Michigan, she was ready to quit. She wanted to teach, but she was having very little success at it; her students interrupted every lesson. But she vowed to finish the school year to "see if I couldn't turn things around."

And turn things around she did.

"I started by observing and defining the behavior of a hostile child who completely disrupted my classroom," Medick says, explaining that she first needed to understand exactly what types of problems she was facing.

Next Medick went to the professional literature on problem behaviors and at-tended a workshop on classroom discipline. She wanted to learn everything she could about what motivated such hostile children.

Back in her classroom, Medick experimented with the strategies she'd learned for helping hostile children improve their behavior. She discovered some that really worked for her and her students. The school year ended successfully.

Not only did Medick continue teaching, but she also started investigating other problem behaviors and classroom man-agement strategies. She later joined a research team for a year at Michigan State University's Institute for Research on Teaching. Eventually she published her own book of classroom management strategies and directed workshops, sharing her insights with colleagues.

"It was so interesting working on these problem behaviors," says Medick. She notes that her research not only solved an immediate problem, it also led to new career opportunities.

That's a typical pattern for teacher

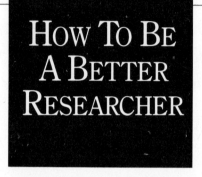

HOW TO BE A BETTER RESEARCHER

Any teacher can formalize and share the research he or she already conducts in the classroom every day.

"Start out by clearly identifying a problem or topic of interest in your own teaching," suggests Jay Sugarman. "Talk to others, do some reading on your topic, then talk to people at the university level who can bring other resources to bear on your own investigations.

"Take the initiative," Sugarman urges. "Make phone calls. Go to local and national conferences. They're a great way to establish networks and enrich your professional knowledge.

"And don't overlook student teachers as research partners," he continues. "It's a partnership that could benefit both of you."

Teacher researchers agree that all teachers can benefit by keeping up with the professional literature. It's impossible to read every journal and magazine, of course, but target a few that you find to be the most helpful. Ask colleagues about their recent readings. This type of sharing also provides a great vehicle for teacher interaction.

Laura Fendel advises would-be teacher researchers to "ask questions and keep seeking answers until you get some satisfaction."

Teachers asking questions and looking for answers in their own classrooms have many research tools at their disposal. One is observing colleagues in action.

"For example, if you decided to use literature to teach reading, you might try watching someone who already does this," Sugarman suggests. "This is valid, genuine research."

Peer Coaching: Many teachers regularly take turns observing and being observed through a process known as peer coaching. Briefly, peer coaching involves teachers choosing "coaches"—trusted colleagues—to help them analyze and focus on a specific problem or teaching strategy. A coach conducts systematic observations, offers feedback in joint problem-solving sessions, and observes again as the teacher experiments with a new approach or strategy. The process continues with new cycles of analysis, problem solving, and experimenting.

Videotape: Videotaping is a valuable tool because it allows teachers to conduct research themselves—right in the classroom.

Susie Davis, a first-grade teacher from Cameron, West Virginia, had never seen a videotape of her own teaching until a parent volunteer taped a reading lesson. As she later viewed the tape, Davis immediately saw one behavior she wanted to change.

"I noticed I never made eye contact with a student who responded correctly to a question," said Davis. "I was already looking ahead to my next question, so I'd just say, 'That's right' and move on. Twenty years of teaching and I wasn't making eye contact!"

Once identified, it was an easy prob-lem to correct. Davis' experience underscores the power of observation. And this tool can be used with students, too.

Michigan teacher educator and former teacher Barbara Diamond offers the example of one child who persistently asked questions. After carefully studying him on videotape, she recognized two patterns to his questions. He asked some questions to gain information, and others to gain control.

Students' patterns and habits in speech, body language, interactions—all things teachers don't have time to analyze in classrooms—reveal a lot when they're analyzed on videotape.

Journals: Keeping a journal, on the other hand, helps you reflect on both thoughts and actions.

If you keep a journal, try to target different aspects of your teaching to study in detail. For example, are you interested in offering equal time and attention to all students? If so, keep track of your personal interactions each day. Make a list of the students you enjoy being around and those you don't. What are the characteristics you like and dislike? Get it down in black and white, then try to assess where and how you can change.

As any teacher researcher will admit, there are always obstacles to overcome whenever the worlds of teaching and research come together: language differences, the slower pace of research compared to that of teaching, and differences in tasks and daily routines represent just a few possible barriers. But teacher researchers help put research in its proper place—the classroom.

researchers. Above all, they illustrate the fact that good teachers never stop learning to teach—and research provides the means to do so.

UNIVERSITY PARTNERSHIP IN PALO ALTO, CALIFORNIA

By forming a partnership with your local university, you can engage in more formal research projects that you may even design and conduct yourself. At the Professional Development Center in Palo Alto, California, teachers do just that.

"My job is to connect people from schools with people from universities," says Don Hill, director of the center. "Here at the center, we're trying to get people to look at school questions in ways they don't usually view them. Teachers conduct research every day of their lives, but they don't always realize it," Hill continues. "Making judgments formed from observations is research."

> *"Teachers make excellent researchers because they have tremendous organizational skills."*

In one formal project, seven teachers and two Stanford researchers studied the California Mentor Teacher Program. They developed a questionnaire, interviewed mentors on a variety of topics, and compiled their findings to present at a state-level forum.

> *"I wanted the knowledge to do the best job I could do for these students, and I'm not intimidated by asking for help."*

The center's Professor in Residence Program matches Stanford faculty members with teachers. For example, one science professor and a group of elementary teachers meet monthly to identify questions they would like to explore, study the research, and demonstrate lessons for each other. The teachers apply what they learn to their own teaching and then share their experiences. They also observe each other's classrooms.

"University researchers no longer use schools for their own purposes; they work with teachers to identify the problems they're experiencing," Hill claims. He also notes an increasing trend among university faculty to return to the classroom periodically for a dose of reality.

JOINING STANFORD UNIVERSITY'S RESEARCH TEAM

"I'm someone who's always kept up with the literature, who's interested in continual learning and being exposed to new ideas," says Jay Sugarman, a fourth-grade teacher at the Runkle School in Brookline, Massachusetts. So when members of the Teacher Assessment Project at Stanford University asked him to join their national research team, he jumped at the chance.

Taking a year's leave of absence from his classroom, Sugarman moved across the country to participate in a major study identifying ways other than paper-and-pencil tests to assess teacher competence. It wasn't just token involvement.

Sugarman conducted a yearlong field test centered on teachers who developed portfolios of their language instruction. The goal was to find out whether teacher portfolios could contribute to a richer, more contextual assessment of teaching. He also managed an assessment center, created by the research team.

"Teacher researchers were treated as equals by the university staff," Sugarman stresses. "They really listened to our voices. Even our teacher subjects—those developing the portfolios in their classrooms—were treated as co-researchers."

That's because research on teaching should be a collaborative process, according to Stanford professor Lee Shulman, who directs the Teacher Assessment Project. In his writings, Shulman refers to the "wisdom of practice" that researchers attempt to identify by interviewing, observing, and working alongside classroom teachers.

"Teachers in our study were encouraged to interact with other teachers at school, as well as with the project staff, as they documented and reflected on their practice," Sugarman explains. "They reported that this interaction was a wonderful growth opportunity. Perhaps one of the best ways for a teacher to grow is to get together with colleagues to talk about teaching," he concludes.

Sugarman's experience enabled him to develop new technical and intellectual skills. Since then, he has presented papers at professional meetings, written articles, and edited a new professional journal called *Reflections* for his district.

"Perhaps most important," Sugarman notes, "research affords us the time and opportunity to think about what we do."

Creating Conditions for Learning: From Research to Practice

Carolyn M. Evertson

Carolyn M. Evertson is professor of education at Peabody College, Vanderbilt University.

Teacher educators have been increasingly admonished to use findings from research on classrooms and teaching in their education of teachers, both preservice and inservice. Indeed one of the most unassailable justifications for including specific content in education programs is in the phrase "research says." Although research is a valid basis for the education of teachers, the issue is not simply one of using research, but of how research is used (Koehler, 1987; Fenstermacher, 1986).

The purpose of this article is to illustrate how research can be used to construct frameworks to guide teachers' inquiry into classroom processes and, hence, their decisions about classroom practice. The article advocates the use of research for identifying features of practice and classroom processes that teachers need to consider. The question of *how* the individual teacher will apply the finding is left to the teacher. The teacher is seen as decision maker and the research as the mirror the teacher uses to reflect that practice. The two parts of this article are written from this perspective. Part one identifies the propositions or the "we know that's" derived from the literature from research on teaching, classroom processes, and staff development.

Part two describes how these bodies of research can be used to create a staff development framework to help teachers reflect on practice and to make informed decisions about their practice (e.g., refine, modify, or change practice). Information

from studies that inform us about how teachers can manage their classrooms effectively is used as a place to begin professional inquiry and to identify teachers' tasks within this framework.

What We Know from Research

Four bodies of research can form the basis for a foundation and set of principles around which teachers can engage, experiment, and improve their practice.

Managing Classrooms

The first area draws on findings from studies conducted in a large number of classrooms that have resulted in the identification of teacher and student variables associated with achievement and other student outcomes (Brophy & Evertson, 1976; Brophy & Good, 1986). These studies provide information about classroom management and the importance of instructional time and student task engagement (Denham & Lieberman, 1980)—areas that have emerged as key features of effective instruction and as necessary conditions for supporting student academic performance.

Other studies show that from the first day of school, advance preparation, planning, and a systematic approach are key factors in influencing effective management and in setting positive conditions for learning; without a well managed environment, students will not gain access to learning (Evertson, Weade, Green, & Crawford, 1985). Specific recommendations for teachers, extracted from work on classroom management, include:

From *Theory into Practice,* Winter 1987, pp. 44-50. Copyright 1987, College of Education, The Ohio State University. Reprinted by permission.

(a) planning rules and procedures for general classroom organization, (b) presenting rules and procedures to students along with expectations for appropriate performance, (c) maintaining a systematic approach through monitoring student academic work and behavior; and (d) providing feedback to students about academic performance and participation. Findings from work on the implementation of these principles indicates that they lead to improved student task engagement, less inappropriate behavior, smoother instructional activities, and generally higher student academic performance (Emmer, Sanford, Clements, & Martin, 1982; Evertson, Emmer, Sanford, & Clements, 1983; Evertson et al., 1985).

Thus this research highlights factors that must be considered in efforts to develop an environment that supports academic activity. What this work does not provide is an understanding of how each of these factors will be applied in a given situation; rather, this work suggests *what* needs to occur. A second body of work identifies how management of classroom processes occurs in individual settings.

Classroom Communication

The second set of findings that can inform practice comes from the sociolinguistic-ethnographic perspective. These studies seek to illustrate not only *what* general classroom processes are, but *how* these processes function on a moment-to-moment basis. They focus on the student as well as the teacher as constructor of the environment in the teaching/learning process.

This work identifies what students need to understand to participate in class lessons. It focuses on ways rules, norms, and expectations function to govern the talk and actions among teacher and students and how these rules, norms, and expectations are signaled.

The teacher's management of how students may gain an opportunity to participate (i.e., answer questions, ask questions, get a turn at reading) is communicated both verbally and nonverbally along with academic instruction. Thus within a lesson a teacher not only presents academic content, but also orchestrates which students can participate, when, how, and for what purposes. This orchestration occurs on a moment-to-moment basis and is often determined by such considerations as maintaining the flow of classroom activity or allocating turns for students who have not had a chance to speak. Through this process students learn not only the academic content but how to participate in class lessons in appropriate ways (Green, 1983).

Studies that have examined how classroom talk functions in educational settings suggest that different rules, norms, and expectations govern different classroom activities and lesson tasks. These activities can be ritualistic (e.g., roll call, collecting assignments) wherein the structure of the activity is predictable and requirements for participation are

familiar. Or they can be novel, requiring students to interpret the requirements for participation as the activity or lesson progresses (Erickson, 1982).

Information students use to interpret the requirements for participation can come from several sources such as observation of their peers' turns at talk or from teachers' responses to student questions about the task to be accomplished (Carter & Doyle, 1982; Morine-Dershimer, 1985). Teachers' evaluations of individual pupils also communicate to peers information about how responses are to be constructed (Edwards & Furlong, 1978; Hammersley, 1974). Individual stages in lessons (i.e., teacher lecturing, checking for understanding, assigning seatwork) have different rules for participating (Cook-Gumperz, Gumperz, & Simons, 1981; Florio & Shultz, 1979; Gumperz, 1977). As lessons progress through phases, what students must understand and do to take part in the lessons also shifts (Erickson, 1982; Green & Harker, 1982; Wilkinson, 1981).

Even though rules and norms for participating exist and are constructed as the lesson or activity proceeds, the exact requirements for taking part in the lesson cannot always be predicted with certainty (Green, 1983). Potential exists for unpredictability and variation in the flow of classroom talk that makes classroom communication a dynamic process. Failure to "read" the requirements correctly can lead to inappropriate performance (Green & Harker, 1982). Such performance can lead to negative evaluation of student ability and achievement by teachers (Michaels & Cook-Gumperz, 1979). As Edwards and Furlong (1978) note:

> Some ways of speaking are associated with particular kinds of situations, and someone who does not know the relevant communicative etiquette risks having what he says ignored, misunderstood, or not taken seriously, however grammatically correct it might be. He also risks being written off himself, or at best having allowances made for him as someone obviously inexperienced in this situation.

The value of this research is that it suggests additional factors to be considered and illustrates *how* the factors are used and the processes occur. The ethnographic approach allows analysis of connections among classroom events and outcomes.

Training Studies

The third area of knowledge comes from training studies of inservice teachers in the area of classroom management and effective instructional practices. The findings from this body of work provide us with the evidence that content from research can be taught and that teachers can use the findings in their classroom practice (Anderson, Evertson, & Brophy, 1979; Borg & Ascione, 1982; Evertson et al., 1983; Evertson et al., 1985; Gage & Needels, in press; Good & Grouws, 1979).

These studies support the usefulness for staff

development of principles such as establishing rules and procedures early in the year, developing systematic ways of managing student academic work, developing explanation portions of mathematics lessons more fully, etc. That is, teachers who were given the opportunity to reflect systematically upon the principles were able to apply and adapt them successfully to their own classrooms.

The key to making this happen is in using the research to provide generalizations that form a global or composite model of effective classroom management. This serves as a framework within which teachers can explore research-based variables within their own classroom and school. Research, then, is used to inform the content of staff development programs. However, planning staff development does not involve consideration of content alone; it also involves consideration of features of effective staff development, which necessitates considering one last area of research.

Staff Development

The fourth area draws on what we know about effective staff development and how this process can function to support teachers in their professional development (Griffin, 1983; Hawley & Rosenholtz, 1984; Joyce & Clift, 1984; Little, 1981).

Griffin (1983) reviewed several studies that he felt were relevant to the planning, conduct, and evaluation of staff development programs. These studies examined staff development from the perspective of (a) the *context* in which it takes place (Bentzen, 1974; Berman & McLaughlin, 1975; Little, 1981); (b) the *assessment* of needs that support a staff development program (Hall, 1979; Hall & Loucks, 1981; Stallings, 1981); (c) the *content* or the body of knowledge, skills, or attitudes that should be introduced in the school setting (Barnes, 1981; Good, 1982); and (d) the *process* by which the content is conveyed to the participants through planning, implementation, and evaluation (Berman & McLaughlin, 1975; Evertson et al., 1983; Griffin, Hughes, & Martin, 1982; Tikunoff, Ward, & Griffin, 1979). From these and other studies he extracted a set of principles that can be used to guide staff development. Table 1 provides a summary of these findings.

This work suggests the need to involve practitioners in examining their practice. The next section builds a case and describes one attempt to accomplish this.

Toward a New Model for Staff Development

While many will accept the four strands of research outlined above as useful for staff development, teachers, researchers, and policy makers have different recommendations and reactions to the "how's"—how to get teachers to use the principles derived from research.

Table 1
Recommendations for Research Based Guidance for Staff Development Programs*

1. Derived as a consequence of systematic problem identification by those most directly related to the program.
2. Interactive: Participants establish a shared language to discuss issues and changes.
3. Mitigate to some degree status differences between administrators and teachers.
4. Depend less on consultants and more on teachers and administrators for substantive and procedural guidance.
5. Formulated and monitored largely according to the perceptions of the participants.
6. Formulated, in part, from careful analyses of the organization and participants.
7. Flexible and responsive to changes in participants and the setting.
8. Situation-specific within reasonable limits.
*From Griffin, 1983.

A Critique of the Generic Teaching Approach

Policy makers and state and local agencies frequently use the findings of classroom research or instructional models to endorse staff development programs that train teachers to implement specific behaviors in the classroom. Too often this is done without significant regard to the contexts or the purposes for which those behaviors are to be implemented.

Such applications of the research on teaching rest on several assumptions: First is the assumption that teaching consists of a succession of separate acts and that those acts can be assessed by evaluation schemes and taught through staff development independently of one another. Second is the assumption that teacher behavior is stable. Third, is the assumption that teacher behavior is context-free. Thus, all one needs to do is to identify in the research the behaviors that correlate with effectiveness and write rules for bridging to practice (Fenstermacher, 1980).

Recent research shows, however, that teaching is more complex than these assumptions suggest. Teaching varies across teachers and for individual teachers across subjects, activities, and students. Further, variations become more significant the more specific our focus on teacher behavior becomes.

Bridging research and practice with rules, therefore, is risky. The findings of research on teaching are easily misinterpreted and applied out of context. One can create, from research findings, rules that govern behavior. However, this restricts teachers' ability to be adaptive and flexible in their classrooms, to think independently, to modify, to adopt, or even to reject behaviors that are inappropriate to the context. Indeed, teacher behaviors that have sometimes been found to relate to student learning when used in moderation have also been found to produce insignificant and even negative results when over- or under-used (Brophy & Evertson, 1976; Peterson & Kauchak, 1982; Soar, 1977) or when applied in the wrong circumstances (e.g., Coker, Medley, & Soar, 1980; McDonald & Elias, 1976). In this way, bridging with rules can have a negligible or even counterproductive effect on efforts to improve teaching.

An Inquiry-based Perspective

If we accept the evidence that teaching is a process involving judgments and decisions that lead to adapting specific behaviors to different contexts in ways most conducive to student learning, we are more likely to focus on different approaches to applying research to improve practice. Fenstermacher (1986) asserts that teaching is a moral, purposeful activity and that teachers' acts result from decisions and judgments grounded in premises and beliefs about teaching, learning, and the context of the classroom. According to this view, teachers cannot be seen as mechanistic implementors of independent behaviors, and efforts to improve teaching cannot be seen as ways to insert specific behaviors in the place of others deemed to be less productive.

This leads to another perspective on the use of knowledge from research on teaching to improve practice. These premises suggest a staff development model that involves teachers and administrators as decision makers, knowledge users, and knowledge producers in local settings. While the teacher-as-decision-maker approach is growing in acceptance, it is not at present the dominant approach to staff development. To understand what is involved in this approach one must understand how it contrasts with the more prevalent model. Although both approaches use research as a basis for identifying what teachers need to know, they differ in what research is used and how one moves between research and practice.

Under the inquiry-based perspective, findings from research are used to create dissonance and to challenge premises and beliefs teachers rely upon to make judgments and decisions in their classrooms. They become points of comparison and new lenses to be used to examine their own practice. In Fenstermacher's (1980) terms, this perspective calls for bridging research and practice with evidence and schemata rather than with rules.

Strategies

The problem facing those interested in staff development becomes—How do we bridge with schema and evidence? To answer this question a series of steps or questions must be addressed. First, the content of the program must be identified. As suggested earlier, bodies of knowledge derived from research done across large numbers of classrooms and research on classroom communication provide a source of constructs that can be used to guide inquiry. Once the content has been identified, consideration must be given to how this content can be delivered to practitioners in ways that allow them to make the decisions about how it will

fit within their settings. In other words activities that bring learner and content knowledge together and also provide opportunities for decision making need to be developed.

As suggested previously, information about effective staff development provides guidelines and recommendations for developing a process to make participants aware of the knowledge and to allow them to reflect, discuss with peers, develop a vocabulary, use knowledge to examine the local situation, and develop a plan that is sensitive to their own context. Finally, a plan for follow through needs to be developed.

To illustrate how these steps can be used, a staff development program focusing on classroom management will be presented. An outline of the program content derived from research on classroom management is presented in Table 2.

Table 2
Content Outline for Developing
Classroom Management System

I. Planning before the year begins
   A. Arranging classroom space and supplies
   B. Choosing classroom rules and procedures
   C. Developing procedures for managing student work (accountability)
   D. Establishing consequences and incentives
   E. Choosing activities for the beginning of school
II. Implementing plans at the beginning of the year
   A. Teaching rules and procedures
   B. Establishing a content focus
   C. Communicating expectations, directions and explanations clearly
III. Maintaining the management system throughout the year
   A. Monitoring student behavior and academic work
   B. Modeling and reinforcing appropriate behavior consistently
   C. Intervening to restore order when necessary
   D. Managing special classroom groups

The information in Table 2 provides the mirror to practice—the "we know that's" that the participants need to think about. This list is a general framework of the teachers' tasks that must be considered in developing a systematic management plan for their classrooms. It is also a framework for identifying aspects of classroom life that can be observed, thus linking observation to planning and delivery.

Once content has been identified, the next question becomes one of how to bring content and the participants together so that teachers can make informed decisions about their classroom practices. As argued above it is not simply a matter of writing specific prescriptions and giving them to the participants; rather the task is one of providing activities from which participants can develop schema to apply to their own settings. Activities listed in Table 3 provide the structure used in the classroom management program.

These activities are designed to respond to teacher need and to guide participants through the decision making process. Thus, decision making is an informed, focused process, not a shotgun approach. The steps in choosing and planning classroom rules and procedures provide an example of how this process can be carried out.

Table 3
Leadership and Participant Activities
for an Inquiry-based Approach
to Professional Development

A. Assessment and problem identification
  1. Use of diagnostic checklists and inventories as self-assessment about aspects of teaching that are of concern (total group)
  2. Identification of concerns to focus direction during workshop (leader)
B. Content presentations and activities that engage participants in examination and analysis of the content: vignettes, case studies, film, simulations (Cycle is repeated for each new topic.)
  1. Presentation based on research findings, including research questions, rationales, procedures, and findings with applications for practice (leader)
  2. Group discussion and problem solving using guidelines, checklists, and case studies of problem situations for analysis and critique (small groups or teams)
  3. Identification of guidelines and approaches applicable to individual classrooms (leader and groups)
  4. Discussion of strategies (small groups and total group)
  5. Feedback on tentative solutions to problems (total group or other small groups)
  6. Individual group reports on results of problem-solving and discussion
  7. Sharing of strategies, techniques, and examples of problem solution (total group)
C. Concluding activities
  1. Reexamination of diagnostic checklists and assessments (individuals)
  2. Focus on a problem participants wish to address (individuals or teams)
  3. Formulation of plans (individuals or teams)
  4. Follow-up on roles, responsibilities, and tasks (teams)
  5. Development of structure for ongoing follow-up and maintenance of the plans (leader, teams)
  6. Development of structure to continue dialogue begun in workshop meetings (teams)

Step I: Selecting the content. Research from two perspectives was used to determine the content. The first body of research (research across classrooms) sets the conditions in which management of actual instruction occurs and defines the broader structure of the classroom. The second body of research (sociolinguistic) allows us to focus in on the social dimension of content and instruction.

Step II: Developing activities. The next step requires construction of activities that help the teacher understand what rules are and how they function so that they can make decisions about the rules in their local contexts. One level of decision making activity focuses on the school level. At this level the faculty makes decisions about whether they want to have a shared set of rules in the school and what these rules will be. In this way, the faculty establishes not only a shared set of rules, but also a shared language to discuss areas of common concern. The activities are, therefore, not prescriptive but descriptive and interactive. They focus on what we know about classrooms and help to make these dimensions visible.

The second type of activity focuses on the classroom, teacher, or team level. In this activity the decision making process is revisited so that the teacher (team) can explore the classroom (grade level) context. In this way the different types of rules needed to build a safe environment for student learning can be made visible, examined, established, refined, and/or modified.

As part of each activity, the participants continue to expand and clarify the knowledge base being developed, ask new questions, discover new relationships between teaching practice and the conditions for student learning, and search for new insights about how those relationships vary across different teaching contexts. Thus, the participants become knowledge producers and evaluators as well as knowledge users. This process enables teachers to continue to increase their analytical decision making capabilities, to examine their own premises and beliefs, to appropriately assess the contexts in which they teach, and to consider, modify, and adapt that knowledge so that the new knowledge becomes incorporated in their frames of reference and actions.

Step III: Sustaining the gains. The final step cannot be accomplished by a staff developer or personnel external to the school. This step requires the school to make a commitment to a sustained program. For example, the participants need to have time to implement the rules and to examine what happens. After a period of time the teachers and administrators will need to reexamine the rules and refine, modify, or change them. Decision making from this perspective is an ongoing cyclical process involving consideration of the research knowledge, reflection on the knowledge and process, implementation of actions based on informed decisions, reconsideration of knowledge gained from observation of classroom/school processes, and modification or change based on reevaluation of decisions made and actions taken.

Conclusion

Skill in organizing, managing, and promoting a productive and stimulating learning environment for students is a complex task and requires time for teachers to think, plan, and reflect in the company of their colleagues. Through this interaction a language for talking about practice can develop (Little, 1981), tacit understandings about classroom processes can become explicit and, hence, can become part of an operating framework against which teachers can view their practice and be supported in changing and refining their skills.

Research supports these principles, but some models of professional development derive rules and enforce teachers' adoption of the rules. Such models ignore context and interactions in school environments. The challenge for staff development is to create dynamic programs that support and stimulate this process. Inquiry-based staff development uses research to provide teachers with frameworks for guiding experimentation, observation, and adoption in ways that allow teachers to make their own discoveries and to become empowered in their work.

References

Anderson, L., Evertson, C., & Brophy, J. (1979). An experimental study of effective teaching in first grade reading groups. *Elementary School Journal, 79,* 193-223.

Barnes, S. (1981). *Synthesis of selected research on teaching findings.* Austin, TX: Research and Development Center for Teacher Education, University of Texas.

Bentzen, M. (1974). *Changing schools: The magic feather principle.* New York: McGraw-Hill.

Berman, P., & McLaughlin, M. (1975). *Federal programs supporting educational change* (Vol. 4). Santa Monica, CA: Rand.

Borg, W., & Ascione, F. (1982). Classroom management in elementary mainstreaming classrooms. *Journal of Educational Psychology, 74,* 85-95.

Brophy, J., & Evertson, C. (1976). *Learning from teaching: A developmental perspective.* Boston, MA: Allyn & Bacon.

Brophy, J., & Good, T. (1986). Teacher behavior and student achievement. In M. Wittrock (Ed.), *Handbook of research on teaching* (3rd ed.) (pp. 328-375). New York: Macmillan.

Carter, K., & Doyle, W. (1982). *Variations in academic tasks in high and average ability classrooms.* Paper presented at the annual meeting of the American Educational Research Association, New York.

Coker, H., Medley, D., & Soar, R. (1980). How valid are expert opinions about effective teaching? *Phi Delta Kappan, 62,* 131-134, 149.

Cook-Gumperz, J., Gumperz, J., & Simons, H. (1981). *School-home ethnography project* (Final report, NIE G-78-0082). Washington, DC: National Institute of Education.

Denham, C., & Lieberman, A. (Eds.). (1980). *Time to learn.* Washington, DC: National Institute of Education.

Edwards, A., & Furlong, V. (1978). *The language of teaching: Meaning in classroom interaction.* London, England: Heinemann.

Emmer, E., Sanford, J., Clements, B., & Martin, J. (1982). *Improving junior high classroom management.* Paper presented at the annual meeting of the American Educational Research Association, Montreal.

Erickson, F. (1982). Classroom discourse as improvisation: Relationships between academic task structure and social participation structure in lessons. In L.C. Wilkinson (Ed.), *Communicating in the classroom* (pp. 153-181). New York: Academic Press.

Evertson, C., Emmer, E., Sanford, J., & Clements, B. (1983). Improving classroom management: An experiment in elementary school classrooms. *Elementary School Journal, 84,* 173-188.

Evertson, C., Weade, R., Green, J., & Crawford, J. (1985). *Effective classroom management and instruction: An exploration of models* (Final report, NIE G-83-0063). Washington, DC: National Institute of Education.

Fenstermacher, G. (1980). On learning to teach effectively from research on teacher effectiveness. In C. Denham & A. Lieberman (Eds.), *Time to learn* (pp. 127-137). Washington, DC: National Institute of Education.

Fenstermacher, G. (1986). Philosophy of research on teaching: Three aspects. In M. Wittrock (Ed.), *Handbook of research on teaching* (3rd ed.) (pp. 37-49). New York: Macmillan.

Florio, S., & Shultz, J. (1979). Social competence at home and at school. *Theory Into Practice, 18,* 234-243.

Gage, N., & Needels, M. (in press). *Essence and accident in process-product research on teaching.* Unpublished manuscript, Stanford University, Stanford, CA.

Good, T. (1982). *Classroom research: What we know and what we need to know.* Austin, TX: Research and Development Center for Teacher Education, University of Texas.

Good, T., & Grouws, D. (1979). The Missouri Mathematics Effectiveness Project. *Journal of Educational Psychology, 71,* 355-362.

Green, J. (1983). Research on teaching as a linguistic process: A state of the art. In E. Gordon (Ed.), *Review of research in education* (Vol. 10) (pp. 151-252). Washington, DC: American Educational Research Association.

Green, J., & Harker, J. (1982). Gaining access to learning: Conversational, social, and cognitive demands of group participation. In L.C. Wilkinson (Ed.), *Communicating in the classroom* (pp. 183-221). New York: Academic Press.

Griffin, G. (1983). Implications of research for staff development program. *Elementary School Journal, 83,* 414-425.

Griffin, G., Hughes, R., & Martin, J. (1982). *Knowledge, training and classroom management.* Austin, TX: Research and Development Center for Teacher Education, University of Texas.

Gumperz, J. (1977). Sociocultural knowing in conversational inference. In M. Saville-Troike (Ed.), *Georgetown University round table on languages and linguistics 1977: Linguistics and anthropology* (pp. 191-211). Washington, DC: Georgetown University Press.

Hall, G. (1979). The concerns-based approach to facilitating change. *Educational Horizons, 57,* 202-208.

Hall, G., & Loucks, S. (1981). Program definition and adaptation. *Journal of Research and Development in Education, 14(2),* 46-58.

Hammersley, M. (1974). The organisation of pupil participation. *Sociological Review, 22,* 355-368.

Hawley, W., & Rosenholtz, S. (1984). Good schools: What research says about improving student achievement. *Peabody Journal of Education, 61,* 1-178.

Joyce, B., & Clift, R. (1984). The Phoenix Agenda: Essential reform in teacher education. *Educational Researcher, 13,* 5-19.

Little, J. (1981). *School success and staff development: The role of staff development in urban desegregated schools.* Boulder, CO: Center for Action Research.

McDonald, F., & Elias, P. (1976). The effects of teaching performance on pupil learning. *Beginning Teacher Evaluation Study* (Phase II, Vol. I). Princeton, NJ: Educational Testing Service.

Michaels, S., & Cook-Gumperz, J. (1979). A study of sharing time with first grade students: Discourse narratives in the classroom. In *Proceedings of the Berkeley Linguistic Society, 5,* 87-103.

Morine-Dershimer, G. (1985). *Talking, listening, and learning in elementary classrooms.* White Plains, NY: Longman.

Peterson, K., & Kauchak, K. (1982). *Teacher evaluation: Perspectives, practices, and promises.* Salt Lake City, UT: University of Utah, Center for Educational Practice.

Soar, R. (1977). Integration of findings from four studies of teacher effectiveness. In G. Borich (Ed.), *The appraisal of teaching* (pp. 96-103). Reading, MA: Addison-Wesley.

Stallings, J. (1981). What research has to say to administrators of secondary schools about effective teaching and staff development. In *Creating conditions for effective teaching.* Eugene, OR: University of Oregon.

Tikunoff, W., Ward, B., & Griffin, G. (1979). *Interactive research and development on teaching: Final report.* San Francisco, CA: Far West Laboratory for Educational Research and Development.

Wilkinson, L.C. (1981). Analysis of teacher-student interaction-expectations communicated by conversational structure. In J.L. Green & C. Wallat (Eds.), *Ethnography and language in educational settings* (pp. 253-268). Norwood, NJ: Ablex Press.

Development

- Childhood (Articles 5-11)
- Adolescence (Articles 12-14)

The study of human development provides us with knowledge of how children and adolescents mature and learn within the family, community, and school environment. Educational psychology focuses on the description and explanation of the developmental processes that make it possible for children to become intelligent and socially competent adults. The idea that cognitive, personal, and social development proceed in stages that are age-related is accepted by most psychologists and educators.

Jean Piaget's theory regarding the cognitive development of children and adolescents is perhaps the best known and most comprehensive. According to this theory, the perceptions and thoughts that young children have about the world are prelogical and premoral. When compared to adolescents and adults, children experience reality in a unique way. Children need to acquire cognitive, moral, and social skills in order to interact effectively with parents, teachers, and peers. If human intelligence encompasses all of the above skills, then Piaget may have been correct in saying that human development is the child's intelligent adaptation to the environment.

Today the cognitive, moral, and social development of children takes place in a rapidly changing society. A child must develop a sense of self-worth and self-reliance, as well as a strong sense of family, in order to cope with these changes and become a competent and socially responsible adult. The contribution of the classroom in fostering social growth and moral development is explored in the articles by Susan Doescher and Alan Sugawara, Thomas Lickona, and W. Dean McCafferty.

Adolescence brings with it the ability to think abstractly and hypothetically and to see the world from the perspective of others. Adolescents strive to form goals and achieve a sense of identity, but they often become frustrated and feel alienated from the adult world. The kinds of adults they want to become and the ideals they want to believe in sometimes lead to conflicts with parents and teachers. Adolescents are also sensitive about espoused adult values versus adult behavior. The articles concerning adolescence in this unit discuss the social and personal problems that confront adolescents, and they suggest ways the school can help meet the needs of adolescents.

Looking Ahead: Challenge Questions

What is an appropriate education for young children? Is childhood still recognized as a unique stage of development? Why is it important for children to have the opportunity to solve problems on their own? How can teachers provide them with these activities?

What are some of the risks and social pressures children face in growing up? How can parents and teachers help children to develop positive self-concepts and high self-esteem?

Describe the societal and personal problems adolescents face. How can the middle school help with these problems? Can we learn something from adolescents who have positive attitudes about their family and friends?

2

Formal Education and Early Childhood Education: An Essential Difference

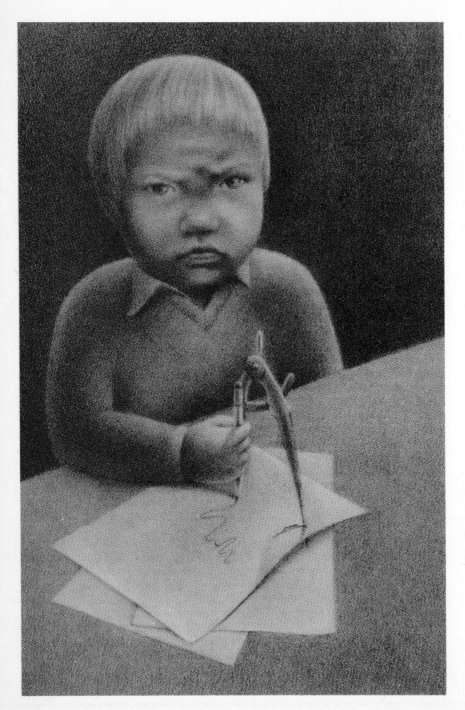

Educational programs devised for school-age children are being applied to the education of younger children, as well. Why is the special character of learning in early childhood being ignored by people who should know better?

David Elkind

DAVID ELKIND is a professor of child study and resident scholar at the Lincoln Filene Center for Citizenship and Public Affairs, Tufts University, Medford, Mass. He is the author of The Hurried Child *(Reading, Mass.: Addison-Wesley, 1981) and* The Miseducation of Children: Superkids at Risk *(New York: A.A. Knopf, 1986). ©1986, David Elkind.*

YOUNG CHILDREN do not learn in the same ways as older children and adults. Because the world of things, people, and language is so new to infants and young children, they learn best through direct encounters with their world rather than through formal education involving the inculcation of symbolic rules. The fact of this difference is rooted in the observations of such giants of child study as Froebel, Montessori, and Piaget, and it is consistently supported by the findings of research in child development.[1] This fact was also recognized by the ancients, who described the child of 6 or 7 as having attained the "age of reason."

Given the well-established fact that young children learn differently, the conclusion that educators must draw is a straightforward one: the education of young children must be in keeping with their unique modes of learning. If we

From *Phi Delta Kappan*, May 1986, pp. 631-636. © 1986, Phi Delta Kappan, Inc.

accept this conclusion, what is happening in the U.S. today is truly astonishing. In a society that prides itself on its openness to research and on its respect for "expert" opinion, parents, educators, administrators, and legislators are blatantly ignoring the facts, the research, and the consensus of experts about how young children learn and how best to teach them.

All across the country, educational programs devised for school-age children are being applied to the education of young children, as well. In such states as New York, Connecticut, and Illinois, administrators are advocating that children enter formal schooling at age 4. The length of many kindergarten programs has been extended to a full day, and nursery school programs have become prekindergartens. Moreover, many of these kindergartens have introduced curricula (including workbooks and papers) once reserved for first-graders. And a number of writers, in books addressed to parents, advocate the teaching of reading and math to infants and very young children.[2]

This transformation of thinking regarding early childhood education raises at least three questions that I will attempt to answer here. First, why is this happening? As we have seen, both theory and research consistently agree that young children learn differently from older children and adults. And no one really questions the principle that education should be adapted to the learning abilities of the students to be instructed. Why is the special character of learning in early childhood being ignored by so many people who should know better?

The second question depends on the first. Even if young children are being taught in the manner of older children, what harm is there in that? After all, it could be that we have merely been coddling young children by not introducing them to a rigorous academic program at an early age. Doesn't the new research on infants and young children substantiate their eagerness to learn and the importance of the early years for intensive instruction? We will see below that this is not quite the case.

The third question follows from the first two. If it can be demonstrated that early, formal instruction does more harm than good, what can we do about it? After all, that is the direction, however mistaken, in which U.S. society as a whole is heading. Formal instructional programs for infants and young children are expanding not only in academic areas but also in sports, the arts, and computer science. To oppose these trends is to ignore the social consensus and to run counter to the culture at large. We live in a democratic society in which the majority rules, so what can a minority do even if it wants to?

WHY BEGIN SO SOON?

In America, educational practice is determined by economic, political, and social considerations much more than it is by what we know about what constitutes good pedagogy for children. Until the 1960s, however, early childhood education was an exception to this general rule. Early childhood education programs were, for the most part, privately run and well adapted to the developmental needs of the children they served. Even kindergartens in public schools had a special status and were generally free of the social pressures that influenced the rest of elementary and secondary education.

All of that changed in the 1960s, however, when early childhood education was abruptly shoved into the economic, political, and social spotlight. At that moment, early childhood education lost its innocence and its special status. Like elementary and secondary education, early childhood education became a ground on which to fight social battles that had little or nothing to do with what was good pedagogy for children. The formal symbol of this mainstreaming of early childhood education came with the passage by Congress of the Head Start legislation in 1964. For the first time, early childhood programs were being funded by the federal government.

What brought about this change during the Sixties? In many ways early childhood education was the scapegoat of the social movements of that turbulent decade. Elementary and secondary education were already under attack on two different fronts. First, such events as the launching of Sputnik I in 1957, the demise of progressive education, and the publication of such books as *Why Johnny Can't Read* focused the spotlight of criticism on American education. One explanation (actually, a rationalization) for the problems that such close scrutiny revealed was that children were poorly prepared for school and that early childhood education should be more academically rigorous so that children could move more rapidly once they entered school.

The second front on which education was trying to fight a rear-guard action was in the arena of the civil rights movement. One of the main issues taken up by this movement was the unequal schooling of minorities. Schools for black children, for example, were obviously inferior in quality to those for white children. Again, one explanation (rationalization) was that black children were poorly prepared for school. It wasn't the schools, the argument ran, but the preparation that led to the lower achievement levels of black children. The Head Start legislation was one response to this claim.

One major consequence of this institutionalization of early childhood education was the introduction of a new conception of infants and young children. Educational practice is not alone in being determined by the social, economic, and political tenor of the times. The conception of the child changes with the times as well. For example, a dominant conception of the child in the 19th century — dictated by the religious orthodoxy of the time — was the notion of the "sinful child." Educating the sinful child necessarily involved "breaking the will" by whatever harsh means were needed to do so.

The advent of Freudian psychology in the early 20th century, along with the continuing secularization and urbanization of American society, gradually replaced the concept of the sinful child with the concept of the "sensual child." Freud's depiction of infantile sexuality and his theories regarding the central role of sexuality in the formation of neuroses focused attention on the development of a "healthy personality."[3] Progressive education had as one of its aims the open, spontaneous expression of feelings and emotions (judged to be healthy) rather than their suppression or repression (judged to be unhealthy). During the reign of the sensual child, there was less concern with the child's intellectual development, which, in an emotionally healthy child, was presumed to take care of itself.

The intellectual importance given early childhood education by the civil rights movement and the education reform movement of the 1960s was inconsistent with the concept of the sensual child. A new concept of infants and young children was, therefore, required. This new concept had to be in keeping with the new significance attached to academic education during the early years. What emerged was the concept of the "competent infant." Unwittingly, perhaps, social scientists of the time, caught up in the emotion of the social movements, fostered this conception through unwarranted reinterpretations of established facts about the cognitive development of young children.

Jerome Bruner, for example, though he was not trained in child development or in education, became a guru of the education reform movement of the day.[4] His totally unsubstantiated claim that "you can teach any child any subject matter at any age in an intellectually honest way" became a touchstone of the new conception of the "competent infant." In the same way, Benjamin Bloom's ambiguous statement that a young child attains half of his or her intellectual ability by the age of 4 (based on well-known correlations between I.Q. scores attained by the same subjects at different ages) was another foundation for the conception of the "competent infant."[5] Finally, James McV. Hunt's idea of the malleability of I.Q. (an idea that had always been accepted by reputable psychometricians) was presented as a new idea that was in opposition to the mental testing establishment's supposed advocacy of a fixed I.Q.[6]

Thus the conception of the competent infant and young child was dictated by social and political forces rather than by any new data or findings about the modes of learning of young children. Whatever psychological theory or educational research that was brought to bear to reinforce this conception had been carefully selected and interpreted to support the notion of early childhood competence. Contrary evidence was ignored. The facts were made to fit the hypothesis rather than the hypothesis being changed to accommodate the facts. In short, our conception of the child at any point in history has been much more dependent on social, political, and economic considerations than on the established facts and theories of child development.

The concept of the competent infant was also congruent with the changing lifestyles of American middle-class families. During the reign of the sensual child, middle-class values dictated that mothers stay at home and rear their children, lend support to their husbands, and run the home. Home economics became a major department for women in most colleges and universities of the time and reflected these values. Within that set of middle-class values, the concept of a sensual infant who was in need of a mother's ministrations fit quite comfortably.

In the past two decades, however,

> # The conception of the competent infant and young child was dictated by social and political forces rather than by any new data or findings.

thanks partly to the women's movement and partly to the shift in U.S. society from an industrial to a postindustrial economy, the middle-class value system has changed dramatically. The women's movement accentuated women's need for choice in the matter of whether to stay home or to pursue a career. At the same time, a postindustrial economy can make use of more women in the workforce than an industrial economy. In the past, factory work required the large muscles of men, but, with the miniaturization of modern technology, the small motor skills and dexterity of women are in greater demand. Likewise, now that our economy is becoming primarily a service economy, the social skills of women are also much in demand.

Another change in the circumstances of the middle class has contributed to the growing number of middle-class women in the workforce. As divorce has become socially acceptable, divorce rates have soared, and it is now expected that more than half of all marriages will end in divorce. In more than 90% of these cases, it is the mother who retains custody of the children. And because alimony and child support are rarely enough to live on, divorced mothers swell the ranks of working women.

One result of these changes in lifestyle and values has been that middle-class women are entering the workforce in ever-increasing numbers. More than 50% of U.S. women are now employed outside the home, and it is estimated that by the year 2000 between 80% and 90% of women will be in the workforce. One consequence of this social movement is that increasing numbers of infants and young children are being cared for outside the home. Current estimates place the number of children under the age of 6 who are receiving one or another form of out-of-home care at six million.

The conception of the competent infant is clearly more in keeping with these contemporary family styles than is the conception of the sensual infant. A competent infant can cope with the separation from parents at an early age. He or she is able to adjust with minimal difficulty to baby sitters, day-care centers, full-day nursery schools, and so on. If some parents feel residual pangs of guilt about leaving their young offspring in out-of-home care, they can place their youngster in a high-pressure academic program. If the child were not in such a program, the parents tell themselves, he or she would fall behind peers and would not be able to compete academically when it is time to enter kindergarten. From this perspective, high-pressure academic preschool programs are for the young child's "own good."

The social dynamics behind the pressure to place young children in educational programs appropriate for school-age children now become painfully clear. The truth is that the many changes in our society have not been accompanied by adequate provisions for the out-of-home care of all the young children who require it. Consequently, parents are putting pressure on elected officials to provide more early childhood care. This has been the primary motivation for full-day kindergartens, starting school at age 4, and so on. Although the avowed reasons for these proposals are to be found in "new" research showing the need for early childhood education, the "new" data consist of nothing more than the "old" (and always dubious) data from the 1960s. The real reason for these programs is that elected officials are feeling pressure from voters to offer out-of-home care for young children.

There is another motive for introducing formal instruction in early childhood programs. This comes from our intuitive psychology regarding technology and human behavior. Much intuitive psychology derives from emotions and feelings rather than from reason and balanced judgment. Nonetheless, such intuitions seem so obviously correct that one thinks it foolish even to question them. (The so-called "gambler's fallacy" is a case in point: the gambler believes that the number of previous losses increases his or her probability of winning, while, in fact, there is no relationship between the two.)

The intuition regarding human behavior and technology is equally fallacious. The intuition is that human potentials are altered by technology. With respect to children, this intuition is often expressed by saying that, thanks to such innovations as television and computers, children today are brighter and more sophisticated than children in the past. This intuition has reinforced and supported the conception of the competent infant and has been used to rationalize the formal instruction of preschool children.

Technology, however, neither changes human potential nor accelerates human development. Technology extends and amplifies our human potentials, but it does not alter them. The telephone extends our hearing; television extends our vision; computers extend our memories. But neither our capacity for hearing, nor our capacity for seeing, nor our capacity for remembering have been changed by the technology. Modern weaponry may have amplified our ability to express our aggression, but it has neither heightened nor lessened our tendency to be aggressive. There is simply no truth in the intuitive belief that technology alters human potential.

Exactly the same holds true with respect to children. Computers have not improved children's intellectual capacities; they have only amplified the limitations of young children's thinking. Consider "turtle geometry," an application of the computer language Logo, created by Seymour Papert for use with preschool and school-age children.[7] Children learn to write programs that move the cursor in different directions to draw figures on a video screen. The sequence of directions then becomes an elementary program for drawing the figure. One instruction, however, gives young children a great deal of trouble. This is the instruction to rotate the cursor in different directions without moving it. Young children do not easily understand that you can change direction while standing still, and they have difficulty grasping this command. Thus the use of the technology only amplifies the limitations of young children's thinking.

Television provides another example. Programs such as "Sesame Street" and "The Electric Company" were supposed to make learning to read easier for young children. However, the rapid presentation of material on these programs is much too fast for the information-processing abilities of young children. It could be that these programs, geared to the information-processing speeds of adults and older children, have amplified the attentional limitations of young children, with negative consequences for their reading abilities.

We miseducate children whenever we put them at risk for no purpose. Formal instruction puts excessive demands on young children.

These programs have been on the air for almost 20 years, and during that time "attentional deficits" have become the leading form of learning disability. Yet most people continue to believe that these programs have improved children's reading abilities. Such intuitive belief that children today are brighter and more sophisticated than previous generations tops off the list of commonly accepted reasons for the formal instruction of young children.

THE HARM OF EARLY INSTRUCTION

What harm is there in exposing young children to formal instruction involving the inculcation of symbolic rules? The harm comes from what I have called "miseducation."[8] We miseducate children whenever we put them at risk for no purpose. The risks of miseducating young children are both short- and long-term. The short-term risks derive from the stress, with all its attendant symptoms, that formal instruction places on children; the long-term risks are of at least three kinds: motivational, intellectual, and social. In each case, the potential psychological risks of early intervention far outweigh any potential educational gain.

Short-term risks. Stress is a demand for adaptation. In this broad sense, of course, stress is coincident with life itself. In a narrower, clinical sense, however, stress refers to any excessive demand for adaptation. What is excessive, in turn, depends on both the individual and the demands made.

Elsewhere I have suggested that each individual has two sources of energy with which to cope with stress.[9] One of these is what I call "clock energy." This

is the energy that we use up in pursuing the tasks of daily living, and it is replenished by food and rest. By contrast, what I call "calendar energy" is the energy involved in growth and development that is given us in a more or less fixed quantity and that determines our total life span.

The early symptoms of stress are those associated with clock energy: fatigue, loss of appetite, and decreased efficiency. When the excessive demands continue without adequate time for replenishment, an individual must draw on his or her calendar energy. When this happens, such psychosomatic stress symptoms as headaches and stomachaches that can injure the organism and shorten the life span begin to appear. In young children exposed to formal instruction, both types of stress symptoms are frequently seen.

The reason for this is not difficult to understand. Formal instruction puts excessive demands on young children. A concrete example may help make this point. The learning of young children is "permeable" in the sense that they do not learn in the narrow categories defined by adults, such as reading, math, science, and so on. At the level at which young children learn, there are no sharp boundaries. When young children make soup, for example, they learn the names of vegetables (language), how to measure ingredients (math), the effects of heat on the hardness and softness of the vegetables (science), and the cross-sectional shapes of the vegetables (geometry). It would be nonsense, however, to single out any one of these learnings as a separate lesson in any of the subjects listed in parentheses.

The focus on a specific learning task, as demanded by formal instruction, is thus at variance with the natural mode of learning of the young child. From the viewpoint of formal instruction, the multiple learning potential of the young child is seen as evidence of distractability or the currently more fashionable phrase, attentional deficit. The pressure to focus on one avenue of learning, such as letter or word identification, is very stressful for young children. Pediatricians around the country report an increase in stress-related symptoms in young children.[10] A pediatrician I met at a meeting of the National Academy of Pediatrics told me that he is treating a 4-year-old who has peptic ulcers.

To be sure, formal instruction is but one of the many demands made on a young child in a formal program of education. The child is also separated from his or her parents, a second stress; is in a new and unfamiliar place with strange children and adults, a third stress; and is required to learn new rules of conduct, still another stress. Although the demands of formal instruction may not be sufficient in themselves to overstrain the young child's reservoir of clock energy, the combination of stresses associated with formal schooling can be sufficient to produce symptoms.

By contrast, young children in a sound program of early childhood education have the support of activities nicely suited to their learning styles. This eliminates the stresses occasioned by the curriculum and the stilted teacher/student interactions inherent in formal instruction.

Long-term effects. One long-term danger of early instruction is the potential harm it can do to the child's motivation to learn. In addition to being permeable, the spontaneous learning of young children is self-directed. Children learn their native language not because anyone "teaches" them that language in a formal way but because they have both the need and the capacity to learn language. They use the language models and verbal interactions provided by their environment to acquire this most complicated skill. Young children have their own set of learning priorities.

Certainly some things need to be taught to very young children. For example, they need to learn what might be called the "healthy" fears: for example, not to touch fire, not to insert fingers in electrical sockets, and not to cross streets without looking both ways. Such learning is not self-directed, but it is necessary for survival. On the intellectual plane, however, children's natural curiosity about the world around them is a strong directive for learning the basic categories and concepts of the physical world. Sound early childhood education encourages children's self-directed learning by providing an environment that is rich in materials to explore, manipulate, and talk about.

When adults intrude in this self-directed learning and insist on their own learning priorities, such as reading or math, they interfere with the self-directed impulse. Children can learn something from this instruction, but it may be something other than what the adults intended. A child may learn to become dependent on adult direction and not to trust his or her own initiative. Erik Erikson has described early childhood as the period when the balance is struck between the sense of initiative

and the sense of guilt.[11] *And this balance has consequences for a lifetime.*

A child whose self-directed learning is encouraged will develop a sense of initiative that will far outweigh a sense of guilt about getting things started. On the other hand, a child whose self-directed learning is interfered with, who is forced to follow adult learning priorities, may acquire a strong sense of guilt about *any* self-initiated activities. One risk of early formal instruction, then, is that it may encourage a sense of guilt at the expense of a sense of initiative.

Let me recount an anecdote to make this risk concrete. Several years ago I met a renowned psychiatrist who told me the following story. In the 1930s, psychologist Myrtle McGraw carried out what has become a classic study of the contributions of nature and nurture to motor development.[12] McGraw's study involved twin boys, Johnny and Jimmy. In her study, McGraw trained one of the twins, Johnny, in a variety of motor tasks, such as riding a tricycle and climbing. Jimmy was not trained. Johnny soon surpassed Jimmy in the skills in which he had been trained. On the other hand, after the training was discontinued, Jimmy quickly caught up with his brother, so that, by the end of the year in which the training was initiated, there was no difference in the motor skills of the twins. In motor learning, maturation appeared to be at least as important as training.

What the psychiatrist told me, however, was that he had seen the twins several years after the investigation had been completed. When he examined the boys, he found a striking difference in their personalities and, particularly, in their approach to learning. Johnny, the twin who had been trained, was diffident and insecure. He seemed always to be looking for adult direction and approval of his activities. Jimmy, the untrained twin, was quite the opposite. Self-confident and self-assured, he undertook activities on his own without looking to adults for guidance and direction. Though this example is anecdotal, it does illustrate the potential risk of too much adult intervention in the self-directed learning of young children.

Early formal instruction also puts the child at intellectual risk. Jean Piaget emphasized the importance of what he called "reflective abstraction" for the mental ability of the child.[13] A child who is engaging in self-directed learning can reflectively abstract from those activities. That reflective abstraction encourages the growth of new mental

abilities. Piaget cited the example of a child who is rearranging 10 pebbles. First, the child makes them into a square, then into a circle, and next into a triangle. What the child discovers, as a result of that activity, is that no matter how he or she arranges the pebbles they still remain 10 in number. In effect, the child has learned the difference between perception and reason. Perceptually, it appears as if there are more pebbles in one configuration than in another. Reason tells the child that they are the same.

When adults intrude on a child's learning, they also interfere with the process of reflective abstraction. Formal instruction presents the child with some content to be learned. Flash cards present the child with a visual configuration that the child must first discriminate and then memorize. Teaching young children phonics is another example of presenting the child with an association that he or she must learn without much active intervention or exploration. Rote learning and memorization, the stuff of much formal education, provide little opportunity for reflective abstraction. Such reflective abstraction, however, is essential for the full realization of a child's cognitive abilities.

Introducing formal instruction too early also puts the child at social risk. One aspect of formal instruction — thankfully absent in sound early childhood education — is the introduction of the notions of "correct" and "incorrect." These notions not only orient the child's thinking but also introduce social comparison. One child gets an answer right, and another gets it wrong. Therefore, one child is smarter, somehow better than the other. Such social comparisons are harmful enough among school-age children, but they are truly damaging among preschoolers.

This damage can occur because the focus on right and wrong turns the child away from self-directed and self-reinforcing sources of self-esteem. Instead, it directs children to look primarily to adults for approval and to social comparison for self-appraisal. This works against the formation of self-esteem that a child attains from successfully completing a self-initiated and self-directed task. From the point of view of socialization, the danger of early instruction is that it can make children too dependent on others for their sense of self-worth. Sound early childhood education encourages children to feel good about themselves as a consequence of their own achievements.

To be sure, the foregoing descriptions

of damage to motivation, intellectual growth, and self-esteem are potential risks that are not always realized in every child who is miseducated. But why put a child at risk in the first place? There is really no evidence that early formal instruction has any lasting or permanent benefits for children. By contrast, the risks to the child's motivation, intellectual growth, and self-esteem could well do serious damage to the child's emerging personality. It is reasonable to conclude that the early instruction of young children derives more from the needs and priorities of adults than from what we know of good pedagogy for young children.

WHAT CAN WE DO?

The miseducation of young children, so prevalent in the United States today, ignores the well-founded and noncontroversial differences between early childhood education and formal education. As educators, our first task is to reassert this difference and insist on its importance. We have to reeducate parents, administrators, and legislators re-

garding what is sound education for young children. And we must make it clear that it is not out-of-home care for young children that is potentially harmful — only the wrong kind of out-of-home care. Sound early childhood education is an extension of the home, not of the school.

As a profession, we have no choice but to go public. Those who are making money from the miseducation of young children are the ones about whom parents hear and read the most. We need to write for popular magazines, speak out on television forums, and encourage newspaper articles about the difference between good early childhood education and miseducation. We are in a war for the well-being of our children, and in this war the media are our most powerful weapon. It is a war we can never absolutely win, no matter how hard we fight. But, unless we fight as hard as we can, it is a war we will certainly lose.

1. Sheldon H. White, "Some General Outlines of the Matrix of Developmental Changes Between 5 and 7 Years," *Bulletin of the Orton Society*, vol. 20, 1970, pp. 41-57.
2. See, for example, Glen Doman, *Teach Your Baby to Read* (London: Jonathan Cape, 1965); Peggy Eastman and John L. Barr, *Your Child Is Smarter Than You Think* (New York: Morrow, 1985); and Sidney Ledson, *Teach Your Child to Read in 60 Days* (Toronto: Publishing Company, Ltd., 1975).
3. Sigmund Freud, "Infantile Sexuality," in A. A. Brill, ed., *The Basic Writings of Sigmund Freud* (New York: Random House, 1938).
4. Jerome Bruner, *The Process of Education* (Cambridge, Mass.: Harvard University Press, 1960).
5. Benjamin S. Bloom, *Stability and Change in Human Characteristics* (New York: Wiley, 1964).
6. James McV. Hunt, *Intelligence and Experience* (New York: Ronald Press, 1961).
7. Seymour Papert, *Mindstorms* (New York: Basic Books, 1980).
8. David Elkind, *The Miseducation of Children: Superkids at Risk* (New York: A.A. Knopf, 1986).
9. David Elkind, *All Grown Up and No Place to Go: Teenagers in Crisis* (Reading, Mass.: Addison-Wesley, 1984).
10. T. Berry Brazelton, quoted in E.J. Kahn, "Stressed for Success," *Boston Magazine*, December 1985, pp. 178-82, 255-57.
11. Erik H. Erikson, *Childhood and Society* (New York: Norton, 1950).
12. Myrtle B. McGraw, *A Study of Johnny and Jimmy* (New York: Appleton-Century-Crofts, 1935).
13. Jean Piaget, *The Psychology of Intelligence* (London: Routledge & Kegan Paul, 1950).

Developmentally Appropriate Education for 4-Year-Olds

David Elkind

David Elkind is professor of child study and senior resident scholar at Tufts University.

The education of 4-year-old children in our public schools is a social experiment with consequences for the entire society. The kind of education young children receive in the early years does make a difference later (Miller & Bizzell, 1983; Schweinhart, Weikart, & Larner, 1986). In my opinion, developmentally appropriate education gives young children the wherewithal to succeed in school and become productive members of society. I believe that teaching young children in a didactic way, as if they were miniature second or third graders, can have lasting negative effects on their academic careers and their successful adaptation to the larger society. Accordingly, in this article I present the developmental approach to early childhood education, which I believe has the best chance of providing children from all walks of life the best start in schooling.

To present this approach, I elaborate on three principles that are the foundation upon which developmental early childhood teaching practices are based. The first principle is multi-age grouping, which derives from the normal variability among young children. The second is nongraded curricular materials, which can be used with profit by children

at different developmental levels. The third is interactive teaching, in which the teacher serves as a matchmaker between child and materials. Effective interactive teaching means the teacher must have a solid understanding of both the intellectual demands of the materials and the cognitive abilities of the children.

The Variability of Young Children

Young children are extremely variable with respect to their levels of intellectual, emotional, and social development. A child learning to walk, for example, may not talk until walking is mastered. Another child may do exactly the reverse. Neither child is really slow in the neglected domain. Young children attend to only one skill at a time and the other will receive its due in good time.

Despite these clear differences, children's age levels are often characterized in an all-encompassing way, such as the "terrible twos." The 4-year-old age has sometimes been called the period of *Trotzalter*,[1] the age of pride. Such catch phrases fail to recognize the variability of young children

D. Elkind, "Developmentally Appropriate Education for 4-Year-Olds," *Theory Into Practice, 28*(1), Winter 1989, pp. 47-52. (Theme is on "Public Schooling At 4?") Copyright © 1989, College of Education, The Ohio State University.

and are counterproductive in planning educational programs for these children. The variability of young children requires a closer look.

In the Darwinian scheme of things, variability plays a crucial role. The variability among members of the same species makes evolution possible. As environmental conditions change, variability permits those members of the species with traits adapted to the new circumstances to survive. A phenomenon called "industrial melanism" is a nice example of how variability within a species enables it to adapt to a rather abrupt change in the environment:

> During the last hundred years many different species of moths have become virtually black in industrial towns, while remaining light and protectively colored in the countryside. In these species, the melanics, or dark forms, are much hardier than the normals, but these—the light ones— are better concealed from their enemies in the unblackened countryside. So they have a selective advantage there, while the melanics are better able to resist the smoke and contamination of the industrial areas. (Huxley, 1953, p. 39)

Variability, then, makes it possible for a species to adapt to changing environmental circumstances. In most cases, this process is a gradual one as the process of variation and natural selection takes place over many generations.

I raise the issue of variability in this way, because putting 4-year-olds in school is a fairly abrupt alteration of their environment. Putting 4-year-olds in school will favor some variations more than others. Children who are socially inclined will respond positively to the availability of same-age peers. Other children, more inclined to solitary pursuits, may find this early entrance to a school setting disruptive and uncomfortable. This situation is neither bad nor good, right nor wrong. Children who are socially inclined, for example, are the ones who are deprived when 4-year-olds are not in school.

Another significant facet of variability for the issue of 4-year-olds at school has to do with certain periods in the development of our species when the range of variability is greater than at other periods. At some point in the evolution of human species, when we were much more subject to environmental control than is true today, this variability made good adaptive sense. A period during which members of the species displayed the full range of variations maximized the options for selection.

The reason for an increased range of variation at early adolescence is easy to fit within evolutionary theory. It is the period prior to sexual activity and procreation. It is thus a critical period for the selection of traits that will be passed on to the next generations. A wide display of traits makes possible the selection of those best suited to survival in the environment at that time. Up until recent times and the increased life span, families were begun in adolescence. Juliet was 13 when she and Romeo shared their fate. The display of variability in early

adolescence is less adaptive today when many couples are waiting until young adulthood and later to form families. On the other hand, other forms of variability such as motivation and intellectual prowess may not emerge until later in life and these may be the adaptive traits necessary to survival in our society.

The wide range of variation at the early childhood level, however, is harder to fit within an evolutionary perspective. Clearly mate selection does not take place at this period, so why the display of variability? It may have to do with another concept within biology, namely, redundance. We are formed with a great deal of potential redundancy. We can survive with one eye, one ear, or with part of our colon removed. Even our brains can make up for early injury according to the principle of vicarious functioning. The display of variation in early childhood may be a form of redundancy, a precursor to variational displays of adolescence, which could serve as a kind of preselection even before adolescence.

Whatever the explanation, the range of variation in early childhood is greater than it will be in later childhood or in adulthood. Children of the same age vary greatly in social, intellectual, and emotional maturity. Although it is convenient to attribute these variations to variations in child rearing practices, this may be too facile an explanation. We have been made aware by infancy research (e.g., Waters, Vaughn, & Egeland, 1980) that children can shape parental behavior as much as parents can shape child behavior. If some children are treated differently from others, they may have evoked different treatments on the part of their parents.

Multi-Age Grouping

I have gone on at considerable length about variability and stressed its biological underpinnings for a reason. As educators, many of us have trouble dealing with variability. We would like all children of a given age to be at a given place intellectually. Then we can proceed with our lesson plans and our course of instruction. Children who are ahead, behind, or somewhere on the outskirts of the group present a problem. They take extra time and effort, both of which are in short supply. While such an attitude may be understandable, given the pressures on teachers, it cannot really be justified at any level of education and is least justified at periods of wide displays of variability.

The alternative to rigid age grading of children and curricula is multi-age grouping. This means having 4-, 5-, and perhaps 6-year-old children in the same classroom. The advantages to this arrangement are many. First, the advanced 4-year-olds can be grouped with the slower 5-year-olds for certain activities. Second, older children can be used to tutor the younger children, an important and beneficial learning experience for both sides. Third, the teacher gets to really know the children and can determine when they are ready to move ahead to more complex learning materials and activities. Much information is lost when, after a year, a teacher has to pass the child to another teacher who has to start from scratch.

Multi-age grouping has drawbacks. One teacher must master the curricula for two or three developmental levels. But since much overlapping occurs at these ages, the problem is not serious. A drawback from the child's point of view is the possibility of having a teacher who is not the best for 2 or 3 years. A third drawback is the resistance of parents who do not mind when their children are the youngest in the class but become concerned when they are the oldest. They wonder whether their children are receiving sufficient intellectual stimulation.

None of these problems are insurmountable and the benefits of multi-age grouping considerably outweigh them. Teachers who have taught this way generally prefer it and are reluctant to go back to single grade teaching.

Multi-age grouping is thus the most effective way of addressing the natural variability of young children. Any program for 4-year-olds that does not take account of the wide range of normal and expectable variations in their physical, social, emotional, and intellectual maturity amounts to developmentally inappropriate practice. Indeed, such practice can result in miseducation for some children to the extent that it puts children at risk for short-term stress and long-term learning difficulties (Elkind, 1987).

Developmentally Appropriate Curricula

As the foregoing discussion indicates, the primary characteristic of developmentally appropriate curricular materials for young children is that they are ungraded and can serve children at different levels of development. Effective early education classrooms are furnished with materials that have appeal for, and can be used with profit by, children at several age levels. What and how these materials are deployed in providing an appropriate environment for young children is described below.

A classroom for young children is usually arranged in interest areas. One such area is the reading or language space. This area usually contains a book rack with a wide range of books including fairy tales, poetry, and good children's fiction. Also to be found in this area are large cushions, perhaps even a child-sized rocker, tape recorder, and record player. This area can be used by individual children, small groups, or the entire class. Such an interest area can serve children at many different levels of language proficiency.

Another area is the block corner. A substantial set of large wooden blocks is an essential curriculum material for young children. Like books, blocks are naturally ungraded materials. Two-year-old children as well as 5-year-olds can enjoy and learn a

great deal from block play. Two-year-olds, for example, gain considerable motor control from handling blocks and placing one on top of another. They also learn spatial concepts such as on top of, behind, and in front of. Later, these concepts will provide the underpinnings for learning the prepositional terms to represent these motor concepts.

Five-year-olds, in contrast, use blocks creatively to express their ordering of the world. Erikson (1951), for example, showed that boys and girls construct different types of block buildings. Boys often build towers and are curious to see how tall they can make them before they topple. In contrast, girls tend to build structures such as enclosed courtyards. For this age group, block play is a way of expressing an emerging sense of self and sexual identity. Inasmuch as 5-year-olds play with blocks in groups, it reinforces their learning of social skills such as cooperation and turn-taking.

Another area that is equally nongraded is the science and math space. Such an area might be outfitted with a water and/or sand table and a cupboard filled with science materials. These materials would include magnets, magnifying glasses, balance scales, different sized weights, and a variety of materials for counting and seriating according to size, color, and thickness. Young children can begin to learn the names of the colors and geometric shapes. Older children can begin to explore which materials float or are attracted by magnets.

Regarding science at the preschool and elementary school levels, a caveat is in order. All science begins with observation. Every science goes through a natural history stage of inquiry where the basic phenomena of the discipline are classified and organized. In some disciplines such as astronomy and paleontology it is hard to go much further. Experimentation, on the other hand, is the most advanced stage of a science and only comes into play once classification has advanced to the point of unit measurement. While experimentation is the most developed stage, it should not be equated with science itself, which includes all levels of a discipline.

This point is necessary because of the tendency in education to rush children into performing "experiments." So long as this term is used in a metaphorical way, such as a teacher putting light and heavy objects into water to determine which float and which do not, no harm is done. This is an experiment in the sense that one is asking a question of nature in a way that can be answered by observation. But this exploration is not a true experiment involving measurement and control of variables in order to test a hypothesis. Yet it is just such experiments that teachers sometimes attempt to convey to children, even at the preschool level.

Attempts to teach experimentation to young children is a good example of age-inappropriate teaching practice and miseducation. Young children do not have a true sense of quantity, so measurement is beyond them. They have difficulty keeping two dimensions in mind simultaneously, so the concept of control is meaningless to them. By presenting children with experiments at an early age, one runs the risk of confusing them and discouraging them from actively exploring materials with the aim of description and classification.

In fact, encouraging children to describe and classify is one of the most important science skills we can teach them. It provides a solid basis for their later science experiences. Moreover, because children are natural observers and classifiers, they enjoy this activity and carry this liking on to more advanced forms of scientific endeavor. In science, as in so many other curricular domains, earlier is not better. When we help children realize their skills as naturalists, we are doing more to encourage their scientific curiosity and enthusiasm for science than they would ever get from observing formal experiments.

From this perspective, the presence of plants and animals in the early childhood classroom is essential. Plants and animals provide materials for children to describe, classify, and draw. In this way they can discover the natural course of growth. Children also learn responsibility when they begin to take care of plants and animals. Having children plant seeds and watch them grow is another concrete science experience for children that is enjoyable as well as instructive. If the animals procreate, this provides still another arena for observation and discussion. Artificial experiments need not be imported into the early childhood classroom. A well outfitted classroom contains a multitude of opportunities for scientific observation, classification, and discussion.

Another nongraded curricular area is a space for dramatic play. This area can have discarded adult clothing such as hats, shirts, shoes, and scarves. Empty food cartons provide materials for playing store, while outdated phones and typewriters can be the starting point for playing office. Children of different age levels can play with and enjoy these materials, although the older children will engage in more elaborate dramas than the younger, whose dramatic play is more imitative.

Although dramatic play has many personal benefits for children as an expression of their competence to play adult roles and work effectively with other children, they learn much else as well. Such play encourages cooperation and role taking, gives children an opportunity to use and display the full range of their vocabularies, and often involves them in active use of their numerical and motor skills. Play for young children is an essential part of the curriculum that allows for personal expression as well as teaching socially adaptive dispositions.

The foregoing description in no way exhausts the range of materials appropriate for young children. Indeed, I have not even ventured to describe the outside play area, which would demand a separate discussion. What I have tried to emphasize is that the criterion for good early childhood education materials is that they be appropriate for children at different age levels. As such the materials are somewhat less structured and more open ended than curricula at later educational levels. What the materials demand, as will be seen in the next section, is a great deal of skill on the part of teachers in using them effectively.

Interactive Teaching

Although the basic trappings of good early childhood education programs have not changed much over the years, our knowledge of how to use those trappings most effectively has grown manyfold. In part this derives from the work of Piaget and Inhelder (e.g., Inhelder & Piaget, 1964) and those who have extended their work to young children (e.g., Kamii & Williams, 1986); and in part it derives from the influence of Montessori education, which has grown extensively and which puts heavy emphasis on training teachers in the use of manipulative materials (e.g., Montessori, 1917/1965).[2]

The effective use of the nongraded materials of the early childhood classroom requires both a knowledge of the intellectual demands and derivatives of the materials and an understanding of the child's cognitive level. With this knowledge the teacher can serve as a kind of matchmaker between the child and the materials. In effect the teacher introduces the child to the materials, gets a "conversation" going between them, and then discreetly moves out of the scene. It is this sort of teaching that I call *interactive*.

To make this concept more concrete, I would like to deal with teaching practices in the domain of number. Familiarity with Piaget's work on the child's conception of number (Piaget, 1952) is basic to effective interactive teaching in this domain. Piaget argued that although we may have only one word for number, there are several different levels of numerical understanding that are obscured by our imprecise language.

The child's first understanding of number is *nominal* in the sense that at this stage number is no more than a name. A number on a football or baseball player's jersey is an example of a nominal number. Next, by the age of 4, most children grasp *ordinal* number, used to designate a rank, e.g., when we say someone came in third in a race. The runner's position tells us nothing with regard to how far behind the other two runners the third runner was, only that the third runner came in behind the first two runners. The runner could have been 2 seconds, 2 minutes, or 2 hours behind the second runner but the numerical rank would remain the same.

Finally, by the age of 6 or 7, most children attain a *true* or *interval* concept of number in the sense that they now have a unit concept of number.

What sets the unit concept apart from the nominal and ordinal number is the awareness of equal intervals. Using an interval scale, a runner who came in third would also have a time designation that would indicate the length of time behind the next runner. Once children understand units as representing equal intervals, they can fully grasp the basic units and operations of arithmetic.

How then does a young child progress to this interval, or unit, concept of number? Piaget's research and that of others (e.g., Kamii, 1982) make clear that the child progresses toward a unit concept of number by engaging in a great deal of classification and seriation (ordering size, intensity, etc.). Young children can classify a few elements and progress to larger numbers of elements as they mature.

What does such classification and seriation have to do with the child's attainment of number? A good deal. A unit concept, the idea of equal intervals, is gleaned from combining the classification and seriation relationships. What children gain from classifying many different things, in addition to the discriminations involved, is the more general notion of sameness, just as they learn the concept of difference from seriating materials that vary in amount. Eventually, they put together the concepts of sameness and difference that together constitute the unit concept. A unit, a number, is both like every other number (the sameness relation) yet different from it (the difference relation). The number 3 is different from every other number in the sense that it is the only number that comes before 4 and after 2. But it is also like every other number in that it is a number.

Armed with this knowledge and a sense of where children are with respect to classification and seriation the teacher is in a position to engage in interactive instruction. The teacher will provide materials for classification and seriation matched to the child's level of ability, and then model how these materials are to be used and provide verbal labels where appropriate. Once children have mastered the classification and seriation skills, they can extend them on their own to a larger number of elements and a wide variety of materials. They can also choose the times when they wish to engage in this activity. The aim of interactive teaching is to get children started in the right way, but then for them to take over and be responsible for their own learning.

Interactive teaching is not easy. Finding materials that are neither too structured nor too open is always a struggle. Materials need enough structure to give children guidance, but also enough openness to pose a challenge to their intelligence. In the same way, the teacher is constantly searching for words and phrasing that will get children started on the activity and give them direction without unduly constraining their manipulations of the materials. Moreover, the teacher has to be aware of individual differences and what types of materials

and verbalizations are most appropriate for particular children or groups of children.

Summary and Conclusion

This article has described three major principles, or goals, with respect to the education of 4-year-old children in the public schools. First, early childhood is a period of increased variability, which is a species characteristic as much or more than a product of diverse child rearing. Any group of young children will be much more variable intellectually, socially, and emotionally than it will be at, say, age 10. The most effective way to deal with this variability is multi-age grouping. Such grouping enables the teacher to move children along at their own pace rather than trying to force them into a rigidly age-graded curriculum.

The second principle is that the curriculum materials and activities for young children should be nongraded in the sense that they can be engaged in with profit by children from 2 to 5. A good set of wooden blocks can be used by 2-year-olds to acquire basic spatial concepts whereas older children can use them to express an emerging sense of identity as well as to learn a number of social skills. Reading materials including fairy tales, poetry, and children's fiction are examples of nongraded material in the sense that children of many different age levels can enjoy and profit from them.

A final principle or goal of educational programs for young children is that the teaching be interactive. In such instruction the teacher serves as a matchmaker between the child and the materials. An effective match depends on the teacher's knowledge of the demands and cognitive derivatives of the materials and the child's cognitive strengths and weaknesses. Once a match is made, the teacher must know how to move to the background and let the relationship between child and materials develop. While these principles may be considered ideal and difficult to achieve, ideals are important to guide us in our efforts to provide the best possible education for the increasing numbers of young children in our schools. A quiet reading corner in a classroom, a bit of matchmaking between a child and a book or puzzle, can mean a lot to a young learner.

In the end, of course, the principles of healthy education at the early childhood level are the principles of sound pedagogy at all grade levels. If we institute solid programs of early childhood education in our schools, perhaps we can improve the quality of schooling for all students.

Notes

1. The term *Trotzalter* is a combination of two German words, *Trotz,* used in the sense of pride, and *alter* or age. The term was used frequently by German child psychologists such as the Buhlers.
2. The Waldorf school movement, which is becoming a force on the national scene, is another early childhood

program that emphasizes manipulatives (e.g., Edmunds, 1979).

References

Edmunds, F. (1979). *Rudolf Steiner education.* London: Rudolf Steiner Press.

Elkind, D. (1987). *Miseducation: Preschoolers at risk.* New York: Knopf.

Erikson, E. (1951). Sex differences in the play configurations of pre-adolescents. *American Journal of Orthopsychiatry, 21,* 667-692.

Huxley, J. (1953). *Evolution in action.* New York: Signet.

Inhelder, B., & Piaget, J. (1964). *The early growth of logic in the young child.* New York: Norton.

Kamii, C. (1982). *Number in preschool and kindergarten: Educational implications of Piaget's theory.* Washington, DC: National Association for the Education of Young Children.

Kamii, C., & Williams, C.K. (1986). How do children learn by handling objects? *Young Children, 42*(1), 23-26.

Miller, L.B., & Bizzell, R.P. (1983). Long term effects of four preschool programs: 6th, 7th and 8th grades. *Child Development, 54,* 725-741.

Montessori, M. (1965). *Spontaneous activity in education.* New York: Schocken. (Original work published 1917)

Piaget, J. (1952). *The child's conception of number.* London: Routledge & Kegan Paul.

Schweinhart, L.J., Weikart, D.P., & Larner, M.B. (1986). Consequences of three preschool curriculum models through age 15. *Early Childhood Research Quarterly, 1,* 15-45.

Waters, E., Vaughn, B.E., & Egeland, B. (1980). Individual differences in infant mother attachment relationships at age one: Antecedents in neonatal behavior in an urban, economically disadvantaged sample. *Child Development, 51,* 208-216.

Societal Influences on Children

Joan Isenberg

Joan Isenberg is Associate Professor of Education, George Mason University, Fairfax, VA.

Today's youth live in a fast-paced, changing world characterized by social pressures that push them to grow up too fast. They are pressured to adapt to changing family patterns, to achieve academically at early ages, and to participate and compete in sports and specialized skills. Moreover, they are pressured to cope with adult information in the media before they have mastered the problems of childhood. Such pressure places increased responsibility and stress on children while simultaneously redefining the essence of childhood itself (Berns, 1985; Postman, 1985; Damon, 1983; Suransky, 1982; Elkind, 1981).

Both educators and psychologists are expressing concern over the impact of these changes on children. In examining the pressures of contemporary society, Elkind (1981) labels today's child "the hurried child," pushed by adults to succeed too soon thereby increasing the likelihood of failure. Others (Winn, 1983; Postman, 1982) contend that the media have contributed to the disappearance of childhood through "adultification" of children in television, films and literature. And Suransky (1982) believes the very concept of childhood is eroding through the institutionalization of early learning environments that deprive children of their right to discover, create and invent by imposing preschool curricula unrelated to their development and interests.

Because children are shaped and molded largely by the expectations of the institutions society creates for them, the social context in which they grow deeply affects their development. Erikson's (1963) theory of studying individuals in their social contexts illustrates the importance of children's interactions and interrelationships with critical agents in their social environment. Within these agents of the family, school, peer group and media, children acquire social skills and behaviors enabling them to participate in society. Recent changes in the patterns of these settings, however, push children out of childhood too fast and threaten their basic social needs at all ages and stages of development.

To best understand how today's youth are influenced by these societal agents, this article will identify children's basic social needs, describe the social pressures affecting those needs and provide suggestions for balancing social priorities for children.

CHILDREN'S SOCIAL NEEDS

Despite the fact that children have their own unique personalities, all children have basic social needs that must be adequately met to develop a healthy sense of self (Erikson, 1963; Bronfenbrenner, 1979). Such needs form the necessary and basic conditions for children from birth through the elementary years and enable them to better meet the lifelong challenges of productive social interaction. Figure 1 outlines the critical ages and conditions for developing children's needs and their subsequent personality outcome.

SOCIAL PRESSURES AFFECTING CHILDREN'S NEEDS

Family

As the United States has moved toward urbanization, industrialization and the information age, significant changes have occurred in the structure and function of families (Bronfenbrenner, 1985a; Elkind, 1984; Umansky, 1983). We have witnessed a rise in single-parent homes, divorce, blended families and working mothers, as well as a decline in extended family homes and the birth

Figure 1—Social Needs

Need	Critical Age	Necessary Conditions	Personality Outcome
Love, Security, Stability	Infancy	Parents and caretakers provide consistent, regular and predictable care.	Develop strong sense of trust and belief in security of world. Foundation for self-confidence.
Independence	Toddlerhood	Parents and caretakers provide encouragement, freedom and choices for children to practice newly developed skills.	Grow self-confident and develop autonomy as they begin to find their own personality and self-will.
Responsi-bility	Preschool	All family members provide opportunities and encouragement for children to self-initiate exploration and discovery of their environment through projects, role-playing and taking time to answer "why" questions.	Develop sense of purpose, goal-directedness, willingness to try new things.
Competence and Success	Elementary School	Family, neighborhood and school provide opportunities for children to learn how things work and become competent and productive "tool-users" in their society.	Develop self-esteem and sense of self. Sense of competence and order.

rate. Today, approximately 20 percent of our youth live in single-parent families. Moreover, each year more than one million children experience divorce in their families (National Center for Health Statistics, 1983; Wallerstein & Kelley, 1980). Yet while the structure of families may have changed, the needs of children are still the same. The family remains their primary socializing agent.

Consequences
The dissolution of the family places additional pressure on children to adjust. Many of these children experience pressure to mature and assume increased adult responsibility (Berns, 1985; Elkind, 1981; Hetherington, 1979).

Preschool children, the most vulnerable to divorce, often do not understand the reasons given and have a strong need to identify with the absent parent. Consequently, they often feel guilty and responsible for the divorce and think that the parent left because they were bad. Elementary children may be very frightened, experience an acute

sense of shame and display anger at one or both parents. They may engage in acting-out behavior (stealing, cheating) or develop physical **symptoms (headaches, stomachaches). Early** adolescents also feel anger and depression and may act out sexually or quickly assume adult roles and responsibilities (Wallerstein & Kelley, 1976). No matter what the age, children experiencing divorce often face additional challenges along with the usual tasks of growing up. Their ability to resolve these tasks depends, in part, on their own resilience and, in part, on parental handling of the separation issues (Papalia & Olds, 1986).

In addition to family changes precipitated by single parenting, the increase in women in the labor force has contributed to the pressure on children to grow up too early. A major problem for working mothers—and, therefore, children—is the availability of adequate child care. The lack of adequate child care has given rise to a group of unsupervised children, commonly referred to as "latchkey" children. At least 7-10 million children between the ages of 7 and 13 are left unattended after school (Seligson et al., 1983). These children spend part of each day alone and take responsibility for themselves Such lack of supervision may lead to physical or psychological harm, contribute to delinquency, or produce feelings of abandonment and fear through lack of adult contact and security (Galambos & Gabarino, 1983; Herzog & Sudia, 1973). As the number of working mothers increases, the need for adequate child care also increases. Without adequate supervision, "latchkey" children are placed at risk.

Because the family is the child's first introduction to societal living, it has primary responsibility for children's socialization. How children learn to relate within the family context strongly affects their developing values, personalities and basic social needs.

Schooling

In addition to affecting the family, societal changes have affected the shape of early education. Today's parents are pushing their children to learn as much as they can earlier than ever (Spodek, 1986; *Newsweek,* 1983; Elkind, 1981). Anxious parents, influenced by mass media, believe that the earlier children begin learning academics, the more successful their school and life experience will be. Publishers are producing popular books such as *Teach Your Child To Read in 20 Minutes a Day* (Fox, 1986) and *Teach Your Child To Read in 60 Days* (Ledson, 1985), better baby videos and "teach your child at home kits." All focus on developing children's intelligence at the expense of their personal and social adjustment. Advertisements promote anxiety in parents, which is then imparted to children: "And by the time they are **2 or 3 years old, another miracle can occur—if you allow it to. They can begin reading"** (Moncure, 1985).

Today public kindergarten is available in every state. Moreover, increases in availability of preschool experiences have made the world of schooling available to children earlier (Spodek, 1986). Unfortunately, in many cases elementary school criteria and programming are being applied to programs for young children (Elkind, 1986; Suransky, 1982). Pressure to provide more formal learning and more rigorous academic content has resulted in refocusing early education: from meeting children's developmental needs in an environment generally free of social pressures to pressuring children to prepare for elementary school and later life. The notion of the "competent infant" fits into our changing lifestyles, along with the idea that children today are more sophisticated and advanced because of the nature of their experiences (Hunt, 1961; Bloom, 1964; Bruner, 1960). New importance has been attached to children's intellectual development as children are placed in high-pressure academic programs for "their own good" (Elkind, 1986).

Consequences

The pressure for early academic achievement has been criticized by child development experts not only because there is no research base to support it but also because it may impede development of other equally important skills (Spodek, 1986; Elkind, 1986; Seefeldt, 1985). Some argue that formal instruction at early ages makes unnecessary demands on children and places them in unnatural learning modes. Others argue that undue emphasis on early formal learning has the potential to diminish children's long-term motivation to learn by interfering with the natural development of their need for self-directed learning. It places children at intellectual risk by interfering with their developing reflective abstraction and at social risk by forcing them to rely on "adults for approval and . . . social comparison for self-appraisal" (Elkind, 1986, p. 636).

Pressure for academic achievement can encourage school failure. Maturity, one factor of development virtually ignored in past years, is now the subject of considerable attention. According to Friesen (1984), there is the "possibility that much of the failure in our schools is the result of overplacement, and that we might reduce the rate of failure by finding a better match between a youngster's grade assignment and his or her developmental age" (p. 14). Research supports the proposition that overplacement can be a significant cause of school failure.

"There is, of course, no evidence to support the value of such early pushing. There is, however, considerable evidence that children are showing more and more serious stress symptoms than ever before" (Elkind, 1984, p. viii). Attempting to force children at early ages to learn specific academic material or develop specific skills may produce a negative attitude toward learning in general, with serious long-term effects evidenced in increased dropout rates and a high rate of cheating (Harris, 1986; Elkind, 1982).

Peers

Peer groups provide yet another critical agent of socialization. Historically, children have relied primarily on informal peer groups, formed and maintained by themselves, to develop social roles and cooperative interests. Today, however,

Marianne Dreyspring

more and more children are engaged in formal group activities, organized and maintained by adults. Activity markers such as organized sports, beauty contests, graduations and specialized arts training—once reserved for the teen years—are rapidly being pushed down to younger and younger children. Elkind (1984) suggests that much of this "premature structuring" stems from parental need rather than concern and understanding for the child. Children pushed too soon into formal and adult organized groups often raise questions in adolescence: "Why am I doing this? Who am I doing this for? When seeking answers to these questions, children revolt in many ways when the answer is for the parent. Delinquency, school dropouts, drugs, alcohol and refusal to perform are some of the behaviors evidenced by children forced to achieve too early" (Elkind, 1982, pp. 178-179). The shift of these activity markers from adolescence to childhood creates unnecessary stress for children, causing them to develop parts of their personality and leaving other parts undeveloped (Elkind, 1984).

Consequences
Unsuccessful children pushed by parents into sports or specialized activities become discouraged and humiliated by not meeting parental expectations and may even end up hating the activity itself. Although the range of pressure is great, some feel rejected by both parents and peers for not achieving (McElroy, 1982).

The notion of competition carries with it negative aspects. Psychological damage can occur when adults stress competition over learning skills and view their children's victories, losses and performances as indicators of their personal successes or shortcomings.

Television
Because television-watching occupies more time than any other single activity except sleeping (Bee, 1985; Gerbner & Gross, 1978; Stein & Friedrich, 1975), it acts as a powerful socializing influence. By the end of high school, the average American child has watched over 20,000 hours of television, more than the number of hours spent in school (Comstock, 1975).

Television programs provide the same information to everyone, regardless of age (Postman, 1985). Information about violence, sexual activity, aggression, and physical and mental abuse is readily available and erodes the dividing line between childhood and adulthood. It places

children and adults in the same symbolic world.... All the secrets that a print culture kept from children—about sex, violence, death and human aberration—are at once revealed by media that do not and cannot exclude any audience. Thus, the media forced the entire culture out of the closet. And out of the cradle. (Postman, 1981, p. 68)

Consequences

The content of prime-time television programming and advertising can cause children to increase their aggressive behavior in the short term (NIMH, 1982) and become desensitized to violence later in life (Thomas, 1982). Viewing violent content through images, characters and plots—whether on prime-time TV, cartoons, MTV or the nightly news—discourages children from cooperating to resolve problems because they come to accept what they see as appropriate behavior (Papalia & Olds, 1986; NIMH, 1982).

Advertisements, on the other hand, glorify instant gratification both explicitly and implicitly. New products and new fads constantly bombard viewers. Advertising directed explicitly at young children can create resentment when parents refuse to purchase products; for older children, it can create unrealistic fantasies that certain products will make them more popular.

Postman (1985) argues that children view one million commercials before age 18 at a rate of 1,000 per week, most of them perpetuating a youth culture, sex and materials as a way of solving problems instantaneously. Elkind (1981) suggests that by treating children as consumers before they are wage earners, children are pressured into a kind of "hucksterism," causing "adults to treat them as more grown-up than they are" and to assume they are able to see through the deceptions of advertising and to make informed choices (p. 79).

Thus, television programming and advertising continue to erode the dividing line between childhood and adulthood by opening secrets once only available to adults, eliminating the innocence of childhood, reducing the concept of childhood, and making the adult's and child's world homogeneous (Postman, 1985, p. 292). In a world where children view adult programming and advertising, how well are our youth being nurtured? Indeed, "the children of the 80's are growing up too fast, too soon. They are being pressured to take on the physical, emotional and social trappings of adulthood before they are prepared to deal with them" (Elkind, 1981, p. xii).

BALANCING PRIORITIES FOR CHILDREN

Pushing children to grow up too early affects the very core of the social fabric that develops, sustains and connects healthy, competent children. There is an urgent need to re-weave the unravelling social fabric of significant social influences (Bronfenbrenner, 1985a, p. 10). This can be accomplished by attending to the following critical agents of socialization at the family, school and policy levels.

Family

Balance concern for academic achievement with equal concern for developing feelings of competence, confidence and self-worth.

Children's successful adjustment to family life affects their ability to adjust to the outside world. The quality of parent/child relationships is built from the means of communication used. As the structure of families changes, there is greater need for positive communication about issues that affect children's self-respect and self-regard. Through empathic listening, talking and responding—setting realistic and honest expectations and talking about fears—families can build a strong foundation for children's positive feelings about themselves.

One context for this communication is the *family meeting*, which provides opportunities for parents and children to talk about concerns, make decisions and suggest ways to solve problems. Children can assume responsibility as family members as well as have a time for "hurried lives" to engage in constructive "family time."

Balance the need for structured and professionalized activity with opportunities for play.

Probably the least understood childhood need is the need for play. Play is vital to children's intellectual, social and physical development and is "seen as a primary mode for a child who is involved in becoming" (Suransky, 1982, p. 12).

Families contribute to children's optimal development by assuring opportunities for children to generate their own play with peers. In so doing, "they are fulfilling a fundamental human activity of intentionality and purposiveness" (Suransky, 1982, p. 173). Denying children the right to play denies them their primary means of learning about themselves and their world. Lack of adequate opportunities to engage in genuine play is evident in our hurried children today (Elkind, 1981, p. 193).

Help children become critical TV-viewers.

Children can develop proper TV-viewing habits with simple guidelines. Adults can view programs with children and talk with them about what they see. In viewing TV, adults should notice those behaviors children can imitate; for example, TV characters who model caring behaviors and programs that depict women as being competent. Moreover, adults should talk to children about the programs and note the differences between make-believe and reality. They should discuss alternate ways to solve problems they see on TV, as well as the effect of commercials.

School

Establish balanced curricula that meet children's needs.

Teachers, administrators and parents must be informed about what children are expected to learn and how they learn best. They need to set high but realistic expectations for children and encourage them to do their best work without pressuring them to perform beyond their level. We need to employ sensitive teachers who promote children's abilities and who recognize the power of their pedagogic task.

Provide inservice support for teachers and administrators about school and community resources.
Schools must take responsibility for educating school personnel about realistic expectations for children and changing family patterns. School counselors must be able to support teachers and help children and families through the varied transitions of schooling and family patterns. In providing this stability and support, counselors must understand current literature and research on the changing fabric of societal institutions.

Provide courses, workshops and training sessions for parents and educators.
Both colleges and communities must provide parenting courses and teaching courses in response to the stresses of contemporary society. Educating parents about parenting is no longer a luxury; it is an imperative.

Policy

Advocate for quality and appropriate child care.
Families with children must demand high quality child care that takes into account the needs of children and their families. Whether the care occurs in or out of the home, children's social patterns and behaviors continue to form in these settings. Young children need settings that integrate play naturally, encourage their active exploration and foster a sense of trust and security. They also need caregivers who enjoy working with young children, understand their growth and development, have realistic expectations for their behavior and are responsive to parents.

School-age children need safe and supervised care in which they are involved in activities appropriate to their stage of development. They also need teachers who understand them, their families and their needs.

Parents and community members must be advocates for quality, comprehensive child care settings. An informed community must develop appropriate programs for children, its most vulnerable group.

CONCLUSION

Pressured by each of the critical socializing agents in their lives, today's children are experiencing shortened childhoods. The sources and consequences of such pressures are clear. Also clear is the urgent need to direct our efforts toward balancing priorities for children at the family, school and policy levels.

References and Other Readings
A healthy personality for each child. (1951). A digest of the factfinding report to the Midcentury White House Conference on Children and Youth. Raleigh, NC: Heath Publications Institute.

Bee, H. (1985). *The developing child,* (4th ed). Cambridge, MA: Harper & Row.

Berns, R.M. (1985). *Child, family and community.* New York: Holt, Rinehart & Winston.

Bloom, B. (1964). *Stability and change in human characteristics.* New York: Wiley.

Bronfenbrenner, U. (1985a). The parent/child relationship and our changing society. In L.E. Arnold, (Ed.), *Parents, children and change.* Lexington, MA: Lexington Books.

Bronfenbrenner, U. (1985b). *The three worlds of childhood.* Principal, 64(5), 7-11.

Bronfenbrenner, U., & Crouter, A.C. (1983). Work and family through time and space. In S.B. Kamerman & C.D. Hayes, (Eds.), *Families that work: Children in a changing world.* Washington, DC: National Academy Press.

Bronfenbrenner, U. (1979). *The ecology of human development.* Cambridge, MA: Harvard University Press.

Bruner, J. (1960). *The process of education.* Cambridge, MA: Harvard University Press.

Coleman, M., & Skeen, P. (1985). *Play, games and sport. Their use and misuse.* Childhood Education, 61(3), 192-197.

Comstock, G.A. (1975). *Effects of television on children: What is the evidence?* Santa Monica, CA: The Rand Corp., #P5412.

Damon, W. (1983). *Social and personality development: Infancy through adolescence.* New York: W.W. Norton.

Elkind, D. (1986). Formal education and early childhood education: An essential difference. *Phi Delta Kappan, 67*(9), 631-636.

Elkind, D. (1984). *All grown up and no place to go: Teenagers in crisis.* Reading, MA: Addison-Wesley.

Elkind, D. (1982, March). *Misunderstandings about how children learn.* Today's Education, 24-25.

Elkind, D. (1981). *The hurried child.* Reading, MA: Addison-Wesley.

2. DEVELOPMENT: Childhood

Erikson, E. (1963). *Childhood and society, (2nd ed.).* New York: W.W. Norton.

Fox, B.J. (1986). *Teach your child to read in 20 minutes a day.* New York: Warner.

Friesen, D. (1984). Too much too soon. *Principal, 6*(4), 14-18.

Galambos, N.L., & Garbarino, J. (1983). Identifying the missing links in the study of latchkey children. *Children Today, 40,* 2-4.

Gerbner, G., & Gross, N. (1978). Demonstration of Power. *Journal of Communication, 29,* 177-184.

Glick, P.C. (1979). Children of divorced parents in demographic perspective. *Journal of Social Issues, 35,* 170-182.

Helms, D.B., & Turner, J.S. (1986). *Exploring child behavior, (3rd ed.).* Belmont, CA: Wadsworth.

Harris, A.C. (1986). *Child development.* New York: West.

Herzog, E., & Sudia, C.E. (1973). Children in fatherless families. In B. Caldwell & H.N. Riccuti (Eds.), *Review of child development research, 3.* Chicago: University of Chicago Press.

Hetherington, E.M. (1979). Divorce: A child's perspective. *American Psychologist, 34,* 851-858.

Hetherington, E.M., Cox, M., & Cox, R. (1978). The aftermath of divorce. In J.H. Stevens, Jr. & M. Matthews (eds.), *Mother-child, father-child relations.* Washington, DC: National Association for the Education of Young Children.

Hofferth, S.L. (1979). Day care in the next decade, 1980-1990. *Journal of Marriage and the Family, 4,* 649-658.

Hoffman, L.W. (1974). Effects of maternal employment on the child: A review of the research. *Developmental Psychology, 10,* 204-228.

Hunt, J. McV. (1961). *Intelligence and experience.* New York: Ronald Press.

Ledson, S. (1985). *Teach your child to read in 60 days.* New York: Berkley.

Martens, R. (1978). *Joy and sadness in children's sports.* Champaign, IL: Human Kinetics.

McElroy, M. (1982). Consequences of perceived parental pressure on the self-esteem of youth sport participants. *American Corrective Therapy Journal, 36*(6), 164-167.

Moncure, J. (1985). *My first steps to reading.* Haddam, CT: Children's Reading Institute.

National Center for Health Statistics. (1983). *Report on marriage and divorce today, 7,* 3-4.

National Institute of Mental Health. (1982). *Television and behavior: Ten years of scientific progress and implications for the eighties.* Washington, DC: U.S. Government Printing Office.

Newsweek. (1983, March). Bringing up superbaby, p. 62.

Papalia, D.E., & Olds, S.W. (1986). *Human development, (3rd ed.).* New York: McGraw Hill.

Postman, N. (1985). The disappearance of childhood. *Childhood Education, 61*(4), 286-293.

Postman, N. (1983, March). The disappearing child. *Educational Leadership,* 10-17.

Postman, N. (1982). *The disappearance of childhood.* New York: Delacorte.

Postman, N. (1982). Disappearing childhood. *Childhood Education, 58*(2), 66-68.

Robinson, S.L. (1985). Childhood: Can it be preserved? An interview with Neil Postman. *Childhood Education, 61*(3), 337-342.

Santrock, J.W., & Wasnak, R.A. (1979). Father custody and social development in boys and girls. *Journal of Social Issues, 35,* 112-125.

Seefeldt, C. (1985). Tomorrow's kindergarten: Pleasure or pressure? *Principal, 64*(5), 12-15.

Seligman, M., Genser, A., Gannett, E., & Gray, W. (1983, December). *School-age child care: A policy report.* Wellesley, MA: Wellesley College Center for Research on Women.

Smith, R.E., & Smoll, F.L. (1978). Sport and the child: Conceptual and research perspectives. In F.L. Smoll & R.E. Smith (Eds.), *Psychological perspectives in youth sports.* New York: Wiley.

Spodek, B. (Ed.). (1986). *Today's kindergarten: Exploring the knowledge base, expanding the curriculum.* New York: Teachers College Press.

Stein, A., & Friedrich, L. (1975). Impact of television on children and youth. In E.M. Hetherington (Ed.), *Review of child development research, 5.* Chicago: University of Chicago Press.

Suransky, V.P. (1982). *The erosion of childhood. Chicago:* University of Chicago Press.

Thomas, M.H. (1982). Physiological arousal, exposure to a relatively lengthy aggressive film, and aggressive behavior. *Journal of Research in Personality, 16,* 72-81.

Umansky, W. (1983). On families and the re-valuing of childhood. *Childhood Education, 59*(4), 260-266.

Wallerstein, J.S., & Kelley, J.B. (1980). *Surviving the breakup: How children actually cope with divorce.* New York: Basic Books.

Wallerstein, J.S., & Kelley, J.B. (1975). The effects on parental divorce: Experiences of the child in later latency. *American Journal of Orthopsychiatry, 46,* 256-269.

Wallerstein, J.S., & Kelley, J.B. (1976). The effects of parental divorce: Experiences of the child in later latency. *Journal of the American Academy of Child Psychiatry, 14,* 600-616.

Winn, M. (1983). *Children without childhood.* New York: Pantheon.

The Development of Self-Concept

Janie says "I can't" a lot, often before she even tries an activity. She seems to need constant encouragement from the teacher just to try.

Timmy speaks so softly that he is rarely heard. Even the teacher sometimes does not respond to his initiatives.

Maria describes all the things she can draw as she completes her picture. She tells the teacher about waiting for her mother in the doctor's waiting room by herself and not being afraid.

Hermine H. Marshall

Hermine H. Marshall, Ph.D., is Associate Professor, Department of Elementary Education, San Francisco State University. For the past 15 years, she has been involved in research concerning self-concept and self-evaluation.

*This is one of a regular series of Research in Review columns. The column in this issue was edited by **Celia Genishi**, Ph.D., Associate Professor of Educational Theory and Practice at The Ohio State University.*

Positive self-image correlates with good mental health, good academic achievement, and good behavior.

Picture Gold

Why is it that some children try new things with enthusiasm and approach peers and adults with confidence, whereas other children seem to believe that they are incapable of succeeding in many situations? Children (and adults) behave consistently with the way they see themselves. Young children's beliefs about whether they can or cannot do things, therefore, influence how they approach new situations. In turn, their success in new situations affects the way they see themselves—in a seemingly circular process (Marsh, 1984).

Our concern with children like Janie and Timmy is justified by research that shows that low self-concept is related to poor mental health, poor academic achievement, and delinquency (e.g., Harter, 1983). But what can we learn from research that will allow us to help children approach new situations and other people with confidence?

To understand the factors that may influence the development of self-concept, we need first to be aware of the difference between such terms as *self-concept, self-image, self-esteem,* and *self-confidence.* We also need to recognize the relationships among self-concept, perceived competence, and locus of control. Based on our knowledge of factors that influence the development of positive self-concept, we can then take steps that will benefit young children.

Definitions and differentiation

We generally think of *self-concept* as the perceptions, feelings, and attitudes that a person has about himself or herself. The terms *self-concept* and *self-image* are often used interchangeably to designate a global conception of self. This global self-concept is made up of many dimensions.

One dimension is *self-esteem* (or self-

Implications and applications

Ways to explore self-concept in young children

The level of self-esteem in some children, such as those cited at the beginning of this article, is more apparent than in others. It is easy to overlook some quiet children. Nevertheless, observing a child's willingness to explore the environment and assume control of events may be a way of assessing self-esteem in preschool children. For example, watch children's responses as they approach or are presented with a new task. Do they hang back or eagerly jump in? Do they say they can't before they try?

Another way to attend to young children's self-concepts is to listen deliberately to spontaneous statements of "I can" and "I am" or "I can't." You might also try open-minded questioning techniques, such as "I would like to write about you. What can I write? . . . What else can I say about you?" Other questions that teachers of young children have found revealing are

- "What can you tell me about yourself? . . . Why is that important?"
- "What can you tell me that is best about you?"
- "What are you good at doing?"

Remember that recent but temporary events influence young children's self-concepts; therefore, judgments about self-concept or self-esteem should not be based on only one or two statements.

Ways to influence self-concept

Because most of the studies reported in this review use correlational methods that do not indicate cause and effect, we need to be cautious in making interpretations. Nevertheless, many of the findings do suggest steps likely to enhance self-concept.

Help children feel they are of value

Listen attentively to what children say. Ask for their suggestions. Soliciting and respecting children's ideas and suggestions helps children feel that they are of value.

Help children identify their own positive and prosocial behavior. When children display cooperation, helpfulness, and other prosocial behavior, give children the words to describe themselves with these terms. For example, "You are being very helpful." They may then come to see themselves in a positive manner and act accordingly. This is a positive use of the self-fulfilling prophecy.

Highlight the value of different ethnic groups. Find ways of demonstrating the value of the cultures of your group's children. Read books that include children of different cultures. Find people of various ethnic groups to share their expertise with the children. Display pictures of women, men, and children of different ethnic groups succeeding in a variety of tasks.

Help children feel they are competent

Provide experiences for children where they can succeed. For some children, we need to provide a series of tasks that can be accomplished initially with little effort but that gradually increase in difficulty. Try to relate the task to something that children already recognize they can do.

Provide new challenges and comment on positive attempts. Some children appear to need a lot of encouragement and verbal reinforcement. Encouragement and statements of confidence in the child's ability to succeed may be necessary at first. However, the effects of verbal praise and persuasion may be short-lived (Hitz & Driscoll, 1988). Children will be more likely to benefit by seeing for themselves that they can, in fact, succeed.

Teach strategies to accomplish tasks. "I can't" sometimes means "I don't know how." Rather than encouragement, children sometimes need specific instruction in par-

ticular strategies to carry out a task. Break down these strategies into smaller steps.

Allow children to carry out and complete tasks by themselves. Because self-concept reflects perceived competence, allowing children to do for themselves whatever they can is important—even when some struggle to accomplish the task is necessary. Avoid the temptation to finish a task or button coats to save time. Help them do it themselves. Doing it for them may convey to children the message that they are not competent.

Help children feel they have some control

Provide opportunities for choice, initiative, and autonomy. Provide opportunities for children to accomplish a variety of tasks at a variety of levels. Give young children simple choices: for example, which task to do first or which of two colors to use. Let children choose which song to sing or game to play next.

Avoid comparison between children. Avoid competition. The self-concept of many children suffers when comparisons between children are made. Comparison and competition point not only to winners, but also to those who have not come out on top. Support each child's accomplishments independently.

Help children learn to evaluate their own accomplishments. Children need to learn to evaluate their own performance so that they will not become dependent on adults for feelings of self-worth. Ask them what their favorite part of their picture or story is, or ask them to look at how their letters compare with those they did last month.

Help children learn interpersonal skills

Help children learn skills to enter interactions with others. Give children the words they need to express their desires and feelings. Help them learn how to enter play and how to resolve conflicts. Knowledge of how to interact appropriately with peers is likely to enhance peer acceptance and liking. This in turn, is related to children's social self-concept.

Become aware of your own expectations for children

Be open to perceiving new information about children and looking at them in new ways. Young children can surprise us. All of a sudden they seem to show new skills. Reappraise your expectations frequently. Let them know you have confidence in their ability to learn new skills.

Be aware of whether your expectations differ for girls and boys. Different expectations for girls and boys may convey cues to children about areas where it is appropriate to become competent. If we expect boys rather than girls to play with the blocks, for example, we may deprive girls of developing positive attitudes and becoming competent in skills needed for success in mathematics and certain types of problem-solving. Initiate activities in all areas that both boys and girls may explore.

worth). Self-esteem refers specifically to our self-evaluations—that is, our judgments about our own worth—whereas self-concept refers to other aspects as well—physical characteristics, psychological traits, and gender and ethnic identity. Our self-esteem may be affected by possessing culturally valued traits, such as helpfulness and honesty. It is also influenced by seeing that others perceive us as significant and worthy or possessing culturally valued traits.

Self-esteem develops in part from being able to perceive ourselves as competent. *Perceived competence* reflects our beliefs about our ability to succeed at particular tasks. According to White (1959), feelings of competence result from being able to act effectively and master one's environment. When our capacities are stretched to new heights, we feel competent.

Self-esteem and feelings of competence are related to acquiring a sense of *personal control* (Harter, 1983)—particularly in mainstream American culture. (In other cultures personal control may not be important for self-esteem.) As children perceive themselves gaining competence in a gradually widening sphere, they begin to see themselves as causal agents and are able to feel that they have greater ability to control more of their environment. This sense of personal control is often referred to as an *internal locus of control.* In contrast, external locus of control means decisions are in the hands of others or of fate.

As children develop, self-concept becomes increasingly differentiated into multiple domains. Perceptions of competence in the social skills domain become differentiated from perceptions of competence in cognitive and physical domains (Harter & Pike, 1984). Self-perceptions about interactions with peers become separated from those about interactions with parents and teachers. Cognitive or academic self-concept gradually further differentiates into math and verbal areas (Marsh, 1984).

Furthermore, the importance of each of these domains differs for individuals and families, and among cultures. A low self-evaluation in one domain, such as athletic ability, may have little effect on the individual if it is not considered important in a particular family or culture. On the other hand, in families or cultures where athletic skills are important or where skills that underpin academic ability are highly valued, low self-esteem in these culturally relevant areas may have increasingly devastating effects as children move through school (Harter, 1986).

Self-concept measurement

Unfortunately, many problems have hampered progress in understanding the development of self-concept. First, different investigators sometimes use different definitions and examine different dimensions of self-concept. This makes it difficult to compare and synthesize results from different studies (Shavelson, Hubner, & Stanton, 1976).

At the early childhood level, problems in measuring self-concept have further hindered progress. Few formal instruments are suitable for children younger than age 8, in part because of the difficulties young children have in understanding and verbalizing abstract ideas and internal processes like self-concept. In addition, the influence of momentary events on young children's self-concepts, such as a temporarily frustrating experience, often causes indicators of self-concept to vary over time and appear "unstable." Children's ability to see characteristics as stable over time develops gradually.

Furthermore, many instruments to measure self-concept have not considered developmental differences in children's levels of understanding and in how children think about themselves (Damon & Hart, 1982). Items appropriate for older elementary school children, such as "I'm not doing as well in school as I'd like to" may be meaningless for preschoolers. Other items, for example

Parents who use an "authoritative"—as opposed to an authoritarian or permissive—childrearing pattern are more likely to have children with high self-esteem.

"I'm pretty sure of myself," may be difficult for preschoolers to understand.

Rather than attempt to adapt for preschoolers instruments designed for older children, one investigation used several types of open-ended questions, asking 3- to 5-year-olds what the experimenter could "write about" each child (Keller, Ford, & Meacham, 1978). Others have used pictures of children succeeding or having difficulty with tasks (Harter & Pike, 1984).

To supplement knowledge based on research conducted with young children, we can also look at studies using older elementary children. At these age levels, self-concept is easier to measure. Although we do not know how early the relationships between self-concept and other variables such as the environment or childrearing practices begin, reviewing studies of preschool and elementary age children can give us clues about what we need to provide for young children so that they can develop a positive self-concept.

One note of caution: Much of the research on self-esteem in children has been conducted within mainstream Anglo culture. Items on self-esteem scales reflect the values of this culture. The childrearing and educational factors that have been found to be correlated with these indexes of self-esteem are, consequently, relative to this culture. Many of today's classrooms include children from diverse cultures with differing values. Therefore, we need to be sensitive to others' values and find ways of minimizing conflicts based on cultural differences.

Cognitive development and self-concept development

Preschool

The level of children's cognitive development influences self-concept development. Preschool children can often use multiple categories to describe themselves, but these categories are not yet very stable or consistent. For example, we may hear a preschooler say, "I am a boy," but "I will be a mommy when I grow up." Preschoolers' self-descriptions are also constrained by the particular events they are experiencing. A girl may say, "I'm strong. I can lift this rock." But she is not bothered if she cannot lift a chair.

In making judgments that may appear to reflect self-esteem, preschoolers' attention is often focused on the value of a specific act. A child who says, "I am a good boy" may mean "I did something good," such as share his candy. Preschoolers also appear to view themselves, as well as others, as either all good or all bad. They do not believe they can be both at the same time. The evaluation may shift to the opposite pole as the child shifts attention to

Self-esteem develops when children possess culturally valued traits and feel competent.

other actions or events (Selman, 1980).

Preschoolers see the self in both physical and action terms (Damon & Hart, 1982). When asked what an observer could "write about you," 3- to 5-year-old children most frequently described themselves in terms of physical actions, such as "I can ride a bike" or "I can help set the table" (Keller et al., 1978). Kindergartners, too, describe themselves largely in terms of activities such as play (Damon & Hart, 1982). Young children seem to see themselves as "good at doing things" or not—without making the distinction between physical and academic competence that older children do (Harter & Pike, 1984). Nevertheless,

about 5% of the responses of the youngest children in the Keller study referred to psychological aspects, such as likes and dislikes.

Primary grades

Primary grade children begin to acquire more mature thinking skills, such as the ability to organize logically and classify hierarchically, and can extend these abilities to their thinking about the self. By age 7 or 8, they are also able to make comparisons between themselves and their peers concerning their abilities (Ruble, Boggiano, Feldman, & Loebl, 1980). By third grade, children still frequently describe themselves in terms of activities, but add comparison with their peers in their self-descriptive statements, such as "I can ride a bike better than my little brother" (Damon & Hart, 1982). They are also able to think inductively and may conclude that "I'm not very smart because I'm in the low group in reading and math."

Primary grade children also acquire new perspective-taking skills that allow them to imagine what other people are thinking, especially what others think of them. Children of this age begin to be more influenced by their perceptions of what significant adults think of them. With further development, what peers think becomes increasingly important.

External factors related to the development of self-concept

Responsiveness of caregivers

Self-concept develops largely within a social context. The interpersonal envi-

Research shows that low self-concept is related to poor mental health, poor academic achievement, and delinquency. But what can we learn from research that will allow us to help children approach new situations and other people with confidence?

ronment that caregivers provide has important influences on the development of self-concept. The quality, consistency, and timing of adults' responses to infants may carry messages about trust, caring, and the value of the infant. Caregiver responsiveness may also convey information about the developing child's capacity to become competent and to control her or his environment (see Honig, 1984). When caregivers respond positively and consistently to infants' cues, infants may come to learn that they are of value and that they can influence their social environment (Harter, 1983). This may contribute to beginning feelings of self-worth, personal control, and competence.

Physical environment

A number of aspects of the physical environment may influence the development of self-concept. For example, if we make developmentally appropriate materials (those that provide both challenge and success) easily accessible to young children for exploration in an encouraging environment, these children are likely to acquire feelings of competence and confidence in approaching new materials (see Bredekamp, 1987).

Other aspects of the environment may influence the development of infants' and toddlers' conceptions of their physical self and of themselves as separate and different from others. Mirrors and similar light-reflecting surfaces, for example, provide opportunities for very young children to learn not only about their physical characteristics but also about themselves as independent agents who can make things happen. When infants can see both themselves and their image moving at the same time, they can learn about the effects of their own actions and their ability to control their world (Lewis & Brooks-Gunn, 1979).

Parental attitudes and childrearing practices

Sears (1970) found that parents who were warm and accepting when their children were young (age 5) had children with high self-esteem measured at age 12. Parents who use an "authoritative"—as opposed to an authoritarian or permissive childrearing pattern (see Honig, 1984)—are also more likely to have children with high self-esteem. These parents make rea-

sonable demands that are accepted by children, but they do not impose unreasonable restrictions and they allow their children some choice and control (Maccoby & Martin, 1983).

Training in effective parenting, where parents learn to be more accepting of their children's feelings and behavior, has led to an increase in kindergarten and second grade children's self-concepts (Summerlin & Ward, 1978). Studies such as these point to the importance of efforts to help parents understand and implement practices that enhance self-esteem.

Feeling in control also helps children develop positive self-esteem.

Expectations

Teachers' and parents' expectations may influence children's self-esteem, both (a) directly through opportunities adults provide for children to learn and become competent and (b) indirectly through more subtle cues that children eventually come to perceive. If adults believe that certain children can learn or do more than others, they may furnish additional materials for these children. In this way, they provide opportunities to become competent in more areas and thus directly influence the children's perceived competence.

In addition, teachers' and parents' expectations influence self-concept in more subtle ways as children gradually become more adept at "reading" environmental cues. Young children are not very accurate in judging adults' expectations for them. They generally hold higher expectations for themselves than their teachers hold for them (Weinstein, Marshall, Sharp, & Botkin, 1987). The discrepancy between young children's expectations and those of their teachers may be due to their relatively undeveloped ability to take the perspective of others. Young children may also have less need to focus on what their teachers expect of them because most preschool and kindergarten classrooms do not emphasize evaluation. However, even at the kindergarten level, if teach-

ers make their evaluations of children salient—such as pointing out the children's best work—children's self-evaluations can show some consistency with those of the teacher (Stipek & Daniels, 1988). Consequently kindergarten and primary teachers need to be aware of subtle ways that their expectations may be conveyed to children and thus influence their self-esteem.

Classroom environments

Classroom structure and teachers' control orientations may influence children's self-concepts as well (Marshall & Weinstein, 1984). This is exemplified in studies comparing the effects of "unidimensional" with those of "multidimensional" classrooms (Rosenholtz & Rosenholtz, 1981). In unidimensional classrooms, teachers emphasize a narrow range of students' abilities (e.g., they value reading ability to the neglect of artistic ability), group students according to ability, assign similar tasks, and publicly evaluate performance. In multidimensional classrooms, in contrast, teachers emphasize multiple dimensions of ability (e.g., artistic and problem-solving skills as well as reading skills), have students work on a variety of different tasks using different materials at the same time, and evaluate students more privately. Although preschools are more often similar to multidimensional classrooms, some kindergarten and "academic" preschools are under pressure to become more unidimensional. In classrooms that emphasized academics, with characteristics similar to unidimensional classrooms, kindergartners' perceptions of their ability were lower than those of kindergartners in more multidimensional classrooms—although the two groups were learning the same skills (Stipek & Daniels, 1988). Teachers need to be aware, therefore, that pressures to prepare children for academics and to include and evaluate more school-like tasks may have detrimental effects on children's self-concepts of ability.

Whether teachers support children's autonomy or tend to control children through external means also affects children's perceptions of competence and self-esteem. Children in classrooms that supported autonomy had higher perceptions of their own cognitive competence, self-worth, and mastery motivation than those in classrooms

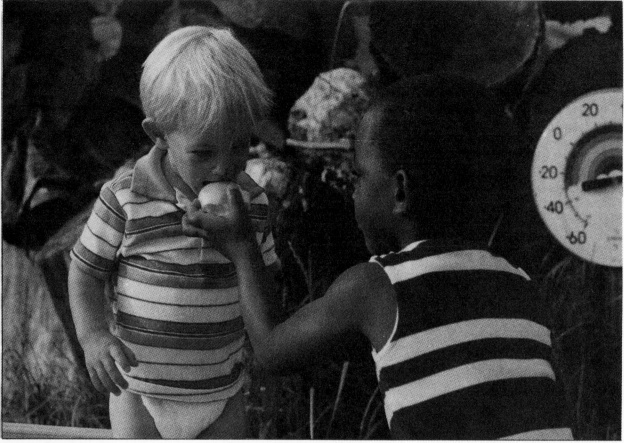

Subjects & Predicates

Is there anything that's more of a priority for teachers than helping each child feel good about himself? People who feel good about themselves are usually good to others.

where teachers retained control (Ryan, Connell, & Deci, 1985). Because this study was conducted with older children, we do not know at what age this effect may begin. We should be aware, nevertheless, that providing opportunities for children to strive toward independence and to develop a sense of personal control is likely to have a positive effect on children's perceptions of competence and self-esteem.

Peers

Some research suggests that peer interactions may have an influence on self-esteem and social self-concept earlier than previously believed. In an attempt to explore sources of esteem, preschoolers were asked the question "Who likes you?" More than 50% of the children mentioned peers and 49% mentioned siblings (Kirchner & Vondraek, 1975).

Older children (third through eighth graders) who have a high self-concept in the social domain have higher status with their peers—as might be predicted (Kurdek & Krile, 1982). Again, we do not

know how early this finding may hold, nor do we know the direction of causality. That is, (a) social self-concept may influence peer relationships, or (b) peer relationships may influence social self-concept, or (c) knowledge of interpersonal skills may affect peer relationships and/or social self-concept. Taken together, these results suggest that helping children learn the skills needed to interact successfully with their peers may ultimately affect their social self-concept.

References

Bredekamp, S. (Ed.). (1987). *Developmentally appropriate practice in early childhood programs serving children from birth through age 8.* Washington, DC: NAEYC.

Damon, W., & Hart, D. (1982). The development of self-understanding from infancy through adolescence. *Child Development, 53,* 841–864.

Harter, S. (1983). Developmental perspectives on the self-system. In E.M. Hetherington (Ed.), *Handbook of child psychology: Vol. 4. Socialization, personality and social development* (4th ed., pp. 275–386). New York: Wiley.

Sensitive parents and teachers may be better able to assess a child's self-concept than researchers are. Differences in definitions and dimensions make it difficult to compare and synthesize studies, but a child with good self-concept radiates it.

Harter, S. (1986). Processes underlying the construction, maintenance, and enhancement of the self-concept in children. In J. Suls & A. Greenwald (Eds.), *Psychological perspectives of the self* (Vol. 3, pp. 137–181). Hillsdale, NJ: Erlbaum.

Harter, S., & Pike, R. (1984). The pictorial scale of perceived competence and social acceptance for young children. *Child Development, 55,* 1969–1982.

Hitz, R., & Driscoll, A. (1988). Praise or encouragement? New insights into praise: Implications for early childhood teachers. *Young Children, 43*(5), 6–13.

Honig, A. (1984). Research in review: Risk factors in infants and young children. *Young Children, 39*(4), 60–73.

Keller, A., Ford, L., & Meacham, J. (1978). Dimensions of self-concept in preschool children. *Developmental Psychology, 14,* 483–489.

Kirchner, P., & Vondraek, S. (1975). Perceived sources of esteem in early childhood. *Journal of Genetic Psychology, 132,* 169–176.

Kurdek, L., & Krile, D. (1982). A developmental analysis of the relation between peer acceptance and both interpersonal understanding and perceived social self-competence. *Child Development, 53,* 1485–1491.

Lewis, M., & Brooks-Gunn, J. (1979). *Social cognition and the acquisition of self.* New York: Plenum.

Maccoby, E., & Martin, J. (1983). Socialization in the context of the family: Parent-child interaction. In E.M. Hetherington (Ed.), *Handbook of child psychology: Vol. 4. Socialization, personality, and social development* (4th ed., pp. 1–102). New York: Wiley.

Marsh, H. (1984). Relations among dimensions of self-attributions, dimensions of self-concept and academic achievement. *Journal of Educational Psychology, 76,* 1291–1308

Marshall, H., & Weinstein, R. (1984). Classroom factors affecting students' self-evaluations. *Review of Educational Research, 54,* 301–325.

Rosenholtz, S.J., & Rosenholtz, S.H. (1981). Classroom organization and the perception of ability. *Sociology of Education, 54,* 132–140.

Ruble, D., Boggiano, A., Feldman, N., & Loebl, J. (1980). Developmental analysis of the role of social comparison in self-evaluation. *Developmental Psychology, 16,* 105–115.

Ryan, R., Connell, J., & Deci, E. (1985). A motivational analysis of self-determination and self-regulation in education. In C. Ames & R. Ames (Eds.), *Research on motivation in education: Vol. 2. The classroom milieu* (pp. 13–52). New York: Academic.

Sears, R. (1970). Relation of early socialization experiences to self-concepts and gender role in middle childhood. *Child Development, 41,* 267–289.

Selman, R. (1980). *The growth of interpersonal understanding.* New York: Academic.

Shavelson, R., Hubner, J., & Stanton, G. (1976). Self-concept: Validation of construct interpretations. *Review of Educational Research, 46,* 407–442.

Stipek, D., & Daniels, D. (1988). Declining perceptions of competence: A consequence of changes in the child or in the educational environment. *Journal of Educational Psychology, 80,* 352–356.

Summerlin, M.L., & Ward, G.R. (1978). The effect of parental participation in a parent group on a child's self-concept. *Psychological Reports, 100,* 227–232.

Weinstein, R., Marshall, H., Sharp, L., & Botkin, M. (1987). Pygmalion and the student: Age and classroom differences in children's awareness of teacher expectations. *Child Development, 58,* 1079–1093.

White, R. (1959). Motivation reconsidered: The concept of competence. *Psychological Review, 66,* 297–333.

For further reading

Young Children has had a continuing series of Ideas That Work With Young Children by Polly Greenberg emphasizing encouraging self-esteem in infants and children. If you missed them, you may want to read:

"Positive Self-Image: More Than Mirrors" (May 1988)

"Avoiding 'Me Against You' Discipline" (November 1988)

"Learning Self-Esteem and Self-Discipline Through Play" (January 1989)

"Parents as Partners in Young Children's Development and Education: A New American Fad? Why Does It Matter?" (May 1989)

Encouraging Prosocial Behavior in Young Children

Susan M. Doescher and Alan I. Sugawara

Susan M. Doescher and Alan I. Sugawara are Professors, Human Development and Family Studies, Oregon State University, Corvallis.

"That's mine!" "I want it!" "Give me that!" In a preschool classroom, two 3-year-old children are fighting over possession of a favorite truck. Moments earlier they were playing side-by-side in the block area, each one building a road. Both go to the truck shelf in search of the dump truck. One child grabs the truck, and the other tries to pull it away. The noise catches the attention of a nearby teacher who quickly approaches. Similar incidents frequently occur in the classroom setting. What can early childhood educators do to minimize such situations and maximize positive social interactions such as cooperating, sharing and helping among children? Often children's prosocial behaviors go unnoticed, while teachers attend to less desirable behaviors.

Defined as acts that aid or benefit another person (Mussen & Eisenberg-Berg, 1977), prosocial behaviors are viewed as central to the development of a child's social competence. Research has indicated that prosocial behavior develops at an early age (Bar-Tal,

Raviv & Leiser, 1980; Hay, 1979; Yarrow & Waxler, 1976). Before the age of 2, children display prosocial actions with their parents such as helping and comforting (Johnson, 1982; Rheingold, 1982). In a school setting, prosocial behaviors occur among most children, although in low amounts (Yarrow & Waxler, 1976). Perhaps young children may not have the ability to accurately perceive and react to the needs of others, or adults may be reinforcing aggressive rather than prosocial actions. Children who have greater role-taking abilities and are more sensitive to the needs of others seem to be more prosocial (Eisenberg-Berg & Hand, 1979; Eisenberg-Berg & Neal, 1979).

Prosocial behaviors are observed in both girls and boys, although research results have not been conclusive. One group of studies found no significant gender differences in prosocial responses among preschoolers (Bar-Tal, Raviv & Goldberg, 1982; Hartup & Keller, 1960; Yarrow & Waxler, 1976). These studies argue that both girls and boys can and do display prosocial abilities equally. On the other hand, another group of studies report significant gender differences in preschool children's prosocial behaviors (Eisenberg, Bartlett & Haake, 1983; Harris & Siebel, 1975; Midlarsky & Bryan,

1972). In these studies girls were found to be more prosocial than boys. The differential socialization experience of girls and boys may help to explain these gender differences. Girls may experience prosocial models and may be expected to demonstrate the prosocial actions they have observed more frequently than boys (Mussen & Eisenberg-Berg, 1977).

Prosocial behavior has also been evidenced in children from various socioeconomic classes. When directly examined, mixed findings have resulted concerning the relationship between the family's socioeconomic class and prosocial actions. Some studies found no significant differences among children from different social classes (DePalma, 1974), while others indicated that lower-economic class children were more cooperative than upper-middle class children (Knight & Kagan, 1977; Madsen, 1967). Perhaps parental expectations and children's experiences can explain the differences in the development of prosocial abilities in children of various socioeconomic classes.

Recently there has been a great deal of research interest in the area of social competence. Current investigations have emphasized the importance of children's social development during the preschool years. Social experiences such as

From *Childhood Education*, Summer 1989, pp. 213-216. Reprinted by permission of the authors and the Association for Childhood Education International, 11141 Georgia Avenue, Suite 200, Wheaton, MD. Copyright © 1989 by the Association.

those preschoolers encounter in a classroom environment can enhance the prosocial skills of young children (Kim & Stevens, 1987; Floody, 1980; Moore, 1977). Early childhood educators have continually sought, therefore, to find effective methods that encourage the development of prosocial behavior in young children. If prosocial behavior occurs among preschoolers, what can teachers do to encourage these behaviors in the classroom setting? This article describes several strategies teachers may use in developing a more prosocial classroom environment for preschool children.

Strategy I: Examining Teacher Attitudes About Prosocial Behavior Among Preschool Children

Awareness of children's developmental levels and abilities. With an understanding of children's developmental levels, teachers are able to recognize that preschoolers are egocentric and have subjective perspective-taking social abilities (Selman & Bryne, 1974). Preschool children are primarily centered within themselves. They are beginning to recognize, however, that others have feelings, too. It is helpful, therefore, to provide young children with descriptions of thoughts and feelings of others different from their own. Teachers can point out how happy a child feels when included in an activity in which the child would like to participate. Imagine the following example: A child approaches a teacher with the request, "I want a trike." With the teacher's help, the child who is riding a tricycle can be asked for a turn by the child in need. "When you are done with the trike, can I use the trike next?" The teacher may add, "That would make Lisa happy for you to share the trike with her." When the trike is traded, a follow-up acknowledgment—e.g. "Lisa likes the way you shared the trike with her"—would reinforce the desired behaviors.

Verbalization of children's thoughts and feelings. Talking about one's own feelings, as well as listening to others describe their feelings, helps children consider other points of view outside themselves. Assistance can be given when children attempt to express their thoughts and feelings to others. Teachers can discuss the feelings of an excluded child to onlooking peers by asking, "How does Todd feel?" "Do you feel sad when someone won't play with you?" "What would make him feel happier?" "What can he be in your house?" Upon admittance into the play, the teacher can mention, "I see Todd is the new uncle in your house." "That must make him feel happy to be playing with you."

Belief in the capabilities of young children. Teachers who have the knowledge, understanding and conviction that all preschoolers are capable of displaying prosocial behavior in the classroom reflect these expectations in their social interactions. Despite gender, race or ethnic origin, all children have the ability to exhibit prosocial behavior. For example, teachers can expect both boys and girls to help one another secure paint smocks, which cannot be done alone. Children can ask one another for help in fastening the backs of their smocks. They can also share art materials such as construction paper, scissors and bottles of glue while working on a collage together.

Strategy II: Examining Teaching Techniques for the Classroom

Use of modeling to facilitate prosocial behaviors. Teachers are powerful models who can be influential in encouraging prosocial behavior among children. Research indicates that children learn while observing the behavior of others (Midlarsky & Suda, 1978). Children who see their teachers sharing or helping are more likely to share or help in return. For instance, when cleaning up materials at the end of activity time, a teacher can hold one end of a small table while two children hold the

other end. The teacher may say, "I like the way we work together to move this table." In another situation, when playing catch with balls, a teacher may simply share a ball with a child and say, "I'll share this ball with you."

Children's responses to encouragement. Modeling and encouraging techniques are effective in eliciting prosocial behavior (Rogers-Warren & Baer, 1976). When children behave prosocially with peers or teachers, expressions of approval (a smile or touch on the arm) or a praising statement ("I like the way you are sharing with me!") will help maintain desired behaviors. Table 1 provides examples of modeling and encouraging strategies useful in facilitating children's prosocial behavior.

Use of reasoning as a guidance technique. When teachers reason rather than use power-oriented strategies to guide children's behavior, prosocial behaviors are more likely to occur. Children receive information to help them understand the consequences of their actions and sharpen their perspective-taking skills. Power-oriented techniques such as strict warnings or punishments do little to model prosocial behavior (Kim & Stevens, 1987). They involve strategies that tend to emphasize satisfying individual needs rather than helping a child empathize with others. When one child wants a truck that another child is using, a teacher can reason or explain how sharing or working together with the vehicle could solve the problem. Taking the truck from the child or providing a second truck for the child in need does not result in the learning of cooperative behavior.

Strategy III: Evaluating the Classroom Environment and Curriculum

Creation of a prosocial environment. Teachers can examine their classroom to see whether the development of prosocial skills is enhanced or hindered by the room setup. For example, is the room divided to separate rather than facilitate interactions between children? Barriers may prevent children from working together in adjacent play areas, such as the block and dramatic play areas. Furthermore, are there enough scissors, paint brushes and tricycles to go around? When materials are available for all children to use individually, a less prosocial environment is created. An environment with a limited but reasonable amount of supplies requires children to work together on projects. For instance, one set of crayons can be shared by three children who are drawing pictures at an art table. By examining the classroom environment and activity setup, teachers are able to evaluate their roles in facilitating prosocial behavior among preschool children.

Selection of appropriate curriculum activities. Children can benefit from the use of prosocial activities. A curriculum encompassing various areas of development can be used to encourage children's involvement in prosocial activities throughout the preschool day (Doescher & Sugawara, 1986). Cooperative cooking projects and dramatic airline play, in which children have limited supplies and need to work together in order to play, are good examples of prosocial experiences. Squeezing oranges for juice with the help of a hand juicer encourages children to cooperate and take turns. One child can hold the juicer while the other squeezes; later these roles may be switched. With airline play, children can take turns acting out the roles of pilot, passenger or travel agent. Turn-taking will encourage the sharing of materials (steering wheel, suitcases and travel brochures).

Summary
Aware that children are capable of displaying prosocial behavior in the preschool classroom, early childhood educators can be instrumental in creating an environment that nurtures their prosocial development. When positive social behavior is modeled and encouraged by teachers, children learn to respect others' needs and to re-

---

Table 1

Application of Teacher Modeling and Encouraging Strategies

Situation	Modeling Techniques	Encouraging Statements
1. "Row, Row, Row Your Boat" sung at group time	1. Demonstrate with one child how to sit facing one another and rock, with legs and arms interlocked.	1. "We need to work together to row our boat." "I like the way you two are cooperating to row your boat."
2. Pegboards at manipulative table	2. Demonstrate the sharing of pegs with a child next to you. Take one peg, and give one to your partner.	2. "I'll share the pegs with you." "I found a red peg." "May I share it with you?"
3. Waterplay at the watertable	3. Demonstrate helping with the child next to you by holding a funnel while he/she tries to fill the container.	3. "I like to help you." "We are working well together." "Can you help me fill this up?"
4. Teeter-totter during outside play	4. Demonstrate cooperative efforts with the child on the seesaw. Push your partner in order for his/her feet to touch the ground.	4. "We need to cooperate to get the teeter-totter to work." "I'll push you down, then you push me down."

spond accordingly. They may seek approval using such statements as, "Look, Jason and I are cooperating!" Or they may encourage each other by expressing such ideas as, "We like to help, don't we, Mary?" Strategies like those provided here can be incorporated effectively by early childhood educators in a variety of preschool settings.

Authors' Acknowledgment: Special thanks to Virginia Adduci and Joanne Sorte for comments on an earlier draft of this manuscript.

References

Bar-Tal, D., Raviv, A., & Goldberg, M. (1982). Helping behavior among preschool children: An observational study. *Child Development, 53*, 396-402.

Bar-Tal, D., Raviv, A., & Leiser, T. (1980). The development of altruistic behavior: Empirical evidence. *Developmental Psychology, 16*, 516-525.

DePalma, D. (1974). Effects of social class, moral orientation and severity of punishment on boys' moral responses to transgression and generosity. *Developmental Psychology, 10*, 890-900.

Doescher, S., & Sugawara, A. (1986). *Prosocial activity guide.* (Available from Dr. Susan M. Doescher, Department of Human Development & Family Studies, Oregon State University, Corvallis, OR 97331.)

Eisenberg-Berg, N., & Hand, M. (1979). The relationship of preschoolers' reasoning about prosocial moral conflicts in prosocial behavior. *Child Development, 50*, 356-363.

Eisenberg-Berg, N., & Neal, C. (1979). Children's moral reasoning about their own spontaneous prosocial behavior. *Developmental Psychology, 15*, 228-229.

Eisenberg, N., Bartlett, K., & Haake, R. (1983). The effects of nonverbal cues concerning possession of a toy on children's proprietary and sharing behaviors. *The Journal of Genetic Psychology, 143*, 79-85.

Floody, D. (1980). An early childhood educator's guide to prosocial development. ERIC document, #ED164 116.

Harris, M., & Siebel, C. (1975). Affect, aggression and altruism. *Developmental Psychology, 11*, 623-627.

Hartup, W., & Keller, E. (1960). Nurturance in preschool children and its relation to dependency. *Child Development, 31*, 681-689.

Hay, D. (1979). Cooperative interactions and sharing between very young children and their parents. *Developmental Psychology, 15*, 647-653.

Johnson, D. (1982). Altruistic behavior and the development of the self in infants. *Merrill-Palmer Quarterly, 28*, 379-388.

Kim, Y-O., & Stevens, J. (1987). The socialization of prosocial behavior in children. *Childhood Education, 63*, 200-206.

Knight, G., & Kagan, S. (1977). Acculturation of prosocial and competitive behaviors among second- and third-generation Mexican-American children. *Journal of Cross-Cultural Psychology, 8*, 273-283.

Madsen, M. (1967). Cooperative and competitive motivation of children in three Mexican sub-cultures. *Psychological Reports, 20*, 1307-1320.

Midlarsky, E., & Bryan, J. (1972). Affect expressions and children's imitative altruism. *Journal of Experimental Research in Personality, 6*, 195-203.

Midlarsky, E., & Suda, W. (1978). Some antecedents of altruism in children: Theoretical and empirical perspectives. *Psychological Reports, 43*, 187-208.

Moore, S. (1977). Research in review: Considerateness and helpfulness in young children. *Young Children, 32*, 73-76.

Mussen, P., & Eisenberg-Berg, N. (1977). *Roots of caring, sharing and helping.* San Francisco: W. H. Freeman.

Rheingold, H. (1982). Little children's participation in the work of adults. *Child Development, 53*, 114-125.

Rogers-Warren, A., & Baer, D. (1976). Correspondence between saying and doing: Teaching children to share and praise. *Journal of Applied Behavior Analysis, 9*, 335-354.

Selman, R., & Byrne, D. (1974). A structural-developmental analysis of levels of role-taking in middle childhood. *Child Development, 45*, 803-806.

Yarrow, M., & Waxler, C. (1976). Dimensions and correlations of prosocial behavior in young children. *Child Development, 47*, 118-125.

Four Strategies for Fostering

CHARACTER DEVELOPMENT

In Children

Elementary students present a constellation of moral strengths and shortcomings, Mr. Lickona points out. But we have the means to bring them to moral maturity — if we can muster the will.

THOMAS LICKONA

THOMAS LICKONA is a professor of education at the State University of New York, College at Cortland. This article was adapted from a chapter in Character Development in Schools and Beyond *(Praeger, 1987), edited by Kevin Ryan and George McClean.*

IT IS A TRUISM that good education, whether for intellect or character, begins by knowing the child. What are children like during their elementary school years? What is their natural stance in the social world? What moral strengths and shortcomings do they present to anyone who would try to foster their character development?

We know that children in elementary school want to be competent — in school subjects, in sports, and in social roles. Furthermore, they want to be *recognized* as competent — hence their emerging concern with how others view them. Through achievement and the recognition of their achievement by peers, parents, and teachers, elementary school children develop a sense of themselves, a self-concept that is the sum of the things they can do.

By nature, children of this age express themselves through competitiveness. They want to do more things and do them better than the next person. They thus put themselves under a lot of pressure and are often extremely hard on themselves and each other. Quick to say "I'm no good" when they do not succeed at a task, they are easily humiliated by any kind of public failure. At least partly because they are not fully secure about their own competence, they are also notoriously intolerant of incompetence in their peers. Spend time on an elementary school playground, and you will wince at the way children routinely heap scorn ("you stink") on age-mates who have the mis-fortune to err in a game or otherwise fail to measure up.

Cliques also begin to form during the middle years in elementary school. Membership in one of these peer groups is both a source of approval for competence ("you've made the grade") and a badge of social success ("we like you"). Those within the "inner circle" frequently affirm their coveted status by denigrating those outside it. I heard a fifth-grade teacher say, "The name-calling in my class is constant. Boys who aren't tough or athletic get called 'fags.' The three Japanese children in the class get called 'egg roll' and 'wonton soup'; one Japanese boy was terrified to come to school. Boys also call girls names — 'fat,' 'pancake face,' and the like."

Name-calling goes hand in hand with

the exclusion of those who are different — from games at recess, from conversation at lunchtime, and from social groups in the classroom. Girls, teachers report, can be even more vicious (though usually more subtle) than boys. Children's reputation for cruelty at this age is well-deserved.

CONTRIBUTIONS OF ENVIRONMENT

Such cruelty, however, is not an inevitable by-product of this developmental period. For better or worse, natural tendencies interact with and are modified by environmental influences. Television violence and snappy put-downs, lack of discipline or love at home, cultural emphasis on self-centered competition, schools that fail to teach caring and cooperation — these factors and more combine to exacerbate the negative developmental tendencies of this age.

But teachers can fashion the school environment, set expectations, and provide moral instruction to channel the natural inclinations of elementary schoolers toward socially constructive ends — and so toward further development. Happily, even in the heyday of the child's callous competition and drive for competence, other developmental forces can be marshaled to check the excesses and to foster the growth of character.

In the cognitive realm, elementary schoolers become increasingly capable of what Piaget calls "decentering" — keeping more than one factor in mind at a time. That means a better ability to consider alternatives and consequences when solving a problem. Robert Selman documents the enormous progress children can make in learning to put themselves in another person's shoes, moving from self-centered egocentrism to a focus on another's viewpoint, to a consideration of two points of view in a dyad, to a mature understanding of the needs of the individual and the group.[1]

In moral judgment, the work of Lawrence Kohlberg shows that, by the end of their elementary school years, children at least begin to apply the Golden Rule. They can understand why trust and mutual helpfulness are essential to human relationships, and they want to be "nice persons" by living up to the expectations of significant others and following the nudge of conscience.[2] Robert Kegan charts the transformation of the strictly autonomous "imperial self" into the more fully integrated "interpersonal self" as the child negotiates the persistent demands of the surrounding social world.[3]

Thus elementary school children, like their older counterparts, are a constellation of strengths and weaknesses. They are independent and competitive to a fault, overeager to succeed, easily hurt by failure or insult; yet they are often extremely insensitive to the ways in which they hurt others. For all of that, their minds and moral potentials are rapidly unfolding, and the classroom is a logical setting to promote positive social growth.

GOALS OF CHARACTER DEVELOPMENT

Given the nature of elementary students, what are reasonable goals for their moral education? Three stand out:
- to promote development away from egocentrism and excessive individualism and toward cooperative relationships and mutual respect;
- to foster the growth of moral agency — the capacity to think, feel, and act morally; and
- to develop in the classroom and in the school a moral community based on fairness, caring, and participation — such a community being a moral end in itself, as well as a support system for the character development of each individual student.

A classroom dedicated to these broad goals would seek to develop in each child the following specific qualities: 1) self-respect that derives feelings of worth not only from competence but also from positive behavior toward others; 2) social perspective-taking that asks how others think and feel; 3) moral reasoning about the right things to do; 4) such moral values as kindness, courtesy, trustworthiness, and responsibility; 5) the social skills and habits of cooperation; and 6) openness to the positive influence of adults.

To do an adequate job of moral education — one that has a chance of making a real impact on a child's developing character — four processes should be going on in the classroom: 1) building self-esteem and a sense of community, 2) learning to cooperate and help others, 3) moral reflection, and 4) participatory decision making. Taken together, these four processes embrace both the formal academic curriculum and the "human" curriculum (the rules, roles, and relationships) that make up the life of the classroom. Let us consider each of these processes individually.

Building self-esteem and sense of community. Building self-esteem in the elementary school years fosters the sense of competence and mastery that is at the core of the child's self-concept. Building self-esteem also teaches children to val-

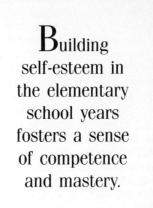

Building self-esteem in the elementary school years fosters a sense of competence and mastery.

ue themselves as persons, to have the kind of respect for themselves that enables them to stand up for their rights and command the respect of others. To build a sense of community is to create a group that extends to others the respect one has for oneself. More specifically, building a community in the classroom allows students to come to know one another as individuals, to respect and care about one another, and to feel a sense of membership in and accountability to the group.

Self-esteem is important to character development because morality begins with valuing one's own person. Loving your neighbor is easier if you love yourself. A sense of community is important because it contributes to self-esteem, partly by creating a norm of mutual respect that inhibits put-downs and partly by helping children to feel known and positively valued by their peers. A sense of community also supplies a vital affective dimension to moral education, a flow of good feeling that makes it easier for children to be good, easier for them to cross the bridge from knowing what is right to doing it. Teachers who take the trouble to build positive "group feeling" know (at least intuitively) that developing virtue is as much an affair of the emotions as of the mind. Finally, for an increasing number of children, a supportive classroom community provides a surrogate "family" that helps to meet important emotional needs that are not being met at home.

Wise teachers begin to foster self-worth and to develop social bonds on day one of the school year. Two team-teachers of second- and third-graders in Brookline, Massachusetts, greet children when they arrive in September with this message: "All of us will be together for

180 days. It will be much happier for everyone if we get along and are able to cooperate. We don't expect you to *like* everybody, but we do expect you to *respect* each other and to take care not to hurt anyone. During the first several weeks of school, we'll be teaching you the skills you'll need to cooperate and to show respect for others."

Over the ensuing weeks, this orientation is followed by simple activities that enable children to get to know each other: playing games, solving puzzles "with someone you don't know very well," writing down "all the ways you and a new partner are alike and different," and so on. "Through the course of the year," the teachers report, "a sense of trust develops. Children begin to reinforce each other's ideas and abilities; they support one another in difficult times. This doesn't happen overnight. It grows slowly and must be openly encouraged."

A fourth-grade teacher rotates "learning partners." Every three weeks students get new partners with whom they work at least once a day on an assigned task. A fifth-grade teacher finds she can reduce the prevalence of exclusive cliques in her class by holding a seating lottery at the end of every week. Because desks in her room are contiguous in a large rectangle, the drawing means that each week each child is almost sure to have two new neighbors — and a chance to make two new friends.

When others give us their time, their attention, their friendship, we are better able to judge ourselves as individuals worthy of love and respect. Feeling good about ourselves, we have an easier time being good to others. That basic truth underlies this first and most fundamental process of moral education: fostering the self-esteem of the individual in and through human community.

Learning to cooperate and help others. Community experience is thin if students come together only in a class discussion to share thoughts and feelings but spend the rest of the day working individually on academic work. Learning to cooperate and help others requires that students *work* together, as well as talk together. If we want them to develop the skill and spirit of cooperation, we must make cooperation a regular feature of classroom life.

Some elementary teachers use the whole academic curriculum as a vehicle for developing cooperation. For example, fourth-graders in Paula Barno's parochial school science class worked in pairs to construct and balance mobiles. In art, they drew group murals, and they

designed and decorated a quiet "meditation corner" for the classroom. But the crowning achievement came in social studies when the whole class collaborated on a unit on Mexico as their contribution to the school's "Festival of Many Lands." Barno writes:

> The children were excited to work on this project. They eagerly settled into their tasks, were able to talk out most disagreements, and objected if one person tried to take over. As they worked on maps, charts, and displays of people, places, and things, it was encouraging for me to hear them discuss new points of view, reconsider their own, and alter their first opinions. . . . We all felt a new unity among us that this cooperative experience had made possible.

> A supportive classroom community provides a surrogate "family" that helps to meet important emotional needs.

Cooperation is also made easier when children learn to support each other. A fifth-grade teacher instituted a practice called "appreciation time," a short session at the end of each day when class members describe something that others have done that they appreciate.

For example, at one meeting a pupil said, "I appreciate Julie for lending me some paper when I forgot mine. All I did was say I didn't have any, and she offered me some of hers." A second student said, "I'd like to appreciate Stan for helping me study for my spelling test. That was the first time I ever got 100!"

The teacher reports that appreciation time has become the most popular activity in her classroom. This fact is all the more impressive when we recall that fifth-graders, left to their own devices, typically trade insults rather than compliments.

Many teachers foster helping relationships in the classroom by taking a further step. They use class problem-solving meetings to crystallize feelings of community and interdependence into a clear sense of collective responsibility. Often such meetings address a problem that affects many or all class members: too much noise, people not helping with clean-up, students taking or otherwise abusing others' property, and so on. But collective responsibility means more; it asserts that we are our neighbor's keepers — that even if only one other person has a problem, that problem belongs to everybody. A new classmate who has no friends or who doesn't know how to get around in the school becomes a classwide concern. The stealing of one person's lunch money is an issue for the entire class.

Social observers often decry "me-first" individualism and lack of concern for the common good among young people. If we wish to strengthen ethical cooperation within society, we should strive to make it a character trait of children, as they live and work in the small society that is the classroom.

Moral reflection. The third process crucial to moral education in the elementary school years is moral reflection. The word *reflection* refers to a wide range of intellectual activities, including reading, thinking, debating moral questions, listening to explanations by the teacher (e.g., why it is wrong to make fun of a handicapped child), and conducting firsthand investigation to increase children's awareness of the complex social system to which they belong.

Of the four processes of moral education, moral reflection aims most directly at developing the cognitive and rational aspects of moral behavior. At the same time, this self-consciously rational aspect of character development can be nurtured in such a way as to foster a union of cognition and affect, so that children come to feel deeply about what they think and value.

One second-grade teacher, for example, saw an opportunity to merge cognition and affect during a science project in which the class was incubating 20 chicken eggs. She had suggested to the class that they might wish to open one egg each week in order to monitor the embryonic development.

Later that day, in his reading group, 7-year-old Nathaniel confided to his teacher, "Mrs. Williams, I've been thinking about this for a long time. It's just too *cruel* to open an egg and kill the chick inside!"

Mrs. Williams listened without comment and said that she would bring the topic up for discussion with the whole class. When she did, there was some agreement that Nat's point was worth considering. But many children said that they were curious to see what the embryo looked like. Nat replied that being curious wasn't a good enough reason for killing a chick. "How would you like it," he said, "if somebody opened your sac when you were developing because they were curious to see what you looked like?" The library must have pictures of chick embryos, he argued. Wouldn't that be a better way of finding out what an embryo looked like?

Some children countered that they wanted to see a *real* chick. "Is it alive?" one asked. Not until it has hatched, some argued. "It's alive now," countered others, "and it's a chicken!"

Mrs. Williams asked the children to think about the issue overnight. She told them that they would reach a decision as a class the following morning. By that time, a majority of the children had come to feel that Nat's objection should be honored; they did not open the eggs.

The potential for moral learning in this episode was tremendous. The children considered the question of whether all life, even that of a chick embryo, is to be taken seriously. They learned that simply wanting to do something isn't a good enough reason for doing it and that a member of the group who has strong feelings about something has a right to express them. They also learned that others have an obligation to listen and that, if possible, a conflict should be resolved in a way that tries to meet the needs of all parties. The class did, in fact, search out pictures of chick embryos in the library.

This intensive moral reflection resulted from Mrs. Williams' taking the time to allow her students to come to grips with a difficult moral dilemma arising from the real life of the classroom. As a side point, real-life dilemmas such as this one are far more effective in engaging children's thinking and feelings than any "canned" dilemmas from a book or kit.

Moral reflection also helps children realize that, while it is often easy to know the right thing, it is usually harder to do it. Children should talk about why they (and other people) sometimes cheat, lie, put people down, or treat others unfairly, even when they know that such things are wrong. What factors — self-interest, peer pressure, anger, anxiety, low self-esteem — lead them to do such things? What helps them stay on the straight and narrow?

Children need practice both as moral psychologists who understand human weakness and wrongdoing and as moral philosophers who declare what is right. They need to be challenged to develop the self-awareness, self-discipline, and strength of will that can help them hew to the right course.

All of this is clearly a tall order. It should come as no surprise that teachers, even the best ones, usually find guiding moral reflection to be the hardest part of moral education. It involves many sophisticated skills: framing moral issues, using Socratic questioning, paraphrasing responses, making connections among the contributions of a variety of students,

> M oral reflection helps children realize that, while it is often easy to know the right thing, it is usually harder to do it.

and drawing out and challenging children's reasoning (rather than settling for mere expression of opinion), to name just a few. Most teachers have rarely seen such skills modeled in their own education and thus will need time, patience, and practice to develop them. But the effort to do so is clearly essential, because moral reflection is at the center of the moral enterprise.

Participatory decision making. Based on his work with high schools, University of Notre Dame professor Clark Power observed that it is easy to get students to agree about such moral rules as "don't steal." But it is much harder to develop moral norms that students feel obligated to follow in their behavior.[4] A true norm is an operative moral standard, one to which children will hold themselves and others accountable. Such norms create a support system that helps students live up to their moral standards. Through

this process of putting belief into practice, a value becomes a virtue.

Participatory decision making, the fourth process of moral education in the elementary school, provides a motivational push from judgment to action. It does so by requiring children to participate in making rules or solving classroom conflicts; they are then held accountable for these decisions, which eventually become operative group norms.

Piaget was one of the first to argue for such participatory governance in the classroom.[5] He reasoned that, if children are truly to understand that people make rules to help themselves live with one another, they must have a hand in discussing and making classroom rules. Otherwise, rules remain external to the child's mind and have little power over behavior. What is essential, however, is not any specific set of procedures, but rather a *spirit* of participation and shared responsibility for the classroom.

There are many ways to foster responsible participation in classroom decision making. Teachers should begin slowly, using whatever they are comfortable with, and gradually branch out. For example, giving children a bigger voice in the classroom can start with something as simple as a suggestion box. It can expand to include teacher/student learning contracts, small-group brainstorming sessions as a means of solving a persistent classroom problem, a "Conflict Corner" where two students can go to work out their differences, a teacher-moderated "fairness committee" to propose solutions to classroom problems, written or oral feedback from students on a curriculum unit (What did you learn? How could it have been improved? How can we make the next unit better?), and regular class meetings.

Class meetings can be held weekly or daily, and they can be run by either consensus or by majority rule. Voting can be open (to encourage public stands) or by secret ballot (to minimize peer pressure). Through any of these methods, teachers can send the message to students that they value each child's viewpoint.

Participatory decision-making contributes to character development by helping children apply their moral reasoning to their own behavior and to the society around them. In a democratic society, participatory decision making has a special value in that it teaches democracy through democracy, training an active citizenry by having children be active citizens in the life of their school.

In summary, not only do these four

Through any of these methods, teachers can send the message to students that they value each child's viewpoint.

processes reinforce one another, but each is also necessary for the full success of the others. Discussion of moral issues, especially debate, is very difficult when the sense of community is weak or when students don't know or like their classmates. Debating moral issues is shallow without opportunities for real-life decision making. Class discussion is "all talk" if children never work together on substantive tasks. Cooperative learning fails to realize its full potential if children never plan and evaluate their joint endeavors. And, without the group spirit that is born of cooperative activity, participatory decision making turns into a forum in which students argue for their "rights" with little thought of their obligations or of the community good.

Taken together, these four processes offer elementary school teachers a way to develop the rational, affective, and behavioral aspects of children's character. Many teachers are already practicing this kind of character education with imagination, dedication, and skill. They have shown us that we have the means to bring our children to moral maturity, if only we can muster the will.

1. Robert Selman, *The Growth of Interpersonal Understanding* (New York: Academic Press, 1980).

2. Lawrence Kohlberg, *Essays on Moral Development, Volume 1: The Philosophy of Moral Development* (San Francisco: Harper & Row, 1981).

3. Robert Kegan, *The Evolving Self* (Cambridge, Mass.: Harvard University Press, 1982).

4. Clark Power, "The Just Community High School," in Kevin Ryan and George McClean, eds., *Character Development in Schools and Beyond* (New York: Praeger, 1987).

5. Jean Piaget, *The Moral Judgment of the Child* (New York: Free Press, 1932).

Prosocial Influences in the Classroom

W. DEAN McCAFFERTY

W. Dean McCafferty is a professor in the Department of Educational Psychology and Counseling at California State University at Northridge.

Instigation, development, and maintenance of prosocial norms and behavior are important aspects of classroom management and student learning. Prosocial norms and behavior commonly refer to concern for the needs, interests, and welfare of others. The intensity and extension of concern can range from a casual positive regard for relatives and friends to an unconditional devotion to all human beings, though it is usually the other way around. Many theorists and researchers include the notion of a mediating altruistic intention to help others in their definitions of prosocial behavior. Other experts restrict themselves to observable behaviors and consequences and are content with pursuing an understanding of how prosocial conduct appears and changes.

At present, no theory encompasses the many findings about prosocial behavior. However, many variables have been studied that can be implemented in classroom procedures with caution and applied research. These variables provide for the instigation of cohesive classroom group norms, ideally with school and community sanctions, which encourage educationally relevant cooperative behavior. Most important among such variables are nurturant teacher and student models who reinforce, expect, advocate, and even preach developmentally appropriate high standards for both learning and prosocial behavior. Learning is accepted as the legitimate outcome of individual and group efforts to achieve, and prosocial behavior is understood to involve strong empathic reasons for helping and accepting responsibility for others in need. The focus of the curriculum, therefore, becomes the academic, personal, and social needs of the teacher, individual students, and the classroom group as a whole. Educational research consistently supports positive outcomes for such a curriculum. Walberg and Anderson (1968) and Schmuck and Schmuck (1988) have demonstrated that interest in an academic task, mutual liking, and shared prestige produce better school performance and cohesive classroom groups as well as students who like school. Low-achieving students in noncohesive classroom groups receive little social acceptance, are aware of their low social status, and are most likely to drop out of school early (Stevens 1971; Oakes 1985).

Cultural and Group Norms

Prosocial behavior has been found to be much higher in cultures and groups that encourage socialization through (a) a group orientation toward helping, (b) an easy to understand social structure, (c) extended family relationships, (d) valued work for women, and (e) valued work for children from an early age (Madsen 1971; Whiting & Whiting 1975).

Recently, at the cultural level, whole school districts and even county districts have agreed upon common goals for teaching a group orientation toward helping with an easy to understand social structure and involving family and community efforts. Such programs usually have been directed at character or moral education. In Baltimore County, Maryland, a Values Education Task Force, representing a wide and diverse community base, cooperatively defined in concrete operational terms a "common core of values" for a K-12 values education curriculum. Concerned about the estrangement of students from traditional value sources, often including their families, the task force based the values program on the Constitution and the Bill of Rights. The study, begun in 1982, obtained commitments from parents, schools, and community organizations to participate in a joint responsibility to teach students, parents, and community members and keep them accountable for the curriculum (Saterlie 1988).

At the group level, prosocial classroom behavior has been promoted by establishing developmentally appropriate and educationally valued work for students, which they clearly understood how to achieve through individual effort and group support. Several recent de-

From *The Clearing House*, Vol. 63, No. 8, April 1990, pp. 367-370. Reprinted with permission of the Helen Dwight Reid Educational Foundation. Published by Heldref Publications, 4000 Albemarle St., N.W., Washington, D.C. 20016. Copyright © 1990.

velopments in cooperative learning have been applied successfully to different academic subjects, to a variety of students, and to many prosocial concerns. In each of these cases, special focus was given to shared individual efforts to help group members achieve both an individual and group academic and/or prosocial goal. For example, in Team Accelerated Instruction (TAI) developed by Robert Slavin (1987), four-member groups of mixed ability and ethnic backgrounds worked on individualized units that teammates checked against answer sheets. Individuals took their own unit test and received both individual credit and contributed to a group grade. Hence, students cooperated on helping each other achieve individualized learning unit. Positive results from cooperative learning approaches, such as TAI, have been documented for rural, urban, and suburban schools in five different countries. The results include grades 2 to 12 in all major subjects, for basic skills, problem solving and critical thinking, for low- and high-achieving students of various ethnic origins, and for student self-esteem, race relations, and mainstreaming (Slavin 1987).

Cognitive Models

Models are imitated by others because they are warm, nurturant, socially responsive, and/or appear competent and powerful. Family members, peers, teachers, students, mass media personalities, and even strangers can serve as potent models for prosocial behavior (Mussen and Eisenberg-Berg 1977). Teachers and peers who are well liked and have earned the reputation for being honest, knowledgeable, and credible are most influential in promoting important academic and prosocial gains in student behavior (Schmuck and Schmuck 1988). Generally, a models' actions speak louder than their words. Such actions accompanied by strongly voiced reasons that provide the student with an appropriate rationale for comforting, sharing with, or helping others are more effective. The rationale should be carefully tuned to the needs of the recipient, whether academic and/or personal-social. The cognitive communications of models should focus attention on important cues for responding, inferences about the beneficiary, and antecedents, processes, and consequences of aiding others. Also, in modeling reasoning techniques, it is crucial to consider the cognitive maturity of participating students. In addition to following the model, the students are explicitly learning to become models themselves. They need to understand how to perform in a variety of situations.

Prosocial reasoning progresses through at least five levels from kindergarten through high school (Eisenberg-Berg and Hand 1979). As children mature, they can develop, with the proper tutelage, clearer reasons and more concrete examples for why and how to help others. With greater maturity, students can understand better what the academic gains and/or personal-social welfare of others entails. Another important consideration is the development of a stable and consistent self-concept. As student's ability to preserve their self-concept and to see themselves consistently as moral persons increases, especially from age eight on, their justifications for prosocial conduct include more internalized self-references (Eisenberg 1983). Besides being able to detect subtle cues and recognize other's needs for academic and prosocial assistance, older children internalize more responsibility and become more competent in helping others (Pearl 1985; Peterson 1983). Hence, as children grow older, teachers and peers can model helping behaviors, such as tutoring, which increasingly refer to more subtle cues. They also can make more appropriate demands for competent academic and/or prosocial responses. More important, peers can refer more frequently to self-referenced values for assisting others.

Increases in prosocial behavior are associated with gains in moral reasoning (Nucci 1987). Mature moral reasoners often will help strangers or even someone they dislike (Eisenberg 1983). Modeling higher moral-reasoning processes should first involve children, especially if they are younger than eight years, in cooperatively constructing moral meanings inherent in moral acts. Children see moral events in terms of characteristics intrinsic to moral acts, such as fairness or harm. However, conventions are viewed as arbitrary rules or social norms. Younger children find the arbitrariness of conventions difficult to understand. They may first affirm rules and/or social norms and then negate them. Hence, effective models help children to clarify distinctions between the moral and conventional realms. As children gain competence in handling the differences between moral and conventional issues, they begin to profit from strong cognitive disagreement over ethical problems. Beginning in the late elementary grades, developmentally appropriate critical thinking, such as extending or refuting another's argument, is associated with improvements in moral reasoning (Nucci 1987).

Affective Models

Good affective models can empathize with students' problems whether they are academic or personal-social. Empathy generally refers to the ability to put one's self in the position (role) of another and experience how it feels. Modeling empathy should involve students in showing genuine concern for others. There is a very strong relationship among empathy, role taking, and prosocial behavior. Gains in prosocial conduct are associated with gains in the reciprocal ability to preserve self-attributes and take the role of others (Barnett, Howard, Melton, and Dino 1982). Children are able to grow out of their natural egocentricities by observing good affective models and performing developmentally appropriate role-taking activities. Switching roles, playing a variety of roles, and generating new roles can help students achieve the perspective of others. Attention should be focused not only on the thoughts, but especially on the feelings, of the role personality in question. Also, self-generated role personalities provide better learning and transfer than role personalities assigned by the teacher (Wittrock 1974). The empathy associated with perspective taking is acquired slowly. First, students should learn to imitate affective models who demonstrate academic performances and/or prosocial conduct. Later, with practice, students can intentionally generate roles for common scripts (Nelson 1981; Selman 1981; Underwood and Moore 1982).

Good affective models can demonstrate positive moods as well as strong empathy. Positive moods generally enhance willingness to assist others, whereas negative moods can generate complex effects. Blue feelings, which derive from personal misfortunes or problems and are focused on one's self are likely to inhibit altruism. Feelings of guilt or sadness, which are focused on the misfortunes and problems of others may increase altruism. If the sad plight of others is clearly understood, and empathy is high, then the impetus to help is strong. Hence, effective teacher and student models can empathize strong feelings for clearly understood social comparisons between needy student beneficiaries and themselves. Also, prosocial gains can be achieved when the model, peer, beneficiary, and social situation give support enough to reduce any fears or hesitations the student may have about generating prosocial conduct. The problems and needs of beneficiaries should be made obvious, and a helper's inward focus should be made less sad or costly (Barnett et al. 1982). Cooperative classroom learning can help provide such support where the problem receives conscious attention and mutual effort (Slavin 1987).

Prosocial Discipline

The focus of prosocial discipline should be *victim-centered* rather than *power-assertive* or *love-oriented* (Hoffman 1975). Power-assertive discipline, which involves coercion, and love-oriented discipline, which involves the withdrawal of affection, expose the student to antisocial punitive models. Coercion and the withdrawal of love elicit resentment in students and force their attention on their own negative consequences. Furthermore, punitive models tend to create tension and anxiety not only in the student being punished, but vicariously in other students in the class. The victim is motivated to "save face" in view of his or her classmates. This can have a very serious direct and vicarious effect on students with low self-esteem. Students with low self-esteem are self-conscious about their social behavior and how others perceive them. They are likely to react negatively and to be sensitive to disapproval or rejection (Fenigstein 1979). Punitive modeling also is frustrating for the teacher who wishes to have a beneficial influence because it begets behavior that is aggressive or withdrawing rather than prosocial.

Punitive models who exhibit cold and rejecting responses, such as the withdrawal of love, are frustrating to students and demonstrate a lack of concern for others by virtue of their aloofness. Also, continuous aggressive student responses, which are difficult to manage, produce fatigue in the disciplinarian. Because of this fatigue, the person modeling discipline often adopts a permissive stance that legitimizes combative behavior (Park and Salby 1983). A major problem with overly aggressive students is their propensity to view—inaccurately—the withdrawal responses of others as being permissive. Furthermore, aggressive students are likely to assign—inaccurately—malicious intent to legitimate assertive retaliations. The best solution for such aggressive behavior is to establish conditions whereby students can receive accurate understandings of the intentions and responses of others (Patterson 1982).

Models who practice victim-centered discipline focus attention on the harm caused to the victim rather than the negative consequences in store for the perpetrator. They attempt to get at the reasons behind the intentions of the harmdoer as well as the consequences for the student that has been harmed (Hartman 1974). In so doing, the disciplinarian models appropriate cognitive and affective prosocial responses. The perpetrators need to be informed about the harm they have caused and encouraged to empathize with the victim. They also need to learn how to respond in a helpful, rather than harmful, manner. Hence, standards of appropriate conduct can be jointly constructed by the disciplinarian and the audience. In the process, students need encouragement to put themselves in the place of the victim and experience that person's discomfort. Subsequently, they can learn, directly and vicariously by imitating models, how to aid the victim through helpful acts of reparation. And finally, students can learn to internalize positive self-values associated with making others feel better.

Conclusion

Prosocial influences in the classroom are concerned with group structure and process that emphasizes responsible cooperative behavior. This procedure is established and maintained by models who expect an appropriate level of academic and/or prosocial performance. Strong empathic cognitive modeling about antecedents, processes, and consequences of behavior seems to work best for all kinds of beneficiaries, including victims of aggression. Attention needs to be focused outwardly on the problems and needs of beneficiaries rather than inwardly on the disappointments of potential helpers.

REFERENCES

Barnett, M. A., H. A. Howard, E. M. Melton, and G. A. Dino. 1982. Effect of inducing sadness about self or other on helping behavior in high and low empathic children. *Child Development* 53:920–23.
Eisenberg, N. 1983. Children's differentiations among potential recipients of aid. *Child Development* 54: 594–602.

2. DEVELOPMENT: Childhood

Eisenberg-Berg, N., and M. Hand. 1979. The relationship of pre-schooler's reasoning about prosocial moral conflicts to prosocial behavior. *Child Development* 50: 356–63.

Fenigstein, A. 1979. Self-consciousness, self-attention, and social interaction. *Journal of Personality and Social Psychology* 37: 75–86.

Hoffman, M. L. 1975. Altruistic behavior and the parent-child relationship. *Journal of Personality and Social Psychology* 31: 937–43.

Madsen, M. C. 1971. Development and cross-cultural differences in the cooperative and competitive behavior of young children. *Journal of Cross-Cultural Psychology* 2: 365–71.

Mussen, P., and N. Eisenberg-Berg. 1977. *Roots of caring, sharing, and helping.* San Francisco: Freeman.

Nelson, K. 1981. In Social cognition in a script framework. *Social cognitive development: Frontiers and possible futures,* ed. by J. H. Flavell and L. Ross. New York: Cambridge University Press.

Nucci, L. 1987. Synthesis of research on moral development. *Educational Leadership* (February) 86–92.

Oakes, J. 1985. *Keeping track: How schools structure inequality.* New Haven, Conn.: Yale University Press.

Parke, R. D., and F. G. Salby. 1983. The development of aggression. In *Handbook of child psychology* Vol. 4, ed. by E. M. Hetherington. New York: Wiley.

Patterson, G. R. 1982. *Coercive family processes.* Eugene, OR: Castilia Press.

Pearl, R. 1985. Childrens understanding of others' need for help: Effects of problem explicitness and type. *Child Development* 56: 735–45.

Peterson, L. 1983. Influence of children's age, task competence, and responsibility focus on children's altruism. *Developmental Psychology* 19: 141–48.

Saterlie, M. E. 1988. Developing a community consensus for teaching values. *Educational Leadership* 45: 44–47.

Selman, R. L. 1981. The child as a friendship philosopher. In *The development of children's friendships,* ed. by S. R. Asher and J. M. Gottman, 242–272. Cambridge: Cambridge University Press.

Schmuck, R. A., and P. A. Schmuck. 1988. *Group processes in the classroom* (5th ed.), Chapter 6.

Slavin, R. E. 1987. Cooperative learning and the cooperative school. *Educational Leadership* (November): 7–13.

Stevens, D. 1971. Reading difficulty and classroom acceptance. *Reading Teacher* 25: 52–55.

Underwood, B., and B. Moore. 1982. Perspective-taking and altruism. *Psychological Bulletin* 91: 143–73.

Walberg, H., and G. Anderson. 1968. Classroom climate and individual learning. *Journal of Educational Psychology* 59: 414–19.

Whiting, B. B., and J. W. M. Whiting. 1975. *Children of six cultures.* Cambridge: Harvard University Press.

Wittrock, M. C. 1974. Learning as a generative process. *Educational Psychologist* 11: 87–95.

Changing Conditions for Young Adolescents:

Reminiscences and Realities

Today's young adolescents face many societal problems in addition to the innate personal problems of their age group. Middle schools—like it or not—must assist with these problems.

Judith A. Brough

JUDITH A. BROUGH is chair of and associate professor in the Department of Education at Gettysburg College, Gettysburg, Pennsylvania. Dr. Brough would like to acknowledge the assistance of Drs. Robert Curtis, Gettysburg College, and George White, Lehigh University, in the preparation of this article.

MY HOW THINGS have changed! Fade back to your days in junior high or middle school. Close your eyes and try to visualize your life back then. What did you look like? What did you most often think about? What activities occupied your time? What did you worry about? I remember worrying about the absence of a boyfriend; about my physical underdevelopment; about a "tough" English teacher. Those are "normal" worries for a thirteen-year-old. Contrast that to the following matters of concern reported by youngsters polled in 1987:

1. Kidnapping (76 percent very concerned; 16 percent sort of concerned).

2. The possibility of nuclear war (65 percent very concerned; 20 percent sort of concerned).

3. The fear of the spread of AIDS (65 percent very concerned; 20 percent sort of concerned).

4. Drug use by professional athletes (52 percent very concerned; 25 percent sort of concerned).

5. Air and water pollution (47 percent very concerned; 38 percent sort of concerned).

6. "Having to fight a war" (47 percent very concerned; 26 percent sort of concerned).

7. Increasing divorce (39 percent very concerned; 33 percent sort of concerned).[1]

My how things have changed. Permit me to particularize further.

Changes in the Family

My personal family situation made me rather a novelty during my middle level school days; I lived in a single-parent home. Today I would be the rule rather than the exception. The population of children involved in family changes has more than doubled over the past twenty-five years.[2] For example, more than one-third of the families in the United States are step-families. And, according to the U.S. census, 59 percent of the children born in 1983 will experience life in a single-parent home.[3]

Beaver Cleaver and his family used to represent the typical American family. Hodgkinson's data show that in 1955, 60 percent of U.S. households consisted of a working father, a housewife mother, and two or more kids (probably a station wagon and a dog, too). By 1980 that number had decreased to 11 percent, and by 1985 only 7 percent of our families could be so described.[4]

With a divorce rate of 50 percent in this country, teachers can no longer assume that a child and his/her parents share a common surname. In increasing instances, through multiple divorces and remarriages, children have come to live in families absent of biological parents.

Often the parents wait to divorce until the kids are "old enough to understand." However, during the middle level stage of development, ten- to fourteen-year-olds must unravel the mysteries of boy/girl relationships, test and study intricacies of adult and peer relationships, establish a sense of belonging as outlined by Maslow, and develop a sense of identity versus role confusion as described by Erikson. What a time to experience the break-up of the family!

The end of a marriage often involves fighting and custody battles. Children often feel guilty and somehow to blame for the break-up. Divorce can also mean

Reprinted with permission of *Educational Horizons*, Vol. 68, No. 2, Winter 1990, pp. 78-81. *Educational Horizons*, quarterly journal published by Pi Lambda Theta, national honor and professional association, Bloomington, IN 47407-6626.

a drop in family income or available money (even if child support payments are made, if a parent moves out s/he must pay additional monies for rent, for example), a move, and/or less adult supervision. Unfortunately, parents are understandably preoccupied at this point in their lives and cannot spend enough time and emotions in dealing with their youngsters. To many, school is the only stable environment and teachers the only stable adult role models. Certainly these youngsters cannot concentrate on subject matter until some of the emotional upheaval is resolved. They need adult guidance to help diminish the self-blame, to regain a sense of optimism about adult relationships, and to learn to accept the divorce and concomitant circumstances.

Other changes have also occurred in the American family. More than 50 percent of women have entered the work force, and that number is expected to increase. Before- and after-school care have become as important an issue as day care.

Kids today, therefore, do not have as much adult supervision as we did in the past. It is not uncommon to see kids in fast food restaurants buying their own suppers and eating with peers in like situations. These same kids go to local malls with credit cards in hand to buy their own clothes and do other shopping. A visit to the video arcade, today's equivalent of the pool hall of yesteryear, is inevitable.

DEALING WITH THE TOUGH TOPICS
Substance Use

When many of us were students, our major social decisions did not have to be made until we were at least sixteen or seventeen years old. In fact, some decisions could be postponed until even later. Despite the "drug culture" of the 1960s, there seemed to be little pressure for junior high or even high school students to become involved in substance abuse. Today, our fifth graders must make difficult decisions about illicit drug use. It's tough to "just say no" when you're ten years old and want to be accepted by your peers. And, unfortunately, these decisions may adversely affect the rest of our youngsters' lives. Deadly drugs like "crack" are now widely used. Children are experimenting with drugs and alcohol. As Packard reported, the extent is alarming:

1. The average age of a child taking his/her first drink of alcohol is now twelve years.

2. Over one million of our youngster aged twelve to seventeen have a serious drinking problem.

3. Arrests of children for drug use or

To many, school is the only stable environment and teachers the only stable adult role models.

dealing rose 4,600 percent in fifteen years.[5]

A survey of over eight thousand youngsters revealed that 12 percent of the fifth-grade students polled had used marijuana over the past year; 10 percent of the sixth graders admitted to use of the drug; 11 percent of the seventh graders; about 12 percent of the eighth graders; and 21 percent of the ninth graders.[6] Further, 40 percent of the fifth graders admitted to worrying about drugs and alcohol "quite a bit" or "very much."[7] Compare those data with your own fifth- through ninth-grade experiences.

Decisions About Sex

Certainly I didn't worry about this topic when I was in junior high school. I don't think I even knew about sex until I was well into my high school years. Nowadays, however, children are reaching puberty earlier—the average age in the U.S. is twelve. There are several theories to explain this phenomenon. Some of the most logical involve our advanced medical technology: better prenatal care, nutritional information and habits, fitness programs, etc. Further, some physicians maintain that the energy once used by the body to fight childhood diseases (e.g., measles, mumps, and whooping cough) is now put toward child growth, since many of these diseases have been eradicated.

Whatever the reason, the fact remains that children now develop reproductive capabilities much earlier. Several implications exist. One centers on the idea that earlier maturation necessarily means more time needed to keep the reins on sexual activity. The body, the hormones, and peers all scream at the young adolescent to "do it," while adults coax, "Don't do it." We're outnumbered three to one.

Second, earlier physical maturation is not necessarily matched by earlier emotional maturation. Therefore, typical thirteen-year-old emotions interject into a decision played out by an "older" body. We expect that if a youngster looks like a seventeen-year-old, s/he will act and reason like a seventeen-year-old. But, to borrow a phrase, it just ain't necessarily so.

So what has occurred as a result of earlier maturation compounded by other societal and familial changes? Kids have sex earlier. Packard reported that one-fifth of all youngster become sexually experienced within one year of reaching puberty.[8] He stated that a series of studies found that "the proportion of sexually experienced teenage girls doubled in less than a decade."[9] A report to the U.S. House Select Committee on Children, Youth and Families included the following statement:

Although the birth rates for all adolescents have actually dropped in recent years, the rates for the youngest "teens" (those from ten to fourteen years old) have actually risen. There are currently between 20 and 29 million adolescent boys and girls in the United States, of whom one-third to one-half are sexually active: this reflects a rate that is not dropping. More and more young adolescents are becoming sexually active and subsequently pregnant at earlier ages.[10]

Such premature sexual behavior has its perils. In addition to the obvious risk of unwanted and/or imprudent teenage pregnancy, as well as its concurrent medical hazards to mother and baby, is the danger of sexually transmitted disease. It has been reported that one-fourth of sexually active youngsters will contract a sexually transmitted disease prior to high school graduation.[11]

Certainly for each of us, decisions regarding sexual activity were serious. For youngsters today, they are critical. Not only are the decisions being made earlier, it has become a matter of life and death because of the advent of the deadly AIDS virus. If youngsters become sexually active during their middle level school years, how many partners will they have before settling into a monogamous relationship? Former Surgeon General Koop stated that "adolescents and pre-adolescents are those whose behavior we wish especially to influence because of their vulnerability when they are exploring their own sexuality (heterosexual and homosexual) and perhaps experimenting with drugs."[12]

When I was thirteen, there was no such threat. How about you?

Mobility

Because of various factors, including divorce, factory shut-downs, and job transfers (now more likely as more women enter the job force), our society has become increasingly mobile. About seven million children must enroll in a new school district each year.[13]

One of the results of this mobility is the dissolution of the extended family. Grandma no longer lives around the block. Therefore, a once-used and effective family support system has been removed. Grandma and grandpa were good "sounding boards." A middle level youngster could ask grandparents questions which couldn't possibly have been addressed to mom or dad. Another result is that extended family members are no longer close by and, therefore, available to baby-sit. Since middle level kids would balk at the idea of a baby-sitter being hired to watch them, often the kids are left home alone.

The middle level school years are a particularly difficult time to adjust to a relocation. It is during this time that belongingness and peer relationships are so important. A move necessitates making new friends in both school and home environments. It is difficult to break into already established young adolescent cliques. Packard concluded that by their teens, children who had frequently moved became "supercool," developed behav-

ior patterns to attract attention, and/or became loners.[14] Being too lonely may be more dangerous than being too boisterous.

*S*ince the world is changing for our students, so must their educational program change.

Suicide

I will never be able to accept the fact that some ten- to fourteen-year-olds feel so beset with problems that they attempt suicide. Although it is presumed that for every suicide there are one hundred unsuccessful attempts, no one can give us reliable statistics. The National Center for Health Statistics reported that in 1984 about 1,900 youngsters aged twelve to nineteen years committed suicide. Of these, 205 were between the ages of twelve and fourteen. "The suicide rate of teens aged 15-19 has more than doubled since 1960..."[15]

And how many accidents aren't really accidental? How many suicides are otherwise recorded on a death certificate?

The Middle Level Mandate

Middle level schools need to respond with programs and activities which help students cope with these changing societal structures. The purpose of any educational organization is to promote healthy physical, social,

emotional, and cognitive growth of the students it serves. Since the world is changing for our students, so must their educational program change. It must evolve continually in order to keep pace with the changing needs and characteristics of our nation's youth. Strategies, such as team planning, comprehensive guidance and counseling, advisor-advisee programs, and decision-making skills, must be components of the all-school program. It doesn't matter if we "turned out okay" without these and other current middle level strategies. How would we "turn out" if we were between ten and fourteen years old in the 1990s? Would we be able to cope with today's society, pressures, and stresses? Fade back. I'm not sure I could.

1. Roper Organization, Inc., *The American Chicle Youth Poll* (Morris Plains, N.J.: Warner-Lambert Co., The American Chicle Group, 1987), p. 19.
2. K. Appel, *Changing Families: A Guide for Educators*, Fastback #219 (Bloomington, Ind.: Phi Delta Kappa, 1985), p. 7.
3. H. Hodgkinson, *All One System: Demographics of Education -- Kindergarten through Graduate School* (Washington, D.C.: Institute for Educational Leadership, Inc., 1985), p. 3.
4. Ibid.
5. V. Packard, *Our Endangered Children: Growing Up in a Changing World* (Boston: Little, Brown and Company, 1983), p. 16.
6. P. Benson, D. Williams, and A. Johnson, *The Quicksilver Years: The Hopes and Fears of Young Adolescents* (San Francisco: Harper and Row, 1987), p. 150.
7. Ibid., p. 70.
8. V.Packard, *Our Endangered Children*, p. 15.
9. Ibid.
10. U.S. Congress, House Select Committee on Children, Youth and Families, *U.S. Children and Their Families: Current Conditions and Recent Trends, 1987* (Washington, D.C.: U.S. Government Printing Office, 1987), p. 71.
11. Carnegie Council on Adolescent Development, *Turning Points: Preparing American Youth for the 21st Century: A Report of the Task Force on Education of Young Adolescents* (Washington, D.C.: Carnegie Council on Adolescent Development, 1989), p. 25.
12. A. Lewis, "A Dangerous Silence," *Phi Delta Kappan* (January 1987): 348.
13. V. Packard, *Our Endangered Children*, p. 53.
14. Ibid., p. 57.
15. U.S. Congress, House Select Committee on Children, Youth and Families, *Infancy to Adolescence: Opportunities for Success*, National Center for Health Statistics, (Washington, D.C.: U.S. Government Printing Office, 1989), p. 53.

Meeting the Needs Of Young Adolescents:
Advisory Groups, Interdisciplinary Teaching Teams, and School Transition Programs

For each of the key practices studied, there is good evidence that strong implementation yields benefits that are educationally significant, Mr. Mac Iver reports. But the movement to implement these practices still has a long way to go.

DOUGLAS J. MAC IVER

DOUGLAS J. MAC IVER is an associate research scientist in the Center for Research on Elementary and Middle Schools and in the Center for Research on Effective Schooling for Disadvantaged Students, Johns Hopkins University, Baltimore.

ACROSS THE nation, a consensus appears to be emerging. Researchers specializing in early adolescent development, leading educators in the middle school movement, state departments of education, and foundations are all recommending similar changes in practice in the middle grades and in the organization of schools that include those grades — changes designed to lessen the current debilitating mismatch between the developmental needs of young adolescents and the characteristics of middle-grade programs.[1] The Carnegie Task Force on Education of Young Adolescents stated the problem succinctly:

> Middle grade schools — junior high, intermediate, and middle schools — are potentially society's most powerful force to recapture millions of youth adrift, and help every young person thrive during early adolescence. Yet all too often these schools exacerbate the problems of young adolescents.[2]

Prominent among the recommended practices are the use of group advisory periods, the establishment of interdisciplinary teacher teams, and the use of "articulation" activities with students, parents, and school staff members to ease students' transition from one level of schooling to the next. In this article I address questions concerning the structure, use, and effects of these practices. To what extent are middle-grade schools currently using these recommended practices? Does the use of these practices differ in schools serving different grade spans, in different locations, and serving different types of student populations? What are the effects of these practices on a school's level of success (e.g., on the overall strength of a school's program or on a school's ability to reduce its retention and dropout rates)?

In addressing these questions I use data from the recent national survey of practices and trends in middle-grade education conducted by the Johns Hopkins University Center for Research on Elementary and Middle Schools (CREMS). These data describe in detail the education of early adolescents in a large, representative sample of public schools that include grade 7.[3]

GROUP ADVISORY PERIODS

One major challenge facing educators in the middle grades is how to provide early adolescents with the social and emotional support they need to succeed as students. As young adolescents strive for autonomy, as they grapple with learning how to regulate their own behavior and make responsible choices, their need for close, caring adult supervision and guidance is paramount.

But how can schools that enroll young adolescents meet this need? The typical organization of instruction in schools that enroll young adolescents interferes with the development of close, trusting relationships between students and teachers.[4] For example, in a worthy attempt to provide students with high-quality instruction from subject-matter experts, many schools that serve middle grades establish departmentalized programs in which students receive instruction from a different teacher for each academic subject. (Even schools with semidepartmentalized programs or interdisciplinary teams often assign students to four or more different teachers.) As students change teachers every period (perhaps six or seven times a day), they may feel that no teacher or other adult in the school really knows them, cares about them, or is available to help them with problems. And their engagement in learning is likely to diminish as they begin to look outside the school for attention and rewards.

To reduce this risk, many schools are developing more responsive support systems, including homerooms, advisory groups, counseling services, and other activities designed to provide guidance and to monitor the academic, social, and emotional welfare of individual students.[5] Group advisory periods assign a small group of students to a teacher, administrator, or other staff member for a regularly scheduled (often daily) meeting to discuss topics important to students.

Sixty-six percent of the schools in the CREMS national survey have one homeroom or group advisory period, and 9% have two such periods. Although advisory or homeroom periods are common, many of the activities that occur during

This article is reprinted from *Phi Delta Kappan*, February 1990, pp. 458-464, with permission of the author.

these periods are the mechanical tasks of keeping school (e.g., taking attendance, distributing notices, making announcements, orienting students to rules and programs) rather than social or academic support activities that use teachers' talents as advisors and that help students feel that someone is looking out for their interests and needs. Social and academic support activities include discussing problems with individual students, giving career information and guidance, developing student self-confidence and leadership, and discussing academic issues, personal or family problems, social relationships, peer groups, health issues, moral or ethical issues and values, and multicultural issues and intergroup relations.

We asked principals to tell us how frequently each of the support activities listed above occurred during group advisory periods at their schools. The principals responded using a five-point scale ranging from "never" (1) to "daily" (5). The overall mean for the nine support activities was 2.3; each activity tended to occur only a few times per year. Only 28% of the schools reported that most support activities occurred at least monthly.

Middle schools (6-8), along with K-8, K-12, and 7-8 schools, provide supportive group advisory activities to their students more frequently than do junior high schools (7-9) and middle/high combination schools (7-12).[6] But junior high schools and middle/high schools are more likely than other schools to have at least one professional guidance counselor on staff. (Every junior high school and 99% of the middle/high schools in our sample had at least one guidance counselor.) Our analyses reveal that, regardless of grade span, schools that have guidance counselors are significantly less likely to use supportive group advisory activities.

On the other hand, our analyses also reveal that grade span predicts a school's use of support activities even after statistically removing the effect of having a guidance counselor.[7] The finding that 7-9 and 7-12 schools use supportive group advisory activities less even after "removing" this effect suggests that including one or more of the high school grades in a school that begins in the middle years makes it less likely that the school will establish a strong group advisory program for its young adolescents. Carnegie unit requirements concerning course offerings (which begin in ninth grade) may limit the number of periods available for group advisory activities in the high school years. Although nothing prevents junior high schools or middle/high schools from offering frequent group advisory activities to their seventh- and eighth-graders (even if they can't offer them to their ninth-graders), these schools usually choose not to differentiate their programs in this way.

Schools serving large numbers of economically disadvantaged students are more likely than other schools to establish group advisory periods that provide social and emotional support for students. Similarly, urban schools or schools serving predominantly black student populations provide more frequent support activities.

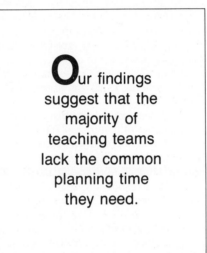

Our findings suggest that the majority of teaching teams lack the common planning time they need.

We also analyzed the measurable benefits obtained by schools that provide frequent support activities during a group advisory period.[8] We wanted to know whether principals are more likely to report that their schools are successfully meeting students' needs for guidance, advice, and counseling when their schools use group guidance activities frequently or whether principals view these activities as pretty much a waste of time. We also wanted to know whether a strong group advisory program helps a school to "rescue" students who are en route to dropping out (e.g., by reducing students' feelings of anonymity and alienation in school). We found that, according to principals' estimates (with other geographic, demographic, and school variables taken into account), schools that have strong group advisory programs are more successful at meeting students' needs for guidance, advice, and counseling and at lowering the proportion of students who will drop out before finishing high school.

Thus the evidence suggests that there are important benefits associated with providing a strong group advisory program. However, the use of group advisory periods should not be viewed as a panacea. The impact of a group advisory program on these indicators of a school's success was significant but modest. For example, our data indicate that a school in which an average of nine supportive group advisory activities occur each month rather than never typically saves 2% of its students from dropping out before high school graduation and raises the principal's rating of the excellence of the schools' guidance services by just over one-fifth of a point on a four-point scale.

INTERDISCIPLINARY TEACHING TEAMS

The recommendations issued by the numerous task forces concerned with reforming education in the middle grades highlight interdisciplinary teams of teachers as a keystone for effective education in the middle grades.[9] Interdisciplinary teams are composed of colleagues who teach different subjects but share the same students. For example, four teachers may share 150 students. Because they share the same students, teachers on a team may be able to respond more quickly, personally, and consistently to the needs of individual students. In theory, teachers on a team know how their students are doing in all subjects, discuss the students' needs for special help with other teachers, arrange extra time for learning, and so on. Teachers on interdisciplinary teams may also meet as a team with each student's parents to review the student's progress and to plan interventions.

Interdisciplinary teams may eliminate the isolation that many teachers feel by providing a working group of colleagues to conduct activities and to discuss and solve mutual problems. In theory, instruction will be more effective in schools that use interdisciplinary teaming because the teachers on a team can plan thematic units that enable students to make connections between ideas in different disciplines. For example, an interdisciplinary unit called "The Day the World Changed" might explore how important rebellions, revolutions, and paradigm shifts in history, science, mathematics, and literature can be seen to fit together.

Students in schools using interdisciplinary teaming become members of a small unit with which they can identify; a stable clustering of peers and teachers allows them to develop close associations. Assignment to interdisciplinary teams theoretically helps students build "team spirit," enhances their motivation to learn, and improves their attitudes toward school because of the closer, more coherent supervision and caring that teams can provide.

About 42% of early adolescents (in 37% of the schools surveyed) receive instruction from interdisciplinary teams of teachers at some time between grades 5 and 9. Teams of teachers range from two to seven or more. More students (34%) have teams of four teachers than teams of other sizes. (However, more schools use two-teacher teams; smaller schools, especially K-8 and K-12 schools, tend to use two-teacher or three-teacher teams.) Although there is great variety in team composition, the most typical four-teacher team consists of one math, one English, one social studies, and one science teacher.

More 6-8 middle schools (just over 40%) use interdisciplinary teaming than do other types of schools included in our survey. However, most schools do not use interdisciplinary teams, including about 60% of the middle schools and about 75% of the schools with other grade organizations. In any case, interdisciplinary teaching teams offer a variety of possibilities and present a variety of challenges.

Common planning time and its use. If teachers on an interdisciplinary team are not given sufficient planning time in common, they cannot do the collaborative work that makes teams successful. Yet about 30% of the schools that use interdisciplinary teaming have a master schedule that contains no officially scheduled common planning time for team teachers, and only 36% of the schools that use interdisciplinary teaming give team members two or more hours of common planning time each week. Without officially scheduled common planning time, interdisciplinary team members must meet before or after school or during lunch period. This makes it much more difficult to coordinate the efforts of the team, to design interdisciplinary units, to meet with parents, and to discuss students needs. Our findings suggest that the majority of teams do not have the common planning time they need to become truly effective.

Even if team members are assigned common planning time, teachers do not always use a meaningful portion of this time for team activities. According to principals' estimates, teachers devote nearly half of their common planning periods to working on their own lessons, tests, and grades rather than to team planning and coordination. Of course, this may be necessary if teachers are provided only one planning or preparation period each day; even teachers who are on teams need time for individual preparation.

The principals in our survey estimated that team members did devote some (rather than little or none) of their common planning time to the following team activities: deciding on common themes and related topics for instruction, discussing the problems of specific students and arranging help, meeting as a team with parents to solve problems and provide assistance for individual students, and arranging assemblies, trips, or other team activities. On the other hand, teams rarely used team planning time for regrouping students (in order to better match lessons to abilities) or for revising schedules (to allow for activities that need more time). In theory, interdisciplinary teaming facilitates flexible grouping and scheduling practices; in reality, regrouping and flexible scheduling seldom occur, even in schools using interdisciplinary teaming.

Finally, the data indicate that increases in the amount of common planning time are strongly associated with increases in the amount of time the team spends coordinating content, diagnosing individual student needs, planning special events, conducting parent conferences, regrouping, and rescheduling. Thus the provision of adequate planning time does make a real difference in how a team functions.

Benefits and problems of teaching teams. Principals were asked to estimate how frequently 10 benefits or problems resulted from the use of interdisciplinary teams of teachers. The most commonly agreed-on benefits were that teachers received social support and understanding from other team members, that instruction was more effective because of increased integration and coordination across subjects and courses, that students' problems were recognized quickly and solved effectively, and that students identified with the team, developed team spirit, and improved both their work and their attitudes.

The most commonly agreed-on problems were that the teams did not have enough planning time, that the teachers were insufficiently trained in the team approach, and that the school schedule prevented flexibility in regrouping students or in varying time for different subjects. Principals did not think that teachers' personality clashes or preferences for identifying with subject-area departments posed problems for the success of interdisciplinary teams. Overall, those principals who were not using interdisciplinary teams in their schools thought that the problems of teaming would be more severe and that the benefits would be smaller than did the principals whose schools were using interdisciplinary teams.

As anticipated, in order to obtain the greatest benefit from interdisciplinary teaming, a school must provide teachers with adequate common planning time. Schools that provide more than two hours per week of common planning time that is regularly used for team coordination report obtaining substantially greater benefits from teaming than do schools that provide little or no common planning time.

Commitment to interdisciplinary teaming. Although 32% of all public schools use interdisciplinary teaming in the seventh or eighth grades, only 10% of schools show a strong commitment to teaming by providing adequate common planning time and by having the team use a significant portion of that time for team planning and activities.[10] Middle schools (6-8) and 7-8 schools have a significantly stronger commitment to interdisciplinary teaming than do K-8, K-12, and junior high (7-9) schools. Schools that serve especially advantaged or disadvantaged populations are also more likely than the average school to make a deep commitment to interdisciplinary teaming. Schools that serve many children whose parents are professionals or managers are the most likely of all to establish well-organized interdisciplinary teaming programs. But schools serving students whose achievement is considerably below national norms and who are at great risk of dropping out before finishing high school are also more likely than the average school to make a strong commitment to interdisciplinary teaming.

Although leaders of the middle school movement have sometimes implied that a departmental organization is incompatible with the use of interdisciplinary teams, the data show that schools that organize their teachers into departments (with department heads or common planning periods for departments) or that use single-subject teaching teams are not significantly less likely than others to make a deep commitment to interdisciplinary teaming. A departmental emphasis and an interdisciplinary emphasis coexist in many of the schools that use interdisciplinary teaming.

Our data support the claim that a well-organized interdisciplinary team approach can strengthen a school's overall program for students in the middle grades. With other geographic, demographic, and school variables taken into account, principals in schools with a deeper commitment to teaming are more likely than other principals to perceive that the present practices at their schools are meeting students' needs effectively and that the schools' overall middle-grade programs are "solid" or "exemplary."[11] Similarly, schools that have a strong commitment to interdisciplinary teaming report obtaining more frequent benefits from their interdisciplinary teams than do schools with less well-organized teaming programs.

Assignment of teachers. In 76% of the schools that use interdisciplinary teams in the seventh or eighth grades, administrators make the team assignments rather than allow teachers to choose the members of their teams. In about 40% of these schools, teams can be adjusted if teachers dislike their team assignment. In junior high schools or middle/high combination schools, where teams are least frequently used overall, it is more often up to teachers to organize their own teams.[12]

Recently, there has been a call to give middle-grade teachers a more significant voice in the decisions that affect them.[13] Does it matter how teachers are assigned to teams? Are teams more effective when teachers choose the other teachers on their teams?

The evidence suggests that the advantages associated with giving teachers a primary role in making team assignments are significant but modest. Teachers on "self-chosen" teams spend more of their common planning time in team planning and coordination. In addition, according to the principals surveyed, self-chosen teams are more likely than administrator-appointed teams to achieve more effective instruction through "integration and coordination across subjects and courses." On the other hand, administrator-appointed teams are as effective as self-chosen teams in building team spirit among students, in recognizing and solving the problems of individual students, and in using other team members as sources of social support.

Establishing team leaders. One might assume that having a team leader — someone who is directly responsible for coordinating and organizing team activities — would help a team to be more successful. However, among schools that use interdisciplinary teams in the seventh or eighth grades, about 40% have no team leaders. In about 28% of the schools, team leaders are appointed by the principal. In still other schools, team leadership is determined by the members of the team: the leader is elected by the other members of the teaching team in 16% of the schools, and the teachers

establish a system in which team leadership rotates among members in 5% of the schools. Finally, in 9% of the schools, principals report that a team leader emerges informally as the team works together.

Our data clearly show that having a formal team leader (whether elected, appointed, or rotating) is better than having no leader at all. Teams with a for-

> **G**iving teachers a primary role in making team assignments has significant but modest advantages.

mal leader spend significantly more of their common planning time on team activities. Similarly, principals report more frequent benefits from interdisciplinary teams in schools where there are formally designated leaders. Our data also suggest that the method by which leaders are selected has a slight impact on a team's effectiveness: teams with elected or rotating leadership devote more of their common planning time to team activities than do teams with appointed leaders.

SCHOOL TRANSITION PROGRAMS

Social scientists have expressed considerable concern about the potential negative effects of school transitions on young adolescents.[14] Our data indicate that more than 88% of the public school students in the U.S. enter a new school when they begin the middle grades, and this transition brings many changes in the school and classroom environments.[15] Furthermore, as students enter the middle grades, they are simultaneously undergoing the social and biological changes associated with early adolescence. Although a transition to a school that has a more appropriate environment may have a positive effect on students,[16] there is clearly a risk that these simultaneous adaptational challenges will overwhelm

the coping skills of some students and have pathogenic effects on their psychological adjustment, self-esteem, and motivation to learn.

We asked principals to report on their use of 10 articulation activities designed to help students make a smooth transition to the middle grades. These included several activities designed to orient incoming students and their parents to the programs and procedures at the middle-grade school and to prepare them for the new responsibilities and the new curricular and social demands they would face (e.g., having elementary students visit the middle-grade school for an assembly, having parents visit the middle-grade school while their children are still in elementary school, or having middle-grade students present information to elementary school students); activities to provide incoming students with sources of social support as they adjust to the new school (e.g., establishing buddy or big brother/big sister programs to pair new students with older ones); and activities that bring elementary and middle-grade educators together so that they can inform one another about the programs, courses, and requirements of their schools.

In our survey the average number of articulation activities used to help students make a smooth transition to the middle grades was 4.5. Even schools that enroll younger students along with early adolescents (e.g., K-8 and K-12 schools) usually conduct at least one or two activities to help students adjust to the middle grades. This indicates that principals recognize that a significant "school transition" occurs between the elementary and middle grades even if the students don't change buildings.

The three most common activities for easing the transition from the elementary to the middle grades (reported by more than 40% of the principals) were: having elementary school students visit the middle-grade school, having the administrators of middle-grade and elementary schools meet to discuss programs and articulation, and having middle-grade counselors meet with elementary counselors or staff members.

Some potentially promising activities were infrequently used, perhaps because they are more difficult to implement. Only 20% or fewer of the principals reported the following practices to ease the transition to a middle-grade school: having elementary school students attend regular classes at the middle-grade school, having summer meetings at the middle-grade school for incoming students, and having a buddy program that pairs new students with older ones.[17]

Which types of middle-grade schools have the most extensive articulation and transition activities in preparing students for entry? Middle schools, junior high schools, and 7-8 schools have similarly extensive articulation programs. Articulation activities are less extensive in 7-12 schools than in schools that enroll only middle-graders. Schools containing a large percentage of students living in poverty have less extensive articulation programs, while schools in populous metropolitan areas, schools serving a large percentage of professional or managerial families, and schools serving a large percentage of high-ability students have more extensive programs.

Principals were asked to rate the quality of their articulation activities. On a four-point scale ranging from "weak — need to design new practices and major changes" (1) to "excellent — practices fit students' needs exactly" (4), the average rating reported was 2.8. This indicates that many principals perceived their articulation programs to be good ones and believed that only minor changes were needed. As might be expected, schools using numerous and diverse articulation activities were more likely than others to earn high ratings from their principals. A more important finding is that fuller and more diversified articulation programs actually do help students succeed in their first year at a middle-grade school. That is, fewer students are retained in the transition grade in schools that have extensive articulation programs, even after taking account of other variables that influence retention rate.[18]

Easing the transition to high school. Not only must middle-grade schools insure that students make a smooth transition to the middle grades, but they must also prepare students for the transition to high school. For schools in our survey, the average number of articulation activities used to help students make a smooth transition to the high school grades was 3.9, significantly less than the average of 4.5 activities used to help students enter the middle grades. Middle schools and 7-8 schools offer the most extensive programs for smoothing the transition to high school; junior high schools offer less help with this transition than do middle and 7-8 schools but offer considerably more help than do K-8 schools. Schools in which the transition to high school does not involve a change of buildings (7-12 and K-12 schools) offer even fewer articulation activities at this transition point. Most K-12 schools provide no special articulation activities to assist stu-

dents with their entry into the high school grades.

Overall, schools with more extensive "elementary to middle grade" articulation programs also have more extensive "middle grade to high school" articulation programs. The most common articulation activities found in school transition programs are similar for both transitions: students visit the school they are about to enter, and administrators or counselors from the sending schools discuss articulation and programs with their counterparts from the receiving schools.

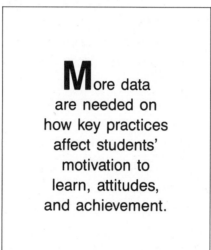

More data are needed on how key practices affect students' motivation to learn, attitudes, and achievement.

Teachers in the middle grades are significantly less likely than counselors and administrators to be given the opportunity to interact with their counterparts in elementary and high schools. Although teachers are expected to prepare their students for the coursework at the next level of schooling, they are typically not given the opportunity to discuss articulation with colleagues at other levels of schooling.

Parent involvement in transition programs. Articulation activities that involve parents at both points of transition are used by many schools, including most middle, 7-8, and junior high schools. Helping parents understand their children's new schools should help the students entering these schools and should also help the schools to maintain parent involvement.

Our data indicate that schools that involve parents in their articulation practices are, indeed, much more likely to maintain a strong partnership with parents (independent of other variables that influence the level of parent involvement found in a school). For example, 45% of the middle-grade schools that involve parents in at least two "elementary to

middle grade" articulation activities also formally recruit and train parents to work as school volunteers (as opposed to only 23% of schools that do not involve parents in the transition activities). Seventy-six percent of the middle-grade schools that involve parents in at least two "elementary to middle grade" articulation practices also have parent/teacher organizations with elected officers and active committees; only 62% of the schools that don't involve parents in articulation activities have similarly active parent/teacher groups. Finally, when parents are taken seriously in a school's articulation activities, the teachers at the school are more likely to continue to involve parents in the education of their children by frequently sending information and ideas to parents on how to help their children with homework and study skills.

SUMMARY AND CONCLUSIONS

The advocates of the middle-grade reform movement (educators, associations, foundations, state boards of education, and researchers) have often recommended the use of interdisciplinary teams, advisory groups, and transition activities as key components of a responsive and responsible educational program for young adolescents. Our analyses of national data from a large representative sample of public schools enrolling seventh-graders explored the use of these components in the "real world" in 1988 and tested the effects of these components on a school's level of success.

Our research essentially answered two key questions: Are the leaders of the reform movement barking up the right trees? (Are these practices effective? Do schools that adopt these practices reap important benefits?) And is anyone paying attention to the barking? (To what extent have middle-grade schools across the nation adopted credible versions of these practices? To what extent have they ignored the suggested reforms or implemented them poorly?) Our data permit at least three clear conclusions.

1. *There are important benefits associated with establishing extensive and well-organized implementations of these practices.* For each of the key practices studied, we found good evidence that strong implementation yields benefits that are educationally significant. For example, by helping a school better meet young adolescents' social and emotional needs, a group advisory program can play an important role in dropout prevention. Based on principals' estimates, a school that provides students with extensive social support and frequent oppor-

tunities to discuss topics that are important to them by means of a regularly scheduled group advisory period is more successful than other schools in increasing the proportion of its students who stay in school until high school graduation.

Likewise, interdisciplinary teams of teachers — if they have an appropriate leader, sufficient common planning time, and the willingness to use this planning time for team activities — were reported to produce a wide variety of benefits. These teams were seen to increase the effectiveness of instruction, to provide teachers with a much-needed support system, to help insure that students' problems will be recognized and solved, to improve students' work and attitudes, and to have a positive impact on the school's overall program for the middle grades.

Finally, school transition programs that use numerous and diverse articulation activities were seen to help students succeed in their first year following a school transition.

2. *If a major goal is to see most schools adopt effective implementations of these practices, the movement to restructure education in the middle grades still has a long way to go.* Although more than two-thirds of the schools that include grade 7 have a group advisory period, these periods are usually short and are focused on taking attendance, distributing notices, making announcements, and so on. Only 28% of the schools have a group advisory program that provides frequent social and academic support activities. Similarly, most middle-grade schools (63%) do not use interdisciplinary teaming at any grade level, and those that do use teaming often provide insufficient common planning time or have groups with no leader to coordinate and organize the team activities. Finally, although most schools do something to try to ease student transitions to and from the middle grades, some of the most

promising articulation activities (e.g., having a buddy program that pairs new students with older ones upon entry to the school) are rarely used.

3. *Additional data are needed to help us understand and improve education in the middle grades.* Although the information I have reported in this article should be useful to middle-grade educators who are making decisions about their schools, more data are needed to study how students' motivation to learn, attitudes, and achievement are directly influenced by these and other key practices. Only by collecting a great deal more information on the diversity of educational approaches and practices in schools for the middle grades and on young adolescents' academic achievement and attachment to school will we be able fully to document and understand the effects of different practices on the progress of students.

1. Jacquelynne Eccles and Carol Midgley, "Stage-Environment Fit: Developmentally Appropriate Classrooms for Young Adolescents," in Carole Ames and Russell Ames, eds., *Research on Motivation in Education*, vol. 3 (New York: Academic Press, 1989), pp. 139-86; Joan Lipsitz, *Growing Up Forgotten* (New Brunswick, N.J.: Transaction Books, 1980); Anne Petersen, "Adolescent Development," *Annual Review of Psychology*, vol. 39, 1988, pp. 583-607; Roberta Simmons and Dale Blyth, *Moving into Adolescence: The Impact of Pubertal Change and School Context* (Hawthorne, N.Y.: Aldine de Gruyter, 1987); William Alexander and Paul George, *The Exemplary Middle School* (New York: Holt, Rinehart & Winston, 1981); John Lounsbury, *Perspectives: Middle School Education, 1964-1984* (Columbus, Ohio: National Middle School Association, 1984); *Caught in the Middle: Educational Reform for Young Adolescents in California Public Schools* (Sacramento: California State Department of Education, 1987); Maryland Task Force on the Middle Learning Years, *What Matters in the Middle Grades?* (Baltimore: Maryland State Department of Education, 1989); and *Making the Middle Grades Work* (Washington, D.C.: Children's Defense Fund, 1988).

2. Carnegie Task Force on Education of Young Adolescents, *Turning Points: Preparing American Youth for the 21st Century* (New York: Carnegie Council on Adolescent Development of the Carnegie Corporation, 1989), p. 8.

3. Joyce L. Epstein and James M. McPartland, *Education in the Middle Grades: A National Survey of Practices and Trends* (Baltimore: Johns Hopkins University Center for Research on Elementary and Middle Schools, 1988). For more details on the sample, participation rates, and survey topics, see Joyce L. Epstein and Douglas J. Mac Iver, *Education in the Middle Grades: Overview of a National Survey of Practices and Trends* (Baltimore: Johns Hopkins University Center for Research on Elementary and Middle Schools, 1989), pp. 2-3.

4. Eccles and Midgley, pp. 165-66.

5. Epstein and Mac Iver, pp. 16-20.

6. Douglas J. Mac Iver and Joyce L. Epstein, *Responsive Education in the Middle Grades: Teacher Teams, Advisory Groups, Remedial Instruction, School Transition Programs, and Report Card Entries* (Baltimore: Johns Hopkins University Center for Research on Elementary and Middle Schools, 1989), pp. 6-8.

7. Ibid., p. 7.

8. Ibid., pp. 8-9.

9. See also Epstein and Mac Iver, pp. 21-28.

10. Mac Iver and Epstein, pp. 10-13.

11. Ibid., pp. 14-16.

12. Epstein and Mac Iver, p. 24.

13. See, for example, Carnegie Task Force . . . , p. 55.

14. See, for example, Dale Blyth, Roberta Simmons, and Steven Carlton-Ford, "The Adjustment of Early Adolescents to School Transitions," *Journal of Early Adolescence*, vol. 3, 1983, pp. 105-20; Eccles and Midgley, op. cit.; Maurice Elias, Michael Gara, and Michael Ubriaco, "Sources of Stress and Support in Children's Transition to Middle School: An Empirical Analysis," *Journal of Clinical Child Psychology*, vol. 14, 1985, pp. 112-18; Simmons and Blyth, op. cit.; and Lisa Crockett et al., "School Transitions and Adjustment During Early Adolescence," *Journal of Early Adolescence*, vol. 9, 1989, pp. 181-210.

15. Jacquelynne Eccles, Carol Midgley, and Terry Adler, "Grade-Related Changes in the School Environment: Effects on Achievement Motivation," in J. G. Nicholls, ed., *The Development of Achievement Motivation* (Greenwich, Conn.: JAI Press, 1984), pp. 283-331.

16. Eccles and Midgley, op. cit.; and L. Mickey Fenzel, "Role Strains and the Transition to Middle School: Longitudinal Trends and Sex Differences," *Journal of Early Adolescence*, vol. 9, 1989, pp. 211-26.

17. Epstein and Mac Iver, pp. 37-38.

18. Mac Iver and Epstein, p. 20.

Respectful, Dutiful Teenagers

Out of TV's wasteland, here's the first generation. They're Global Villagers.

BY ROBERT ATKINSON

Robert Atkinson, Ph.D., is an assistant professor of human development at the University of Southern Maine. A full report of this study appears in The Teenage World: Adolescent Self-Image in Ten Countries *(Plenum Press, 1988).*

TWENTY YEARS AGO Marshall McLuhan predicted that television would create an electronic global village. If so, many felt, it would be a wasteland. Two events in the summer of 1985, the Live Aid Concert and the hijacking of a TWA jet in Beirut, both witnessed by a worldwide television audience, seemed to bear out McLuhan's thesis. But has the unifying power of television created the predicted wasteland of shallow and degenerate viewers? If a look at the first generation reared on television is the measure, the answer is no.

A new international data base of adolescents that my colleagues and I have just completed tests McLuhan's forecast. A global village has indeed sprung up among this generation of teenagers, who share common values and attitudes. But they are anything but delinquent products of the wasteland.

At the Center for the Study of Adolescence in Chicago, psychiatrists Daniel Offer and Eric Ostrov, psychologist Kenneth Howard and I found that psychological maturation follows a common process worldwide. It consists of increased introspection and self-evaluation, leading to the formation of personal identity, ambitions and goals. The profiles we collected of nearly 6,000 adolescents from 10 nations have given us a sense of how teenagers in different countries see themselves.

Far outweighing the expected gender, age and nationality differences in self-image is the finding that young people of similar socioeconomic backgrounds throughout the world are more alike than different. The attitudes of the world's teenagers are remarkably uniform. For example, the overwhelming majority of teenagers surveyed from Australia, Bangladesh, Hungary, Israel, Italy, Japan, Taiwan, Turkey, West Germany and the United States hold very positive attitudes toward their families. The popular image of adolescents as alienated from their parents was not verified. Instead, we found that today's youth have great respect for their parents. Very few teenagers expressed dislike for or carried grudges against their parents. Few thought their parents were ashamed of them and almost all felt assured of their parents' continued support and pride in them.

Another teenage stereotype, being directionless and self-centered, was also disproved. At least 90 percent of the teenagers we polled agreed with the statements "A job well done gives me pleasure" and "At times I think about what kind of work I will do in the future." Only a small percentage endorsed the statement "I would rather be supported for the rest of my life than work."

A common portrait emerged of a very peer-oriented group. Most teenagers were interested in developing and maintaining social ties and also seemed committed to their friends. They said that being with others gave them good feelings and that they tried to help their friends whenever they could.

Overall, nearly three-quarters of those surveyed appear to be well adjusted. They are generally happy, self-controlled, caring toward others, concerned with the repercussions of their actions, sociable, comfortable thinking and talking about sex and realistic and effective in their approaches to problem-solving. They are confident that they will be able to assume responsibilities for themselves in the future.

On the dark side, however, one-quarter of the adolescents tested said they are frequently sad and lonely and feel empty emotionally, as well as overwhelmed by life's problems. A few even admitted suicidal thoughts and leanings. This depressed, or "quietly disturbed," group had difficulty coping with life's surprises and was strapped with a poor self-image.

Adolescents' general mood can be accounted for, in part, by their country's economic and demographic conditions. For example, the relatively high rate of depression we found among Bengali youth may be related to severe poverty. But the relatively high rate of depression found among Japanese youth may be due to the social pressure to achieve.

Another factor that may contribute to both poor mental health and a lower self-image is the proportion of adolescents in the total population. Turkey and Bangladesh have the highest proportion of 14-to-18-year-olds among the countries studied, and teenagers in those two countries reported a lower self-image. The amount of money a country spends on education, on the other hand, shows a positive correlation. In the United States and West Germany, which are the countries spending the most money on education per capita, teenagers scored the

From *Psychology Today*, October 1988, pp. 22, 26. Copyright © 1988 by PT Partners, L.P.

The Universal Teenager: Common Concerns

PERCENT WHO AGREE	Australia	Bangladesh	Hungary	Israel	Italy	Japan	Taiwan	Turkey	United States	West Germany	International Average
A job well done gives me pleasure.	95	95	96	98	96	98	97	96	97	94	96
My parents are ashamed of me.	11	7	4	3	4	15	10	8	7	2	7
I like to help a friend whenever I can.	94	92	92	93	91	90	94	93	94	91	92
Very often I feel that my mother is no good.	11	10	9	9	9	17	15	6	13	6	9
At times I think about what kinds of work I will do in the future.	91	93	87	85	87	91	91	90	94	91	90
My parents will be disappointed in me in the future.	14	10	9	6	7	23	22	13	7	6	11
Being together with other people gives me a good feeling.	93	84	93	88	87	78	76	91	95	94	88
Very often I feel that my father is no good.	19	12	13	6	15	14	18	8	15	9	13
I feel empty emotionally most of the time.	27	39	12	20	29	29	47	42	18	8	27
I often feel that I would rather die than go on living.	30	38	17	19	15	20	14	25	19	19	22
I feel so lonely.	22	43	14	17	20	39	33	32	18	11	25
I find life an endless series of problems—without solution in sight.	27	39	11	23	13	39	31	37	15	18	25
I frequently feel sad.	27	36	24	28	25	55	26	34	25	17	29

Teenagers agreed or disagreed with each statement from the Offer Self-Image Questionnaire. The teens were surveyed in two age groups, 13 to 15 and 16 to 19, except in Japan, where only the older group responded.

highest in ability to cope effectively with life's uncertainties.

We found that traditional sex-role patterns — in which men are associated with power and women are invested in relationships and emotions — were consistent across the 10 nations that we studied. Boys appeared to be more self-centered, even self-indulgent, while girls appeared more other-oriented and more emotionally open.

The shared attitudes we found indicate that there is a common adolescent experience worldwide. This may be due partially to a common developmental process. But it is also likely that the modern teenager is a product of the electronic revolution. This generation's growth toward maturity has coincided with the world growing smaller.

Undoubtedly, teenagers, the age group most easily swayed by peer pressure and outside influences, have been affected by the unifying power of television. We may be witnessing a global cohort of teenagers influenced by information and images that have a common origin. This generation of teenagers may be the first to have experienced a world culture and the first really to have felt a connection with their age-mates from around the world.

Learning

- Information Processing/Cognitive Learning (Articles 15-18)
- Behavioristic Learning (Article 19)
- Humanistic/Social Psychological Learning (Articles 20-21)
- Instructional Strategies (Articles 22-26)

Learning can be broadly defined as a relatively permanent change in behavior due to experience. Learning is not a result of change due to maturation or drugs. Changes in behavior result from a complex interaction between individual characteristics of students and environmental factors. One of the continuing challenges in education is understanding these interactions so that learning results can be predicted. This section focuses on approaches within educational psychology that represent unique ways of viewing the learning process. Each approach emphasizes a different set of personal and environmental factors that influence certain behaviors. While no one approach can fully explain learning, each is a valuable contribution to our body of knowledge about the process.

The discussion of each learning approach includes suggestions for specific techniques and methods of teaching to guide teachers in understanding student behavior and in making decisions about how to teach. The articles in this section reflect a recent emphasis on applied research conducted in schools rather than in laboratories. The relatively large number of articles on information processing/cognitive learning and instruction, as opposed to behaviorism, also reflects a change in emphasis. Behaviorism, however, remains very important in our understanding of learning and instruction.

Researchers have recently made significant advances in understanding the way our minds work. Information processing refers to the way that the mind receives sensory information, stores it as memory, and recalls it for later use. This procedure is basic to all learning, no matter what teaching approach is taken, and we know that the method used in processing information determines to some extent how much and what we remember. The articles in this subsection present some of the fundamental principles of information processing, and examine concepts of thinking.

In cognitive learning, new knowledge is obtained as existing knowledge is reorganized and altered. This process is often stimulated when we are presented with information that disagrees or is incompatible with knowledge we already possess. Cognitive learning is practiced continually by children as they learn about their world; they make discoveries by perceiving things that pique their curiosity or raise questions in their minds. The third article in this subsection describes discovery learning as an effective approach to integrating the principles of cognitive learning with instruction.

Behaviorism is probably the best-known approach to learning. Most prospective teachers are familiar with concepts such as classical conditioning, reinforcement, and punishment, and there is no question that behaviorism has made significant contributions to understanding learning. But behaviorism has also been subject to much misinterpretation because it seems so simple. In fact, the effective use of behavioristic principles is complex and demanding, as the article in this subsection points out.

Humanistic/social psychological learning emphasizes the affective, social, and personal development of students. Humanistic learning involves an acceptance of the uniqueness of each individual, and stresses human feelings, values, and self-worth. To the humanist, learning is the personal discovery of the meaning of information, not simply a change in behavior or thinking. A central theme in humanistic learning is the development of self-concept and self-esteem through self-perception.

Social psychology is the study of the nature of interpersonal relationships in social situations. In education, this approach looks at teacher-pupil relationships and group processes to derive principles of interaction that affect learning. One of this area's most significant contributions to learning is the understanding of how teacher expectations affect student behavior. The first article in this subsection reviews how expectations are expressed, and maintains that teachers need to monitor their interactions carefully to communicate the appropriate expectations. The second article summarizes research about a specific method of instruction—cooperative learning—that is based on social psychological principles.

Instructional strategies are the methods of conveying

information and teacher behaviors that affect student learning. Teaching methods or techniques can vary greatly, depending on objectives, group size, types of students, and personality of the teacher. For example, discussion classes are generally more effective for enhancing thinking skills than are individualized sessions or lectures. For this subsection, we have selected some major instructional strategies to illustrate the variety of approaches. Most effective teaching strategies are based on learning principles. The first article summarizes research on effective teaching to indicate instructional strategies that promote student learning. How controversy can be used to enhance critical thinking and other important outcomes is addressed in the second article. The third article examines principles of best practice in asking questions. The fourth article suggests methods of instruction that match learning styles of students, while the last article discusses methods to encourage student creativity.

Looking Ahead: Challenge Questions

Compare and contrast the different approaches to learning. What approach do you think is best? What factors are important to your answer (e.g., objectives, types of students, setting, personality of the teacher)?

What are some teaching strategies that you could use to promote greater student retention of material? What is the best way to attract and keep students' attention? Is it necessary for a teacher to be an entertainer?

What are some advantages and disadvantages to discovery learning?

How can a teacher promote positive self-concepts, values, and attitudes? Is this more important than cognitive achievement?

How do teacher expectations affect student learning? How much emphasis should be put on cultivating positive student interactions? Do you think cooperative learning is feasible? Why or why not?

The Celebration of Thinking

Elliot W. Eisner

ELLIOT W. EISNER is professor of education and art at Stanford University.

Celebration has a spirit that is rare in discussions of American schooling. Celebration connotes joy, ceremony, something special in experience. Celebrations are events we look forward to and prize. The celebration of thinking suggests an honoring of, and a joy in, a process we all consider central to education. Yet those of us who work in education today are admonished to get serious, to tighten up, to excise the so-called soft side of school programs. One way to do this is to specify a common curriculum. Another is to prescribe to teachers the steps that should be taken to teach the students in our classrooms. The former solution neglects student idiosyncrasy and aptitude differences by assuming that in curricular matters one size fits all. Both Allan Bloom, in *The Closing of the American Mind*, and E. D. Hirsch, in *Cultural Literacy: What Every American Needs to Know*, come close to such solutions, the former in the name of intellect, the latter in the name of culture.

The specification of teaching method appeals to our sense of techne, a technology of practice that is deduced from research that aims to assure, if not guarantee, results. The most common pedagogical procedure for such a technology is the breaking up of content into small units, prescribing a uniform sequence among those units, and using an objective, multiple-choice test to measure learning. Both approaches to school improvement have little place in their lexicons for celebration. Both, if they celebrate anything, celebrate standardized content, standardized method, and standardized objectives measured by standardized tests.

The idea that education is best served by standardizing method, content, goals, and evaluation procedures leads to another consequence. It tends to convert education into a race. Those who achieve goals most quickly win. This attitude is expressed in the proliferation of preschools, the academic formalization of kindergarten, the creation of "better baby" institutes, and the all-too-common syndrome that David Elkind refers to as the hurried child (see his book *The Hurried Child*, Addison-Wesley, 1981). At more-advanced levels, this attitude is represented in the growth of Stanley Kaplan schools and the special high school courses on the SATs. Yet speed in accomplishing tasks is not particularly compatible with the concept of celebration. Events that we celebrate are events that we like to prolong. Efficiency and speed in completing a task are characteristics of tasks that are distasteful. We like to clean our kitchen or the toilet bowl efficiently, but who likes to eat a great meal efficiently? What we enjoy we wish to savor.

> "Getting through the curriculum in the shortest possible time is a virtue primarily when the program is noxious."

My argument here is not to slow up teaching and learning for its own sake but rather to recognize that speed is no necessary virtue. Getting through the curriculum in the shortest possible time is a virtue primarily when the program is noxious. Thinking, which we celebrate here today, should be prized not only because it leads to attractive destinations but also because the journey itself is satisfying.

Language and Knowledge. It is the nature of thinking and the forms through which it occurs that I wish to focus upon. In American schools, like their counterparts in Europe, thinking is often conceptualized as a process that is both abstract and linguistic in nature. Thinking, like knowledge itself, is argued by some to depend upon language. To truly have knowledge, one must be able to make a claim about the world that is capable of being verified. The truth or falsity of a belief can be determined only if the belief can be stated in words; and not just any words, but propositions. Without propositions, there is no claim. Without a claim, there is no test; without a test, there is no verification. Without verification, there is no knowledge. (For elaboration of this point, see Denis Phillips's "After the Wake: Postpositivistic Educational Thought," *Educational Researcher*, May 1983.)

The argument goes further. To state propositions, one must be able to think in a propositional form. Indeed, some claim that language itself makes thinking possible. Consider the following statement by Adam Scaff, a prominent student of language:

When we adopt the monistic standpoint, we reject the claim that language and thinking can exist separately and independently of one another. Of course, we are talking about specifically *human* thinking, in other words about *conceptual* thinking. Thus we assert that in the process of cognition and communication, thinking and using a language are inseparable elements of one and the same whole.

What such a view has meant for schools is that language has been assigned a place of privilege in our educational priorities, in our time allocations, and in our concept of

From *National Forum*, Spring 1988, pp. 30-33. Originally from *Educational Horizons*, Fall 1987, quarterly journal published by Pi Lambda Theta national honor and professional association, Bloomington, IN 47407-6626. Reprinted by permission of *Educational Horizons*, and the author.

intelligence itself. I need not remind you that the best predictor of IQ is the vocabulary subtest on the IQ test. The SATs have two sections, verbal and mathematical. So do the GREs. Human intellectual ability, the ability to think, is made almost isomorphic with the ability to use language or number.

My aim is to challenge that view. I wish to portray a conception of mind, of thinking, of intelligence that is not restricted to language. Any view of intellect that is limited in scope will penalize those students whose aptitudes reside outside of its boundaries. If schools are aimed at the cultivation of intellect, those students whose aptitudes lie in forms of thinking excluded from the accepted conception of intellect will themselves be excluded from a place in our educational sun. So, too, will others whose aptitudes are in the use of language; for language itself, I will argue, depends upon forms of thinking and intelligence that relate to the qualitative aspects of our experience.

A Biological Basis for Thinking and Learning. I start with the claim that humans do not enter the world with minds, but with brains. The task of education, acculturation, and socialization is to convert brains into minds. Brains are born and minds are made, and one of the privileges of the teaching profession is to have an important part to play in the shaping of minds.

The major means through which this feat is accomplished is through the programs we offer in schools—the curriculum—and the quality of the process through which it is mediated—teaching.

When we define school curricula, our definition reflects views of mind that we believe are important. Our culture regards language skills as important and defines intelligence as being able to handle abstract, language-based tasks. I wish to develop another view of thinking and intelligence and, hence, another basis for deciding about the content and goals of our school programs.

Traditionally we have separated mind from body. The separation is Platonic. For Plato mind was lofty and body was base. Working with one's head was different and more noble than working with one's hands. Today we have manual trade schools for those who are good with their hands, but the really bright take physics. This separation, this unfortunate dichotomy, is philosophically naive, psychologically ill-conceived, and educationally mischievous. There is no competent work of the hand that does not depend on the competent use of the mind. The mind and senses are one, not two.

Consider the world in which we live. It is first and foremost a qualitative world: that is, a world consisting of qualities we are able to experience; color, texture, smell, sounds are qualities that permeate our world. Becoming conscious of that world or some aspect of it depends upon a skilled and intact sensory system. I emphasize *skilled*. We often do not think of the senses as being skilled; they are just there. But if you think about it, the qualities of the world are not simply given to human experience; they must be won. Experience is not simply an act or event; it is an achievement. We learn to see and hear. We *learn* to read the subtle qualitative cues that constitute the environment. We learn to distinguish and differentiate between the small furry creatures we call kittens, squirrels, and puppies. Eventually, if we care enough, we are able to see qualities in Irish setters, golf clubs, fine wines, antique cabinets, Japanese pots, and the complex nuances of American football that others miss. If we care enough and work hard enough, we *achieve* experience. We become connoisseurs of some aspect of the world.

It is through cultivated or refined sensibilities that the nuances and pleasures of a Beethoven quartet are experienced; the differences between a smile and a smirk are noticed; the achievements of a fine craftsman are appreciated. It is through a cultivated and refined sensibility that patterns in nature and culture are distinguished. It is from these patterns that the works of science and art are built.

Remembering and Imagining. The development of the sensibilities not only provides us with access to the qualities of the world. It is through the content of such experience that we are able to perform two very important cognitive operations: we are able to remember and we are able to imagine.

Recall, or remembering, is the ability to reconstruct in our mind's eye images encountered earlier. The sensibilities, a part of our *minding*, provides recall with its content. What we have noticed we are more likely to be able to recall. What we have not experienced we cannot under normal circumstances remember. The ability to remember, therefore, is significantly influenced by the qualities of the world we are able to experience in the first place. The differentiation of the sensibilities is a key process in providing the mind with a content.

The ability to remember is clearly a crit-

> ### *"The task of education, acculturation, and socialization is to convert brains into minds."*

ical aspect of our cognitive capabilities, but to remember without the ability to imagine would leave us with a static culture. The engine of social and cultural progress is our ability to conceive of things that never were, but that might become. The central term in the word imagination is *image*. To imagine is to create new images, images that function in the development of a new science, the creation of a new symphony, and the invention of a new bridge. It is a process critical for the creation of poetry and for innovation in our practical lives. But imagination, like recall, works with qualities we have experienced. What was not first in the hand cannot be later in the head. Try to imagine something you have never experienced. You will find that while you are able to imagine new forms of animals, autos, devices for seating, and the like, the components of these entities are qualities you once encountered. Our imaginative life is built out of experience.

One would think, given the importance of imagination, that it would be regarded as one of the basics of education. It is not on anyone's list of basics, at least not in any national report on the state of our schools. We are far more concerned with the correct replication of what already exists than with cultivating the powers of innovation or the celebration of thinking. Perhaps a little parity among these educational goals would be appropriate.

Everything that I have said thus far about the sensibilities and about recall and imagination pertains to events that occur inside our heads. Recall and imagination are qualities of human experience that are internal and private. I can enjoy my own fantasies and you can enjoy yours, but you cannot access mine, nor I yours. If things were left that way, culture would be static; even worse, it would eventually cease to exist, because culture depends on communication. Communication requires the externalization of what is internal, a shift through which what is private is made public.

Using Forms of Representation. This process of making the private public is a process we take too much for granted. It is an extraordinary achievement, one that is still evolving and, although language is our prime vehicle, we have over time found it necessary to create other means through which what we have thought, felt, and imagined could be given a public face. In my book *Cognition and Curriculum* (Longmans, 1982), I have called these means "forms of representation." Becoming acculturated means acquiring the multiple forms of literacy that enable one to encode or decode such forms of representation.

Forms of representation are visual, auditory, tactile, gustatory, and even olfactory. They manifest themselves in pictures, speech, the movements of dance and gesture, in words, and in number. Each of these social devices carries meanings that represent qualities we have experienced directly or through recall or imagination. Hence, experience that is visual may be uniquely represented by forms of representation that exploit the visual; if we want to know what someone looks like, a picture is better than a paragraph. If we want to know about a sequence of events over time, a story is usually better than a picture. If we want to convey the vital and dynamic experience of our emotional life, dance and music are probably better than a string of numbers. Our curricula could be designed to help children acquire the multiple forms of literacy.

The use of any form of representation has at least four important educational functions. First, it is important to recognize that there is nothing so slippery as a thought. Working with a form of representation provides the opportunity to stabilize what is ephemeral and fleeting. Second, it gives students an opportunity to hold onto their thinking. Thoughts in one's head are difficult to edit. Thoughts written on a paper, portrayed on a canvas, arrayed in a notation, or reproduced on a recorded tape can be edited, and the process of editing allows one to refine one's thinking, to make it clearer and more powerful, and, not least, to appreciate the happy achievements created.

The editing process, whether in writing, painting, or making music, is not much emphasized in our schools. Students typically write not to communicate what they care about but to answer questions, posed by the teacher, that the teacher already has answers to.

The third function of using a form of representation to externalize the internal is to makes communication possible. For our thoughts to be known, they must be given public status: they must, somehow, be made public. Imagine how impoverished our musical life would be if Mozart at age 13 decided not to notate his magnificent music, or if Cézanne simply enjoyed the views of Mount St. Victoire rather than painting them, or if Isaac Newton decided not to tell. The history of art and Western science would have been ineluctably altered.

The fourth function of using a form of representation is to provide opportunities for discovery. The creation of anything is more like a dialogue than a monologue. The act of making something is not only an occasion for expressing or representing what you already know, imagine, or feel; it is also a means through which the forms of things unknown can be uncovered. The creative act is an act of exploration and discovery.

Thinking should be celebrated by giving students opportunities to try to represent what they think they know. And because what they know cannot always be pro-

jected in a single form of representation— say, the logical use of language—they should have a variety of options available and the skills with which to use them.

Forms of Representation Have a Syntax. There is one other feature about forms of representation that is relevant to our discussion concerning the celebration of thinking. All forms of representation have a syntactical structure. The term syntax comes from the Latin *syntaxis*, which means to arrange. For example, forms of representation used in painting or drawing require the student to arrange the qualities within the work so that they cohere. The same is true of musical composition or choreography. What the individual seeks is a coherent, satisfying form. Other forms of representation, such as the use of word and number, must also be arranged. However, mathematics and much of language, particularly in the early grades, is more rule abiding than structure seeking. (For a discussion of this distinction see G.L. Rico's *Writing the Natural Way*.) That is, there are strict conventions that work within these forms must meet. To use the English language correctly requires that one obey the rules for language use. To spell correctly requires that one put letters in the proper order. To calculate correctly requires that operations be performed according to rule.

However, the problem in our schools is that activities whose syntactical structure is rule-abiding dominate the curriculum to the virtual exclusion of figural or structure-seeking activities. As we all know, students never learn one thing at a time. While they are learning to write and to compute they are also learning to be good rule followers. They are also learning that for most tasks, and especially the most important ones, the correct answer is known. The teacher knows it or, if not, it can be found in the back of the book.

I believe we should be concerned about a curriculum that places such a heavy emphasis on such limited forms of learning and thinking. When these forms of learning dominate a curriculum, they also cultivate a disposition, and that disposition is one that does not match the kinds of problems with which most people must deal in life outside of school. Life's problems are seldom solved by following rules or applying algorithms. They almost always have more than one solution, and they typically require judgment and trade-off. They are problems that more often demand a satisfying sense of closure than a single correct answer. The paucity of such problems in our programs creates a disjuncture between what we emphasize in the short-term and what we seek as the long-term goals of schooling. Ironically, one area of thinking that has the most to offer is often the most neglected in our schools. I speak of the arts. The arts are models of work that do

emphasize the creation of coherent structure, that do encourage multiple solutions to problems, that do prize innovation, that do rely upon the use of judgment, and that do depend upon the use of sensibility. In short, the arts, a realm of thinking typically neglected in our school programs, constitute our potentially most important means of celebrating thinking.

Now I am painfully aware that the current educational climate for the ideas I have expressed is not as hospitable as it might be. As I indicated when I began, we do not typically pay much attention to celebrating thinking, or curiosity, or imagination, or creativity in our schools. In addition, we have a strong tendency to want to monitor the quality of schooling by implementing a common program and applying common standards to determine who comes in first. The results, like the results at the Belmont race track and the Kentucky Derby, are published in the newspapers.

Developing Multiple Forms of Literacy in Our Schools. Consider the matter of content and the ways in which students display what they have learned. The content that we care about, let's say, is helping students understand the life and times of the slaves just prior to and during the Civil War. This material, as you know, is common fare for fifth-graders in many elementary schools in our country. What students learn about slavery will be shaped by the kind of messages they are given. In turn, these messages are shaped by the forms of representation that we choose to use. If the students read an artistically crafted historical text, not only will they be given access to facts, but the language itself, its style and form, will enable them to learn something about how the slaves felt and what those who kept slaves felt about their own lives. Through narrative and prose that exploit the capacity of language to generate images and to foster feeling, an effective picture of the period can be rendered and secured. Of course, to secure this picture students must know how to read. They must know how to read not only clipped, factual accounts but also literary accounts. They must be sensitive to the melody, cadence, and metaphor of language if the text contains them.

But even when students possess such high levels of reading comprehension, literary text cannot tell all. The music of the period, the hymns, the chants, the rhythms of Africa can also help students gain access to the period. And so can Matthew Brady's photos and Lincoln's Emancipation Proclamation and Gettysburg Address. So, too, can the mythology of the slaves and their homespun stories. Further, it would be useful for students to create their own plays about the period and to act them out. It might be useful for them to perform the dances and to eat what the slaves of the period ate.

A model of curriculum that exploits various forms of representation and that utilizes all of the senses helps students learn what a period in history feels like. Reality, whatever it is, is made up of qualities: sights, smells, images, tales, and moods. First-hand experience is simply a way of getting in touch with reality. In our schools we often rely upon conceptually dense and emotionally eviscerated abstractions to represent what in actuality is a rich source of experience. To compound things further, we require students to tell us what they have learned by trying to fit it into one of four alternatives to a multiple-choice question.

The use of multiple forms of representation in the construction of curriculum is not limited to social studies; good math teachers use them in the teaching of math.

Graphics, charts, histograms, and number diagrams are ways of helping students access mathematical ideas through forms that many find easier to grasp. The fact that charts, diagrams, schematics, and spreadsheets are very useful ways to display information has been quickly understood by IBM, Apple, and Toshiba. They waste no time pointing out to prospective customers how much more readable and saleable their products will be if they use graphics. In this respect, they are far ahead of educators.

The hegemony of language on our curriculum, and a narrow version at that, limits what students can come to know and restricts thinking processes to those mediated mainly by language. What language can carry is not all that we can know. Ultimately, what we know is rooted in qualities encountered or images recalled and imagined.

The celebration of thinking should be returned to our classrooms. It should be given a seat of honor in its own right, for its own rewards. The forms in which thinking occurs should not be subjected to the status differences and inequities of our society. Is a first-rate piece of science really better or more important than a first-rate symphony? Is knowledge of geometry more important than understanding and appreciating poetry? I am not urging a displacement of science for art or math for poetry. I am not arguing for the creation of a new privileged class, but rather for a decent conception of what our students are entitled to. Without opportunities to acquire multiple forms of literacy, children will be handicapped in their ability to participate in the legacies of their culture. Our children deserve more than that.

Putting Learning Strategies to Work

By increasing students' repertoires of tactics for learning, we can prepare them to develop their own strategies for problem solving in the classroom and beyond.

SHARON J. DERRY

Sharon J. Derry is Associate Professor and Chair, Cognitive and Behavioral Sciences, Department of Psychology, Florida State University, Tallahassee, FL 32306-1051.

Recent research in cognitive and educational psychology has led to substantial improvements in our knowledge about learning. Researchers have identified certain mental processing techniques—learning strategies—that can be taught by teachers and used by students to improve the quality of school learning. Let me illustrate.

As a professor of educational and cognitive psychology, I often begin the semester with a simulation exercise designed to illustrate major principles about the role of learning strategies in classroom instruction. For example, recently I presented my students with the following scenario:

You are a high school student who has arrived at school 20 minutes early. You discover that your first-period teacher is planning to give a test covering Chapter 5. Unfortunately, you have prepared the wrong chapter, and there is no one around to help you out. Skipping class is not the solution, since this results in an automatic "F," and you would never dream of cheating. So you open your book and use the next 15 minutes as wisely as you can.

I gave my students 15 minutes to study. They then took a quiz with eight main idea questions and two application questions. At the end of the quiz, I asked them to write in detail exactly what they did when they studied. Quizzes (without names) were collected and then distributed randomly to the class for scoring and for analyz-

Learning is a form of problem solving that involves analyzing a learning task and devising a strategy appropriate for that particular situation.

ing the study strategies reported in them.

Few people performed well on this test. A student who did wrote the following:

There wasn't enough time for details. So I looked at the chapter summary first. Then I skimmed through the chapter and tried to understand the topic paragraphs and the summary paragraphs for each section. I also noticed what the headings said, to get the organization, and I noticed certain names that went with each heading, figuring they did something related to each topic, a study or something. I started to do some memory work on the headings, but time was up before I finished.

By comparison, most students answered only two or three of the main idea questions, reporting a study strategy something like the following.

Panic. There was not enough time! I started going over the chapter and got as far as I could, but it was hopeless. I assume you do not plan to grade this quiz, because that would be unfair!

As illustrated in these two examples, the differences between successful and unsuccessful learning

strategies often are clear and striking. Whereas the successful learners assessed the learning situation and calmly developed a workable plan for dealing with it, the less successful learners were occupied with fruitless worries and vague strategies but little planning effort.

Such an exercise serves to introduce the following important principles about self-directed learning:

1. The plan that one uses for accomplishing a learning goal is a person's learning strategy. Learning strategies may be simple or complex, specific or vague, intelligent or unwise. Obviously, some learning strategies work better than others.

2. Learning strategies require knowledge of specific learning skills, or "tactics" (e.g., Derry and Murphy 1986), such as skimming, attending to chapter structure, and memorization techniques. The ability to devise appropriate learning strategies also requires knowledge about when and when not to use particular types of learning tactics.

3. Learning is a form of problem solving that involves analyzing a learning task and devising a strategy appropriate for that particular situation. Different learning situations may call for different strategies.

Further, I asked my students to determine whether any reported learning strategy had produced useful knowledge. Alas, no participant had applied the knowledge acquired in the 15-minute study session to the two application questions on the quiz. Even when learning strategies are apparently successful according to one form of measurement, the resultant learning is not necessarily usable later

Sharon J. Derry, "Putting Learning Strategies to Work," *Educational Leadership*, December 1988/January 1989, pp. 4-10.

Category	Examples	Some Conditions of Use	Strengths or Weaknesses
Attentional Focusing			
Simple focusing	Highlighting. Underlining.	Structured, easy materials. Good readers.	No emphasis on importance or conceptual relations of ideas.
Structured focusing	Looking for headings, topic sentences. Teacher-directed signaling.	Poor readers. Difficult but considerate materials.	Efficient, but may not promote active elaboration, deep thinking.
Schema Building	Use of story grammars, theory schemas. Networking.	Poor text structure. Goal is to encourage active comprehension.	Inefficient, but develops higher-order thinking skills.
Idea Elaboration	Some types of self-questioning. Imagery.	Goal is to comprehend and remember specific ideas.	Powerful, easy to combine. Difficult for some students unassisted. Will not ensure focus on what is important.

Fig. 1. Tactics for Learning Verbal Information

in problem solving. Thus, we added a fourth principle to our list:

4. In most school learning situations, strategies should be devised with the aim of creating usable, rather than inert, knowledge. Clearly, not all learning strategies will lead to the formation of usable knowledge structures.

Next I will elaborate these principles in greater detail, suggesting how they can influence classroom practice.

Strategies as Learning Plans

There is much confusion about the term *learning strategy*. The term is used to refer to (1) specific learning tactics such as rehearsal, imaging, and outlining (e.g., Cook and Mayer 1983, Levin 1986); (2) more general types of self-management activites such as planning and comprehension monitoring (e.g., Pressley et al. in press a); and (3) complex plans that combine several specific techniques (e.g., Derry and Murphy 1986, Snowman and McCown 1984).

To clarify the uses of the term, I distinguish between the specific tactics and the learning strategies that combine them. Thus, a learning strategy is a complete plan one formulates for accomplishing a learning goal; and a learning tactic is any individual processing technique one uses in service of the plan (Derry and Murphy 1986, Snowman and McCown 1984). That is,

a learning strategy is the application of one or more specific learning tactics to a learning problem. Within this definition, the plethora of learning techniques (popularly called "strategies") being promoted by various researchers and practitioners can be viewed as potentially useful learning tactics that can be applied in various combinations to accomplish different learning jobs.

This definition points to the need for two distinct types of strategies instruction: specific tactics training and training in methods for selecting and combining tactics into workable learning plans. Teachers can incorporate both types of training into regular classroom instruction by thoughtfully combining different study tactics—outlining plus positive self-talk, for example—and assigning them along with regular homework.

Learning Strategies Employ Specific Learning Tactics

In this section I discuss tactics in three major categories: (1) tactics for acquiring verbal knowledge, that is, ideas and facts fundamental to disciplines such as science, literature, and history; (2) tactics for acquiring procedural skills such as reading, using language, and solving problems that underlie various curriculum disciplines; and (3) support tactics for self-motivation,

which are applicable to all types of learning situations. (For a more thorough treatment of these topics, see the reviews by Derry and Murphy 1986, Weinstein and Mayer 1985, Levin 1986, and Pressley et al. in press b.)

Verbal learning tactics

Strategies aimed at improving comprehension and retention of verbal information should build upon tactics that enhance these mental processes: (1) focusing attention on important ideas, (2) schema building, and (3) idea elaboration (see fig. 1).

Attentional focusing. Two types of attention-focusing tactics are simple focusing and structured focusing. In the simple focusing category, highlighting and underlining are common examples. Unfortunately, the use of simple focusing procedures does not necessarily ensure identification of important information. I have often confirmed this point by requesting to see the textbooks of students who are having academic problems. Frequently I find almost every word in their texts highlighted.

Students, weaker ones in particular, should be taught to combine simple focusing with structured focusing, whereby the learner directs primary attention to headings, topic sentences, or other signals provided by the instructional presentation. The teaching

3. LEARNING: Information Processing/Cognitive

Category	Examples	Some Conditions of Use	Strengths or Weaknesses
Pattern Learning			
Hypothesizing	Student reasons and guesses why particular pattern is or isn't example of concept.	Goal is to learn attributes of concepts and patterns.	Inefficient unless feedback given. Encourages independent thinking.
Seeking reasons for actions	Student seeks explanations why particular actions are or are not appropriate.	Goal is to determine which procedures are required in which situations.	Develops meta-cognitive knowledge. Inefficient if not guided. If too guided, might not promote thinking skills.
Reflective Self-Instruction	Student compares reification of own performance to expert model.	Goal is to tune, improve complex skill.	Develops understanding of quality performance. May increase self-consciousness, reduce automaticity.
Practice			
Part practice	Student drills on one specific aspect of performance.	A few specific aspects of a performance need attention.	Develops subskill automaticity. Doesn't encourage subskill integration.
Whole practice	Student practices full performance without attention to subskills.	Goal is to maintain or improve skill already acquired or to integrate subskills.	May consolidate poorly executed subskills. Helps develop smooth whole performance.

Fig. 2. Tactics for Learning Procedural Knowledge

of structured focusing is a well-established practice in English classes, and it can profitably be reinforced in other courses to help students identify information they need to learn. However, the success of structured focusing depends heavily on well-structured, considerate instructional presentations (as well as on considerate teachers who test for the main ideas). And the use of these tactics does not ensure that the ideas identified will actually be remembered.

Schema building. A more powerful type of verbal-learning tactic is schema building, which encourages active analysis of an instructional presentation and formation of a synthesizing framework. One well-known form of schema building is networking (Dansereau 1985, Dansereau et al. 1979), whereby a student draws a node-link map representing the important ideas in a text and the interrelationships among them. This technique is powerful, but it is difficult to teach and time-consuming to apply (McKeachie 1984). Simpler forms of schema building include the use of teacher-suggested schemas, such as the well-known tactic of requiring students to

analyze stories in English literature by identifying the theme, setting, plot, resolution, and so on. Similar assignments can facilitate verbal learning in other courses of study. For example, Dansereau (1985) improved students'

A learning strategy is a complete plan one formulates for accomplishing a learning goal; and a learning tactic is any individual processing technique one uses in service of the plan.

performance on science tests by teaching them to use a theory schema as a study aid for scientific text.

Schema building encourages in-

depth analysis and is particularly useful if instruction is inconsiderate or unclear. Schema-building strategies are generally employed as comprehension aids; however, they also aid memory through the organization and elaboration of ideas.

Idea elaboration. Idea elaboration is a memory-enhancing process whereby students link each important new idea with prior knowledge so as to connect them. These linkages can be based on an image, a logical inference, or on anything else that serves to connect new ideas to prior knowledge (Gagne 1985).

Many elaboration tactics capitalize on imagery, a powerful memory-enhancing technique. For example, the key-word method for acquiring foreign vocabulary involves creating a mental image (prior knowledge) representing the sound of a foreign word (new information), and relating that image to another image (prior knowledge) representing the meaning of the word's English equivalent. Many types of elaboration tactics facilitate memorization (e.g., Bransford and Stein 1984), and these can be employed to great advantage in many courses.

Category	Examples	Some Conditions of Use	Strengths or Weaknesses
Behavioral Self-Management	Student breaks task into sub-goals, creates goal-attainment plan, rewards.	Complex, lengthy task; low motivated students.	Promotes extrinsic, rather than intrinsic, motivation. Very powerful.
Mood Management			
Positive self-talk	Student analyzes, avoids negative self-statements, creates positive self-statements.	Preparation for competitive or difficult performance; presence of negative ideas.	Good intrinsic motivator; requires conscious attention during performance.
Relaxation techniques	Student uses deep breathing, counting, other clinical relaxation methods.	Text anxiety; highly anxious students.	Techniques controversial in some districts.
Self-Monitoring	Student stops self during performance to consciously check mood, progress, etc.	Goal is to increase conscious awareness and control of thinking process.	May interrupt concentration.

Fig. 3. Tactics for Developing Motivation

Procedural learning tactics

Most learning strategies research has examined tactics for acquiring verbal information. However, some strategy researchers are developing techniques for acquiring procedural skills. Procedural learning has three aspects (Anderson 1983, Gagne 1985): (1) learning how to carry out basic actions such as performing long division or executing a tennis lob; (2) learning to recognize the conceptual patterns that indicate when it is appropriate to perform particular actions (such as recognizing that a word problem is a division situation or that a tennis lob is required); and (3) learning to combine many pattern-action pairs into a smooth overall system of response. Consider, for example, the complex combining of subskills that underlies the actual playing of a tennis match.

Based on this view, Figure 2 presents three categories of mental tactics for procedural learning: (1) tactics for learning conceptual patterns that cue applicability of associated actions; (2) tactics for acquiring the component actions (performance subskills) themselves; and (3) tactics for perfecting and tuning complex overall performance.

Pattern-recognition tactics. Pattern recognition plays an important role in the development of procedural performance; however, students are probably not aware of this. Thus, developing students' procedural learning abilities includes both conveying the important function of pattern recognition and helping students develop tactics for acquiring performance-related patterns.

Examples of tactics in the patterns-acquisition category include hypothesizing and seeking reasons for actions. In applying these tactics, the learner attempts to discover the identifying features of a pattern or concept through guesswork, reasoning, and investigation. For example, while watching a tennis pro at work, the student might hypothesize about the features of play that cause the pro to execute a lob or a groundstroke. Hypotheses are confirmed or altered through continued observation, until the pattern features are known. Alternatively, the student might seek reasons by consulting the tennis pro directly. Seeking information overcomes the major weakness of the hypothesizing tactic, inefficiency. However, the virtue of hypothesizing is that it can be used in situations where expert advice is not available.

Practice tactics. Other aspects of procedural learning include the acquisition of basic component actions (subskills) and, ultimately, the development of smooth complex performances that combine those subskills. There are learning tactics that can help students derive maximum benefit from their practice sessions. One example is part practice, whereby the student attempts to improve a complex performance by perfecting and automating an important subcomponent of that performance. For example, a student might greatly improve performance on mathematics tests by memorizing and practicing square-root tables. Or performance in tennis might be improved by concentrating practice on service and smashes. Part practice should be alternated with whole practice (Schneider 1985), whereby the student practices the full complex performance with little attention to individual subskills.

Reflective self-instruction. Another class of procedural learning tactics is reflective self-instruction, whereby the student attempts to improve personal performance by studying an expert model. For example, a student might videotape her tennis swing and compare that to a tape of an expert's swing. Or the student might critically compare her homework solution for a geometry proof to the teacher's expert solution presented on the board. Reflective self-instruction can concentrate either on specific component subskills or on whole complex performances. One key to successful self-instruction is the availability of adequate performance models. By providing models of expert performance and guiding students in how to benefit from those models while learning, teachers can provide training in the valuable technique of reflective self-instruction.

Mental support tactics

Acquiring useful knowledge in school is a lengthy and difficult process demanding a great investment of time and effort on the part of the student. Thus, tactics are needed for helping learners maintain a positive attitude and a high state of motivation during learning and practice. Researchers (e.g., Dansereau et al. 1979, 1985; Meichenbaum 1980; McCombs 1981-82) recommend several types of support tactics: (1) behavioral self-management, (2) mood management, and (3) self-monitoring (see fig. 3).

The behavioral self-management category includes such tactics as breaking a complex learning chore into subgoals, developing a schedule for meeting subgoals, devising a reporting procedure for charting progress, and devising a self-reward system for completing major subgoals. Mood management tactics include concentration and relaxation techniques (useful for combating test anxiety); and positive self-talk, used to establish and maintain a positive frame of mind before and during learning and performance (e.g., Meichenbaum 1980). Finally, an example of self-monitoring is the technique of stopping periodically during learning and practice to

Verbal information is likely to be called into service only if it is understood when learned and only if it is stored in memory within well-structured, well-elaborated networks of meaningfully related ideas.

check and, if necessary, readjust strategy, concentration, and mood.

Frequently used by professional athletes, mental support tactics can also be used by students to increase academic performance and motivation

and to decrease tension associated with evaluation. They are applicable to all types of learning situations and can be combined with both verbal and procedural learning tactics in study assignments. For example, to study for a history test, a student might devise a learning strategy that orchestrates several specific tactics, such as positive self-talk with self-checking (to maintain motivation), networking (to help organize facts in a meaningful way), and use of imagery or mnemonics (to help with memorization).

Strategy-Building as Problem Solving

The ultimate aim of tactics training is to provide students with tools that will enable them, as autonomous learners, to devise their own strategies. Unfortunately, a persistent problem in strategy training has been students' failure to apply tactics in situations outside the class in which they were learned originally.

However, several training techniques can alleviate these problems. A large number of researchers (e.g., Baron 1981, Bransford and Stein 1984) suggest teaching students to respond to all learning tasks using a general problem-solving model. For example, Derry, Jacobs, and Murphy (1987) taught soldiers to use the "4C's" to develop plans for study reading. The 4C's stood for: clarify learning situation, construct a learning strategy, carry out the strategy, and check results.

One presumed advantage of such plans is that they remind students to stop and think reflectively about each learning situation prior to proceeding with the task (Baron 1981). Also, such plans may serve as mnemonic devices that help students recall previously learned tactics associated with each step. There is some empirical support for the idea that problem-solving models enhance tactics transfer (Belmont et al. 1982).

Another procedure for inducing tactics transfer is informed training (Campione et al. 1982, Pressley et al. 1984). This procedure enhances direct tactics instruction with explicit information regarding the effectiveness of various tactics, including how and when they should be used. As Levin (1986) points out, there are different learning tools for different learning jobs. With informed training,

students learn that tactics selection is always influenced by the nature of the instructional material as well as the nature of the learning goal. For example, if a text is not highly struc-

Two distinct types of strategies instruction are needed: specific tactics training and training in methods for selecting and combining tactics into workable learning plans.

tured and the primary aim of study is to comprehend and remember important ideas, a strategy that combines networking with idea elaboration would be appropriate. However, if the aim is primarily comprehension rather than retention, a schema-building technique alone would suffice. Informed training is superior to "blind training" in producing transfer and sustained use of specific learning tactics (Pressley et al. 1984, Campione et al. 1982).

Previously I suggested that teachers can help develop students' learning skills by devising, assigning, and explaining learning strategies and by providing feedback on strategy use. Such established classroom practices are excellent vehicles for informed training.

Learning Strategies Should Produce Useful Knowledge

Cognitive psychology has taught us much about the nature and structure of usable knowledge. Verbal information is likely to be called into service only if it is understood when learned and only if it is stored in memory **within well-structured, well-elaborated networks of meaningfully related ideas. Procedural skills, on the other hand, are likely to be accessed and accurately executed only if they have been devel-**

oped through extensive practice and only if the environmental patterns that indicate their applicability are well learned. If the primary aim of schooling is the creation of useful knowledge, then strategy application should result in the deliberate creation of a well-structured knowledge base, whether verbal, procedural, or both.

It is unlikely that reliance on any single learning tactic alone will ensure the creation of well-constructed knowledge. Rather, multiple tactics are usually required. For example, if an elaboration technique is applied for the purpose of enhancing individual ideas, another schema-building tactic may be needed to tie related ideas together. Or if practice is used to perfect a specific aspect of procedural performance, a pattern-learning tactic may still be needed to ensure that the skill is executed only when appropriate. Thus, useful knowledge is most likely to evolve through a dynamic process requiring, first, an informed analysis of each learning problem, then selection and combining of all the learning tactics needed to produce a well-formed mental structure.

Not every learning strategy produces useful knowledge. Some strategies lead to isolated, unstructured bits of learning that will remain forever inert. For this reason, both teachers and students should be aware of the nature and form of useful knowledge and of learning strategies that are likely to facilitate its creation.

Strategy Training for Lifelong Learning

Students who receive good strategy training during their years in school can acquire a form of knowledge especially useful in coping with the wide variety of learning situations they will encounter throughout their lives. Given the amount of time that people spend in school, in job-related training, and in acquiring knowledge associated with their interests and hobbies, the ability to find good solutions to learning problems may be the most important thinking skill of all.

References

Anderson, J.R. (1983). *The Architecture of Cognition*. Cambridge, Mass.: Harvard University Press.

Baron, J. (1981). "Reflective Thinking as a Goal of Education." *Intelligence* 5: 291-309.

Belmont, J.M., E.C. Butterfield, and R.P. Ferretti. (1982). "To Secure Transfer of Training Instruct Self-Management Skills." In *How and How Much Can Intelligence Be Increased*, edited by D.K. Detterman and R.J. Sternberg, pp. 147-154. Norwood, N.J.: ABLEX.

Bransford, J.D., and B.S. Stein. (1984). *The Ideal Problem Solver: A Guide For Improving Thinking, Learning, and Creativity*. New York: Freeman.

Campione, J.C., A.L. Brown, and R.A. Ferrara. (1982). "Mental Retardation and Intelligence." In *Cognitive Strategy Research: Educational Applications*, edited by R.J. Sternberg, pp. 87-126. New York: Springer-Verlag.

Cook, L.K., and R.E. Mayer. (1983). "Reading Strategies Training for Meaningful Learning from Prose." In *Cognitive Strategy Research: Educational Applications*, edited by M. Pressley and J.R. Levin, pp. 87-126. New York: Springer-Verlag.

Dansereau, D.F. (1985). "Learning Strategy Research." In *Thinking and Learning Skills*, edited by J. W. Segal, S.F. Chipman, and R. Glaser, vol. 1, pp. 209-240. Hillsdale, N.J.: Erlbaum.

Dansereau, D.F., K.W. Collins, B.A. McDonald, C.D. Holley, J.C. Garland, G.M. Diekhoff, and S.H Evans. (1979). "Development and Evaluation of an Effective Learning Strategy Program." *Journal of Educational Psychology* 79: 64-73.

Derry, S.J., J. Jacobs, and D.A. Murphy. (1987). "The JSEP Learning Skills Training System." *Journal of Educational Technology Systems* 15, 4: 273-284.

Derry, S.J., and D.A. Murphy. (1986). "Designing Systems That Train Learning Ability: From Theory to Practice." *Review of Educational Research* 56, 1: 1-39.

Gagne, E.D. (1985). *The Cognitive Psychology of School Learning*. Boston: Little, Brown and Company.

Levin, J.R. (1986). "Four Cognitive Principles of Learning-Strategy Instruction." *Educational Psychologist* 21, 1 and 2: 3-17.

McCombs, B.L. (1981-82). "Transitioning Learning Strategies Research in Practice: Focus on the Student in Technical Training." *Journal of Instructional Development* 5: 10-17.

McKeachie, W.J. (1984). "Spatial Strategies: Critique and Educational Implications." In *Spatial Learning Strategies: Techniques, Applications, and Related Issues*, edited by C.D. Holley and D.F. Dansereau, pp. 301-312. Orlando, Fla.: Academic Press.

Meichenbaum, D.H. (1980). "A Cognitive-Behavioral Perspective on Intelligence." *Intelligence* 4: 271-283.

Pressley, M., J.G. Borkowski, and J.T. O'Sullivan. (1984). "Memory Strategy Instruction Is Made of This: Metamemory and Durable Strategy Use." *Educational Psychologist* 19: 94-107.

Pressley, M., J.G. Borkowski, and W. Schneider. (In press a). "Cognitive Strategies: Good Strategy Users Coordinate Metacognition and Knowledge." In *Annals of Child Development*, edited by R. Vasta and G. Whitehurst, vol. 4. Greenwich, Conn.: JAI Press.

Pressley, M., F. Goodchild, J. Fleet, R. Zajchowski, and E.D. Evans. (In press b). "The Challenges of Classroom Strategy Instruction." In *The Elementary School Journal*.

Schneider, W. (1985). "Training High-Performance Skills: Fallacies and Guidelines." *Human Factors* 27: 285-300.

Snowman, J., and R. McCown. (April 1984). "Cognitive Processes In Learning: A Model for Investigating Strategies and Tactics." Paper presented at the annual meeting of the American Educational Research Association, New Orleans.

Weinstein, C.E., and R.E. Mayer. (1985). "The Teaching of Learning Strategies." In *Handbook of Research on Teaching*, 3rd ed., edited by M.C. Wittrock. New York: Macmillan.

Rediscovering Discovery Learning

RAY T. WILCOX

Dr. Wilcox is a professor of secondary education at Brigham Young University in Provo, Utah.

Ever since the 1960s, when Jerome Bruner focused attention on the process of learning by discovery, teachers have been bombarded with suggestions to forsake direct, expository teaching in favor of indirect, discovery methods. Along with many teachers, I used to be fearful about holding back answers and possibly abandoning students to their own devices so that they might discover meanings for themselves. Discovery methods seemed risky, much like throwing youngsters into the deep end of a swimming pool so they would learn to swim. Furthermore, discovery methods appeared to be complicated and overly time-consuming.

It was only recently that I began rereading a few articles and books about discovery teaching, where I found some suggestions that motivated me to try again. Now, I have introduced discovery methods into my own classes with excellent results. Most of the techniques have not proven to be complicated or unusually time-consuming. And I have had good feedback from my students. They really like these discovery methods, which are a diversion from the steady routine of show and tell, tell, tell, and they seem to have an increased excitement for learning.

I hasten to add that I have not abandoned expository approaches. Current curriculum requirements and my own lack of ingenuity do not afford me that choice. Instead, I use discovery methods to supplement regular direct, frontal teaching. By using techniques from both ends of the expository-discovery continuum, there is more variety in my classroom, and I have proven to myself that teaching does not have to be an either/or situation. Educators can use many teaching approaches to suit their own requirements. This article discusses ten of the discovery methods that I have found to be the most helpful supplements.

Warm-Ups

Warm-ups are short practice exercises to get students in the mood to participate fully in indirect, discovery-type lessons. Warm-ups represent an anticipatory set—an obvious shifting of gears from expository-type lessons. Students are given responsibility for asking questions and are invited to take an active part in each warm-up activity.

"Twenty questions" is an excellent warm-up. This activity is like the parlor game in which a riddle is given and the students must figure out the answer by asking the teacher only yes/no questions. An example is the following riddle: "The man who made it didn't want it. The man who bought it didn't need it. The man who used it didn't know it. What is it?" Answer: "A coffin." Variations of this exercise are "Animal, vegetable, or mineral?" or "I'm thinking of a noun."

Public interviews are also good warm-ups. A student is selected to be interviewed, and the class is allowed to ask questions about his or her personal life and past experiences. If the interviewee does not want to answer a particular question, he or she simply says, "I pass," and another question is asked. After the allotted time is gone, the teacher concludes the session.

Incomplete sentences provide a warm-up that can be done individually, like the public interview, or with the entire class as a group. Incomplete sentences such as "If I were president, the first thing I would do is . . . ," "I like people who . . . ," or "The one thing I want most to accomplish is . . . ," are given out for completion; completed versions may be read aloud later.

Class meetings have been recommended by William Glasser to involve the teacher and individual class members. I like to use such meetings as warm-up activities. In a circle, students talk to me and to each other about a variety of topics. The subject is relatively unimportant as long as all students participate. Thus they learn from each other as well as from the teacher. They also practice taking increased responsibility for their own learning.

Another warm-up activity is working simple problems in rapid-fire order. The teacher starts the process by putting a math problem on the board, giving a spelling word, or asking a question. A student is called on at random for the answer. The teacher quickly presents another problem. The student who correctly answered the preceding problem chooses another student. This process continues until someone makes a mistake. Then the chain can be started again by the teacher calling on another student. The object of the game is to see how many problems can be worked correctly in a given period of time. Variations are to divide the class into two teams that compete against each other, or to have students come up with the problems.

Student Questions

In using the "ask me about . . . " method, once a topic has been introduced, the teacher answers only those questions that students ask. If the pump has been primed through various warm-up activities, students quickly recognize that they have a responsibility for how the lesson develops. "Ask me about behavioral objec-

---

If all the student needs to do is follow a "recipe" and fill in the blanks, discovery opportunities will be minimal.

---

tives," I might begin. The rest is up to the students. I have found that students are usually quite willing to ask relevant questions once they understand they control how much I tell them and, thus, how much they learn. Sometimes I am disappointed with how little they want to know, and so I revert to telling or try another discovery method, but often I am impressed with the quality and quantity of the questions asked. Occasionally, questions come up that I cannot answer without doing additional reading. In those cases, I try to bring back more information the next day, which usually prompts even further questions.

Examples and Non-examples

For different concepts or important generalizations, a list of examples and corresponding non-examples can usually be identified in advance of the planned teaching episode. By simply presenting these examples and non-examples and nothing more, I have been pleasantly sur-

prised at how often students can discover the concept I am trying to teach. They usually have trouble naming the concept, so I either tell them or play the game of "hangman," in which all the letters are represented by short lines on the chalkboard and the students guess letters that go on the lines.

Examples should be broad enough to include special cases unless inclusion of the exceptional case would confuse students and detract from correct identification and naming of the concept. Normally, if students can succeed in discovering the concept, special cases can be pointed out later through more traditional expository approaches.

A variation on providing examples and non-examples is to give good examples and bad examples. In a speech class, for instance, an oration is presented using clear organization, proper English, and attractive gestures. A second oration follows, and this time the speaker uses improper organization, poor English, and distracting gestures. Without any preaching at all, it is relatively easy for the class to discover that proper organization, use of English, and suitable gestures add to the persuasiveness of an oration.

Class Discussion

There can be several forms of class discussion. On a continuum, these forms will range from narrow, teacher-directed questions and answers to freewheeling, almost out-of-control, shoot-the-breeze sessions with everyone asking questions and interjecting opinions. The closer a teacher can come to conducting the latter type of class discussion without totally losing control, the better the opportunity for discovery learning to take place.

Open-ended or divergent questions usually stimulate more student involvement in the discussion. I've started class sessions by saying, "What is learning?" English teachers might ask, "What is poetry?" and so on.

Set Induction

Set induction is used mainly to teach an object lesson. The attention of the class is focused on a physical object or an experience that is common to all class members. Then the lesson shifts to an abstract concept. Through the use of analogy and student discovery, the abstraction is interpreted as being like the physical object or the common experience. This comparison to what is already known and perceived by the students makes the abstraction more meaningful and understandable to them.

For example, by comparing a group of people to a pile of books, it is possible to show that one cannot really judge people by their appearance any more than one can judge a book by its cover.

Solving Problems

Almost any kind of problem will do to begin the process of student thinking, whether the problem be mathematical, scientific, creative, or value-laden.

Mathematical problem solving will not always be relevant outside of science and mathematics classes. However, regardless of subject, many teachers will find that judicious use of story problems and puzzles may serve to set the stage and develop an interest in the general mechanics of problem solving.

In solving a mathematical problem, students discover that it is important to classify the problem so it can be related to similar problems with known solutions. Or they find that it is usually appropriate to draw a picture and then work forward or even backward. They might even learn that it is best to widen the conditions or to simply guess and test the answer.

Scientific problem solving helps students learn that they must gather and analyze relevant information, formulate a hypothesis, test the hypothesis, draw conclusions, and make possible recommendations. For example, a homemaking teacher might ask students to vary the amount of water added to one cup of pancake flour and observe the product under standard cooking conditions.

Creative problem solving begins with raising new questions and possibilities, or by viewing old problems from a different angle. For example: "How can educators have quality education programs without asking for more money?" "Please find another way of doing long division other than the one taught in the textbook." A good brainstorming session in which all ideas are welcomed is beneficial in delving into these kinds of problems.

Value-laden problem solving deals with examining both sides of any controversial issue. Debates might be conducted in class to make sure that both sides of the issue get a fair hearing. Or students might be charged with the responsibility of investigating both sides in an issue probe and then reporting their findings to the class. The teacher may need to play the devil's advocate if students are leaning completely to one side or the other.

Student discovery is encouraged as they listen to the differing opinions expressed. The disequilibrium that normally follows an issue probe requires students to do some cognitive restructuring, which might take the form of a new awareness or a new value different from what they have believed in the past. Or it might take the form of confirming already established values.

Some value-laden problems I have used in my classes are: "Should senior high school students be required to pass a minimum competency test for graduation from high school?" "Should schools allow students to rate teachers?" "Should parents be permitted to teach their children at home rather than send them to the public schools?" "Should special education students be mainstreamed?"

Socratic Questions

Since this style of questioning began with Socrates, teachers should read some of the dialogues attributed to him to get a feel for the kinds of questions he asked.

Socratic questioning, as it is used today, leads the students to recognize a predetermined concept by focusing on a few carefully selected examples. Then, when the students believe they have discovered the intended generalization, the teacher surprises them with a mind-boggling counter-example. Thus trapped by the teacher, students are left to extricate themselves from the dilemma as best they can. After the discussion has ended, it is hoped the students begin to recognize the larger dimensions of the concept or debate. Perhaps they will conclude that the dilemma has no pat answers, as they might have expected, for example, from a discussion of the question, "Who is the educated man or woman?"

Appropriate Laboratory Exercises

Unfortunately, simply conducting an exercise in a laboratory does not ensure discovery. If all the student needs to do is follow a "recipe" and fill in the blanks, discovery opportunities will be minimal.

To make a laboratory exercise become a discovery experience, the teacher must hold something back, either answers or directions or both. The student must then try to figure out what has been left out.

Ideally, the student should be given the opportunity to form his or her own hypothesis and design an experiment to test this hypothesis. The student must then conduct the experiment, analyze data, and accept or reject the hypothesis.

Laboratory exercises are designed to be a part of most science classes, but other subject teachers, with a little forethought, can use this approach also. For example, I asked my students to keep a "teaching journal" for a one-week period in which they recorded an assignment to teach a friend about the concepts they were learning in my class. I then asked them to let me check their journals, which I deliberately kept for almost a full week. After the second week, I gave them a test that was divided equally between the concepts taught during the first week and the second week. I scored the papers and returned them along with the question, "Which concepts were learned the best, those for week one or those for week two?" Considering the time factor, those for week two should have been remembered the best. But it turned out that the concepts taught when the students had been forced to teach them to another person were remembered the best. Although the difference was not large, the class members nonetheless concluded that teaching a concept to another person helped them learn the concept better.

Suitable Class Demonstrations

The same principle applies to class demonstrations as

to laboratory exercises. Something must be held back if students are to discover. Teachers must show and not tell. Or, they must show and not tell all.

As the teacher conducts the demonstration, students are provided clues to help them recognize and hence find regularities and solutions that fit the experiment or demonstration. The teacher carefully directs the students so they discover the main concepts. Actual generalizations might even be left for students to formulate, the teacher eventually endorsing them as correct.

For example, I observed a student teacher in a junior high school general science class who conducted a discovery-oriented demonstration. He had filled a number of coke bottles (which are hard to break) with varying proportions of oxygen and hydrogen by displacing water from the bottles by bubbling gas into them from two compressed tanks, one of oxygen and the other of hydrogen. He set each bottle upside-down in a pan of water to keep the gases from escaping. He then refreshed the students' memories by recording on the chalkboard the exact percentage of oxygen and the exact percentage of hydrogen in each coke bottle. Finally, he asked the class members to predict which bottle would make the loudest noise and spray the contents the farthest. The students voted for the winning bottle and served as judges when the teacher aimed each bottle at the class and held it to an open candle flame. The bottle with 67 percent hydrogen and 33 percent oxygen was declared the actual winner. The class members went on to determine that they had discovered the formula for water, H_2O.

Some of the students told me they really liked the student teacher's lesson and thought he was doing a great job.

Individualized Study Assignments

In this type of activity, each student works at his or her own speed on a planned assignment that is common to the class or designed solely for the single student.

Individualized study assignments are given to heighten student activity levels both in and out of class. To make a study assignment a discovery activity, the student's activity must be focused and meaningful. The teacher might ask a student to do almost any of the things already suggested: to find out about a particular subject, to look for examples or even non-examples, to compare an abstract concept with a physical object, to solve problems, or to conduct a special laboratory exercise.

The purpose of a discovery study assignment should be to expand on what students have already learned and to integrate new insights with previous information and knowledge. There probably will be built-in opportunities for students to experience insightful moments when they see for themselves what is right or wrong, how something works, or what the solution to a problem may be ("Ah hah, I get it!").

For example, I have asked my students to view and evaluate their previously made micro-teaching videotapes and tell me what they liked and disliked about their teaching and what they would change if they were able to reteach that particular lesson. Most students discover some things they would like to change.

Conclusion

Undoubtedly there are still other excellent discovery approaches that I have not mentioned. However, these ten methods have been the most useful for me.

Robert M. Gagné has defined discovery learning as "something the student does, beyond merely sitting in his [sic] seat and paying attention" (1966, p. 135). Ideally, students accept increased responsibility for their own education, discovering and learning through their own activities, both mental and physical, and not necessarily through the teacher's activities.

Today, we are living through an incredibly accelerated and unprecedented explosion of knowledge. That fact, along with the frighteningly complex economic, social, and political problems our world faces, leave educators no logical alternatives but to try to produce students who can think for themselves, who see education as a process and not merely a product, who know how to learn, and who are adept at solving problems. Are not these kinds of students the ones for whom discovery methods are designed?

By whatever name, we need these methods in today's schools: warm-ups, student questions, examples and non-examples, class discussions, set induction, problem solving, Socratic questions, laboratory exercises, class demonstrations, and individualized study assignments. All of us need to rediscover discovery learning.

REFERENCE

Gagné, R. M. 1966. Varieties of learning and the concept of discovery. In *Learning by discovery: A critical appraisal,* edited by L. S. Shulman and E. R. Keislar. Chicago: Rand McNally.

Linking Metacognition to Classroom Success

Martin N. Ganz
Incarnate Word College

Barbara C. Ganz
Pima Community College

Traditionally, the task of teaching students the fundamentals of study strategies has been in the domain of elementary educators. For the most part, their efforts have been satisfactory for students at this stage of intellectual growth. However, problems begin to arise as elementary students enter secondary education and begin their transition to the next developmental stage. The study strategies they developed in the elementary school are often incomplete for the secondary school setting with its more formalized learning environment.

In response to this, and to the ever-increasing problem of retaining students in school by preventing failure, secondary teachers are showing interest in helping their students master skills necessary to study and learn. Teachers and administrators who recognize the importance of learning skills also understand the importance of going beyond the classroom framework to develop the whole person. To these professionals, helping students develop useful study habits and positive attitudes and ultimately graduate is as important as the subject matter that may be their expertise.

Secondary teachers must realize that students were not likely taught how to adapt their study habits to a variety of learning situations during the elementary years. In fact, any attempt to do so would probably have met with little success, given the nature of children at that stage of intellectual development. It is therefore critical for secondary teachers to help students mature the learning skills they need for success. While the goal of improving study habits and further developing the skills the students already have is important, current methods used to reach desired outcomes must be modified and enhanced if success is to be achieved. Success should not be defined solely from the standpoint of student mastery of subject matter, but rather from the perspective of helping students develop a major self-control process, metacognitive skills processing.

Metacognitive skills are related to thinking about thinking, and more precisely, thinking about one's own learning. Teaching about this process should not be random or capricious. It can be accomplished in any classroom with a teacher who understands the learning process and wants to help students achieve. Students who develop metacognitive skills are far more likely to be able to make the changes needed in their own study habits and learning strategies when faced with unfamiliar tasks or challenges than students who do not.

What Is Metacognition?

Metacognition, or the act of thinking about one's own thinking, is necessary to ensure efficient learning. Dirkes (1985) points out that students who direct their own thinking commonly do three things: connect new information to former knowledge; select thinking abilities directly; and relate time and degrees to certainty of purpose. Dirkes refers to these activities as executive strategies and defines awareness of them as metacognition. Costa (1984) defines metacognition as the ability to know what one doesn't know. He further states, "Some people are unaware of their own thinking process. They are unable to describe the steps or strategies they use during the act of problem-solving. They cannot transform into words the visual images held in their minds. They seldom evaluate the quality of their own thinking skills" (p. 198).

The importance of spending effort on the development of thinking-about-thinking skills in all young people becomes especially clear when it is realized that students who are able learners develop these skills intuitively. The simplest example of a metacognitive skill is when students realized that after doing poorly on a test, they are not learning through the use of one study technique and will therefore need to try a different one. Brown and DeLoache (1977) believe that determining a desired goal and planning the steps required to achieve that goal are desirable metacognitive skills.

Many students have a goal of improving a grade at some point in their education. Fulfilling that goal can become a source of serious frustration. There are several causes for the lack of academic success many students experience, including immature metacognitive knowledge and strategies as well as the lack of motivation, attention, and effort to employ strategic activity (Ryan, 1982). Failing to determine a goal for learning or failing to think about the steps required to achieve that goal may also be included here. Students often realize that they do not understand what was read or heard, but then fail to act on this understanding. This practice can reinforce an existing negative view of their ability or lead them to believe that they are poor learners. A more precise explanation would be that they are too passive in their learning attempts. They do not practice the self-control and self-correction necessary to become better learners. It is interesting to note that at a time when these skills should be developing, the drop-out problem drops in.

Developing Metacognition

Self-interrogation is an important metacognitive technique. By asking questions of themselves, students can monitor themselves, predict and hypothesize, assess feelings of understanding or lack of understanding in order to choose and employ a self-correction strategy, and integrate new information with existing information. Examples of questions that monitor learning or comprehension include the following: Should I slow down here? Can I skip the additional clarifying explanation? Can I picture this situation or information in my mind? To predict and hypothesize, students might ask themselves such questions as, What do I think will happen next? Do I think this is fiction or nonfiction? Was that piece of information related to what I read on the last page or paragraph?

Assessing one's feelings of understanding is also important for comprehension and learn-ing. Students could ask, Did this make sense? Can I say this in my own words? Can I make a judgment now? To assess their lack of understanding, students might ask, Is this part harder than previous information? Do I get what the author is saying here? What does this word mean? Will this make sense later? This type of introspection is critical because the selection and employment of correction strategies is based upon it. Students need to know if they should reread, continue, slow their speed, find assistance, or choose a different strategy.

After learning new information, the self-interrogation should not stop. Students should continue to reflect on their information by asking themselves such questions as, Can I make some generalizations, and are they fitting? Can I draw some conclusions, and are they plausible? Is this similar to anything that I already know?

The development of metacognitive skills is not inherited; nor is it achieved through passive attendance at school each day. It is a process that must be presented to adolescents with a cohesive, carefully planned strategy. Those who have experienced the intrinsic satisfaction that comes from being in control of their own educational success know the motivational factor that is directly connected with that control.

Using Metacognitive Skills

To examine metacognitive abilities, it is important to look at the difference between what efficient, mature learners do and what less proficient, immature learners do during their study process. Most basic is the notion that mature learners treat studying as a purposeful, attention-directing, self-questioning act, while less mature learners possess naive theories about what it takes to learn new information and to meet certain task and text demands (Brown et al., 1982). Mature learners engage in purposeful strategic learning activities tailored specifically to the demands of each task. If necessary, they develop new strategies. Less mature learners, on the other hand, do not necessarily introduce appropriate learning strategies. If they do, they may be inflexible in adapting these strategies to different text or task situations. Furthermore, they are often impeded by inferior, inefficient strategies which result in only partial success but are consistently applied in a variety of situations. Such inflexibility of approach may stem from the fact that students feel most comfortable using one kind of strategy, do not know any other strategies, or fail to realize it may be their strategic action, rather than their lack of ability, impeding their learning.

As learners mature, they become increasingly able to predict the essential elements of the text (Brown and Smiley, 1977). Evidence of this was seen during research with young through college-age learners. Some of the students spontaneously began to underline or take notes. Not only was this study strategy used spontaneously, the ideas highlighted were also considered the important elements of the text. Students induced to adopt a note-taking strategy, however, were not as sensitive to the main elements; their notations were more random. The very immature learners underlined almost all of the text when told to underline. Their skill did improve with instruction but never reached the level of the spontaneous user.

Students who are able to extract main ideas will benefit from study time. They know what to attend to first so that more detailed information may be built upon basic ideas. Mature learners use this building process to flesh out meaning. Developing learners also use it but take more trials to come upon the strategy themselves (Baker, 1980). Unless basic ideas are extracted, study time becomes an exercise in passive rereading or in rote memorization without understanding.

Self-testing, or rehearsal, is another appropriate study technique for all learners because it helps them realize what has not been learned and acts as a rehearsal procedure for learning. Rehearsal allows a transfer of information from short-term to long-term memory (Bransford, 1979). The more rehearsal attempts, the greater the probability of retention of information. The success of information retrieval for an exam or a problem-solving task depends on how specifically the information was encoded during the time of acquisition and on the quality of the retrieval schemes in the mind of the learner. Questioning gives practice in retrieving information and thus reduces the amount of forgetting. Therefore, self-interrogation is an effective study technique for recall of information and is more efficient than other techniques such as passive, desperate rereading. It is important for students to engage in self-interrogation because they often don't realize that they have inadequate preparation for a test or other similar task until it is too late.

Deciding what information needs further attention before a detailed understanding is achieved can also be accomplished through attempts to summarize materials. Baker and Brown (1980) suggest five operation for effective summarizing: delete redundancy; delete trivia; provide superordinate terms or labels for items that can be grouped; select topic sentences; and invent topic sentences where missing. Summarizing can be taught and is an important check that a student both understands and remembers the material. Some students find that studying from a summary is easier than returning to the complete text.

Learning information does not always mean that the learner will be able to transfer it to different contexts, problems, or roles. Effective learners hypothesize different contexts in which information may be used. Experiences in multiple contexts increase the probability of effective transfer (Brown et al., 1982). Another element that plays a role in effective transfer is acknowledging that certain information, formulas, or concepts are meant to be applicable to various situations. Students need to see how things can be applied generally so that they too learn to put their learning in different contexts. Students also need to see how a new situation is related to one previously encountered. An understanding of situational relationships can aid information transfer.

Research Findings

Subject-matter teachers are aware of the importance of fostering good reading and study habits among students if their own efforts in the classroom are to be fruitful. Accordingly, much of the early research in the teaching of metacognitive skills has come from reading. Andre and Anderson (1979) determined that the metacognitive technique of self-generated questions during study led to improved performance on tests requiring comprehension. A recent study by Stevens (1988) demonstrated that training remedial reading students in metacognitive strategies improved their ability to identify the main idea of expository paragraphs.

Research in a variety of disciplines supports the need for metacognitive training for general classroom success. As an example, Bean et al. (1986) reported on the effect of metacognitive instruction on a tenth-grade world history class. Their study showed that the use of graphic organizer construction (a technique that expands study strategies beyond outlining) was enhanced by metacognitive training. The authors further noted that "secondary students are eager to expand their metacognitive strategies" (p. 167). Some students reported using the strategies in their biology class, especially on difficult sections of the text.

Research also suggests that metacognitive strategies training can help students be successful as young adults. Mikulecky and Ehlinger (1986) studied the higher level literacy demands placed on young people competing in today's workplace by investigating the effects of metacognitive instruction on electronic technicians. Electronic technicians, according to the study, spend nearly 2.5 hours daily in job-related reading and writing. Results indicate that "metacognitive aspects of literacy did consistently and significantly correlate to job performance" (p. 41). Also significant for students directed toward a profession requiring higher education is a study by Lundeberg (1987). This study centered on the reading strategies used by lawyers and law professors, since "legal educators profess to build minds rather than fill them" (p. 409). Lundeberg's findings indicated that metacognitive strategies significantly improved comprehension, especially of beginning law students.

As these studies suggest, waiting for students to mature into skilled learners is not an educationally viable position. There are many strategies to be learned, and while some students may discover them intuitively, others will require induced learning.

Conclusion

The key to better education for the complex world of the future is producing more efficient, independent learners who can complete their educational goals. It is only through a combination of three kinds of knowledge — strategic learning-to-learn skills, metacognitive abilities, and factual information from content courses — that students will develop self-direction and self-regulation abilities for learning. All teachers, at all levels, need to show students that successful learning is a continually active process requiring internal monitoring and control over a learning situation. Students can be shown strategies for improvements; moreover, they can be encouraged to develop them for themselves.

Individuals play the central role in their own learning. Students who do not take responsibility for their thinking and learning may exhibit symptoms of learned helplessness. If they see no relation between effort and the attainment of their goals, they may become lethargic (Thomas, 1979). Their efforts could be curtailed and their self-esteem might suffer. Sometimes after acquiring this helpless attitude, students fail to perform tasks that they could do at a previous time. Therefore, aside from the academic advantages of the learning-to-learn skills, there may be social and emotional advantages in affording students the opportunity to reduce passive, helpless attitudes that result in only a minimal effort to avoid a failing grade or even dropping out.

Considering that forgetting occurs rather quickly after exposure to material, content-area teachers who just fill students with factual knowledge soon find that students are left with very little of anything important. Thoughtful teaching professionals must move away from antiquated approaches toward a credible pedagogical alternative of teaching students to control their own learning. However, as was pointed out by Porter and Brophy (1988), "...helping students is not sufficient by itself to insure mastery of those strategies" (p. 79). Teachers need to incorporate these strategies into their lesson structure and encourage their use for class so that the strategies can be mastered. Teachers can determine if their efforts to teach and improve metacognitive skills have been successful by asking specific questions about what is going on in their students' minds as they think through various problems. Students who are developing metacognitive skills will be able to describe their thinking process, mental organization, and future strategies when coping with a problem.

As Wiens (1983) points out, "As students enter adolescence, their ability to engage in abstract thinking increases and their 'self-consciousness' takes on new meanings with real implications for being able to control their own thinking and behavior. An understanding of metacognitive skills can greatly enhance an adolescent student's ability to use appropriate strategies in learning" (p. 144).

References

Andre, M.E., and Anderson, T.H. (1970). "The Development and Evaluation of a Self-Questioning Study Technique." *Reading Research Quarterly, 14,* 605-623.

Baker, L., and Brown, A. (1980). "Metacognitive Skills and Reading." *Tech. Report 188* (November). Center for the Study of Reading, University of Illinois, Urbana-Champaign.

Bean, T.W., Singer, H., Sorter, J., and Frazee, C. (1986). "The Effect of Metacognitive Instruction in Outlining and Graphic Organizer Construction on Student's Comprehension in a Tenth-Grade World History Class."

Journal of Reading Behavior, 28(2), 153-169.

Bransford, J. (1979). "Human Cognition: Learning, Understanding, and Remembering." Belmont, Calif.: Wadsworth Publishing.

Brown, A., Bransford, J., Ferrara, R., and Campione, J. (1982). "Learning, Remembering and Understanding." *Tech. Report 244* (June). Center for the Study of Reading, University of Illinois, Urbana-Champaign.

Brown, A., and DeLoache, J. (1977). "Skills, Plans, and Self-Regulation." *Tech. Report 48* (July). Center for the Study of Reading, University of Illinois, Urbana-Champaign.

Brown, A., and Smiley, S. (1977). "Development of Strategies for Studying Prose Passages." *Tech. Report 48* (October). Center for the Study of Reading, University of Illinois, Urbana-Champaign.

Costa, A. (1984). "Thinking: How Do We Know Students Are Getting Better at It?" *Roeper Review, 6*(4), 197-199.

Dirkes, M. (1985). "Metacognition: Students in Charge of Their Thinking." *Roeper Review, 8*(2), 96-100.

Lundeberg, M.A. (1987). "Metacognitive Aspects of Reading Comprehension: Studying Understanding in Legal Case Analysis." *Reading Research Quarterly, 22*(4), 407-432.

Mikulecky, L., and Ehlinger, J. (1986). "The Influence of Metacognitive Aspects of Literacy on Job Performance of Electronic Technicians." *Journal of Reading Behavior, 18*(1), 41-62.

Porter, A.C., and Brophy, J. (1988). "Synthesis of Research on Good Teaching: Insights From the Work of the Institute for Research on Teaching." *Educational Leadership, 45*(8), 74-85.

Ryan, E.B. (1982). "Two Causes of Underachievement." *Forum, 3*(2), Winter. The English Composition Board, University of Michigan.

Stevens, R.J. (1988). "Effects of Strategy Training on the Identification of the Main Idea of Expository Passages." *Journal of Educational Psychology, 80*(1), 21-26.

Thomas, A. (1979). "Learned Helplessness and Expectancy Factors: Implications for Research in Learning Disabilities." *Review of Educational Research, 49*(2), 208-221.

Wiens, J.W. (1983). "Metacognition and the Adolescent Passive Learner." *Journal of Learning Disabilities, 16*(3), 144-149.

Practicing Positive Reinforcement

Ten Behavior Management Techniques

THOMAS R. McDANIEL

Dr. McDaniel is a professor of education and director of graduate education studies at Converse College in Spartanburg, South Carolina.

Almost all teachers know something about behavior modification. Somewhere in their training they have learned the importance of positive reinforcement. That "praise is better than punishment" in managing behavior has become almost trite. And yet, negativism abounds in public school classrooms today. For most practicing teachers it is a long step between knowing the principles of positive reinforcement and using them consistently, frequently, and successfully.

One reason that day-to-day practices of teachers do not demonstrate familiarity with behavioral psychology is that the practices often run counter to their growing-up experiences. Like their parents, teachers tend to *assume* good behavior, to accept it as commonplace, and to ignore it on the grounds that this communicates the normal expectation for good behavior. "Let sleeping dogs lie" is a common principle of child rearing. A second reason for the infrequent use of behavioral principles in classrooms is that teachers learn to intervene quickly to squelch misbehavior. Since students will test the teacher's alertness, the vigilant teacher often learns from students to apply "desist statements," which often start with negative terms: "Stop," "Don't," "No." A third reason that teachers do not frequently use positive reinforcement is that their teacher education courses seldom teach them how to apply such principles to improve discipline and classroom management. We teacher-educators often tell prospective teachers that they *should* be positive, but neglect to give them specific training to show them *how to* apply the principles in specific situations.

I list ten practical and specific techniques that are derived from behavioral psychology. Each of the ten rests on solid research of Neo-Skinnerian educators and psychologists. Each principle contains a suggestion for how to put positive reinforcement to work for more effective classroom discipline.

Teach Specific Directions

Few teachers realize how many of their discipline problems are a consequence of poor, vague, or unspecific directions. We make the mistake, especially in elementary school, of assuming that students know how to perform all kinds of instructional and behavioral assignments. It is not enough to tell students to begin work on their math assignment, to line up for lunch, and to get ready for dismissal. To maximize good behavior, teachers should teach students exactly what is required. This takes some forethought and at least a little effort, but it is well worth the time it takes.

Example: "Class, it is now time to begin work on your math assignment. When I give you the signal, I want you to (1) put all your supplies away, (2) take out your math books and two pencils, and (3) quietly open your books to page 12 and do the first five problems on that page. . . . I see that everyone is ready. Mary Lou, what are the three things you are going to do when I give you the signal? Very good. All right, begin." At this point the teacher should watch to see that every student is following the three simple steps to beginning the math work. The wise teacher will maximize good behavior by

From *The Clearing House*, May 1987, pp. 389-392. Reprinted with permission of Helen Dwight Reid Educational Foundation. Published by Heldref Publications, 4000 Albemarle, St., N.W., Washington, D.C. 20016. Copyright © 1987.

making expectations for behavior so clear, direct, and unambiguous that every student will know precisely what is expected. Such expectations increase the likelihood that students will behave the way you want them to.

Look for Good Behavior

This is the "catch 'em being good" principle so central to positive reinforcement. If the first principle asks you to communicate specific expectations, the second requires you to follow through by looking for those who are complying with the expectation. Here is a good opportunity to use "positive repetitions." You repeat each of your specific directions as you see students following them. If one seems *not* to be following the directions, use a positive repetition on the student closest to him or her if you can. This technique is called "proximity praise."

Example: You have just given directions for the assignment and then you say, "Freddy has put all his materials away; Claudette has her math book and two pencils; Clarence is starting quietly to work on the first five problems on page 12." The effect that such positive repetitions can have is sometimes amazing. It is important that you remember to find the examples of good behavior rather than criticizing those who are not following the expectations. Many students get special attention and special service by *mis*behaving so that teachers will provide them extra attention in the classroom. The message you want to give students is that your attention is always focused on those who are doing what you expect them to do.

Praise Effectively

Much research has been done on effective praise. Verbal praise can be a powerful tool if teachers understand the requirements of effective praise. One of these requirements is that the teacher give descriptive details, as in the second example. The teacher should describe the specific thing he or she likes about the student's behavior. Too often we are too general in our praise. So, a teacher should not merely say, "You are doing a good job on your drawing," but should provide specific details to give meaning to the general term "good job." Another important element of effective praise is to concentrate on the behavior rather than on the person. The phrase, "I like the way . . . " is one specific teacher assertion that can help the teacher focus on what students do rather than on who they are.

Example: "Class, you are doing a good job on your drawing. I like the way that so many of you are using the entire page for your work. I also like the way you are using contrasting colors to make your picture more interesting. I see that some of you are working hard to put details on your pictures of people. I like the way these details make the people look so real."

Praise can be overdone, of course, and it should be sincere. I suspect that teachers could use more praise,

especially to compliment students on how they came into the room quietly and promptly, how they started to work efficiently, how they took turns at the pencil sharpener, how they raised their hands to ask for permission to contribute in class, and how they kept the classroom free of trash. Some teachers even use what is called "anticipatory praise" to encourage students to behave in the way that the teacher would like. "We are about to go to lunch, class. I really appreciate your picking up the scrap paper around your desk before we leave for the lunch room." This praising *before* the fact can be much more effective than the normal practice of complaining about the messiness of the room.

Model Good Behavior

Most teachers realize that a student's behavior is learned more from example than from admonitions. Because students "do as we do" rather than "do as we say," it is important that we provide appropriate models. The teacher should demonstrate how things ought to be done. Explicit modeling is found frequently in art rooms, gymnasiums, and automotive shops. Appropriate modeling should be found more frequently in all academic classrooms. Teachers might, for example, model their thinking processes as they explain a math problem or a literary question. In the area of classroom management, a teacher can demonstrate how to move from center to center, how to enter and exit the room, how to do such simple things as sit in chairs and raise hands for permission to move. A quick review of the three previous principles might suggest that what good behavior modifiers do is set up situations that allow the teacher to use students as models.

Example: Consider your own behavior. Are you prompt and well organized when you come to class? Do you keep your voice level low and calm? When students are working quietly at their seats, do you tiptoe around and whisper softly to individuals to show that you respect their need for quiet? You should be the best example of the behavior you expect from your students. Also, consider your use of student models. Do you train demonstration groups that can be used to show how a small group discussion should be conducted? Do you select competent students to role-play good manners in a classroom? Do you take opportunities to role-play conflict resolutions so that students can demonstrate effective ways to solve interpersonal problems? If not, consider ways by which you might more effectively use the modeling principle.

Use Nonverbal Reinforcement

You can go beyond modeling to use a variety of practices that show approval for the kind of behavior you want in a classroom. Facial expressions are especially meaningful for nonverbal reinforcement. Most teachers eventually learn to use smiles, nods, and touch to show approval. Truly effective behavior modifiers use a great deal of nonverbal reinforcement. As they teach, they look at students and smile as if to say, "I see you are paying attention."

Example: "Class, I have this empty jar. Whenever I see you behaving well, I will drop a marble in the jar. At first I may tell you exactly why I am doing that, or on certain days I may tell you that I will only drop a marble in when I see examples of a particular behavior, such as concentration on your work, efficiency in completing assignments, or following the hand-raising rule." This allows you to teach students to respond to your nonverbal reinforcement system. This requires that you pair verbal and nonverbal reinforcement initially, but over time you gradually phase out the verbal part of the process.

Establish Token Economies

Students can quickly learn that each marble in the jar is a token that may represent, for example, free time. Each token might be worth fifteen seconds of free time to be cashed in at the end of the day. Or the teacher might indicate that each marble counts toward a record-playing session (music of the students' choice) to be cashed in when the students have earned 100 marbles. If your classes are small, token economies can be highly

---

. . . If you have been following the principles outlined so far, a total system of positive reinforcement is already operating in your classroom.

---

individualized. Special education teachers frequently are able to establish complex and sophisticated token economies, rewarding each student on his or her individual reinforcement card. That is more difficult to do in regular classrooms, but sometimes can be arranged with those few students who need extra structure and extra incentive. The underlying behavior principle here is contingency management. Rewards or reinforcers are contingent upon the students' demonstrating a specific behavior. This is sometimes called "Grandma's rule": if you eat your spinach, then you can have peach cobbler. Token economies are ways by which students can see their progress toward some longer range goal that is contingent upon the accumulation of successive approximations toward the goal. Tokens mark the small steps —and reward them.

Example: "Students, if you get every answer correct on this quiz, you will not have any homework tonight" (Grandma's rule). "Class, I am keeping a record of who has handed in every homework assignment during the week. Those of you who have a perfect record at the end of the week will get a special certificate. Students who get four certificates will get a special field trip" (token economy).

Premack

Premacking (a technique named after David Premack, who first described this idea in detail) asks the teacher to let students determine the reinforcers for appropriate behavior. Premacking reminds us that a reinforcer is in the eye of the beholder. The teacher must give students the opportunity to identify what they want for rewards and to exercise choice in setting up a token economy.

Example: You might observe what students prefer to do during free time when given the opportunity to exercise choice. Keep a record of which students use their free time to (a) converse with other students, (b) do their homework, (c) sleep or rest, (d) play games, (e) read comic books. If you can identify several reinforcers that motivate your students, use them to set up a reward system that the whole class will embrace.

Teach Kids to Reinforce One Another

While an effective teacher knows how to reinforce students and knows how to identify the rewards (verbal, nonverbal, token) that can be used for reinforcing expected behavior, effective teachers also teach students to praise one another. Actually, if you have been following the principles outlined so far, a total system of positive reinforcement is already operating in your classroom. If you are an effective reinforcer, you are also a good model of how people might interact with one another in positive ways. You should give students an opportunity to practice what you have been modeling in the classroom. Some teachers, following the "One-Minute Manager" prescription, ask students to take one minute to tell another student what they like about his or her behavior. Students can be not only negative toward their classmates but downright cruel. Providing opportunities for students to describe *good* things they see in their classmates can be a valuable practice. What you can do with one-minute praisings is to train students to be positive and to use the principles of positive reinforcement in their relationships with other students.

Example: "Students, we have a few minutes now at the end of the day to think about our behavior. I would like you to work in pairs to tell one of your classmates what he or she has done today that is praiseworthy. Do not discuss character or personality—only those things that your partner has done during the day that you think deserve a compliment. This should take no more than one minute. When you finish, reverse the process and let your partner compliment you on specific things you have done today that might be complimented." This can be awkward and unnatural; however, handled skillfully, these could be some of the most important minutes in the class day. This teaches students to look for good behavior in their classmates.

3. LEARNING: Behavioristic

Teach Kids to Reinforce Themselves

Students can benefit from observing their own behavior and complimenting themselves on their performance. The practice forces them to look for their strengths and can improve self-concept. This should be a serious, but not somber, enterprise. Just as we parents and teachers often do, students tend to ignore good behavior. Setting up explicit opportunities to identify one's own good behavior can counteract that tendency.

Example: "Students, we are at the end of another successful day. I would like each of you to write down on a piece of paper as many responses as you can to this phrase: 'Today I learned. . . .' When you get home be sure to share your list with a parent. Next, write down as many responses as you can to this phrase: 'My behavior was successful today because. . . .' Here, students, you should list as many kind things that you have done for yourself or others as you can. Now, get started."

Vary Positive Reinforcement

There are many practices that you can use to keep your reinforcement practices changing and improving. New techniques, new reinforcers, and new ideas can help keep your classroom sparkling.

Example: Vary any typical practices you may have by having some surprise reinforcers. If you are using the marble jar, for example, announce that the class has won some bonus marbles because of especially good behavior at the assembly program. Or, as a surprise reinforcement, cancel a homework assignment because the students have done so well on the in-class drill. Use positive notes either to parents or to students themselves. A simple personal hand-written note to a student that says, "Johnny, I certainly do appreciate how hard you have been trying to remember to bring your books to class" may do more than all of your reprimands combined. Establish a "rewards committee" to come up with some suggestions for reinforcers that would appeal to the class. Being on the rewards committee itself could be an important reward. Ask students to stop their work and to imagine themselves successfully performing a given task. Athletes frequently go through the mental process of reinforcing their imagined success on the tennis court or basketball court or track. Why not give your students an opportunity to do the same?

Example: "Students, we are getting ready to go out to the buses for the field trip. I want you to imagine yourself walking quietly down the hall in single file, getting on the bus in an orderly fashion, and conversing quietly as we move. When we get back, we will compare your mental image with your actual performance. Now, is everybody ready to go?"

These ten principles of positive reinforcement can help you practice what has been so often preached to you. If you successfully apply the principles of positive reinforcement in your day-to-day work with students, you will find that you not only develop your own skills of reinforcement but that you can help students develop theirs as well. Positive reinforcement in practice can build a positive self-concept, develop an attitude of success, and enhance instructional motivation for students. Practicing positive reinforcement principles takes work, but it is work that pays dividends for the teacher who wants to make the classroom a better place in which to live.

Teacher Expectations: A Model for School Improvement

C. Patrick Proctor
Connecticut State Department of Education

□ C. Patrick Proctor is coordinator of the School Effectiveness Unit/State Chapter 1 Program in the Bureau of School and Program Development of the Connecticut State Department of Education.

Over the past decade, research on classroom and school effects has presented considerable evidence of a positive link between teacher expectations and student achievement. Drawing from this research base, the model employed by the Connecticut Department of Education to help schools improve their effectiveness acknowledges high expectations as one of the principal characteristics that differentiate more effective from less effective schools in terms of promoting children's academic achievement (Gauthier 1982). Moreover, high expectations appear to be among the most salient of the characteristics and thus represent for the department one of its most promising areas for school intervention and improvement.

Viewing school improvement from the perspective of teacher expectations, this paper (1) summarizes the classroom and school literature on expectation effects, (2) proposes a school-based model for the influence of teacher expectations on student performance, and (3) describes applications of this model in Connecticut's school improvement efforts.

Classroom research

Early studies

Since the publication of *Pygmalion in the Classroom* (Rosenthal & Jacobson 1968), classroom research on teacher expectations has proliferated. In that study, teachers of an experimental group of students were informed that the children had obtained high scores on a test that predicted intellectual "blooming" and therefore could be expected to show a significant increase in intellectual competence. In actuality, given random selection of the experimental group, there was no reason to assume that the children would excel. Eight months later, children were readministered the test and, according to the researchers, showed significantly greater gains in total IQ than a control group. In explaining their findings, the researchers posed the existence of a self-fulfilling expectancy bias that led to teachers' differential treatment of experimental children, resulting in their improved intellectual performance. Criticized severely on methodological grounds (Barber 1973; Snow 1969; Thorndike 1968), the study sparked considerable controversy in the education community and stimulated numerous research inquiries into expectancy effects.

The results of these early inquiries were mixed. While some researchers failed to replicate the Rosenthal-Jacobson findings (Claiborne 1969; Fleming & Anttonen 1971; José & Cody 1971), others, using teachers' naturally formed expectations (as determined by teacher ratings and predictions of student performance), reported positive expectancy effects on student achievement (Doyle, Hancock, & Kifer 1971; Palardy 1969). This pattern continued throughout the early 1970s, with studies of experimentally induced expectations consistently failing to replicate

Pygmalion, and the results of naturalistic studies, though mixed, showed mounting evidence of positive expectancy effects.

Brophy-Good model

In their comprehensive review of these early efforts, Brophy and Good (1974) noted the difficulty of interpreting the negative findings of experimental studies in that it was impossible to determine whether experimenters had actually induced the desired expectations. Viewing the results of naturalistic studies as far less ambiguous, the authors concluded that the notion that teacher expectations can operate as self-fulfilling prophecies appears to be an established fact rather than a mere hypothesis. The mixed results of these studies, however, suggested to the authors that, although the self-fulfilling prophecy clearly operated in some classrooms, it was less widespread than had originally been assumed.

Their model of the self-fulfilling prophecy, first proposed in 1970 (Brophy & Good 1970) and reiterated in a recent publication (Good 1981), may be summarized as follows:

1. From a variety of sources and influences, teachers form differential expectations regarding the behavior and achievement of students in their classrooms.
2. Because of these expectations, teachers behave in different ways toward various students.
3. The different treatment will communicate to students what teachers expect from them and will begin to affect their self-perception and motivation and to decrease their opportunities to learn.
4. If this treatment continues over time, and if neither teachers nor pupils are successful at changing it, it will shape students' achievement and behavior. High-expectation students will achieve at high levels, and the achievement of low-expectation students will decline.
5. Differential achievement on the part of high and low achievers will continue.

This model has directly or indirectly informed much of the research on teacher expectations during recent years. This research has examined influences on the formation of expectations, identified specific teacher behaviors and student-teacher interaction patterns associated with differential expectations, and investigated the relationship of these to student performance outcomes. The remainder of this section reviews the research in these key areas.

Influences on the formation of teacher expectations

As the Brophy and Good model suggests, teachers form expectations on the basis of the group and individual characteristics of their students. Numerous student characteristics have been identified as influences on expectations—for example, race, social class, gender, personality, physical features, speech patterns, and prior academic achievement. Low expectations are generally associated with minority group membership, low SES, male gender, nonconforming personality, physical unattractiveness, nonstandard speech patterns, and low achievement. Moreover, researchers note the complex relationships among these characteristics (Cooper, Baron, & Lowe 1975; Kehle, Bramble, & Mason 1974) and suggest that response to them varies greatly from teacher to teacher (Brophy & Good 1974).

Among the most influential of these characteristics appear to be race, social class, and prior achievement. Early research findings suggest that, without evidence of students' actual capabilities, teachers formulate expectations for young children on the basis of social and physical characteristics related to race and class, and that such expectations lead to differential, negative treatment of low-SES and minority-group children (Leacock 1969; Rist 1970). Later research (Crano & Mellon 1978) and the substantial literature on social inequality as reflected in school grouping and sorting practices (Bowles & Gintis 1977; Persell 1977) lend considerable support to the thesis that race and social class are powerful determinants of teacher expectations and treatment of children.

Children's prior achievement also exerts substantial influence on expectations. Virtually all of the research examining the relationship between prior achievement and expectations reports high positive correlations between the two (Cooper 1979). In fact, there is evidence that, as students move up the grade-level hierarchy, prior academic achievement replaces all other characteristics as the predominant influence on teacher expectations (Lockheed 1976).

However, considering the strong interactive relationships among race, social class, and student achievement, it makes little difference from the point of view of low-income and minority children which characteristic exerts the most influence; the net effect in terms of teacher expectations is approximately the same. Thus, although researchers have identified many expectation influences and have suggested that response to these varies greatly among teachers, the characteristics of race, social class, and prior achievement appear to be the most influential, with teachers responding to them as much on a normative as on an individualistic basis.

Student-teacher interaction patterns associated with differential teacher expectations

No area of expectation research has been more thoroughly investigated than the identification of classroom interaction patterns associated with differential expectations (Braun 1976; Brophy & Good 1974; Cooper 1979; Good 1981). The findings of this research, simply stated, are that students for whom teachers have low expectations are taught much less effectively than their high-expectation classmates.

In the area of curriculum and instruction, low-expectation students in general receive fewer opportunities to learn, spend less time on instruction-related activities, and receive less curricular content (or receive content that has been "diluted"). Teachers are less apt to direct instruction to low-expectation students, are less likely to be aware of, or more likely to tolerate, nonattending behavior on the part of such students, and tend to place fewer demands on them for classroom performance, homework assignments, and overall academic effort. Available instructional time for low-expectation students may be replaced disproportionately by control-oriented, discipline-related teacher behavior.

Teacher questioning and feedback patterns also differ for high- and low-expectation students. In general, low-expectation students are asked fewer questions and given less time to respond to questions. They receive (1) inadequate feedback, in terms of quantity, accuracy, and specificity, (2) less praise for successful performance (but more for marginal performance), and (3) more criticism for incorrect responses.

Finally, low-expectation students receive from the teacher fewer positive, nonverbal communications of warmth and personal regard.

Table 1 provides a more comprehensive listing of these treatment patterns for low-expectation students and integrates the typologies of various researchers. The table categorizes patterns according to instructional input, instructional feedback, and personal communications. These will be among the key descriptors in the model presented in a later section of this paper.

The effects of such differential treatment on students may be described along two dimensions. The first is a cognitive dimension relating to learning opportunities in the classroom. For low-expectation students, the interaction patterns described above are likely to result in less academic learning time (with lower success rates during that time) and less (and lower-quality) coverage of curricular content—two classroom variables that have received considerable attention in recent years in terms of their positive relationship to student achievement (Cooley & Leinhardt 1980; Fisher, Berliner, Filby, Marliave, Cahen, & Dishaw 1980).

One affective consequence for the low-expectation student appears to be an increasingly negative self-perception, with declining self-expectations for success. According to Braun (1976), there is a close relationship among the teacher's expectations for the learner, the teacher's treatment of the learner, and ultimately, the child's self-expectation. This expectation of self is inseparable from self-image. This link between teacher and student expectations has been consistently demonstrated in recent research (Brattesani, Weinstein, Middlestadt, & Marshall 1981; Lockheed 1976), indicating that low teacher expectations are closely tied to low self-expectations of students, and together, in mutual reinforcement, they have a substantial influence on student learning outcomes.

The consequences of differential expectations for students in terms of learning opportunities and self-expectations appear to be the intermediate links between

TABLE 1. Student-Teacher Interaction Patterns Associated with Low-Expectation Students

A. Instructional input (quantity and quality):	B. Instructional feedback (quantity and quality):	C. Personal communications:
1. Paying less attention to "lows" in academic situations 2. Ignoring comments of "lows" 3. Calling on "lows" less often 4. Waiting less time for "lows" to answer questions 5. Not staying with (prompting, cueing) "lows" in failure situations 6. Providing fewer curricular statements to "lows" 7. Interrupting performance of "lows" more often 8. More discussion with "lows" of nonacademic activities 9. More time spent in control-oriented disciplinary contacts with "lows" 10. Demanding less work and effort from "lows" 11. Accepting poor performance of "lows" 12. Providing "lows" fewer opportunities to learn new materials 13. Not giving "lows" as much responsibility 14. Using ideas of "lows" less often	1. Directing less reward-oriented behavior to "lows" 2. Criticizing "lows" more frequently for incorrect responses 3. Praising "lows" less frequently for successful performance 4. Praising "lows" for marginal or inadequate responses 5. Providing less frequent feedback to "lows" 6. Providing less accurate or detailed feedback to "lows"	1. Seating "lows" farther from teacher 2. Providing "lows" fewer positive affective communications (smiling, eye contact, courtesy, interest, warmth, personal contact, etc.)

SOURCES.—Braun 1976; Brophy & Good 1974; Cooper 1979; Good 1981; Leacock 1969; Rist 1970; Weinstein & Middlestadt 1979.

student-teacher interaction patterns and student academic achievement.

Teacher expectations and student achievement

The link between teacher expectations and student achievement is firmly established by classroom research. In his recent review of expectations research, Good (1981) notes that research efforts that have examined the relationship between student achievement and teacher expectations have consistently demonstrated positive relationships. The problem with studies of naturalistic expectations, however, is that all the evidence that relates expectations to achievement is correlational, leading some researchers to raise the question of directional causality (West & Anderson 1976). It would, they maintain, be as plausible to argue that prior achievement produces teacher expectations as it would be to argue the reverse. Addressing this problem of "causal ambiguity," Cooper (1979) argues that, rather than altering student performance, teacher expectations primarily act to sustain preexisting achievement differences among students. Good (1981) concurs with this position.

Other researchers, however, present evidence that teacher expectations do more than simply "sustain" achievement differences. In their 4-year longitudinal study of 5,200 elementary school children, Crano and Mellon (1978) found that, for children in the early elementary grades, teacher expectations based on social characteristics unrelated to academic capabilities had a strong impact on children's achievement, indicating the "causal primacy" of teacher expectations on chil-

dren's later performance. This study lends support to similar findings reported earlier by Leacock (1969) and Rist (1970).

Lockheed (1976) found that teacher expectations "consistently and significantly" related to achievement outcomes even when the effects of prior achievement had been partialled out. For average students, high teacher expectations were estimated to increase achievement as much as 1 SD when compared with similar students for whom teachers held low expectations.

Similarly, Brattesani et al. (1981) found that, in classrooms where students perceived high differential treatment of low and high achievers, teacher expectations accounted for an additional 9%–18% of the variance in student achievement when the effects of prior achievement were eliminated. The authors suggest that their results contradict the argument that teacher expectations only sustain the preexisting achievement variations among students.

In sum, then, the foregoing review suggests that, in the early years of schooling, where teachers make assumptions about children's capabilities that are not related to observed or documented performance, teacher expectations can act to produce achievement variations among children. Furthermore, as children progress through the grades, teacher expectations generally act to sustain and solidify preexisting achievement differences among children. In instances where teacher expectations are not congruent with children's prior achievement, teacher expectations can act to alter student performance further, beyond what earlier achievement would predict.

Research on school effectiveness

Building on findings that schools can have a positive impact on student achievement regardless of the socioeconomic backgrounds of their pupils (Brookover, Schweitzer, Schneider, Beady, Flood, & Wisenbaker 1976; Edmonds & Frederiksen 1978), recent research on school effectiveness attempts to identify characteristics of schools that are instructionally effective for poor children (Edmonds 1978; Mann 1980). As it relates to teacher expectations, this research converges with the classroom research in several specific areas.

First, school research, like classroom research, reports positive correlations between teacher expectations and student achievement. Defining "effectiveness" operationally in terms of student performance, nearly all the school studies identify high teacher expectations as a primary correlate of instructional effectiveness (Edmonds 1978; Lezotte, Hathaway, Miller, Passalacqua, & Brookover 1980; Mann 1980).

Second, the differential behavior of teachers in schools identified as more or less effective approximates the differential student-teacher interaction patterns for low- and high-expectation students reported in the classroom literature. Compared with teachers in less effective schools, teachers in more effective schools spend more time in direct instruction, emphasize the completion and mastery of curricular objectives, and make a greater effort to monitor and assess students' academic progress (Brookover & Lezotte 1979). These behaviors are the converse of those treatment patterns reported for low-expectation students in the classroom research.

Third, school researchers report that one factor that appears to account for the greatest amount of school-to-school and pupil-to-pupil difference in achievement is a construct identified as "student sense of academic futility" (Lezotte et al. 1980). Equivalent to the construct of student self-expectation reported in the classroom research, this factor is viewed by school and classroom researchers alike as a primary intermediate link between teacher expectations and student achievement.

Finally, the concept of "teacher efficacy" emerges in both the school and classroom literature. School researchers report that teachers in effective schools not only hold high expectations for students but also for themselves, with the belief that they have the capability to deliver the required program of instruction (Lezotte 1979). Similarly, classroom research indicates that successful teachers have beliefs that reflect positive attitudes that they can teach and students can learn (Brophy & Evertson 1976).

Despite this convergence, the different approach employed by the school effectiveness research yields a broader conception of the expectation phenomenon than is currently envisioned in the classroom literature. Focusing on the school rather than the classroom as its unit of analysis, school effectiveness research employs a social systems approach in its investigation of expectancy effects. From the perspective of this approach, expectancy is viewed as an organizational phenomenon in dynamic interaction with the expectations of individual teachers. It is viewed, moreover, as a critical element of a school's learning climate, with "climate" defined as the configuration of "norms, beliefs and attitudes reflected in institutional patterns and behavioral practices that enhance or impede student achievement" (Lezotte et al. 1980, p. 4). School climate, according to researchers, accounts for a substantial portion of the variance in student achievement from school to school and is thus viewed as a key factor in differentiating schools in terms of instructional effectiveness (Brookover et al. 1976; Rutter, Maughan, Mortimore, Ouston, & Smith 1979).

As a core element of school climate, organizational expectation exerts a potent influence on the individual members of the school's social system. An overall analysis of the literature cited in this section suggests that its influence operates in the following way. First, it communicates predictions for student performance, as well as beliefs regarding teachers' instructional capacities vis-à-vis the presumed learning capabilities of the student population. These communications mediate teachers' responses to the characteristics of their students, help shape the expectations of individual teachers, and influence classroom practices and achievement outcomes.

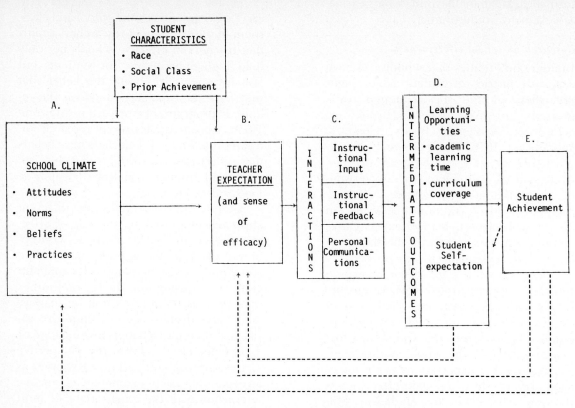

FIG. 1.—A school-based model for teacher expectations

Finally, information on student achievement is interpreted in a way that validates institutional predictions and beliefs. Where learning climate differs for individuals and groups within a school, patterns of differential expectations will emerge, with differential outcomes in student achievement.

The above construct exactly mirrors, at an organizational level, the "prophecy" model in the classroom research. In the context of the social systems approach, however, the self-fulfilling prophecy is a more powerful and widespread institutional phenomenon, with more compelling implications for teaching and learning than its counterpart in the classroom literature.

A school-based model for teacher expectations

Adopting the social systems perspective of the school effectiveness research, the Connecticut model for teacher expectations (see figure 1) provides a conceptualization of school-based expectancy effects, showing hypothesized causal and feedback influences. The model attempts to integrate the findings of the school and classroom research presented earlier in this paper. From school research, it shows the dominant influence of school climate on classroom expectations and behavior, and it indicates how information on student performance is fed back into the system to perpetuate the institutional "prophecy" cycle. From classroom research, it shows the elements, with their causal linkages, connecting teacher expectations to student achievement. It also demonstrates the internal feedback influences that maintain the classroom cycle on an ongoing basis. Teacher expectation and "sense of efficacy" are combined in the model, reflecting their correlative relationship as reported in both the school and classroom literature. Finally, student characteristics are viewed by the model as not only influencing the individual expectations of teachers but also the overall learning climate of the school. This aspect of the model reflects the implication of school effectiveness research that it is not so much the characteristics of students that determine student performance as it is the school's response to those characteristics. The model provides a useful theoretical framework within which to view Connecticut's school improvement efforts as they relate to influencing expectations in classrooms and schools.

Applications of the model for school improvement

Connecticut's school improvement process approaches its intervention activities with a dual focus on school- and classroom-level variables. A school staff is helped to view its school as a social system with unique norms, values, and attitudes and to examine the influence of this system on the attitudes and behavior of individual students and teachers within the school.

The teacher expectations model reflects this dual focus and thus is applicable to a variety of Connecticut's improvement efforts. Moreover, the cyclical, interactive aspects of the model suggest that improvement efforts can occur at various points along the model to influence the expectations of teachers and schools. The two major areas in which the model is applicable are (1) school assessment, planning, and implementation, and (2) staff training and development. In both areas, school and classroom variables are probed and school staff are helped to understand and act on the relationship between the two.

School assessment, planning, and implementation

As Gauthier (1982) states, the Connecticut school improvement process is a voluntary, school-based approach that assists a school in examining itself introspectively in relation to school effectiveness characteristics and in developing and implementing an action plan that is meaningful to the faculty and principal of the school. Introspective examination occurs through a schoolwide assessment (Villanova 1982). The assessment is conducted through use of a questionnaire and an interview survey designed by the Department of Education (Villanova, Gauthier, Proctor, Shoemaker, Sirois, & Gotowala 1982) and through analysis of a school's archival and achievement data.

The interview and questionnaire probe faculty perceptions of the degree of existence in the school of various behaviors, practices, and attitudes assumed to be associated with effective schools.[1] A number of the areas assessed by the instruments directly or indirectly related to expectations in the school. These areas are summarized in table 2, with an indication of the point where each connects with the expectations model.

Archival data—information on a school that is readily available and does not require a formal data collection instrument—are also gathered. Archival data relevant to our expectations model include (1) written curriculum objectives (model point A), (2) mastery requirements (point A), (3) promotion/retention policies and data (point A), (4) grouping practices (points A and C), (5) allotted time periods for instruction (points A and C), (6) testing policies and data analysis (point A), and (7) formal reports of student progress (points A and C). Finally, student achievement data are gathered to show differential achievement patterns in relation to the income status ("low" or "other") of pupils in a school (point E on the model).

The principal and faculty of the school receive a comprehensive analysis of the assessment data; with this information, they develop and implement one or more "action plans" for school improvement. The assessment itself, apart from subsequent planning and implementation activities, may promote changes in a school, which may themselves influence expectations in a school. Our expectations model predicts that action plans successfully implemented in any of the assessment areas outlined in table 2 will influence expectations in a school—either directly through changes in beliefs and attitudes (points A and B on the model) or indirectly through changes in school and classroom practices (points A and C). Our goal is ultimately to have an effect at point E of the model (student achievement) and thereby disrupt the negative feedback cycles for low-achieving children in a school.

Staff training and development

As part of its improvement plan, a school may opt to participate in one or more formal training programs currently offered to schools participating in the Effective Schools Project. These include programs in mastery learning, teacher expectations and student achievement (TESA), and time on task. The following is a description of each of these programs with a statement of its relationship to our expectations model.

Mastery learning model. Mastery learning is based on the assumption that, given appropriate conditions for learning (particularly enough time), all students can master at least minimal subject matter objectives (Bloom 1976). This program, offered in Connecticut by staff of the University of Hartford, promotes student mastery by helping teachers to (1) organize subject matter into manageable learning units, (2) develop specific learning objectives for each unit, (3) develop appropriate formative and summative assessment measures, and (4) plan and implement group teaching strategies, with sufficient time allocations, practice opportunities, and corrective reinstruction. (Mastery learning connects at point C of the expectations model.)

Teacher expectations and student achievement. Developed by Kerman (1979) and Martin (1973), the TESA program sensitizes teachers to their often subtle and unintended negative treatment of low-achieving children in classrooms and provides teachers with specific behavior alternatives to counteract such treatment. Teachers learn and practice new behavior through direct classroom observation and feedback techniques. Developers of the program claim widespread success in changing teacher attitudes and improving student achievement (Kerman 1979). (The TESA program connects at points B and C of the expectations model.)

Time on task. Developed by the Basic Skills Component of Research for Better Schools (1980–81), this program instructs teachers on how to (1) gather information on students' use of classroom time through systematic classroom observation techniques, and (2) select and implement strategies to increase students' instructional engagement rates and to maximize academic learning time in the classroom. (The time-on-task training connects at point C of the expectations model.)

The three staff development interventions described above are primarily aimed at changing teachers' classroom behavior. Our expectations model predicts, because of internal feedback influences, that successful changes in teachers' behavior (i.e., those linked to improvement in student achievement) will result in more positive teacher expectations for students, which in turn will promote further achievement growth.[2]

Evaluation

A design for the evaluation of Con-

TABLE 2. Areas Assessed by Faculty Interviews and Questionnaire

Assessment Area	Model Point
1. High expectations:	
Percentage of students expected to master basic skills	B
Percentage of students expected to complete high school	B
Beliefs regarding the relationship between home background and student achievement	B
Patterns of response to classroom questions	C
Grouping patterns in the classroom	C
General level of building expectations	A
Discipline problems with low achievers	C
Teacher acceptance of responsibility for student achievement	B
Differential retention practices for low-income children	A
2. Clear school mission:	
Existence of written, sequential learning objectives in basic skills	A
Policy regarding student student mastery of objectives	A
Use of objectives to guide classroom instruction	C
3. Frequent monitoring of student progress:	
Nature and frequency of classroom monitoring of student progress	C
Nature and frequency of school monitoring of student progress	A
Use of classroom progress information for student diagnosis and instructional improvement	C
Use of school progress information for school and program improvement	A
4. Opportunity to learn and student time on task:	
School policy on time allotments for basic skills instruction	A
Amount of classroom time allocated to basic skills instruction	C
Student interruptions of class time	D
School interruptions of class time	A
Student success rate on practice assignments	D

necticut's improvement activities is currently being developed. The design will include at least three elements: (1) the degree to which schools have successfully implemented action plans for school improvement, (2) the extent to which teachers' perceptions and attitudes (including expectations) have changed as a result of the intervention, and (3) the effect of improvement activities on student academic achievement.

The evaluation will include periodic readministration of the School Effectiveness Questionnaire (Villanova, Gauthier, Proctor, & Shoemaker 1982), review by a panel of external evaluators of the nature and extent of action plan implementation and the effects of such implementation on school and classroom practices, and collection and analysis of longitudinal student achievement data, with specific examination of the differential performance of low-income children.

Preliminary evaluation data will be available during the 1983–84 school year.

Summary and conclusion

Overall, the Connecticut school improvement process is an attempt to influence school characteristics assumed to be associated with instructional effectiveness. Considering the interdependent nature of these characteristics (Gauthier 1982), our improvement efforts may be viewed from a variety of perspectives. This paper, however, views them from the particular perspective of teacher and school expectations. We predict that certain of our initiatives in assessment, planning, implementation, and staff development will have a positive influence on expectations and achievement in schools. The expectations model we present provides us with a theoretical framework for understanding and predicting this influence. We hope, therefore, that other practitioners find the model useful as they undertake their own improvement efforts.

Notes

The article was originally written as a paper presented at the annual meeting of the American Educational Research Association, New York, March 19–23, 1982.

1. For a complete description of the research-based characteristics of effective schools and how they are assessed in Connecticut, see Gauthier (1982), Shoemaker (1982), and Villanova (1982).

2. For research evidence linking successful instructional change (mastery learning techniques) to positive changes in teacher expectations, see Guskey (1981).

References

Barber, T. Pitfalls in research: nine investigator and experimenter effects. In R. M. W. Travers (Ed.), *Second handbook of research on teaching.* Chicago: Rand McNally, 1973.

Bloom, B. S. *Human characteristics and school learning.* New York: McGraw-Hill, 1976.

Bowles, S., & Gintis, H. *Schooling in capitalist America.* New York: Basic, 1977.

Brattesani, K.; Weinstein, R.; Middlestadt, S.; & Marshall, H. Using student perceptions of teacher behavior to predict student outcomes. Paper presented at the annual meeting of the American Educational Research Association, Los Angeles, 1981.

Braun, C. Teacher expectation: socio-psychological dynamics. *Review of Educational Research,* 1976, **46,** 185–213.

Brookover, W. B.; Schweitzer, J. H.; Schneider, J. M.; Beady, C. H.; Flood, P. K.; & Wisenbaker, J. M. Elementary school climate and school achievement. East Lansing: Michigan State University, Institute for Research in Teaching, 1976.

Brookover, W. B., & Lezotte, L. Changes in school characteristics coincident with changes in student achievement. East Lansing: Michigan State University, Institute for Research on Teaching, 1979.

Brophy, J., & Evertson, C. *Learning from teaching: a developmental perspective.* Boston: Allyn & Bacon, 1976.

Brophy, J., & Good, T. Teachers' communication of differential expectations for children's classroom performance: some behavioral data. *Journal of Educational Psychology,* 1970, **61,** 365–374.

Brophy, J., & Good, T. *Teacher-student relationships: causes and consequences.* New York: Holt, Rinehart & Winston, 1974.

Claiborne, W. Expectancy effects in the classroom: a failure to replicate. *Journal of Educational Psychology,* 1969, **60,** 377–383.

Cooley, W., & Leinhardt, G. The instructional dimensions study. *Educational Evaluation and Policy Analysis,* 1980, **2,** 7–25.

Cooper, H. Pygmalion grows up: a model for teacher expectation communication and performance influence. *Review of Educational Research,* 1979, **49,** 389–410.

Cooper, H.; Baron, R.; & Lowe, C. The importance of race and social class information in the formation of expectancies about academic performance. *Journal of Educational Psychology,* 1975, **67,** 312–319.

Crano, W., & Mellon, P. Causal influence of teachers' expectations on children's academic performance: a cross-lagged panel analysis. *Journal of Educational Psychology,* 1978, **70,** 39–49.

Doyle, W.; Hancock, G.; & Kifer, E. Teachers' perceptions: Do they make a difference? *Journal of the Association for the Study of Perception,* 1971, **7,** 21–30.

Edmonds, R. A discussion of the literature and issues related to effective schooling. Paper prepared for the National Conference on Urban Education, St. Louis, 1978.

Edmonds, R., & Frederiksen, J. R. Search for effective schools: the identification and analysis of city schools that are instructionally effective for poor children. Unpublished manuscript, Harvard University, 1978.

Fisher, C.; Berliner, D.; Filby, N.; Marliave, R.; Cahen, L.; & Dishaw, M. Teaching behaviors, academic learning time, and student achievement: an overview. In C. Denham & A. Lieberman (Eds.), *Time to learn.* Washington, D.C.: National Institute of Education, 1980.

Fleming, E., & Anttonen, R. Teacher expectancy or my fair lady. *American Educational Research Journal,* 1971, **8,** 241–252.

Gauthier, W. Connecticut perspectives on instructionally effective schools: a model and process. Paper presented at the annual meeting of the American Educational Research Association, New York, 1982.

Good, T. Teacher expectations and student perceptions: a decade of research. *Educational Leadership,* 1981, **38,** 415–421.

Guskey, T. The influence of change in instructional effectiveness upon the relationship of teacher expectations and student achievement. Paper presented at the annual meeting of the American Educational Research Association, Los Angeles, 1981.

José, J., & Cody, J. Teacher-pupil interaction as it relates to attempted changes in teacher expectancy of academic ability. *American Educational Research Journal,* 1971, **8,** 39–49.

Kehle, T.; Bramble, W.; & Mason, E. Teachers' expectations: ratings of student performance as biased by student characteristics. *Journal of Experimental Education,* 1974, **43,** 54–60.

Kerman, S. Teacher expectations and student achievement. *Phi Delta Kappan,* 1979, **60,** 716–718.

Leacock, E. *Teaching and learning in city schools.* New York: Basic, 1969.

Lezotte, L. A policy prospectus for urban education. Paper prepared for the Connecticut State Board of Education, Hartford, 1979.

Lezotte, L.; Hathaway, D.; Miller, S.; Passalacqua, J.; & Brookover, W. *School learning climate and student achievement.* Tallahassee: Florida State University, SSTA Center, 1980.

Lockheed, M. Some determinants and consequences of teacher expectations concerning pupil performance. In *Beginning Teacher Evaluation Study: phase II.* Princeton, N.J.: Educational Testing Service, 1976.

Mann, D. The politics and administration of the "instructionally effective school." Remarks prepared for the National Graduate Research Seminar in Educational Administration, sponsored by the National Institute of Education and the American Educational Research Association, Boston, 1980.

Martin, M. *Equal opportunity in the classroom, ESEA, title III: session A report.* Los Angeles: County Superintendent of Schools, Division of Compensatory and Intergroup Programs, 1973.

Palardy, M. What teachers believe—what children achieve. *Elementary School Journal,* 1969, **69,** 370–374.

Persell, C. *Education and inequality: the roots and results of stratification in America's schools.* New York: Free Press, 1977.

Research for Better Schools. *Time leader's guide.* Philadelphia: Research for Better Schools, 1980–81.

Rist, R. Student social class and teacher expectations: the self-fulfilling prophecy in ghetto education. *Harvard Educational Review,* 1970, **40,** 411–451.

Rosenthal, R., & Jacobson, L. *Pygmalion in the classroom.* New York: Holt, Rinehart & Winston, 1968.

Rutter, M.; Maughan, B.; Mortimore, P.; Ouston, J.; & Smith, A. *Fifteen thousand hours.* Cambridge: Harvard University Press, 1979.

Shoemaker, J. What are we learning? Evaluating the Connecticut school effectiveness project. Paper presented at the annual meeting of the American Educational Research Association, New York, March 1982.

Snow, R. Unfinished Pygmalion. *Contemporary Psychology,* 1969, **14,** 197–199.

Thorndike, R. Review of *Pygmalion in the classroom* by Robert Rosenthal & Lenore Jacobson. *American Educational Research Journal,* 1968, **5,** 708–711.

Villanova, R. Measuring and validating the characteristics of instructionally effective schools in Connecticut. Paper presented at the annual meeting of the American Educational Research Association, New York, 1982.

Villanova, R.; Gauthier, W.; Proctor, C.; & Shoemaker, J. *The Connecticut School Effectiveness Questionnaire.* Hartford: Connecticut State Department of Education, 1982.

Villanova, R.; Gauthier, W.; Proctor, C.; Shoemaker, J.; Sirois, H.; & Gotowala, M. *The Connecticut School Effectiveness Interview.* Hartford: Connecticut State Department of Education, 1982.

Weinstein, R., & Middlestadt, S. Student perceptions of teacher interactions with male high and low achievers. *Journal of Educational Psychology,* 1979, **71,** 421–431.

West, C., & Anderson, T. The question of preponderant causation in teacher expectancy research. *Review of Educational Research,* 1976, **46,** 613–630.

Cooperative Learning and the Cooperative School

The availability of models that can be used in math, reading, and writing at every grade level has made it possible to plan an elementary school around the concept of everyone's working together to improve all aspects of the school.

ROBERT E. SLAVIN

Robert E. Slavin is Director of the Elementary School Program at the Center for Research on Elementary and Middle Schools, Johns Hopkins University, 3505 N. Charles St., Baltimore, MD 21218.

Photograph by Barbara Bennett

The Age of Cooperation is approaching. From Alaska to California to Florida to New York, from Australia to Britain to Norway to Israel, teachers and administrators are discovering an untapped resource for accelerating students' achievement: the students themselves. There is now substantial evidence that students working together in small cooperative groups can master material presented by the teacher better than can students working on their own.

The idea that people working together toward a common goal can accomplish more than people working by themselves is a well-established principle of social psychology. What is new is that practical cooperative learning strategies for classroom use have been developed, researched, and found to be instructionally effective in elementary and secondary schools. Once thought of primarily as social methods directed at social goals, certain forms of cooperative learning are considerably more effective than traditional methods in increasing basic achievement outcomes, including performance on standardized tests of mathematics, reading, and language (Slavin 1983a, b; Slavin in press a).

"There is now substantial evidence that students working together in small cooperative groups can master material . . . better than can students working on their own."

Recently, a small but growing number of elementary and secondary schools have begun to apply cooperative principles at the school as well as the classroom level, involving teachers in cooperative planning, peer coaching, and team teaching, with these activities directed toward effective implementation of cooperative learning in the classroom. Many of these schools are working toward institutionalization of cooperative principles as the focus of school renewal.

This article reviews the research on cooperative learning methods and presents a vision of the next step in the progression of cooperative learning: the cooperative school.

What Is Cooperative Learning and Why Does It Work?

Cooperative learning refers to a set of instructional methods in which students work in small, mixed-ability learning groups. (See p. 114 for a vignette about one day in the life of a hypothetical cooperative school.) The groups usually have four members—one high achiever, two average achievers, and one low achiever. The students in each group are responsible not only for learning the material being taught in class, but also for helping their groupmates learn. Often, there is some sort of group goal. For example, in the Student Team Learning methods developed at Johns Hopkins University (Slavin 1986), students can earn attractive certificates if group averages exceed a pre-established criterion of excellence.

For example, the simplest form of Student Team Learning, called Student Teams-Achievement Division (STAD),

consists of a regular cycle of activities. First, the teacher presents a lesson to the class. Then students, in their four-member mixed-ability teams, work to master the material. Students usually have worksheets or other materials; study strategies within the teams depend on the subject matter. In math, students might work problems and then compare answers, discussing and resolving any discrepancies. In spelling, students might drill one another on spelling lists. In social studies, students might work together to find information in the text relating to key concepts. Regardless of the subject matter, students are encouraged not just to give answers but to explain ideas or skills to one another.

At the end of the team study period, students take brief individual quizzes, on which they cannot help one another. Teachers sum the results of the quizzes to form team scores, using a system that assigns points based on how much individual students have improved over their own past records.

The changes in classroom organization required by STAD are not revolutionary. To review the process, the teacher presents the initial lesson as in traditional instruction. Students then work on worksheets or other practice activities; they happen to work in teams, but otherwise the idea of practice following instruction is hardly new. Finally, students take a brief, individual quiz.

Yet, even though changes in classroom organization are moderate, the effects of cooperative learning on students can be profound. Because one student's success in the traditional classroom makes it more difficult for others to succeed (by raising the curve or raising the teacher's expectations), working hard on academic tasks can cause a student to be labeled as a "nerd" or a "teacher's pet." For this reason, students often express norms to one another that discourage academic work. In contrast, when students are working together toward a common goal, academic work becomes an activity valued by peers. Just as hard work in sports is valued by peers because a team member's success brings credit to the team and the school, so academic work is valued by peers in cooperative learning classes because it helps the team to succeed.

In addition to motivating students to

do their best, cooperative learning also motivates students to help one another learn. This is important for several reasons. First, students are often able to translate the teacher's language into "kid language" for one another. Students who fail to grasp fully a concept the teacher has presented can often profit from discussing the concept with peers who are wrestling with the same questions.

Second, students who explain to one another learn by doing so. Every teacher knows that we learn by teaching. When students have to organize their thoughts to explain ideas to teammates, they must engage in cognitive elaboration that greatly enhances their own understanding (see Dansereau 1985).

Third, students can provide individual attention and assistance to one another. Because they work one-on-one, students can do an excellent job of finding out whether their peers have the idea or need additional explanation. In a traditional classroom, students who don't understand what is going on can scrunch down in their seats and hope the teacher won't call on them. In a cooperative team, there is nowhere to hide; there *is* a helpful, nonthreatening environment in which to try out ideas and ask for assistance. A student who gives an answer in a whole-class lesson risks being laughed at if the answer is wrong; in a cooperative team, the fact that the team has a "we're all in this together" attitude means that, when they don't understand, students are likely to receive help rather than derision.

Under What Conditions Is Cooperative Learning Effective?

Cooperative learning is always fun; it almost always produces gains in social outcomes such as race relations; and it

"Students are often able to translate the teacher's language into 'kid language' for one another."

has never been found to reduce student achievement in comparison to traditional methods. However, a substantial body of research has established that two conditions must be fulfilled if cooperative learning is to enhance student achievement substantially. First, students must be working toward a group goal, such as earning certificates or some other recognition. Second, success at achieving this goal must depend on the individual learning of all group members (see Slavin 1983a, b; in press a).

Simply putting students into mixed-ability groups and encouraging them to work together are not enough to produce learning gains: students must have a reason to take one another's achievement seriously, to provide one another with the elaborated explanations that are critical to the achievement effects of cooperative learning (see Webb 1985). If students care about the success of the team, it becomes legitimate for them to ask one another for help and to provide help to each other. Without this team goal, students may feel ashamed to ask peers for help.

Yet team goals are not enough in themselves to enhance student achievement. For example, classroom studies in which students complete a common worksheet or project have not found achievement benefits for such methods.. When the group task is to complete a single product, it may be most efficient to let the smartest or highest achieving students do most of the work. Suggestions or questions from lower-achieving students may be ignored or pushed aside, as they may interfere with efficient completion of the group task. We can all recall being in lab groups in science class or in project groups in social studies in which one or two group members did all the work. To enhance the achievement of all students, then, group success must be based not on a single group product, but on the sum of individual learning performances of all group members.

The group's task in instructionally effective forms of cooperative learning is almost always to prepare group members to succeed on individual assessments. This focuses the group activity on explaining ideas, practicing skills, and assessing all group mem-

"In a cooperative team, there is nowhere to hide; there *is* a helpful, nonthreatening environment in which to try out ideas and ask for assistance."

bers to ensure that all will be successful on learning assessments.

When cooperative learning methods provide group goals based on the learning of all members, the effects on student achievement are remarkably consistent. Of 38 studies of at least four weeks' duration comparing cooperative methods of this type to traditional control methods, 33 found significantly greater achievement for the cooperatively taught classes, and 5 found no significant differences (Slavin in press a). In contrast, only 4 of 20 studies that evaluated forms of cooperative learning lacking group goals based on group members' learning found positive achievement effects, and 3 of these are studies by Shlomo Sharan and his colleagues in Israel that incorporated group goals and individual accountability in a different way (see Sharan et al. 1980, Sharan et al. 1984).

Successful studies of cooperative learning have taken place in urban, rural, and suburban schools in the U.S., Canada, Israel, West Germany, and Nigeria, at grade levels from 2 to 12, and in subjects as diverse as mathematics, language arts, writing, reading, social studies, and science. Positive effects have been found on such higher-order objectives as creative writing, reading comprehension, and math problem solving, as well as on such basic skills objectives as language mechanics, math computations, and spelling. In general, achievement effects have been equivalent for high, average, and low achievers, for boys and girls, and for students of various ethnic backgrounds. As noted earlier, positive effects of cooperative learning have also been found on such out-

comes as race relations, acceptance of mainstreamed academically handicapped classmates, and student self-esteem and liking of class (see Slavin 1983a).

Comprehensive Cooperative Learning Methods

The cooperative learning methods developed in the 1970s—Student Teams-Achievement Divisions and Teams-Games-Tournaments (Slavin 1986); Jigsaw Teaching (Aronson et al. 1978); the Johnsons' methods (Johnson and Johnson 1986); and Group Investigation (Sharan et al., 1984)—all are generic forms of cooperative learning. They can be used at many grade levels and in many subjects. The broad applicability of these methods partly accounts for their popularity. A one- or two-day workshop given to a mixed group of elementary and secondary teachers of many subjects can get teachers off to a good start in most of the methods, which makes this an ideal focus of staff development.

However, because the early cooperative learning methods are generally applicable across grade levels and subjects, they tend not to be uniquely adapted to any particular subject or grade level. Also, the methods developed earlier are mostly curriculum-free; they rarely replace traditional texts or teaching approaches. As a result, these methods are most often applied as supplements to traditional instruction and rarely bring about fundamental change in classroom practice.

Since 1980, research and development on cooperative learning conducted at Johns Hopkins University has begun to focus on comprehensive cooperative learning methods designed to replace traditional instruction *entirely* in particular subjects and at particular grade levels. Two major programs of this type have been developed and successfully researched: Team Accelerated Instruction (TAI) in mathematics for grades 3–6, and Cooperative Integrated Reading and Composition (CIRC) in reading, writing, and language arts for grades 3–5. The main elements of these programs are described below.

Team Accelerated Instruction (TAI). Team Accelerated Instruction shares with STAD and the other Student Team Learning methods the use of four-member mixed-ability learning teams and certificates for high-performing teams. But where STAD uses a single pace of instruction for the class, TAI combines cooperative learning with individualized instruction. TAI is designed to teach mathematics to students in grades 3–6 (or older students not ready for a full algebra course).

In TAI, students enter an individualized sequence according to a placement test and then proceed at their own rates. In general, team members work on different units. Teammates check each other's work against answer sheets and help one another with any problems. Final unit tests are taken without teammate help and are scored by student monitors. Each week, teachers total the number of units completed by all team members and give certificates or other rewards to teams that exceed a criterion score based on the number of final tests passed, with extra points for perfect papers and completed homework.

Because students are responsible for checking each other's work and managing the flow of materials, the teacher can spend most class time presenting lessons to small groups of students drawn from the various teams who are working at the same point in the mathematics sequence. For example, the teacher might call up a decimals group, present a lesson, and then send the students back to their teams to work on decimal problems. Then the teacher might call the fractions group, and so on.

In TAI, students encourage and help one another to succeed because they want their teams to succeed. Individual accountability is assured because the only score that counts is the final test score, and students take final tests without teammate help. Students have equal opportunities for success because all have been placed according to their level of prior knowledge; it is as easy (or difficult) for a lower achiever to complete three subtraction units in a week as it is for a higher-achieving classmate to complete three long division units.

However, the individualization that is part of TAI makes it quite different from STAD. In mathematics, most concepts build on earlier ones. If the earlier concepts were not mastered, the later ones will be difficult or impossible to learn—a student who cannot subtract or multiply will fail to master

A Visit to a Cooperative School

It is Friday morning at "Cooper Elementary School." In Ms. Thompson's third-grade, the students are getting ready for reading. They are sitting in teams at small tables, four or five at each table. As the period begins, Ms. Thompson calls up the "Rockets." Pairs of students from several of the small groups move to a reading group area, while the remaining students continue working at their desks. In Ms. Thompson's class the students at their desks are working together on activities quite different from the usual workbooks. They are taking turns reading aloud to each other; working together to identify the characters, settings, problems, and problem solutions in stories; practicing vocabulary and spelling; and summarizing stories to one another. When Ms. Thompson finishes with the Rockets, they return to their groups and begin working together on the same types of activities. Ms. Thompson listens in on some of the students who are reading to each other and praises teams that are working well. Then she calls up the "Astros," who leave their teams to go to the reading group.

Meanwhile, in Mr. Fisher's fifth-grade, it is math period. Again, students are working in small teams, but in math, each team member is working on different materials depending on his or her performance level. In the teams students are checking one another's work against answer sheets, explaining problems to one another, and answering each other's questions. Mr. Fisher calls up the "Decimals" group for a lesson. Students working on decimals leave their teams and move to the group area for their lesson. When the lesson is over, the students return to their teams and continue working on decimals.

In Mr. Fisher's class there are five learning disabled students, who are distributed among the various teams. The special education resource teacher, Ms. Walters, is teaming with Mr. Fisher. While he is giving lessons, she is moving through the class helping students. At other times, Ms. Walters gives math lessons to groups of students who are having difficulties in math, including her five LD students, while Mr. Fisher works with students in their team areas.

In Mr. Green's fourth-grade class it is writing time. Mr. Green starts the period with a brief lesson on "and disease," the tendency to write long sentences connected by too many "ands." Then the students work on compositions in teams. They cooperatively plan what they will write and then do a draft. The students read their drafts to their teammates and receive feedback on what their teammates heard, what they liked, and what they wanted to hear more about. After revising their drafts, students hold editing conferences with teammates focusing on the mechanics of the composition.

While the students are writing, Mr. Green is moving from team to team, listening in on what they are saying to each other and conferencing with individual students to help them. Also in the class is Ms. Hill, another fourth-grade teacher. She and Mr. Green began using writing process methods at the same time and are coaching each other as they use them in their classes. At the end of the day the two teachers will meet to discuss what happened, and to plan the next steps jointly. On other days, a substitute will cover Mr. Green's class while he visits Ms. Hill's writing class.

All over Cooper Elementary School, students are working in cooperative teams, and teachers are working together cooperatively to help students learn. In the first grades, students are working in pairs taking turns reading to each other. In the sixth grades students are doing team science projects in which each team member is responsible for a part of the team's task. Second-graders are working in teams to master capitalization and punctuation rules.

At the end of the day, teachers award certificates to teams that did outstanding work that week. Those teams that met the highest standards of excellence receive "Superteam" certificates. Throughout the school the sounds of applause can be heard.

After the students have gone home, the school steering committee meets. Chaired by the principal, the committee includes representatives of teachers at several grade levels, plus two parent representatives. The committee discusses the progress they are making toward their goal of becoming a cooperative school. Among other things, the committee decides to hold a school fair to show what the school is doing, to display the students' terrific cooperative work in writing, science, and math; and to encourage parents to volunteer at the school and to support their children's success at home.

—Robert E. Slavin

long division, a student who does not understand fractional concepts will fail to understand what a decimal is, and so on. In TAI, students work at their own levels, so if they lack prerequisite skills they can build a strong foundation before going on. Also, if students can learn more rapidly, they need not wait for the rest of the class.

Individualized mathematics instruction has generally failed to increase student mathematics achievement in the past (see Horak 1981), probably because the teacher's time in earlier models was entirely taken up with checking work and managing materials, leaving little time for actually teaching students. In TAI, students handle the routine checking and management, so the teacher can spend most class time teaching. This difference, plus the motivation and help provided by students within their cooperative teams, probably accounts for the strong positive effects of TAI on student achievement.

Five of six studies found substantially greater learning of mathematics computations in TAI than in control classes, while one study found no differences (Slaven, Leavey, and Madden 1984; Slavin, Madden, and Leavey 1984; Slavin and Karweit 1985). Across all six studies, the TAI classes gained an average of twice as many grade equivalents on standardized measures of computation as traditionally taught control classes (Slavin in press b). For example, in one 18-week study in Wilmington, Delaware, the control group gained .6 grade equivalents in mathematics computations, while the TAI classes gained 1.7 grade equivalents (Slavin and Karweit 1985). These experimental-control differences were still substantial (though smaller) a year after the students were in TAI.

Cooperative Integrated Reading and Composition (CIRC). The newest of the Student Team Learning methods is a comprehensive program for teaching reading and writing in the upper elementary grades. In CIRC, teachers use basal readers and reading groups, much as in traditional reading programs. However, students are assigned to teams composed of pairs from two different reading groups. While the teacher is working with one reading group, students in the other groups are working in their pairs on a series of cognitively engaging activities, includ-

ing reading to one another; making predictions about how narrative stories will come out; summarizing stories to one another; writing responses to stories; and practicing spelling, decoding, and vocabulary. Students also work in teams to master main idea and other comprehension skills. During language arts periods, a structured program based on a writing process model is used. Students plan and write drafts, revise and edit one another's work, and prepare for publication of team books. Lessons on writing skills such as description, organization, use of vivid modifiers, and on language mechanics skills are fully integrated into students' creative writing.

In most CIRC activities, students follow a sequence of teacher instruction, team practice, team pre-assessments, and a quiz. That is, students do not take the quiz until their teammates have determined they are ready. Certificates are given to teams based on the average performance of all team members on all reading and writing activities. Two studies of CIRC (Stevens et al. in press) found substantial positive effects from this method on standardized tests of reading comprehension, reading vocabulary, language expression, language mechanics, and spelling, in comparison to control groups. The CIRC classes gained 30 to 70 percent of a grade equivalent more than control classes on these measures in both studies. Significantly greater achievement on writing samples favoring the CIRC students was also found in both studies.

A New Possibility

The development and successful evaluation of the comprehensive TAI and CIRC models has created an exciting new possibility. With cooperative learning programs capable of being used all year in the 3 Rs, it is now possible to design an elementary school program based upon a radical principle: students, teachers, and administrators can work *cooperatively* to make the school a better place for working and learning.

There are many visions of what a cooperative elementary school might look like, but there is one model that my colleagues and I have begun to work toward in partnership with some

innovative practitioners. Its major components are as follows.

1. *Cooperative learning in the classroom.* Clearly, a cooperative elementary school would have cooperative learning methods in use in most classrooms and in more than one subject. Students and teachers should feel that the idea that students can help one another learn is not just applied on occasion, but is a fundamental principle of classroom organization. Students should see one another as resources for learning, and there should be a schoolwide norm that every student's learning is everyone's responsibility, that every student's success is everyone's success.

2. *Integration of special education and remedial services with the regular program.* In the cooperative elementary school, mainstreaming should be an essential element of school and classroom organization. Special education teachers may team-teach with regular teachers, integrating their students in teams with nonhandicapped students and contributing their expertise in adapting instruction to individual needs to the class as a whole. Similarly, Chapter I or other remedial services should be provided in the regular classroom. If we take seriously the idea that all students are responsibile for one another, this goes as much for students with learning problems as for anyone else. Research on use of TAI and CIRC to facilitate mainstreaming and meet the needs of remedial readers has found positive effects on the achievement and social acceptance of these students (see Slavin 1984, Slavin et al. in press).

3. *Peer coaching.* In the cooperative elementary school, teachers should be responsible for helping one another to use cooperative learning methods successfully and to implement other improvements in instructional practice. Peer coaching (Joyce et al. 1983) is perfectly adapted to the philsophy of the cooperative school; teachers learn new methods together and are given release time to visit one another's classes to give assistance and exchange ideas as they begin using the new programs.

4. *Cooperative planning.* Cooperative activities among teachers should not be restricted to peer coaching. In addition, teachers should be given time to plan goals and strategies together, to prepare common libraries of instructional materials, and to make decisions

about cooperative activities involving more than one class.

5. *Building-level steering committee.* In the cooperative elementary school, teachers and administrators should work together to determine the direction the school takes. A steering committee composed of the principal, classroom teacher representatives, representatives of other staff (e.g., special education, Chapter I, aides), and one or more parent representatives meets to discuss the progress the school is making toward its instructional goals and to recommend changes in school policies and practices to achieve these goals.

6. *Cooperation with parents and community members.* The cooperative school should invite the participation of parents and community members. Development of a community sense that children's success in school is everyone's responsibility is an important goal of the cooperative school.

The Cooperative School Today

To my knowledge, there is not yet a school that is implementing all of the program elements listed here, but a few enterprising and committed schools are moving in this direction. In Bay Shore (New York) School District, teachers in two intermediate schools are using CIRC in reading, writing, and language arts, and STAD in math. In Alexandria, Virginia, Mt. Vernon Community School is working with the National Education Association's Mastery in Learning project to build a cooperative school plan. At Mt. Vernon, a building steering committee is planning and helping to implement a gradual phasing in of the TAI math program and CIRC reading, writing, and language arts programs. Several schools throughout the U.S. that have successfully implemented TAI math are now planning to add CIRC for reading and writing instruction, and are looking toward full-scale imple-

mentation of a cooperative school plan. Most schools that have focused school renewal efforts on widespread use of cooperative learning are at the elementary level; but several middle, junior high, and high schools have begun to work in this direction as well.

In a time of limited resources for education, we must learn to make the best use of what we have. Cooperative learning and the cooperative school provide one means of helping students, teachers, and administrators work together to make meaningful improvements in the learning of all students.□

References

Aronson, E., N. Blaney, C. Stephan, J. Sikes, and M. Snapp. *The Jigsaw Classroom.* Beverly Hills, Calif.: Sage, 1978.

Dansereau, D. F. "Learning Strategy Research." In *Thinking and Learning Skills: Relating Instruction to Basic Research, Vol. 1,* edited by J. Segal, S. Chipman, and R. Glaser. Hillsdale, N.J.: Erlbaum, 1985.

Horak, V. M. "A Meta-analysis of Research Findings on Individualized Instruction in Mathematics." *Journal of Educational Research* 74 (1981): 249–253.

Johnson, D. W., and R. T. Johnson. *Learning Together and Alone.* 2d ed. Englewood Cliffs, N.J.: Prentice-Hall, 1986.

Joyce, B. R., R. H. Hersh, and M. McKibbin. *The Structure of School Improvement.* New York: Longman, 1983.

Sharan, S., R. Hertz-Lazarowitz, and Z. Ackerman. "Academic Achievement of Elementary School Children in Small-Group vs. Whole Class Instruction." *Journal of Experimental Education* 48 (1980): 125–129.

Sharan, S., P. Kussell, R. Hertz-Lazarowitz, Y. Bejarano, S. Raviv, and Y. Sharan. *Cooperative Learning in the Classroom: Research in Desegregated Schools.* Hillsdale, N.J.: Erlbaum, 1984.

Slavin, R. E. *Cooperative Learning.* New York: Longman, 1983a.

Slavin, R. E. "When Does Cooperative Learning Increase Student Achievement?" *Psychological Bulletin* 94 (1983b): 429–445.

Slavin, R. E. "Team Assisted Individualization: Cooperative Learning and Individualized Instruction in the Mainstreamed Classroom." *Remedial and Special Education* 5, 6 (1984): 33–42.

Slavin, R. E. *Using Student Team Learning.* 3d ed. Baltimore, Md.: Center for Research on Elementary and Middle Schools, Johns Hopkins University, 1986.

Slavin, R. E. "Cooperative Learning: A Best-Evidence Synthesis." In *School and Classroom Organization,* edited by R. E. Slavin. Hillsdale, N.J.: Erlbaum. In press a.

Slavin, R. E. "Combining Cooperative Learning and Individualized Instruction." *Arithmetic Teacher.* In press b.

Slavin, R. E., and N. L. Karweit. "Effects of Whole-Class, Ability Grouped, and Individualized Instruction on Mathematics Achievement." *American Educational Research Journal* 22 (1985): 351–367.

Slavin, R. E., M. Leavey, and N. A. Madden. "Combining Cooperative Learning and Individualized Instruction: Effects on Student Mathematics Achievement, Attitudes, and Behaviors." *Elementary School Journal* 84 (1984): 409–422.

Slavin, R. E., N. A. Madden, and M. Leavey. "Effects of Team Assisted Individualization on the Mathematics Achievement of Academically Handicapped and Non-handicapped Students." *Journal of Educational Psychology* 76 (1984): 813–819.

Slavin, R. E., R. J. Stevens, and N. A. Madden. "Accommodating Student Diversity in Reading and Writing Instruction: A Cooperative Learning Approach." *Remedial and Special Education.* In press.

Stevens, R. J., N. A. Madden, R. E. Slavin, and A. M. Farnish. "Cooperative Integrated Reading and Composition: Two Field Experiments." *Reading Research Quarterly.* In press.

Webb, N. "Student Interaction and Learning in Small Groups: A Research Summary." In *Learning to Cooperate, Cooperating to Learn,* edited by R. E. Slavin, S. Sharan, S. Kagan, R. Hertz-Lazarowitz, C. Webb, and R. Schmuck. New York: Plenum, 1985.

Author's note: This article was written under funding from the Office of Educational Research and Improvement, U.S. Department of Education (Grant No. OERI-G-86–006). However, the opinions expressed are mine and do not necessarily reflect OERI positions or policy.

Productive Teaching and Instruction: Assessing The Knowledge Base

HERBERT J. WALBERG

HERBERT J. WALBERG (University of Chicago/DePaul University Chapter) is an educational psychologist and a research professor of education at the University of Illinois, Chicago. ©1990, Herbert J. Walberg.

Mr. Walberg surveys the vast literature on the effects of various instructional methods, enabling readers to consider the advantages and disadvantages of different techniques — including some effective ones that are no longer popular.

SOME TEACHING techniques have remarkable effects on learning, while others confer only trivial advantages or even hinder the learning process. Over the past decade, there has been an explosion of research activity centering on the question of what constitutes effective teaching. Ten years ago, several psychologists observed signs of a "quiet revolution" in educational research. Five years later, nearly 3,000 studies of effective teaching techniques existed. By 1987 an Australian/U.S. team was able to assess 134 reviews of 7,827 field studies and several large-scale U.S. and international surveys of learning.[1]

In this article I will give an overview of the findings to date on elementary and secondary school students and will evaluate the more recent and definitive reviews of research on teaching and instruction. Surveying the vast literature on the effects of various instructional methods allows us to consider the advantages and disadvantages of different techniques — including some effective ones that are no longer popular.

I will begin by considering the effects of the psychological elements of teaching, and I will discuss methods and patterns of teaching that a single teacher can accomplish without unusual arrangements or equipment. Then I will turn to systems of instruction that require special plan-

From *Phi Delta Kappan*, February 1990, pp. 470-478. Reprinted by permission of the author and *Phi Delta Kappan*.

ning, student grouping, and materials. Next I will describe effects that are unique to particular methods of teaching reading, writing, science, and mathematics. Finally, I will discuss special students and techniques for dealing with them and the effects of particular types of training on teachers. It is important to bear in mind that, when we try to apply in our own classrooms the methods we have read about, we may attain results that are half — or twice — as good as the average estimates reported below. Our success will depend not only on careful implementation but also on our purposes. The best saw swung as a hammer does little good.

PSYCHOLOGICAL ELEMENTS

A little history will help us to understand the evolution of psychological research on teaching. Even though educators require balance, psychologists have often emphasized thought, feeling, or behavior at the expense of the other two components of the psyche. Today, thinking or cognition is sovereign in psychology, but half a century ago behaviorists insisted on specific operational definitions (and they continue to do so). In particular, Yale psychologists John Dollard and Neal Miller, stimulated by E. L. Thorndike and B. F. Skinner, wrote about cues, responses, and positive reinforcement, especially in psychotherapy. Later Miller and Dollard isolated three components of teaching — cues, engagement, and reinforcement — that are similar to the elements of input, process, and output in physiology.[2] Their influential work led researchers to consider what teachers *do* instead of focusing on their age, experience, certification, college degrees, or other factors not directly connected to what their students learn.[3]

The behavioral model emphasized 1) the quality of the instructional cues impinging on the learner, 2) the learner's active engagement, and 3) the reinforcements or rewards that encourage continuing effort over time. Benjamin Bloom recognized, however, that in cycles of cues and effort learners may fail the first time or even repeatedly. Thus they may practice incorrect behavior, and so they cannot be reinforced. Therefore, he emphasized feedback to correct errors and frequent testing to check progress. Inspired by John Carroll's model of school learning, Bloom also emphasized engaged learning time and stressed that some learners require much more time than others.[4]

The effects of cues, engagement, re-inforcement, and corrective feedback on student learning are enormous.[5] The research demonstrating these effects has been unusually rigorous and well-controlled. Even though the research was conducted in school classes, the investigators helped to insure precise timing and deployment of the elements and relied on short-term studies, which usually lasted less than a month. Similar effects are difficult to sustain for long time periods.

Cues. As operationalized, cues show students what is to be learned and explain how to learn it. Their quality depends on the clarity, salience, and meaningfulness of explanations and directions provided by the teacher, the instructional materials, or both. Ideally, as the learners gain confidence, the salience and number of cues can be reduced.

Engagement. The extent to which students actively and persistently participate in learning until appropriate responses are firmly entrenched in their repertoires is known as engagement. Such participation can be indexed by the extent to which the teacher engages students in overt or covert activity. A high degree of engagement is indicated by an absence of irrelevant behavior and by concentration on tasks, enthusiastic contributions to group discussion, and lengthy study.

Corrective feedback. Corrective feedback remedies errors in oral or written responses. Ideally, students should waste little time on incorrect responses, and teachers should detect difficulties rapidly and then remedy them by reteaching or using alternative methods. When necessary, teachers should also provide students with additional time for practice.

Reinforcement. The immense effort elicited by athletics, games, and other cooperative and competitive activities illustrates the power of immediate and direct reinforcement and shows that some endeavors are intrinsically rewarding. By comparison, classroom reinforcement may seem crass or jejune. The usual classroom reinforcers are acknowledgment of correctness and social approval, typically expressed by praise or a smile. More unusual reinforcers include providing contingent activity — for example, initiating a music lesson or other enjoyable activity as a reward for 90% correctness on a math test. Other reinforcers are tokens or check marks that are accumulated for discrete accomplishments and that can be exchanged for tangible reinforcers such as cookies, trinkets, or toys.

In special education programs, students have been reinforced not only for academic achievement but also for minutes spent on reading, for attempts to learn, and for the accuracy with which they perform tasks. Margo Mastropieri and Thomas Scruggs have shown that results can be impressive when the environment can be rigorously controlled and when teachers can accurately gear reinforcement to performance, as in programs for unruly or emotionally disturbed students. Improved behavior and achievement, however, may fail to extend past the period of reinforcement or beyond the special environment.[6]

Educators ordinarily confine reinforcement to marks, grades, and awards because they must assume that students work for such intangible, long-term goals as pleasing parents, furthering their education, achieving success in later life, and the intrinsic satisfaction of learning itself. Even so, when corrective feedback and reinforcement are clear, rapid, and appropriate, they can powerfully affect learning by efficiently signaling students what to do next. In ordinary classrooms, then, the chief value of reinforcement is informational rather than motivational.

METHODS OF TEACHING

The psychological elements just discussed undergird many teaching methods and the design of most instructional media. Techniques to improve the affective or informational content of cues, engagement, correctives, and reinforcement have shown a wide range of effects.

Cues. *Advance organizers* are brief overviews that relate new concepts or terms to previous learning. They are effective if they connect new learning and old. Those delivered by the teacher or graphically illustrated in texts work best.

Adjunct questions alert students to key questions that should be answered — particularly in texts. They work best when questions are repeated on posttests, and they work moderately well when posttest questions are similar or related to the adjuncts. As we might expect, however, adjunct questions divert attention from incidental material that might otherwise be learned.

Goal setting suggests specific objectives, guidelines, methods, or standards for learning that can be spelled out explicitly. Like the use of adjunct questions, goal setting sacrifices incidental for intended learning.

Learning hierarchies assume that instruction can be made more efficient if the facts, skills, or ideas that logically or psychologically precede others are presented first. Teaching and instructional media sequenced in this way appear to be slightly more effective. However, learners may adapt themselves to apparently ill-sequenced material, and it may even be advantageous to learn to do so, since human life, as Franz Kafka showed, may depart from logic.

Pretests are benchmarks for determining how much students learn under various methods of teaching. Psychologists have found, however, that pretests can have positive cuing effects if they show students what will be emphasized in instruction and on posttests.

Several principles follow from surveying the effects of these methods. To concentrate learning on essential points and to save time (as would be appropriate in training), remove elaborations and extraneous oral and written prose. To focus learners on selected questions or to teach them to find answers in elaborated prose, use adjunct questions and goal setting. To encourage the acquisition of as much undifferentiated material as possible, as in college lecture courses, assign big blocks of text and test students on randomly selected points.

Although the means of producing certain results may seem clear, reaching a consensus on educational purposes may be difficult. Clarity at the start saves time and helps learners to see things the teacher's way, but it limits individual autonomy and deep personal insights. Zen masters ask novices about the sound of one hand clapping and wait a decade or two for an answer. Hiroshi Azuma and Robert Hess find that Japanese mothers use more indirection and vagueness in teaching their young children than do assertive American mothers, and I have observed Japanese science teachers asking questions and leaving them long unresolved. Do the Japanese cultivate initiative and perseverance by these methods?

Engagement. *High expectations* transmit teachers' standards of learning and performance. They may function both as cues and as incentives for students to put extended effort and perseverance into learning.

Frequent tests increase learning by stimulating greater effort and providing intermittent feedback. However, the effects of tests on performance are larger for quizzes than for final examinations.

Questioning also appears to work by promoting engagement and may encourage deeper thinking — as in Plato's accounts of Socrates. Questioning has bigger effects in science than in other subjects. Mary Budd Rowe and Kenneth Tobin have shown that *wait time* — allowing students several seconds to reflect rather than the usual .9 of a second — leads to longer and better answers.

> **P**raise may pale in comparison with the disincentives to achievement afforded by the youth culture.

Correctives and reinforcement. *Corrective feedback* remedies errors by reteaching, either with the same or with a different method. This practice has moderate effects that are somewhat higher in science — perhaps because learning science often involves more conceptualizing while learning other subjects may allow more memorizing.

Homework by itself constructively extends engaged learning time. Correctives and reinforcement in the form of grades and comments on homework raise its effects dramatically.

Praise has a small positive effect. For young or disturbed children, praise may lack the power of the tangible reinforcers used in psychological experiments. For students who are able to see ahead, grades and personal standards may be more powerful reinforcers than momentary encouragement. Moreover, praise may be under- or oversupplied; it may appear demeaning or sardonic; and it may pale in comparison with the disincentives to academic achievement afforded by youth culture in the form of cars, clothing, dating, and athletics.

None of this is to say that encouragement, incentives, and good classroom morale should be abandoned; honey may indeed be better than vinegar. Yet, as cognitive psychologists point out, the main classroom value of reinforcement may lie in its capacity to inform the student about progress rather than in its power to reward.

PATTERNS OF TEACHING

As explained above, methods of teaching enact or combine more fundamental

psychological elements. By further extension, *patterns* of teaching integrate elements and methods of teaching. The process of determining these more inclusive formulations was another step in the evolution of psychological research on education. Behavioral research evolved in the 1950s from psychological laboratories to short-term, controlled classroom experiments on one element at a time. In the 1970s educational researchers tried to find patterns of effective practices from observations of ordinary teaching.

Thus behaviorists traded educational realism for theoretical parsimony and scientific rigor; later psychologists preferred realism until their insights could be experimentally confirmed. Fortunately, the results of both approaches appear to converge. Moreover, it seems possible to incorporate the work of cognitive psychologists of the 1980s into an enlarged understanding of teaching.

Explicit teaching. Explicit teaching can be viewed as traditional or conventional whole-group teaching done well. Since most teaching has changed little in the last three-quarters of a century and may not change substantially in the near future,[7] it is worth knowing how to make the usual practice most productive. Since it has evolved from ordinary practice, explicit teaching seems natural to carry out and does not disrupt conventional institutions and expectations. Furthermore, it can incorporate many previously discussed elements and methods.

Systematic research was initiated in the early 1960s by N. L. Gage, Donald Medley, and others who employed "process-product" investigations of the association between what teachers do and how much their students learn. Jere Brophy, Carolyn Evertson, Thomas Good, and Jane Stallings later contributed substantially to this effort. Walter Doyle, Penelope Peterson, and Lee Shulman put the results into a psychological context. Barak Rosenshine has periodically reviewed the research, and Gage and Margaret Needels recently measured the results and pointed out their implications.

The various contributors to the knowledge base do not completely agree about the essential components of explicit teaching, and they refer to it by different names, such as process-product, direct, active, and effective teaching. The researchers weigh their own results heavily, but Rosenshine, a long-standing and comprehensive reviewer, has taken an eagle's-eye view of the results.[8]

In his early reviews of the correlational studies, Rosenshine discussed the traits of effective teachers, including clarity, task orientation, enthusiasm, and flexibility, as well as their tendency to structure their presentations and occasionally to use student ideas. From later observational and control-group research, Rosenshine identified six phased functions of explicit teaching: 1) daily review, checking of homework, and reteaching if necessary; 2) rapid presentation of new content and skills in small steps; 3) guided student practice with close monitoring by teachers; 4) corrective feedback and instructional reinforcement; 5) independent practice in seatwork and homework, with a success rate of more than 90%; and 6) weekly and monthly review.

Comprehension teaching. The heirs of Aristotle and of the Anglo-American tradition of Bacon, Locke, Thorndike, and Skinner objected to philosophical "armchair" opinions; mid-century behaviorists, particularly John Watson, constructively insisted on hard empirical data about learning. But they also saw the child's mind as a blank tablet and seemed to encourage active teaching and passive acquisition of isolated facts. Reacting to such atomism and to William James' "bucket" metaphor, cognitive psychologists in the early 1980s revived research on student-centered learning and "higher mental processes," in the tradition of Plato, Socrates, Kant, Rousseau, Dewey, Freud, and Piaget. In American hands, however, this European tradition has sometimes led to vacuity and permissiveness, as in the extremes of the "progressive education" movement of the 1930s.

Oddly, the Russian psychologist Lev Vygotsky hit on an influential compromise: emphasizing the two-way nature of teaching, he identified a "zone of proximal development," which extends from what learners can do independently to the maximum that they can do with the teacher's help.[9] Accordingly, teachers should set up "scaffolding" for building knowledge and then remove it when it becomes unnecessary. In mathematics, for example, the teacher can give prompts and examples, foster independent use, and then withdraw support. This approach is similar to the "prompting" and "fading" of the behavioral cues, and it seems commonsensical. It has revived interest in granting some autonomy to students.

During the 1980s cognitive research on teaching sought ways to encourage self-monitoring, self-teaching, or "metacognition" to foster independence. Skills were seen as important, but the learner's monitoring and management of them had

priority, as though the explicit teaching functions of planning, allocating time, and reviewing were partly transferred to the learner.

For example, David Pearson outlined three phases: 1) modeling, in which the teacher exhibits the desired behavior; 2) guided practice, in which students perform with help from the teacher; and 3) application, in which students perform independently of the teacher — steps that correspond to explicit teaching functions. Anne Marie Pallincsar and Anne Brown described a program of "reciprocal teaching" that fosters comprehension by having students take turns in leading dialogues on pertinent features of a text. By assuming the kind of planning and executive control ordinarily exercised by teachers, students learn planning, structuring, and self-management. Perhaps that is why tutors learn from teaching and why we say that to learn something well, one should teach it.

Comprehension teaching encourages students to measure their progress toward explicit goals. If necessary, they can reallocate their time to different activities. In this way, self-awareness, personal control, and positive self-evaluation can be increased.[10]

LEARNER AUTONOMY IN SCIENCE

The National Science Foundation sponsored many studies of student inquiry and autonomy that showed that giving students opportunities to manipulate science materials, to contract with teachers about what to learn, to inquire on their own, and to engage in activity-based curricula all had substantial positive effects. Group- and self-direction, however, had smaller positive effects, and pass/fail and self-grading had small negative effects. Methods of providing greater learner autonomy may also work well in subjects other than science, as in the more radical approach that I discuss next.

OPEN EDUCATION

In the late 1960s, open educators expanded autonomy in the primary grades by enabling students to join teachers in planning educational purposes, means, and evaluation. In contrast to teacher- and textbook-centered education, open education gave students a voice in deciding what to learn — even to the point of writing their own texts to share with one another. Open educators tried to foster cooperation, critical thinking, constructive attitudes, and self-directed lifelong

learning. They revived the spirit of the New England town meeting, Thoreau's self-reliance, Emerson's transcendentalism, and Dewey's progressivism. Their ideas also resonate with the "client-centered" psychotherapy of Carl Rogers, which emphasizes the "unconditional worth" of the person.

Rose Giaconia and Larry Hedges' synthesis of 153 studies showed that open education had worthwhile effects on creativity, independence, cooperation, attitudes toward teachers and schools, mental ability, psychological adjustment, and curiosity. Students in open programs had less motivation for grade grubbing, but they differed little from other students in actual achievement, self-concept, and anxiety.

However, Giaconia and Hedges also found that the open programs that were more effective in producing the positive outcomes with regard to attitudes, creativity, and self-concept sacrificed some academic achievement on standardized tests. These programs emphasized the role of the child in learning and the use of individualized instruction, manipulative materials, and diagnostic rather than norm-referenced evaluation. However, they did not include three other components thought by some to be essential to open programs: multi-age grouping, open space, and team teaching.

Giaconia and Hedges speculated that children in the most extreme open programs may do somewhat less well on conventional achievement tests because they have little experience with them. At any rate, it appears that open classrooms enhance several nonstandard outcomes without detracting from academic achievement unless they are radically extreme.[11]

INSTRUCTIONAL SYSTEMS

All the techniques discussed thus far can be planned and executed by a single teacher. They may entail some extra effort, encouragement, or training, but they do not call for unusual preparation or materials. In contrast, instructional systems require special arrangements and planning, and they often combine several components of instruction. Moreover, they tend to emphasize the adaptation of instruction to individual students rather than the adaptation of students to a fixed pattern of teaching. A little history will aid our understanding of current instructional systems.

Programmed instruction. Developed in the 1950s, programmed instruction presents a series of "frames," each one of which conveys an item of information and requires a student response. *Linear programs* present a graduated series of frames that require such small increments in knowledge that learning steps may be nearly errorless and may be continuously reinforced by progression to the next frame. Able students proceed quickly under these conditions. *Branched programs* direct students back for reteaching when necessary, to the side for correctives, and ahead when they already know parts of the material. The ideas of continuous progress and branching influenced later developers, who tried to optimize learning by individualization, mastery learning, and adaptive instruction.

Individualization adapts instruction to individual needs by applying variations in speed or branching and by using booklets, worksheets, coaching, and the like. Perhaps because they have been vaguely defined and poorly operationalized, individualized programs have had small effects. Other systems (discussed below) appear more effective for adapting instruction to the needs of individual learners.

Mastery learning. Combining the psychological elements of instruction with suitable amounts of time, mastery learning employs formative tests to allocate time and to guide reinforcement and corrective feedback. In the most definitive synthesis of research on mastery learning, James Kulik and Chen-Lin Kulik reported substantial positive effects. Mastery programs that yielded larger effects established a criterion of 95% to 100% mastery and required repeated testing to mastery before allowing students to proceed to additional units (which yielded gigantic effects of one standard deviation). Mastery learning yielded larger effects with less-able students and reduced the difference between their performance and that of abler groups.

The success of mastery learning is attributable to several factors. The Kuliks, for example, found that when control groups were provided feedback from quizzes, the mastery groups' advantage was smaller. As Bloom pointed out, mastery learning takes additional time; the Kuliks found that mastery learning required a median of 16% (and up to 97%) more time than conventional instruction. The seven studies that provided equal time for mastery and control groups showed only a small advantage for mastery learning on standardized tests. However, the advantage was moderate on experimenter-made, criterion-referenced tests for nine equal-time studies. These results illustrate the separate contribu-

tions to mastery learning of cuing, feedback, and time.

Mastery learning yielded larger effects in studies of less than a month's duration than in those lasting more than four months. Retention probably declines sharply no matter what the educational method, but the decline can be more confidently noted with regard to mastery learning since it has been more extensively studied than other methods.

Bloom and his students have reported larger effects than has Robert Slavin, who reviewed their work. Thomas Guskey and S. L. Gates, for example, reported an average effect size of .78 estimated from 38 studies of elementary and secondary students. In response to Slavin, Lorin Anderson and Robert Burns pointed out two reasons for larger effects in some studies, especially those under Bloom's supervision. Bloom has been more interested in what is possible than in what is likely; he has sought to find the limits of learning. His students, moreover, have conducted tightly controlled experiments over time periods of less than a semester or less than a year.[12]

Adaptive instruction. Developed by Margaret Wang and others, adaptive instruction combines elements of mastery learning, cooperative learning, open education, tutoring, computer-assisted instruction, and comprehension teaching into a complex system whose aim is to tailor instruction to the needs of individuals and small groups. Managerial functions — including such activities as planning, allocating time, delegating tasks to aides and students, and quality control — are carried out by a master teacher. Adaptive instruction is a comprehensive program for the whole school day rather than a single method that requires simple integration into one subject or into a single teacher's repertoire. Its effects on achievement are substantial, but its broader effects are probably underestimated, since adaptive instruction aims at diverse ends — including student autonomy, intrinsic motivation, and teacher and student choice — which are poorly reflected by the usual outcome measures.

COMPUTER-ASSISTED INSTRUCTION

Ours is an electronic age, and computers have already had a substantial impact on learning. With the costs of hardware declining and with software becoming increasingly sophisticated, we may hope for still greater effects as computers are better integrated into school programs.

Computers show the greatest advan-

tage for handicapped students — probably because they are more adaptive to their special needs than teachers might be. Computers may also be more patient, discreet, nonjudgmental, or even encouraging about progress. Perhaps for the same reasons, computers generally have bigger effects in elementary schools than in high schools or colleges.

Another explanation for the disparate results is also plausible. Elementary schools provide less tracking and fewer differentiated courses for homogeneous groups. Computers may be better adapted to larger within-class differences among elementary students because they allow them to proceed at their own pace without engaging in invidious comparisons.

Simulations and games, with or without computer implementation, require active, specific responses from learners and may strike a balance between vicarious book learning and the dynamic, complicated, and competitive "real world." The interactiveness, speed, intensity, movement, color, and sound of computers add interest and information to academic learning. Unless geared to educational purposes, however, computer games can also waste time.

STUDENT GROUPING

Teaching students what they already know and teaching them what they are yet incapable of learning are equally wasteful practices and may even be harmful to motivation. For this reason, traditional whole-class teaching of heterogeneous groups can present serious difficulties — a problem that is often unacknowledged in our egalitarian age. Outside of universities, however, most educators recognize that it is difficult to teach arithmetic and trigonometry at the same time. (Even some English professors might balk at teaching phonics and deconstructionism simultaneously.) If we want to teach students as much as possible rather than to make them all alike, we need to consider how they are grouped and try to help the full range of students.

Acceleration. Accelerated programs identify talented youth (often in mathematics and science) and group them together or with older students. Such programs provide counseling, encouragement, contact with accomplished adults, grade skipping, summer school, and the compression of the standard curriculum into fewer years. The effects are huge in elementary schools, substantial in junior high schools, and moderate in senior high schools. The smaller effects at more ad-

For Japanese students, long-term adult rewards reinforce educational effort.

specific subject-matter needs rather than according to I.Q., demeanor, or other irrelevant characteristics.

Well-defined subject matter and student grouping may be among the chief reasons why Japanese students lead the world in academic achievement: the curriculum is explicit, rigorous, and nationally uniform. In primary schools, weaker students, with maternal help, study harder and longer to keep up with these explicit requirements. Subject-matter tests are administered to screen students for "lower" and "upper" secondary schools and for universities of various gradations of rigor and prestige. Each such screening determines occupational, marital, and other adult prospects; long-term adult rewards thus reinforce educational effort.[13]

There are some successful precedents for the use of media-based instruction.

vanced levels may be attributable to the smaller advantage of acceleration over the tracking and differentiated course selection already practiced in high schools.

The effects of acceleration on educational attitudes, vocational plans, participation in school activities, popularity, psychological adjustment, and character ratings have been mixed and often insignificant. These outcomes may not be systematically affected in either direction.

Ability grouping. Students are placed in ability groups according to achievement, intelligence test scores, personal insights, and subjective opinions. In high school, ability grouping leaves deficient and average students unaffected, but it has beneficial effects on talented students and on attitudes toward the subject matter. In elementary school, the grouping of students with similar reading achievement but from different grades yields substantial effects. Within-class grouping in mathematics yields worthwhile effects, but generalized ability grouping does not.

Tutoring. Because it gears instruction to individual or small-group needs, tutoring is highly beneficial to both tutors and tutees. It yields particularly large effects in mathematics — perhaps because of the subject's well-defined scope and organization.

* * *

In whole-group instruction, teachers may ordinarily focus on average or deficient students to insure that they master the lessons. When talented students are freed from repetition and slow progression, they can proceed quickly. Grouping may work best when students are accurately grouped according to their

SOCIAL ENVIRONMENT

Cooperative learning programs delegate some control of the pacing and methods of learning to groups of between two and six students, who work together and sometimes compete with other groups within classes. Such programs are successful for several reasons. They provide relief from the excessive teacher/student interaction of whole-group teaching, they free time for the interactive engagement of students, and they present opportunities for targeted cues, engagement, correctives, and reinforcement. As in comprehension teaching, the acts of tutoring and teaching may encourage students to think for themselves about the organization of subject matter and the productive allocation of time.

Many correlational studies suggest that *classroom morale* is associated with achievement gains, with greater interest in subject matter, and with the worthy outcome of voluntary participation in nonrequired subject-related activities. Morale is assessed by asking students to agree or disagree with such statements as "Most of the students know one another well" and "The class members know the purpose of the lessons."

Students who perceive the atmosphere as friendly, satisfying, focused on goals, and challenging and who feel that the classroom has the required materials tend to learn more. Those who perceive the atmosphere as fostering student cliques, disorganization, apathy, favoritism, and friction learn less. The research on morale, though plausible, lacks the specificity and causal confidence of the controlled experiments on directly alterable methods.

READING EFFECTS

Comprehension teaching, because it may extend to several subjects in elementary school, has already been discussed as a pattern of teaching. Several other methods have substantial effects on reading achievement.

Adaptive speed training involves principles that are similar to those of comprehension training. Students learn to vary their pace and the depth of their reflection according to the difficulty of the material and their reading purposes.

Reading methods vary widely, but their largest effects seem to occur when teachers are systematically trained, almost irrespective of particularities of method. Phonics or "word-attack" approaches, however, have a moderate advantage over guessing and "whole-word" approaches in the teaching of beginning reading — perhaps because early misconceptions are avoided. Phonics may also reduce the need for excessive reteaching and correctives.

Pictures in the text can be very helpful, although they add to the cost of a book and occupy space that could otherwise be used for prose. In order of their effectiveness, several types of pictures can be distinguished. Transformative pictures recode information into concrete and memorable form, relate information in a well-organized context, and provide links for systematic retrieval. Interpretive pictures, like advance organizers, make the text comprehensible by relating abstract terms to concrete ones and by connecting the unfamiliar and difficult to previously acquired knowledge. Organizational pictures, including maps and diagrams, show the coherence of objects or events in space and time. Representational pictures are photos or other concrete representations of what is discussed in the text. Decorative pictures present (possibly irrelevant or conflicting) information that is incidental to intended learning (although decoration may add interest if not information).

Pictures can provide vivid imagery and metaphors that facilitate memory, show what is important to learn, and intensify the effects of prose. Pictures may sometimes allow students to bypass the text, but memorable, well-written prose may obviate pictures.[14]

WRITING EFFECTS

Sixty well-designed studies of methods of teaching writing compared 72 experimental groups with control groups. The methods below are presented in the order of their effectiveness.

The inquiry method requires students to find and state specific details that convey personal experience vividly, to examine sets of data to develop and support explanatory generalizations, or to analyze situations that present ethical problems and arguments.

Scales are criteria or specific questions that students can apply to their own and others' writing to improve it.

Sentence combining shows students how to build complex sentences from simpler ones.

Models are presentations of good pieces of writing to serve as exemplars for students.

Free writing allows students to write about whatever occurs to them.

Grammar and mechanics include sentence parsing and the analysis of parts of speech.

SCIENCE EFFECTS

Introduced in response to the launch of Sputnik I, the "new" science curricula, sponsored by the National Science Foundation, yielded substantial effects on learning. They efficiently added value by producing superior learning on tests of their intended outcomes and on tests of general subject-matter goals. The new curricula also yielded effects ranging from small to substantial on such often-unmeasured outcomes as creativity, problem solving, scientific attitudes and skills, logical thinking, and achievement in non-science subject matter.

Perhaps these advantages are attributable to the combined efforts of teachers, psychologists, and scientists, who collaborated to insure that the curricula would be based on modern content and would foster effective teaching practices. The scientists may have been able to generate enthusiasm for teaching scientific methods, for laboratory work, and for other reforms.

The new science curricula worked well in improving achievement and other outcomes. Ironically, they are often forgotten today, despite the fact that, by international standards, U.S. students score poorly in mathematics and science.

Inquiry teaching. Often practiced in Japan, this method requires students to formulate hypotheses, reason about their credibility, and design experiments to test their validity. Inquiry teaching yields substantial effects, particularly on the understanding of scientific processes.

Audio-tutorials. These are tape-recorded instructions for using laboratory equipment, manipulatives, and readings for topical lessons or whole courses. This simple approach yields somewhat better results than conventional instruction, allows independent learning, and has the further advantage of individual pacing — allowing students to pursue special topics or to take courses on their own.

Original source papers. This method derives from the Great Books approach of the late Robert Maynard Hutchins, former president of the University of Chicago, and his colleague Mortimer Adler. They saw more value in reading Plato or Newton than in resorting to predigested textbook accounts. The use of original sources in science teaching trades breadth for depth in the belief that it is better to know a few ideas of transcending importance than to learn many unconnected bits of soon-forgotten information. Advocates of this approach have shown that such knowledge can be acquired by studying and discussing original scientific papers of historical or scientific significance.

Other methods of teaching science have effects that are near zero — that is, close to the effects of traditional methods of teaching. They include team teaching, departmentalized elementary programs, and media-based instruction. The equal results for media methods, however, suggest that choices can be based on cost and convenience. Since television programs and films can be broadcast, they can provide equally effective education in different and widespread locations (even in different parts of the world by satellite). Moreover, students today can interact "on-line" with teachers and fellow students who are far away.

There are some successful precedents for the use of media-based instruction. For a decade, the Chicago community colleges provided dozens of mainly one-way television courses to hundreds of thousands of students, who did most of their studying at home but participated in discussion and testing sessions at several sites in the metropolitan area. The best lecturers, media specialists, and test constructors could be employed, and tapes of the courses could be rebroadcast repeatedly.

In several Third World countries that are gaining in achievement and school enrollments, ministries of education make efficient and successful use of such low-cost, effective "distance education" for remote elementary and secondary schools.

The Oklahoma and Minnesota state departments of education apparently lead the nation in providing small high schools in rural areas with specialized television teachers and interactive courses in advanced science, mathematics, foreign language, and other subjects.

MATHEMATICS EFFECTS

In the heyday of its Education Directorate, the National Science Foundation sponsored considerable research not only on science but also on mathematics. Some worthwhile effects were found.

Manipulative materials. The use of Cuisenaire rods, balance beams, counting sticks, and measuring scales allows students to engage directly in learning instead of passively following abstract presentations by the teacher. Students can handle the materials, see the relation of abstract ideas and concrete embodiments, and check hypothesized answers by quick empirical testing without having to wait for quiz results or feedback from the teacher. This method apparently results in enormous effects.

Problem solving. In mathematics teaching, a focus on problem solving yields worthwhile effects. Such an approach requires comprehension of terms and their application to varied examples. It may motivate students by showing them the application of mathematical ideas to "real-world" questions.

New math. The so-called new math produced beneficial results, although it was not as successful as the new science curricula. Both reforms probably gained their learning advantages partly by testing what they taught.

SPECIAL POPULATIONS AND TECHNIQUES

We can also gain insights from programs that lie outside the usual scope of elementary and secondary classrooms.

Early intervention. Programs of early intervention include educational, psychological, and therapeutic components for handicapped, at-risk, and disadvantaged children from the ages of one month to 5½ years. Studies of these programs found that the large, immediate effects of these programs declined rapidly and disappeared after three years.

Preschool programs. Preschool programs also showed initial learning effects that were not sustained. It appears that young children can learn more than is normally assumed, but, like other learners, they can also forget. The key to sustained gains may be sustained programs and effective families — not one-shot approaches.

Programs for the handicapped. Students classified as mentally retarded, emotionally disturbed, or learning disabled have been subjects in research that has several important implications. When they serve as tutors of one another and of younger students, handicapped students can learn well — a finding similar to those in comprehension-monitoring and tutoring studies of nonhandicapped children. Moreover, handicapped students are often spuriously classified, and we may underestimate their capacities.

Mainstreaming. Studies show that mildly to moderately handicapped students can prosper in regular classes and thereby avoid the invidious "labeling" that is often based on misclassification.

Psycholinguistic training. Providing psycholinguistic training to special-needs students yields positive effects. This approach consists of testing and remedying specific deficits in language skills.

Patient education. Educating patients about diseases and treatments can affect mortality, morbidity, and lengths of illness and hospitalization. In studies of the acquisition of knowledge regarding drug usage for hypertension, diabetes, and other chronic conditions, one-to-one and group counseling (with or without instructional material) produced greater effects than providing instruction through labels on bottles or package inserts for patients.

Labels, special containers, memory aids, and behavior modification were successful in minimizing later errors in drug usage. The most efficacious educational principles were: specification of intentions; relevance to the needs of the learner; provision of personal answers to questions; reinforcement and feedback on progress; facilitation of correct dosage, e.g., the use of unit-dose containers; and

instructional and treatment regimens suited to personal convenience, e.g., prescribing drugs for administration at mealtimes.

Inservice training of physicians. Such training shows large effects on doctors' knowledge and on their classroom or laboratory performance but only moderate effects on the outcomes of treating actual patients. Knowledge and performance, even in practical training, may help, but they hardly guarantee successful application in practice. Can an accomplished mathematician handle the intricacies of federal income tax?

Panaceas and shortcuts. At the request of the U.S. Army, the National Academy of Sciences evaluated exotic techniques for enhancing learning and performance that are described in popular psychology (and presumably are being exploited in California and the USSR).[15] However, little or no evidence was found for the efficacy of learning during sleep; for mental practice of motor skills; for "integration" of left and right hemispheres of the brain; for parapsychological techniques; for biofeedback; for extrasensory perception, mental telepathy, and "mind over matter" exercises; or for "neurolinguistic programming," in which instructors identify the students' modes of learning and mimic the students' behaviors as they teach.

The Greeks found no royal road to geometry; even kings, if they desired mastery, had to sweat over Euclid's elements. Perhaps brain research will eventually yield a magic elixir or a panacea, but for proof of its existence educators should insist on hard data in refereed scientific journals.

EFFECTS ON TEACHERS

Programs to help teachers in their work have had substantial effects — notwithstanding complaints about typical inservice training sessions. Do physicians complain about the medical care they get?

Microteaching. Developed at Stanford University in the 1960s, microteaching is a behavioral approach for preservice and inservice training that has substantial effects. It employs the explanation and modeling of selected teaching techniques; televised practice with small groups of students; discussion, correctives, and reinforcement while watching playback; and recycling through subsequent practice and playback sessions with new groups of students.

Inservice education. Inservice training for teachers also proves to have substantial effects. Somewhat like the case

> **K**nowledge from the field of psychology alone is not sufficient to prescribe practices.

of inservice training of physicians, the biggest effects are on the teacher's knowledge, but effects on classroom behavior and student achievement are also notable.

For inservice training, authoritative planning and execution seem to work best; informal coaching by itself seems ineffective. Allowing the instructor to be responsible for the design and teaching of the sessions works better than relying on presentations by teachers and group discussions. The best techniques are observation of classroom practices, video/audio feedback, and practice. The most effective training combines lectures, modeling, practice, and coaching. The size of the training group, ranging from one to more than 60, makes no detectable difference.

Some apparent effects may be attributable to the selectivity of the program rather than to its superior efficacy. For example, federal-, state-, and university-sponsored programs appear more effective than locally initiated programs. Competitive selection of participants and the granting of college credit apparently work better as incentives than extra pay, renewal of certification, or no incentives. Independent study seems to have larger effects than workshops, courses, minicourses, and institutes.

PSYCHOLOGICAL research provides first-order estimates of the effects of instructional means on educational ends under various conditions. But some instructional practices may be costly — not in terms of dollars but in terms of new or complicated arrangements that may be difficult for some teachers and districts to adopt. Thus estimates of effects are only one basis for decision making. We need to consider the productivity or value of effects in relation to total costs, including the time and energies of educators and students.

Knowledge from the field of psychology alone is not sufficient to prescribe practices, since different means bring about different ends. Educators must decide whether the learning effort is to be directed by teachers, by students, or by the curriculum. They must choose among a range of facts and concepts, breadth and depth, short- and long-term ends, academic knowledge and knowledge that has direct application in the real world, equal opportunity and equal results. They must decide which aspect of Plato's triumvirate of thinking, feeling, and acting will take precedence. Once these choices are made, educators can turn to the researchers' estimates of effects as one basis for determining the most productive practices.

1. Herbert J. Walberg, Diane Schiller, and Geneva D. Haertel, "The Quiet Revolution in Educational Research," *Phi Delta Kappan*, November 1979, pp. 179-83; Herbert J. Walberg, "Improving the Productivity of America's Schools," *Educational Leadership*, vol. 41, 1984, pp. 19-27; and Barry J. Fraser, Herbert J. Walberg, Wayne W. Welch, and John A. Hattie, "Syntheses of Educational Productivity Research," *International Journal of Educational Research*, vol. 11, 1987, pp. 73-145.

2. Neal Miller and John Dollard, *Social Learning and Imitation* (New Haven, Conn.: Yale University Press, 1941); and John Dollard and Neal Miller, *Personality and Psychotherapy* (New York: McGraw-Hill, 1950).

3. Eric A. Hanushek, "Throwing Money at Schools," *Journal of Policy Analysis and Management*, vol. 1, 1981, pp. 19-41; and Herbert J. Walberg and William F. Fowler, "Expenditure and Size Efficiencies of Public School Districts," *Educational Researcher*, vol. 16, 1987, pp. 515-26.

4. Benjamin S. Bloom, *Human Characteristics and School Learning* (New York: McGraw-Hill, 1976); and John B. Carroll, "A Model of School Learning," *Teachers College Record*, vol. 64, 1963, pp. 723-33.

5. The effects are expressed as differences between experimental and control groups in units of standard deviations. For further details and references, see my chapter in Merlin C. Wittrock, ed., *Handbook of Research on Teaching* (New York: Macmillan, 1986), and the research monograph by Fraser, myself, and others cited above. For a time I will send a table of effects and number of studies, as well as a graphic display, to readers who send a self-addressed, stamped envelope (two first-class stamps) to me at the University of Illinois, College of Education, P.O. Box 4348, Chicago, IL 60680.

6. Margo A. Mastropieri and Thomas E. Scruggs, *Effective Instruction for Special Education* (Boston: Little, Brown, 1987).

7. John Hoetker and William P. Ahlbrand, "The Persistence of the Recitation," *American Educational Research Journal*, vol. 6, 1969, pp. 145-67.

8. For a full account of most views, see Penelope L. Peterson and Herbert J. Walberg, eds., *Research on Teaching* (Berkeley, Calif.: McCutchan, 1979); and Wittrock, op. cit.

9. Lev Vygotsky, *Mind in Society* (Cambridge, Mass.: Harvard University Press, 1978).

10. Anne Marie Pallincsar and Anne Brown, "Reciprocal Teaching of Comprehension-Fostering and Comprehension-Monitoring Activities," *Cognition and Instruction*, vol. 1, 1984, pp. 117-76; David Pearson, "Reading Comprehension Instruction: Six Necessary Steps," *Reading Teacher*, vol. 38, 1985, pp. 724-38; and Paul R. Pintrich et al., "Instructional Psychology," *Annual Review of Psychology*, vol. 37, 1986, pp. 611-51.

11. Rose M. Giaconia and Larry V. Hedges, "Identifying Features of Effective Open Education," *Review of Educational Research*, vol. 52, 1982, pp. 579-602.

12. James A. Kulik and Chen-Lin Kulik, "Mastery Testing and Student Learning," *Journal of Educational Technology Systems*, vol. 15, 1986, pp. 325-45; Lorin W. Anderson and Robert B. Burns, "Values, Evidence, and Mastery Learning," *Review of Educational Research*, vol. 57, 1988, pp. 215-23; Thomas R. Guskey and S. L. Gates, "Synthesis of Research on the Effects of Mastery Learning in Elementary and Secondary Classrooms," *Educational Leadership*, May 1986, pp. 73-80; and Robert E. Slavin, "Mastery Learning Reconsidered," *Review of Educational Research*, vol. 57, 1988, pp. 175-213.

13. Herbert J. Walberg, "What Can We Learn from Japanese Education?," *The World and I*, March 1988, pp. 661-65.

14. Joel R. Levin, Gary J. Anglin, and Russell N. Carney, "On Empirically Validating Functions of Pictures in Prose," in D. M. Willows and H. A. Houghton, eds., *Illustrations, Graphs, and Diagrams* (New York: Springer-Verlag, forthcoming).

15. Daniel Druckman and John A. Swets, eds., *Enhancing Human Performance* (Washington, D.C.: National Academy Press, 1988).

Critical Thinking Through Structured Controversy

Through controlled argumentation, students can broaden their perspectives, learn material more thoroughly, and make better decisions.

DAVID W. JOHNSON
AND ROGER T. JOHNSON

David W. Johnson is Professor of Educational Psychology, and **Roger T. Johnson** is Professor of Curriculum and Instruction, both at the University of Minnesota, Cooperative Learning Center, 202 Pattee Hall, 150 Pillsbury Dr., S.E., Minneapolis, MN 55455.

Have you learned lessons only of those who admired you, and were tender with you, and stood aside for you?

Have you not learned great lessons from those who braced themselves against you and disputed the passage with you?

—Walt Whitman, 1860

Using academic conflicts for instructional purposes is one of the most dynamic and involving, yet *least-used* teaching strategies. Although creating a conflict is an accepted writer's tool for capturing an audience, teachers often suppress students' academic disagreements and consequently miss out on valuable opportunities to capture their own audiences and enhance learning.

Teachers generally avoid and subdue students' academic conflicts for several reasons. For instance, they may view conflicts as divisive, alienating students from each other, with the least capable feeling defeated and humiliated (Collins 1970, DeCecco and Richards 1974). Another reason is that teachers do not have an instructional model for structuring and controlling academic controversies to stimulate learning.

Over the past 10 years, we have developed and tested a theory about how controversy promotes positive

"Controversies must be defined as interesting problems to be solved rather than as win-lose situations."

outcomes (D. Johnson 1979, 1980; Johnson and Johnson 1979, 1985). Based on our findings, we have developed a series of curriculum units on energy and environmental issues structured for academic controversies. We have also worked with schools and colleges throughout the United States and Canada to field-test and implement the units in the classroom.

We will review these efforts by discussing the process of controversy, how teachers can organize and use it, and the advantages of using it to enhance both cognitive and affective learning.

A Model for the Process of Controversy

Controversy is a type of academic conflict that exists when one student's ideas, information, conclusions, theories, and opinions are incompatible with those of another and the two seek to reach an agreement. Structured academic controversies are most commonly contrasted with concurrence-seeking, debate, and individualistic learning (fig. 1). For instance, students

David W. Johnson and Roger T. Johnson, "Critical Thinking Through Structured Controversy," *Educational Leadership*, Vol. 45, No. 8, May 1988, pp. 58-64. Reprinted with permission of the Association for Supervision and Curriculum Development.

can inhibit discussion to avoid any disagreement and compromise quickly to reach a consensus while they discuss the issue (concurrence-seeking). Or students can appoint a judge and then debate the different positions with the expectation that the judge will determine who presented the better position (debate). Finally, students can work independently with their own set of materials at their own pace (individualistic learning).

When teachers structure controversy, students must rehearse orally the information they are learning; advocate a position; teach their knowledge to peers; analyze, critically evaluate, and rebut information; reason deductively and inductively; and synthesize and integrate information into factual and judgmental conclusions that are summarized into a joint position to which all sides can agree.

Consider the following illustration. A teacher assigns students to groups of four composed of two-person advocacy teams and asks them to prepare a report entitled "The Role of Regulations in the Management of Hazardous Waste." One team is given the position that more regulations are needed, and the other team, that fewer regulations are needed. During the first hour, both teams receive materials supporting their assigned positions. The teacher instructs them to plan how best to support their assigned positions so that they *and* the opposing team learn the information and the perspective within the materials so well that the opposing team is convinced.

During the second hour, the two teams present their positions to each other and then engage in general discussion in which they advocate their positions, rebut the opposing side, and seek to reach the best decision possible about the need to regulate hazardous waste management. This discussion continues during the third hour, and each team spends 30 minutes arguing for the opposing position.

During the fourth hour, the four group members reach consensus about the issue, synthesize the best information and reasoning from both sides, write a report on the role of regulations in hazardous waste management, and individually take a test on the factual information contained in the reading materials.

"Heterogeneity among group members leads to spirited and constructive argumentation . . . "

This illustration represents the structured use of academic controversy, a six-step process through which students advance from factual learning to reasoned judgment (fig. 2). During such a sequence, students realize that their conclusions are being contested by others who hold different views. They then become uncertain about the correctness of their own ideas, and an internal state of conceptual conflict is aroused. To resolve their uncertainty, students search for more information, new experiences, improved reasoning, and a more nearly adequate cognitive perspective. They try to understand their opponents' conclusion and rationale. The cognitive rehearsal of their own position and their attempts to understand their opponents' position result in a reconceptualization of their position. This new level of comprehension is characterized by understanding the opposing perspective, incorporating the opponents' information and reasoning, changing their own attitude and position if warranted, and using higher-level reasoning strategies. This process is repeated until the differences in conclusions among students have been resolved, a synthesis is achieved, an agreement is reached, and the controversy has ended.

Structured academic controversies require students to invest physical and

"Students must value and respect one another."

psychological energy in their educational experiences. This investment takes many forms: absorption in academic work, epistemic curiosity, effort expended toward academic achievement, and the like. Student time and energy, of course, are finite resources, and educational success can be evaluated in terms of increasing the time and energy students willingly commit to their education.

Use of Controversy in the Classroom

For the past several years, we have been training teachers to use structured academic controversies, which they are now using in a wide variety of grade levels and subject areas. At the University of Minnesota, we are using controversies in several engineering courses and with undergraduate and graduate education and psychology students. The basic format teachers use for organizing structured academic controversies consists of four steps.

1. *Choosing the discussion topic.* The choice of topic depends on the interests of the instructor and the purposes of the course. That two well-documented positions can be prepared and that students are able to manage the content are criteria for selection. Most environmental, energy, public policy, social studies, literary, and scientific issues are appropriate.

2. *Preparing instructional materials.* The following materials are needed for each position:
- a clear description of the group's task;
- a description of the phases of the controversy procedure and the collaborative skills to be used during each;
- a definition of the position to be advocated with a summary of the key arguments supporting the position;
- resource materials (including a bibliography) to provide evidence for and elaboration of the arguments supporting the position to be advocated.

3. *Structuring the controversy.* The principal requirements for a successful structured controversy are a cooperative context, skillful group members, and heterogeneity of group membership. Teachers establish a cooperative context by assigning students randomly to groups and by requiring each group to reach consen-

Controversy	Debate	Concurrence-Seeking	Individualistic
Deriving conclusions by categorizing and organizing information and experiences	Deriving conclusions by categorizing and organizing information and experiences	Deriving conclusions by categorizing and organizing information and experiences	Deriving conclusions by categorizing and organizing information and experiences
Being challenged by opposing views	Being challenged by opposing views	Quick compromise to one view	Presence of only one view
Uncertainty about the correctness of own view, cognitive conflict	Uncertainty about the correctness of own view, cognitive conflict	High certainty	High certainty
High epistemic curiosity	Moderate epistemic curiosity	Absence of epistemic curiosity	No epistemic curiosity
Active representation and elaboration of position and rationale	Active representation and elaboration of position and rationale	Active restatement of original position	No oral statement of position
High reconceptualization	Moderate reconceptualization	No reconceptualization	No reconceptualization
High productivity	Moderate productivity	Low productivity	Low productivity
High positive cathexis	Moderate positive cathexis	Low positive cathexis	Low positive cathexis

Fig. 1. Four Learning Processes

> ## "Students must feel safe enough to challenge each other's ideas and reasoning."

sus on an issue and submit a report on which all members will be evaluated. Heterogenenity among group members leads to spirited and constructive argumentation and increases appreciation of different views. (In the next section we discuss five strategies for promoting constructive controversy.)

4. *Conducting the controversy*. To guide a controversy, the teacher gives students specific instructions in five phases.

● *Learning positions*. Plan with your partner how to advocate your position effectively. Read the materials supporting your position, and plan a persuasive presentation. Make sure you and your partner master the information supporting your assigned position and present it in a way to ensure that the opposing pair will comprehend and learn the information.

● *Presenting positions*. As a pair, present your position forcefully and persuasively. Listen carefully and learn the opposing position. Take notes, and clarify anything you do not understand.

● *Discussing the issue*. Argue forcefully and persuasively for the posi-

tion, presenting as many facts as you can to support your point of view. Listen critically to the opposing pair's position, asking them for the facts that support their viewpoint, and then present counter-arguments. Remember this is a complex issue, and you need to know both sides to write a good report.

● *Reversing perspectives*. Working as a pair, present the opposing pair's position as if you were they. Be as sincere and forceful as you can. Add any new facts you know. Elaborate their position by relating it to other information you have previously learned.

● *Reaching a decision*. Summarize and synthesize the best arguments for *both* points of view. Reach consensus on a position that is supported by the facts. Change your mind only when the facts and the rationale clearly indicate that you should do so. Write your report with the supporting evidence and rationale for your synthesis that your group has agreed on.

Instruct the students to follow specific discussion rules during the controversy (see fig. 3). After the controversy, spend some time processing how well the group functioned and how its performance may be enhanced during the next controversy. It is a good idea to highlight and discuss the specific conflict management skills students need to master.

Prerequisites to Promoting Constructive Controversy

Positive outcomes do not automatically appear every time students disagree intellectually. To produce them, teachers need to know how to initiate, nurture, and manage controversies

constructively. This involves five strategies.

1. *Structuring learning activities cooperatively*. For controversies to be constructive—neither competitive nor destructive—the following conditions must be met.

● Controversies must be defined as interesting problems to be solved rather than as win-lose situations.

● Controversies must be valued as opportunities and challenges.

● Similarities as well as differences between positions must be recognized.

● Information must be accurately communicated.

● Feelings as well as information have to be communicated and responded to.

● Students must value and respect one another.

● Students must feel safe enough to challenge each other's ideas and reasoning.

2. *Ensuring that groups are heterogeneous*. Differences among students—in personality, sex, attitude, background, social class, reasoning strategies, cognitive perspective, information, ability level, and skills—

> ## "A balanced presentation should be given for each side of the controversy."

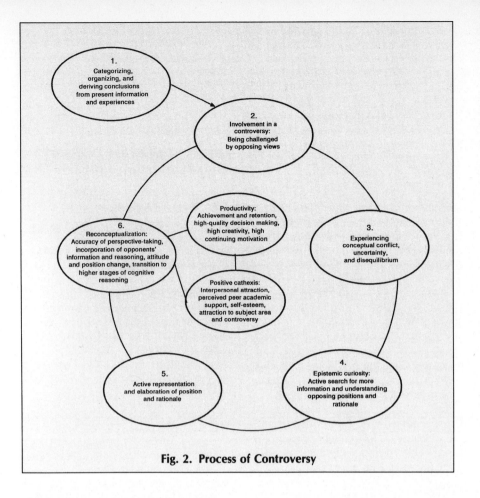

Fig. 2. Process of Controversy

1. Categorizing, organizing, and deriving conclusions from present information and experiences

2. Involvement in a controversy: Being challenged by opposing views

3. Experiencing conceptual conflict, uncertainty, and disequilibrium

4. Epistemic curiosity: Active search for more information and understanding opposing positions and rationale

5. Active representation and elaboration of position and rationale

6. Reconceptualization: Accuracy of perspective-taking, incorporation of opponents' information and reasoning, attitude and position change, transition to higher stages of cognitive reasoning

Productivity: Achievement and retention, high-quality decision making, high creativity, high continuing motivation

Positive cathexis: Interpersonal attraction, perceived peer academic support, self-esteem, attraction to subject area and controversy

> **"Engaging in structured academic controversies increases students' perspective-taking abilities."**

lead to differing styles of processing information, which in turn actually begin the cycle of controversy. Such differences promote learning and increase the amount of time spent in argumentation.

3. *Distributing information relevant to both sides.* A balanced presentation should be given for each side of the controversy. The more information students have about an issue, the greater their learning tends to be. Having relevant information available, however, does not mean that students will use it. They need the interpersonal and group skills necessary to ensure that all participants contribute pertinent information and synthesize data effectively.

4. *Teaching conflict management skills.* To manage controversy constructively, students need collaborative and conflict management skills (D. Johnson 1981, Johnson and Johnson 1982). One of the most important is the ability to challenge another's ideas while at the same time confirming that individual's personal competence. Students can learn to value disagreements as interesting opportunities to learn something new, not as personal attacks.

Perspective taking is another important ability for exchanging information and opinions within a conflict (D. Johnson 1971). Additional information, both personal and impersonal, can be disclosed and is more often accurately comprehended when stu-

dents engage in perspective-taking behaviors (e.g., paraphrasing).

A third set of skills involves the cycle of differentiation of positions and their resultant integration. Students need to perform several cycles of *differentiation* (seeking out and clarifying differences among ideas, information, conclusions, theories, and opinions) and *integration* (combining information, reasoning, theories, and conclusions of others into one new, creative solution).

5. *Teaching the procedures of rational argument.* During a controversy, students must follow the canons of rational argument. They should generate ideas, collect and organize relevant information, reason logically, empathetically enter into the perspective of their opponents, and make tentative conclusions based on current understanding. After presenting their perspectives and the rationales for their positions, as well as their conclusions, students should ask their opponents for proof that their analyses and conclusions are accurate. Students should keep an open mind, changing their conclusions if their opponents present persuasive rationales, proofs, and logical reasoning.

How Students Benefit

When students interact, conflicts among their ideas, conclusions, theories, information, perspectives, opinions, and preferences are inevitable. Teachers who capitalize on these differences find that academic conflicts can yield highly constructive dividends. Over the past 10 years, we have conducted systematic research to discover the consequences of structured controversy (Johnson and Johnson 1979, 1985). One of the most interest-

> **"To produce [positive outcomes], teachers need to know how to initiate, nurture, and manage controversies constructively."**

██████████████████

"Students should keep an open mind, changing their conclusions if their opponents present persuasive rationales, proofs, and logical reasoning."

---

1. I am critical of ideas, not people.
2. I focus on making the best decision possible, not on "winning."
3. I encourage everyone to participate and master all the relevant information.
4. I listen to everyone's ideas, even if I do not agree.
5. I restate (paraphrase) what someone has said if it is not clear.
6. I first bring out *all* the ideas and facts supporting both sides and then try to put them together in a way that makes sense.
7. I try to understand both sides of the issue.
8. I change my mind when the evidence clearly indicates that I should do so.

Fig. 3. Discussion Rules for Participating in an Academic Controversy

---

ing findings is that engaging in structured academic controversies increases students' perspective-taking abilities. Within structured academic controversies, students practice adopting a perspective, advocating it, then enlarging their view to include the opposing position as well.

Other interesting findings relate to student achievement and attitudes. For instance, compared with concurrence-seeking, debate, and individualistic learning efforts, structured controversy results in:

● greater student mastery and retention of the subject and greater ability to generalize the principles learned to a wider variety of situations;

● higher-quality decisions and solutions to problems;

● the promotion of creative insights by influencing students to view a problem from different perspectives and reformulate it in ways that allow the emergence of new orientations to the problem;

● an increase in the number and quality of students' ideas, feelings of

stimulation and enjoyment, and originality of expression in problem solving, resulting in greater emotional commitment to solving the problem, greater enjoyment of the process, and more imaginative solutions.

Within controversies are elements of disagreement, argumentation, and rebuttal that could result in divisiveness among peers and the promotion of negative attitudes. The research, however, indicates that compared with the other three learning processes, structured controversy promotes a greater liking among participants, greater perceived peer academic support, higher academic self-esteem, and more positive attitudes toward both the subject and the process of controversy.

A Generic Problem-Solving Strategy

If students are to become citizens capable of making reasoned judgments about the complex problems facing society, they must learn to use the higher-level reasoning and critical thinking processes involved in effective problem solving, especially problems for which different viewpoints can plausibly be developed. With structured controversy, students of all ages are learning how to find high-quality solutions to complex problems.

References

Collins, B. *Social Psychology*. Reading, Mass.: Addison-Wesley, 1970.

DeCecco, J., and A. Richards. *Growing Pains: Uses of School Conflict*. New York: Aberdeen Press, 1974.

Johnson, D. W. "Students Against the School Establishment: Crisis Intervention in School Conflicts and Organization Change." *Journal of School Psychology* 9 (Winter 1971): 84–92.

Johnson, D. W. *Educational Psychology*. Englewood Cliffs, N.J.: Prentice-Hall, 1979.

Johnson, D. W. "Group Processes: Influences of Student-Student Interaction on School Outcomes." In *The Social Psychology of School Learning*, edited by J. McMillan. New York: Academic Press, 1980.

Johnson, D. W. *Reaching Out: Interpersonal Effectiveness and Self-Actualization*. 2d ed. Englewood Cliffs, N.J.: Prentice-Hall, 1981.

Johnson, D. W., and F. Johnson. *Joining Together: Group Theory and Group Skills*. 2d ed. Englewood Cliffs, N.J.: Prentice-Hall, 1982.

Johnson, D. W., and R. Johnson. "Conflict in the Classroom: Controversy and Learning." *Review of Educational Research* 49 (Winter 1979): 51–61.

Johnson, D. W., and R. Johnson. "Classroom Conflict: Controversy vs. Debate in Learning Groups." *American Educational Research Journal* 22 (Summer 1985): 237–256.

Whitman, W. *Leaves of Grass*. New York: Viking Press, 1860.

Questioning: An Effective Teaching Method

Imogene Ramsey, Carol Gabbard, Kenneth Clawson, Lynda Lee, and Kenneth T. Henson

Imogene Ramsey is a professor, Carol Gabbard is an associate professor, Kenneth Clawson is a professor, Lynda Lee is an associate professor, and Kenneth Henson is a professor and dean, all at the College of Education, Eastern Kentucky University, Richmond, Kentucky.

The value of using questions to teach has been recognized for centuries. As early as 200 B.C., Socrates used questions to provoke his students and make them listen carefully, analyze their thoughts, and think critically. In this country, questioning has a long history of use in education. In 1912 Stevens (see Dean 1986) reported that teachers used approximately 80 percent of the school day to ask questions and receive student answers. Clegg (1971) found that, on the average, today's high school teachers ask 395 questions each day (Dean 1986, 184).

Educators recognize that teachers need to have expertise in the skill of asking questions. As early as 1906, Hamilton was quoted as saying that questions are the core of effective teaching. Ornstein (1987) said that "the essence of good teaching is related to good questioning" (71). Questioning serves a number of essential functions in teaching. If students are to participate in the nation's social structure, they must learn to think and act independently (Dean 1986). Questioning can play an important role in this development. In general, questioning is closely related to the accomplishment of the school's educational goals (Frager 1986). This is true because questions are effective tools that teachers use to guide student thinking.

Historically, teachers have focused their attention primarily on meeting the needs of the school. In recent years, however, teachers have been concerned with meeting student needs as well. Dean (1986) explained: "Questions must be used to stimulate student thinking and enhance class participation. The effective use of questions automatically causes a shift from teacher domination toward student involvement." As one author (Kloss 1988) said: "Asking questions, then, can help the teacher step back a little and allow those who should be most involved in learning—the students—to come forward as full and equal participants in the collaborative adventure of the mind" (248).

Recent research to determine whether teachers are asking higher-level questions showed the answer to be an unqualified and resounding no. Kloss (1988, 245) quoted a 1986 study by Daines, which reported that 93 percent of the questions asked by elementary and secondary teachers were at the literal level of comprehension, and 88 percent of the students' answers—regardless of the teaching style and grade level—were also at the lowest level of cognitive skills. Clearly, attention should be given to preparing teachers to ask more higher-level questions that will elicit more thinking and analysis.

Teachers should also be concerned with the questions their students ask. In many classrooms, students ask few questions.

Limitations

Asking and answering questions is a common human activity and one of the most frequently practiced teaching strategies. Yet teachers do not appear to be using this teaching strategy adequately. Skillful questioning must be constant and consistent so that it becomes an art. However, few teachers are willing to devote time and energy to cultivate this teaching strategy (Kloss 1988).

Most of the questions asked in a typical classroom require only recitation of memorized material and are on the lowest cognitive level. Teachers appear to be unaware of the extent to which they are omitting meaningful, well-phrased, and higher-order questions from their teaching. Only "20% of the questions asked in the elementary and secondary classrooms require critical thinking skills" (Hamblen 1988, 200).

An additional limitation of the question-and-answer strategy practiced by teachers is that teachers often answer their own questions. Dantonio (1987, 48) stated that "answering your own questions also stifles thinking, not only by inhibiting the discussion but by cluing students that you will give them the answer if they are silent long enough. If you repeatedly rephrase your question, the students get confused and discussion drifts away from the focused thinking you are trying to foster."

Ainley (1986) referred to the asking of questions to which one already knows the answers as a very odd linguistic activity that appears to be almost entirely restricted to classrooms. "It is part of the 'school games,' and teachers and students both know its purpose: the teacher does not want to find out information, but rather to ascertain whether or not the students know the answers" (Ainley 1986, 24).

Teachers very often ask multiple follow-up questions of students before a response can be given. Yet this "quantity of questions asked does not necessarily demand quality responses on the part of the learner" (Dean 1986, 184). Follow-up questions should be used by the teacher to move students through learning steps from lower-level to higher-level thinking, and to "usher the habit of an intellectual pause in the discussion, refreshing both leaders and participants" (Will 1987, 34).

"Asking questions is a slower means of teaching than lecturing" (Kloss 1988, 247). It should be emphasized that time and planning are needed in preparing questions for the classroom. "Teachers must develop and present proper questions in order to receive the appropriate response" (Dean 1986, 185). "Teachers need to spend time coding and analyzing their own questions, student answers, and student questions" (Hamblen 1988, 199). "One must keep in mind that the nature of the question has a remarkable impact on the progression of thought in the class" (Dean 1986, 185). Sometimes teachers rely too heavily on questions. For example, rather than beginning each lesson with questions, "research shows that it is far more effective to wait until a knowledge base has been established before initiating questioning" (Henson 1988, 99).

The Teacher's Role

A well-known teaching principle suggests that the academic achievement of students is positively correlated with the number of clear academic questions posited by the teacher. Teachers' questions often follow a structured, repetitive pattern. The pattern consists of (a) establishing the framework, background, or context of the question; (b) asking the question, and (c) reacting to the question by correcting, clarifying, expanding, and praising (Clark, Gage, Marx, Peterson, Staybrook, and Winne 1979).

On the average, teachers ask 395 questions per day (Gall 1970). Woolfolk and McCune-Nicolich (1984) said that these questions might be asked in accordance with one of six levels of Bloom's cognitive taxonomy of objectives. Questions might elicit responses that are con-

vergent (only one correct answer) or divergent (many possible correct answers) (Woolfolk and McCune-Nicolich 1984).

There are four types of questions that may help teachers assess students' understanding. These four types are (1) silent questions, (2) oral questions, (3) written questions, and (4) student questions (Lindquest 1988).

The research is controversial as to which type of question fosters the greatest academic achievement among students. Woolfolk and McCune-Nicolich (1984) suggest that several types of questions can be effective. The types of questions asked by the teacher should depend on the instructional objectives and the student's age, socioeconomic background, and ability. For lower-ability students, simple knowledge or comprehension questions requiring more convergent responses are more successful. For these students, teachers should phrase questions that result in high frequency of correct responses followed by much praise and encouragement. For high-ability students, teachers should ask more difficult questions that elicit fewer correct responses. For these higher-ability students, teachers should also quicken the pace and limit encouragement, praise, and discussion. Discussion should be limited to clarifying, correcting, or criticizing students' responses. For those classes composed of mixed-ability students or students with fragile self-esteems, a mix of higher- and lower-level questions should be posed, followed by criticism or praise and encouragement as deemed appropriate considering the instructional goals and needs of the student (Medley 1977; Ward and Tikunoff 1976).

Questioning in the classroom can have many purposes. To begin a lesson, questions of evaluation may be asked. To end the lesson, teachers may ask knowledge-level questions. Teachers who are skilled at questioning may use questions to develop lesson structure (Kloss 1988). Questions may be used to probe the students' understanding of the lesson (Lindquist 1988). Given this framework, the following tips are offered to help teachers ask more successful questions in the classroom.

1. Ask knowledge-level questions when assessing students' ability to recall, recognize, or repeat information as it was learned.

2. When assessing students' higher-level thinking, use terms such as *how, why, what if* to encourage deeper thought.

3. Prepare questions in advance.

4. Ask questions in a logical sequence.

5. Ask specific questions that students can answer silently.

6. As direct questions are asked, sprinkle the questioning with direct statements.

7. Request that students repeat the teacher's question before answering.

8. When a specific student is asked a question, have another student repeat the question before allowing a response.
9. Allow students to converse with each other in a directed manner after a question is asked or answered.
10. Request that students express their own questions fully and specifically.
11. Name specific students in a random order to respond to questions.
12. Provide adequate waiting time after naming a respondent. Rowe (1974) found that waiting approximately three to five seconds after naming a respondent before eliciting a response brought better responses from more students.

Asking successful questions in the classroom is a skill that requires knowledge of questioning techniques, planning, and creativity. The art of successful questioning in the classroom can be cultivated through practice.

The Student's Role

Much has been said about the teacher's role in using questions effectively. But what of the role of students? Generally students are thought of as responders—teachers ask questions and students respond.

Accordingly, the student may benefit from a systematic approach to answering, which includes attending to the question, deciphering its meaning, generating a silent answer, and answering overtly. Answers can be revised as needed (Kloss 1988, 247). The process described here involves time—time to listen to or read questions, time to analyze questions, time to consider possibilities and select answers, and, finally, time to share answers through spoken or written language. There is evidence that "low ability students need more time" (Ornstein 1988, 75).

The process described here suggests other roles for students: thinker, speaker, writer. And if the question to which students are responding cannot be answered from their reservoirs of information, then they may become researchers.

In assuming the latter role, the student becomes a questioner. "There is a popular belief that children learn from asking questions" (Comber 1988, 147). Students who ask thoughtful, focused questions may secure valuable information and, at the same time, help others gain new insights and knowledge. Such questions reflect the thinking ability of the students who ask them, and also reveal something about their self-confidence. Be-

cause asking questions can leave students vulnerable, able thinkers sometimes hesitate to raise questions. Dillon (1982) has pointed out that the social rules of the classroom may make students' questions inappropriate. In a secure atmosphere, questions can become powerful catalysts for learning and provide excellent models for other students.

The potential of questions to unveil students' confusions and understandings is barely tapped in many classrooms. Students must first trust that they can ask questions without being criticized. It is important that teachers listen to students' questions, so that students who might be ignored, or who are at risk of failure, do not escape their attention.

REFERENCES

Ainley, J. 1987. Telling questions. *Mathematics Teaching* 118: 24–26.

Clark, C. M., N. L. Gage, R. W. Marx, P. L. Perterson, N. G. Staybrook, and P. H. Winne. 1979. A factorial experiment on teacher structuring, soliciting, and reacting. *Journal of Educational Psychology* 71: 534–50.

Clegg, A. A. 1971. Classroom questions. In *The encyclopedia of education,* ed. L. C. Deighton. New York: Macmillan.

Dantonio, M. 1987. Develop concepts, question by question. *The Science Teacher* 54: 46–49.

Dean, D. 1986. Questioning techniques for teachers: A closer look at the process. *Contemporary Education* 57: 184–85.

Dillon, J. T. 1982. Cognitive correspondent between question/statement and response. *Educational Research Journal* 19: 540–51.

Frager, A. M. 1986. How can we improve teacher questioning?—A good question. *Reading Improvement* 23: 145–51.

Gall, M. D. 1970. The use of questions in teaching. *Review of Educational Research* 40: 707–21.

Hamblen, K. A. 1977. A golden source: Armstrong and Armstrong. *Studies in art education* 29: 198–202.

Henson, K. T. 1988. *Methods and strategies for teaching in secondary and middle schools.* White Plains, N.Y.: Longman.

Kloss, R. J. 1988. Toward asking the right questions: The beautiful, the pretty, and the messy ones. *The Clearing House* 61: 245–48.

Lindquist, M. M. 1988. Assessing through questioning. *Arithmetic Teacher* 35: 16–18.

Medley, D. M. 1977. *Teacher competence and teacher effectiveness: A review of process-product research.* Washington, D.C.: American Association of Colleges for Teacher Educators.

NASSP Bulletin 1988. Pp. 72–80.

Ornstein, A. C. 1987. Questioning: The essence of good teaching. *NASSP Bulletin* 71: 71–79.

Rowe, M. 1974. Wait time and rewards as instructional variables, their influence on language, logic and fate control: Part I: Wait time. *Journal of Research in Science Teaching* 11: 81–99.

Ward, B., and W. Tikunoff. 1976. The effective teacher education problem: Application of selected research results and methodology to teaching. *Journal of Teacher Education* 27: 48–52.

Will, H. C. 1987. Asking good follow-up questions (Junior Great Books program). *Gifted Child Today* 10: 32–34.

Woolfolk, A. E., and L. McCune-Nicolich. 1984. *Educational psychology for teachers.* 2d ed. Englewood Cliffs, N.J.: Prentice-Hall.

Survey of Research on Learning Styles

A number of studies conducted during the last decade have found that students' achievement increases when teaching methods match their learning styles—biological and developmental characteristics that affect how they learn.

RITA DUNN, JEFFREY S. BEAUDRY, AND ANGELA KLAVAS

Rita Dunn is Professor, Division of Administrative and Instructional Leadership, and Director, Center for the Study of Learning and Teaching Styles; **Jeffrey S. Beaudry** is Assistant Professor, Division of Administrative and Instructional Leadership; and **Angela Klavas** is Assistant Director, Center for the Study of Learning and Teaching Styles, and a doctoral student in the Instructional Leadership Program—all at St. John's University, Grand Central and Utopia Parkways, Jamaica, NY 11439.

Research on learning styles has been conducted at more than 60 universities over the past decade. These investigations have yielded useful findings about the effects of environmental, emotional, sociological, physiological, and cognitive preferences on the achievement of students. Learning style is a biologically and developmentally imposed set of personal characteristics that make the same teaching method effective for some and ineffective for others.

Every person has a learning style—it's as individual as a signature. Knowing students' learning styles, we can organize classrooms to respond to their individual needs for quiet or sound, bright or soft illumination, warm or cool room temperatures, seating arrangements, mobility, or grouping preferences. We can recognize the patterns in which people tend to concentrate best—alone, with others, with certain types of teachers, or in a combination thereof. We become aware of the senses through which people remember difficult information most easily—by hearing, speaking, seeing, manipulating, writing or notetaking, experiencing, or, again, a combination of these.

Learning style also encompasses motivation, on-task persistence versus the need for multiple assignments simultaneously, the kind and amount of structure required, and conformity versus nonconformity. When a National Association of Secondary School Principals (NASSP) Task Force (1983) examined all the characteristics that influence student achievement, intake preferences (individual needs for eating and/or drinking while concentrating) achieved the highest reliability. Chronobiology is also part of style: some people are "morning people"; some are "night owls."

There are only three comprehensive models of learning style (Hill et al. 1971, Keefe et al. 1986, Dunn et al. 1975, 1979, 1981, 1985); others address only one to four elements, usually on a bipolar continuum. Although various scholars define the concept differently, only a few learning style identification instruments are reliable and valid (Curry 1987).

Correlational Studies

To investigate connections between individual preferences and other influences on learning, researchers have conducted correlational studies to establish the relationships between learning style and birth order, cognitive development, maturation, hemisphericity, field dependence/independence, global/analytic processing, temperament, and self-concept. Their comparisons examined learners at all levels from primary school through adulthood. They differentiated among gifted, musically and artistically talented, average, underachieving, at-risk, nontraditional, reading-disabled, special education, dropout, and adolescent psychiatric populations. Researchers further tested consistency of style over subject matter and time. In addition, the researchers determined the responsiveness of basal readers to style differences, and they also examined the extent to which teacher training programs complemented their student candidates.

Correlational studies also explored the similarities and differences between and among diverse groups. Thus, researchers developed profiles of the styles of a wide range of learners, including students at various levels of achievement in diverse age groups; gifted, learning disabled, and mentally retarded students; supervisors and their supervisees; teachers and their students; Southeast Asian and American Caucasian college registrants; and numerous other groups. In addition, comparisons were made of the learning styles of Bahamians and Jamaicans; Afro-Americans and Caucasians; and Afro-, Chinese, Greek, and Mexican Americans (*Annotated Bibliography* 1988; *Learning Styles Network Newsletter* 1980-1988).

Correlations Between Learning Style and Hemisphericity

As new findings about left/right brain functions appeared, researchers investigated the connections between learning style and hemisphericity. The terms *left/right, analytic/global,* and *inductive/deductive* have been used interchangeably in the literature; descriptions of these pairs of variables parallel each other. Lefts/analytics/inductives appear to learn successively, in small steps leading to understanding; rights/globals/deductives more easily learn by obtaining meaning from a broad concept and then focusing on details.

Studies that examined the similarities and differences between hemispheric style and other elements of learning style revealed that, when concentrating on difficult academic material:

1. High school students who were less motivated than their classmates and who preferred working with *distracters* (music, low illumination, informal or casual seating, peers rather than alone or with the teacher, tactile rather than auditory or visual instructional resources) scored right-hemisphere significantly[1] more often than left-hemisphere. Also, students who scored high on persistence invariably scored high as left processors (Dunn et al. 1982). (The latter data may have implications for time-on-task research.)

2. Left-hemisphere youngsters in grades 5-12 preferred a conventional formal classroom seating design, more structure, less intake, and visual rather than tactile or kinesthetic resources during learning significantly more often than their right-preferred classmates (Cody 1983).

3. Right-hemisphere 5th through 12th graders disliked structure and were not adult motivated but *were* strongly peer motivated. Gifted and highly gifted students were significantly more often right or integrated than left processors (Cody 1983).

4. Right-hemisphere community college adult math underachievers preferred learning with sound and intake.

They wanted tactile and kinesthetic instructional resources and mobility significantly more often than their left-hemisphere counterparts, who preferred bright light and a formal design. [When the predominantly right-hemisphere students were taught alternately with both global and analytic lessons, they achieved statistically higher test scores through the global, rather than through the analytic, resources (Bruno 1988).]

Thus, correlational studies revealed sets of traits among students within the same age or grade and among those with similar talents, achievement, and interests. Even when culturally diverse groups were examined, there were as many within-group as between-group differences. Within each family, the parents, their offspring, and the siblings tend to be more different from than similar to each other.

Experimental Research

These correlational findings prompted

Researcher/Date	Sample	Subject Examined	Element Examined	Significant Effects Achievement	Attitudes
DeGregoris 1986	6th, 7th, 8th graders	Reading comprehension	Kinds of sound needed by sound preferences	+ With moderate talking	Not tested
DellaValle 1984	7th graders	Word recognition memory	Mobility/passivity needs	+	Not tested
Hodges 1985	7th, 8th graders	Mathematics	Formal/informal design preferences	+	+
Krimsky 1982	4th graders	Reading speed and accuracy	Bright/low lighting preferences	+	Not tested
MacMurren 1985	6th graders	Reading speed and accuracy	Need for intake while learning	+	+
Miller 1985	2nd graders	Reading	Mobility/passivity needs	+	Not tested
Murrain 1983	7th graders	Word recognition/ memory	Temperature preference	0	Not tested
Pizzo	6th graders	Reading	Acoustical preference	+	+
Shea 1983	9th graders	Reading	Formal/informal design preferences	+	Not tested
Stiles 1985	5th graders	Mathematics testing	Formal/informal design preferences	0	Not tested

Note: Price (1980) reported that the older students became, the less they appeared able to adapt to a conventional setting. Thus, design may be far more crucial to secondary students' ability to concentrate than to 4th graders, who may be better able to adjust to this element. Dunn and Griggs (1988) described the importance of design to high schoolers throughout the United States.
(+) = significant positive findings at p<.01 or greater; (0) = no differences or slight trend.

Fig. 1. Experimental Research Concerned with Learning Styles and Instructional Environments

researchers to conduct experimental studies to determine the effects of individual learning style on achievement, attitudes, and/or behavior.

On Instructional Environments

The extent to which classrooms appear either to stimulate or to inhibit learning for students with selected learning style characteristics has been documented in terms of individuals' needs for quiet versus sound, bright or soft lighting, warm or cool temperatures, and formal versus informal seating designs (Dunn 1987, Dunn et al. 1985; see fig. 1). These four elements affect from 10 to 40 percent of students, dependent upon age, gender, hemisphericity, and achievement. For example, the need for sound remains fairly consistent during the elementary school years but increases as adolescence begins and, as that stage passes, appears to return to its previously normal level. The younger children are, the less light they need; but about every five years most children require significantly more light than previously. Boys tend to require more mobility than girls and, thus, find sitting for any length of time difficult (Price 1980). However, teachers often view negatively the children who squirm in their seats, tap their pencils,

The need for sound remains fairly consistent during the elementary school years but increases as adolescence begins and, as that stage passes, appears to return to its previously normal level.

complain about the temperature, or become hyperactive (in some cases because of too much illumination).

On Perceptual Preferences

In addition to the instructional environment, sensory preferences influence the ways in which students learn. Eight studies within the past decade reveal that when youngsters were taught with instructional resources that both matched and mismatched their preferred modal-

ities, they achieved statistically higher test scores in modality-matched, rather than mismatched, treatments (Dunn 1988; see fig. 2). In addition, when children were taught with multisensory resources, but *initially through their most preferred modality* and then were reinforced through their secondary or tertiary modality, their scores increased even more.

Perceptual preferences affect more than 70 percent of school-age youngsters. High school teachers who have translated their curriculum into electroboards, Flip chutes, multipart task cards, and Pick-A-Holes reported increased achievement and interest when such manipulatives were available for highly tactual students (Dunn and Griggs 1988).

Data from studies conducted before the late '70s concerned with perceptual strengths often were conflicting because of inappropriate statistical designs, poor analyses, misinterpretations of the findings, and/or faulty conclusions. Those investigators examined *group* mean gain scores—which are inappropriate for determining whether individuals achieve better, the same, or less well in comparison with their own baseline data when they are taught through their preferences. In addition, the words *tactile* and *kinesthetic* often

Researcher/Date	Sample	Subject Examined	Perceptual Preference Examined	Significant Effects Achievement	Attitude
Carbo 1980	Kindergartners	Vocabulary	Auditory, visual, "other" (tactile)	+	Not tested
Jarsonbeck 1984	4th grade underachievers	Mathematics	Auditory, visual, tactile	+	Not tested
Kroon 1985	9th, 10th graders	Industrial Arts	Auditory, visual, tactile, sequenced	+	Not tested
Martini 1986	7th graders	Science	Auditory, visual, tactile	+	+
Urbschat 1977	1st graders	CVC Trigram Recall	Auditory, visual	+	Not tested
Weinberg 1983	3rd graders	Mathematics	Auditory, visual, tactile	+	Not tested
Wheeler 1980	Learning disabled 2nd graders	Reading	Auditory, visual, tactile, sequenced	+	Not tested
Wheeler 1983	Learning disabled 2nd graders	Reading	Auditory, visual, tactile	+	Not tested
(+) = significant positive findings.					
Fig. 2. Experimental Research Concerned with Perceptual Learning Styles					

were used interchangeably. *Tactile* suggests learning with hands through manipulation of resources, but writing is not tactile enough for children below 4th grade. *Kinesthetic* implies whole-body involvement, such as taking a trip, dramatizing, interviewing, or pantomiming. However, even when older studies identified tactile strengths, their treatments did not *introduce* the new material that way. Finally, studies that employed many diverse instruments, populations, methods, and statistical designs and that confused the terminology could not yield solid data.

On Sociological Preferences

The influence of students' social preferences also affects their achievement in school. Figure 3 shows that, in four of five studies, when students' sociological preferences were identified and the youngsters then were taught in multiple treatments both responsive and unresponsive to their diagnosed learning styles, they achieved significantly higher test scores in matched conditions and significantly lower test scores when mismatched.

How do sociological preferences interface with cooperative learning? The higher the grade level, the less teacher-motivated students become (Price 1980). Thus, there are more peer-oriented youngsters able to work in well-organized small groups than there are students willing to learn directly from their teachers. Nevertheless, in every class we have ever tested, there are students who prefer to learn by themselves with appropriate resources, others who prefer to learn with peers, and some who wish to work directly with their teachers (Price 1980).

From practical experience, educators generally consider the junior high school years a period of strong peer influence. By the beginning of grade 9, however, educators should expect movement away from that preference; Price (1980) found that students in grades 9-12 experience a greater need to learn and study alone than during any other interval. The gifted also prefer to learn alone unless the material to be mastered is difficult for them; when that happens, they prefer to learn with other gifted children (see fig. 3). Thus, except among the gifted, many students in grades 3-8 will learn better in small, well-organized groups

Learning Styles and Student Diversity

Sue Loper

As a young teacher, I inherited a junior high classroom from a teacher who left in midyear. The students were totally out of control. I made it through the year, but I was not pleased with my performance.

I unloaded my feelings of frustration on Margaret Payne, who taught next door. She had a reputation for being able to teach even the worst students. In fact, she often accepted problem students during the year when other teachers could no longer tolerate them. Students liked learning in her class; she made them feel special and successful. Each time they succeeded, they wanted to try again.

Ms. Payne listened to my complaints, made sympathetic sounds, and proceeded to offer practical advice: that I teach my students the way they learned best; in other words, that I determine my students' preferred learning styles and provide activities to match them. She suggested that I use several methods of presenting material and include a variety of activities—individual and group projects—ranging from the replicative to the highly creative. Ms. Payne understood that different students learn in different ways, while teachers often teach as they have been taught (Dunn and Dunn 1978).

This was certainly true in my own case. Because I learn well auditorily, I tended to teach in a lecture format. Unfortunately, this tendency shortchanged the visual, kinesthetic, and tactile learners in my classroom. Because I am a self-directed learner, I assigned mostly individual projects to be completed by a certain date. These assignments were difficult for students who learned best in a group or with the help of an adult, or who needed encouragement, assistance, or prodding to finish a project. Furthermore, I didn't like gum chewing, foot tapping, or other extraneous movements or noise, yet I had students who *needed* those activities in order to learn (Dunn and Dunn 1978).

If a teacher teaches and evaluates in only one cognitive mode, he or she is adequately serving only those students who prefer to learn in that mode. To give every learner the opportunity to succeed, teachers can expand their repertoires to include a variety of cognitive modes. Teachers should also become aware of their own learning style preferences and of how those preferences affect their teaching methods. Yet another goal is to help students move from one preferred learning mode to a base of mixed preferences, so they can benefit from various instructional modes.

If we make these changes, we will improve our chances of success at educating a diverse student population.

Reference
Dunn, R., and K. Dunn. (1978). *Teaching Students Through Their Individual Learning Styles: A Practical Approach.* Reston, Va.: Reston Publishing.

Sue Loper is Media Center Specialist, Moore County High School, Lynchburg, TN 37352.

than either alone or with the teacher. After grade 8, however, more will learn better alone.

In a small group structure, children who are frequently chastised for not sitting quietly can move about and relieve the discomfort they experience because of mobility needs or hard chairs. This structure also permits youngsters to read together, discuss items, reason out answers, and use multisensory interactions. The various contributors may enjoy different processing styles; thus, they can help each other, especially when the teacher's dominant hemispheric style is incongruent with theirs. Despite the advan-

Except among the gifted, many students in grades 3-8 will learn better in small, well-organized groups than either alone or with the teacher. After grade 8, however, more will learn better alone.

3. LEARNING: Instructional Strategies

tages to group work, students who feel constrained by the slower group pacing or who enjoy the challenge of solving problems by themselves do not learn most easily through small-group instructional strategies, nor do they enjoy the experience.

Research on Time-of-Day Preferences

It is common knowledge that morning people and night owls function better at their respective times of day. The research supports our easy acceptance of these preferences. For example,

two junior high school principals revealed that the math underachievers in both their schools preferred learning in the afternoon but had been scheduled into morning math classes. When those youngsters were rescheduled into afternoon classes, they evidenced higher motivation, better discipline, and an increase in achievement. Three years later, a New York high school reported that time preference was a crucial factor in the reversal of initial and chronic truancy patterns among secondary students (Dunn et al. 1987). Similar data were reported by the di-

rector of five alternative high schools in Washington (Dunn and Griggs 1988).

In 1983, the matching of elementary students' time preferences with their instructional schedules resulted in significant achievement gains in both reading and math over a two-year period. One year later, *teachers'* time preferences were identified, and staff development was conducted during their preferred and nonpreferred times (early morning and immediately after school). Interestingly, those teachers implemented innovative in-

Researcher/Date	Sample	Subject Examined
Cholakis 1986	106 underachieving, inner-city, parochial school 7th and 8th graders	Vocabulary development was provided through three strategies—by the teacher, alone by themselves, and in a peer group treatment.
Findings: Those who preferred learning alone, scored significantly higher (.01) than those who preferred learning either with peers or the teacher. However, all students attained significantly higher achievement (.001) and attitude (.01) scores when learning with an authority figure.		
DeBello 1985	236 suburban 8th graders	Students wrote social studies compositions and then experienced revision strategies that were congruent *and* incongruent with their sociological preferences.
Findings: Peer learners scored significantly higher when matched with the peer-conferencing technique (.01). Authority-oriented learners, when revising through the teacher-conference, achieved statistically higher (.01) than when revising either through peer conferencing or self-review. And those who preferred to learn alone scored significantly higher (.01) when matched, rather than mismatched, with self-review. No learning style group achieved better than any other, but a significant interaction occurred between individual sociological style and the matched method of revision (.001). In addition, the attitudes of students who preferred to learn alone or with an adult were significantly more positive (.01) when they were assigned to approaches that matched their styles.		
Giannitti 1988	104 suburban, parochial and public school 6th, 7th, and 8th graders	Social studies taught through both a mini-Contract Activity Package (CAP) and a small-group strategy, Team Learning
Findings: Peer-oriented students achieved significantly higher test and attitudes scores when learning through Team Learning than through the mini-Cap (.01). Learning-alone preferents attained significantly higher test and attitude scores (.01) through the mini-Cap than with their peers. Non-preferred students achieved better through the mini-Cap than through the Team Learning and liked working alone better than in groups. A significant interaction occurred between learning alone and peer-preferred learning and the method of learning (mini-Cap and Team Learning).		
Miles 1987	40 inner-city 5th and 6th graders	Twenty-two who preferred to learn alone and 18 who preferred to learn with peers were assigned randomly to two instructional groups that taught career awareness and career decision-making concepts in conditions both congruent and incongruent with their preferences.
Findings: The matching of sociological preference with complementary grouping patterns increased achievement significantly on career awareness (.01) and career decision making (.01). In addition, students' attitude scores were statistically higher when they were taught career awareness (.01) and career decision-making concepts (.05) in patterns accommodating their sociological preferences. With the exception of career awareness achievement, neither sociologically preferred group achieved better than the other but learning-alone preferents scored higher (.05) than peer-preferenced individuals.		
Perrin 1984	104 gifted and nongifted, suburban 1st and 2nd graders	Problem solving and word recognition through both individual- and peer-group strategies. Learning with the teacher was eliminated as a strategy when not a single gifted child preferred to learn that way.
Findings: Analysis of the mean gain scores revealed that achievement was significantly higher (.05) whenever students were taught through approaches that matched their diagnosed sociological preferences. Although the gifted tended to prefer to learn alone in their heterogeneously grouped classes, a small group of seven gifted, who previously had known each other from participation in a special, part-time program for the gifted, actually performed best when learning in isolation with other gifted children.		

Fig. 3. Experimental Research Concerned with Sociological Preferences

structional techniques significantly more often (as reported by their supervisors' evaluations) when *they* were taught during their most preferred hours. Then an elementary school principal in Kansas administered the *Iowa Basic Skills Tests* in reading and math to groups whose time preferences matched their test schedules—either early morning or afternoon. She reported significantly higher test gains in both subjects as compared with each youngster's previous two years' growth (Dunn et al. 1987.)

Studies of dropouts, underachievers, at-risk (Griggs and Dunn 1988), and vocational education (Tappenden 1983) students indicate that, as a group, they are *not* morning people; neither were the truants in the New York experiment. For each of these groups, learning in late morning, afternoon, or evening significantly increased achievement.

Among the more interesting findings of research with time preferences is that *most* students are *not* morning-alert. At the elementary school level, approximately 28 percent appear to be "early birds"; many do not begin to be capable of concentrating on difficult material until after 10:00 a.m., and many are at their best in the early afternoon. Only about one-third of more than a million students we have tested prefer learning in the early morning, and the majority prefer late morning or afternoon. At the high school level, almost 40 percent are early morning learners, but a majority remain most alert in the late morning and afternoon; and, for the first time identifiable after early childhood, almost 13 percent are "night owls," able to concentrate on difficult material in the evening (Price 1980). However, most teachers are early morning, high-energy people but often experience lows after 1:00 p.m. Another large group of educators merely get by much of the day and become mentally alert toward evening.

Mobility Needs

One element of learning style is the need for physical activity, and a review of this research reveals how this need can be confused with other, more alarming diagnoses. For example, Fadley and Hosler (1979) noted that children often were referred to psychologists because of their consistent

| | Means | |
	Passive b_1	Active b_2
Passive a_1	8.70	5.45
Active a_2	7.15	9.10

Note: a = preference; b = environment. N = 20.

Fig. 4. Analysis of Preference X Environment Interaction

hyperactivity; their teachers complained that such youngsters were unable to sit quietly and pay attention during lessons. Those psychologists reported that most students sent to them were not at all clinically hyperactive; instead, they were normal children in need of movement. In addition, the less interested they were in the lesson, the more mobility the children required.

During the same period, Restak (1979) substantiated that "over 95 percent of hyperactives are males" (p. 230) and that the very same characteristic, when observed in girls, correlated with academic *achievement*. He deplored that boys were required to be passive in school and were rejected for aggressive behaviors there, but were encouraged societally to engage in typical male aggressions in the world at large; this paradox could lead to role conflict. Restak added that conventional classroom environments did not provide male students with sufficient outlets for their normal needs. He warned that schools actually *caused* conflict with societal expectations that boys not be timid, passive, or conforming.

Other researchers corroborated Restak's admonitions and chastised educators for believing that physical activities prevented, rather than enhanced, learning. Indeed, when previously restless youngsters were reassigned to classes that did not require passivity, their behaviors were rarely noticed. Eventually, teachers began to report that although certain students thrived in activity-oriented environments that permitted mobility, others remained almost exclusively in the same area despite frequent attempts to coax them to move (Dunn et al. 1986). That led to Fitt's (1975) conclusions that no amount of persuasion increased certain

children's interest in movement, whereas others found it impossible to remain seated passively for extended periods. "These are cases of a child's style . . . governing his interaction with and within the environment" (p. 94).

DellaValle's (1984) research documented that almost half the 7th graders in a large urban racially mixed but predominantly black junior high school could not sit still for any length of time. Twenty-five percent could but only when interested in the lesson, and the remaining 25 percent *preferred* passivity. When preference and environment were matched, students' performance yielded significantly higher test scores than when they were mismatched. Figure 4 reports the post hoc analysis used to determine exactly where the interaction occurred. This analysis was conducted after the initial repeated measures design indicated a significant interaction at the .001 level.

Everyone Has One

Every person has a learning style—all have at least some preferences—the result of many influences. Certain learning style characteristics are biological, whereas others are developed through experience (Restak 1979, Thies 1979). Individual responses to sound, light, temperature, design, perception, intake, chronobiological highs and lows, mobility needs, and persistence appear to be biological; whereas sociological preferences, motivation, responsibility (conformity), and need for structure are thought to be developmental. The significant differences among diverse cultures tend to support this theory (*Learning Styles Network Newsletter* 1980-1988). Despite cultural influences, however, within each culture, socioeconomic strata, and classroom *there are as many within-group differences as between-group differences*. Indeed, each *family* includes parents and offspring with styles that differ.

Those who suggest that children should learn to adapt to their teachers' styles disregard the biological nature of style. They also disregard Cafferty's (1980) findings that the closer the match between each student's and the teachers' styles, the higher the grade point average; and the reverse. In addition, Kagan (1966) reported that his "success" with training impulsive students to become more reflective was

Those who suggest that children should learn to adapt to their teachers' styles disregard the biological nature of style.

evidenced only when adults were present. In addition, although Kagan's subjects learned to respond more reflectively, *their accuracy on tasks was decreased*. Thus, educators can see that learning styles are not lightly held; they demonstrate remarkable resistance to change.

Identifying learning styles as a basis for providing responsive instruction has never been more important than now, as educators meet the needs of a diverse student population. To identify their students' learning styles (Beaty 1986, Dunn et al. 1977, Marcus 1977), teachers must use a reliable and valid learning style preference instrument (Curry 1987). When permitted to learn difficult academic information or skills through their identified preferences, children tend to achieve statistically higher test and attitude scores than when instruction is dissonant with their preferences.

No learning style is either better or worse than another. Since each style has similar intelligence ranges, a student *cannot* be labeled or stigmatized by having any type of style. Most children can master the same content; *how* they master it is determined by their individual styles.

1. When we use the terms *significant* and *significantly*, we mean in a statistical sense.

Authors' note: Space limitations required the reduction from 163 primary references to the following list.

References

Annotated Bibliography. (1988). New York: Center for the Study of Learning and Teaching Styles, St. John's University.

Beaty, S.A. (1986). "The Effect of Inservice Training on the Ability of Teachers to Observe Learning Styles of Students." Doctoral diss., Oregon State University. *Dissertation Abstracts International* 47: 1998A.

Bruno, J. (1988). "An Experimental Investigation of the Relationships Between and Among Hemispheric Processing, Learning Style Preferences, Instructional Strategies, Academic Achievement, and Attitudes of Developmental Mathematics Students in an Urban Technical College." Doctoral diss., St. John's University.

Cafferty, E. (1980). "An Analysis of Student Performance Based Upon the Degree of Match Between the Educational Cognitive Style of the Teachers and the Educational Cognitive Style of the Students." Doctoral diss., University of Nebraska.

Carbo, M. (1980). "An Analysis of the Relationship Between the Modality Preferences of Kindergartners and Selected Reading Treatments as They Affect the Learning of a Basic Sight-Word Vocabulary." Doctoral diss., St. John's University, New York. *Dissertation Abstracts International* 41: 1389A.

Cholakis, M. M. (1986). "An Experimental Investigation of the Relationships Between and Among Sociological Preferences, Vocabulary Instruction and Achievement, and the Attitudes of New York, Urban Seventh and Eighth Grade Underachievers." Doctoral diss., St. John's University, New York. *Dissertation Abstracts International* 47: 4046A.

Cody, C. (1983). "Learning Styles, Including Hemispheric Dominance: A Comparative Study of Average, Gifted, and Highly Gifted Students in Grades Five Through Twelve. Doctoral diss., Temple University. *Dissertation Abstracts International* 44: 1631-6A.

Curry, L. (1987). *Integrating Concepts of Cognitive Learning Style: A Review with Attention to Psychometric Standards*. Ontario, Canada: Canadian College of Health Service Executives.

DeBello, T. (1985). "A Critical Analysis of the Achievement and Attitude Effects of Administrative Assignments to Social Studies Writing Instruction Based on Identified Eighth Grade Students' Learning Style Preferences for Learning Alone, with Peers, or with Teachers." Doctoral diss., St. John's University, New York. *Dissertation Abstracts International* 47: 68A.

DeGregoris, C. N. (1986). "Reading Comprehension and the Interaction of Individual Sound Preferences and Varied Auditory Distractions." Doctoral diss., Hofstra University, *Dissertation Abstracts International* 47: 3380A.

DellaValle, J. (1984). "An Experimental Investigation of the Word Recognition Scores of Seventh Grade Students to Provide Supervisory and Administrative Guidelines for the Organization of Effective Instructional Environments." Doctoral diss., St. John's University. *Dissertation Abstracts International* 45: 359-02A.

Dunn, R. (1987). "Research on Instructional Environments: Implications for Student Achievement and Attitudes." *Professional School Psychology* 11, 2: 43-52.

Dunn, R. (1988). "Commentary: Teaching Students Through Their Perceptual Strengths or Preferences." *Journal of Reading* 31, 4: 304-309.

Dunn, R., D. Cavanaugh, B. Eberle, and R. Zenhausern. (1982). "Hemispheric Preference: The Newest Element of Learning Style." *The American Biology Teacher* 44, 5: 291-294.

Dunn, R., J. DellaValle, K. Dunn, G. Geisert, R. Sinatra, and R. Zenhausern. (1986). "The Effects of Matching and Mismatching Students' Mobility Preferences on Recognition and Memory Tasks." *Journal of Educational Research* 79, 5: 267-272.

Dunn, R., K. Dunn, and G. E. Price. (1975, 1979, 1981, 1985). *Learning Style Inventory*. Price Systems, Box 1818, Lawrence, KS 66044-0067.

Dunn, R., K. Dunn, and G.E. Price. (1977). "Diagnosing Learning Styles: A Prescription for Avoiding Malpractice Suits Against School Systems." *Phi Delta Kappan* 58, 5: 418-420.

Dunn, R., K. Dunn, L. Primavera, R. Sinatra, and J. Virostko. (1987). "A Timely Solution: A Review of Research on the Effects of Chronobiology on Children's Achievement and Behavior." *The Clearing House* 61, 1: 5-8 (Heldreff Publications, Washington, D.C.).

Dunn, R., and S.A. Griggs. (1988). *Learning Style: Quiet Revolution in American Secondary Schools*. Reston, Va.: National Association of Secondary School Principals.

Dunn, R., J. Krimsky, J. Murray, and P. Quinn. (1985). "Light Up Their Lives: A Review of Research on the Effects of Lighting on Children's Achievement." *The Reading Teacher* 38, 9: 863-869 (The International Reading Association, Newark, Delaware).

Fadley, J.L., and V.N. Hosler. (1979). *Understanding the Alpha Child at Home and at School*. Springfield, Ill.: Charles C Thomas.

Fitt, S. (1975). "The Individual and His Environment." In *Learning Environments,* edited by T.G. David and B.D. Wright. Chigago: University of Chicago Press.

Giannitti, M. C. (1988). "An Experimental Investigation of the Relationships Among the Learning Style Sociological Preferences of Middle-School Students (Grades 6, 7, 8), Their Attitudes and Achievement in Social Studies, and Selected Instructional Strategies." Doctoral diss., St. John's University, New York.

Griggs, S.A., and R. Dunn. (September/October 1988). "High School Dropouts: Do They Learn Differently from Those Who Remain in School?" *The Principal* 35, 1: 1-8 (Board of Jewish Education of Greater New York).

Hill, J., et al. (1971). *Personalized Education Programs Utilizing Cognitive Style Mapping*. Bloomfield Hills, Mich.: Oakland Community College.

Hodges, H. (1985). "An Analysis of the Relationships Among Preferences for a Formal/Informal Design, One Element of Learning Style, Academic Achievement, and Attitudes of Seventh and Eighth Grade Students in Remedial Mathematics Classes in a New York City Junior High School." Doctoral diss., St. John's University, New York. *Dissertation Abstracts International* 45: 2791A.

Jarsonbeck, S. (1984). "The Effects of a Right-Brain and Mathematics Curriculum on Low Achieving Fourth Grade Students." Doctoral diss., University of South Florida. *Dissertation Abstracts International* 45: 2791A.

Kagan, J. (1966). "Reflection-Impulsivity: The Generality and Dynamics of Conceptual Tempo." *Journal of Abnormal Psychology* 71: 17-24.

Keefe, J., M. Languis, C. Letteri, and R. Dunn. (1986). *Learning Style Profile*. Reston, Va.: National Association of Secondary School Principals.

Krimsky, J. (1982). "A Comparative Analysis of the Effects of Matching and Mismatching Fourth Grade Students with Their Learning Style Preference for the Environmental Element of Light and Their Subsequent Reading Speed and Accuracy Scores." Doctoral diss., St. John's University, New York. *Dissertation Abstracts International* 43: 66A.

Kroon, D. (1985). "An Experimental Investigation of the Effects on Academic Achievement and the Resultant Administrative Implications of Instruction Congruent and Incongruent with Secondary Industrial Arts Students' Learning Style Perceptual Preference." Doctoral diss., St. John's University, New York. *Dissertation Abstracts International* 46: 3247A.

Learning Styles Network Newsletter. (Winter 1980-Autumn 1988). New York: National Association of Secondary School Principals and St. John's University.

MacMurren, H. (1985). "A Comparative Study of the Effects of Matching and Mismatching Sixth-Grade Students with Their Learning Style Preferences for the Physical Element of Intake and Their Subsequent Reading Speed and Accuracy Scores and Attitudes." Doctoral

diss., St. John's University, New York. *Dissertation Abstracts International* 46: 3247A.

Marcus, L. (1977). "How Teachers View Learning Styles." *NASSP Bulletin* 61, 408: 112-114.

Martini, M. (1986). "An Analysis of the Relationships Between and Among Computer-Assisted Instruction, Learning Style Perceptual Preferences, Attitudes, and the Science Achievement of Seventh Grade Students in a Suburban New York School District." Doctoral diss., St. John's University, New York. *Dissertation Abstracts International* 47: 877A.

Miles, B. (1987). "An Investigation of the Relationships Among the Learning Style Sociological Preferences of Fifth and Sixth Grade Students, Selected Interactive Classroom Patterns, and Achievement in Career Awareness and Career Decision-Making Concepts." Doctoral diss., St. John's University, New York. *Dissertation Abstracts International* 48: 2527A.

Miller, L. M. (1985). "Mobility as an Element of Learning Style: The Effect Its Inclusion or Exclusion Has on Student Performance in the Standardized Testing Environment." Master's thesis, University of North Florida.

Murrain, P. G. (1983). "Administrative Determinations Concerning Facilities Utilization and Instructional Grouping: An Analysis of the Relationships Between Selected Thermal Environments and Preferences for Temperature, an Element of Learning Style, as They Affect Word Recognition Scores of Secondary Students." Doctoral diss., St. John's University, New York. *Dissertation Abstracts International* 44: 1749A.

NASSP National Task Force. (Summer 1983). "National Task Force Defines Learning Style Operationally and Conceptually." *Learning Styles Network Newsletter* 4, 2: 1 (National Association of Secondary School Principals and St. John's University).

Perrin, J. (1984). "An Experimental Investigation of the Relationships Among the Learning Style Sociological Preferences of Gifted and Non-Gifted Primary Children, Selected Instructional Strategies, Attitudes, and Achievement in Problem Solving and Rote Memorization." Doctoral diss., St. John's University, New York. *Dissertation Abstracts International* 46: 342A.

Pizzo, J. (1981). "An Investigation of the Relationships Between Selected Acoustic Environments and Sound, an Element of Learning Style, as They Affect Sixth Grade Students' Reading Achievement and Attitudes." Doctoral diss., St. John's

University, New York. *Dissertation Abstracts International* 42: 2475A.

Price, G.E. (1980). "Which Learning Style Elements are Stable and Which Tend to Change Over Time?" *Learning Styles Network Newsletter* 1, 3: 1.

Restak, R. (1979). *The Brain: The Last Frontier*. New York: Doubleday.

Shea, T. C. (1983). "An Investigation of the Relationship Among Preferences for the Learning Style Element of Design, Selected Instructional Environments, and Reading Achievement with Ninth Grade Students to Improve Administrative Determinations Concerning Effective Educational Facilities." Doctoral diss., St. John's University, New York. *Dissertation Abstracts International* 44: 2004A.

Stiles, R. (1985). "Learning Style Preferences for Design and Their Relationship to Standardized Test Results." Doctoral diss., University of Tennessee. *Dissertation Abstracts International* 46: 2551A.

Tappenden, V. J. (1983). "Analysis of the Learning Styles of Vocational Education and Nonvocational Education Students in Eleventh and Twelfth Grades from Rural, Urban, and Suburban Locations in Ohio." Doctoral diss., Kent State University. *Dissertation Abstracts International* 44: 1326a.

Thies, A.P. (1979). "A Brain-Behavior Analysis of Learning Style." In *Student Learning Styles: Diagnosing and Prescribing Programs*. Reston, Va.: National Association of Secondary School Principals, pp. 55-61.

Urbschat, K. S. (1977). "A Study of Preferred Learning Models and Their Relationship to the Amount of Recall of CVC Trigrams." Doctoral diss., St. John's University, New York. *Dissertation Abstracts International* 38: 2536-5A.

Weinberg, F. (1983). "An Experimental Investigation of the Interaction Between Sensory Modality Preference and Mode of Presentation in the Instruction of Arithmetic Concepts to Third Grade Underachievers." Doctoral diss., St. John's University, New York. *Dissertation Abstracts International* 44: 1740A.

Wheeler, R. (1980). "An Alternative to Failure: Teaching Reading According to Students' Perceptual Strengths." *Kappa Delta Pi Record* 17, 2: 59-63.

Wheeler, R. (1983). "An Investigation of the Degree of Academic Achievement Evidenced When Second Grade Learning Disabled Students' Perceptual Preferences Are Matched and Mismatched with Complementary Sensory Approaches to Beginning Reading Instruction." Doctoral diss., St. John's University, New York. *Dissertation Abstracts International* 44: 2039A.

Fostering Creativity: The Innovative Classroom Environment

The standard classroom environment contains major barriers to the development of creativity in students, the author contends. He suggests methods for removing the barriers and for fostering creativity.

Randall P. Pruitt

RANDALL P. PRUITT is an instructor in the Department of Interpersonal and Public Communication at Bowling Green State University, Bowling Green, Ohio.

> Sometimes, nothing short of "a whack on the side of the head" can dislodge the assumptions that keep us thinking "more of the same."
>
> —Roger Von Oech[1]

FROM INITIAL WORK by Wallas, who classified the creative process into the four steps of preparation, incubation, illumination, and verification, to later work by Osborn, Maslow, and Arieti, the creative process has been examined from a wide variety of perspectives.[2]

In the classroom, environmental factors greatly influence the creative process. While the environment could be considered a small piece of the creative puzzle, it is, nonetheless, of vital importance with respect to how it affects innovative and creative instructor-student interaction in the classroom setting. For the purpose of this article, the instructor will be considered part of the classroom environment. The term environment itself will be defined as the aggregate of surrounding things or conditions.

Considering the teacher as part of the creative environment, J.P. Guilford, former president of the American Psychological Association, drew a direct link between the classroom instructor and the students' creativity development when he suggested that poor teaching inhibits development of creativity and that the normal conditions of mass education generally impede the development of creative individuals.[3] Arieti, Gowan and Olson, and Walker support the notion that creativity is encouraged by certain features in the environment.[4] Arieti also suggests that certain cultures have encouraged creative climates more than others. Before considering some of the advantages of a creative classroom environment, however, let us examine how to overcome some of the barriers to developing such an environment.

Overcoming Barriers to an Innovative Classroom Environment

The four major factors which impede the development of a creative classroom environment are classroom

Reprinted with permission of *Educational Horizons*, Vol. 68, No. 1, Fall 1989, pp. 51-54. *Educational Horizons*, quarterly journal published by Pi Lambda Theta, national honor and professional association, Bloomington, IN 47407-6626.

*T*orrence states that a major shortcoming in the educational system today is that too much emphasis is placed on conformity to behavioral norms and too little time is spent on encouraging original work.

control, habitual behavior, dealing with time as it relates to the creative process, and student assessment. Each is important in establishing a healthy environment for the creative process.

The Control Factor

Instructors fear that they will not be able to control the classroom in a creative learning situation. Control, in this case, does not refer to discipline, but to the process of learning within the context of the classroom. Among educators, there is often a desire to tie learning experiences into tidy little packages, but as Torrence explains, learning does not always conform to the expectations of instructors. Torrence states that a major shortcoming in the educational system today is that too much emphasis is placed on conformity to behavioral norms and too little time is spent on encouraging original work. He warns against the temptation to become confined to set patterns in learning situations and suggests that an atmosphere of "released control" be present in the classroom. "Released control" means that some control is present, but that students feel more freedom to experiment with creative alternatives because the principle of deferred judgment is practiced by the instructor.[5]

Iverson also supports the concept of a creative classroom environment, suggesting that flexibility can stimulate creative thinking in students.[6] Parnes conducted four years of research at the University of Buffalo studying the deliberate development of creative problem solving.[7] His research suggests that a "free wheeling" classroom atmosphere which includes the principle of deferred judgment can provide students with invaluable practice in viewing problems from varying vantage points. In seeking this type of environment, Parnes encouraged the creative process by giving students the freedom to apply imagination, enthusiasm, and individual creative ability in the environment where judgment of ideas was not immediate, but deferred. For some instructors, the relinquishment of immediate feedback may seem strange, but the advantage of such an atmosphere is that students can offer a great number of suggestions without the fear of immediate scrutiny by peers and superiors.

*V*AUGHAN discusses creativity as adventure and contends that for the creative process to develop its own direction and end, some kind of surrender of central control must be made.[8] For classroom instructors, this surrender might involve a decision to release control over expectations regarding how students should think, respond, and form ideas. To glean the advantages of a freewheeling environment, instructors may need to rethink attitudes toward students who respond and think in nonconforming ways. As Torrence suggests, students may feel more freedom to respond in creative ways if they perceive an attempt by the instructor to be open to a variety of individual learning/response styles.

In summary, the creative process can be encouraged and nurtured if instructors are willing to: (1) avoid an emphasis on conformity; (2) utilize the principle of released control; and (3) develop and practice the concept of deferred judgment.

The Habit Factor

A second barrier to a creative classroom environment is what could best be termed the habit factor. It is simply the tendency for instructors to rely on the techniques, styles, and patterns with which they are more familiar, and with which certain responses and outcomes are more predictable. Though some instructors find comfort in familiarity, the advantages of breaking the habit factor can be seen clearly in creativity research.

The Vermont Alliance for Arts in Education addressed the issue of fostering creativity in schools and communities in Vermont.[9] One of the findings of the study was that creativity needs a variety of settings. The key, according to the report, is that instructors and educators need to have a flexible attitude toward the environment.

If creativity is to flourish, the environment could not, according to the alliance, be thought of as inert and immutable. Raudsepp and Hough contend that part of the reason individuals view change with considerable anxiety is because of the pressure that sometimes accompanies the change process. He contends that the only way individuals can face change is by becoming more "creatively flexible and imaginative."[10] Stanish supports the idea that for creative thinking to be encouraged, randomness and risk taking in teaching experiences and personal examples must be present in the classroom.[11]

Though instructors may use different models to foster a creative environment in the classroom, research indicates that flexibility, randomness, change, and risk taking may be important parts of breaking the habit barrier.

The Time Factor

Nicholas Murray Butler, former president of Columbia University, once said, "Time was invented by Almighty God in order to give ideas a chance." One of the biggest enemies of any instructor is time. Some instructors may find it difficult to make the time commitment that innovation and creativity demands.

*T*hough instructors may use different models to foster a creative environment in the classroom, research indicates that flexibility, randomness, change, and risk taking may be important parts of breaking the habit barrier.

Historically, many of the major models of the creative process include at least one stage involving the careful use of time. Wallas called this stage the incubation stage.[12] Rossman called it the birth of a new idea, or the invention stage.[13] Osborn referred to it as ideation.[14] And Von Oech labeled it the germination phase.[15] The emphasis is not time as it relates to preparation by the educational professional, but as it relates to the creative process itself. For students to receive the benefits of an innovative environment, it is necessary for instructors to prevent the barrier of time from rushing the birth of new ideas and approaches.

The Assessment Factor

A fourth barrier to a creative environment is the assessment factor. An assessment barrier is formed whenever judgment or assessment become a controlling factor in classroom interaction. This factor is usually present in any situation where there is the fear or actual presence of ridicule or rebuke. The object of the fear may be peers or superiors, but the result is usually an inhibition of individual willingness to risk, to question, and to fail.

Maslow asserted that the presence of a psychologically safe environment would greatly enhance creativity.[16] The Vermont Alliance for the Arts supports the need for delaying judgment in the classroom in order to encourage student creativity. One example of a delayed judgment technique is the act of brainstorming. Ideas are offered without immediate judgment or evaluation. The participants have the freedom to be creative without the fear of ridicule, failure, or rejection. The result is usually the generation of a wide variety of innovative ideas stemming from the flow of the creative process. Lobuts and Pennewell suggest the use of a classroom environment known as the open system: "The system allows students to feel comfortable trying new concepts and asking naive questions. This system facilitates learning by encouraging students to be inquisitive without feeling intimidated."[17]

The Benefits of an Innovative Environment

The Freedom to Fail

There is a great motivation to try new things and think new thoughts when the pressure of failure is removed from classroom settings. When instructors practice the principle of deferred judgment in the classroom, they encourage students to go beyond failure to innovation. It has been said that prior to Thomas Edison's patenting of the first commercially practical incandescent lamp (the light bulb), he failed over one hundred times in his attempts to find a filament that would provide a high enough degree of resistance within a vacuum. In much the same way, in-

structors need to overcome the *control and assessment factor*s by allowing enough room for themselves and their students to fail in the creative process.

Mark McCormack, one of the most successful entrepreneurs in American business and author of the best-selling book, *What They Don't Teach You at Harvard Business School*, emphasizes the value of being able to face personal mistakes and failures. He considers it important for individuals to be able to admit mistakes and move on. He states that the ability to say "I was wrong" is vital to success.[18]

STUDENTS AND instructors need to be taught that rejection and failure are an important part of the creative process. And since students and instructors are likely to face setbacks and criticism when attempting to experiment, high doses of encouragement are necessary within the classroom setting to keep the creative process alive.

In *The Craft of Teaching*, Eble describes the role of the instructor as an encourager. He says that when conversing with students, "no utterances are wrong, though they may be false, off the mark, vague, wandering, irritating or whatever...all answers are good answers."[19] Instructors desiring to nurture a creative environment should be aware of the fears and setbacks associated with trying new ideas and approaches in the classroom. When students feel the freedom to experiment without the fear of failure, the creative process can become a positive experience for both students and instructors.

The Freedom to Change

By fostering creativity in the classroom through the freedom to change, instructors and students will avoid many of the pitfalls associated with stagnation. By altering the *habit factor* through cultivation of randomness, change, and risk taking, instructors and their students can move toward increased freedom in the learning environment.

CHANGE IN THE learning environment can take any number of forms. The use of guest speakers; the encouragement of student participation in course goals and planning; the use of films, videos, or music; the possibility of team teaching a course; a physical change in the

classroom environment; or the use of new subject matter and discussion techniques are all possible avenues for breaking new creative ground. Without a concerted effort to break through the habit barrier, however, educational professionals and their students may find the classroom environment mundane and the creative process limited.

The Freedom to Enjoy and Create

One of the benefits of a creative environment is the freedom to enjoy the creative process itself. The teaching techniques of Jearl Walker, an award-winning teacher of physics at Cleveland State University, have been described as a combination of Evel Knievel, Mr. Wizard, and Saturday Night Live.[20] Walker's antics have included lying on a bed of nails, breaking bricks with his bare hands, and plunging his hand into hot lead to demonstrate varying principles of physics. The point is not that instructors need to go to the extremes practiced by Walker, but that the freedom to enjoy the creative process enhances the learning experience for both instructors and their students.

The freedom to enjoy and create can also be encouraged through increasing individuals' abilities to dream and imagine in new and creative ways. Weaver and Cotrell refer to the process as imaging.[21] It is the practice of creating specific, material pictures as a source for new thoughts and feelings. Parnes calls a similar process visioneering.[22]

The Freedom to Wait

To be creative requires time; not only preparation time for instructors, but time for the creative process to germinate. Roger von Oech, who is a creative thinking consultant for Apple Computers, Colgate-Palmolive, DuPont, International Business Machines, and a host of other major industries, divides the creative process into two main phases. One of those phases, the germinal phase, involves taking the time to sprout and grow new ideas based on looking at common situations in new ways. He describes this phase as "soft thinking" and says that it involves taking the time to look at things by using ambiguity, humor, fantasy, generalization, and approximation. The environment is not pressured for time, requiring logical, precise, immediate decisions; rather, time is given to wait, to ponder, and to germinate ideas.

For instructors, this may mean taking an extra five minutes to consider a class problem in a new light or taking time to incorporate ideas that encourage students to be creative. Above all, it involves careful planning and consideration for germination of the creative process when planning course objectives, in-class discussions, and classroom activities. One example of an activity could be as simple as dividing the class into groups for the purpose of listing as many unconventional uses for a paper clip as they can think of in a two-minute period. Though the exercise may have little to do with an instructor's lesson plan for the day, the exercise can help students to begin thinking in creative ways. To overcome the *time factor*, instructors need to become sensitive to the flow of the creative process and allow enough time for its development.

The freedom to wait can also be helpful when it is applied to the *assessment factor*. In some cases, instructors might consider giving feedback but no grades on assignments in the early part of a course as a way for students to experiment with ideas and gain experience without the fear of poor grades.

The benefits associated with an innovative environment are both practical and realistic. They come as a result of overcoming the barriers of control, habit, time, and assessment and by embracing the freedom to fail, the freedom to change, the freedom to enjoy and create, and the freedom to wait. In doing so, instructors and students may realize their full creative potential and take advantage of a tremendous opportunity to revitalize the classroom environment.

1. R. Von Oech, *A Whack on the Side of the Head* (New York: Warner Books, 1983).
2. G. Wallas, *The Art of Thought* (New York: Harcourt Brace, 1926); A.F. Osborn, *Applied Imagination* (New York: Charles Scribner's Sons, 1953); A.H. Maslow, "A Holistic Approach to Creativity," in *Climate for Creativity*, ed. C.W. Taylor (New York: Pergamon Press, 1972), pp. 287-293; S. Arieti, *Creativity the Magic Synthesis* (New York: Basic Books, Inc., 1976).
3. J.P. Guilford as cited in S.J. Parnes and H.F. Harding, *A Source Book for Creative Thinking* (New York: Charles Scribner's Sons, 1962).
4. Arieti, "Creativity" pp. 293-294; J.C. Gowan and M. Olson, "The Society Which Maximizes Creativity," *Journal of Creative Behavior* (3rd Qtr. 1979): 194-210; W.J. Walker, "Creativity: Fostering Golden Environments," *The Clearing House* (January 1986): 220-222.
5. E.P. Torrence, "Developing Creative Thinking Through School Experiences," in *A Source Book*, ed. S.J. Parnes and H.F. Harding (New York: Charles Scribner's Sons, 1962), pp. 31-47.
6. B.K. Iverson, "Haha, aha, ah: A Model for Playful Curricular Inquiry and Evaluation" (Paper presented at the Annual Meeting of the American Educational Research Association, Los Angeles, Cal., September 1981).
7. Parnes and Harding, *A Source Book*.
8. T. Vaughan, "On Not Predicting the Outcome: Creativity as Adventure," *The Journal of Creative Behavior* (4th Qtr. 1987): 300-310.
9. "First Steps: Fostering Creativity in Vermont's Schools and Communities" (Montpelier, Vt.: Vermont Alliance for Arts in Education, 1982).
10. E. Raudsepp and G.P. Hough, Jr., *Creative Growth Games* (New York: Harcourt Brace Jovanovich, 1977), p. 7.
11. B. Stanish, "The Underlying Structures and Thought About Randomness and Creativity," *The Journal of Creative Behavior* (2nd Qtr. 1986): 110-114.
12. Wallas, *The Art of Thought*.
13. J. Rossman, *The Psychology of the Inventor* (Washington, D.C.: Inventors Publishing, 1931).
14. Osborn, *Applied Imagination*.
15. Von Oech, *A Whack*.
16. Maslow, "A Holistic Approach."
17. J.F. Lobuts and C.L. Pennewell, "Do We Dare Restructure the Classroom Environment?" *The Journal of Creative Behavior* (4th Qtr. 1984): 244-246.
18. M.H. McCormack, *What They Don't Teach You at Harvard Business School* (New York: Bantam Books, 1984), p. 71.
19. K.E. Eble, *The Craft of Teaching* (San Francisco, Jossey-Bass: 1976), p. 60.
20. R. Wolkomir, "Old Jearl Will Do Anything to Stir an Interest in Physics," *Smithsonian* (October 1986): 112-120.
21. R.L. Weaver, II and H.W. Cotrell, "Imaging Can Increase Self Concept and Lecturing Effectiveness," *Education* (Spring 1985): 264-270.
22. S.J. Parnes, "Visioneering—State of the Art," *The Journal of Creative Behavior* (4th Qtr. 1987): 283-299.
23. Von Oech, *A Whack*. **EH**

Motivation and Classroom Management

- Approaches to Motivation (Articles 27-30)
- Classroom Management and Discipline (Articles 31-34)

The term *motivation* is used by educators to describe the processes of initiating, directing, and sustaining goal-oriented behavior. Motivation is a complex phenomenon, involving many factors that affect an individual's choice of response and perseverance in completing tasks. Furthermore, the reasons why people engage in particular behaviors can only be inferred; motivation cannot be directly measured.

Several theories of motivation, each highlighting different reasons for sustained goal-oriented behavior, have been proposed. We will discuss three of them—behavioral, humanistic, and cognitive. The behavioral theory of motivation suggests that an important reason for engaging in behavior is that reinforcement follows the action. If the reinforcement is controlled by someone else and is arbitrarily related to the behavior (such as money, a token, or a smile), then the motivation is extrinsic. In contrast, behavior may also be initiated and sustained for intrinsic reasons such as curiosity or mastery.

Humanistic approaches to motivation are concerned with the social and psychological needs of individuals. Humans are motivated to engage in behavior to meet these needs. Abraham Maslow proposes that there is a hierarchy of needs that directs behavior, beginning with physiological and safety needs and progressing to self-actualization. Some other important needs that influence motivation are affiliation and belonging with others, love, self-esteem, influence with others, recognition, status, competence, achievement, and autonomy.

Motivation in the classroom is a primary concern of teachers, especially beginning teachers. As long as students are on task, learning is maximized and misbehavior is lessened. Because students have different needs, interests, and backgrounds, teachers must know each student personally. They must also set appropriate, clear goals, direct and sustain attention, communicate accurate expectations, and provide meaningful feedback and incentives. The article on research of motivational strategies by Jere Brophy summarizes the general principles of motivation.

Students with high efficacy ultimately are motivated toward mastery of skills. Students who blame their failures on their inadequate abilities have low self-efficacy and will be discouraged and at risk for dropping out. Richard Sagor discusses the problems of discouraged learners and describes techniques for improving their motivation.

M. Kay Alderman next presents a model for building the efficacy of students. She suggests that teachers can help students acquire responsibility for their own learning by setting goals, and then determining the learning strategies to help them reach those goals. As students reach their learning goals, their success is attributed to their ability and effort.

The article by Margaret Clifford argues that while the principles outlined by cognitive motivation theorists are well known and accepted in educational psychology, many well-established practices of schools directly contradict those principles. It is these practices, she argues, that lead students to drop out of school.

No matter how effectively students are motivated, teachers always need to exercise management of behavior in the classroom. Classroom management is an approach to controlling behavior in order to establish a favorable learning environment. As T. R. Ellis observes, "effective teachers have the fewest discipline problems." They prevent misbehavior by setting reasonable rules and adjusting to different learning styles. Steven Grubaugh suggests that teachers can achieve considerable classroom control nonverbally through proxemics, silence, body language, expressions, etc.

Effective teachers also have a plan for responding to students who do misbehave. Assertive discipline, developed by Lee Canter according to principles of behavioral learning theory, is one such plan. Canter describes in detail how to implement assertive discipline. David Hill, on the other hand, argues that some critics consider assertive discipline "dehumanizing," and "humiliating." Taken together, these two articles encourage students to think about the goals of discipline.

Looking Ahead: Challenge Questions

What is the most effective way to motivate learners? Are at-risk students motivated by the same techniques as typical students? What can teachers do to increase students' self-efficacy? Can failure be motivating?

How are classroom management and motivation related? What is the difference between classroom management and discipline? Do you agree with Ellis that programs such as assertive discipline are a crutch for ineffective teachers? What are the advantages and disadvantages of the behavioral view of motivation and discipline?

Unit 4

Synthesis of Research on Strategies for Motivating Students to Learn

Students are more likely to want to learn when they appreciate the value of classroom activities and when they believe they will succeed if they apply reasonable effort.

JERE BROPHY

Jere Brophy is Co-Director, Institute for Research on Teaching, and Professor of Teacher Education, Michigan State University, Erickson Hall, East Lansing, MI 48824-1023.

This article synthesizes the conclusions drawn from a review of the literature on motivation conducted to identify principles suitable for use by teachers, especially principles for motivating students to learn during academic activities. To begin with, student *motivation to learn* can be conceptualized either as a general trait or as a situation-specific state. The *trait* of motivation to learn is an enduring disposition to strive for content knowledge and skill mastery in learning situations. The *state* of motivation to learn exists when student engagement in a particular activity is guided by the intention of acquiring the knowledge or mastering the skill that the activity is designed to teach.

Several conceptual distinctions implied by these definitions of student motivation to learn guided my review of the literature. Student motivation to learn is an acquired competence developed through general experience

Illustration by Lori Oxendine

but stimulated most directly through modeling, communication of expectations, and direct instruction or socialization by significant others (especially parents and teachers). If activated in particular learning situations, motivation to learn functions as a scheme or script that includes not only affective elements but also cognitive elements such as goals and associated strategies for accomplishing the intended learning. According to this view, teachers are not merely reactors to whatever motivational patterns their students had developed before entering their classrooms but rather are *active socialization agents* capable of stimulating the general development of student motivation to learn and its activation in particular situations.

However, teachers work within certain restrictions. Schools are formal institutions that students are required to attend in order to learn a prescribed curriculum, and classrooms are public settings where performance is monitored by peers and graded by teachers. If teachers were recreation program directors, they could solve motivation problems merely by finding out what their clients like to do and arranging for them to do it. Instead, like supervisors in work settings, teachers must find ways to motivate their students voluntarily to try to do well what is required of them.

Schools are not ordinary work settings, however; they are settings for learning. With a few exceptions (penmanship, zoology dissection skills), school learning is covert and conceptual, not overt and behavioral. We need a clear distinction between learning and performance: *learning* refers to the information-processing, sense-making, and comprehension or mastery advances that occur during the acquisition of knowledge or skill; *performance* refers to the demonstration of such knowledge or skill after it has been acquired. The term *motivation to learn* refers not just to the motivation that drives later performance but also to the motivation underlying the covert processes that occur during learning. Therefore, strategies for motivating students to learn apply not only to performance on tests or assignments, but also to information-processing activities (paying attention to lessons, reading for understanding, paraphrasing ideas) initially involved in learning the content or skills. The

emphasis is not merely on offering students incentives for good performance later but on stimulating them to use thoughtful learning. Thus, strategies for stimulating motivation to learn differ from strategies for supplying extrinsic motivation for performance.

They also differ from strategies for capitalizing on students' intrinsic motivation, because intrinsic motivation is not the same as motivation to learn. *Intrinsic motivation* usually refers to the affective aspects of motivation— liking for or enjoyment of an activity. Intrinsic motivation, even for academic activities, does not necessarily imply motivation to learn. For example, students may enjoy participating in an educational game without trying to derive any academic benefit from it. Similarly, students can try to learn the knowledge or skills that an activity is designed to teach without enjoying the activity.

Guided by these distinctions concerning the nature of schooling and of student motivation, I have searched the literature for theory and research that suggest principles suitable for application by teachers in classrooms. This review and synthesis work has yielded the strategies summarized in the "Highlights" box (Ames and Ames 1984, 1985, Brophy 1983, Corno and Rohrkemper 1985, Deci and Ryan 1985, Keller 1983, Kolesnik 1978, Lepper and Greene 1978, Maehr 1984, Malone and Lepper in press, McCombs 1984, Nicholls 1984, and Wlodkowski 1978). For additional discussion and examples beyond this brief listing, see Brophy (1986a, b) or Good and Brophy (1986, 1987).

Development and organization of the list of strategies has been guided by *expectancy x value* theory (Feather 1982), which posits that the effort people will expend on a task is a product of: (1) the degree to which they *expect* to be able to perform the task successfully if they apply themselves; and (2) the degree to which they *value* participation in the task itself or the benefits or rewards that successful task completion will bring to them. This theory assumes that no effort will be invested in a task if either factor is missing entirely, no matter how much of the other factor may be present. People do not invest effort on tasks that do not lead to valued outcomes even if they know they can perform the tasks successfully, and they do not invest effort

"The simplest way to ensure that students expect success is to make sure they achieve it consistently."

on even highly valued tasks if they are convinced that they cannot succeed no matter how hard they try.

The *expectancy x value* theory of motivation implies that, in order to motivate their students to learn, teachers must both help them to appreciate the value of academic activities and make sure that they can achieve success on these activities if they apply reasonable effort. The "Highlights" box is organized according to these *expectancy x value* theory ideas. First, it lists the preconditions necessary if teachers are to motivate their students. Second, it enumerates strategies that involve establishing and maintaining success expectations in the students. Third, it offers strategies that enhance the subjective value students place on school tasks. The latter strategies are subdivided into those that involve offering extrinsic incentives, taking advantage of intrinsic motivation, or stimulating student motivation to learn.

Essential Preconditions

No motivational strategies can succeed with students if the following preconditions are not in effect.

1. *Supportive environment*. If the classroom is chaotic or if the students are anxious or alienated, then students are unlikely to be motivated to learn academic content. Thus, in order to motivate students to learn, the teacher must organize and manage the classroom as an effective learning environment. This includes encouraging students, patiently supporting their learning efforts, and allowing them to feel comfortable taking intellectual risks without fear of being criticized for making mistakes.

2. *Appropriate level of challenge/difficulty*. Students will be bored if tasks are too easy and frustrated if tasks are too difficult. They will be

"If teachers were recreation program directors, they could solve motivation problems merely by finding out what their clients like to do and arranging for them to do it."

optimally motivated by tasks that allow them to achieve high levels of success when they apply reasonable effort.

3. *Meaningful learning objectives.* Teachers should select academic activities that teach some knowledge or skill that is worth learning, either in its own right or as a step toward a higher objective. It is not reasonable to expect students to be motivated to learn if they are continually expected to practice skills already thoroughly mastered, memorize lists for no good reason, copy definitions of terms that are never used in readings or assignments, or read material that is not meaningful to them because it is too vague, abstract, or foreign to their experience.

4. *Moderation/optimal use.* Motivational attempts can be overdone, and any particular strategy can lose its effectiveness if it is used too often or too routinely.

Motivating by Maintaining Success Expectations

Much of the best-known research on motivation is focused on the role of success expectations in determining performance. Research on *achievement motivation* (Dweck and Elliott 1983) has shown that effort and persistence are greater in individuals who set goals of moderate difficulty level, who seriously commit themselves to pursuing these goals, and who concentrate not on avoiding failure but on achieving success. Research on *efficacy perceptions* (Bandura and Schunk 1981) has shown that effort and persistence are greater in individuals who believe that they have the efficacy (competence) needed to succeed on a task than in individuals who lack it.

Research on *causal attributions* for performance suggests that effort and persistence are greater in individuals who attribute their performance to internal or controllable causes rather than to external or uncontrollable ones (Weiner 1984). In particular, better performance is associated with a tendency to attribute success to a combination of sufficient ability with reasonable effort and a tendency to attribute failure either to insufficient effort (if this has been the case) or to confusion about what to do or reliance on an inappropriate strategy for doing it. The literature on motivation suggests that the following strategies (nos. 5–8) will help students maintain success expectations and associated goal setting behaviors, efficacy perceptions, and causal attributions.

5. *Program for success.* The simplest way to ensure that students expect success is to make sure they achieve it consistently. Teachers can accomplish this by beginning instruction at their level, moving in small steps, and preparing students sufficiently for each new step so that they can adjust to it without much confusion or frustration. Note that students' success levels will depend not only on task difficulty, but on the degree to which the teacher prepares the students for the task through advance instruction and assists their learning efforts through guidance and feedback.

6. *Teach goal setting, performance appraisal, and self-reinforcement skills.* Help students learn to set and commit themselves to goals that are: (1) near rather than far (they refer to tasks to be attempted here and now rather than to ultimate goals in the distant future); (2) specific (complete a page of math problems with no more than one error) rather than global (work carefully and do a good job); and (3) challenging rather than too easy or too hard. Provide specific, detailed feedback and help students use appropriate standards for judging their performance (i.e., to compare it with absolute standards or with their own previous progress rather than with the performance of peers), so that they can recognize their successes and reinforce themselves for their efforts.

7. *Help students to recognize linkages between effort and outcome.* Use modeling, socialization, and feedback to make students aware that the amount and quality of effort that they put into an activity determines what they get out of it. Portray effort as an investment, which will produce knowledge or skill development and thus empower students, rather than as a risk of failure or embarrassment. Portray skill development as incremental (open to improvement in small steps rather than fixed) and domain specific (students possess a great many different kinds of skills rather than a single IQ that determines performance in everything). Last, focus on mastery of instructional objectives rather than comparisons with the achievements of peers.

8. *Provide remedial socialization.* With discouraged students, use performance contracts, Mastery Learning Principles (additional instruction, practice opportunities, and make-up exams to allow struggling students to overcome initial failures through persistent efforts), and attribution retraining (teach students to concentrate on doing the task at hand rather than to become distracted by fears of failure; to cope with frustration by retracing their steps to find their mistake or analyzing the problem to find a better way to approach it; and to attribute failures to insufficient effort, lack of information, or reliance on ineffective strategies rather than to lack of ability).

"People do not invest effort on tasks that do not lead to valued outcomes even if they know they can perform the tasks successfully, and they do not invest effort on even highly valued tasks if they are convinced that they cannot succeed no matter how hard they try."

Teachers can shape the ways students view their performance—what they see as achievable with reasonable effort, whether they define this achievement as successful, and whether they attribute their performance to their own efforts. Empty reassurances or a few words of encouragement will not do the job. Rather, a combination of appropriately challenging demands with systematic socialization designed to make students see that success can be achieved with reasonable effort should be effective.

The strategies described in this section have addressed the *expectancy* term of the *expectancy x value* formulation. The strategies explained in the next three sections address the *value* term.

Motivating by Supplying Extrinsic Incentives

Strategies for supplying extrinsic motivation do not attempt to increase the value that students place on the task itself but rather to link successful task performance with access to valued rewards.

9. *Offer rewards for good (or improved) performance.* In addition to grades, these may include: (1) material rewards (prizes, consumables); (2) activity rewards and special privileges (play games, use special equipment, engage in self-selected activities); (3) symbolic rewards (honor rolls, displays of good work); (4) praise and social rewards (teacher or peer attention); and (5) teacher rewards (opportunities to go places or do things with the teacher). Teachers should offer and deliver rewards in ways that call attention to developing knowledge and skills rather than in ways that encourage students to focus just on the rewards.

10. *Structure appropriate competition.* The opportunity to compete for prizes or recognition either as an individual or as a member of a team can add incentive to classroom activities. In addition to structuring competition based on test scores or other performance measures, teachers can build competitive elements into instruction by including activities such as argumentative essays, debates, or simulation games that involve competition (Keller 1983). Use handicapping systems such as those devised by Slavin (1983) to ensure that everyone has a good (or at least an equal) chance to

win. It is also helpful to depersonalize the competition and emphasize the content being learned rather than who wins and who loses.

Extrinisic incentives and competition are more effective for stimulating intensity of effort than for inducing thoughtfulness or quality of performance. Thus, rewards and competition are best used with practice tasks designed to produce mastery of specific skills rather than with incidental learning or discovery tasks, and with tasks where speed of performance or quantity of output is of more concern than creativity, artistry, or craftsmanship.

11. *Call attention to the instrumental value of academic activities.* Where possible, note that the knowledge or skills developed by an academic task will enable students to meet their own current needs, provide them with a "ticket" to social advancement, or prepare them for success in an occupation or in life generally. Help students to see academic activities not as imposed demands to be resisted but rather as enabling opportunities to be valued.

Extrinsic motivational strategies are effective under certain circumstances, but teachers should not rely on them. When students are preoccupied with rewards or competition, they may not attend to or appreciate the value of what they are learning.

Motivating by Capitalizing on Students' Intrinsic Motivation

Teachers can capitalize on intrinsic motivation by planning academic activities that students will engage in willingly because they are interested in the content or enjoy the task. Opportunities to do this are limited by several features inherent in the nature of schooling—compulsory attendance, externally prescribed curriculum, public monitoring, and grading of performance. Further, students differ in what they find interesting or enjoyable. Even so, teachers can schedule activities that incorporate elements that most students will find rewarding.

12. *Adapt tasks to students' interests.* Whenever curriculum objectives can be accomplished using a variety of examples or activities, incorporate content that students find interesting or activities that they find enjoyable. When giving examples or applications of concepts being learned, include

> **"Extrinsic incentives and competition are more effective for stimulating intensity of effort than for inducing thoughtfulness or quality of performance."**

people, fads, or events prominent in the news or in the youth culture.

13. *Include novelty/variety elements.* Make sure that something about each activity (its form or content, the media involved, or the nature of the responses it demands) is new to the students or at least different from what they have been doing recently. Do not allow a steady diet of routine lessons followed by routine assignments to become "the daily grind."

14. *Allow choices or autonomous decisions.* Within the constraints imposed by the instructional objectives, offer students alternative ways to meet requirements and opportunities to exercise autonomous decision making and creativity in determining how to organize their time and efforts. If children make poor decisions when left completely on their own, provide them with a menu of choices or require them to get their choices approved before going ahead.

15. *Provide opportunities for students to respond actively.* Most students prefer activities that allow them to respond actively by interacting with the teacher or with one another, by manipulating materials, or by doing something other than just listening or reading. Provide students with opportunities to participate, for example, in projects, experiments, role-playing, simulations, educational games, and creative applications of what is being learned.

16. *Provide immediate feedback to student responses.* Students especially enjoy tasks that allow them not only to respond actively but to get immediate feedback they can use to guide subsequent responses. Automatic feedback features are built into programmed

---

Highlights of Research on Strategies for Motivating Students to Learn

Research on student motivation to learn indicates promising principles suitable for application in classrooms, summarized here for quick reference.

Essential Preconditions
1. Supportive environment
2. Appropriate level of challenge/difficulty
3. Meaningful learning objectives
4. Moderation/optimal use

Motivating by Maintaining Success Expectations
5. Program for success
6. Teach goal setting, performance appraisal, and self-reinforcement
7. Help students to recognize linkages between effort and outcome
8. Provide remedial socialization

Motivating by Supplying Extrinsic Incentives
9. Offer rewards for good (or improved) performance
10. Structure appropriate competition
11. Call attention to the instrumental value of academic activities

Motivating by Capitalizing on Students' Intrinsic Motivation
12. Adapt tasks to students' interests
13. Include novelty/variety elements
14. Allow opportunities to make choices or autonomous decisions

15. Provide opportunities for students to respond actively
16. Provide immediate feedback to student responses
17. Allow students to create finished products
18. Include fantasy or simulation elements
19. Incorporate game-like features
20. Include higher-level objectives and divergent questions
21. Provide opportunities to interact with peers

Stimulating Student Motivation to Learn
22. Model interest in learning and motivation to learn
23. Communicate desirable expectations and attributions about students' motivation to learn
24. Minimize students' performance anxiety during learning activities
25. Project intensity
26. Project enthusiasm
27. Induce task interest or appreciation
28. Induce curiosity or suspense
29. Induce dissonance or cognitive conflict
30. Make abstract content more personal, concrete, or familiar
31. Induce students to generate their own motivation to learn
32. State learning objectives and provide advance organizers
33. Model task-related thinking and problem solving

—Jere Brophy

---

learning and other "self-correcting" materials as well as into computerized learning programs. Teachers can incorporate feedback features into typical activities by leading the group through an activity and then circulating to supervise students' progress during seatwork. Teachers can arrange for alternative sources of feedback when they cannot be available themselves by providing answer keys or instructions about how to check work, designating student helpers, or having students review their work in pairs or small groups.

17. *Allow students to create finished products.* Students prefer tasks that have meaning or integrity in their own

> "Students prefer tasks that have meaning or integrity in their own right over tasks that are mere subparts of some larger entity."

right over tasks that are mere subparts of some larger entity. They are likely to experience a satisfying sense of accomplishment when they finish such tasks. Ideally, task completion will yield a finished product that students can use or display such as a map, an essay, a scale model, or something other than just another ditto or workbook page.

18. *Include fantasy or simulation elements.* Where more direct applications of what is being learned are not feasible, introduce fantasy or imagination elements that will engage students' emotions or allow them to experience events vicariously. In addition to full-scale drama, role-play, simulation games, and other "major productions," incorporate more modest simulation activities into everyday instruction. For example, stimulate students to think about the motives of a literary author or scientific discoverer or to imagine themselves living in the historical time or geographical place under study.

19. *Incorporate game-like features into exercises.* Transform ordinary assignments into "test yourself" challenges, puzzles, or brain teasers that:
- require students to solve prob-

lems, avoid traps, or overcome obstacles to reach goals;
- call for students to explore and discover in order to identify the goal itself in addition to developing a method for reaching it;
- involve elements of suspense or hidden information that emerges as the activity is completed (puzzles that convey a message or provide the answer to a question once they are filled in); or
- involve a degree of randomness or uncertainty about what the outcome of performance is likely to be on any given trial (e.g., knowledge games that cover assorted topics at a variety of difficulty levels and that are assigned according to some random method, such as in Trivial Pursuit).

Although many teachers associate "games" with team competitions, the term "game-like feature" has a much broader meaning; most of these features involve presenting intellectual challenges appropriate for use by individuals or by groups working cooperatively.

20. *Include higher-level objectives and divergent questions.* Most students soon become bored by a steady diet of knowledge- and comprehension-level questions. Therefore, in-

"When the topic is familiar, counter students' tendency to think they already know everything there is to know about it by pointing out unexpected, incongruous, or paradoxical aspects. . . ."

clude questions that address higher cognitive levels (application, analysis, synthesis, or evalution) and encourage students to make sense of what they are learning by processing it actively, paraphrasing it, and relating it to their prior knowedge and experience. Also, ask questions that elicit divergent thinking (opinions, predictions, suggested courses of action, or solutions to problems) in order to generate student responses that are more personal and creative.

21. *Provide opportunities to interact with peers.* Students enjoy activities that allow interaction with their peers. Build such opportunities into whole-class activities by scheduling discussion, debate, role-play, or simulation. In addition, plan follow-up activities that permit students to work together in pairs or small groups to tutor one another, discuss issues, or develop suggested solutions to problems, or to work as a team preparing for a competition, participating in a simulation game, or producing some group product. Peer interactive activities are likely to be most effective if teachers: (1) make them worthwhile learning experiences rather than merely occasions for socializing by structuring them around curriculum objectives; and (2) arrange conditions so that every student has a substantive role to play and must participate actively (Slavin 1983).

Strategies for Stimulating Student Motivation to Learn
The strategies just described for capitalizing on intrinsic motivation should increase students' enjoyment of classroom activities; however, these strategies will not directly increase students' motivation to learn the content or skills being taught. The literature on motivation suggests that the following strategies will stimulate students to take academic activities seriously and to acquire the knowledge or skills that they were designed to develop. The first three strategies are general ones describing pervasive features of the learning environment that should be established in the classroom.

22. *Model interest in learning and motivation to learn.* Routinely model interest in learning by showing students that you value learning as a rewarding, self-actualizing activity that produces personal satisfaction and enriches your life. Share with students your interests in books, articles, TV programs, or movies on the subjects you teach. Mention applications of the subjects to everyday living, the local environment, or current events.

23. *Communicate desirable expectations and attributions about students' motivation to learn.* Routinely project attitudes, beliefs, expectations, and attributions concerning reasons for students' behavior which imply that you expect them to be curious, to want to understand concepts and master skills, and to see what they are learning as meaningful and applicable to their lives.

24. *Minimize students' performance anxiety during learning activities.* Protect students from premature concern about performance adequacy by structuring most activities to promote learning rather than to evaluate performance. When activities do include test-like items, treat these as opportunities for students to apply the material rather than as a chance for you to see who does or doesn't know the material. Combat test anxiety by minimizing time pressures, by portraying tests as opportunities to assess progress rather than as measures of ability, by giving pretests to accustom students to "failure" and provide a basis for marking progress, and by teaching stress management and test-taking skills (Hill and Wigfield 1984).

In addition to fostering a supportive learning environment through these general strategies, use the following strategies to stimulate student motivation to learn during specific activities.

25. *Project intensity.* Project a level of intensity that tells students that the material deserves close attention either by saying so or by using rhetorical devices (slow pacing, step-by-step presentation with emphasis on key words, unusual voice modulations or exaggerated gestures, scanning the group intensely at each step to look for signs of understanding or confusion). Projecting intensity is especially useful when introducing new content, demonstrating skills, or giving instructions for assignments.

26. *Project enthusiasm.* Present topics or assignments in ways that suggest they are interesting or worthwhile by identifying your own reasons for finding the topic meaningful, and then communicate these reasons when teaching it.

27. *Induce task interest or appreciation.* Where relevant, elicit student appreciation for an activity by noting its connections with things that students already recognize as interesting or important, by mentioning applications of the knowledge or skills to be learned, or by specifying challenging or exotic aspects that the students can anticipate.

28. *Induce curiosity or suspense.* Put students into an active information-processing or problem-solving mode by posing questions or doing "set-ups" that introduce curiosity or suspense elements and motivate students to engage in the activity in order to answer some question, resolve an ambiguity, or fill in gaps in their knowledge.

"[Teachers can] portray effort as an investment, which will produce knowledge or skill development and thus empower students, rather than as a risk of failure or embarrassment."

29. *Induce dissonance or cognitive conflict.* When the topic is familiar, counter students' tendency to think that they already know everything there is to know about it by pointing out unexpected, incongruous, or paradoxical aspects; calling attention to unusual or exotic elements; noting exceptions to general rules; or challenging students to solve the "mystery" that underlies a paradox.

30. *Make abstract content more personal, concrete, or familiar.* Promote personal identification with content by relating experiences or telling anecdotes illustrating how the content applies to the lives of individuals (especially persons whom the students are interested in and likely to identify with). Make abstractions concrete by showing objects or pictures or by conducting demonstrations. Help students relate new or strange content to their existing knowledge by using examples or analogies referring to familiar concepts, objects, or events. Where a text is too abstract or sketchy, elaborate by filling in sufficient detail to enable students to visualize what is being described and explain it in their own words.

31. *Induce students to generate their own motivation to learn.* Do this by asking them to list their own interests in particular topics or activities, to identify questions that they would like to have answered, or to note things that they find surprising as they read.

32. *State learning objectives and provide advance organizers.* Stimulate motivation to learn when introducing activities by stating their objectives and by providing advance organizers. Prepare students to get more out of lectures, films, or reading assignments by clarifying what you want them to concentrate on as they process the information; distributing outlines or study guides; making suggestions about notetaking; or calling attention to structural features of the presentation that can help students to remember it in an organized way.

33. *Model task-related thinking and problem solving.* The information-processing and problem-solving strategies used when responding to academic tasks will be invisible to students unless teachers make them overt by showing students what to do and thinking out loud as they demonstrate. Such *cognitive modeling* is an important instructional device. It is also an effective way to stimulate student motivation to learn because, through modeling, teachers expose students to the beliefs and attitudes associated with such motivation (e.g., patience, confidence, persistence in seeking solutions through information processing and rational decision making, benefiting from the information supplied by mistakes rather than giving up in frustration).

A Starter Set

Although student motivation to learn cannot be taught as directly as a concept or a skill, it can be developed in children by teachers who systematically socialize their students using the strategies listed here as part of a larger package of appropriate curriculum and instruction. Further research will undoubtedly identify additional strategies and qualifications on the use of ones described here. Nevertheless, the list provides a "starter set" of strategies to select from in planning motivational elements to include in instruction. In particular, these strategies remind us that students need not only incentives for applying themselves and activities they will enjoy but also motivation to learn the knowledge and skills being taught.

References

Ames, C., and R. Ames, eds. *Research on Motivation in Education, Vol. II: The Classroom Milieu.* Orlando: Academic Press, 1985.

Ames, R., and C. Ames, eds. *Research on Motivation in Education, Vol. I: Student Motivation.* New York: Academic Press, 1984.

Bandura, A., and D. Schunk. "Cultivating Competence, Self-Efficacy, and Intrinsic Interest Through Proximal Self-Motivation." *Journal of Personality and Social Psychology* 41 (1981): 586–598.

Brophy, J. "Conceptualizing Student Motivation." *Educational Psychologist* 18 (1983): 200–215.

Brophy, J. "On Motivating Students." Occasional Paper No. 101, Institute for Research on Teaching. East Lansing: Michigan State University, 1986a.

Brophy, J. "Socializing Student Motivation to Learn." In *Advances in Motivation and Achievement*, vol. 5, edited by M. L. Maehr and D. A. Kleiber. Greenwich, CT: JAI Press, 1986b.

Corno, L., and M. Rohrkemper. "The Intrinsic Motivation to Learn in Classrooms." In *Research on Motivation in Education, Vol. II: The Classroom Milieu*, edited by C. Ames and R. Ames. Orlando: Academic Press, 1985.

Deci, E., and R. Ryan. *Intrinsic Motivation and Self-Determination in Human Behavior.* New York: Plenum, 1985.

Dweck, C., and E. Elliott. "Achievement Motivation." In *Handbook of Child Psychology*, edited by P. Mussen. New York: Wiley, 1983.

Feather, N., ed. *Expectations and Actions.* Hillsdale, N.J.: Erlbaum, 1982.

Good, T., and J. Brophy. *Educational Psychology: A Realistic Approach.* 3d ed. New York: Longman, 1986.

Good, T., and J. Brophy. *Looking in Classroom.* 4th ed. New York: Harper and Row, 1987.

Hill, K. T., and A. Wigfield. "Test Anxiety: A Major Educational Problem and What Can Be Done About It." *Elementary School Journal* 85 (1984): 105–216.

Keller, J. "Motivational Design of Instruction." In *Instructional-Design Theories and Models: An Overview of Their Current Status*, edited by C. Reigeluth. Hillsdale, N.J.: Erlbaum, 1983.

Kolesnik, W. *Motivation: Understanding and Influencing Human Behavior.* Boston: Allyn and Bacon, 1978.

Lepper, M., and D. Greene, eds. *The Hidden Costs of Reward: New Perspectives on the Psychology of Human Motivation.* Hillsdale, N.J.: Erlbaum, 1978.

Maehr, M. "Meaning and Motivation: Toward a Theory of Personal Investment." In *Research on Motivation in Education, Vol. I: Student Motivation*, edited by R. Ames and C. Ames. Orlando: Academic Press, 1984.

Malone, T., and M. Lepper. "Making Learning Fun: A Taxonomy of Intrinsic Motivation for Learning." In *Aptitude, Learning, and Instruction, Vol. III: Conative and Affective Process Analysis*, edited by R. Snow and M. Farr. Hillsdale, N.J.: Erlbaum, in press.

McCombs, B. "Processes and Skills Underlying Continuing Intrinsic Motivation to Learn: Toward a Definition of Motivational Skills Training and Interventions." *Educational Psychologist* 19 (1984): 199–218.

Nicholls, J. "Conceptions of Ability and Achievement Motivation." In *Research on Motivation in Education, Vol. I: Student Motivation*, edited by R. Ames and C. Ames. Orlando: Academic Press, 1984.

Slavin, R. *Cooperative Learning.* New York: Longman, 1983.

Weiner, B. "Principles for a Theory of Student Motivation and Their Application Within an Attributional Framework." In *Research on Motivation Education, Vol. I: Student Motivation.* Orlando: Academic Press, 1984.

Wlodkowski, R. J. *Motivation and Teaching: A Practical Guide.* Washington, D.C.: National Education Association, 1978.

Motivation for At-Risk Students

"Helpless" students need to learn to link their successes and failures to their own efforts.

M. Kay Alderman

M. Kay Alderman is Professor, Department of Educational Foundations, University of Akron, Akron, OH 44325.

Student motivation for learning is a major concern of most teachers, but especially for teachers of low-achieving or "at risk" students, whose numbers are on the rise (Hodgkinson 1985). In today's classrooms, motivational inequality prevails: some students persist and work on their own for their own intrinsic interest, while others work because they are required to and do not believe their actions are related to success and failure (Nicholls 1979). The encouraging news, however, is that motivation research (e.g., Alderman and Cohen 1985, Ames and Ames 1989) and cognitive learning research (e.g., Weinstein and Mayer 1986) offer teachers an abundant repertoire of strategies to foster student success and self-worth.

Understanding Motivation Levels

The motivation theory of attribution has helped us to understand students who have a pattern of failure. The reasons one assigns for achieving success or failure are called *attributions* (Weiner 1979). Students' attributions affect their future expectations and actions. The following four attributions are used most frequently:

> Some students persist and work on their own for their own intrinsic interest, while others work because they are required to and do not believe their actions are related to success and failure.

1. Not having the ability ("I'm just not a writer");
2. Not expending enough effort ("I could do it if I really tried");
3. Task difficulty ("the test was too hard");
4. Luck ("I guessed right").

These attributions have been further categorized into two dimensions, stable-unstable and internal-external. Stable-unstable refers to the consistency of a student's pattern of failure. Internal-external refers to the student's beliefs that the cause for failure lies either within or outside the student. For example, Teresa fails an exam on reading comprehension—she has done this many times. Her attributions for her failure are that she can never answer those kinds of questions and that she is just not a good reader. These attributions have internal/stable characteristics: the student blames herself rather than an outside force for her failure, and she characterizes herself as someone who can never succeed.

Students with such internal/stable attributions for failure consider themselves "helpless"—they believe they can do nothing to prevent failure or assure success (Dweck and Goetz 1978). The "helpless" student actually expends less effort after failure, while a "mastery" student increases effort and looks for better strategies. Failure attributed to internal/stable ability is one of the most difficult motivational problems to remedy. And for the helpless student, simply experiencing success is not enough to ensure motivation.

For example, a student may not attribute his success to anything that he did—he attributes it to luck—so he does not expect success again. Or another student attributes her failure to "stupidity," so failure becomes a self-fulfilling prophecy. The task for teachers is to help these students break this failure/low expectation/helpless cycle.

Efficacy and Expectations

Teachers who are successful in reach-

M. Kay Alderman, "Motivation for At-Risk Students," *Educational Leadership*, Vol. 48, No. 1, September 1990, pp. 27-30.

ing low-achieving students combine a high sense of their own efficacy with high, realistic expectations for student achievement. *Teacher efficacy* refers to teachers' confidence in their ability to influence student learning and motivation. This sense of efficacy, in turn, affects teachers' expectations concerning students' abilities. Teachers with a high sense of efficacy are more likely to view low-achieving students as reachable, teachable, and worthy of their attention and effort (Ashton and Webb 1986).

The effects of teacher expectations on student achievement are well documented (Good and Brophy 1987): the key attitudes for teachers are confidence and determination. This does not mean that they are idealistic in their expectations. Instead, it means that, although teachers are realistic—aware that students have learning problems—they look for ways to overcome the learning problems (Brophy and Evertson 1976). They let students know they want them to succeed and that they will be expected to achieve the objectives. Then they assure them that they will be taught the skills or learning strategies necessary for achieving them.

"Links" to Success

It is not enough that the student achieve success; in order to acquire a high degree of motivation, the student must know how he or she personally contributed to this success. In other words, there must be a link between what the student did and the outcome. Drawing from research on motivation and learning strategies, I have developed the "Links" for helping the "helpless" student become successful and, in turn, develop an increased sense of self-worth. These links are shown in Figure 1.

Link One: proximal goals. The first link to success is the setting of goals for performance. Goals play an important role in the cultivation of self-motivation by establishing a target or personal standards by which we can evaluate or monitor our performances (Bandura 1986). Goal setting provides the mechanism for self-assessment. Morgan (1987) concluded that there is a reciprocal relationship between goal setting and self-monitoring: either process will lead to the other. For example, Harris and Graham's (1985) instruction and training program for teaching composition skills to learning disabled students requires students to set a criterion for performance and then keep graphs to show their progress toward their goals.

But all goals are not equally effective in providing standards for self-evaluation. To be effective, the goal should be specific rather than general; harder rather than easier (but attainable); and proximal (close at hand) rather than long term (Locke 1968). It is especially important for students with a history of failure to have proximal goals so they won't be overwhelmed. Bandura and Schunk (1981) found that children who had proximal goals performed better than those with distal or long-term goals.

How do we establish a starting point to forge this proximal goal link? First, we have to find out where students are so that we can establish a baseline. The baseline can be determined by pretests (formal or informal) and analyses of student errors. Teachers and students can then jointly decide on the proximal goals.

Goal setting seems to benefit everyone: it has been found to have a positive effect on elementary and secondary students (Gaa 1973, 1979), as well as learning disabled students (Tollefson et al. 1984) and college students (Morgan 1987). Figure 2 shows a form that can be used and adapted to teach students to set effective goals.

I have used adaptions of these steps for students of various ages and ability and have found that most students need considerable practice in learning to make goals specific.

Link Two: learning strategies. Low-achieving students usually can be described as "inefficient learners" (Pressley and Levin 1987); that is, an inefficient learner fails to apply a learning strategy that would be bene-

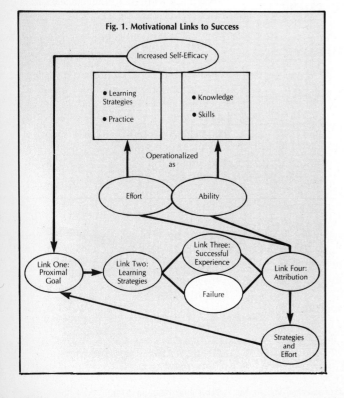

Fig. 1. Motivational Links to Success

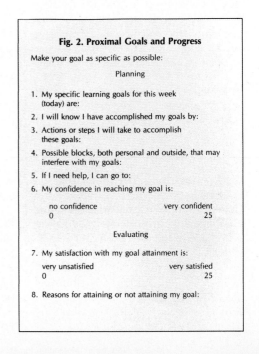

Fig. 2. Proximal Goals and Progress

Make your goal as specific as possible:

Planning

1. My specific learning goals for this week (today) are:

2. I will know I have accomplished my goals by:

3. Actions or steps I will take to accomplish these goals:

4. Possible blocks, both personal and outside, that may interfere with my goals:

5. If I need help, I can go to:

6. My confidence in reaching my goal is:

   no confidence   very confident
   0   25

Evaluating

7. My satisfaction with my goal attainment is:

   very unsatisfied   very satisfied
   0   25

8. Reasons for attaining or not attaining my goal:

ficial. In Link Two, the students identify the learning strategies that will help them accomplish their goals. Examples of learning strategies are: basic and complex rehearsal strategies; comprehension-monitoring strategies (Weinstein and Mayer 1986); task-limited and across-domains strategies, with metacognitive knowledge about when to use them (Pressley et al. 1989); and various reading comprehension strategies, including summarization, question asking, clarification, and prediction. In the latter example, Palincsar and Brown (1984) reported improved reading comprehension scores after students were taught the four comprehension skills.

Link Three: successful experience. A learning goal rather than a performance goal is the key to success in Link Three (Dweck 1986). The focus in a learning goal is on "how much progress I made," not on "how smart I am," a performance goal. The student measures his or her success using the proximal goal as the criterion. As teachers, we may think that success is the final link. However, consider the student who is successful but still has low expectations for future performance. It is the *attribution* the student makes for the successful experience that affects expectation: the student must link his or her personal effort or strategy to the successful outcome.

Link Four: attribution for success. In Link Four, students are encouraged to attribute success to their personal effort or abilities. The teacher's role is to help the student make the appropriate attribution. The attributions most easily changed are the internal and unstable. Thus, since students control their own effort, this is the likely starting place to influence their attributions for success. Teachers can ask, "What did you do when you tried?" Examples of student effort might be: completing all homework, correcting errors, extra practice, redoing an assignment, going to a "help" or review lesson, or using appropriate learning strategies.

Schunk (1984) concluded that for difficult tasks, attributional feedback should begin with effort, then shift to ability as skills develop. Researchers have found that effort attributions were often less valued by students than attributions for ability (Covington and Omlich 1979, Nicholls 1976). Students, especially adolescents, may not

> **When we help students take responsibility for their learning, we have taken a giant step in promoting motivational equality in the classroom.**

view themselves as "smart" if they "tried hard." However, it is important that the student see "ability" as skills that can be learned (e.g., writing composition skills).

The teacher's role in Link Four is to model and give feedback about why the student succeeded or failed at the task. Attributional feedback is information (oral or written) about effort, strategies, or ability. Examples of feedback are: "Jenny, look at your test score, that extra practice really paid off" (effort); "Martin, the latest revision of your story shows you have really learned to use action words" (ability); "Tom, your reading scores improved because you have learned to summarize and find main ideas" (strategies).

This model then goes "full circle." Students who have succeeded and attributed the success to their own effort or ability (and not to task ease or luck) have concrete performance feedback that in turn will lead to increased self-efficacy. Self-efficacy is most enhanced by prior successful performance (Bandura 1977). This increased self-efficacy then leads to increased confidence about goal accomplishment.

In this "Links" model, we have focused on a successful experience. However, failure will occur; and when it does, students' attributions for it are important determinants of their future expectations for success. Students who attribute failure to not using the proper strategy, for example, are more likely to try again than students who attribute failure to lack of intelligence. This latter attribution for failure results in a dead end for the student. Teachers should be cautious in assigning lack of effort as the cause of failure; they should only

use this attribution when they are sure the task was within the student's capability. Often students don't know why they failed (Alderman et al. 1989). When students indicate they don't know why they failed, the teacher can provide them with a new strategy for accomplishing the task.

Classroom Structure to Support Success

To foster optimum motivation, classroom structure must support student goals, effort, and use of effective strategies. A "mastery orientation" structure fosters optimum student motivation (Ames and Archer 1988). A mastery classroom emphasizes learning and progress (Link Three) over performance and ability. Thus, errors are viewed as a natural and important part of the learning process, not as an indication that one lacks ability. Teachers in mastery classrooms give students opportunities to relearn concepts and correct errors. Low-achieving students in particular need to know exactly what they are expected to do and the criterion for measuring their success (Covington and Beery 1976). This criterion takes the focus off ability in comparison to other students as the reason for failure.

Progress, Not Miracles

The Links-To-Success model is not an algorithm but rather a guide for fostering students' motivation for success and self-worth. It is flexible: any link of the chain can be the starting point. For example, when a student fails, the cycle can begin with attributing the failure to lack of effort or use of ineffective strategies and returning to Link One: proximal goals.

This model also serves to enhance the teacher's motivation as well, through the same dynamics used with the students. When teachers see progress in their at-risk students, their teaching efficacy increases.

Finally, I make no claim that these links will work miracles with at-risk students. They only provide teachers and students with a framework for beginning the cycle of progress that fosters self-responsibility for learning. When we help students take responsibility for their learning, we have taken a giant step in promoting motivational equality in the classroom. This type of motivational intervention takes time and patience; our focus is progress, not miracles.

References

Alderman, M.K., and M.W. Cohen. (1985). *Motivation Theory and Practice for Preservice Teachers* (Teacher Education Monograph No. 4). Washington, D.C.: ERIC Clearinghouse on Teacher Education.

Alderman, M., R. Klein, M. Sanders, and S. Keck. (1989). "Metacognitive Self-Portraits: Preservice Teachers as Learners in Formation," Paper presented at the annual meeting of the American Educational Research Association, San Francisco.

Ames, C., and R. Ames. (1989). *Research on Motivation in Education: Goals and Cognition* (Vol. 3). San Diego, Calif.: Academic Press.

Ames, C., and J. Archer. (1988). "Achievement Goals in the Classroom: Students' Learning Strategies and Motivation Processes." *Journal of Educational Psychology* 80: 260–267.

Ashton, P.T., and R.B. Webb. (1986). *Making a Difference: Teachers' Sense of Efficacy and Student Achievement*. N.Y.: Longman.

Bandura, A. (1977). "Self-Efficacy: Toward a Unifying Theory of Behavioral Change," *Psychological Review* 84: 191–215.

Bandura, A., and D. Schunk. (1981). "Cultivating Competence, Self-Efficacy, and Intrinsic Interest Through Proximal Self-Motivation." *Journal of Personality and Social Psychology* 41: 586–598.

Bandura, A. (1986). *Social Foundations of Thought and Action*. Englewood Cliffs, N.J.: Prentice Hall.

Brophy, J., and C. Evertson. (1976). *Learning From Teaching: A Developmental Perspective*. Boston: Allyn & Bacon.

Covington, M. V., and R. M. Beery. (1976). *Self-Worth and School Learning*. N.Y.: Holt, Rinehart, and Winston.

Covington, M.V., and C. Omlich. (1979). "Effort: The Double-Edged Sword in School Achievement." *Journal of Educational Psychology* 71: 169–182.

Dweck, C.S., and T. Goetz. (1978). "Attributions and Learned Helplessness." In *New Directions in Attribution Research*, Vol. II. Hillsdale, N.J.: Erlbaum.

Dweck, C.S. (1986). "Motivational Processes Affecting Learning." *American Psychologist* 41: 1040–1048.

Gaa, J.P. (1973). "Effects of Individual Goal-Setting Conferences on Achievement, Attitude, and Goal-Setting Behavior." *Journal of Experimental Education* 42: 22–28.

Gaa, J.P. (1979). "The Effects of Individual Goal-Setting Conferences on Achievement, Attitudes, and Modification of Locus of Control." *Psychology in the Schools* 16: 591–597.

Good, T.L., and J.E. Brophy. (1987). *Looking in Classrooms* (4th ed.). N.Y.: Harper & Row.

Harris, K.R., and S. Graham. (1985). "Improving Learning Disabled Students' Composition Skills: Self-Control Strategy Training." *Learning Disability Quarterly* 8: 27–36.

Hodgkinson, H.L. (June 1985). *All One System: Demographics of Education— Kindergarten Through Graduate School*. Washington, D.C.: Institute for Educational Leadership.

Locke, E.A. (1968). "Toward a Theory of Task Motivation and Incentives." *Organizational Behavior and Human Performance* 3: 157–189.

Morgan, M. (1987). "Self-Monitoring and Goal Setting in Private Study." *Contemporary Educational Psychology* 12: 1–6.

Nicholls, J.G. (1976). "Effort is Virtuous, But It's Better to Have Ability: Evaluative Responses to Perceptions of Effort and Ability." *Journal of Research in Personality* 10: 306–315.

Nicholls, J. (1979). "Quality and Inequality in Intellectual Development: The Role of Motivation in Education." *American Psychologist* 34: 1071–1084.

Palincsar, A.M., and A.L. Brown. (1984). "Reciprocal Teaching of Comprehension Fostering and Monitoring Activities." *Cognition and Instruction* 1: 117–125.

Pressley, M., F. Goodchild, J. Fleet, R. Zajchowski, and E. Evans. (1989). "Classroom Strategy Instruction." *The Elementary School Journal* 89: 301–342.

Pressley, M., and J. Levin. (1987). "Elaborative Learning Strategies for the Inefficient Learner." In *Handbook of Cognitive, Social, and Neuropsychological Aspects of Learning Disabilities*, edited by S.J. Ceci. Hillsdale, N.J.: Erlbaum.

Schunk, D. (1984). "Sequential Attributional Feedback and Children's Achievement Behavior." *Journal of Educational Psychology* 76: 1159–1169.

Tollefson, N., D.B. Tracy, E.P. Johnson, A. W. Farmer, and B. Buenning. (1984). "Goal Setting and Personal Responsibility Training for LD Adolescents." *Psychology in the Schools* 21: 224–232.

Weiner, B. (1979). "A Theory of Motivation for Some Classroom Experiences." *Journal of Educational Psychology* 71: 3–25.

Weinstein, C.E., and R.E. Mayer (1986). "The Teaching of Learning Strategies." In *Handbook of Research on Teaching* (3rd ed.), edited by M. Wittrock. New York: Macmillan.

TEEETERING

...on the edge of failure

More than 10 million of today's students are walking a tightrope. They're discouraged learners—at risk of becoming tomorrow's dropouts. We *can* steady their course and give them a chance at success in school, but we have to start early—in the primary grades.

RICHARD SAGOR

Richard Sagor is assistant superintendent of the West Linn, Ore., school district. He was principal of the West Linn High School when it was recognized for excellence by the U.S. Department of Education. A former classroom teacher, he also conducts workshops on motivating students for the Learning Institute.

hey're easy to spot. They slump in their chairs, never contribute to class discussions, and don't have anything to say when you call on them. They daydream, visit with their neighbors, rarely hand in homework. Some are shy; others defiant. But all the students who consistently display these kinds of behaviors have one thing in common. They are discouraged learners. And, whatever their background or problems outside of school, they are at risk of ending up as one of the approximately 700,000 American teenagers who drop out of school every year. In some communities, the drop-out rate is now approaching a staggering 50 percent.

The outcry over this nationwide crisis is reaching a crescendo. National meetings have been held; the presidential candidates are being called to account for their views on the topic; state and local governments are seeking answers.

Of course there are no simple solutions to stemming the tide. But grass roots evidence—from individual schools and classrooms that are putting new research into practice—is encouraging. It suggests that if we notice the signs of trouble as early as the primary grades and address the symptoms rather than decry the causes, we'll have a good chance of reversing the current statistics.

The discouraged learner: A profile
These children are not the abused, the severely emotionally disturbed, or those that need in-depth therapy or crisis intervention. These are the students who could succeed at school, but who don't think they have a reason to try. They don't believe school offers them anything to make their lives better. They don't see that what they're being asked to do at school has any point, and they get constant feedback on their academic *in*competence. They feel out of place at school—not part of the "in" group.

Students held back a grade are up to four times more likely to dropout than those who are not.

Source: *Dropouts in America*

©VOLK

The connection between grade promotion and dropping out of school begins as early as kindergarten.

Source: *Dropouts in America*

And most discouraging, they don't feel they have any control over their lives at school.

Our at-risk students are confirmed externalizers: They interpret successes or failures as beyond their control—the consequences of luck. When they get in trouble, it's always someone else's fault—the mean teachers, the unfair principal. Some externalizers are spoiled children, who are given everything they want and are rarely held accountable for misbehavior—the kids who think that rewards are a birthright rather than something to be earned. Other externalizers are the children of poverty who don't see their parents' hard work rewarded, but instead hear about lucky lottery winners and see neighborhood criminals apparently doing well. No wonder these kids think success has more to do with luck than with hard work and perseverance.

Most of our defeated and discouraged learners have been externalizers for so long, and have developed such an investment in their misplaced beliefs, that they've lost whatever faith in the future they may once have had. They rarely see any reason to deny immediate gratification as a reasonable price to pay for achieving a long-range goal. Instead, their feelings of inadequacy and hopelessness cause them to finally withdraw from the classroom—both psychologically and literally.

What can a teacher do?

Can we teachers, armed with an understanding of the perspective, experience, and orientation of the at-risk student, develop classrooms and lessons that will change his view of himself and school and put him on a path to academic success? Given hard work, and dedication, the answer is yes.

Certainly the task isn't easy. This child is not attractive. He stands in stark contrast to the enthusiastic, bright student whose successes continually reaffirm that we teachers are doing a great job. We must force our way through the negatives to help the discouraged learner succeed. That is the challenge for teachers now and into the nineties. And the rewards and benefits will be tremendous.

Here are some approaches to helping the discouraged learner. Together

with understanding and perseverance, they're already working in many classrooms and schools.

● *Have high expectations and set attainable goals.* Discouraged learners must be educated in classrooms where academic success is both expected and demanded. Ironically, in a humanistic attempt to make school more comfortable for our alienated students, we frequently make matters worse. We tend to make a big fuss over the mastery of low-level objectives. But a child won't gain a sense of pride by accomplishing a "Mickey Mouse" task no matter what we say about it.

On the other hand, a child who has felt underappreciated as a learner will feel great about a real success—achieving something he had to stretch for. Bill Purkey, University of North Carolina expert on student self-concept, said it well: "If you can only teach one thing, make it something tough."

● *Use mastery learning techniques.* Defeated and discouraged learners may be low on skills, but that doesn't mean they're low on intelligence. Building on their strengths can work wonders; these students are all too accustomed to having their weaknesses pointed out. By using mastery learning techniques, we can create an environment where everyone is successful and everyone develops self-esteem.

A few failures to properly implement the mastery technique, notably the Chicago Public Schools project, have given the strategy a bad name. But research has shown that when teachers are faithful to the basic principles of mastery learning, improvements in learning and self-concept can be astounding. The idea is to set a single high performance standard, and expect—in fact demand—that *every* student meet it. Then provide all the support, motivation, alternative learning strategies, and practice students need to reach that standard.

For mastery learning to work, it's essential to remember that learning rates do differ. For example, some students will need to spend more time on homework than others. Although papers and tests may have to be redone until the standard is met, it should never be altered. The trick is

That's what friends are for

Become an advocate for an at-risk student—one who's not in your class—and help him flourish. Here are the stories of three educators who made the commitment and succeeded.

Helping hugs

Curriculum director Sandra King met kindergartner Brian Ellis on his first day at school. It was *not* love at first sight. In fact, she'd been called to help his teacher calm him when he began cussing, shoving furniture around, and kicking anyone who came near. But King took a special interest in this troubled boy, and she's been an important part of his school life ever since.

The teachers soon found out that Brian has terrible problems at home. His father not only has a criminal record a mile long, but has physically abused both Brian and his mother. The father has even made threats toward school officials. Repeated referrals to child protective services and the police had failed to help so far. Brian was going to need lots of understanding.

That first day, King took Brian down to her office, and he kept up his wild behavior—the same kicking, hitting, and cussing. But, over the next few weeks, after he'd been forcibly returned to King's office several times, he began to settle down. She let him know he could talk to her—that she was his friend and that she wanted to help him get along better at school. After a few visits to King's office, he even began *asking* to go and see her. Now, he stops by whenever he can. And hardly a day goes by without at least a walk or a talk with "Mrs. King." There are plenty of hugs, too.

Because she cared and took the trouble to find out about Brian's particular situation, King was able to get social services help for his family. At school, she provides a safe harbor for him. Most important, Brian likes school and he's doing a lot better!

Literary leaps

It was a guidance counselor who brought librarian Sharon Landis together with 7th grader Kristin Phillips. And what a difference it made!

Kristin was seen in the school as bright, but "an awfully tough kid." She was an only child of a middle-class family, and her parents couldn't seem to control her. She had run away from home several times and, when she associated with anyone, she hung out with the identifiable misfits—the "druggies." Still, at this point, she wasn't a serious drug user.

Kristin's counselor found her to be bored and unresponsive. Though she maintained average grades, she seemed to see herself as a loser. Determined to get her seriously involved wtih some activities outside of school, the counselor asked her to identify some interests. She chose track, piano, and reading.

The reading was what opened the door to a continuing relationship between Kristin and Sharon Landis. Through suggesting books and talking about them, the librarian got to know Kristin. She found more books on topics such as ESP, mystery, and romance that intrigued Kristin and kept her reading. Eventually, Landis was able to use examples from books and personal experience to show Kristin some ways of getting along with difficult people (for Kristin this included peers, teachers, and even her parents).

Over a period of several months, Kristin has gradually improved her grades and her self-image. She's become independent enough to keep her old friends but not be sucked into their drug culture. She's making new friends, and she's growing closer to her parents. These large gains stem to a great extent from one adult taking a special interest in one child.

Rewarding work

Jim Salvatore was a freshman in high school when Steve Johanson, the athletic director, first took him under his wing. The coach realized right away that Jim was clumsy—socially *and* physically. The youngster had no friends and was unlikely to shine at any sport. Johanson offered Jim friendship and a chance to help out with athletic department affairs

Thrilled to be doing something of real value, Jim worked tirelessly over the next 4 years in the shadows of the locker room and on the sidelines as a team manager and student aide. Jim never did have a lot of friends. But he came to see himself as a very important person in the life of the school, and he was recognized as such. He was even chosen by the faculty to receive both the "School Services" and "Inspirational Senior" awards in his senior year.

When Jim went to the stage to accept his awards, the standing ovation he got was as much a surprise to him as it was to his parents, who were in the audience. But the joy, pride, and tears in Steve Johanson's eyes said more than any words could about the importance of friendship.

Jim is now equipment manager for the football team at the major southwestern university he attends. He still visits Johanson and writes him. Theirs will probably be a lifelong friendship. —R.S.

The names of teachers and students in these stories have been changed to protect their privacy.

---

to organize the classroom and offer out-of-school support to accommodate the needs of the slower as well as the faster learners.

Classroom experience and laboratory research have demonstrated that with these techniques, 90 percent to 95 percent of our students *can*

master a tough universal curriculum. Retarded and LD students *can* meet the same goals as gifted learners. And classroom experience has also validated Benjamin Bloom's University of Chicago research showing that slow learners' learning rates increase gradually as their confidence grows.

• *Keep up a fast pace.* This advice goes against conventional wisdom: If a kid isn't learning something, slow things down to be sure he gets it. But since discouraged learners lack a faith in the future, they tend to be extreme in their love for present stimulation and excitement. And they are impatient with routine. Many of them also have short attention spans. Downtime can breed the very passivity and complacency that keeps the discouraged learner from experiencing success.

Athletic coaches, who are frequently successful with the very students who fail in the classroom, maintain a feverish pace in practice ("keep it up," "let's go," "do it again, faster"). If we give short, lively assignments, the kids are more likely to come through—especially if we expect good things of them. But if kids have to go over and over the same thing, they're very likely to tune out because they're bored.

● *Minimize ability grouping.* Just as we judge others by the company they keep, our children judge themselves by the groups to which they are assigned. If a child perceives that we think he has low ability, he'll internalize that stigma. Even worse, the evidence suggests that once he's accepted the label, that child will lose any desire he may have had to show he can do better.

Research drawn from several major studies, including John Goodlad's monumental "Study of Schooling," demonstrates that in low-ability classes less time is spent on task, less learning occurs, and the quality of teaching is lower than in heterogeneous classes. Analogous findings have emerged in the related areas of athletics (where we've seen that participants and teams play better when the competition is better) and juvenile corrections (where the more children are treated like offenders, the greater the chance of recidivism).

It may be impossible and even unwise to eliminate all vestiges of ability grouping from our schools, but we should reconsider all of our grouping strategies in light of the impact they may have on a student's self-esteem.

● *Encourage cooperative learning:* Cooperative learning in mixed-ability groups is a promising strategy that meets the needs of discouraged as well as motivated learners. The classroom may be organized for circles of learning, as developed by David and Roger Johnson at the University of Minnesota; for cooperative team learning, as developed by Robert Slavin at The

Johns Hopkins University; or for another system. (See *Learning88*, February, for details on these programs.) In any case, a truly cooperative classroom allows every student to demonstrate competence, to feel a sense of belonging, usefulness, and personal potency. And, most significant, the research shows that in cooperative-learning classrooms academic and affective performance improves for both the advantaged *and* the disadvantaged learners.

● *Pay attention to learning styles.* Educators have been talking about the relevance of learning-style research to classroom practice for a long time. And it seems that no group of students benefits more from our recognition that different students learn in different ways than the defeated and discouraged learners. Recent research by Jerry Conrath, author of *Our Other Youth* and an expert on drop-out prevention, shows that at-risk students are disproportionately experiential, practical, hands-on learners. Ironically, most teachers are abstract and sequential learners who tend to teach the way they learned.

Consequently, teachers inadvertently ask students to work in ways that feel unnatural and set these students up to fail. Such failures can be embarrassing—especially when they happen in front of peers. And they intensify the already low self-esteem of these students. On the other hand, nothing makes a student feel more at home than a chance to show off those skills which come naturally.

If we make a point of frequently designing lessons to meet the practical learner's needs—models and demonstrations instead of essays, for example—we'll ensure that our discouraged learners have chances to feel that they and their learning strengths fit in. And they'll be better able to master truly meaningful academic objectives—precisely the kinds of achievements that build self-esteem.

● *Teach behavior management and cause and effect.* If low academic expectations are counterproductive for the at-risk student, lax behavioral expectations may be even worse. Remember, this student may have seen

More than 3,500 American teenagers drop out of school each day.

Source: *Dealing With Dropouts*

An estimated 25 percent of Chicago elementary school graduates never show up for high school.

Source: *Dropouts in America*

himself as a victim for so long that he doesn't even know what he's doing wrong when he interrupts or acts up in class. So he has to have a discipline system that provides immediate feedback on inappropriate behavior. Any other response will only reinforce the externalizing child's view that it's the authority figure or "lady luck"—not his behavior—that triggers consequences.

First, it's important to gain the child's trust so he'll know he's getting help rather than criticism. Then tell him exactly what he did wrong and why it caused a problem. When properly administered, the most effective discipline programs—whether they focus on logical consequences, assertive discipline, reality therapy, or some other theory—help an externalizer understand the connection between behavior and consequence. This understanding helps the child learn personal responsibility.

Recognizing cause and effect is one of those thinking skills we're so interested in teaching these days. And whenever we teach children about it—whether in science, history, politics, or in personal behavior—we're increasing the likelihood that they'll ultimately be able to control their own lives.

• *Become an advocate.* A disproportionate number of students at risk come to us from "fragile" families. Don't mistake "fragile" as a synonym for "single parent" or "low income." Such assumptions are dangerous because they can produce a self-fulfilling prophesy. Instead, fragile families can be defined as those in which quality nurturing is frequently lacking due to an array of stresses, traumas, and concerns which the child cannot control. It's important to recognize that, as teachers, we can rarely change a student's home life, but we can supplement it in enriching ways.

Invariably, our successful students have parents or other adults in their lives who serve as advocates for them and their interests and stand by them if they get into trouble. Almost all at-risk students lack such support.

At some schools the teachers, counselors, and administrators provide discouraged learners with advocates through discrete "adopt-a-kid" programs. First, a counselor, principal, or interdisciplinary inter-

vention team prepares a confidential list of students, which is then shared at a faculty meeting. A faculty member, preferably not the at-risk student's current classroom teacher, signs up to "adopt" one of the kids. The adopting teacher then commits to taking a personal interest in that child. For example, the teacher may agree to have at least three personal contacts per week with her adoptee. These can be anything from a brief "How's it going?" exchange in the hallway to a longer get-together such as a brown bag lunch. Many such seemingly insignificant relationships have continued for years and provided a crucial support for a child in need of unconditional adult love.

Before promising to take on such a responsibility, it's important to remember that a true advocate, like a true friend, stays involved for the long run. But being a true friend doesn't mean we should make excuses for our at-risk child. To the contrary, like a good parent, we should express displeasure at his misdeeds, but be constant and steadfast in our time, love, and support.

What schools can be
Successful adults are those who have

grown to feel confident in their strengths, at ease in their communities, of value to their society, and in charge of their lives. Those positive feelings begin early in life and can either be reinforced or refuted by school experiences. Each year, increasing numbers of our students lose faith in themselves, their skills, and their communities. They begin to develop a pessimism about the future and to distrust the very people who seek to help them. Gradually, those perspectives become ingrained, and the child finally thinks of himself as a powerless victim of a hostile society.

This grim scenario need not continue. Teachers and schools can provide the love and support these children need. Collaborative classrooms can give them the victories they need to feel good about themselves. And carefully planned curriculum and management practices can show them how to wield power over their own lives. Schools can be places where *everyone* succeeds. We have the techniques and theories. Now it's up to us to put them together—for *all* our kids' sake.

If you want to know more...

The following books and article will give you more information about the strategies described on these pages.

• *Assertive Discipline: A Take-Charge Approach for Today's Educator* by Lee Canter and Marlene Canter (Canter and Associates, Inc., P.O. Box 2113, Santa Monica, CA, 90406, 1978.)
• "Basketball's John Wooden: What a Coach Can Teach a Teacher," *Psychology Today*, January 1976
• *Circles of Learning: Cooperation in the Classroom* by David Johnson, Roger Johnson, et al (Association for Supervision and Curriculum Development, 225 N. Washington St., Alexandria, VA, 22314, 1986.)
• *Human Characteristics and School Learning* by Benjamin Bloom (McGraw Hill, 1982; pb).
• *Inviting School Success* by William Purkey (Wadsworth Publishing, 10 Davis Dr., Belmont, CA, 94002, 1984; pb)
• *Keeping Track: How Schools Structure Inequality* by Jeannie Oakes (Yale University Press, 1985)
• *Mastery Learning and Classroom Instruction* by James Block (MacMillan, 1975)

• *Psychology in the Classroom: A Manual for Teachers* by Rudolf Driekurs (Harper and Row, 1968)
• *Our Other Youth* by Jerry Conrath (3301 77th Ave., Gig Harbor, WA, 98335, 1987)
• *Schools and Delinquency* by Kenneth Polk and Walter Schafer (Prentice-Hall, 1972)
• *Student Team Learning* by Robert Slavin (National Education Association, 1983)

The following booklets will provide facts and figures about the dropout problem:
• *Dealing With Dropouts: The Urban Superintendents' Call to Action*, Office of Educational Research and Improvement, (U.S. Department of Education, 1987; Available from the U.S. Government Printing Office, Washington, DC 20402)
• *Dropouts in America* by Andrew Hahn, et al (Institute for Educational Leadership, 1001 Connecticut Avenue, N.W., Suite 310, Washington DC 20036, 1987)
• *School Dropouts: Everybody's Problem*, (Institute for Educational Leadership, Inc., 1986 [see address above])

Students Need Challenge, Not Easy Success

Only by teaching students to tolerate failure for the sake of true success can educators control the national epidemic of "educational suicide."

MARGARET M. CLIFFORD

Margaret M. Clifford is Professor of Educational Psychology, University of Iowa, College of Education, Iowa City, IA 52242.

Hundreds of thousands of apathetic students abandon their schools each year to begin lives of unemployment, poverty, crime, and psychological distress. According to Hahn (1987), "Dropout rates ranging from 40 to 60 percent in Boston, Chicago, Los Angeles, Detroit, and other major cities point to a situation of crisis proportions." The term *dropout* may not be adequate to convey the disastrous consequences of the abandonment of school by children and adolescents; *educational suicide* may be a far more appropriate label.

School abandonment is not confined to a small percentage of minority students, or low ability children, or mentally lazy kids. It is a systemic failure affecting the most gifted and knowledgeable as well as the disadvantaged, and it is threatening the social, economic, intellectual, industrial, cultural, moral, and psychological well-being of our country. Equally disturbing are students who sever themselves from the flow of knowledge while they occupy desks, like mummies.

Student apathy, indifference, and underachievement are typical precursors of school abandonment. But what causes these symptoms? Is there a remedy? What will it take to stop the waste of our intellectual and creative resources?

We must encourage students to reach beyond their intellectual grasp and allow them the privilege of learning from mistakes.

To address these questions, we must acknowledge that educational suicide is primarily a motivational problem—not a physical, intellectual, financial, technological, cultural, or staffing problem. Thus, we must turn to motivational theories and research as a foundation for examining this problem and for identifying solutions.

Curiously enough, modern theoretical principles of motivation do not support certain widespread practices in education. I will discuss four such discrepancies and offer suggestions for resolving them.

Moderate Success Probability Is Essential to Motivation

The maxim, "Nothing succeeds like success," has driven educational practice for several decades. Absolute success for students has become the means *and* the end of education: It has been given higher priority than learning, and it has obstructed learning.

A major principle of current motivation theory is that tasks associated with a moderate probability of success (50 percent) provide maximum satisfaction (Atkinson 1964). Moderate probability of success is also an essential ingredient of intrinsic motivation (Lepper and Greene 1978, Csikszentmihalyi 1975, 1978). We attribute the success we experience on easy tasks to task ease; we attribute the success we experience on extremely difficult tasks to luck. Neither type of success does much to enhance self-image. It is only success at moderately difficult or truly challenging tasks that we explain in terms of personal effort, well-chosen strategies, and ability; and these explanations give rise to feelings of pride, competence, determination, satisfaction, persistence, and personal control. Even very young children show a preference for tasks that are just a bit beyond their ability (Danner and Lonky 1981).

Consistent with these motivational findings, learning theorists have repeatedly demonstrated that moderately difficult tasks are a prerequisite for maximizing intellectual development (Fischer 1980). But despite the fact that moderate challenge (implying considerable error-making) is essential for maximizing learning and optimizing motivation, many educators attempt to create error-proof learning environments. They set minimum criteria and standards in hopes of ensuring success for all students. They often reduce task difficulty, overlook errors, de-emphasize failed attempts, ignore faulty performances, display "perfect papers," minimize testing, and reward error-free performance.

It is time for educators to replace easy success with challenge. We must encourage students to reach beyond their intellectual grasp and allow them the privilege of learning from mistakes. There must be a tolerance for error-making in every classroom, and gradual success rather than continual success must become the yardstick by which learning is judged. Such transformations in educational practices will not guarantee the elimination of educational suicide, but they are sure to be one giant step in that direction.

External Constraints Erode Motivation and Performance

Intrinsic motivation and performance deteriorate when external constraints such as surveillance, evaluation by others, deadlines, threats, bribes, and rewards are accentuated. Yes, even rewards are a form of constraint! The reward giver is the General who dictates rules and issues orders; rewards are used to keep the troops in line.

Means-end contingencies, as exemplified in the statement, "If you complete your homework, you may watch TV" (with homework being the means and TV the end), are another form of external constraint. Such contingencies decrease interest in the first task (homework, the means) and increase interest in the second task (TV, the end) (Boggiano and Main 1986).

Externally imposed constraints, including material rewards, decrease task interest, reduce creativity, hinder performance, and encourage passivity on the part of students—even pre-schoolers(Lepper and Hodell 1989)! Imposed constraints also prompt individuals to use the "minimax strategy"—to exert the minimum amount of effort needed to obtain the maximum amount of reward (Kruglanski et al. 1977). Supportive of these findings are studies showing that autonomous behavior—that which is self-determined, freely chosen, and personally controlled—elicits high task interest, creativity, cognitive flexibility, positive emotion, and persistence (Deci and Ryan 1987).

We face the grim reality that our extraordinary efforts to produce "schools without failure" have not yielded the well-adjusted, enthusiastic, self-confident scholars we anticipated.

Unfortunately, constraint and lack of student autonomy are trademarks of most schools. Federal and local governments, as well as teachers, legislate academic requirements; impose guidelines; create rewards systems; mandate behavioral contracts; serve warnings of expulsion; and use rules, threats, and punishments as routine problem-solving strategies. We can legislate school attendance and the conditions for obtaining a diploma, but we cannot legislate the development of intelligence, talent, creativity, and intrinsic motivation—resources this country desperately needs.

It is time for educators to replace coercive, constraint-laden techniques with autonomy-supportive techniques. We must redesign instructional and evaluation materials and procedures so that every assignment, quiz, test, project, and discussion activity not only allows for, but routinely *requires*, carefully calculated decision making on the part of students. Instead of minimum criteria, we must define multiple criteria (levels of minimum, marginal, average, good, superior, and excellent achievement), and we must free students to choose criteria that provide optimum challenge. Constraint gives a person the desire to escape; freedom gives a person the desire to explore, expand, and create.

Prompt, Specific Feedback Enhances Learning

A third psychological principle is that specific and prompt feedback enhances learning, performance, and motivation (Ilgen et al. 1979, Larson 1984). Informational feedback (that which reveals correct responses) increases learning (Ilgen and Moore 1987) and also promotes a feeling of increased competency (Sansone 1986). Feedback that can be used to improve future performance has powerful motivational value.

Sadly, however, the proportion of student assignments or activities that are promptly returned with informational feedback tends to be low. Students typically complete an assignment and then wait one, two, or three days (sometimes weeks) for its return. The feedback they do get often consists of a number or letter grade accompanied by ambiguous comments such as "Is this your best?" or "Keep up the good work." Precisely what is good or what needs improving is seldom communicated.

But, even if we could convince teachers of the value of giving students immediate, specific, informational feedback, our feedback problem would still be far from solved. How can one teacher provide 25 or more students immediate feedback on their tasks? Some educators argue that the solution to the feedback problem lies in having a tutor or teacher aide for every couple of students. Others argue that adequate student feedback will require an increased use of computer technology. However, there are less expensive alternatives. First, answer keys for students should be more plentiful. Resource books containing review and study activities should be available in every subject area, and each should be accompanied by a key that is available to students.

Second, quizzes and other instructional activities, especially those that supplement basic textbooks, should be prepared with "latent image" processing. With latent image paper and pens, a student who marks a response to an item can watch a hidden symbol emerge. The symbol signals either a correct or incorrect response, and in some instances a clue or explanation for the response is revealed. Trivia and puzzle books equipped with this latent image, immediate feedback process are currently being marketed at the price of comic books.

Of course, immediate informational feedback is more difficult to provide for composition work, long-term projects, and field assignments. But this does not justify the absence of immediate feedback on the learning activities and practice exercises that are aimed at teaching concepts, relationships, and basic skills. The mere availability of answer keys and latent image materials would probably elicit an amazing amount of self-regulated learning on the part of many students.

Moderate Risk Taking Is a Tonic for Achievement

A fourth motivational research finding is that moderate risk taking increases performance, persistence, perceived competence, self-knowledge, pride, and satisfaction (Deci and Porac 1978, Harter 1978, Trope 1979). Moderate risk taking implies a well-considered choice of an optimally challenging task, willingness to accept a moderate probability of success, and the anticipation of an outcome. It is this combination of events (which includes moderate success, self-regulated learning, and feedback) that captivates the attention, interest, and energy of card players, athletes, financial investors, lottery players, and even juvenile video arcade addicts.

Risk takers continually and freely face the probability of failing to attain the pleasure of succeeding under specified odds. From every risk-taking endeavor—whether it ends in failure or success—risk takers learn something about their skill and choice of strategy, and what they learn usually prompts them to seek another risk-taking opportunity. Risk taking—especially moderate risk taking—is a mind-engaging activity that simultaneously consumes and generates energy. It is a habit that feeds itself and thus requires an unlimited supply of risk-taking opportunities.

Moderate risk taking is likely to occur under the following conditions.

● The success probability for each alternative is clear and unambiguous.

● Imposed external constraints are minimized.

● Variable payoff (the value of success increases as risk increases) in contrast to fixed payoff is available.

● The benefits of risk taking can be anticipated.

My own recent research on academic risk taking with grade school, high school, and college students generally supports these conclusions. Stu-

Risk takers continually and freely face the probability of failing to attain the pleasure of succeeding under specified odds.

dents do, in fact, freely choose more difficult problems (a) when the number of points offered increases with the difficulty level of problems, (b) when the risk-taking task is presented within a game or practice situation (i.e., imposed constraint or threat is minimized), and (c) when additional opportunities for risk taking are anticipated (relatively high risk taking will occur on a practice exercise when students know they will be able to apply the information learned to an upcoming test). In the absence of these conditions we have seen students choose tasks that are as much as one-and-a-half years below their achievement level (Clifford 1988). Finally, students who take moderately high risks express high task interest even though they experience considerable error making.

In summary, risk-taking opportunities for students should be (a) plentiful, (b) readily available, (c) accompanied by explicit information about success probabilities, (d) accompanied by immediate feedback that communicates competency and error information, (e) associated with payoffs that vary with task difficulty, (f) relatively free from externally imposed evaluation, and (g) presented in relaxing and nonthreatening environments.

In today's educational world, however, there are few opportunities for students to engage in academic risk taking and no incentives to do so. Choices are seldom provided within tests or assignments, and rarely are variable payoffs made available. Once again, motivational theory, which identifies risk taking as a powerful source of knowledge, motivation, and skill development, conflicts with edu-

cational practice, which seeks to minimize academic risk at all costs.

We must restructure materials and procedures to encourage moderate academic risk taking on the part of students. I predict that if we fill our classrooms with optional academic risk-taking materials and opportunities so that all students have access to moderate risks, we will not only lower our educational suicide rate, but we will raise our level of academic achievement. If we give students the license to take risks and make errors, they will likely experience genuine success and the satisfaction that accompanies it.

Using Risk Can Ensure Success

Both theory and research evidence lead to the prediction that academic risk-taking activities are a powerful means of increasing the success of our educational efforts. But how do we get students to take risks on school-related activities? Students will choose risk over certainty when the consequences of the former are more satisfying and informative. Three basic conditions are needed to ensure such outcomes.

● First, students must be allowed to freely select from materials and activities that vary in difficulty and probability of success.

● Second, as task difficulty increases, so too must the payoffs for success.

● Third, an environment tolerant of error making and supportive of error correction must be guaranteed.

The first two conditions can be met rather easily. For example, on a 10-point quiz, composed of six 1-point items and four 2-point items, students might be asked to select and work only 6 items. The highest possible score for such quizzes is 10 and can be obtained only by correctly answering the four 2-point items and any two 1-point items. Choice and variable payoff are easily built into quizzes and many instructional and evaluation activities.

The third condition, creating an environment tolerant of error making and supportive of error correction, is more difficult to ensure. But here are six specific suggestions.

First, teachers must make a clear distinction between formative evaluation activities (tasks that guide instruction during the learning process) and summative evaluation activities (tasks used to judge one's level of achievement and to determine one's grade at the completion of the learning activity). Practice exercises, quizzes, and skill-building activities aimed at acquiring and strengthening knowledge and skills exemplify formative evaluation. These activities promote learning and skill development. They should be scored in a manner that excludes ability judgments, emphasizes error detection and correction, and encourages a search for better learning strategies. Formative evaluation activities should generally provide immediate feedback and be scored by students. It is on these activities that moderate risk taking is to be encouraged and is likely to prove beneficial.

Major examinations (unit exams and comprehensive final exams) exemplify summative evaluation; these activities are used to determine course grades. Relatively low risk taking is to be expected on such tasks, and immediate feedback may or may not be desirable.

Second, formative evaluation activities should be far more plentiful than summative. If, in fact, learning rather than grading is the primary objective of the school, the percentage of time spent on summative evaluation should be small in comparison to that spent on formative evaluation (perhaps about 1:4). There should be enough formative evaluation activities presented as risk-taking opportunities to satisfy the most enthusiastic and adventuresome learner. The more plentiful these activities are, the less anxiety-producing and aversive summative activities are likely to be.

Third, formative evaluation activities should be presented as optional; students should be enticed, not mandated, to complete these activities. Enticement might be achieved by (a) ensuring that these activities are course-relevant and varied (e.g., scrambled outlines, incomplete matrices and graphs, exercises that require error detection and correction, quizzes); (b) giving students the option of working together; (c) presenting risk-taking activities in the context of games to be played individually, with competitors, or with partners; (d) providing immediate, informational, nonthreatening feedback; and (e) defining success primarily in terms of

improvement over previous performance or the amount of learning that occurs during the risk-taking activity.

Fourth, for every instructional and evaluation activity there should be at least a modest percentage of content (10 percent to 20 percent) that poses a challenge to even the best students completing the activity. Maximum development of a country's talent requires that *all* individuals (a) find challenge in tasks they attempt, (b) develop tolerance for error making, and (c) learn to adjust strategies when faced with failure. To deprive the most talented students of these opportunities is perhaps the greatest resource-development crime a country can commit.

Fifth, summative evaluation procedures should include "retake exams." Second chances will not only encourage risk taking but will provide good reasons for students to study their incorrect responses made on previous risk-taking tasks. Every error made on an initial exam and subsequently corrected on a second chance represents real learning.

Sixth, we must reinforce moderate academic risk taking instead of error-free performance or excessively high or low risk taking. Improvement scores, voluntary correction of errors, completion of optional risk-taking activities—these are behaviors that teachers should recognize and encourage.

Toward a New Definition of Success

We face the grim reality that our extraordinary efforts to produce "schools without failure" have not yielded the well-adjusted, enthusiastic, self-confident scholars we anticipated. Our efforts to mass-produce success for every individual in every educational situation have left us with cheap reproductions of success that do not even faintly represent the real thing. This overdose of synthetic success is a primary cause of the student apathy and school abandonment plaguing our country.

To turn the trend around, we must emphasize error tolerance, not error-free learning; reward error correction, not error avoidance; ensure challenge, not easy success. Eventual success on challenging tasks, tolerance for error making, and constructive responses to failure are motivational fare that

school systems should be serving up to all students. I suggest that we engage the skills of researchers, textbook authors, publishers, and educators across the country to ensure the development and marketing of attractive and effective academic risk-taking materials and procedures. If we convince these experts of the need to employ their creative efforts toward this end, we will not only stem the tide of educational suicide, but we will enhance the quality of educational success. We will witness self-regulated student success and satisfaction that will ensure the intellectual, creative, and motivational well-being of our country.

References

Atkinson, J.W. (1964). *An Introduction to Motivation.* Princeton, N.J.: Van Nostrand.

Boggiano, A.K., and D.S. Main. (1986). "Enhancing Children's Interest in Activities Used as Rewards: The Bonus Effect." *Journal of Personality and Social Psychology* 51: 1116-1126.

Clifford, M.M. (1988). "Failure Tolerance and Academic Risk Taking in Ten- to Twelve-Year-Old Students." *British Journal of Educational Psychology* 58: 15–27.

Csikszentmihalyi, M. (1975). *Beyond Boredom and Anxiety.* San Francisco: Jossey-Bass.

Csikszentimihalyi, M. (1978). "Intrinsic Rewards and Emergent Motivation." In *The Hidden Costs of Reward*, edited by M.R. Lepper and D. Greene. N.J.: Lawrence Erlbaum Associates.

Danner, F.W., and D. Lonky. (1981). "A Cognitive-Developmental Approach to the Effects of Rewards on Intrinsic Motivation." *Child Development* 52: 1043-1052.

Deci, E.L., and J. Porac. (1978). "Cognitive Evaluation Theory and the Study of Human Motivation." In *The Hidden Costs of Reward*, edited by M.R. Lepper and D. Greene. Hillsdale, N.J.: Lawrence Erlbaum Associates.

Deci, E.L., and R.M. Ryan. (1987). "The Support of Autonomy and the Control of Behavior." *Journal of Personality and Social Psychology* 53: 1024-1037.

Fischer, K.W. (1980). "Learning as the Development of Organized Behavior." *Journal of Structural Learning* 3: 253–267.

Hahn, A. (1987). "Reaching Out to America's Dropouts: What to Do?" *Phi Delta Kappan* 69: 256–263.

Harter, S. (1978). "Effectance Motivation Reconsidered: Toward a Developmental Model." *Human Development* 1: 34–64.

Ilgen, D.R., and C.F. Moore. (1987). "Types and Choices of Performance Feedback." *Journal of Applied Psychology* 72: 401–406.

Ilgen, D.R., C.D. Fischer, and M.S. Taylor. (1979). "Consequences of Individual Feedback on Behavior in Organizations." *Journal of Applied Psychology* 64: 349–371.

Kruglanski, A., C. Stein, and A. Riter. (1977). "Contingencies of Exogenous Reward and Task Performance: On the 'Minimax' Strategy in Instrumental Behavior." *Journal of Applied Social Psychology* 2: 141–148.

Larson, J.R., Jr. (1984). "The Performance Feedback Process: A Preliminary Model." *Organizational Behavior and Human Performance* 33: 42–76.

Lepper, M.R., and D. Greene. (1978). *The Hidden Costs of Reward*. Hillsdale, N.J.: Lawrence Erlbaum Associates.

Lepper, M.R., and M. Hodell. (1989). "Intrinsic Motivation in the Classroom." In *Motivation in Education, Vol. 3*, edited by C. Ames and R. Ames. N.Y.: Academic Press.

Sansone, C. (1986). "A Question of Competence: The Effects of Competence and Task Feedback on Intrinsic Motivation." *Journal of Personality and Social Psychology* 51: 918–931.

Trope, Y. (1979). "Uncertainty Reducing Properties of Achievement Tasks." *Journal of Personality and Social Psychology* 37: 1505-1518.

GOOD TEACHERS DON'T WORRY ABOUT
DISCIPLINE

Behavior is rarely a problem when effective teaching is taking place.

T. R. Ellis

T. R. Ellis is curriculum coordinator of the Lawrenceburg Community Schools in Lawrenceburg, Indiana. This article is adapted from a presentation delivered at the Indiana Department of Education's Prime Time Fair in New Albany, Indiana, August 1988.

Discipline in the classroom has become big business. Many companies are marketing workshops, audiocassettes, videocassettes, filmstrips, workbooks, and texts, each designed to instruct teachers how to control student behavior so that effective teaching can occur.

They just may have that backwards!

Eleven years as an elementary school principal taught me many things, but no lesson clearer than this: the most effective teachers have the fewest discipline problems.

Control of student behavior *is* important. No one can teach well when students have their own agenda, and you will find no argument here in favor of disbanding whatever discipline programs you or your school have adapted. Structured discipline programs do accomplish an important educational goal: they make ineffective teachers less ineffective. But they do little to help teachers who are already effective, because those teachers need very little help.

Of all the sad stories circulating about the state of public school education today, the saddest may be the ascendancy of student discipline gurus. Their very popularity serves as a severe indictment of our profession. When Lee Canter claims that 500,000 educators use his assertive discipline methods, we must ask why so many of our peers need such a crutch to gain control over students.

A much more positive emphasis is found in the work being done in the area of effective teaching and mastery learning by John B. Carroll, Benjamin Bloom, Madeline Hunter, Marie Carbo, and many others. In their efforts to describe effective teaching, they make little mention of student discipline. There is an inherent understanding that when the learning is meaningful, the motivation provided, and the teaching appropriate, discipline problems seldom occur.

Controlling student behavior through effective teaching requires skills that are developed through a two-step process: knowledge followed by practice. Unfortunately, most educators perform those steps backwards; they learn by trial and error—mostly the latter. How much better for their students if they followed the correct procedure: first learn what effective teaching is, then practice until they become skillful.

As a supervising principal in two different school systems, I have observed and evaluated scores of teachers over the years. Three of them were so inept they were fired. Several others received strongly worded directives to shape up or ship out. Most of the others, however, were very effective teachers and I learned something from each of them.

Getting Started

Getting the lesson off to a good start is as important in teaching as being on the first horse out of the gate at the Kentucky Derby. Yet, legions of teachers start every lesson with a fizzle like this: "All right, class. Open your books to page 39. Who will read first?" The most highly motivated student in the class cannot get very excited about page 39 after an introduction like that.

Madeline Hunter suggests the use of an anticipatory set for motivation and a written objective for the lesson that provides a reason for learning. One teacher who uses this technique starts every lesson with a challenge like, "Think of an important thing we learned in yesterday's lesson, then whisper it to your neighbor." While this thinking and telling is going on, the

The Dos and Don'ts of Teaching

Effective Practices	Ineffective Practices
Start every lesson with an anticipatory set (motivation to learn) and a written list of objectives (reason to learn).	"Ok, class, it's time for health. Open your books to page 39. Who remembers where we left off?"
Target individual students for performance. ("Johnny, you think about that question and try to remember. I want you to answer that before we finish.")	"Johnny, what's the answer?" (Pause two seconds.) "Sara, can you tell us?" (Pause one second.) "Hasn't anyone been paying attention in here?"
Ask How, Why, and If questions.	Ask only Who, What, When, and Where questions.
Check frequently for learning. Examples: Have each student write the answer to a question and pass it to a neighbor for checking. Or, call five or six students at random to write their answers on the board simultaneously.	Just keep plodding along in order to cover the material. Assign seatwork, paperwork, workbook pages, and unreadable ditto papers that keep the students quiet and out of your hair.
Be confident and welcome observation, particularly if constructive feedback follows.	Keep the door closed and direct very hard stare at anyone brave enough to enter, including the principal. Never ask for advice or help.
Be positive. Have high expectations for all students. ("Everyone will learn in this class, including me.")	Be negative. ("No one could teach those bozos. When's our next holiday?")
Give appropriate, personalized praise. ("Mary, you raised an interesting point. I like the connection you made.")	Give either the same praise ("Good," "OK," "Great"), undeserved praise, or no praise at all.
Provide constructive criticism and direction. Be polite while being assertive.	Use sarcasm and insults. Make punishment humiliating. Yell and scream your expectations of polite behavior.
Catch students being good and give them public recognition.	Catch students being bad and publicly embarrass them.
Expect all students to perform every day. Provide opportunities for success.	Expect only your best students to perform. Don't call on the slow learners.
Energize the class. Move around the room. Be ready to provide immediate feedback on written work.	Sit at your desk. Supervise by yelling out names. Make seatwork an individual activity with no teacher assistance.
Show personal regard for all students.	Make a big deal about Mary's vacation in Hawaii. Ignore Sam's camping trip.

teacher writes on the board one or two clear objectives for that day's lesson. Then, signaling quiet with one word—"Ready?"—she reads what she has written: "Today we will learn, starting on page 39, why . . ."

Students in that class expect a connection between thinking, recalling, anticipating, and learning. They know that learning is an overt activity and that it takes more effort than simply opening their books to the current page. They also know that the teacher expects *everyone* to recall an important part of yesterday's lesson, not just the class apple shiners with their hands raised.

Raising Expectations

For educators, the expression, "What you see is what you get," needs to be rephrased to read: "What you *expect* is what you get." We typically have low levels of expectation for many of our students. We get what we expect.

And yet, Benjamin S. Bloom says, ". . . it is difficult to conceive of any single learning task which is beyond the capabilities of most human beings who wish to learn it and who have been properly prepared for it" (Bloom 1982).

Japanese parents *expect* their chil-

dren to achieve. When they don't, their parents blame lack of *effort*.

American parents *hope* their children will achieve. When they don't, their parents blame lack of *aptitude*.

I have observed a teacher who expects all students in his class to master each learning task and who conducts the process of instruction to guarantee that outcome. It's amazing the amount of learning mastered by the "slow" students in that class. The teacher is not a magician; he is a master teacher, as these observation notes attest:

Billy seems confused and cannot respond. The teacher keeps him after the others have gone to recess. He gives individual tutoring, then lets Billy practice the skill at the board. Then, while the others are still away, he teaches Billy the next lesson and lets him know that he will be the first student called upon to respond the next day and that Billy will be his "star" pupil, since the others have not learned the lesson yet. Billy's performance the next day recovers his peer image as a worthy learner and motivates him for further success.

Meeting Student Needs

The most useless piece of furniture in an effective classroom is the teacher's chair. Teaching from the seat of one's pants is not teaching at all, but uttering.

I have seen a teacher who never pulls her chair away from the desk unless she has to open the top drawer. Once the lesson is delivered and independent practice assigned, she flitters around the room, assisting here, checking there, questioning this one, and encouraging that one. Her students see effort being modeled and they are secure in their belief that the teacher will help.

B. F. Skinner calls such behavior "immediate feedback." Bloom calls the same behavior "feedback and corrective instruction," a critical part of the quality of instruction portion of his learning model. As far as the teacher is concerned, she is simply meeting her students' needs.

Motivating and Reinforcing

Teaching in a classroom where little effort is applied to motivation and reinforcement is like pulling teeth, without the blood.

Students are curious creatures who love to learn. The trick is getting them to learn what the teacher is teaching. To succeed in that task requires motivation and reinforcement.

Motivation is complex. What motivates one student bores another. The same is true of reinforcement. Although the standard tricks of the trade include individual praise and recognition, too many teachers limit themselves to such expressions as "Good," "OK," "Great," "Nice job."

Praise and recognition must be personal to be effective: "Mary, that was a unique interpretation. Thank you for that insight." Even more effective is praise that specifically reminds the class of the lesson: "Bob just explained in his own words that a country is a political division of land, while a continent is a geographical division of land."

Madeline Hunter carries this point of reinforcement even further with her idea of "dignifying errors." Thus, even wrong answers can be accepted—and add to the learning—by correcting with dignity: "The answer you gave, Helen, correctly answers the question of why Columbus sailed west to go to the East Indies. But how did he discover America? Will you try again?"

Another common practice by teachers to reinforce student effort is their habit of displaying student papers on the walls. Unfortunately, this practice stops being reinforcing with overuse. Recognition should be special. Call everyone's attention to Susie's perfect paper. Make a big deal out of Rob's rock collection.

One teacher, after reading *Tom Sawyer* to the class, found that his students were intrigued by the idea of Tom earning "white tickets" for memorizing bible verses. That was a perfect introduction to a motivation and reinforcement program that kept his students energized all year.

Students earned white tickets for perfect papers, extra projects, special effort, and unexpected good deeds. The tickets could be "cashed in" for various prizes or entitlements. For instance, for a white ticket a child could move his desk to another location, or have one practice assignment canceled, or line up first for lunch, or leave two minutes early for recess, or get a piece of hard candy.

Five white tickets could be traded for one yellow ticket, five yellows for a green, five greens for a red, and five reds for a blue. The tickets became extremely coveted tokens. Monetarily, a white ticket was worth one cent, a yellow worth a nickel, and so on up to the $6.25 value blue ticket. Only three students managed to earn blue tickets over

the course of the year, and two of those three elected *not* to cash them in on the last day of school. They wanted them as keepsakes of a happy, successful school year.

Madeline Hunter refers to such extrinsic rewards as the lowest form of positive reinforcement, and many teachers think of them as a form of bribery. Both points of view have merit, within reason. Students should be taught the pleasure of intrinsic rewards, for example, knowledge, good grades, praise, recognition, and pride. At the same time, however, an appropriate extrinsic reward can go a long way toward motivating student effort.

Using Learning Styles

Students are not all alike. We cannot make them alike, nor should we try. Students have suffered many injustices over the years from teachers unwilling to tolerate differences. Because they are different, and not because they are handicapped in any way, hundreds of students are labeled under one or another special education category each year.

Teachers often impose ridiculous rules that reduce many students to nervous wrecks. Marie Carbo presents a typical example: "Although many of us tell children to sit up and pay attention, there is no direct relationship between how one sits and the amount of concentration devoted to what is being studied" (Carbo, Dunn, and Dunn 1986). So why hassle the kid?

Tactile learners probably suffer the most humiliation in our schools. They need to touch. They count on their fingers. Teachers hate kids who count on their fingers. They believe it represents ignorance. All it represents is a learning style.

I had a teacher who repeatedly berated a boy for counting on his fingers. "Put your hands flat on your desk," she would say. The child started bouncing his fingers. "Hold those fingers still," she yelled. The child started tapping his feet. "Hold your feet still," she shrieked.

The child's mother eventually brought him to me for after-school tutoring. He could not, said his mother, learn his math facts. As I flashed the facts cards to this nervous boy I was fascinated and saddened to watch his facial contortions. He looked to be in pain.

Do you know what he was doing? He was counting his teeth with his tongue! He could figure 8 times 9 in a few seconds by tapping his thumb against the fingers of his right hand. Can you do that? I can't! Yet we had turned this handsome youngster into a facial contortionist because we could not tolerate his learning style.

There are several learning styles programs that deserve your attention. *The 4 MAT System* by Bernice McCarthy is very thorough and Carbo's book, *Teaching Students to Read Through*

Their Individual Learning Styles, co-authored with Rita and Kenneth Dunn, is great.

Even without a formal learning styles program, teachers should lighten up and be tolerant of different preferences. Allow children to learn in whatever way is least painful to them. Then, both teachers and students will suffer fewer frustrations.

∽

Students consistently behave better in classrooms where effective teachers rule, and it goes without saying that students deserve effective teachers. As Bloom has written, ". . . the schools can provide the best of education for virtually all of their students—if the schools choose to do so" (Bloom 1982).

We cannot humanely choose any alternative.

REFERENCES

Bloom, Benjamin S. *Human Characteristics and School Learning.* New York: McGraw-Hill, 1982.

Bloom, Benjamin S. "The New Direction in Educational Research: Alterable Variables." *Phi Delta Kappan,* February 1980.

Carbo, Marie; Dunn, Rita; and Dunn, Kenneth. *Teaching Students to Read Through Their Individual Learning Styles.* Englewood Cliffs, New Jersey: Prentice-Hall, 1986.

Carroll, J. B. "A Model of School Learning." *Teachers College Record,* May 1963.

Holly, William J. "Students' Self-Esteem and Academic Achievement." *Research Roundup* (NAESP), November 1987.

McKeachie, W. J. "The Decline and Fall of the Laws of Learning." *Educational Researcher,* March 1974.

Kerman, Sam; Kimball, Tom; and Martin, Mary. *Teacher Expectations and Student Achievement.* Bloomington, Ind.: Phi Delta Kappa, 1980.

Assertive Discipline — More Than Names on the Board and Marbles in a Jar

Mr. Canter explains the background of the program and addresses some of the issues that are frequently raised about Assertive Discipline.

LEE CANTER

LEE CANTER is president of Lee Canter & Associates, Santa Monica, Calif. He is the author of many books on behavior management and is the developer of the Assertive Discipline program.

ABOUT A YEAR ago I was on an airline flight, seated next to a university professor. When he found out that I had developed the Assertive Discipline program, he said, "Oh, that's where all you do is write the kids' names on the board when they're bad and drop marbles in the jar when they're good."

The university professor's response disturbed me. For some time I've been concerned about a small percentage of educators — this professor apparently among them — who have interpreted my program in a way that makes behavior management sound simplistic. More important, I'm concerned with their misguided emphasis on providing only negative consequences when students misbehave. The key to dealing effectively with student behavior is not negative — but positive — consequences. To clarify my views for *Kappan* readers, I would like to explain the background of the program and address some of the issues that are often raised about Assertive Discipline.

I developed the program about 14 years

> **The key to Assertive Discipline is catching students being good — and letting them know that you like it.**

ago, when I first became aware that teachers were not trained to deal with student behavior. Teachers were taught such concepts as "Don't smile until Christmas" or "If your curriculum is good enough, you will have no behavior problems." Those concepts were out of step with the

reality of student behavior in the 1970s.

When I discovered this lack of training, I began to study how effective teachers dealt with student behavior. I found that, above all, the master teachers were assertive; that is, they *taught* students how to behave. They established clear rules for the classroom, they communicated those rules to the students, and they taught the students how to follow them. These effective teachers had also mastered skills in positive reinforcement, and they praised every student at least once a day. Finally, when students chose to break the rules, these teachers used firm and consistent negative consequences — but only as a last resort.

It troubles me to find my work interpreted as suggesting that teachers need only provide negative consequences — check marks or demerits — when students misbehave. That interpretation is wrong. The key to Assertive Discipline is catching students being good: recognizing and supporting them when they behave appropriately and letting them know you like it, day in and day out.

From *Phi Delta Kappan*, September 1989, pp. 57–61. Reprinted by permission of *Phi Delta Kappan* and the author.

THE DISCIPLINE PLAN

It is vital for classroom teachers to have a systematic discipline plan that explains exactly what will happen when students choose to misbehave. By telling the students at the beginning of the school year what the consequences will be, teachers insure that all students know what to expect in the classroom. Without a plan, teachers must choose an appropriate consequence at the moment when a student misbehaves. They must stop the lesson, talk to the misbehaving student, and do whatever else the situation requires, while 25 to 30 students look on. That is not an effective way to teach — or to deal with misbehavior.

Most important, without a plan teachers tend to be inconsistent. One day they may ignore students who are talking, yelling, or disrupting the class. The next day they may severely discipline students for the same behaviors. In addition, teachers may respond differently to students from different socioeconomic, ethnic, or racial backgrounds.

An effective discipline plan is applied fairly to all students. Every student who willfully disrupts the classroom and stops the teacher from teaching suffers the same consequence. And a written plan can be sent home to parents, who then know beforehand what the teacher's standards are and what will be done when students choose to misbehave. When a teacher calls a parent, there should be no surprises.

MISBEHAVIOR AND CONSEQUENCES

I suggest that a discipline plan include a maximum of five consequences for misbehavior, but teachers must choose consequences with which they are comfortable. For example, the first time a student breaks a rule, the student is warned. The second infraction brings a 10-minute timeout; the third infraction, a 15-minute timeout. The fourth time a student breaks a rule, the teacher calls the parents; the fifth time, the student goes to the principal.

No teacher should have a plan that is not appropriate for his or her needs and that is not in the best interests of the students. Most important, the consequences should never be psychologically or physically harmful to the students. Students should never be made to stand in front of the class as objects of ridicule or be degraded in any other way. Nor should they be given consequences that are inappropriate for their grade levels. I also feel strongly that corporal punishment

should *never* be administered. There are more effective ways of dealing with students than hitting them.

Names and checks on the board are sometimes said to be essential to an Assertive Discipline program, but they are not. I originally suggested this particular practice because I had seen teachers interrupt their lessons to make such negative comments to misbehaving students as, "You talked out again. I've had it. You're impossible. That's 20 minutes after school." I wanted to eliminate the need to stop the lesson and issue reprimands. Writing a student's name on the board would warn the student in a calm, non-degrading manner. It would also provide a record-keeping system for the teacher.

Unfortunately, some parents have mis-

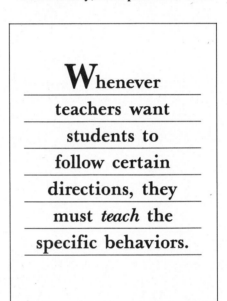

> **W**henever teachers want students to follow certain directions, they must *teach* the specific behaviors.

interpreted the use of names and checks on the board as a way of humiliating students. I now suggest that teachers instead write an offending student's name on a clipboard or in the roll book and say to the student, "You talked out, you disrupted the class, you broke a rule. That's a warning. That's a check."

In addition to parents, some teachers have misinterpreted elements of the Assertive Discipline program. The vast majority of teachers — my staff and I have probably trained close to 750,000 teachers — have used the program to dramatically increase their reliance on positive reinforcement and verbal praise. But a small percentage of teachers have interpreted the program in a negative manner.

There are several reasons for this. First, Assertive Discipline has become a generic term, like Xerox or Kleenex. A number of educators are now conducting training in what they call Assertive Dis-

cipline without teaching *all* the competencies essential to my program. For example, I have heard reports of teachers who were taught that they had only to stand in front of their students, tell them that there were rules and consequences, display a chart listing those rules and consequences, and write the names of misbehaving students on the board. That was it. Those teachers were never introduced to the concept that positive reinforcement is the key to dealing with students. Such programs are not in the best interests of students.

Negative interpretations have also come from burned-out, overwhelmed teachers who feel they do not get the support that they need from parents or administrators and who take out their frustrations on students. Assertive Discipline is not a negative program, but it can be misused by negative teachers. The answer is not to change the program, but to change the teachers. We need to train administrators, mentor teachers, and staff developers to coach negative teachers in the use of positive reinforcement. If these teachers cannot become more positive, they should not be teaching.

POSITIVE DISCIPLINE

I recommend a three-step cycle of behavior management to establish a positive discipline system.

First, whenever teachers want students to follow certain directions, they must *teach* the specific behaviors. Teachers too often assume that students know how they are expected to behave. Teachers first need to establish specific directions for each activity during the day — lectures, small-group work, transitions between activities, and so forth. For each situation, teachers must determine the *exact* behaviors they expect from the students.

For example, teachers may want students to stay in their seats during a lecture, focusing their eyes on the lecturer, clearing their desks of all materials except paper and pencil, raising their hands when they have questions or comments, and waiting to be called on before speaking. Once teachers have determined the specific behaviors for each situation, they must teach the students how to follow the directions. They must first state the directions and, with younger students, write the behaviors on the board or on a flip chart. Then they must model the behaviors, ask the students to *restate* the directions, question the students to make sure they understand the directions, and immediately engage the students in the activity to make sure that they understand the directions.

Second, after teaching the specific directions, teachers — especially at the elementary level — must use *positive repetition* to reinforce the students when they follow the directions. Typically, teachers give directions to the students and then focus attention only on those students who do *not* obey. ("Bobby, you didn't go back to your seat. Teddy, what's wrong with you? Get back to work.") Instead, teachers should focus on those students who do follow the directions, rephrasing the original directions as a positive comment. For example, "Jason went back to his seat and got right to work."

Third, if a student is still misbehaving after a teacher has taught specific directions and has used positive repetition, only then should the teacher use the negative consequences outlined in his or her Assertive Discipline plan. As a general rule, a teacher shouldn't administer a disciplinary consequence to a student until the teacher has reinforced at least two students for the appropriate behavior. Effective teachers are always positive first. Focusing on negative behavior teaches students that negative behavior gets attention, that the teacher is a negative person, and that the classroom is a negative place.

An effective behavior management program must be built on choice. Students must know beforehand what is expected of them in the classroom, what will happen if they choose to behave, and what will happen if they choose not to behave. Students learn self-discipline and responsible behavior by being given clear, consistent choices. They learn that their actions have an impact and that they themselves control the consequences.

I wish teachers did not need to use negative consequences at all. I wish all students came to school motivated to learn. I wish all parents supported teachers and administrators. But that's not the reality today. Many children do not come to school intrinsically motivated to behave. Their parents have never taken the time or don't have the knowledge or skills to teach them how to behave. Given these circumstances, teachers need to set firm and consistent limits in their classrooms. However, those limits must be fair, and the consequences must be seen as outcomes of behaviors that students have *chosen*.

Students need teachers who can create classroom environments in which teaching and learning can take place. Every student has the right to a learning environment that is free from disruption.

Students also need teachers who help them learn how to behave appropriately in school. Many students who are categorized as behavior problems would not be so labeled if their teachers had taught them how to behave appropriately in the classroom and had raised their self-esteem.

WHY ASSERTIVE DISCIPLINE?

The average teacher never receives in-depth, competency-based training in managing the behavior of 30 students. No one teaches teachers how to keep students in their seats long enough for teachers to make good use of the skills they learned in their education classes. In most in-

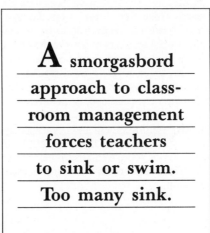

A smorgasbord approach to classroom management forces teachers to sink or swim. Too many sink.

stances, behavior management is taught through a smorgasbord approach — a little bit of William Glasser, a little bit of Thomas Gordon, a little bit of Rudolf Dreikurs, a little bit of Lee Canter. The teachers are told to find an approach that works for them.

Such an approach to training teachers in behavior management is analogous to a swimming class in which nonswimmers are briefly introduced — without practice — to the crawl stroke, the breast stroke, the back stroke, and the side stroke; then they are rowed to the middle of a lake, tossed overboard, and told to swim to shore, using whatever stroke works for them. In effect, we're telling teachers to sink or swim, and too many teachers are sinking.

The lack of ability to manage student behavior is one of the key reasons why beginning teachers drop out of teaching. Teachers must be trained thoroughly in classroom management skills. It is not sufficient for them to know how to teach content. They will never get to the content unless they know how to create a

positive environment in which students know how to behave.

Assertive Discipline is not a cure-all. It is a starting point. Every teacher should also know how to use counseling skills, how to use group process skills, and how to help students with behavioral deficits learn appropriate classroom behaviors. In addition, classroom management must be part of an educator's continuing professional development. Teachers routinely attend workshops, enroll in college courses, receive feedback from administrators, and take part in regular inservice training to refine their teaching skills. Classroom management skills deserve the same attention. Unfortunately, some educators view training in Assertive Discipline as a one-shot process; they attend a one-day workshop, and that's supposed to take care of their training needs for the rest of their careers.

One day is not enough. It takes a great deal of effort and continuing training for a teacher to master the skills of classroom management. A teacher also needs support from the building administrator. Without an administrator backing a teacher's efforts to improve behavior management, without an administrator to coach and clinically supervise a teacher's behavior management skills, that teacher is not going to receive the necessary feedback and assistance to master those skills.

Parental support for teachers' disciplinary efforts is equally important. Many teachers become frustrated and give up when they don't receive such support. We must train teachers to guarantee the support of parents by teaching teachers how to communicate effectively with parents. In teacher training programs, participants are led to believe that today's parents will act as parents did in the past and give absolute support to the school. That is rarely the case. Today's teachers call parents and are told, "He's your problem at school. You handle it. You're the professional. You take care of him. I don't know what to do. Leave me alone."

RESEARCH AND ASSERTIVE DISCIPLINE

Over the last several years, a number of dissertations, master's theses, and research projects have dealt with Assertive Discipline. The results have consistently shown that teachers dramatically improve student behavior when they use the skills as prescribed. Teachers who use Assertive Discipline reduce the frequency of disruptive behavior in their classrooms, greatly reduce the number of students they refer to administrators, and dramatically increase their students' time-on-task.[1] Other research has demonstrated that student teachers trained in Assertive Discipline are evaluated by their master teachers as more effective in classroom management.[2] Research conducted in school districts in California, Oregon, Ohio, and Arizona has shown that an overwhelming majority of teachers believe that Assertive Discipline helps to improve the climate in the schools and the behavior of students.[3]

No one should be surprised that research has verified the success of the program when teachers use the skills properly. Numerous research studies have shown that teachers need to teach students the specific behaviors that they expect from them. Research also shows that student behavior improves when teachers use positive reinforcement effectively and that the pairing of positive reinforcement with consistent disciplinary consequences effectively motivates students to behave appropriately.[4]

Any behavior management program that is taught to teachers today must have a solid foundation in research. Many so-called "experts" advocate programs that are based solely on their own opinions regarding what constitutes a proper classroom environment. When pressed, many of these experts have no research validating their opinions or perceptions, and many of their programs have never been validated for effectiveness in classrooms. We can't afford to train educators in programs based only on whim or untested theory. We have an obligation to insure that any training program in behavior management be based solidly on techniques that have been validated by research and that have been shown to work in the classroom.

Research has demonstrated that Assertive Discipline works and that it isn't just a quick-fix solution. In school districts in Lennox, California, and Troy, Ohio, teachers who were trained 10 years ago still use the program effectively.[5] The program works because it is based on practices that effective teachers have followed instinctively for a long time. It's not new to have rules in a classroom. It's not new to use positive reinforcement. It's not new to have disciplinary consequences.

Teachers who are effective year after year take the basic Assertive Discipline competencies and mold them to their individual teaching styles. They may stop using certain techniques, such as putting marbles in a jar or writing names on the board. That's fine. I don't want the legacy of Assertive Discipline to be — and I don't want teachers to believe they have to use — names and checks on the board or marbles in a jar. I want teachers to learn that they have to take charge, explain their expectations, be positive with students, and consistently employ both positive reinforcement and negative consequences. These are the skills that form the basis of Assertive Discipline and of any effective program of classroom management.

1. Linda H. Mandlebaum et al., "Assertive Discipline: An Effective Behavior Management Program," Behavioral Disorders Journal, vol. 8, 1983, pp. 258-64; Carl L. Fereira, "A Positive Approach to Assertive Discipline," Martinez (Calif.) Unified School District, ERIC ED 240 058, 1983; and Sammie McCormack, "Students' Off-Task Behavior and Assertive Discipline" (Doctoral dissertation, University of Oregon, 1985).

2. Susan Smith, "The Effects of Assertive Discipline Training on Student Teachers' Self Concept and Classroom Management Skills" (Doctoral dissertation, University of South Carolina, 1983).

3. Kenneth L. Moffett et al., "Assertive Discipline," California School Board Journal, June/July/August 1982, pp. 24-27; Mark Y. Swanson, "Assessment of the Assertive Discipline Program," Compton (Calif.) Unified School District, Spring 1984; "Discipline Report," Cartwright (Ariz.) Elementary School District, 10 February 1982; and Confederation of Oregon School Administrators, personal letter, 28 April 1980.

4. Helen Hair et al., "Development of Internal Structure in Elementary Students: A System of Classroom Management and Class Control," ERIC ED 189 067, 1980; Edmund Emmer and Carolyn Everston, "Effective Management: At the Beginning of the School Year in Junior High Classes," Research and Development Center for Teacher Education, University of Texas, Austin, 1980; Marcia Broden et al., "Effects of Teacher Attention on Attending Behavior of Two Boys at Adjacent Desks," Journal of Applied Behavior Analysis, vol. 3, 1970, pp. 205-11; Hill Walker et al., "The Use of Normative Peer Data as a Standard for Evaluating Treatment Effects," Journal of Applied Behavior Analysis, vol. 37, 1976, pp. 145-55; Jere Brophy, "Classroom Organization and Management," Elementary School Journal, vol. 83, 1983, pp. 265-85; Hill Walker et al., "Experiments with Response Cost in Playground and Classroom Settings," Center for Research in Behavioral Education of the Handicapped, University of Oregon, Eugene, 1977; Thomas McLaughlin and John Malaby, "Reducing and Measuring Inappropriate Verbalizations," Journal of Applied Behavior Analysis, vol. 5, 1972, pp. 329-33; Charles Madsen et al., "Rules, Praise, and Ignoring: Elements of Elementary Classroom Control," Journal of Applied Behavior Analysis, vol. 1, 1968, pp. 139-50; Charles Greenwood et al., "Group Contingencies for Group Consequences in Classroom Management: A Further Analysis," Journal of Applied Behavior Analysis, vol. 7, 1974, pp. 413-25; and K. Daniel O'Leary et al., "A Token Reinforcement Program in a Public School: A Replication and Systematic Analysis," Journal of Applied Behavior Analysis, vol. 2, 1969, pp. 3-13.

5. Kenneth L. Moffett et al., "Training and Coaching Beginning Teachers: An Antidote to Reality Shock," Educational Leadership, February 1987, pp. 34-46; and Bob Murphy, "Troy High School: An Assertive Model," Miami Valley Sunday News, Troy, Ohio, 12 March 1989, p. 1.

ORDER in the CLASSROOM

Some teachers swear by Lee Canter's Assertive Discipline system. But if it's so good, why do critics call it "dehumanizing," "humiliating," even "dangerous"?

DAVID HILL

LINDA DARLING-HAMMOND HAD never heard of Assertive Discipline until her daughter, Elena, entered kindergarten two years ago. When she came home from school, Elena had plenty of stories to tell her mother, but they weren't the kind of stories Darling-Hammond expected to hear. Instead of being about new friends and new things to learn, Elena's accounts of her first days at Takoma Park (Md.) Elementary School focused on which kids in her class were being punished—and how. The teacher, Elena told her mother, wrote the names of the "bad" kids on the blackboard, which meant they could have certain privileges taken away from them. Elena wasn't among the "bad" kids; in fact, she brought home happy-face stickers because she had been "good." Yet she was frightened of what could happen if she played with the kids who had been punished.

"She was so terrified by the prospect of having her name placed on the board, being held in from recess, or being excluded from class activities that she stopped participating in class," says Darling-Hammond, an educational researcher for the RAND Corporation at the time and now a professor at Columbia University's Teachers College.

When Darling-Hammond went to observe her daughter's classroom, she learned that the teacher was using a system called Assertive Discipline, developed in the 1970's by Lee and Marlene Canter and now used in many schools across the country. The highly structured system, a mixture of common sense and behavior-modification techniques, stresses rewards and punishments as a way for teachers to "take charge" of their classrooms. Many teachers and administrators swear by it, but Darling-Hammond was appalled by what she witnessed:

"I saw a group of small children trying hard not to move or speak; a young, inexperienced, and unmentored teacher trying religiously to apply rewards and consequences. The list of names on the board grew

From *Teacher Magazine*, April 1990, pp. 70-73, 75-77. Copyright © 1990 by Editorial Projects in Education. Reprinted by permission.

whenever someone wiggled or spoke. The children appeared unhappy and confused. The stickers did not do much to offset their distress, since many of the children who got them felt bad about the children who didn't. Virtually all of the 'offenders' that day were boys; most of them were black. None of them had done anything that I could term 'misbehaving' during my visit. But they had broken rules forbidding talking and moving; i.e., normal 5-year-old behavior."

Takoma Park Elementary School no longer uses Assertive Discipline. And Lee Canter no longer advocates the discipline technique of writing down names on the blackboard. "People such as Linda Darling-Hammond interpret that as something that could be psychologically harmful to the kids," says Canter. "Personally, I don't think it is, but I have come out in all my latest materials saying that teachers should not use it. I think especially with kindergarten kids, I would not write their names on the board."

Darling-Hammond isn't the only critic of Assertive Discipline. In recent years, many educators and child psychologists have spoken out against the technique, calling it, among other things, "dehumanizing," "humiliating," and "dangerous." Yet it remains popular; Canter says that more than 750,000 teachers have been trained in Assertive Discipline during the last 15 years, and his company, Lee Canter & Associates, has grown from a mom-and-pop operation to a multimillion-dollar enterprise, with 75 full- and part-time employees. Proponents of Assertive Discipline speak of it as if it were the greatest thing since sliced bread. The bottom line, they say, is that it works. One middle school principal who recently began using Assertive Discipline at his school goes so far as to call it "a godsend."

I N A MODEST, WINDOWLESS office in Santa Monica, Calif., Lee Canter is explaining to a visitor the genesis of Assertive Discipline. If Canter were a student, he would no doubt get a happy-face sticker, his office is so tidy. On one wall, between two shelves of neatly arranged books, is a cartoon that depicts the kind of fantasy a teacher might have after an especially bad day. In it, a plump, innocent-looking teacher with glasses faces her wide-eyed students and says: "Good morning, children. My name is Miss Applegate. One false move and I'll kill you."

Despite waking up with a stomach virus, Canter, 43, is animated and energetic, constantly emphasizing his points with his hands. He often gives motivational speeches to teachers and principals, and his speaking experience shows, even in a one-on-one situation.

Canter received a master's degree in social work from the University of Southern California in 1970, and says he got most of the ideas for Assertive Discipline while working as a guidance counselor, helping parents and teachers deal with problem children. "I saw what was going on in the classroom," he says. "I saw teachers coming home every night so frustrated, kids not getting the opportunity they needed to learn, and I just sat down with my wife and said, 'We've got to do something about it.' And we came up with ideas that obviously worked.

"I think they probably worked because they're based upon nothing really new. I get a lot of credit for Assertive Discipline, and I get a lot of blame for it from people who don't like it. But there's nothing really brand new in this program. Throughout history, teachers have told kids what they wanted them to do, have had rules for the classroom, have established consequences if you break the rules, and have had positive consequences when you're good. All I really did was to put it together in a package.

"I watched a lot of effective teachers. I went into classrooms, and I sat down and watched teachers who did not have discipline problems. Number one, they were assertive. That meant they clearly and firmly told their kids what they wanted. They were positive with the kids, very straightforward. When the kids were good, the teachers would give them a lot of positive support. If the kids chose not to behave, the teachers would discipline them."

Canter and his wife, Marlene, a former special-education teacher, published *Assertive Discipline: A Take-Charge Approach For Today's Educator* in 1976. The book, now in its 26th printing, remains the basic text for the discipline technique, but Canter's company also publishes a number of other materials for teachers and parents, such as *Positive Reinforcement Activities*, *Homework Without Tears*, and *Assertive Discipline For Parents*. Canter's 25 instructors offer Assertive Discipline workshops all over the country, and there's something for everyone: teachers (K-12), administrators, parents, paraprofessionals, even bus drivers.

Canter says that, in the past, most of the training was done on a schoolwide or districtwide basis, usually in one-day, inservice seminars. (Teachers at Takoma Park Elementary, in fact, were required to be trained in the Assertive Discipline method.) But recently, he says, there has been increased interest in his five-day graduate-level course called "Beyond Assertive Discipline," for which teachers may earn college credit.

Canter promises results, too. Teachers who take the basic one-day training (at an average cost of $28 per person) are told that they will see "an 80 percent reduction in classroom disruptions," "fewer students in the principal's office," "a calm, positive classroom climate conducive to teaching and learning," and "more success in dealing with parents on behavior problems."

Here's how Assertive Discipline works: "Assertive" teachers should (in Canter's words) establish a "systematic discipline plan that explains exactly what will happen when students choose to misbehave." The key, says Canter, is consistency: "An effective discipline is applied fairly to all students."

Canter suggests that the plan include a maximum of five consequences for misbehavior. "For example, the first time a student breaks a rule, the student is warned. The second infraction brings a 10-minute time out [isolation]; the third infraction, a 15-minute time out. The fourth time a student breaks a rule, the teacher calls the parents; the fifth time, the student goes to the principal." Canter says he initially suggested that teachers write students' names on the board because he wanted to eliminate their need to stop the lesson and issue reprimands.

"Writing a student's name on the board would warn the student in a calm, nondegrading manner," Canter says. "It would also provide a record-keeping system for the teacher. Unfortunately, some parents have misinterpreted the use of names and checks on the board as a way of humiliating students. I now suggest that teachers instead write an offending student's name on a clipboard or in the roll book and say to the student, 'You talked out, you disrupted the class, you broke a rule. That's a warning. That's a check.' "

At the same time, Canter says that teachers should reward those students who obey the rules. He suggests, for example, that teachers drop marbles into a jar every time a student does something positive; when the jar is full, the entire class is rewarded by, say, 10 minutes of free time at the end of the day. Canter suggests that students be rewarded with material objects, such as cookies, ice cream, or even a hamburger from McDonald's.

"An effective behavior-management program must be built on choice," Canter has written. "Students must know beforehand what is expected of them in the classroom, what will happen if they choose to behave, and what will happen if they choose not to behave. Students learn self-discipline and responsible behavior by being given clear, consistent choices. They learn that their actions have an impact and that they themselves control the consequences."

Canter often makes the point that Assertive Discipline is not a cure-all. "This is not a perfect program," he says. "This is not the answer. And I keep saying that, because there are people out there who say, 'This is the answer.' "

Teachers and administrators who use Assertive Discipline *do* tend to gush about its benefits. Charles Warner, principal of Jackie Robinson Middle School in New Haven, Conn., has nothing but praise for the system. "It's fantastic," he says. "We're looking at it as a godsend for us."

Warner says that Jackie Robinson and two New Haven elementary schools (which "feed" students into Jackie Robinson) began using Assertive Discipline last

September. The middle school, he says, is located in a neighborhood with a lot of drug activity, an atmosphere that created "a fair amount of discipline problems" and "hostile children." Teachers at the school used to have their own individual discipline plans. "But we felt that we needed to do something different," says Warner.

Now, students at all three schools know exactly what is expected of them—and what will happen to them if they disobey the rules. "Assertive Discipline gave us consistency," Warner says. "That's one of its highlights." He says there has been "a drastic decrease" in discipline problems since the plan was implemented. "I'm sold on it. I had my reservations at first. I thought it was just another thing to spend money on. But once we had our first training session, I realized it was worth doing."

Henry Rhodes, who teaches 7th grade social studies at Jackie Robinson, agrees. "I couldn't wait to try it," he says. "It's easy to use. It's all spelled out for you."

Critics, however, contend that Assertive Discipline is harmful—to students *and* to teachers—precisely *because* of its apparent simplicity. "It totally dehumanizes the teacher by putting the control into a system," says educator Richard Curwin, co-author (along with Allen Mendler) of *Discipline with Dignity*. "Where's the teacher's judgment? For teachers who are insecure, it has a lot to offer."

Assertive Discipline's main objective, say Curwin and Mendler, is to teach kids to be obedient, not to be responsible for their actions. In their book, they write: "We define obedience as following rules without question, regardless of philosophical beliefs, ideas of right and wrong, instincts and experiences, or values. A student 'does it' because he is told to do it. In the short term, obedience offers teachers relief, a sense of power and control, and an oasis from the constant bombardment of defiance. In the long run, however, obedience leads to student immaturity, a lack of responsibility, an inability to think clearly and critically, and a feeling of helplessness that is manifested by withdrawal, aggressiveness, or power struggles. . . . Obedience models are far more interested in keeping students in line rather than maintaining their dignity."

(Curwin also says that the use of Assertive Discipline is "dying out," a charge that Canter disputes. "Every year, more and more teachers go through the program," Canter says. He estimates that his company will train 85,000 teachers this year; 50,000 of them will take the one-day seminar, while 35,000 of them will take the five-day graduate-level course.)

Linda Darling-Hammond believes that Assertive Discipline is especially harmful to children in the early grades, when they are still developing self-regulatory behavior and social skills. For one thing, she says, the rules Canter recommends are "inappropriate for young children" because "they suggest a curriculum in which conversing and moving about in the classroom are inappropriate and punishable activities." In addition, she says, "Designating children's behavior as 'bad' results for young children in them believing they themselves are bad. Under the age of 11, children cannot generally separate attributions about their behavior from attributions about themselves."

Darling-Hammond also cites research showing that the use of rewards actually *decreases* intrinsic motivation among students. Assertive Discipline, she concludes, "replaces the teaching of values and the development of intrinsic motivation for learning with a control-oriented system of rules and penalties stressing compliance, sanctions, and external motivation."

Canter is accustomed to such criticism. "The whole *point* of Assertive Discipline," he says, "is teaching children responsibility. The way you teach kids to be responsible is by telling them exactly what is expected of them and then giving them a choice. One thing that I've always talked about in my work is that children need to be given a choice." He pauses, assumes the role of an assertive teacher, and addresses me as a student. "Dave, you have a choice. If you choose to yell and stop me from teaching someone else, you choose to have this consequence. On the other hand, if you choose to behave, I will recognize that behavior."

He continues: "So Assertive Discipline is based upon choice. Curwin can say that he views it as an obedience model, but I think it's clearly spelling out to kids what's expected and then giving them a choice. Because how else do you learn responsibility but by making choices, and realizing there are choices in life, and that we have to be responsible for our actions?"

The concept of student choice in Assertive Discipline, contends Vincent Crockenberg, professor of education at the University of California-Davis, is "utterly muddled. It is fraudulent." In a 1982 article in the *California Journal of Teacher Education* titled "Assertive Discipline: A Dissent," Crockenberg pointed out that the notion of "choice" is distorted when children have only two options. "The Canters simply stack the deck in favor of the teachers. They give teachers a simple way out of their difficulties, but at the price of miseducating children by deeply misrepresenting to them what it means to choose to do something which affects others, what it means to act morally."

Crockenberg concluded: "Assertive Discipline is too simple. It 'works,' if it works at all, only by distorting moral language, by pandering to the defensiveness of teachers about their work, and by ignoring or even denying that children have any significant rights or needs that are independent of the needs of the adults who are their teachers. That is just too high a price to pay for order in the classroom."

"The thing that I've found," responds Canter, "is that kids need limits. It's not like you're doing something to harm a child when you give him some structure. We're not talking about hitting kids. We're not talking about verbally degrading kids. We're not talking about saying to kindergarten kids, 'You're going to sit on the rug for an hour.' We're saying there should be some general rules so the kids know there's an adult there who really cares about them. That's what we're after."

Canter claims that Assertive Discipline is "based solidly on techniques that have been shown to work in the classroom," and he even distributes a publication titled *Abstracts of Research Validating Effectiveness of Assertive Discipline*. One study cited, for example, surveyed 129 teachers and 12 principals at three Indiana schools during the 1982-83 school year. Of the respondents, 86 percent said that they liked using Assertive Discipline, and 82 percent said that student behavior at the schools had improved. Yet critics contend that such evidence is scant and, further, that Canter has selectively reported it.

Gary Render, a professor of education at the University of Wyoming, along with Ph.D. candidates Je Nell Padilla and Mark Krank, conducted a study of the existing research on Assertive Discipline and found "a surprising lack of investigation of a program that is being so widely used. The literature supporting Assertive Discipline is not strong or generalizable. Much of it is based on perceptions of teachers, students, parents, and administrators." Their conclusion: "We can find no evidence that Assertive Discipline is an effective approach deserving schoolwide or districtwide adoption."

One of the most troubling aspects of Assertive Discipline is its abuse by some teachers and school districts. In 1983, parents of five children attending Germantown Elementary School in Annapolis, Md., sued the Anne Arundel County Board of Education for $17.3 million, claiming that their children's civil rights were violated when they were placed in solitary confinement for misconduct in 1980 and 1981. One student, 11-year-old Michyle Davis, testified that she was confined for five consecutive days during school hours in a "storage room" with a desk, after she was accused of laughing in class and throwing a chair. The suit also alleged that the children, aged 7 to 12, were discriminated against because they are black.

Ralph McCann Jr., the elementary school's principal at the time, testified that his policy of confining unruly children in isolation rooms was part of Canter's Assertive Discipline program, implemented in 1980 to stem runaway discipline problems at the school. Canter, however, said at the time that Assertive Discipline does not recommend isolating students without adult supervision. When an attorney for the children asked the principal, "Didn't you know that Lee Canter recommended no more than two consecutive hours of in-school suspension for elementary school students?" McCann replied, "No, sir." He also said that he had used Canter's basic concepts but had modified them to "suit our particular needs."

A $30,000 out-of-court settlement was reached in 1984. As part of the settlement, school officials agreed that students placed on in-school suspension would be supervised by an adult at all times.

Milton Shore, a Silver Spring, Md., child psychologist who testified on behalf of the five children, says that he asked Canter to testify in court that the Maryland school was using a "distortion" of his system, but Canter said his lawyer had told him he had "nothing to gain" by doing so. "His comment to me was, 'I wouldn't have approved it,'" Shore says. "Why he wouldn't say it in court is something I've never been able to understand."

Canter says that *both* sides wanted him to testify in the case, and that he was ready and willing to testify on behalf of the children. "Absolutely," he says. "What went on in that district was unconscionable." His lawyer, however, told him not to get involved. "He said, 'Don't get caught in the middle of this thing. You are being set up.'"

Canter admits that Assertive Discipline has taken on a life of its own. "It has become a generic term, like Xerox or Kleenex," he says. "A number of educators are now conducting training in what they call Assertive Discipline without teaching *all* the competencies essential to the program. For example, I have heard reports of teachers who were taught that they had only to stand in front of their students, tell them that there were rules and consequences, display a chart listing those rules and consequences, and write the names of misbehaving students on the board. That was it. Those teachers were never introduced to the concept that positive reinforcement is the key to dealing with students."

To Canter, the problem isn't with the system; rather, it's with the people who don't understand how to use it: "Negative interpretations have also come from burned-out, overwhelmed teachers who feel they do not get the support that they need from parents or administrators and who take out their frustrations on students. Assertive Discipline is not a negative program, but it can be misused by negative teachers. The answer is not to change the program, but to change the teachers. We need to train administrators, mentor teachers, and staff developers to coach negative teachers in the use of positive reinforcement. If these teachers cannot become more positive, they should not be teaching."

At the same time, Canter insists that the teachers who most effectively use Assertive Discipline are the ones who mold the system to their individual teaching styles. "That's fine," he says. "I don't want the legacy of Assertive Discipline to be—and I don't want teachers to believe they have to use—names and checks on the board or marbles in a jar. I want

teachers to learn that they have to take charge." Or, as he also has said: "The children must know that something will happen when they break a rule. The form it takes is not as important as the reality of a negative consequence."

In other words, don't take Canter's suggestions too literally. When Canter's son, Josh, was 13, his father sent him to his room after he had misbehaved. "An hour later," Canter says, "he comes out reading *Assertive Discipline for Parents*, and he says, 'Dad, how many times did you warn me about yelling and screaming?' And I said, 'Two.' And he said, 'But in your book, it says two warnings, maximum half-hour in the room. You sent me in for an hour! You can't even follow your own program!'" Canter laughs about the incident: "It's very hard to practice what you preach."

LINDA DARLING-HAMMOND wasn't the only parent upset over the use of Assertive Discipline at Takoma Park Elementary and other schools in the Montgomery County (Md.) school district. When a group of them began voicing their concerns about the system, they found an ally in school board member Blair Ewing, who had done some research of his own. "I thought [Canter's] materials were dreadful," he says. "Assertive Discipline doesn't examine the reasons *why* children are misbehaving. It values conformity above everything, and that's dangerous."

Ewing says he raised the issue "over and over" with School Superintendent Harry Pitt, who eventually issued a policy statement recommending that prepackaged discipline systems not be accepted wholesale by the district. "Assertive Discipline is not prohibited, but it's understood that it's not to be used," says Ewing. "I haven't seen it rear its ugly head again."

Darling-Hammond didn't wait around to see what would happen; she removed her daughter from the school. When she took her to look at another school, one that didn't use Assertive Discipline, Elena said, "Mom, I want to stay in this school, because they don't punish the kids."

Non-verbal Language Techniques for Better Classroom Management and Discipline

Steven Grubaugh
University of New Orleans

According to *What Works* (1987), "Schools that encourage academic achievement focus on the importance of scholastic success and on maintaining order and discipline" (p. 58). Of course, good discipline, to an extent, is a byproduct of interesting, exciting, and engaging instruction. But achieving good classroom control, in most cases, involves much more than good instruction. The attributes of a good disciplinarian and classroom manager can include confidence, a demeanor, a stature, an aura of personal power, and a variable of position power, as well as a degree of charisma, all of which add up to a personal presence. Certainly, discipline is a combination of qualities, the interactions of which are difficult to describe or discuss outside the context of specific teaching situations. It is, therefore, difficult to teach or tell someone how to be a good disciplinarian since each teacher faces a unique set of students in specific circumstances, and all teachers must test, practice, and hone their skills of management and control in the classroom. However, a study of the characteristics of effective discipline, focused upon through a teacher's use of language, can reveal many insights into how good classroom management and discipline are achieved by good disciplinarians (Calabrese, 1985; Kise, 1982), thereby highlighting many language variables, each of which can be adjusted to improve classroom control.

It is important to realize that there are many communication variables, or as Williams (1982) says, "low profile controls," which can be manipulated to the teacher's advantage for discipline. The instructional setting and the teacher's non-verbal (body) language give students extremely strong impressions about a teacher's management and disciplinary intentions, tolerances, strengths, and weaknesses. Verbal language delivers the content and specifics of discipline. Students read clear messages from both language mediums, speculate on possible consequences of their behavior, and respond accordingly as they develop their behavior patterns. Recognizing that most classroom language should be devoted to instruction, a teacher's language use for instruction can, and should simultaneously, function as the language of management and discipline, conveyed through the metalanguage of non-verbal meanings and verbal innuendo.

A teacher can adjust the non-verbal, as well as the verbal language variables, to relax control or exert increasing control over the management and behavior of the class. Hence, all of the non-verbal language related variables discussed here can range from a low degree of use, to moderate use, to extensive application as each class control device becomes necessary to apply in specific situations. Some of the variables considered, such as maintaining good eye contact, are overt and easily utilized, but many more, such as controlling facial expressions or using non-responses, are more subtle and can be mastered with use. The more extensively each one of these variables is applied, the more control the teacher gains. Using more and more of the variables extensively, and in combination with one-another, gives the teacher the potential for enormous control over a class. However, even though it is advisable to begin tough, overtightening these controls for prolonged periods is not recommended since today's students will not tolerate working for an absolute authoritarian in a boot camp atmosphere.

Empowerment Using Effective Body Language: Surprisingly, research studies indicate that 40% of common classroom disruptions can be curbed by effective use of body language (Shrigley, 1985). Thus, teachers should learn to provide clear messages through their body movements, stance, and facial expressions to communicate their intentions non-verbally. According to Woolfolk (1985), non-verbal expressions function to provide information, regulate interactions, express intimacy or liking, exercise social control, and facilitate service or task goals. Using a full range of body language — from power movements such as standing up to tower over a student when taking to him, to more subtle movements, such as arching a brow to prevent an anticipated misbehavior, opening arms palm upwards to express acceptance, or raising the head when asking a question to gesture for a response — is an important form of communication in the classroom and should be used to reinforce messages to students.

There are implicit messages, such as the body posture and body orientation, which also provide clear messages to students. Body orientation is the degree to which the speaker's legs and shoulders are facing the listener and is a powerful indicator of status and liking. The more direct the orientation, the more positive the attitude being displayed. Not only are many body language movements read, but a lack of gestures, a lack of movement, and a lack of facial expressions and eye contact are also interpreted by students and referenced in with what is actually said.

Of course, students read the body language and facial expressions of the classroom leader who is before them day after day. Indeed, non-verbal messages are likely to be genuine expressions of the teacher's feelings; students can detect the teacher's attitude toward them and toward the subject as well as feelings of frustration, embarrassment, and indifference and other important messages which will contribute to the formation of the teacher's relationship with the group and students' perception of him or her (Bowman, 1983; Wagner, 1983).

Expression with body language forms a separate communication channel and can help transmit complex messages (Miller, 1986). Teachers can learn to send effective non-verbal messages to students which are congruent with verbal messages. According to Miller (1986), 82 percent of teacher messages are non-verbal and only 18 percent are verbal. The non-verbal and verbal messages can confirm each other or reflect a confusing mismatch of communication. For example, teachers can sound confident and look confident or can sound weak and express insecurity in their body language. In cases where the non-verbal and verbal messages mismatch, the non-verbal might show confidence or style but the verbal may be weak or void of content. Of course, the opposite situation is possible where the verbal message is strong but non-verbal signals, such as shifty eyes or the body turned away from the audience, contradict the verbal message. When the teacher's verbal communication conflicts with the non-verbal message, students become confused but tend to trust more in the non-verbal message (Miller, 1986).

Explicit body language messages, such as pointing, which accent or augment verbal messages, can be developed into aids for more stylistic teaching. These gestures may be interpreted different ways in different cultures. A teacher's explicit non-verbal communications can be dynamic and should invite success. Expression of emotion, such as enthusiasm, is communicated non-verbally through frequent demonstrative gestures with dramatic body movements and emotive facial gestures (Hasselbring, Hawley and Rosenholtz, 1984). Other commonly identified emotions, such as disgust, fear, happiness, anger, surprise, and combinations of these, can be read on the face — the place where people look for information. Learning to replace involuntary facial expressions with calculated practiced expressions can give students clear messages and can be used to alter behavior.

On the face, the eyes are perhaps the most important feature to watch and to use for non-verbal expression. Good speakers and class-room managers sweep the room with their gaze and maintain a high percentage of steady eye contact with students (Brooks, 1985; Guthrie, 1983). Eye contact can indicate a willingness to communicate or learn. Lack of contact might show a lack of interest or indicate that a student does not know the answer to a question. For the teacher, intentionally breaking eye contact can be an indication to students to break off their overtures to developing a too familiar relationship (such as being best friends), or a sexual relationship (when a student's crush begins to be a problem), or other student behaviors which should be discouraged but which students may, in their immature ways, desire. Shifty eyes express everything from a lack of confidence to dishonesty. A teacher's steady, unwavering eye-contact with a class gives students the impression that they are being monitored and helps keep them on task and behaving.

Teachers can learn to become better interpreters of student messages by reading students' body language and facial expressions to judge class mood, to determine whether students understand the lesson, and to anticipate disturbances and discipline problems before they happen. Students with arms and legs folded into the body might be closed to the teacher or exhibiting passive rebellion due to a negative impression of the teacher. A confusing or angry look on a student's face often indicates frustration. Students wiggling around in their seats, or exhibiting an inability to concentrate, often indicate frustration. This may be an indication of trouble with the lesson or trouble with a non-school factor, and it is a mistake to interpret negative body language, such as a student with arms crossed, as having a negative attitude toward the teacher without verbal confirmation of the body language. The student with arms folded tight might be cold or just more comfortable with arms folded. In this vein, it is especially important not to misinterpret the body language of students from other cultural backgrounds. The younger the students are, the less guarded they are with their facial expressions and body language, and these messages can be read like a book.

Empowerment Through Proxemics: The invasion of body space, or the teacher's proximity to students, is another factor which can influence behavior (Etscheidt, Stainback, and Stainback, 1984). Every student and teacher has a deep rooted and culturally established sense of personal territory. Since most classroom behavior problems occur furthest from the teacher (Fiber, 1986), moving about becomes an important management technique.

In the average classroom, teachers and students are separated by 12 or more feet (Miller, 1986). A public zone is 12-25 feet and is used for one way communication, such as a lecture. Keeping a public zone distance from potentially violent students is a safety measure all teachers should keep in mind. When lecturing from the public zone, moving into the social zone (4-12 feet) — which is commonly used for interaction between strangers, business acquaintances, and teachers and students — is a good way to curb minor student misbehavior, simply by being closer to the offensive students. But for even greater control, breaking other zone conventions and moving into a student's personal space can be used in conjunction with a verbal message to accentuate a point or catch a misbehaving student by surprise. This might include moving into the personal zone (1 1/2-4 feet) for informal conversations or even touching the student to encroach intentionally upon what is termed the intimate zone. Knowing when and when not to touch a student requires experience. One prerequisite for effectively using space proxemics is that the physical setting should be arranged so that the teacher can move around continually to change the degree of proximity, thus maintaining contact with all students. Employing various instruction methods, such as using an overhead projector (to face students) rather than the chalkboard (back to students) to display lessons, enables the teacher to monitor the group and maintain eye contact and proximity with students.

Cultural Meanings of Non-verbal Messages: Teachers must be aware of non-verbal communication when teaching students from various cultures because it is perhaps the most important form of communication. For instance, in the Vietnamese and American Indian cultures it is not considered polite for students to have prolonged eye contact with adults; in fact, the head may also be bowed as a gesture of respect to the adult. Chinese students and other Asians may misinterpret or dislike being touched. What a Caucasian teacher might consider public space, a black student may consider his personal space. Hispanic students tend to be comfortable defining their social zone with less distance to the speaker (O'Donnell, 1982). According to Wolfgang (1979, 1984) teachers must learn to communicate on a cultural level, for not being familiar with the verbal and non-verbal language rules and mores of the cultures of students in the classroom can put teachers at a disadvantage and make them poor communicators with students whose backgrounds differ from their own. This communication breakdown between teacher and students from different cultures can destroy the professional relationship between the instructional leader and the learners.

The Sounds of Silence: There are precise psychological moments to say nothing! Even though it is difficult to master, teachers should consider the non-verbal variable of using the sound of silence in the classroom. S.I. Hayakawa (1972) makes the point that people talk to prevent silence, for silence is so very uncomfortable to endure in a social situation. For example, persons often experience discomfort when not speaking to strangers in an elevator as they ride up or down with their eyes on the floor indicator dial. Students have an easier time dealing with a frazzled teacher shouting and screaming at them than with a teacher who is staring at them in absolute silence with a foreboding look on the face. James Dobson (1970) tells about the teacher who talked louder and louder each time her students became louder and louder until she finally climbed onto the desk and shouted "shut up" at them. Dobson says that the students had one unified goal the remainder of the year which was to get their teacher back on top of the desk. On the other hand, there is something dangerous, forbidding, and even intimidating about a teacher purposefully removing his voice from the din of classroom noise, especially when combined with an appropriate body pose and warning facial expression. Creating this uncomfortable silence is a tactic that can be used as an effective disciplinary tactic.

In order to set "quiet" as a tone, there are several instructional strategies which help establish silence for learning with discipline as a byproduct. Javernick (1985) recommends a technique where the teacher raises a hand with finger to lips. As students miss the teacher's voice in the room and turn to see her silently signaling for quiet, the "shh" sign sweeps the room until everyone has responded to the quiet sign. Also, teaching students a few sign language symbols is an effective and fun way to signal for silence in the room and can greatly increase students' attentiveness to directions. To quiet a class down, one teacher challenged students to see how long they could hold their breath, which of course prevented them from talking. Prolonged periods of silence, where students are engaged in instructional practice, can be used to calm a rowdy group of students. Silence can be established and maintained by methods designed so that group peer pressure works on those inclined to be noisy. Sustained Silent Reading (SSR), for instance, is a school-wide program which has teachers enforce 5-20 minutes of silence each day while students, teachers, and others in the school read for enjoyment. This program can be implemented at a time of day, following lunch, for instance, to calm a rowdy group and engage students in subject matter (Grubaugh, 1986). To establish this silence, provide students with a forced choice: "Class, would you prefer free reading today or this worksheet?" Students are left with little choice in the matter. However, when a silent activity is underway, someone inevitably breaks the silence by talking. In this instance, it is appropriate to stop the silent activity and move back to the worksheet alternative. The other students will complain to the one who has broken the silence, and within a week students will be reading in silence. Once students are reading, make sure all students have something they are able to read at their independent level and are interested in. Within two weeks, everyone will be enjoying the silent reading period. In math, silence may be established by "do nows," which are problems on the board that students work once the late bell has rung. Writing time can also be a time for silence, concentration, and desk work. Activities like these in any content area serve to establish the content area learning set and to give students a chance to settle down.

In nearly all instances, the volume of the sound of a group of people speaking rises and falls in patterns or waves. For a teacher, it is best to time one's opening remarks at the trough of a wave of sound in the classroom so as to begin speaking in a softer voice to set a more quiet tone. Nothing is more tiring than trying to shout down groups of students throughout the day.

Students have tremendous imaginations, and allowing students to interpret silence and a menacing look on the teacher's face allows them to interpret the teacher's response to their behavior and translate it into an expectation of a fitting punishment. In their minds (most youngsters have an acute sense of fairness), the punishment should fit the crime. When dealing with a particularly tough discipline problem, a more active use of this silent technique might be to stop the class, walk to the student's desk, and begin writing on a pad. This note writing will be an anecdotal record of the student's transgressions. The student can infer what the teacher will do with this "documentation," and if the student openly asks, the teacher can explain that these are notes for a referral to the appropriate place befitting his actions. As in the film, "Scared Straight," where juvenile delinquents visited penitentiary inmates to get a glimpse of their own future lives, this is a powerful technique and should be used as a last resort with the intention of making the referral if the misbehavior is not curbed.

Empowerment through Non-response: History is full of sayings about the wisdom of keeping one's mouth shut. A non-response to a student is also an effective discipline technique to use in certain circumstances. Often it is better to ignore a student's action if a confrontation can be avoided and the offense is not too objectionable to students or teachers. According to Orlich, et. al (1985), over 90% of classroom problems — including gumchewing, missing homework, or just being social — are minor. Yet, beginning teachers, or ineffective disciplinarians, have problems putting out each fire which ignites and, as such, can be easily baited by the students. A non-response signals the misbehaving student that the infraction will not get attention through negative reinforcement, was poor judgment on the student's part in the first place, and is not worthy of consideration or the time to deal with it. Shrigley (1985) suggests that teachers ignore spontaneous off-track behavior not meant to attract others and only then using stronger measures, such as expressing an appropriate facial expression to give students fair warning. Moving near to the student and using proximity control is Shrigley's final step before verbal measures are used.

Using silence effectively, a teacher can allow inferences to work with students. One beginning teacher I taught with in a particularly

tough situation used the rumor mill to allow the word to spread that he had a black belt in karate. This rumor gave him tremendous respect with the students but could have begun to work against him, like a gunfighter's reputation, if one of the tough students had been looking for a challenge and called his bluff.

Defusing anger and keeping impulsive thoughts to oneself are two more virtues associated with silence. When one is angry, feeling sick, or likely to be unfair or overreact, it is prudent to keep one's silence rather than react in anger. Students have hard days, too, and often what is said in anger is not meant. Of course, major classroom confrontations should be avoided and dealt with at a time when student and teacher can meet outside of class. Sometimes, listening patiently and allowing an angry student to blow off steam are effective ways to defuse hostility. Administrators often defuse explosive situations by simply allowing students or angry parents to vent their frustrations. Two or three minutes is usually all it takes for an angry person to vent frustration. Often, hostile people just want to say what bugs them, and that gets it off their chest. As difficult as it is, experienced teachers and administrators will listen to angry persons, letting them erupt to blow off their anger (about two minutes), and then address their concerns point-by-point dealing objectively and fairly with the problem. Teachers should recognize that defusing administrator anger is accomplished in the same way.

When used instructionally, a teacher's intentional silence, as in the concept of wait time, can be used to encourage students to think for themselves as well as talk to classmates for answers and solutions to problems. Another silence variable is the decision of when to say what. One example of using the variable of time to shape student behavior is to provide the answer to a test question during the first three minutes after the bell rings. This will encourage students to be on time to class, seated with notebooks open and ready to listen.

Summary: All the non-verbal variables of language can be used as strategies to establish and reinforce the disciplinary message to the students. Without using one word, the empowered teacher can say: "I am fully aware that students read my body language. What I tell you verbally is strongly reinforced with my body movements and facial expressions. As you read these impressions, you'll see that I enjoy teaching this subject, and I accept you and will work with you. I also use gestures as part of my speaking style so my enthusiasm shows. My steady eye contact with you is an indication that I monitor what you do in here and read your non-verbal communications to me. I like to move around the classroom, and I will come especially close to you if you are misbehaving. I do, however, understand and respect your culture and the manner in which you communicate non-verbally with me. I will not yell over your voices, so when my voice is missing from the room, beware! I also provide times of silence for us to settle down and learn in a quiet atmosphere. If you are one of those students who expects me to acknowledge mildly irritating behavior, I simply do not have time for such nonsense. I will not interrupt the momentum of my lesson with someone trying to bait me or irritate me. Let's not either one of us say anything in anger that we would later regret. However, if you do, I'll not take it personally, but rather, I'll try to be objective and fair. In this way, we will maintain an attitude of cooperation and fairness toward each other and develop a good climate for learning."

References

Anderson, T.H. and Armbruster, B.B. (1984). "Studying." In P. David Pearson (Ed.), *Handbook of Reading Research* (pp. 657-680). New York: Longman.

Bowman, R. (1983). "Effective Classroom Management: A Primer for Practicing Professionals." *Clearing House, 57,* 116-118.

Boynton, P., Geronimo, J.D., and Gustafson, G. (1985). "A Basic Survival Guide for New Teachers." *Clearing House, 59,* 101-103.

Brooks, D.M. (1985). "The Teacher's Communicative Competence: The First Day of School." *Theory into Practice, 24,* 63-70.

Calabrese, R.L. (1985). "Communication is the Key to Good Discipline." *NASSP Bulletin, 69,* 109-110.

Dobson, J. (1970). *Dare to Discipline.* Wheaton, Illinois: Tyndale House Publishing.

Etscheidt, S. Stainback, S. and Stainback, W. (1984). "The Effectiveness of Teacher Proximity as an Initial Technique of Helping Pupils Control their Behavior." *Pointer, 28,* 33-35.

Fifer, F.L. (1986). "Twelve Tips for Better Discipline." *Contemporary Education, 12,* 401-410.

Guthrie, J.T. (1983). "Classroom Management." *The Reading Teacher, 36,* 606-608.

Grossnickle, D.R. (1981). "Dress for Success." *The Clearing House, 54,* 205-206.

Grubaugh, S.J. (1986). "Sustained Silent Reading: What's in It for 'Them'?" *Clearinghouse, 60,* 160-174.

Hayakawa, S.I. (1972). *Language in Thought and Action.* New York: Harcourt, Brace & Jovanovich, Inc.

Hasselbring, T., Hawley, W., and Rosenholtz, S. (1984). "Good Schools: What Research Says about Improving Student Achievement." *Peabody Journal of Education, 61,* 118-128.

Javernick, E. (1985). "Silent Discipline." *Momentum, 16,* 38-39.

Kise, J.D. (1982). "Languages Usage as a Means of Maintaining Classroom Discipline." *Clearinghouse, 56,* 12-15.

Lovell, R.B. (1980). *Adult Learning.* New York: John Wiley & Sons.

Miller, P.W. (1986). *Non-verbal Communication.* Washington, D.C., National Education Association.

O'Donnell, H. (1982). "Do You Read Me?" *Language Arts, 59,* 630-633.

Orlich, D.C., Harder, R.J., Callahan, R.C., Kravas, C.H., Kauchak, D.P., Pendergrass, R.A., and Keogh, A.J. (1985). *Teaching Strategies. (Second Edition),* Boston: D.C. Health and Company, 345.

Rosenfield, P., Lambert, N., and Black, A. (1985). "Desk Arrangement Effects on Pupil Classroom Behavior." *Journal of Educational Psychology, 77,* 101-108.

Russell, D., Purkey, W., and Siegel, B.L. (1982). "The Artfully Inviting Teacher: A Hierarchy of Strategies." *Education, 103,* 35-38.

Shrigley, R.L. (1985). "Curbing Student Disruption in the Classroom — Teachers Need Intervention Skills." *NASSP Bulletin, 69,* 26-32.

Stefanich, G.P. and Bell, L.C. (1985). "A Dynamic Model for Classroom Discipline." *NASSP Bulletin, 69,* 19-25.

Wagner, H. (1983). "Discipline in Schools Is Inseparable from Teaching." *Education, 103,* 390-394.

(1987). *What Works: Research about Teaching and Learning.* (2nd Edition). United States Department of Education.

Wilcox, R.T. (1983). "Discipline Made Gentle." *Clearinghouse, 57,* 30-35.

Wolfgang, A. (1979). *Non-verbal Behavior Applications and Cultural Implications.* New York: Academic Press.

Wolfgang, A. (1984). *Non-verbal Behavior-Perceptions, Applications and Intercultural Insights.* Lewiston, New York: C.J. Hogrefs, Inc.

Woolfolk, A. and Nicolich, L. (1984). *Educational Psychology for Teachers* (2nd Edition). New Jersey: Prentice-Hall, Inc.

Exceptional Children

- **Educationally Disadvantaged (Articles 35-37)**
- **Gifted and Talented (Articles 38-40)**
- **Culturally Different (Articles 41-42)**

The Equal Educational Opportunity Act For All Handicapped Children (Public Law 94-142) gives disabled children the right to an education in the least restrictive environment, due process, and an individualized educational program specifically designed to meet their needs. Professionals and parents of exceptional children are responsible for developing and implementing an appropriate educational program for each child. The application of these ideas to classrooms across the nation at first caused great concern among educators and parents. Classroom teachers whose training did not prepare them for working with the exceptional child expressed negative attitudes about mainstreaming. Special resource teachers also expressed concern that mainstreaming would mitigate the effectiveness of special programs for the disabled and would force cuts in services. Parents feared that their children would not receive the special services they required because of governmental red tape and delays in having their children properly diagnosed and placed.

It has now been more than a decade since the implementation of Public Law 94-142. Many of the above concerns have been studied by psychologists and educators, and their findings have often influenced policy. For example, research has indicated that mainstreaming is more effective when regular classroom teachers and special resource teachers work cooperatively with disabled children.

The articles concerning the educationally disadvantaged confront many of these issues. Sally Smith discusses the characteristics of learning disabled students. Teachers who have worked with learning disabled children share their observations and teaching strategies. Howard Margolis and Elliot Schwartz discuss the positive effects of cooperative learning in mainstreamed classes, and Gary Adkins addresses the benefits of integrated programs for the handicapped.

Another dimension of exceptional children is the gifted and talented. These children are rapid learners who can absorb, organize, and apply concepts more effectively than the average child. They often have IQs of 140 or more and are convergent thinkers (that is, they give the correct answer to teacher or test questions). Convergent thinkers are usually models of good behavior and academic performance and they respond to instruction easily; teachers generally value such children and often nominate them for gifted programs. There are other children, however, who do not score well on standardized tests of intelligence because their thinking is more divergent (they can imagine more than one answer to teacher or test questions, for example). These gifted divergent thinkers may not respond to traditional instruction, may become bored, may respond to questions in unique and disturbing ways, and may appear uncooperative and disruptive. Many teachers do not understand these unconventional thinkers and fail to identify them as gifted. In fact, such children are sometimes labeled as emotionally disturbed or mentally retarded because of the negative impressions they make on their teachers. Because of the differences between these types, a great deal of controversy surrounds programs for the gifted. Such programs should enhance the self-esteem of all gifted and talented children, motivate and challenge them, and help them realize their creative potential. The three articles in this subsection on gifted and talented children discuss the nature of giftedness and explain how to identify gifted students and provide them with an appropriate education.

The third subsection of this unit concerns the culturally different. Just as labeling may adversely affect the disabled child, it can also affect the child who comes from a minority ethnic background where the language and values are quite different from those of the mainstream culture. The term "disadvantaged" is often used to describe these children, but it is negative, stereotypical, and may result in a self-fulfilling prophecy whereby teachers perceive such children as incapable of learning. Teachers should provide culturally different children with experiences that they have missed in the restrictive environment of their homes and neighborhoods. The articles in this subsection address cultural and language differences and suggest strategies for teaching culturally different children.

Looking Ahead: Challenge Questions

Can mainstreaming have a positive effect on the intellectual and social development of disabled children?

What are the characteristics of children with learning disabilities? What are some strategies that teachers can use to help students deal with their disabilities?

Who are the gifted and talented? How can knowledge of their learning needs help in providing them with an appropriate education?

What are some of the cultural differences that exist in our society? How can teacher expectations affect the culturally different child? Would multicultural education help teachers deal more effectively with these differences?

Unit 5

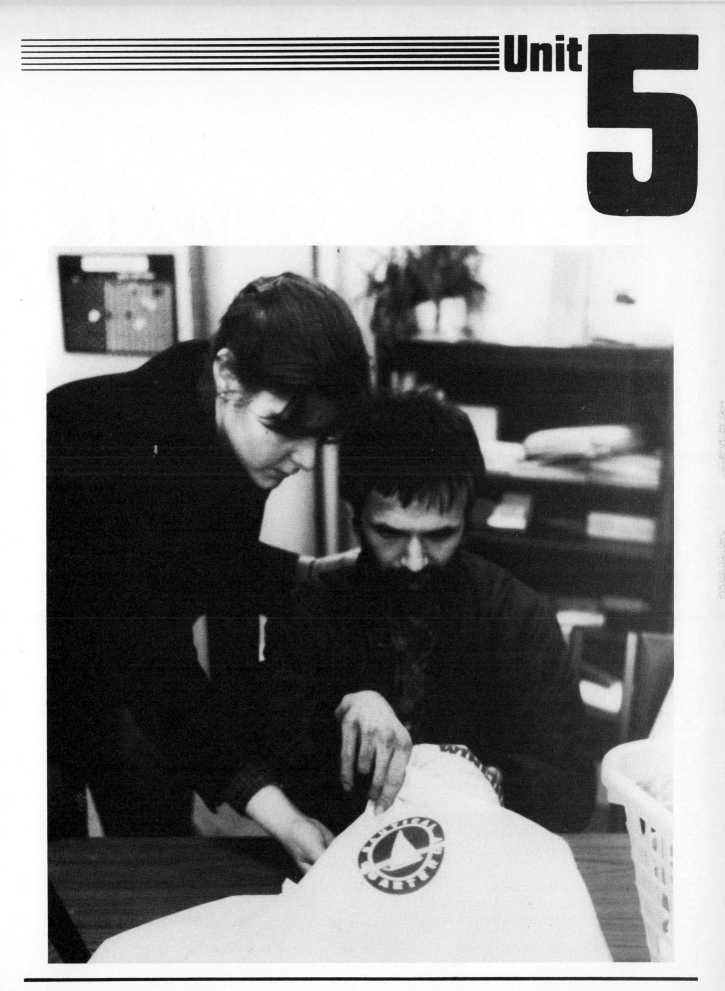

THE MASKS STUDENTS WEAR

Recognizing the behaviors learning disabled students use to hide their problems helps you to help them

Sally L. Smith

Sally L. Smith is the founder/director of The Lab School of Washington, a full professor and director of the graduate program in learning disabilities at The American University in Washington, D.C. and the author of the book, No Easy Answers: The Learning Disabled Child at Home and at School.

Learning disabled adults are telling educators what learning disabled children can't. What we learn from these adults can improve the teaching of children and the training of teachers.

There are many types of learning disabilities including auditory, vision and language disabilities. And students can have combinations of different learning disabilities.

One of the most important messages learning disabled adults are giving is that the greatest challenge learning disabled children face is the battle for self-esteem. These adults say they felt stupid and were treated in school as though they were. They felt defeated, worthless and "dumb." Over the years, these adults learned to mask their hurts.

"I learned to act a certain way so I couldn't be teased. I would appear bored, tired, eager to be of help, all-knowing or funny, depending upon what was going on. In other words, I would do anything but let them know I couldn't read the material," confesses one learning disabled adult.

"I faked my way all through school," says another. "I had the gift of gab and an excellent memory."

Unfortunately, many dyslexic and learning disabled adults started to develop masks in first or second grade when they could not read what others could. Few ever received special education. They were not identified as learning disabled or dyslexic. Instead, their teachers often labeled them "lazy," "willful," "poorly disciplined" and "spoiled" when actually they were trying their hardest.

These students were called "retarded" if they had any speech and language problems and "disturbed" if they were hyperactive, impulsive or had any of the behavioral manifestations of a learning disabled child. Often these children were gifted, above average in intelligence, and unable to bear their inability to accomplish the simplest academic task.

Think of the energy many learning disabled students spend hiding their disabilities and masking the feeling of being stupid. The masks are an elaborate subterfuge that make students feel worse about themselves. The masks protect the students from being thought of as "stupid," but isolate them from others. Often the masks interfere with students' ability to learn.

Recognizing the masks learning disabled students sometimes wear to hide their inabilities will help you take action to have the problem treated. Masking behavior comes in many variations. The following types are among the most common masks students wear.

The mask of super competence

"Easy!" "Oh, sure! Everyone knows that!"

With a great deal of bravado, this student tries to make everything look simple. He knows he can talk his way

Characteristics of a learning disabled child

- Looks typical but doesn't learn typically.
- Is intelligent, often gifted.
- Has reading, spelling, writing and/or math achievements that are significantly below child's capability level.
- Has a short attention span.
- Is easily distracted.
- Has poor listening skills.
- Has trouble following directions.
- Doesn't seem to be trying, acts lazy or is defiant.
- Sometimes uses immature speech and language.
- Confuses left and right.
- Sometimes uses immature movements, is awkward, clumsy. Shows poor motor coordination (i.e., reaches one hand out and the other hand follows).
- Exhibits immature behavior.
- Displays general disorganization, poor organization of time and space.
- Often has difficulty with tasks employing paper and pencil.
- Produces many reversals (i.e., "b" instead of "d") and rotations (i.e., "b" instead of "q") in written work.
- Is inconsistent in behavior and work.
- Frequently displays exceptional ability in the arts, sports, science and verbalization.

Steps you can take if you suspect a student is learning disabled

1. List the child's personal and academic strengths and areas of weakness. Back up the list with anecdotal records after a week of careful observation and listening.
2. Check student's recent eye and hearing test records as well as general physical health records to rule out physical problems.
3. Confer with parents to discuss the list; ask them if they see similar strengths and weaknesses at home.
4. Recommend an evaluation by a school psychologist. In some schools, initial referral is to the pupil personnel worker; in others it is to the interdisciplinary team or principal.
5. Inform parents about Public Law 94–142, the *Education for All Handicapped Children Act.* Specify parents' rights to have their child evaluated, and if not satisfied with the evaluation results to seek a second evaluation.

If a child is diagnosed as being learning disabled, the child is entitled by law to appropriate services.

These range from support in the classroom to resource assistance to placement in self-contained classrooms. These services may or may not include speech and language therapy, occupational therapy and adaptive physical education.

Resources

Organizations

Association for Children with Learning Disabilities (ACLD)
This grassroots organization serves parents, teachers and other professionals. It provides needed support and information to help follow the latest educational and medical research and supports legislation for special education classes and teachers in the field. To find the organization nearest you, write the National ACLD, 4156 Library Road, Pittsburgh, PA 15234, or call (412) 341–1515.

Council for Exceptional Children (CEC)
This organization for professionals publishes books, media, journals, periodicals and research findings. Low-cost informational flyers are available. For a catalog or more information, write to CEC, 1920 Association Drive, Reston, VA 22091, or call (703) 620–3660.

Foundation for Children with Learning Disabilities (FCLD)
This organization for parents and professionals is a source of information for publications concerning the learning disabled child. It also provides grants. For more information, write to FCLD, 99 Park Ave., New York, NY 10016, or call (212) 687–7211.

The Orton Society
This organization for professionals is also open to parents. It studies preventive measures and treatment for children with specific language disabilities, sponsors research, and shares its findings. For more information, write to The Orton Society, 724 York Road, Baltimore, MD 21204, or call (301) 296–0232.

Books
Smith, Sally L. *No Easy Answers: The Learning Disabled Child at Home and at School,* Bantam Books, New York, 1981.
Stevens, Suzanne. *Classroom Success for the Learning Disabled,* John Blair Publisher, 1984.

through anything. His logic is impeccable. He's good with people, numbers, problem solving and trouble shooting.

Gen. George S. Patton, a dyslexic, assured his daughter that Napoleon couldn't spell, either, and quoted Jefferson Davis as saying, "A man must have a pretty poor mind not to be able to think of several ways to spell a word."

The mask of helplessness

"I don't know." "I don't understand." "I can't do anything."

Through pity, this person gets everyone around to help her do her work and assume responsibilities so she never fails. She refuses to risk failure, but feels even worse because she knows she didn't do any of the work.

The mask of invisibility

"I would hide in my shell, hold my neck in like a turtle, almost pleading with the teacher not to call upon me."

By looking frightened, whispering to teachers and acting terrified with peers, this person gets everyone else to do his work for him.

The student realizes he can get through school by not talking, just repeating when necessary, taking a low profile, and making no waves. With his head down and sitting quietly for a long time, nobody bothers him. He has the talent of melting into the crowd. Teachers and supervisors later realize they never got to know this student or acknowledge he was there.

The mask of the clown

"Isn't that a riot!" "Ha, ha, ha." "What a joke!"
Everything is funny when this student is around. Laughter, however, hides the real issue—a learning disability.

Cher, the Academy Award-winning actress/singer, admits she was the "class clown" to divert attention from her inability to read, write or do arithmetic in school. Despite her problems, she was exceedingly verbal and outstanding in the arts. A teacher proclaimed that she was not working hard enough. Feeling stupid, she dropped out of school at 16 and wasn't tested for learning disabilities until after she was 30.

The mask of the victim

"It's not fair." "Everyone picks on me." "There's no justice anywhere."

Injustice is a basic theme with this person. Often called a "jailhouse lawyer" because he has an argument for everything, this student feels victimized and takes on a "poor me" attitude. He assumes no responsibility for anything. He angers others around him.

The mask of not caring

"I don't care." "Nothing matters." With this mask, the student is never vulnerable, and risks no failure. If she tries to succeed and fails, she says she never tried and it doesn't matter. The mask is a way of keeping others at a distance, making her feel woefully inadequate. If nothing matters, it's very difficult to change or motivate this person.

The mask of boredom

"This is boring!" *Yawn.* "What time is it now?" *Yawn.*

With big yawns, loud sighs, tapping fingers and toes, this person lets the teacher know how bored he is. This behavior puts the teacher on the defensive. Usually this person is not bored, but frustrated, and can't do what he's been asked to do.

Thomas Edison was kicked out of schools for not following instructions. He probably did not understand the instructions due to his auditory problems. Severe learning disabilities prevented him from being able to write what he was told.

The mask of activity

"Gotta run." "Sorry, I'm in a hurry, I can't talk." "I'm busy now, I'll do whatever you want later."

This student is always on the move. Standing still may bring her close to others, and she precludes any intimacy. Constant activity wards away others and keeps her from having to perform.

The mask of outrageousness

"I'm way out." "I don't like being a conformist." "I believe in individualism to the extreme." Through wild clothing, hair style and color, wigs, extraordinary glasses, stockings, boots, and so on, this student projects eccentricity and hides his problems.

Robert Rauschenberg, a famous artist who had extreme difficulty with math and spelling, did outrageous, unheard of things in school and in his career. Many artists feel he expanded the definition of art for a generation of Americans by daring to innovate.

The mask of the Good Samaritan

"Let me help you." "What can I do for you?"

This student wants to please at any cost. Frequently, she is too nice and too accommodating. She will echo what you say, work longer hours than necessary and be overly helpful to get out of doing what she can't do.

The mask of contempt

"They don't know how to teach." "This whole place sucks."

Negativity encompasses this mask. This joyless student has a negative word for everything. If it's sunny out, it could be sunnier. He wears out the people around him because nothing is ever good enough. He takes no pleasure in small successes. He's angry at the world for making him feel stupid and believes the world owes him something. He puts everyone around him on the defensive.

The mask of the strong silent type

"I'm Joe Cool." "Nobody comes too close to me, but they follow me everywhere." "Get out of my face. Nobody moves on me." "Every sport is for me. I live for sports."

Personified by a sleek body and prowess in sports, this student is revered by many and endowed, in her own mind, with every fine feature.

Bruce Jenner, Olympic decathlon champion who is dyslexic, says sports gave him his self-esteem. Jenner says reading aloud in the classroom was much harder and more frightening for him than competing in the decathlon.

The mask of perfection

"If they don't recognize my talents, that's their problem." "Good artists don't have to read really well, anyhow."

Proclaiming loudly that there are machines to spell and write, secretaries to take dictation and lawyers to read for him, this student presents himself as perfection. He tolerates no mistakes in himself or others. He often carries an impressive book or magazine he can't read and saunters into a room looking completely pleased with life. He makes everyone around him miserable.

The mask of illness, frail health and vulnerability

"My head." "My stomach." "My side." "My bladder." "My migraine."

To receive extra attention and get out of the work she can't do, this student calls in sick, leaves sick, constantly pretends to be sick and talks about her frailties.

Given something to read, she uses her illnesses and frailties as an excuse or cries if necessary. Expecting special attention, special privileges, while avoiding what she can't do, this student confuses everyone around her and usually gets by with this behavior.

The mask of seduction

"Hey, woman, write this down for me. Men don't write." The "macho man" often gets a female to do for him what he can't do. He hides behind his macho mask, making himself appear sexy.

"Math is men's work, girls can't do it." The "helpless female" asks a "macho man" to do what she can't do and hides behind her female mask to make it appear sexy.

The mask of being bad

"Don't mess with me. You'll be sorry." "I threw the book at him, so what?" "I'd rather be thought of as bad than dumb."

Losers at school often become winners on the street.

This student feels stupid, powerless and useless at school and often directs his frustration and anger towards his teachers. His peers enjoy his bad behavior and encourage more of it.

Billionaire Dallas real estate manager Rick Strauss changed schools several times, always suffering the humiliation of not learning to read or write due to his severe dyslexia. He compounded his problems by cutting up. Doing so diverted his teachers' attention away from his poor work. It wasn't until he was a high school senior that he learned that his inability to read and write resulted from his learning disabilities.

The mask of fantasy

"I'm going to be a millionaire by the time I'm 30!" "The world will understand me soon." "I'll have a Ph.D. once I learn to read."

Characterized by a fertile imagination and a great deal of creativity, this student tends to live more in her hopes and fantasies than in reality, which is filled with daily frustrations.

Hans Christian Andersen didn't learn to read and write, even with the help of 10 royal tutors of the Danish Court. He dictated his wonderful fairy tales to a scribe. His mask of fantasy protected him from the pain of facing reality, even though glimpses of his suffering appear in some of his stories, such as "The Ugly Duckling."

Removing the masks

The masks can be removed when students reach a certain comfort level. This usually happens when a student realizes he is not stupid, but suffers from a learning disability. The student experiences enormous relief when he discovers why he has been having difficulties learning.

What learning disabled adults have to say about the masks they wore in school alerts educators to the need to reach children in their early years, identify those children who have trouble learning before they begin to wear the masks, and teach them in ways that will help them succeed.

Focus: Making Schools Do More

Educating the Handicapped in the Regular Classroom

Gary Adkins

Gary Adkins is Contributing Editor, Illinois School Board Journal, *Springfield.*

SCHOOL districts that segregate large proportions of their handicapped students from the regular classroom are probably doing more harm than good for many of those students, say a growing number of experts. What's more, they may be breaking the law.

"Special education" has meant labeling students ever since federal law first established a mandate in 1975. The Education for All Handicapped Children Act requires school districts to identify—and label—children with special needs. But it has never mandated separate programs, although such programs become a practical necessity for certain severe handicaps.

In fact, both federal and state laws have been amended in recent years to insist on placing special needs students in the "least restrictive envi-

ronment." The least restrictive environment, of course, is the regular classroom, unless solid evidence shows otherwise.

The biggest objections to separate special education programs revolve around the hazards of labeling. To qualify for special education services, a child's dysfunction must be identified and given a name. (The four most common labels—learning disabled, speech/language impaired, mentally handicapped, and emotionally disturbed—cover 95 percent of all students classified as handicapped.)

Labels are hazardous in part because they are not consistently interpreted and applied. For example, a typical school district may classify from 6 to 12 percent of its pupils as handicapped—a rather narrow range. Yet, some large city districts reportedly classify from zero to 73 percent of their handicapped pupils as "learning disabled." Probability suggests that such districts are not finding all of their children with learning disabilities or, conversely, that the label is

being used to get some difficult students out of the regular classroom.

Just as important, student labels can create worse problems for the student than the handicap itself, say many psychologists. Labeling and removing students from the regular classroom limit student expectations of success and lower student self-esteem, peer acceptance, and academic performance.

Separate programs may even damage the disabled student's life beyond high school, particularly in the job market. A recent poll shows most parents of disabled students rate their schools poorly in preparing their kids for the years after high school. Yet, disabled kids must eventually interact with their "regular" peers. They must cope with the real world because there are few special education jobs in real life.

Educators are finding there's a way around the hazards of labeling. A number of programs around the country are achieving immense success by putting "handicapped" children into

From *The Education Digest,* September 1990, pp. 24-27. Condensed from *Illinois School Board Journal, 88,* March/April 1990, pp. 20-23, 25-27.

classrooms with other students, then giving children the individual attention they need. The benefits include higher academic achievement and, to an even greater extent, improved social skills.

Integrated settings have already proven successful in preparing severely disabled students to find competitive jobs. For example, 44 percent of the severely disabled graduates of San Francisco's integrated programs found jobs in regular work places.

Even though the programs have reported considerable success, some parents and educators oppose returning kids with special needs to regular classrooms. They fear, primarily, that needed special services won't follow.

Funding problems are at the root of most such concerns. Under state special education funding regulations, integrated classes generally cost schools more. For example, Illinois won't pay for a special education teacher's salary if the teacher works with regular students half of the time or more. This may help discourage team teaching in integrated classrooms, where both regular and special education teachers instruct all students alike and disabled students are in the minority.

Faced with inflexible state funding mechanisms, time-consuming reporting requirements, and the need to maximize state aid, most school districts approach special education through pull-out programs—using a self-contained separate class or a resource room to work with special

---

Educators are finding out that there is a way around the hazards of labeling.

---

students for a portion of the day. Although research discredits this approach, all but a few districts cling to it.

The state pays about 54 percent of the average per-pupil cost of special education, and localities pay only about 37 percent nationwide. Federal law promised to pay 40 percent of the cost of the federally mandated special services by 1982 and thereafter. But the feds have never chipped in more

than 13 percent, and they now contribute less than 8.5 percent nationally.

With so much of the cost of special needs education being paid locally, school boards need to know whether integrated classes can be cost effective compared to "pull-out" programs. A study conducted in New York City public schools from 1981 to 1983 found that pull-out programs cost more.

Savings can accrue because integration removes the need for separate facilities. The Christina public school district in Delaware, a K-12 district of more than 20 schools, needed 80 fewer classrooms after switching to integrated, team-taught classes in 1984.

Costs aside, however, a more profound misgiving about integrating special education programs concerns the possible effect on the quality of education. Will it hold back regular students, for example, if instructors pace lessons for the slowest learners? What would be the educational effect of bringing the most severely disabled students—particularly those who may be disruptive in some way—into regular classrooms?

One promising approach to serving the vast majority of special education students without using labels has been to restructure general classroom instruction. This means offering most classroom instruction one-on-one or in small groups, regrouping students according to academic abilities in each area of study.

Some teachers may oppose integration because it would require changes in the way classrooms are structured and lessons are planned. Others may fear a change in the number and status of teaching jobs— although integration should not affect these matters. Some may resist because they fear that either special services or regular education will suffer— something which has not happened in full-scale programs.

All of these concerns need to be addressed by school boards and administrators before integration can succeed. With proper assurances and preparation, however, integrated programs have proved relatively easy to implement, once the initial resistance has faded.

Many special education teachers

have expressed concern that the regular education initiative will move too far too fast. "It won't work if it sets up false expectations that something concretely different is happening for a student placed in regular classes all day, if in fact no plan of action exists. Often the barriers to individualizing

---

Special education students can be served without labeling by restructuring general classroom instruction.

---

are greater than one regular educator can overcome," said one special education teacher.

But George Diamond, director of the Cooperative Education Association for Special Education in Lombard, Illinois, believes collaborative consultation can overcome this objection, even without team teaching. "We have not only duplicated the special education and service program, but added to it in a regular setting." As a result, "special needs kids and their so-called 'regular' peers eat lunch and play on the same playgrounds. They go to classes together, form friendships, and many walk home together," Diamond said.

Programs like these demonstrate that the disabilities of some are less significant than the abilities and concerns all children share. Every student has pressing special needs at times, and schools often must serve those needs first in order to educate. The question is, for how many students is a separate setting really necessary to meet special needs? Growing evidence has convinced many school officials to reexamine and, ultimately, to integrate special education programs—usually through team teaching or consultation. It looks like a promising long-term development.

Federal court rulings require that placement decisions begin with a presumption in favor of integration. One precedent-setting U.S. appellate court case, *Roncker* v. *Walter*, set down "more aggressive standards by which school districts can measure their degree of compliance," according to Colleen B. Wilcox, superintendent of the Northern Suburban Special Education District in Highland Park, Illinois. In this case, Wilcox said, "the five most frequent justifications for placing students in a more restrictive environment were held to be unacceptable."

These were the unacceptable justifications: (1) Related services were more easily provided in the separate setting; (2) special equipment was available in a separate facility, or there was a specially designed separate facility; (3) better-qualified professional and support staff were available in a separate facility; (4) a particular program or curriculum was offered only in a separate facility; and

Integration of these students takes careful planning, training of staff, and application of effective-schools research.

(5) more intensive services were available in a separate facility because of lower teacher-pupil ratios.

Thus, Wilcox said, courts have required that the individual needs of students should be emphasized over

"the types of placements available." Many more school districts may soon be asked to integrate special and regular education. Illinois is proceeding with caution, however, to make sure special needs students aren't simply dumped back into regular classes without the necessary supports and teacher preparation.

Experience shows that, although integration can be a sound approach, it won't work without careful planning, staff training, and the application of effective-schools research. The latter element may be the most crucial if schools expect to improve the quality of the offerings for all students.

Facilitating Mainstreaming Through Cooperative Learning

Howard Margolis

Queens College of the City University of New York

Elliot Schwartz

August Martin High School, Jamaica, New York

Regardless of their philosophical stance toward mainstreaming, teachers are often apprehensive at the prospect of having mildly handicapped students (for example, learning disabled, educable mentally retarded, and emotionally disturbed students) placed in their classes (Kavanagh, 1977; Knoff, 1985). Many already consider their classes extremely difficult to teach because of the wide range of competencies and diverse needs of their students. Teachers find it difficult to address the needs of mildly handicapped students in heterogeneous classrooms without inviting disorder or depriving their other students of needed attention (Knoff, 1985; Madden & Slavin, 1983). These concerns often prompt teachers' reluctance "to mainstream students for whom they must alter basic instruction" (Salvia & Munson, 1985, p. 126). Nonetheless, given current mainstreaming trends, many subject area teachers will be responsible for educating mildly handicapped students in their classes.

Fortunately, easy-to-understand instructional methodology, such as cooperative learning, can be highly effective as a way to assimilate mildly handicapped students into the mainstream. Cooperative learning can help teachers meet the individual needs of handicapped and nonhandicapped students without significantly altering the curriculum (Johnson & Johnson, 1986). Through the use of carefully structured group assignments, cooperative learning strategies help (a) individualize instruction in a time-efficient manner that avoids dependency on recurrent teacher-student dyads (which, paradoxically, reduce the amount of direct instruction per student); (b) guide planning; (c) teach essential cooperative skills and promote positive social interaction; and (d) increase understanding of

disabilities and respect for differences. After reviewing the research on cooperative learning, Johnson and Johnson (1986) concluded that compared to competitive or individualistic learning:

> Cooperative learning experiences result in higher achievement and greater retention of learning. . . . Students in cooperative learning situations tended to use higher level thought processes, engaged in more higher level oral rehearsal, and discovered higher level strategies more frequently. . . . (Moreover, cooperative learning) promoted greater achievement motivation, more intrinsic motivation, more persistence in completing tasks, and greater continuing motivation to learn. . . . (It) also resulted in more positive attitudes toward the subject area and instructor (p. 556).

Cooperative learning activities are highly structured "so that students work together to achieve a shared academic goal (Schniedewind & Salend, 1987, p. 22)." Each student is viewed as having something important to offer other members of the group, which will contribute to the group's success. Students stimulate or complement each other. According to Cohen (1972), cooperative learning activities can be categorized as either (a) consensus-oriented tasks, in which the group reaches agreement on a common answer to some shared question; (b) a collegial model, in which group members share resources or teach each other to master a specific topic; or (c) divided labor, in which each group member has a specific, clearly delineated task(s) that helps satisfy a communal assignment when completed. To realize the benefits of cooperative learning, teachers must assign tasks that legitimately require cooperation and that tap the diverse skill and knowledge of the different group members. For example, writing and performing a play analyzing the causes of the Civil War from the perspectives of well-known historical figures—as opposed to adding columns of figures that students find simple, tedious and commonplace—would be an appropriate task. In addition, teachers need to monitor individual accountability, offer incentives based on group rather than individual performance, and foster student beliefs that cooperation will enhance accomplishment.

Success in most adult activities requires the cooperation of diverse individuals or groups. Cooperative learning attempts to prepare students for this challenge. At the core of cooperative learning is the premise that learning how to work effectively and efficiently with neighbors to achieve what cannot be accomplished alone is valuable in and of itself. For mildly handicapped and their nonhandicapped peers, cooperative learning also provides opportunities for individuals to contribute to the group's success and the achievement of its members regardless of their level of individual skills. It offers mildly handicapped students a chance to enhance their self-esteem by providing help, rather than only receiving it. For example, in English class, Doug, a highly intelligent, mildly handicapped adolescent with a severe reading problem, could be assigned a group task in which success depends on his strengths rather than on his poor reading ability. He may have the job of (a) collecting magazine pictures to illustrate the major themes of the group's report; (b) using a tape recorder to interview the school's principal to assess the principal's opinions about some controversial subject; (c) roleplaying a critical character in a group play; (d) sharing with the group his expertise on a relevant topic he learned about through personal experience (for example, what it's like working on a family fishing boat); (e) editing a videotape of relevant news events supporting the group's consensus position on some public issue; or (f) orally summarizing the group's conclusions to the class and enumerating potential implications. In a resource room, Lucy, a fourteen-year-old mildly handicapped student of average intellect, who reads at a third-grade level, may be assigned to teach match concepts she has mastered to Keith, a nonhandicapped student from another class who is having difficulty with a math concept that he missed due to an extended illness. Keith, in turn, has the responsibility of teaching Lucy ten basic sight words she needs to learn. When they have finished instructing each other and think that their partner is prepared for a test, the teacher assesses both on criterion-referenced measures which he discussed with them before initiating peer tutoring. Lucy is given a test on the sight words that Keith taught her, and Keith is given a test on the arithmetic concepts that Lucy taught him. Their grades are averaged and each receives the mean grade for the pair as the individual's grade. As the mildly handicapped student makes crucial contributions to the group, nonhandicapped peers have direct, structured, personal, and experiential opportunities to learn that although the mildly handicapped student has severe academic problems, the mildly handicapped student is not necessarily lower in intelligence, importance, personality, or human worth. In other words, given the right

situation, we all are capable of making valuable contributions and learning from each other. Thus the teacher's challenge is how to structure cooperative learning situations to bring out the best in all students.

Schniedewind and Salend (1987) identified peer teaching, group projects, the "jigsaw" and the combination "jigsaw-counterpart" group as the basic formats for cooperatively-structured learning. In the example given above, Lucy and Keith performed peer teaching by instructing each other in their areas of competence. Group projects are often more ambiguously structured and the tasks less discrete. Students are asked to combine their knowledge and skill to develop a project or complete an assignment. This format makes maximum demands on student ability to analyze task requirements and assign responsibilities. If more structure is needed, Schniedewind and Salend recommend using the "jigsaw" format. This design assigns specific tasks to individual group members. All groups in class may work on the same project, with each having members assigned the same distinct task. For example, one member in each group is assigned task "A," another member task "B," and so on. The combination "jigsaw-counterpart" takes this one step further by having all students in class with the same assignment work with each other as well as with their original group. Counterparts work together to improve their skill, knowledge, or product. In some situations, they continue instructing and offering assistance to one another until a predetermined criterion is met. Counterpart participation usually improves contributions to the original group and helps instill confidence.

Expectancy theory (Hackman & Oldham, 1982) suggests that cooperative learning will yield success when students have the competence to perform whatever aspects of a group's work they are assigned, to believe in their ability to succeed at given tasks, to realize that they are in a productive interdependent relationship, and to value the outcomes or rewards associated with success. It is likely to work even better when students have a predilection for the topic and activities and are given adequate time and guidance. When group members realize that a mildly handicapped student has the prerequisite knowledge and skill to make positive contributions to the group, they may, for the first time, view the mildly handicapped student as a resource rather than a liability. Involvement in situations in which success depends on the mildly handicapped student's strengths, rather than his weaknesses, have the potential to increase achievement and peer acceptance, which, in turn, may enhance self-esteem.

Guidelines for Implementation: Conceptually, cooperative learning is relatively easy to understand. Individuals with a common goal form a group to achieve their goal, which can be accomplished only by working together. Tasks and responsibilities are identified and assigned by the teacher or by the students themselves.

Each student is dependent upon other group members for success. Individual grades are assigned on the basis of group achievement, product, and cooperative effort. Grades take into account the quality of team efforts at working together, as well as academic accomplishment.

Initially, implementing cooperative learning is often more complex than anticipated. With practice over time, and teacher analysis of what contributed to previous successful experiences, and an understanding of what still must be improved, cooperative learning becomes easier and easier for teachers to manage. The key is to start small with relatively easy tasks and gradually expand the program's scope as teacher and student facility with cooperative learning strategies increases. Adherence to the following guidelines should facilitate successful implementation.

1. Choose both academic and social learning objectives appropriate for the grade and skill levels of the group. Assignments and responsibilities for students of various achievement levels, experiential backgrounds, and predilections should be designed for success.

2. Explain assignment objectives and procedures clearly, explicitly, and completely. Ask group members to paraphrase what they are supposed to do and why. Use roleplaying and practice assignments to prevent misunderstandings.

3. Emphasize the importance of specific social-cooperative skills in attaining success. Explain to students which of these skills will be observed and the reasons for doing so. Discuss these before initiating academic activities. Make sure students can articulate the reasons for stressing these skills and working together.

4. Have students initially work on highly discrete tasks in groups of two or three. As they become more comfortable and skilled in group work, progressively less-distinct tasks may be assigned, giving students a greater role to play in defining tasks for themselves and in determining "who does what." Similarly, group size may gradually be increased, commensurate with student ability to handle larger groups. Groups of more than five should be avoided, since larger groups offer fewer opportunities for participation. When increasing the group size, do not simultaneously diminish the specificity of individual assignments or roles. Initially assign mildly handicapped students to groups with students most likely to be sensitive to the feelings of others.

5. Plan for group diversity. The greater the variety of skill, knowledge, and opinion, the greater the potential for interesting and creative groups. Discussion of how particular differences are strengths fosters an appreciation for differences. Providing positive feedback, on visible individual and group behavior that demonstrates how student differences helped produce success, promotes respect for individuality.

6. Make sure that each student ultimately has a well-defined role and clearly articulated responsibilities on which he can obtain feedback. Provide regular oral and written feedback to students on academic and group interaction efforts. This can be done by writing individual students, and the group as a whole, letters enumerating which of their actions positively influenced progress. Structure reinforcement (grades) so that group members realize that accomplishment depends on the cooperation of all group members. For example, if everyone in the group gets at least a 'B' on his assignment, then every group member could receive an 'A' for the project. Such linkage encourages members to help each other, if afforded ample opportunities to do so. Regular monitoring helps identify students who continue to experience difficulty. These students should be given individual or small group instruction. If necessary, modify assignments to more accurately reflect student abilities.

7. Monitor group collaborative processes as well as individual academic achievement. Make it clear that you are available to clarify instructions, review procedures, offer suggestions, conduct mini-lessons, and provide feedback on both academic and collaborative matters. If appropriate, review rating forms with students, forms that delineate distinct behaviors you will focus on during observations (for example, listening while others speak, asking clarification questions, soliciting suggestions, integrating different positions). This underscores the importance of these behaviors and encourages their use. Assigning students to particular roles often facilitates group productivity. Roles may include consensus seeker, academic coach, summarizer, and process observer. Before delegating students to roles, be sure they have the knowledge, sensitivity, and desire to handle the assignment. This may require coaching, roleplaying, and supervised practice. Reinforce students for new cooperative behaviors by giving verbal reinforcement that indicates which behaviors were beneficial and why.

8. Pay particular attention to the physical arrangement and sound level of the classroom. A circle usually works best for individual groups (Johnson & Johnson, 1986). Circles require members to face each other and establish eye contact. This promotes dialogue and cooperation. Provide members with safe places to keep their work. Although talk should be encouraged, extraneous noise should be kept to a minimum. It is often helpful to discuss this in advance and to assign one member of each group the task of monitoring the group's sound level.

9. Use materials and assignments that promote interdependence while respecting differences in student abilities. For example, if there are four students per group and four riddles to figure out to solve a mystery, "jigsaw" the assignment by giving each group member a different riddle. Students with lower reading

abilities could be given riddle sheet "A," written at a fourth grade readability level, and higher-functioning students could be assigned riddle sheets that make greater demands on their reading abilities. Thus, the teacher needs to prepare only four different riddle sheets for an entire class. Separate assignments, designed to help students achieve a shared goal, allow for differentiation according to ability levels while avoiding embarrassment. In another situation, two students per group may jointly write a script for the remaining three group members to perform.

10. Use reinforcement procedures that promote intergroup cooperation to prevent groups from becoming isolated, competitive entities. The teacher may say: "We'll begin videotaping the play after each group gets 80 points."

11. Before beginning the autonomous-group phase of a cooperative learning assignment, provide whatever critical information or instruction students need to be successful. Instruction on how to use a thesaurus, for example, may be necessary. Remember that a primary purpose of cooperative learning is to maximize individual student learning.

12. Periodically hold plenary class discussions in which students describe group or individual actions that fostered or hindered cooperation. Be careful to establish ground rules that preclude blaming. These might include: "Discuss specific behaviors, not personalities. . . . Before suggesting behaviors which possibly need improvement, first indicate what you liked about the student's cooperative efforts. . . . Before speaking, ask yourself if what you want to say is likely to improve the situation. . . . Avoid using names or identifying people who exhibited behaviors you thought needed improvement. . . . Speak in terms of improvement rather than 'blame' or 'fault.' " A common mistake is not allowing sufficient time for these mutual feedback sessions.

Conclusion: Mildly handicapped students need every opportunity possible to succeed in mainstreamed environments. Given the innumerable responsibilities of regular classroom teachers, the presence of mildly handicapped students often complicates their jobs and makes teaching difficult. Cooperative learning strategies offer one potentially productive and satisfying way to help individualize instruction, foster social responsibility, teach group skills, and promote interpersonal sensitivity within heterogeneous classes by using an organized framework that can enhance teacher effectiveness and student creativity. Careful planning and step-by-step implementation offer the promise of making cooperative learning strategies a valuable resource for both teachers and students.

REFERENCES

Cohen, E. G. (1972). *Designing Groupwork: Strategies for the Heterogeneous Classroom.* New York: Teachers College Press.

Hackman, J. R. and Oldman, G. R. (1982). "Motivation Through the Design of Work." In D. A. Nadler, M. L. Tushman, and N. G. Hatvany, (Eds.), *Managing Organizations: Reading and Cases* (pp. 158–172). Boston: Little Brown.

Johnson, D. W. and Johnson, R. T. (1986). "Mainstreaming and Cooperative Learning Strategies." *Exceptional Children, 52,* 553–561.

Kavanagh, E. (1977). "A Classroom Teacher Looks at Mainstreaming." *The Elementary School Journal, 77,* 318–322.

Knoff, H. M. (1985). "Attitudes Toward Mainstreaming: A Status Report and Comparison of Regular and Special Educators in New York and Massachusetts." *Psychology in the Schools, 22,* 410–418.

Madden, N. A. and Slavin, R. E. (1983). "Mainstreaming Students with Mild Handicaps: Academic and Social Outcomes." *Review of Educational Research, 53,* 519–569.

Salvia, J. and Munson, S. (1985). "Attitudes of Teachers in Regular Education Toward Mainstreaming Mildly Handicapped Students." In C. J. Meisel (Eds.), *Mainstreaming Handicapped Children: Outcomes, Controversies, and New Directions* (pp. 111–128). Hillsdale, NJ: Lawrence Erlbaum.

Schniedewind, N. and Salend, S. J. (1987). "Cooperative Learning Works." *Teaching Exceptional Children, 19*(2), 22–25.

Synthesis of Research on Gifted Youth

The research on identifying and educating gifted youth supports the use of multiple identification measures, accelerated instruction, and ability grouping.

JOHN F. FELDHUSEN

John F. Feldhusen is Director, Gifted Education Resource Institute, Purdue University, South Campus Courts–G, West Lafayette, IN 47907.

What is giftedness? What is talent? What should schools and parents do for gifted and talented youth? What are desirable short-term and long-range goals for their development? While definitive answers to these questions are not yet available to guide us, research and evaluation projects during the past 20 years have given us some insights about how to structure and conduct educational services for gifted and talented students.[1]

Conceptions of Giftedness

Educators often view giftedness as something calling for a label (Guskin et al. 1986). The most troubling report on conceptions of gifted and talented youth was presented by Richert, Alvino, and McDonnel in 1982. They conducted a national survey of school personnel and concluded that there is "a labyrinth of confusion" (p. 89) about what giftedness is.

Sternberg and Davidson (1986) made a major contribution to theory in their excellent compilation, *Conceptions of Giftedness*, which presents the views of 29 researchers. This work offers the clearest delineation of what is known and what remains unknown about giftedness and presents the conclusion that giftedness is often seen as cognitive processing capacity, following models of information processing.

Gagne (1985) presented one of the first major attempts to delineate talent as distinct from giftedness. He suggested that talent is an ability focus that emerges out of general ability. He proposed four domains of general ability or giftedness: intellectual, creative, socio-emotional, and sensorimotor. In individuals, these abilities develop differentially; they interact with environmental circumstances and personality factors in the child and emerge as talent in specific fields, such as leadership, art, natural science, dance, or photography. Schooling is essential in the development of specific talents from general giftedness.

Major determiners of school-based conceptions of giftedness are Renzulli (1986) and Stanley and Benbow (1986). Renzulli's three-ring concept of giftedness was first presented in 1978 and has been elaborated and updated in a chapter in *Conceptions of Giftedness* (Sternberg and Davidson 1986). This model proposes three interlocking sets of traits: above-average abilities, creative capacities, and task commitment. Renzulli stressed that it is more productive to focus on gifted behaviors than to attempt to determine whether or not children are gifted. He also emphasized the idea that giftedness is a set of traits that can grow with nurturance, not just a condition bestowed on some and denied to others. Major support for the three-ring model has been presented by Monks and colleagues (1985) from research conducted in Europe. Monks extended the three-ring concept to include the social context in which giftedness manifests itself (family, school, and peers).

Identification

Educators must, of course, identify gifted students before they can provide special enrichment and accelerated services. Many states make identification a prerequisite for receiving special funding for the gifted. Moreover, good identification procedures yield information about students that can guide program development.

Nevertheless, identification of signs of giftedness, of potential for high-quality creative achievement, remains a relatively inexact science. There is great variation in the procedures used to detect giftedness. Many practitioners search for the gifted *child*, not for *signs* of giftedness, of potential. They typically pay little attention to diagnosing children's particular strengths or talents. Most researchers and theorists agree that multiple measures should be used in identifying the gifted, but multiple data sources are rarely used to specify alternate types of giftedness or to specify appropriate program services. Often multiple scores are simply added up to identify the "all purpose" gifted child.

Interpreting the results of their national survey, Richert, Alvino, and McDonnel (1982) concluded that the "state of the art of identification of gifted and talented youth is in some disarray" (p. 39). They found that a wide variety of test instruments, many of them lacking any standardization, are used to identify gifted students, and are often used quite inappropriately.

Yarborough and Johnson (1983) surveyed the 50 state departments of education concerning identification of the gifted. They found that standardized achievement tests and tests of intelligence are widely used, in spite of prevailing pessimism that either form of testing really reflects giftedness.

More recently, Klausmeier, Mishra, and Maker (1987) surveyed school psychologists in the United States concerning their views and practices in identifying the gifted. Their first choices of tests were the Wechsler Scales and the Stanford-Binet. Very few used creativity tests or achievement tests. The school psychologists surveyed also viewed themselves as poorly trained for identification of the gifted.

The work of Stanley and colleagues on the identification and nurturance of mathematically and verbally talented youth has been presented in dozens of articles and a number of books. For example, in *Mathematical Talent, Discovery, Description, and Development* (1974), Stanley, Keating, and Fox presented a series of papers by themselves and others. In *The Gifted and Creative, A Fifty-Year Perspective*, Stanley, George, and Solano (1977) presented new research; and Stanley set forth the rationale for his Study of Mathematically Precocious Youth (SMPY) and its use of the Scholastic Aptitude Test (SAT) as a primary identification tool. Later research presented by Benbow and Stanley in *Academic Precocity, Aspects of Its Development* (1983) confirmed the value of the SAT as an identification tool and the efficacy of high-level, fast-paced instruction for the gifted. Van Tassel-Baska (1984) has presented a more specific rationale for use of the SAT and talent searches to identify gifted children.

Feldhusen, Baska, and Womble (1981) discussed problems in the way test scores are combined in identification systems, and Feldhusen, Asher, and Hoover (1984) reviewed the many technical problems that can arise in the identification process. Hoover and Feldhusen (1987) presented a comprehensive model for the identification of the gifted at the secondary level.

Despite this catalog of research, serious problems remain in identifying giftedness, especially in finding talent among children from poverty and minority backgrounds (Baldwin 1987, McKenzie 1986, Chambers et al. 1980), among very young children (Hollinger and Kosek 1985), and among those who are underachievers in school (Butler-Por 1987). Some promise has been shown in the SOI (Structure Of Intellect) tests and research by Meeker and colleagues (1985), which focus on the assessment of several factors of intelligence; but Clarizio and Mehrens (1985) have criticized the SOI tests as lacking adequate norms and having questionable reliability and validity. Heller and Haeny (1985) at the University of Munich are conducting a major research project on identification of the gifted, funded by the Federal Republic of Germany.

Acceleration

Acceleration means different things to its proponents and its opponents. To proponents it means providing instruction at a level and pace appropriate to the child's level of achievement or readiness. In a series of experiments,[2] my colleagues and I showed that if an effort is made to assess children's readiness level for learning a new task, and if a new task is then taught at that proper level, children will retain the new learning in both short- and long-term memory; and they will transfer the new learning to other related learning tasks. A host of other studies reviewed by Daurio (1979) confirmed the short- and long-term values of all forms of acceleration, ranging from early admission to school to early admission to college, and the absence of problems resulting from acceleration in the lives of accelerated youth.

From the point of view of proponents, *acceleration* is a misnomer; the process is really one of bringing gifted and talented youth up to a suitable level of instruction commensurate with their achievement levels and readiness so that they are properly challenged to learn the new material. Proponents of acceleration also argue that gifted children spend much time in school encountering new material at far too slow a pace or being instructed in things they already know. They argue that an excess of such experience demotivates the gifted and talented, and is at the heart of the widespread problem of underachievement among the gifted (Whitmore 1980).

Opponents of acceleration view it as rushing children through the curriculum without concern for their social and emotional development. Although Kulik and Kulik (1984) showed in their analysis of the research that acceleration does not cause social-emotional problems, critics—especially school personnel—fear that gifted and talented youth will suffer from social immaturity in an accelerated setting and hence experience emotional difficulty. However, a recent review of the social-emotional adjustment and maturity of gifted and talented youth by Janos and Robinson (1985b) concluded that:

● Gifted and talented youth are often precocious or advanced in their social adjustment; as a result, they often prefer older playmates.

● They are socially and emotionally well adjusted.

● Extremely gifted children have more social and emotional adjustment problems than those who are moderately gifted.

Major changes in educators' views of acceleration of the gifted and talented came from the work of Stanley at Johns Hopkins University in the Study of Mathematically Precocious Youth and the later Study of Verbally Precocious Youth.[3] This research clearly established the value of accelerated instruction for gifted youth, the validity of using the Scholastic Aptitude Test as an identification tool for gifted youth at the middle school level, and the effectiveness of a diagnostic/prescriptive teaching methodology to test gifted youth in the classroom and place them at appropriate levels of readiness. Brody and Benbow (1987) reviewed the research from the acceleration projects at Johns Hopkins University and concluded:

This study investigated the relationships between acceleration and academic achievement, extra-curricular activities, goals and aspirations, and social and emotional adjustment for highly able students who have selected accelerative options to varying degrees. This study did not reveal any harmful effects as a result of acceleration (p. 109).

On the contrary, they reported that accelerated students earned more state and national awards than non-accelerated students and more attended highly selective colleges. Brody and Benbow (1987) stress that accelerated students gain in being able to select challenging learning experiences in their special interests.

Several researchers have reviewed studies of early admission to school and grade advancement of precocious children.[4] They agree on the positive value of such acceleration for children of high achievement and ability and the relative absence of personal or social problems, if the advancement is made after careful examination of the individual circumstances. These researchers presented guidelines to help school personnel make decisions regarding candidates for early admission or grade advancement.

Several researchers have reported on studies in which middle school and high school students received advanced high school or college level courses while still enrolled as secondary students (Benbow and Stanley 1983), and additional research is reported on the effects of College Board Advanced Placement (AP) Courses on high school students (Willingham and Morris 1986). Compared to students of equal ability who did not take AP courses, students who did so in high school had better academic records in college, graduated from college with more honors, engaged in more leadership activities, and took more advanced courses in college. Benbow and· Stanley (1983) reported on an eight-year follow-up of students who took accelerated classes in high school. They concluded:

Findings from the eight-year follow-up of the participants in SMPY's first fast-paced precalculus classes and equally able nonparticipants revealed that the most successful students in the mathematics classes achieved much more in high school and college than the equally able students who had not participated. The students were satisfied with their acceleration, which they felt did not detract from their social and emotional development. Furthermore, there appeared to be no evidence to justify the fear that accelerated rate of learning produces either gaps in knowledge or poor retention (p. 208).

Several researchers have also conducted studies of the progress and success of students who enter college early.[5] Compared to unaccelerated peers matched for ability, accelerated students earned higher GPAs, earned more honors, associated with older and more intellectual students, were more satisfied with the academic climate, and were equal in psychosocial adjustment to unaccelerated peers. Clearly, students who are ready for the college experience thrive on the opportunity to enter college early.

Kulik and Kulik (1983, 1984) have done major syntheses of the research on acceleration of the gifted. They concluded that accelerated students perform as well academically as equally able students who are already in the advanced grade(s), and accelerated students show a year's advancement over nonaccelerants of the same age. Long-range performance indicators produced less clear findings but suggested that accelerants earned more advanced degrees, earned top salaries, and were viewed favorably by superiors. The Kuliks (1984) concluded that:

Together experimental and correlational studies provide strong evidence that acceleration leads to greater student achievement in school and in life for talented students (p. 89).

Given the evidence of superior achievement in school and in performance beyond school and an absence of evidence suggesting social-emotional problems due to acceleration, my colleagues and I conclude that, to provide for the gifted, we must upgrade the level and pace of instruction to fit their abilities, achievement levels, and interests. Further, for gifted youngsters, the only suitable enrichment—defined as extended learning beyond the regular curriculum—is instruction on special enriching topics at a high level and a fast pace.

Grouping

Providing special services for the gifted and talented almost inevitably requires some special grouping. Grouping the gifted for all or part of the school day accommodates achievement and readiness levels and can serve other purposes as well. Gifted and talented children complain a great deal about the boredom of their classroom experiences (Feldhusen and Kroll 1985); they are forced to spend a lot of time being taught things they already know, doing repetitive drill sheets and activities, and receiving instruction on new material at too slow a pace. These experiences probably cause gifted youth to lose motivation to learn, to get by with minimum effort, or to reject school as a worthwhile experience.

Grouping gifted and talented youth for all or part of the school day or week also serves as a stimulus or motivator. Interaction with other students who are enthusiastic about astronomy, robotics, Shakespeare, or algebra motivates gifted and talented students. DeLisle reports (1984) that gifted children must often hide or suppress their special interests or their enthusiasms for academic topics or else face ridicule; peer pressure prohibits excitement about academics in many schools. In special classes for the gifted and talented, the reverse is true: mutual reinforcement of enthusiasm for academic interests and activities prevails.

For gifted and talented youth, grouping also confirms the legitimacy of their personal identity. Some of them worry about being viewed as outcasts because of their scholarly or bookish natures. Through interaction with other gifted or talented youth in special programs, however, they discover others who are like themselves and learn that it is legitimate to have strong intellectual interests and enthusiasm for reading and study. Thus, the sense of being abnormal is alleviated, and a new, positive self-image can emerge.

The Kuliks reported two meta-analytic evaluations of the research literature on ability grouping (1982, 1987). They found (1982) the average effect size for educational achievement to be small but significant, favoring grouped classes. However, when high-ability youth were grouped in special classes *and* given enriched or accelerated instruction, effect sizes were large. Grouped high-ability students also developed more favorable attitudes toward the subject matter than did high-ability students in ungrouped classes. And achievement of low- and average-ability students did not decline when high-ability students were removed to the special classes.

In a more recent meta-analytic study of the research on grouping, the Kuliks (1987) included a wider variety of studies. They concluded that the strongest and clearest effects of grouping came from programs designed especially for talented students. The talented students in these programs gained more academically than they would have in heterogeneous classes (p. 28). Special within-class grouping designed for talented students raised academic achievement substantially. The Kuliks (1987) concluded that "grouping can be a powerful tool in the education of gifted and talented students" (p. 29).

A frequent complaint from regular classroom teachers is that any special grouping of the gifted that removes them from the regular classroom will deprive children of low and average ability of role models to motivate them to higher achievement. Conversely, some teachers have reported positive effects when the gifted leave; they no longer dominate the classroom, and children of low and average ability get a chance to be leaders or top performers. Nevertheless, the idea that the gifted are needed to inspire other students is ubiquitous.

In a comprehensive review of the literature on peer role models in the classroom, Shunk (1987) concluded that the more alike observers and models are, the greater the probablity that the model affects observer behavior. In other words, watching someone of *similar ability* succeed at a task raises the observers' feelings of efficacy and motivates them to try the task: hence the superiority of "coping" role models over "mastery" role models. Coping models gradually improve their performance after some effort, and are thus effective models for peers who will also have to struggle to achieve academically. Mastery models (often the gifted), on the other hand, demonstrate perfect performance from the outset.

Overall, my colleagues and I conclude that grouping of gifted and talented students in special classes with a differentiated curriculum, or as a cluster group in a regular heterogeneous classroom (but again with differentiated curriculum and instruction), leads to higher academic achievement and better academic attitudes for the gifted and leads to no decline in achievement or attitudes for the children who remain in the regular heterogeneous classroom.

Meeting the Needs of the Gifted

Gifted and talented youth need accelerated, challenging instruction in core subject areas that parallel their special talents or aptitudes. They need opportunities to work with other gifted and talented youth. And they need highly competent teachers who both understand the nature and needs of gifted youth and are deeply knowledgeable in the content they teach.

If we fail to meet the needs of gifted students, we are harming not only those children but all of society, which benefits from their contributions. We must enable all students to realize their potential, including the gifted.

---

1. The research and evaluation evidence has been reported mainly in articles in the *Roeper Review*, the *Journal for the Education of the Gifted*, and the *Gifted Child Quarterly*, while evaluation and development projects have been reported in *Gifted Child Today*, *Gifted International*, and *Gifted Education International*. A number of books and technical reports have also documented the findings of researchers, developers, and evaluators.

2. Feldhusen and Klausmeier 1959; Klausmeier and Feldhusen 1959; Klausmeier, Check, and Feldhusen 1960; and Feldhusen, Check, and Klausmeier 1961.

3. Stanley 1978; Stanley 1980; Stanley, Keating, and Fox 1974; Stanley, George, and Solano 1977; Stanley and Benbow 1982; Benbow and Stanley 1983; Stanley and McGill 1986.

4. Feldhusen, Proctor, and Black 1986; Proctor, Black, and Feldhusen 1986; Proctor, Feldhusen, and Black 1988.

5. Janos and Robinson 1985a, Janos 1987, Janos et al. 1988.

References

Baldwin, A.Y. (1987). "I'm Black, but Look at Me, I Am Also Gifted." *Gifted Child Quarterly* 31, 4: 180-185.

Benbow, C.P., and J.C. Stanley. (1983). "An Eight-Year Evaluation of SMPY: What Was Learned?" In *Academic Precocity, Aspects of Its Development*, edited by C.P. Benbow and J.C. Stanley. Baltimore: Johns Hopkins University Press, 205-214.

Brody, L.E., and C.P. Benbow. (1987). "Accelerative Strategies: How Effective Are They for the Gifted?" *Gifted Child Quarterly* 31: 105-109.

Butler-Por, N. (1987). "*Underachievers in School*. New York: John Wiley and Sons.

Chambers, J.A., F. Barron, and J.W. Sprecher. (1980). "Identifying Gifted Mexican-American Students." *Gifted Child Quarterly* 24, 3: 123-128.

Clarizio, H.F., and W.A. Mehrens. (1985). "Psychometric Limitations of Guilford's Structure-of-Intellect Model for Identification and Programming of the Gifted." *Gifted Child Quarterly* 29, 3: 113-120.

Daurio, S.P. (1979). "Educational Enrichment Versus Acceleration: A Review of the Literature." In *Educating the Gifted, Acceleration and Enrichment*, edited by W.C. George, S.J. Cohn, and J.C. Stanley. Baltimore: Johns Hopkins University Press, 13-63.

DeLisle, J.R. (1984). *Gifted Children Speak Out*. New York: Walker Company.

Feldhusen, J.F., J.W. Asher, and S.M. Hoover. (1984). "Problems in the Identification of Giftedness, Talent, or Ability." *Gifted Child Quarterly* 28: 149-156.

Feldhusen, J.F., L.K. Baska, and S.R. Womble. (1981). "Using Standard Scores to Synthesize Data in Identifying the Gifted." *Journal for the Education of the Gifted* 4: 177-185.

Feldhusen, J.F., J. Check, and H.J. Klausmeier. (1961). "Achievement in Subtraction." *The Elementary School Journal* 61: 322-327.

Feldhusen, J.F., and H.J. Klausmeier. (1959). "Achievement in Counting and Addition." *The Elementary School Journal* 59: 388-393.

Feldhusen, J.F., and M.D. Kroll. (1985). "Parent Perceptions of Gifted Children's Educational Needs." *Roeper Review* 1: 240-252.

Feldhusen, J.F., T.B. Proctor, and K.N. Black. (1986). "Guidelines for Grade Advancement of Precocious Children." *Roeper Review* 9, 1: 25-27.

Gagne, F. (1985). "Giftedness and Talent." *Gifted Child Quarterly* 29: 103-112.

Guskin, S.L., C. Okolo, E. Zimmerman, and C.Y.J. Ping. (1986). "Being Labelled Gifted or Talented: Meanings and Effects Perceived by Students in Special Programs." *Gifted Child Quarterly* 30: 61-65.

Heller, K.A., and E.A. Haeny. (1985). "Identification, Development, and Analysis of Talented Children." In *Identifying and Nurturing the Gifted*, edited by K.A. Heller and J.F. Feldhusen. Toronto: Hans Huber, 67-82.

Hollinger, C.L., and S. Kosek. (1985). "Early Identification of the Gifted and Talented." *Gifted Child Quarterly* 29, 4: 168-171.

Hoover, S.M., and J.F. Feldhusen. (1987). "Integrating Identification, School Services, and Student Needs in Secondary Gifted Programs." *Arkansas Gifted Educators' Magazine* 1: 8-16.

Janos, P.M. (1987). "A Fifty-Year Follow-Up of Terman's Youngest College Students and IQ-Matched Agemates." *Gifted Child Quarterly* 31, 2: 55-58.

Janos, P.M., and N.M. Robinson. (1985a). "The Performance of Students in a Program of Radical Acceleration at the University Level." *Gifted Child Quarterly* 29, 4: 175-179.

Janos, P.M., and N.M. Robinson. (1985b). "Psychosocial Development in Intellectually Gifted Children." In *The Gifted and Talented, Developmental Perspectives*, edited by F.D. Horowitz and M. O'Brien. Washington, D.C.: American Psychological Association, 149-195.

Janos, P.M., N.M. Robinson, C. Carter, A. Chapel, R. Cufley, M. Curland, M. Daily, M. Guilland, M. Heinzig, H. Kehl, S. Lu, D. Sherry, S. Stotoff, and A. Wise. (1988). "A Cross-Sectional Developmental Study of the Social Relations of Students Who Enter College Early." *Gifted Child Quarterly* 32, 1: 210-215.

Klausmeier, H.J., J.F. Check, and J.F. Feldhusen. (1960). "Relationships Among Physical, Mental, Achievement, and Personality Measures in Children of Low, Average, and High Intelligence at 125 Months of Age." *American Journal of Mental Deficiency* 65: 69-78.

Klausmeier, H.J., and J.F. Feldhusen. (1959). "Retention in Arithmetic Among Children of Low, Average, and High Intelligence at 117 Months of Age." *Journal of Educational Psychology* 50, 88-92.

Klausmeier, K., S.P. Mishra, and C.J. Maker. (1987). "Identification of Gifted Learners: A National Survey of Assessment Practices and Training Needs of School Psychologists." *Gifted Child Quarterly* 31, 3: 135-137.

Kulik, C.C., and J.A. Kulik. (1982). "Effects of Ability Grouping on Secondary School Students: A Meta-Analysis of Evaluation Findings." *American Educational Research Journal* 19, 3: 415-428.

Kulik, J.A., and C.C. Kulik. (1983). "Effects of Accelerated Instruction on Students." *Review of Educational Research* 54: 409-425.

Kulik, J.A., and C.C. Kulik. (October 1984). "Synthesis of Research on Effects of Accelerated Instruction." *Educational Leadership* 42, 2: 84-89.

Kulik, J.A., and C.C. Kulik. (1987). "Effects of Ability Grouping on Student Achievement." *Equity and Excellence* 23, 1-2: 22-30.

McKenzie, J.A. (1986). "The Influence of Identification Practices, Race, and SES on the Identification of Gifted Students." *Gifted Child Quarterly* 30, 2: 93-95.

Meeker, M., R. Meeker, and G. Roid. (1985). *Structure-of-Intellect Learning Abilities Test (SOI-LA)*. Los Angeles: Western Psychological Services.

Monks, F.J., H.W. VanBoxtel, J.J.W. Roelofs, and M.P.M. Sanders. (1985). "The Identification of Gifted Children in Secondary Education." In *Identifying and Nurturing the Gifted*, edited by K.A. Heller and J.F. Feldhusen. Toronto: Hans Huber Publishers, 39-65.

Highlights of Research on Gifted Youth

The voluminous research on gifted and talented students provides educators with guidelines for serving this special population.

Identification. Schools are often ineffective in identifying gifted students, especially in finding talent among children from poverty and minority backgrounds, among very young children, and among underachievers. Identification is most often based on intelligence tests; use of creativity tests or achievement tests is rare. Multiple data sources should be used to identify alternate types of giftedness and to specify appropriate program services.

Acceleration. Acceleration motivates gifted students by providing them with instruction that challenges them to realize their potential. Accelerated students show superior achievement in school and beyond. Despite the fears of some educators, acceleration does not damage the social-emotional adjustment of gifted youth.

Grouping. Grouping gifted and talented youth for all or part of the school day or week serves as a motivator. In special classes or cluster groups for the gifted, mutual reinforcement of enthusiasm for academic interests prevails. Removing gifted students from regular classrooms does not deprive other students of role models; instead, it allows them to be leaders and top performers.

Overall, to provide for the gifted, we must upgrade the level and pace of instruction to fit their abilities, achievement levels, and interests. The only suitable enrichment is instruction on special enriching topics at a high level and a fast pace. We must also provide them with highly competent teachers and with opportunities to work with other gifted and talented youth.

Proctor, T.B., K.N. Black, and J.F. Feldhusen. (1986). "Early Admission of Selected Children to Elementary School: A Review of the Literature." *Journal of Educational Research* 80, 2: 70-76.

Proctor, T.B., J.F. Feldhusen, and K.N. Black. (1988). "Guidelines for Early Admission to Elementary School." *Psychology in the Schools* 25: 41-43.

Renzulli, J.S. (1986). "The Three-Ring Conception of Giftedness: A Developmental Model for Creative Productivity." In *Conceptions of Giftedness*, edited by R.J. Sternberg and J.E. Davidson. New York: Cambridge University Press, 53-92.

Richert, E.S., J.J. Alvino, and R.C. McDonnel. (1982). *National Report on Identification: Assessment and Recommendations for Comprehensive Identification of Gifted and Talented Youth*. Sewell, N.J.: Educational Improvement Center–South.

Shunk, D.H. (1987). "Peer Models and Children's Behavioral Change." *Review of Educational Research* 52, 2: 149-174.

Stanley, J.C. (1978). "SMPY's DT-PI Model: Diagnostic Testing Followed by Prescriptive Instruction." *ITYB* 4, 10: 7-8.

Stanley, J.C. (1980). "On Educating the Gifted." *Educational Research* 9, 3: 8-12.

Stanley, J.C., and C.P. Benbow (1982). "Educating Mathematically Precocious Youth: Twelve Policy Recommendations." *Educational Researcher* 11, 5: 4-9.

Stanley, J.C., and C.P. Benbow (1986). "Youths Who Reason Exceptionally Well Mathematically." In *Conceptions of Giftedness*, edited by R.J. Sternberg and J.E. Davidson. New York: Cambridge University Press, 361-387.

Stanley, J.C., W.C. George, and C.H. Solano. (1977). *The Gifted and Creative: A Fifty-Year Perspective*. Baltimore: Johns Hopkins University Press.

Stanley, J.C., D.P. Keating, and L.H. Fox. (1974). *Mathematical Talent: Discovery, Description, and Development*. Baltimore: Johns Hopkins University Press.

Stanley, J.C., and A.M. McGill. (1986). "More About Young Entrants to College, How Did They Fare?" *Gifted Child Quarterly* 30, 2: 70-73.

Sternberg, R., and J. Davidson, eds. (1986). *Conceptions of Giftedness*. New York: Cambridge University Press.

VanTassel-Baska, J. (1984). "The Talent Search as an Identification Model." *Gifted Child Quarterly* 28, 4: 172-176.

Whitmore, J.R. (1980). *Giftedness, Conflict, and Underachievement*. Boston: Allyn Bacon.

Willingham, W.W., and M. Morris. (1986). "Four Years Later: A Longitudinal Study of Advanced Placement Students in College." *College Board Reports No. 86-2*. New York: College Entrance Examination Board.

Yarborough, B.H., and R.A. Johnson. (1983). "Identifying the Gifted: A Theory-Practice Gap." *Gifted Child Quarterly* 27, 3: 135-138.

Gifted Child Education

MYRLISS HERSHEY

Dr. Hershey is an associate professor of education and directs the Gifted Program teacher preparation at Wichita State University in Wichita, Kansas.

"They are our most precious natural resource, but like most minorities they are neglected," admonishes the speaker. "When their general level of instruction is compared to their measured ability, they could be called our most 'retarded' school population."

The audience of professional gifted child advocates nods and claps in agreement. For the most part, they represent innovative educators who desire an opportunity to practice their craft with a "degree of freedom" from lockstep expectations, rigid curriculum parameters, and administrative tyrannies. These educators are generally child-centered and understand that manifested abilities and preferred styles of learning vary considerably from student to student, and that these variations require personalized learning approaches. They also believe that mainstream classroom teachers have too little time, energy, and (sometimes) knowledge and skills to meet adequately the wide continuum of needs in their overpopulated classrooms. Special education essentially grows out of the assumption that regular classroom teachers need help in meeting the needs of handicapped children.

Recent federal laws (PL94–142, 1975) guarantee every child, regardless of handicap, the right to a free public school education in the least restrictive environment. The federal laws do not include the gifted student, but approximately twenty states have included the gifted in a mandate that offers them essentially the same special education provisions as other exceptional children. These provisions follow the rationale that classroom teachers, unable to meet the educational needs of handicapped students who function below standard grade level expectations, would also have difficulty serving the unique needs of the academically precocious. Typically, traditional schools do not offer differentiated educational programs based on individual needs and abilities. Curriculum is usually textbook based, even when the adopted texts are far off the mark for the majority of students in a given classroom. Even in classrooms where wise teachers differentiate curriculum for diverse needs, high teacher-student ratios and little planning time are limiting factors.

Would it not follow that classroom teachers, many of whom feel frustrated by these limitations, would welcome special educational provisions for exceptional students? Not necessarily. Most willingly accept relief from the time-consuming task of teaching basic academic skills to educationally handicapped or disabled students. But many seem reluctant to support special education programs for the gifted. Even those selfless teachers who subscribe to the Jeffersonian concept of democracy (there is nothing as unequal as the equal treatment of the unequal) express legitimate concerns about special educational provisions for the gifted. Their reservations cluster around three problem areas: scheduling, teaming, and labeling.

Most special education provisions for the gifted evolve as "pull-out" programs that take the students labeled gifted from the regular classroom for from one hour a week to half-day sessions daily. Some skilled learning managers are able to personalize their schedules so that pull-out programs do not pose any threat to their daily plans. In these well-managed classrooms each child has at least a partially individualized schedule. These flexible teachers team with the special education providers to develop an effective, integrated program for all students including those identified for special education services. When the facilita-

From *The Clearing House,* February 1988, pp. 280-282. Reprinted with permission of the Helen Dwight Reid Educational Foundation. Published by Heldref Publications, 4000 Albemarle, St., N.W., Washington, D.C. 20016. Copyright © 1988.

tor (consultant, teacher) for the gifted works as an adjunct to such teachers, the results are usually positive. The specialist provides appropriate enrichment and/or accelerative learning material that the classroom teacher implements in designated content areas. The gifted students are occasionally pulled out for activities that give them opportunities to interact with other gifted students.

In states where identified gifted students must have Individualized Educational Programs (IEPs) along with all other identified special education students, it seems imperative that the major educational provider (in most cases the classroom teacher) have a strong voice in IEP planning. The effective classroom teacher/special education facilitator team can deal effectively with the

---

One mature, socially responsible sixth grader refuses to go on special field trips because his friends (whom he considers also gifted) resent his special privileges.

---

often-negative stigma of labeling. Then identified special education students, including the gifted, do not suffer for being deviant.

Identifying Gifted Students

In states where gifted education is mandated under stringent special education guidelines, the identification process is heavily reliant on Intelligence Quotient cut-offs. Identified gifted students are subjected to a reevaluation after three years just as handicapped special education students. These reevaluation guidelines assure handicapped students due process. When and if their educational handicaps are remediated, they deserve an opportunity to be phased into the regular school population. Remediation is not the purpose of special education for the gifted. Thus, the mirror-image interpretation of the law is not only redundant but may be harmful.

There are documented cases of students who, indeed, had their giftedness "remediated." One twelve-year-old girl whose initial I.Q. score was over 150 received a score of 128 on her retest three years later (the established cut-off score was 130). This discrepant performance might have been caused by high anxiety (she was afraid she might not qualify this time around), by the expected regression to the mean when the initial score is high, by standard (and not-so-standard) testing errors, or by a prejudiced psychometrist.

It is not logical to fit gifted students into procedures that are fully appropriate for educationally handicapped students. It would, in fact, make more sense to determine whether the gifted student is benefiting from his or her special education placement, rather than focus on whether he or she consistently scores high on

mental tests. When the letter of the law takes precedence over the intent of the law, however, students will be subjected to these anomalies.

Even a highly cooperative mainstream teacher may have misgivings about a program that seems to be so exclusionary. Highly creative students who would likely benefit from additional enrichment opportunities and advanced critical thinking opportunities may not achieve the appropriate I.Q. score. The I.Q. score cut-off has several limitations: The I.Q. test has a heavy cultural bias; it does not measure divergent thinking ability; and it cannot detect job-related talents such as communication skills, forecasting ability, and task commitment.

It is a myth that

- special education identification, placement, and review processes appropriate for handicapped students are fully appropriate for gifted students;
- gifted students always need special provisions outside the mainstream classroom;
- the curriculum needs of the gifted are adequately met by enrichment programs;
- identified gifted students do not have weak academic areas;
- the "gifted" label is always positive;
- gifted child educators are elitist;
- gifted child educators have no interest in the potential enhancement of all children;
- any gifted program is better than none;
- regular educators need not be concerned about the needs of the gifted students in special education programs; and that
- acceleration is inappropriate for most gifted students.

Implications for Gifted Education

1. There are deviant students who need special provisions in school. Most classroom teachers do not have the time, energy, and sometimes, the knowledge and skills to work effectively with deviant students.
2. Those students who are capable of working beyond grade level should not be held back.
3. I.Q. scores are not adequate as sole identifiers of students who will receive gifted programming.
4. State departments of education should appropriately modify special education regulations for gifted students.
5. Consultation with a gifted education specialist may help a mainstream teacher work more effectively with identified gifted students.
6. Elitism is an attitude, not a program.
7. Gifted child education can promote flexible, differentiated instruction that will have a ripple effect to all students.
8. Gifted child education can enhance the level of

awareness among educators of the unique learning needs of highly able students.

9. Special education for the gifted can demonstrate the efficacy of individual educational planning for all students.

10. Radical acceleration will meet the learning needs of some high-achieving gifted students.

11. Gifted child education can demonstrate the importance of advocacy from all sectors for highly talented students.

Outcomes of Labeling Students

When a student is labeled, he or she must cope with the implications of that label. Socially able students identified as gifted seem capable of taking it in their stride; ''nerd'' does not fit them. Their families usually provide warmth, support, and balance. Other students who have been labeled are confused by the altered reactions of teachers, friends, family, and neighbors. Some begin to hear, ''If you're so gifted, why can't you figure it out?'' or ''You're gifted, but you don't finish your work.'' Many who feel no handicap before being formally identified as gifted know they catch on faster than most of their classmates and recognize that they sometimes know more than the teacher. Now they feel the weight of a different, more burdensome ambiguity. They wonder how to react. One possibility is for them to call on their mature human relations skills to help them cope. But some students have not developed these skills. Another option is to withdraw—to hide gifted behavior. Still another possibility is to act out, to be the clown, idiosyncratic, a know-it-all.

One mature, socially responsible sixth grader refuses to go on special field trips because his friends (whom he considers also gifted) resent his special privileges. He also notes that some of the underprivileged students need these extracurricular experiences more than he does.

Other identified gifted students may reject pull-out opportunities because they have to make up all work missed in the regular classroom as a kind of penance for their special privileges. It finally is not worth it for some of the students.

Parental feedback indicates that enrichment opportunities, while welcome and often suitable, cannot overcome a lack of meaningful and challenging course content. It is irrefutable that highly gifted, achieving students require radical acceleration—anathema to most public school teachers.

Some parents defend inadequate programs for the gifted just for the status it gives their child. Others see the program as a way to have input into their child's education through IEPs. The latter motivation seems defensible. Maybe these personalized procedures can become pilot endeavors that will be adopted for parents of students on all levels. Indeed, it is surprising that parents of ''average'' students have not demanded the same due process rights given those of ''exceptional'' students.

Conclusions

All children are special. Each child brings to the world a gift worthy of enhancement. All children would benefit from gifted classrooms (personalized learning environments).

We should accept that some highly deviant gifted students need more than a pull-out program in the name of ''special'' education. Gifted child education can be a pattern for appropriately differentiated instruction. When the learning needs of students become the first priority of the educational system and are reflected in budgets, class size, training, and support systems, all education will be gifted.

Learning Strategies Can Help

Mary E. Scott

Mary E. Scott *(CEC Chapter #182) is Adjunct Associate Professor, University of Oklahoma, Norman.*

■People employ certain styles or strategies as they go about learning (Griggs & Dunn, 1984), some of which are more effective than others. Research has indicated that most academic failures can be attributed to surmountable strategy difficulties rather than limitations in capacity (Baron, 1978). Although learning entails some intellectual factors that are not modifiable, nonintellectual factors such as learning styles and strategies can foster or inhibit the full use of a person's ability (Tannenbaum, 1983), and studies have shown that students who are taught learning strategies can greatly improve their overall academic performance (Scruggs, Mastroperi, Monson, & Jorgensen, 1985).

Gifted students in general show a certain cluster of learning strategy patterns unique to their group (Griggs & Dunn, 1984). Since they employ learning strategies most successfully, exploration of how they go about learning can help teachers understand how to guide *all* students toward becoming more effective learners.

Learning Strategies of Gifted Students

Although some of the traits that vary in gifted versus nongifted students are unmodifiable or genetically determined, others are modifiable (Mann & Sabatino, 1985). The following six traits of gifted learners have been selected from among many to serve as examples of traits that may be modified in students with learning difficulties:

1. Superior concentration skills—are able to tune in and stay on task.
2. Field independence—are not distracted by the environment around them.
3. Reflection—have a tendency to ponder, observe, and take time to think.
4. Internal locus of control—feel in charge and responsible for what is accomplished.
5. Active learning—take a vigorous part in the learning process.
6. Persistence—keep on task until a way is found to complete a task (Dunn & Price, 1980; Klatzky, 1980; Steinberg, 1981).

While successful gifted learners possess this cluster of traits, students with learning difficulties often show a cluster of traits that are nearly opposite; that is, they lack concentration skills, are distractible and impulsive, feel others control them, depend on others to direct them, and give up easily. In fact, one study of cognitive strategies found that students who used nearly all the strategies attributed to gifted students fell in the top 15% to 18% of the population while those who lacked the majority of these strategies fell in the bottom 15% to 18% of the population in terms of achievement (Letteri, 1985). If students were taught successful strategies for learning, improvement could be tremendous, and strategies such as the six discussed here are indeed teachable (Mann & Sabatino, 1985).

Superior Concentration Skills

Sustained concentration is essential if learning is to occur. Many gifted learners can tune in and stay on task successfully; some learners, including gifted underachievers (Whitmore, 1980), cannot. Since attention and concentration significantly affect the operations of other cognitive processes, their lack is a major cause of faulty information processing.

Given the opportunity, students can learn to concentrate (Vail, 1979). One way to teach this is an exercise called "power of concentration" (Whitmore, 1980). Students bring to school an interesting object that they must try to focus their undivided attention on for as long as possible. They keep track of their own increases in the amount of time they can focus with undivided attention, and they must evaluate sources of interference with concentration.

Unfortunately, schools usually break concentrated study or thought with a bell, a signal to move on, and parents often interfere with concentration as well. Considering how vital concentration is to learning, it may be important to reschedule broken days into more extended learning opportunities, especially for students who have difficulty concentrating because of distractions.

Many students can concentrate better with a background of music or other consistent noise (Ostrander &

Reprinted from *Teaching Exceptional Children*, Spring 1988, pp. 30-34, by permission of The Council for Exceptional Children.

Schroeder, 1979). Headsets and music can be a tremendous learning aid for some students who have difficulty concentrating. Being allowed to draw or doodle on a sketch pad while attending to a lecture also can aid attention and concentration (Cordell & Cannon, 1985).

Games can help students learn to slow down and concentrate on one thing (Graham, 1985). Through games, students who are mentally retarded can learn to concentrate and see patterns, while students who are emotionally disturbed can learn to practice self-control, which will help with concentration. Chess, Mastermind, and Concentration are excellent games for this purpose. For students requiring even more basic help with concentration, the materials described by Douglas, Parry, Martin, and Garson (1976) and by Wittrock (1985) may be of interest.

Field Independence

Successful gifted students are very field independent (Steinberg, 1981). This means they can deal with all the input from the environment and still concentrate on the task at hand. This ability to decide just what is important and what is not is often the first and most important step in problem solving. Poor learners often lack this skill (Zeaman & House, 1963). They tend to see all tasks as global, and they seem unable to analyze what is crucial to the task at hand. They appear disorganized in their search for the information needed for a task.

Teaching segmentation skills can help students be more field independent and therefore more successful learners. They must be taught to take a global picture and break it into parts which can then be analyzed. They must learn to look from top to bottom or left to right or develop other methods of breaking large problems into small portions.

For example, a teacher could take a six-petaled flower and direct the students to look at each petal, count them, and notice how they are connected to the center circle and stalk. Having the students try to match the flower with others similar to it and discriminate those which are different (e.g., five petals, no stalk, etc.) will help them learn how to analyze and segment. Matching and differentiating geometric forms provide an even more basic exercise, but as this skill is learned it can be transferred to other tasks and problems (Letteri, 1985).

Another program, which has been used successfully with students as old as college age (Heiman, 1985) and is now being piloted at grades 6 through 12, is called "Learning to Learn." This program takes assignments, breaks the ideas into small segments, and helps the student step by step through the thinking, questions, and other steps that must be gone through in order to complete the work.

Another way to help students develop field independence is to make use of page cutting of assignments. The teacher takes a workbook page and cuts it into fourths or thirds, at first giving the students only one segment to concentrate on. As they become more skilled, they are given half pages and finally a full page. Alternatively, cardboard markers may be used to block out surrounding materials either by cutting out an inner space to reveal the task at hand or by placing the marker below the line to be worked on. After skill is gained, clear markers can provide a step toward independence from this aid.

Reflection

Successful gifted learners take time to ponder and reflect (Clark, 1986). This is an important learning strategy that often is not used by inefficient learners. Impulsive learners tend to make decisions based on partial and unorganized analysis of a task. They give responses quickly, but are often not correct. These learners need to be "encouraged not to give a quick answer (often the first thought or guess) but to carefully compare each choice. . ." (Letteri, 1985).

The "Learning to Learn" program helps develop reflection by encouraging students to stop and ask questions about new materials, engage in a covert dialogue with the lecturer or author, form hypotheses, and then read or listen for confirmation (Heiman, 1985). This helps them to reflect and think about the material to be learned and become personally involved in the learning process.

Schools appear to be training students to be "lightning thinkers." Rowe (1974) found that teachers allow students approximately 1 second to answer questions. Yet, since reflective students are the more successful learners, teachers may well have to analyze how they teach and what they reward. Teachers should consider how much time children will need to solve a problem and allow sufficient time before calling on them to present an answer or solution.

The game of chess can be one route to help learners slow down and think (Graham, 1985). Students should play with someone who will instruct them to look at the board and think before moving. Activities such as the hidden pictures and mazes in *Highlights* magazine also can help students learn to slow down and reflect. Activities that involve careful selection from among alternatives and lists of words that rhyme or have the same beginning sound will help transfer the skills of reflection to schoolwork (Letteri, 1985).

Cognitive behavior modification also can help impulsive students become more reflective. By simply reminding themselves to think before doing, students learn to control their impulsiveness (Hobbs, Moguin, & Troyler, 1980). Using this self-talk or verbal control strategy, teachers first model how students should perform; they act while describing what they are doing. Then the students repeat the actions and description. Gradually the students progress through whispered self-direction to self-direction through silent speech (Merchenbaum, 1980).

Another approach to impulse control is haptic discrimination training, in which students examine an object using touch only. The single-sense examination forces them to slow down and proceed more deliberately, and the improvement in impulse control is retained when the other senses are later reintroduced (Locher, 1985).

Internal Locus of Control

Successful gifted learners feel that they are in charge and are responsible for what is accomplished. They take responsibility for successes and failures and do not attribute these to luck or to others. This attitude is crucial for learning. Unsuccessful or underachieving learners often do not accept their responsibility in the outcome of events, and they blame others (Rimm, 1985);

they have an external locus of control. This lack of responsibility influences many areas of learning from interest to motivation and perseverance (Wittrock, 1985). Self-concept or confidence is also robbed when students do not take responsibility (Rimm, 1985). They develop a learned helplessness or dependence or a feeling of "everything is against me" (Whitmore, 1980).

Since internal locus of control is an attitude rather than a skill, improvement will come about as the result of how teachers interact with such students rather than through specific activities (Dinkmeyer & McKay, 1982). Encouragement and positive feedback are important if students are to become self-confident and responsible for their own behavior and focus on internal evaluation. It is also important for teachers not to provide too much help, because this can be seen as a vote of no confidence. Situations must be set up that require effort but also ensure the possibility of success. Teachers should insist on independent activity and reward finished products with stickers, stars, privileges, and so forth, but avoid giving sympathy or one-to-one help. Only students who can perceive the relationship between their efforts and the outcomes will achieve (Rimm, 1985).

Teachers should also be aware that if their classroom and lesson organization incorporates only competition or external criteria in grading, external locus of control will be developed. The students will sense no control, may feel they are helpless, and will not be motivated to learn. In order to develop an internal locus of control, students must have some opportunities to make decisions and choose from alternatives. More detailed discussion of internal locus of control can be found in Clark (1986).

Two additional programs that can retrain students not to attribute success to luck, task difficulty, or ability are by de Charms (1972) and McCombs (1982). Suggestions for help with this problem are also available in the form of activity books that structure positive, successful games and activities (Canfield & Wells, 1976).

Active Learning

Successful gifted learners demand to take a vigorous part in the learning process. Internal locus of control helps them want to choose, explore, and manipulate factors within their surroundings (Brooks & Hounshell, 1975). If they see that they are responsible, they then take steps to go out and accomplish tasks, while students who feel no internal locus of control often take a passive role.

Anything that inspires students will help them remain in a state of high energy and do whatever needs to be done to achieve the desired end (Fletcher, 1978). Teachers should show students how to look at a topic from all angles. For example, in studying about Halley's Comet, teachers should not just have students read about it, they should let them see a film, go to the planetarium, talk to astronomers, use a telescope, draw a picture, write a story, or construct a comet. By teaching this way, they offer students chances to learn via all different modalities.

Perhaps the most crucial element of active learning is structuring classes so that students have the opportunity to be an active force in the learning process. Teachers should allow students to make some decisions about what will be learned and in what way the topic will be studied. They should allow students a role in setting expectations and class rules. They should encourage more independent study, hands-on practice, and student participation by contracting for projects and determining with the students expectations as to what will be done, how it will be done, and by what date it will be done.

Persistence

Successful gifted learners are well known for the persistence they show when working on a task (Clark, 1986). Persistence requires learners to face the prospect of failure as well as success. In order to persist on a task, students must learn to be tolerant of ambiguity and to sort through even that which contradicts and confuses (Letteri, 1985). If they cannot tolerate the flow of input learning requires, they will not succeed.

Materials and strategies have been developed that help students modify their cognitive structures to accommodate and assimilate new information and better persist with tasks (Letteri, 1985). Teaching students to persist involves getting them to understand that tasks take time. It can be fostered by starting them on tasks that take shorter times and as persistence improves, changing to tasks requiring more time.

Tracking programs, in which a student must find all the symbols in a row or on a page that match an initial symbol, may be of value. They can start with a single row, and later the number of rows can be increased until the exercise involves an entire page. Jigsaw puzzles can also be useful in helping students persist. They should be started on simple puzzles with few pieces and go on to more complex ones. Teachers can also offer nearly completed puzzles and have the students finish them. This enables the students to see the end and the real possibility of success. The game Mastermind can also be used to foster persistence by first using only a couple of holes and two or three colors of pegs and later increasing the number of holes and colors as skill increases.

Just talking to students about sticking with tasks can also help. They need to know that perfecting a project requires reading, editing, and re-reading until the project is done well. Students whose lack of persistence is due to past failure might also be helped by teaching by means of questions rather than assertions. Students who are led to discover a solution by means of well-chosen questions can develop the confidence in their own ability that is needed for persistence.

Implementation

These ideas for enhancing learning have been used in a variety of combinations depending on student needs. For example, during a summer program, an 8-year-old gifted child who was unable to attend to a task was given the power-of-concentration exercise on a daily basis. Even a student this young was able to keep track of increases in the amount of time he could focus and identify sources of interference. This particular student was distracted by nearly everthing, and awareness of this was the first step toward addressing the problem. Then a stereo headset, at first with calming music but later without any music, was used to block auditory distraction. A carrel was also used at first to block out visual distractions. The child was able to increase concentration time from less than a minue to over a one-half hour and maintain that concentration even without the use of a headset or carrel. But the biggest benefit of all was that he improved in most other areas as a result of being able to concentrate. He felt that he was in charge of his success, was more active, persisted longer, and was able to reflect and focus better over all. The example illustrates just one way teachers can design an effective program based on a particular student's weaknesses and needs.

Teachers and Learning Strategies

Since teachers must help students develop and use learning strategies, it is vital that they become more familiar with these strategies themselves. Since students often learn by example, it may also be important for teachers to *use* the strategies. As a first step they should analyze their own learning and teaching strategies and styles and devise ways to adapt them to different learners' needs. According to Mann and Sabatino (1985), this entails being able to

1. Describe accurately the strategies that pupils need to solve a problem (cognitive task analysis can apply).

2. Measure a student's use or nonuse of strategies.

3. Help students implement selected strategies and adjust and revise as tasks demand.

4. Monitor how well the strategy is progressing.

5. Motivate students to use the strategies once learned. (p. 216)

With these steps in mind, teachers can organize their instruction more around teaching important strategies. Whenever students are being taught strategies, it will help to discuss with them the effectiveness of those strategies and the importance of using them (Cordell & Cannon, 1985). Effective use of learning strategies can help all students to be more successful.

References

Baron, J. (1978). Intelligence and general strategies. In G. Underwood (Ed.), *Strategies of information processing* (pp. 403-450). London: Academic Press.

Brooks, M., & Hounshell, P. B. (1975). A study of locus of control and science achievement. *Journal of Research in Science Teaching, 12,* 175-181.

Canfield, J., & Wells, H. C. (1976). *100 ways to enhance self concept in the classroom.* Englewood Cliffs, NJ: Prentice-Hall.

Clark, B. (1986). *Growing up gifted.* Columbus, OH: Charles E. Merrill.

Cordell, A., & Cannon, T. (1985). Gifted kids can't always spell. *Academic Therapy, 21*(2), 143-152.

de Charms, R. (1972). Personal causation training in the schools. *Journal of Applied Social Psychology, 2,* 95-113.

Dinkmeyer, D., & McKay, G. (1982). *Systematic training for effective parenting.* Circle Pines, MN: Am. Guidance Svc.

Douglas, V. S., Parry, P., Martin, P., & Garson, C. (1976). Assessment of a cognitive training program for hyperactive children. *Journal of Abnormal Child Psychology, 4,* 389-410.

Dunn, R. S., & Price, G. E. (1980). The learning style characteristics of gifted students. *Gifted Child Quarterly, 24,* 33-36.

Fletcher, J. S. (1978). The outer limits of human educability: A proposed research program. *Educational Researcher, 7,* 13-18.

Graham, A. (1985). Chess makes kids smart. *Parents,* 112-116.

Griggs, S., & Dunn, R. (1984). Selected case studies of the style preferences of gifted students. *Gifted Child Quarterly, 28,* 115-119.

Heiman, M. (1985, Summer). Learning to learn. *Educational Leadership,* 20-24.

Hobbs, S. A., Moguin, L. E., & Troyler, N. (1980). Parameters of investigations of cognitive behavior therapy with children. *Catalog of Selected Documents in Psychology, 10,* 62-63.

Klatzky, R. L. (1980). *Human memory: Structures and process.* San Francisco: W. H. Freeman.

Letteri, C. (1985). Teaching students how to learn. *Theory into Practice, 24*(2), 112-122.

Locher, P. J. (1985). Use of haptic training to modify impulse and attention control deficits of learning disabled children. *Journal of Learning Disabilities, 18*(2), 89-93.

Mann, L., & Sabatino, D. (1985). *Foundations of cognitive process in remedial and special education.* Rockville, MD: Aspen Systems.

McCombs, B. C. (1982). Transitioning learning strategies research into practice: Focus on the student in technical training. *Journal of Instructional Development, 5,* 10-17.

Merchenbaum, D. (1980) Cognitive behavior modification with exceptional children: A promise yet unfulfilled. *Exceptional Educational Quarterly, 1,* 83-88.

Ostrander, S., & Schroeder, L. (1979). *Superlearning.* New York: Delacorte Press.

Rimm, S. B. (1985, September). How to reach the underachievers. *Instructor,* 73-76.

Rowe, M. B. (1974). Wait-time and rewards as instructional variables, their influence on language, logic, and fate control: Part I, Fate control. *Journal of Research in Science Teaching, 11,* 81-94.

Scruggs, T. E., Mastroperi, M. A., Monson, J., & Jorgensen, C. (1985). Maximizing what gifted students can learn: Recent findings of learning strategy research. *Gifted Child Quarterly, 29*(4), 181-185.

Steinberg, R. J. (1981). A componential theory of intellectual giftedness. *Gifted Child Quarterly, 25*(2), 86-97.

Tannenbaum, A. J. (1983). *Gifted children.* New York: MacMillan.

Vail, P. L. (1979). *The world of the gifted child.* New York: Walker.

Whitmore, J. R. (1980). *Giftedness, conflict and underachievement.* Boston: Allyn & Bacon.

Wittrock, M. C. (1985). Teaching learners generative strategies for enhancing reading comprehension. *Theory into Practice, 24*(2), 123-126.

Zeaman, D., & House, B. J. (1963). An attention theory of retardate discrimination learning. In N. R. Ellis (Ed.), *Handbook of mental deficiency* (pp. 159-223). New York: McGraw Hill.

Educating Language-Minority Children: Challenges And Opportunities

Teachers facing the challenge of teaching children from different cultural communities find themselves hard pressed to decide what constitutes an appropriate curriculum. Ms. Bowman identifies a few developmental principles that can provide a conceptual framework.

BARBARA T. BOWMAN

BARBARA T. BOWMAN is director of graduate studies at the Erikson Institute, which is affiliated with Loyola University, Chicago, where she teaches courses in public policy administration and early childhood curriculum. She is a past president of the National Association for the Education of Young Children and currently serves on a committee on early education for the National Association of State Boards of Education and on a committee on day care for the National Research Council.

HY CAN'T all Americans just speak standard English? This plaintive question reflects the distress that many citizens feel about the linguistic diversity that has become a source of divisiveness in society and a source of failure in the schools. In many school districts, the number of languages and dialects spoken by children and their families is staggering, as the languages of Central and South America, Africa, and Asia mix with various American dialects to create classrooms in which communication is virtually impossible. Across America, language-minority children are not learning the essential lessons of school and are not fully taking part in the economic, social, and political life of the country.

And the problem will soon become even more serious. Over the next decade or two, language-minority children will become the *majority* in our public schools, seriously straining the capacity of those institutions to educate them.

In a nation that is increasingly composed of people who speak different languages and dialects, the old notion of melting them together through the use of a common language is once again attractive. Requiring all children to speak the same language at a high level of proficiency would make the task of educating them a good deal easier. Unfortunately, what seems quite simple in theory is often difficult to put into practice. One of the most powerful reasons in this instance is the interrelationship of culture, language, and the children's development.

CULTURE, LANGUAGE, AND DEVELOPMENT

Christian men show respect for their religion by removing their hats but keeping their shoes on in church, while Muslim men show similar respect by keeping their hats on and removing their shoes in a mosque. But differences in how groups think and act are more than a matter of using different words or performing different actions for the same purposes. Differences in culture are more substantial than whether members of a community eat white bread, corn pone, or tortillas. The behavior of people varies, and the beliefs, values, and assumptions that underlie that behavior differ as well. Culture influences both behavior and the psychological processes on which it rests; it affects the ways in which people perceive the world — their physical environment, the events that surround them, and other people. Culture forms a prism through which members of a group see the world and create "shared meanings."

Child development follows a pattern similar to culture. The major structural changes in children — changes that arise from the interaction of biology and experience, such as language learning — are remarkably similar in kind and sequence across cultural groups. However, the specific knowledge and skills — the cultural learning — that children acquire at different ages depend on the children's family and community.

Learning a primary language is a developmental milestone for young children and is, therefore, a "developmentally appropriate" educational objective. Moreover, the informal, social method by which children learn their primary language is also "developmentally appropriate." However, the specific uses to which that language is put are determined by the culture.

As the ideas from a child's social world are brought to bear through the guidance of the older members of the community, children come to know, to expect, and to share meanings with their elders. Children acquire *scripts* (sequences of actions and words) for various interactions with people and things, and the adults in their families and communities structure these scripts for children to help them learn. Gradually, children internalize the adult rules for "making meaning."

From *Phi Delta Kappan*, October 1989, pp. 118-120. Reprinted by permission of the author and *Phi Delta Kappan*.

Classroom discourse presents a challenge to children to learn new rules for communication. The use of formal language, teacher leadership and control of verbal exchanges, question-and-answer formats, and references to increasingly abstract ideas characterize the classroom environment, with which many children are unfamiliar. To the extent that these new rules overlap with those that children have already learned, classroom communication is made easier. But children whose past experience with language is not congruent with the new rules will have to learn ways of "making meaning" all over again before they can use language to learn in the classroom.

When teachers and students come from different cultures and use different languages and dialects, the teachers may be unaware of the variations between their own understanding of a context and that of their students, between their own expectations for behavior in particular contexts and the inclinations of the children they teach. When children and adults do not share common experiences and do not hold common beliefs about the meaning of experiences, the adults are less able to help children encode their thoughts in language.

Children are taught to act, believe, and feel in ways that are consistent with the mores of their communities. The goals and objectives presented, the relationships available, and the behavior and practices recommended by family and friends are gradually internalized and contribute to a child's definition of self. Language is an integral part of a group's common experience. Speaking the same language connects individuals through bonds of common meaning and also serves as a marker of group membership; it is the cement for group members' relationships with one another. The shared past and the current allegiances of the group are the bedrock for the "common meanings" taught to children through language.

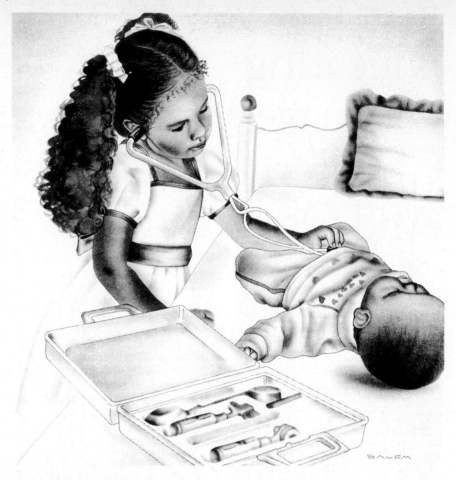

TEACHING CULTURALLY DIFFERENT CHILDREN

The idea of a developmentally appropriate curriculum is inherently attractive. It evokes a vision of classrooms in which experiences are synchronized with each child's levels of maturity and experience, so that what is taught is consistent with the child's capacity to learn.

But teachers facing the challenge of teaching children from different cultural communities find themselves hard pressed to decide what constitutes an appropriate curriculum. If the children speak different languages and dialects, how should teachers communicate with them? If children from some groups are hesitant to speak up in school, how can teachers organize expressive language experiences? If children from some groups are dependent on nonverbal cues for meaning, how can teachers stress word meaning? If different groups have different ways of expressing themselves, how can teachers know what children mean to say or what children understand of what teachers and other children say? How can teachers test for mastery of the curriculum if children do not speak a standard language or use the same styles of communication? Cultural diversity makes it hard for teachers to assess each child's developmental status, to find common educational experiences to promote further growth, and to measure the achievement of educational objectives.

Given the complexity of the interaction between culture and development, is it possible to design a developmentally appropriate curriculum at all? If that question implies that the same curriculum can be used for all children, the answer must be no. Children who have been socialized in different worlds will not understand material in the same ways. On the other hand, recognizing a few developmental principles can provide a conceptual framework for the culturally sensitive teacher. The following list of principles is not meant to be exhaustive; it merely provides a beginning for teachers who are trying to bridge the gap between children's cultural backgrounds and the school's objectives.

First, teachers need to learn to recognize developmentally equivalent patterns of behavior. Before they come to school, all children have learned many of the same things — a primary language, categorizing systems, interpersonal communication styles. Although these developmental accomplishments may look quite different, they can be said to be developmentally equivalent. There are a number of "equally good" ways to shape development. When a child does not respond to the social and cognitive expectations of the school, the teacher should look first for a developmentally equivalent task to which the child will respond. For instance, a child who does not talk in the classroom can be observed on the playground or at home. A child who does not separate buttons correctly can be asked to sort car logos or other personally rele-

amily values should reinforce school expectations; interpreting the school's agenda for parents is one of the teacher's most important tasks.

vant artifacts. A child who does not listen to stories about the seasons may be spellbound by a story about a basketball player.

Teachers who have doubts about the development of culturally different children should assume that the children are normal and look at them again, recognizing that their own vision may be clouded by cultural myopia. By assuming the developmental equivalence of a variety of tasks, adults can begin the search for the mismatch between their own and a given child's understanding of a situation or of a task to be performed.

Second, it is essential not to value some ways of achieving developmental milestones more highly than others, because young children are particularly sensitive to the ways in which adults view them. Asa Hilliard and Mona Vaughn-Scott point out that, because the behavior of African-American children is so different from that of their white peers, such children are often judged to be deficient in their development, rather than just different. The result is that normal, healthy children are sometimes diagnosed as sick or retarded.*

Speaking a common language is the cement that binds individuals to groups. Thus young children who speak languages other than English (or nonstandard dialects) are reluctant to give up this connection to the members of their own

*Asa Hilliard and Mona Vaughn-Scott, "The Quest for the Minority Child," in Shirley G. Moore and Catherine R. Cooper, eds., *The Young Child: Reviews of Research*, Vol. 3 (Washington, D.C.: National Association for the Education of Young Children, 1982).

group. When such children find that the way they talk and act is not understood or appreciated in school, they are apt to become confused or disengaged. And their rejection by the school presages their rejection of school.

Third, teachers need to begin instruction with interactive styles and with content that is familiar to the children. Whether this entails speaking in the child's primary language, using culturally appropriate styles of address, or relying on patterns of management that are familiar to and comfortable for children, the purpose is to establish a basis for communication. While fluency in a child's primary language may not be an achievable goal for many teachers, they can nonetheless become more adept at understanding, planning, and implementing a culturally sensitive curriculum. Such a curriculum must encompass more than tasting parties and colorful ethnic costumes; it must be more than shopworn introductions to the odd and amusing practices of people from different nations or different racial groups. In order to teach such a curriculum, teachers must have come to grips with their own ethnocentricity and must be able to deal with themselves and others fairly; teachers must know the difference between style and substance.

Fourth, school learning is most likely to occur when family values reinforce school expectations. This does not mean that parents must teach the same things at home as teachers do in school. However, it does mean that parents and other community members must view achievement in school as a desirable and attainable goal if the children are to build it

into their own sense of themselves. This means that interpreting the school's agenda for parents is one of the most important tasks for teachers.

Fifth, when differences exist between the cultural patterns of the home and community and those of the school, teachers must deal with these discrepancies directly. Teachers and children must create shared understandings and new contexts that give meaning to the knowledge and skills being taught. The challenge is to find personally interesting and culturally relevant ways of creating new contexts for children, contexts in which the mastery of school skills can be meaningful and rewarding. Learning mediated by teachers who are affectionate, interested, and responsive — teachers who are personally involved in the lives of young children — has greater "sticking power" than learning mediated by an adult who is perceived as impersonal and socially distant.

Sixth, the same contexts do not have the same meanings to children from different racial and ethnic groups. The meanings of words, of gestures, and of actions may be quite different. The assessment of learning outcomes presents a formidable problem when children misunderstand the meaning of the teacher's requests for information and for demonstrations of knowledge and skills. The same instructional materials and methods may take on meanings different from those that the teacher intended. Formal assessment should be delayed until teachers and children have jointly built a set of new meanings, so that the children understand the language and behavior called for in school.

A developmentally appropriate curriculum can never be standardized in a multicultural community. Thoughtful teachers, however, can use the principles of child development to make the new context of school meaningful, to attach new kinds of learning to what children have already achieved, and to safeguard the self-image and self-confidence of children as their knowledge and skills expand. It is not easy, but it is the only workable system.

Teaching to the Distinctive Traits of Minority Students

JAMES A. VASQUEZ

James A. Vasquez is an associate professor in the College of Education at the University of Washington, Seattle.

Researchers report that students at all levels find greater motivation and perform at higher levels academically when instructional methods complement student learning characteristics (Gentry and Ellison 1981). Yet it is not uncommon to find that many teachers, both minority and mainstream, are unable to identify distinctive traits among ethnic minority youths that require a unique set of instructional strategies if acceptable levels of learning are to be experienced by these youths. Equally disturbing is that, once such cultural traits have been identified, teachers have no idea how to adapt classroom instruction to these traits.

In this article I will identify several traits in each of three minority student groups and will show their notable distinctiveness when contrasted with traits commonly believed to characterize students from mainstream society. I will then suggest a procedure for adapting teaching to fit the distinctive traits of ethnic minority students.

Hispanic Students

An abundance of literature suggests that many Hispanic students are distinguished by a sense of loyalty to the family (Montalvo, Lasater, and Garza 1981; Vasquez 1979a; Ramirez and Castaneda 1974). Children from such homes are brought up with the notion that to bear the family name is a very important responsibility, that their behavior at all times reflects on the honor of the family, and that the family is to be their basic support group throughout their lives. Socialization of this type cannot help but produce in the individual a sense of motivation that is other-directed, one that seeks its impetus from a basically external source—the family. (Other minority groups seem also to imbue in their youth a sense of loyalty directed outwardly, although not necessarily toward the family.)

In contrast to this is the strong sense of individualism (Adams 1988; Brandt 1987) that is found in many typical mainstream families where young people are taught that life is in their hands, that they can go as far in life as they want, and that they will have only themselves to blame or to thank for what they have achieved at life's end. This concept is referred to as "rugged individualism" in textbooks. It is a deeply rooted value in American mainstream society, one that is said to have been of major importance in the move westward by Anglo-Americans when families lived in isolation and had to learn to depend largely on themselves.

Hispanic and mainstream students also differ significantly along the dimensions of cooperation and competition. The literature on Hispanic students abounds with reports on the preference of many of these youths, especially Chicanos, for activities in which they can achieve a goal with other students, not in isolation from them or in competition with them (Avellar and Kagan 1976; Kagan and Madsen 1971). The author remembers well his refusal to participate in a school activity in which he excelled simply because the teacher put him in a competitive position vis-à-vis his classmates. The experience is not uncommon among Hispanic students, as many will testify. In contrast, we find that mainstream youths are said to learn early on to be competitive (Elleson 1983; Nelson and Kagan 1972), that it is important to strive to be "numero uno," and that it is okay to achieve in school at someone else's expense. Because classes are essentially taught by mainstream, middle-class individuals, it is not surprising that such a high percentage of activities in the classroom require that students compete with one another.

A third trait of Hispanic youths in our schools (and one in which they are again in contrast with their mainstream peers) is their continual need for ethnic role models. Data from the U.S. Bureau of the Census (1980), for example, show that in a number of selected professions (computer specialist, engineer, math specialist, life scientist, physics scientist, psychologist, social scientist), Spanish-surnamed individuals are virtually nonexistent. This point must be well understood by teachers if they are to adequately serve students from

From *The Clearing House*, Vol. 63, No. 7, March 1990, pp. 299–304. Reprinted with permission of the Helen Dwight Reid Educational Foundation. Published by Heldref Publications, 4000 Albemarle St., N.W., Washington, D.C. 20016. Copyright © 1990.

this, and other, minority groups. Its importance is easily noted when we consider that the young persons' professional aspirations are so profoundly influenced by the presence or absence of role models in their awareness. Consider, for example, that mainstream children never have to ask themselves the question, "Can I really be a doctor (engineer, mayor, principal, etc.)? I've never seen one who looks like me." No, mainstream children are surrounded at all times by role models from their own ethnic backgrounds. That is the situation we would wish for all American children. Such is not the case, however, for many Hispanic children who have yet to see, or hear about, the first successful Hispanic in many of the professions in our society.

Black Students

Shade (1982) wrote that research has found black students, from an early age, to be significantly more person-centered than mainstream children who are characterized by an object-centered approach to learning. According to Young, the tendency of socialization techniques in the black community to orient the child toward persons tends "to frustrate the child's interest in the 'object world'" (in Shade 1982). Shade (1982) also reported that Yarrow, Rubenstein, Peterson, and Kowski found that preferences of black children for these two aspects of the environment (humans and inanimate objects) were "strikingly independent."

The roots of the person-centered preference may be found in historical settings that required that blacks, for survival purposes, be highly sensitive to the moment-by-moment moods of others, especially those who exercised total control over black people, and found in the enduring interpersonal relationships that existed between blacks and others in their social milieu. This distinction between black and white children takes on considerable importance when we become aware of the requirement in typical classrooms to focus on objects (mathematics, natural phenomena, letters of the alphabet, rules, etc.), not people, for extended periods of time in order to learn well.

Some research also suggests that many black children learn better when multiple stimuli are present. Following Young (1974), Shade (1982) noted that Afro-American children apparently "are taught to concentrate on many stimuli at one time rather than learning to concentrate on one." Shade also reported that Boykin (1979) concluded that although Euro-American children were apparently socialized to "tolerate monotony or unvaried presentation of material," black children "did markedly better if the formats had high variability" in problem-solving tasks.

Yet most classroom instruction apparently provides single or limited stimuli to students. If, as research suggests, single stimulus conditions are more conducive to learning among mainstream students than black students, we may be dealing, at this point, with an example

of typical classroom practice that favors one American ethnic group (the mainstream) at the expense of another.

Finally, black children may be more receptive to learning that allows them to use their skills in the oral tradition (a trait Barwell [1981] also reports among native Americans), although mainstream children are thought to have a stronger orientation to the written word as a major source of gathering information. Britto (1983), for example, cites Smitherman: "The crucial difference in American culture lies in the contrasting modes in which black and white Americans have shaped their language . . . a written mode for whites, having come from a European, print-oriented culture; a spoken mode for blacks, having come from an African, orally oriented background." Britto urges teachers of black youth to pursue "this avenue of understanding and study" in their teaching.

Native American Students

Some native American students are said to be characterized by a deductive, or holistic, approach to learning (Barwell 1981), which is sometimes referred to as the field-dependent style (the terms *field sensitive* and *field attentive* are sometimes used). This approach to learning proceeds from the general to the particular. Students so characterized are thought to be more responsive to an overview or "big picture" presented at the beginning of a lesson. They presumably are in need of an early orientation to the entire field of information to be covered (thus the term *field dependent*), after which they can proceed to more specific details of the lesson. So important is this learning preference among some native American students that one researcher (Barwell 1981) has stated that, in teaching these students, "above all, the course should be taught holistically."

In contrast to this learning style is the field-independent learning style, believed by some researchers to describe many, if not most, mainstream students (Ramirez and Castaneda 1974; Witkin 1967; Witkin et al. 1962). This trait requires a more inductive approach to learning, meaning that the student learns better when details are presented first and the direction of learning is from the particulars of a lesson to the more general concepts. Although neither learning style is unduly difficult to conceptualize, the significant differences in teaching strategies each requires for maximal learning among students are obvious.

An important additional (but infrequently discussed) trait of some native American students is their preference for engaging in trial-and-error learning by means of private rather than public experiences such as those the classroom provides. Kleinfeld (1975), for example, notes the difficulty some native American students have in coping with the direct type of criticism that failure in classroom activities inevitably brings. Researchers reporting this trait suggest that in some native American communities, learning among youth often takes place as the learner practices the skill to be mastered privately, and only after an acceptable degree of mastery is attained in that context will he or she attempt to publicly demonstrate it.

Yet traditional practice in the public classroom assumes no difference in this area among students, and teachers regularly employ activities that make failure an inevitable experience in the classroom. Indeed, many teachers believe that failure is an important and necessary learning experience for students. It would seem that the competitive nature of so many mainstream students (Vasquez 1979a; Avellar and Kagan 1976) would better prepare them for trial-and-error learning in our classrooms. The emphasis on keeping one's errors within one's own private experience as much as possible, combined with a relative lack of competitive spirit among native American students (Barwell 1981; Kleinfeld 1975), seems to work to their disadvantage at this point, considering the present nature of many of our classrooms.

Bridging Traits and Instructional Strategy

I will not in this article fall prey to the temptation to compare the merits of values within different American groups, but I cannot help but point out the important implications that differing values have for teachers in our classrooms. Recall, for the moment, the sense of family loyalty that characterizes many Hispanic youth from traditional homes. Now consider a common phrase any teacher might say to a student: "Good work, Mary. You should be proud of yourself." In an effort to reinforce the student for high performance, the teacher will use this phrase on the assumption that Mary has within her value system the belief that she should be proud of herself for doing good academic work.

But what if this is Maria, and not Mary? What if the student in question comes, not from a traditional mainstream value system with its high sense of individualism, but from a traditional Hispanic value system where children are not taught so much to perform for the sake of pride in their own work as for the pride their family will have in them? In such a case the teacher's efforts to reinforce the student will be largely ineffective.

Our attempts to reinforce must be based on values the student holds (Gentry and Ellison 1981; Vasquez 1979b; Vasquez and Wainstein n.d.), and these often differ depending on the particular ethnic (and social class) background of the student. It is for this reason that teachers who boast that they "treat all students the same" are not showing their democratic disposition, but rather that they are not yet prepared to teach in the pluralistic classrooms of American schools where already more than one in every four students is an ethnic minority student (U.S. Bureau of the Census 1986).

Or, again, consider the ease with which instruction could be made culturally suitable for black children if the teacher would keep in mind a person-oriented approach to teaching. Even concepts dealing with naturalistic phenomena (math, science) can be couched in terminology that involves people interacting with people. Is that too much to ask of a teacher who has black children in the classroom?

And what about the notion that the black culture has a strong oral tradition? Is this not also a unique strength that teachers should be quick to capitalize on for the purpose of enhancing learning among these students? It is a fact that a strong oral tradition characterized the Jewish people for many centuries, and it served them well.

Native American students, too, will be better served in our schools as teachers learn to adapt instruction to their learning propensities. It is not difficult, after all, to teach in a manner that makes use first of the larger concepts, to "set the field" with broad strokes right from the beginning of the lesson, to proceed from the general to the specific in communicating a set of facts to students. Nor should it be difficult to reduce the number of classroom activities involving a public display (from the perspective of these students) of failure, for the sake of allowing native American students to fail privately so that they might succeed publicly.

Are there not some basic guiding concepts that will help teachers learn a practical procedure for adapting teaching to cultural traits for the purpose of enhancing learning among ethnic minority students? I believe there are. Rather than considering specific traits of each minority group in turn, it would be more helpful to discuss a few practical procedures that can assist us in bridging the gap between an observed student trait and an instructional strategy that is founded upon the trait.

Adapting Instruction to Cultural Traits

Earlier I stated that teachers do not generally know the cultures of ethnic minority students sufficiently to identify those traits that require an appropriate adaptation of instructional strategies to assure effective teaching. I suggested several such traits for students from three ethnic groups and indicated how they stand in clear contrast with common traits among many students of Anglo-American background. If teachers are willing to train themselves as close observers of student behavior (a trait recommended for teachers at all levels, including those in higher education) and to avail themselves of the sources of information on minority students (reading, workshops, academic courses, etc.), there is no reason why they cannot attain an adequate knowledge of their students in terms of cultural distinctives.

I also stated that once teachers do become aware of certain cultural traits in their students, they are often at a loss as to what to do with those traits. To resolve difficulties at this point, it would be helpful to keep in mind three elements of good teaching, each of which may become the means for moving from an observed student trait to an appropriate instructional strategy for that trait. The three teaching elements are content, context, and mode.

Content, of course, refers to the material that is taught. It is the information or data the teacher wishes to communicate to the students. *Context,* in this sense, refers to the physical and psychological environment of the classroom and may include such factors as the kind of teacher expectations projected by the teacher, the degree of feminization of the classroom, whether a spirit of cooperation or competition is dominant, whether students generally feel that their own efforts are effective in getting the reinforcements they desire in the classroom, and student perceptions regarding how much the teacher really cares about them. There are other contextual factors as well (Vasquez 1988). The *mode* refers to how the information is treated or presented. It can include the method, form, style, or manner of delivery used by the teacher. Aspects of the mode include the degree of globalism, complexity, and abstractness used, as well as the sequence and length of the presentation.

It would seem that teachers are somewhat more inclined to think in terms of the first element—the content—when a change in instructional strategy is needed and to avoid thinking in terms of the context in which teaching takes place or the mode of teaching. Although efforts that focus on adapting content to specific cultural traits of minority students are helpful, this approach greatly reduces the range of instructional adaptations needed for providing students with culturally appropriate instruction. Teachers must be aware of the ways in which both context and mode may also be changed for the sake of enhancing learning among non-mainstream students.

The approach to adapting instruction to student traits involves three steps. The first is to identify the particular student trait that may require some adaptation in the teacher's normal way of teaching. As stated earlier, this may come from direct observation on the part of the teacher. It may also be information that the teacher has learned from some other source. Although information characterizing groups should not be considered as infallible when applied to individuals, such information at least serves the teacher well as a starting point in adapting instruction to the cultural needs of minority students.

The second step, once a trait has been identified, is to pass the trait through the filter of several questions, each one relating to the content, context, or mode of instruction that might be required. For example, the teacher must ask whether any aspect of the student trait has implications for the content that should be taught. Similar questions are then asked with regard to the context in which teaching should take place, and with regard to the mode that should be used in teaching. The result of this activity may, of course, identify more than

one aspect of teaching that could be appropriately changed for the purpose of assuring culturally appropriate teaching. A given trait—high motivation for the sake of pleasing the family, for example—may suggest to the teacher the need to both reinforce the student by making reference to the student's family (changing the psychological context for the student), and to teach more about the family's specific expectations for students in the classroom (changing the content of what is taught).

Although the practice of reexamining one's teaching in terms of the effect particular student traits should have on it (at the points of content, context, and mode) may seem new and even peculiar, this practice is at the heart of culturally appropriate instruction, and the dividends will be quickly evident for those who take it seriously.

Third, the teacher must define the new instructional strategy that will be used as a consequence of the first two steps. It would be helpful to actually write out the strategy. Assume, for example, that Carlos is the student in whom a high regard for pleasing his family has been observed. The procedure described above must end in some articulated strategy such as: "I'm going to tell Carlos that I will send his best work home to his parents." Although the actual final adaptation of instruction may take many forms, the importance of carrying the process through to this last step cannot be emphasized too strongly, for final success in teaching in culturally appropriate ways is dependent on reaching this practical point. Figure 1 illustrates the proposed steps in sequence, with several beginning points (student traits) developed to the point of an appropriate instructional strategy.

Conclusion

One might well ask why I do not suggest that culturally appropriate instruction could and should be provided by teachers who themselves are ethnic minorities. Two important facts argue convincingly against this solution. The first is that at present the enrollment in our teacher training institutions is proceeding in a direction quite opposed to that required by this strategy. Minority students simply are not choosing teaching as their preferred vocation. Those who enroll in college are quite aware that, at present, teaching as a profession is not one of the highly paid professions, nor does it enjoy particularly high regard in the public eye. These facts, combined with the phenomenon of a rapidly increasing minority student population in the public elementary and secondary schools, mean that a sufficient number of minority teachers is simply nowhere to be found in the foreseeable future.

A second argument against this solution is that some evidence suggests that ethnic minority teachers are not better teachers of minority youth than are mainstream (Anglo) teachers (U.S. Commission on Civil Rights

---

FIGURE 1
Three-Step Procedure for Adapting Instruction to Cultural Traits

Step 1	Step 2	Step 3
Teacher observes/ identifies student trait	Trait is passed through "filter" of three questions to identify which aspect of teaching (content, context, mode) should be affected.	Teacher verbalizes/writes out the new instructional strategy

Step 2 questions:

Content
a. Does any aspect of the trait suggest the kind of material I should be teaching?

Context
b. Does any aspect of the trait suggest the physical or psychological setting I should create in the classroom?

Mode
c. Does any aspect of the trait suggest the manner in which I should be teaching?

Step 1:

1. Carlos is very concerned about pleasing his family.

2. Sammy and Joanna seem disinterested when given individual work and more "turned on" when interacting with others.

3. Ben seems intimidated and shy when I ask him questions to which he might not know the answer.

4. Charlotte does better when the material I teach involves people interacting with one another; she is not strongly "object" oriented.

Step 3:

1. I'll tell Carlos that I'll inform his parents when he does really good work. (Carlos should work with greater effort and expectation and thus for him the context is changed.)

2. I'll provide more activities that allow Sammy and Joanna to work on projects with others in small groups. (Mode is changed since the means of instruction has shifted to include more student input.)

3. I'll focus on asking Ben questions in class that I'm fairly sure he can answer correctly, and work with him individually in areas in which he is less knowledgeable. (This strategy affects both the mode of instruction and the psychological context for Ben.)

4. I will teach more math concepts in the context of people dealing with one another, as in buying, trading, borrowing. (The mode is basically changed to suit Charlotte's preferred style of learning.)

1973). It seems clear that, although minority teachers indeed serve in the capacity of role models for minority students, both groups—minority and mainstream teachers—are in need of special training if instruction in the classroom is to be appropriately adapted to the distinctive cultural traits of minority students.

The problem of insufficient knowledge on the part of teachers with regard to the distinctive learning characteristics of many minority students is one that is largely in the hands of teachers themselves to resolve. Teachers must become good observers of student behavior in the classroom. This practice in itself can be of significant help to teachers at this point. Then teachers can avail themselves of research and other educational literature to further their knowledge of value systems, reinforcement needs, cognitive styles, and other learning-related traits of these students.

The problem of not knowing what to do once minority student traits have been identified is a little more difficult to resolve, for, to my knowledge, proven models that will guide teachers through the practical steps needed in such a procedure has not yet been published. I have proposed here a basic three-step procedure that, it is hoped, will be of help to some who wish to move ahead in this pedagogical area.

This procedure is clearly student centered, for the teacher is required to begin with observed student traits, and the whole intention is to ultimately produce an instructional strategy that is uniquely fitted to those student traits. It is also a procedure that encourages continual professional growth for the teacher because revision of instructional strategies will be an ongoing practice given the changing nature of students in the classroom year by year.

Finally, it is a procedure that measures good teaching, not in terms of a set of traits we might observe in the teacher, but in terms of the teacher's response to student characteristics, for the basic point in seeking to implement culturally appropriate instructional strategies is to assure that the strengths students bring into the classroom are the factors that give shape to the content, context, and mode of instruction employed by the teacher.

REFERENCES

Adams, D. W. 1988. Fundamental considerations: The deep meaning of native American schooling, 1880–1900. *Harvard Educational Review* 58(1): 1–28.

Avellar, J., and S. Kagan. 1976. Development of competitive behaviors in Anglo-American and Mexican-American children. *Psychological Reports* 39: 191–98.

Barwell, J. 1981. Strategies for teaching composition to native Americans. Paper presented at the Annual Meeting of the Conference on College Composition and Communication, March, in Dallas, Texas. ERIC Document No. ED 199 761.

Brandt, R. 1987. Is cooperation un-American? *Educational Leadership* 45(3).

Boykin, A. W. 1979. Psychological/behavioral verve: Some theoretical explorations and empirical manifestations. In *Research directions of black psychologists,* edited by A. W. Boykin, A. J. Franklin, and J. F. Yates. New York: Russell Sage Foundation.

Britto, N. 1983. Teaching writing to minority students. Paper presented at the Annual Meeting of the Midwest Regional Conference on English in the Two-Year College, February, in Overland Park, Kansas. ERIC Document No. ED 233 343).

Elleson, V. J. 1983. Competition: A cultural imperative? *Personnel and Guidance Journal* (December): 195–98.

Gentry, R., and V. G. Ellison. 1981. Instructional strategies that challenge black college students in the area of exceptional child education. Paper presented at the Council for Exceptional Children Conference on the Exceptional Black Child, February, in New Orleans, Louisiana. ERIC Document No. ED 204 906.

Kagan, S., and M. Madsen. 1971. Cooperation and competition of Mexican, Mexican-American, and Anglo-American children of two ages under four instructional sets. *Developmental Psychology* 5(1).

Kleinfeld, J. S. 1975. Effective teachers of Eskimo and Indian students. *School Review* (February): 301–44.

————. 1973. Intellectual strengths in culturally different groups: An Eskimo illustration. *Review of Educational Research* 43(3), 341–59.

Montalvo, F. F., T. T. Lasater, and N. Garza. 1981. *Mexican American culture simulator for child welfare, trainer's manual.* San Antonio, Tex.: Our Lady of the Lake University.

Nelson, L., and S. Kagan 1972. Competition: The star-spangled scramble. *Psychology Today* 6(4).

Ramirez, M., and A. Castaneda. 1974. *Cultural democracy, bicognitive development, and education.* New York: Academic Press.

Shade, B. J. 1982. Afro-American cognitive style: A variable in school success? *Review of Educational Research* 52(2): 219–44.

U.S. Bureau of the Census. 1980. *Population statistics in the U.S.* Washington, D.C.: The Bureau.

————. 1986. *Population statistics in the U.S.* Washington, D.C.: The Bureau.

U.S. Commission on Civil Rights. 1973. *Teachers and students.* Report V: Mexican American Education Study.

Vasquez, J. A. 1979a. Bilingual education's needed third dimension. *Educational Leadership* (November): 166–68.

Vasquez, J. A. 1979b. Motivation and Chicano students. *Bilingual Resources* 2(2), 2–5.

Vasquez, J. A. 1988. Contexts of learning for minority students. *Educational Forum* 52(3): 243–53.

Vasquez, J. A., and N. Wainstein. n.d. *The responsibilities of college faculty to minority students.* Unpublished manuscript, College of Education, University of Washington, Seattle.

Witkin, H. A. 1967. A cognitive style approach to cross-cultural research. *International Journal of Psychology* 2(4), 233–50.

Witkin, H., R. B. Dyk, H. F. Faterson, D. R. Goodenough, and S. A. Karp. 1962. *Psychological differentiation.* New York: John Wiley.

Young, V. H. 1974. A black American socialization pattern. *American Ethnologist* 1: 405–13.

Measurement and Evaluation

In which reading group does John belong? How do I construct multiple-choice tests? How do I know when my students have mastered the objectives? How can I explain test results to Mary's parents? Each of these questions, and many more questions that educators ask, are answered by applying principles of measurement. College students in education often groan when they come to the part of a course that deals with tests and measurements. They believe they will be forced to learn material that is unimportant and unrelated to teaching but is at the same time difficult. Yet the principles of measurement constitute a universal, generally agreed-upon set of concepts that are integral to the teaching-learning process. Indeed, it seems that with accountability and the stress on basic skills, testing has become more prevalent and more important than ever before.

Measurement provides a foundation for making sound evaluative judgments about students' learning and achievement. Teachers need to use fair and unbiased criteria in order to objectively and accurately assess student learning and make appropriate decisions about student placement. For example, in assigning John to a reading group, the teacher will use John's test scores as an indication of his ability and skill level. Are the tests valid for the school's reading program? Are his test scores consistent over several years? Are they consistent with his performance in class? How does John compare with other pupils in the class? These questions should be asked and then answered by the teacher before he or she can make intelligent decisions about John. On the other hand, will knowledge of the test scores affect the teacher's perception of classroom performance and create a self-fulfilling prophecy? Teachers also evaluate students in order to assign grades, and the question is how to balance test scores with subjective evaluation. Both kinds of evaluative information are necessary, but both can be inaccurate and are frequently misused. What the field of measurement provides is a set of principles to improve all types of evaluation.

The first two articles in this section focus on grading. Teachers need to be aware of grading practices and procedures that are counterproductive for students, such as the indiscriminate use of zeros and averages, and the failure to understand the impact of measurement error in interpreting test scores. Teachers also need to differentiate between criterion-referenced grading for minimal objectives, and using norms to evaluate the achievement of higher-order objectives. The third article introduces a new type of measurement, performance-based testing, which has great potential for more effectively integrating assessment of higher order skills with learning. The last article examines characteristics and limitations of standardized aptitude tests.

Looking Ahead: Challenge Questions

Many educators believe that schools should identify the brightest, most capable students. What are the implications of this philosophy for low-achieving students? Does the overall achievement of students matter?

What conditions need to be considered in deciding whether to use criterion-referenced or norm-referenced testing?

What principles of measurement should teachers adopt for their own classroom testing? Is it necessary or feasible to develop a table of specifications for each test?

How can teachers grade thinking skills such as analysis, application, and reasoning? How should objectives for student learning and grading be integrated? What are some practices to avoid in grading students? Why? What are appropriate teacher uses of standardized test scores?

It's a Good Score!
Just a Bad Grade

With 15 million children at risk of academic failure, the schools must shift their focus from sorting and selecting to teaching and learning, Mr. Canady and Ms. Hotchkiss maintain.

ROBERT LYNN CANADY AND

PHYLLIS RILEY HOTCHKISS

ROBERT LYNN CANADY is an associate professor in the Department of Educational Leadership and Policy Studies, Curry School of Education, University of Virginia, Charlottesville. PHYLLIS RILEY HOTCHKISS is an associate professor in the Division of Education, Midwestern State University, Wichita Falls, Tex. Both are members of the University of Virginia Chapter of Phi Delta Kappa.

ALGEBRA WAS quite a struggle for Amy. One afternoon she came home excited about her performance on an algebra test and announced, "I made a good score, an 80 — just a bad grade." For Amy an 80 was indeed a good score, the highest she had earned all semester. Translated into a letter grade, however, Amy had earned a D.

Amy's situation is but one example of the many common grading practices that make it difficult for many youngsters to feel successful in school.

One reason why the schools have not succeeded with students like Amy is that the schools have been reluctant to give up their traditional roles of sorting and selecting. Perhaps identifying and teaching the best students was once a valid function of the schools. After all, until fairly recently the American economy did not need large numbers of highly educated workers. However, when 15 million children are at risk of academic failure and of joining the ranks of the chronically unemployed, that time has clearly passed.[1] To help such children become productive citizens, schools must shift their focus from sorting and selecting to teaching and learning.

As a first step, we suggest that teachers reflect on grading policies and practices that might be counterproductive for students at all ability levels. For each grading procedure discussed below, we present a single illustration, which is a composite of many observations.

1. *Varying grading scales.* Martha, a high school freshman, and her brother David, a junior, moved from a highly rated private school in the South to a public high school in a mid-Atlantic state. Their mother and father held professional positions, and Martha and David shared similar ambitions for professional training at good universities. Martha and David liked their new school and were pleased to get grades in the 80s and 90s — as good as those they had received in private school. They were pleased, that is, until report cards were distributed. Then they discovered that their 80s and 90s no longer translated into A's and B's, but rather into B's and C's. Their performance had not changed, but the grading scale had.

In most schools it is common practice to establish grading scales with a passing range of 25 to 30 points. (Table 1 shows three examples.) Obviously, students in those schools that use a 10-point range for each letter grade have more opportunities to feel successful than do students in other schools. Depending on the grading scale employed, an 80 could be a B, a C, or a D.

Moreover, the ranges of failing grades on these three scales differ greatly: from 59 points to 74 points. We recommend strongly that, if teachers are going to play the "numerical averaging game," the

From *Phi Delta Kappan*, September 1989, pp. 68-71. Reprinted by permission of *Phi Delta Kappan* and the authors.

TABLE 1.
Three Typical Grading Scales

Numerical Range			Letter Grade
95-100	93-100	90-100	A
88-94	85-92	80-89	B
81-87	77-84	70-79	C
75-80	69-76	60-69	D
0-74	0-68	0-59	F

range of passing grades be expanded and the grade of F have the same range as the other four letter grades.

2. *Worshipping averages.* Dale made A's in mathematics and scored at the 99th percentile on standardized tests. In seventh grade, he took the math section of the Scholastic Aptitude Test (SAT) as part of the Johns Hopkins Talent Search and scored 480. One day, while he was enrolled in Algebra I in the eighth grade, Dale had an argument with his best friend *and* a jammed lock on his locker. He arrived 15 minutes late for an algebra test. Consequently, he was unable to finish the test and scored 68, which translated into an F. This was his only score below 97 for the marking period, but it lowered his average to B. Although admitting that the grade did not reflect Dale's ability or knowledge, the teacher refused to consider his previous record and give him an opportunity for a retest.

Dale would have found it to his advantage to have faked illness and so postponed taking the test. At times, this strict devotion to averaging grades is practiced even when the "average" is inconsistent with what is known about a student's background, performance, and ability. No one works at peak efficiency at all times, and that includes students. A number of ways exist to make allowances for off days. For example, students can be permitted to drop their lowest grade or to repeat one test during a marking period. It seems to us that a teacher has an obligation to use professional judgment and occasionally decide to make an exception.

3. *Using zeros indiscriminately.* Bill's teacher had recently attended a workshop on direct instruction. After she presented each day's lesson, she asked a series of questions to "check for understanding." The students were to raise their hands if they could answer the questions. Bill liked the subject, studied hard, and knew the answers to most questions. However, after a week of having his raised hand ignored, he ceased to respond. What he did

not know was that his teacher had recorded zeros for him on the three occasions when he failed to raise his hand. At the end of the marking period these three zeros lowered Bill's grade from a B to a D. Had he merely been absent for three days, his grade would have stayed high.

One of the most punitive and damaging weapons in a teacher's grading arsenal is the use of zeros. We find this practice objectionable for at least two reasons. First, zeros are usually given for incomplete or missing homework. But far too many students go home to situations in which they have no place to work and no materials to use; other complications can also make completing assignments difficult. Second, homework should be assigned for independent practice to give students the opportunity to reinforce skills or concepts learned in class. If students are capable of performing well in class and on tests without completing homework, the students should not be penalized with zeros. Instead, teachers should examine their own teaching and assigning practices, which may not be challenging enough for the students.

Zeros have a devastating effect on students' grade-point averages. For example, assume that a student has the following numerical grades: 90, 92, 88, 90, 91, 89, and 91. The student's average grade is then 90.1. Add a single zero, and the average drops to 78.9. Add two zeros, and the student's average drops to 70.1 — a failing grade in many school districts. Clearly, a student who has learned 90% of the material on which he is tested has benefited from being in class. Can we justify giving that student a D or an F for the entire grading period?

We know of cases in which the zeros given to students were not related to academics. For instance, some teachers give zeros for late work — regardless of its quality. Behavior, class participation, respect for the teacher, and punctuality are among the nonacademic factors that influence grading in some classrooms. If teachers believe that students should be

judged in these areas, we recommend that separate grades from the academic grade be used.

4. *Following the pattern of assign, test, grade, and teach.* During the late spring, Mr. Slepp became concerned about covering all the remaining material in the textbook for his two honors classes in biology. Admonishing the students to move faster, he assigned a difficult chapter to read on Monday night. He promised the students a test on the following day on material that would have challenged college biology students. When the students arrived in class on Tuesday, they were given a true/false test. Mr. Slepp graded the test that evening and recorded the grades. On Wednesday he told the students that more than half of them had made C's, D's, or F's. He spent the entire period discussing the test and the material in the chapter, but it was too late for the students.

Far too often, students are told to read the next chapter and to be prepared for a test on the material. After they have been tested and their tests have been graded, the real teaching and discussion begin. In spite of all the emphasis that has been placed on effective instruction, we continue to an alarming extent to follow this pattern of assign, test, grade, and teach. Wouldn't it be far more logical to teach before testing and grading?

5. *Failing to match testing to teaching.* Bobby, who was interested in becoming a doctor, worked hard in his advanced chemistry class. Bobby felt comfortable with the material covered in class presentations and discussions. His teacher made straightforward presentations and then asked questions requiring mostly simple recall. Bobby read the assigned material in the text but concentrated on studying his class notes in preparation for the first test.

The test questions came as quite a shock to Bobby and his classmates. The items required application and synthesis and were based totally on the textbook. The students believed that they had received inadequate preparation for making the transition from recalling facts to synthesizing information. "He always does that," former students told Bobby. "You have to get used to it."

In this case, the quality of the test, the presentation, and the questioning strategies employed by the teacher are not in question. Rather, there was an obvious mismatch among the three. Students were given no instruction and no practice in answering the high-level questions that appeared on the test. If students are to have a fair chance to succeed, teachers need to monitor closely the match between teaching and testing.

6. *Ambushing students.* Ms. Romney frequently used pop quizzes "to keep the students on their toes." Confidential discussions with her students revealed that those who cared about grades were learning as much about how to cheat on the quizzes as about the material. Other students decided that they could not win at Ms. Romney's game and simply gave up. Her colleagues regarded Ms. Romney as a tough teacher who maintained high standards. No one asked the students.

No teaching and learning takes place when pop quizzes are given, nor can they be justified as "motivational." Pop quizzes are simply punitive measures that teachers employ when they suspect that their students have not learned the material. Rather than spend class time determining what the students have not learned and why, many teachers assume that students have not studied and decide to "get even." The validity of these quizzes, which are usually short and often composed on the spot, is questionable. Such tests will change the distribution of grades for the marking period. However, unless our primary focus is sorting and selecting rather than teaching and learning, we must question whether such practices represent the best use of teachers' and students' time.

7. *Suggesting that success is unlikely.* Ms. Brannet taught students in their first year of high school. At the beginning of the year she repeatedly told her students, "Remember that you are in high school now. Those middle school teachers gave more A's than we do. The fact that you got an A in middle school doesn't mean you'll get one in high school." After hearing this warning a few times, Judy, who had always been an A student, decided, "I'm going to let her keep her A's. She wants them more than I do." Judy got A's in all her other classes, but in Ms. Brannet's class Judy had decided that the deck was stacked against her. Think about the effect that Ms. Brannet's behavior could have on students who were less motivated to succeed than Judy.

Teachers employ other means of conveying to students the notion that success is unlikely. Consider the following statements, which we have heard in classrooms.

• "I can tell you right now, at the beginning of the second six weeks, that your grade is so low that you cannot possibly pass this course."

• "Your grade was so low last semester that you cannot pass the course for the year, regardless of your performance this

If the emphasis on sorting and selecting is to continue, we suggest that a formal appeals process for contested grades be set up.

semester. However, you keep coming to class, behaving, and trying. You're doing better!"

• "You almost earned an A. You needed a 95 average, and your average was 94.48. Maybe next time you'll make it!"

• "I had to change your B to an F. The three days you missed because you were suspended for shoving Mary while you were downtown last Saturday meant that you missed a vocabulary quiz, a homework assignment, and the test on *Beowulf*. Those three zeros really hurt you, but the school policy does not permit any makeup work for suspended students. My hands are tied."

8. *Practicing "gotcha" teaching.* Mr. Telly recently had a conference with his son's English teacher. Mr. Telly's son, John, had been an above-average, hardworking student prior to taking this English course. Even though he took copious notes in class and studied them diligently, John was making C's and D's on assignments and tests. Mr. Telly explained that John seemed to have difficulty discerning what was important in the lectures. The teacher explained that he always paused briefly before discussing the topics that would appear on the tests. "John must learn to read those pauses," said the teacher.

A nearly foolproof way to lower students' grade-point averages is to practice what we have come to call "gotcha" teaching. Teachers who have mastered this practice are skilled at keeping the objectives of their classes secret. Students are kept in the dark about what is important and what should be studied for tests. The students have to find out what it is that the teacher wants them to learn, and

the tests are ways of finding out how well students have read the teacher's mind. Wouldn't it be more reasonable to use pointed verbal markers and to share with the students those points that are worth stressing? What is wrong with letting students know what is expected of them?

9. *Grading first efforts.* Students in Tom's fifth-grade classroom were told to write an essay on the person they most admired. Tom wrote an eloquent essay on his older brother, Rob. He painted a vivid picture of his brother's free spirit. The paper was returned with a grade of F. Spelling and punctuation errors accounted for the points deducted. Yet mechanics had not been discussed as a factor to be graded. No comments appeared on Tom's paper regarding its excellent content. Tom is unlikely to bare his soul in writing again.

The standard practice, from kindergarten through college, seems to be to assign grades first and then to give feedback. (This happens frequently when teachers grade homework while students are still learning.) When are students given the opportunity to find out what we want them to learn? We have observed a few secondary English teachers and elementary language arts teachers who are providing feedback through a series of drafts of student writing. But we have not observed similar practices in other content areas.

10. *Penalizing students for taking risks.* Cynthia loved English. This was one subject in which she excelled. With the encouragement of her teachers, she decided to elect a "level 5" English course in her junior year. Her parents cautioned her that the course would be extremely difficult, because her previous experience had been in "level 4" classes. After four weeks of school and four difficult papers, Cynthia admitted that the class was "over her head." She asked to move to a lower-level class but was told that she could not do so. "What a fool I was to give this a try," Cynthia lamented to her friends. "There is no way out!"

Taking risks is not rewarded in most schools. From time to time, some students wish to take classes that may be too difficult for them. If they find that they are doing poorly, however, those students are given one of two options: take a low or failing grade with them to a lower-level class, or remain in the difficult class and continue to perform poorly. Many schools do not allow students to change classes once they have enrolled. Provisional placements without penalties might encourage students to risk trying more challenging work without jeopardizing their grade-point averages.

11. *Failing to recognize measurement error.* Ms. Corder proudly presented her grade book to Martha's mother, who had expressed concern about her daughter's grade. "Look, I have all the scores recorded," said Ms. Corder. "I carried them out to two decimal places when I averaged them, just to insure accuracy. Martha's average was 75.67, which gives her a D." This teacher's arithmetic may have been accurate, but she assigned equal weight to grades on homework, pop quizzes, papers, and tests. Is that likely to be appropriate?

12. *Establishing inconsistent criteria.* Judy and Stacey were reviewing their assignments on the way home from school. Judy was preparing to stay up all night to finish her social studies term paper. "Oh, don't bother," Stacey told her. "Mr. Kellogg will accept it a day late with no penalty." Judy thought that the grades for late papers would be lowered, but Stacey said, "No, that's what Ms. Trenton does. Mr. Kellogg takes papers late if you have a good excuse."

In some schools, each teacher establishes his or her own criteria for grading. Furthermore, these criteria may change from day to day or from grading period to grading period. We have seen a single school in which some teachers allowed students to drop one homework score per grading period, other teachers allowed students to drop one test score, and still other teachers insisted on counting all grades. Some teachers averaged all homework grades and counted this average as equal to one test grade; others averaged all grades as recorded. In other words, we could find no consensus among these teachers regarding grading practices.

If the emphasis on sorting and selecting is to continue, we suggest that, at the least, a formal appeals process for contested grades be established. The common practice of allowing the principal to arbitrate is unsatisfactory, because principals are placed in an untenable position: those who find for students are sure to be accused of not supporting teachers; those who find for teachers will certainly be accused of unfairness to students.

We propose that schools or school districts consider establishing appeals boards, each made up of a representative of the central office, a building-level administrator, a parent, and several teachers. Such boards would remove the burden of taking sides from principals and, more important, would focus the attention of teachers on the complexities of grading.

The student population served by the public schools continues to change. If demographic predictions for the next 20 years hold up, there will be a growing number of at-risk students. And these youngsters will remain in school *only* if there is more emphasis on teaching and learning and less emphasis on sorting and selecting. We are not advocating lowering standards. Rather, we wish to raise expectations for success by expanding students' chances to succeed. As long as schools insist on a narrow range of grading practices, educators will adopt curriculum materials and grouping practices that exclude many students from the best educational opportunities. Traditionally, the curriculum has been diluted — rather than the grading scale expanded — so that larger numbers of students will fit the narrow passing range.

The learning deficits that so trouble the recent crop of school critics[2] appear to support the need to enrich the existing curriculum in many schools. Changing grading practices to allow more students to succeed may help prevent students from dropping out even as opportunities for learning are enriched for all students. When educators cease to focus on sorting and selecting and begin to replace adversarial and inequitable grading policies with teaching and learning practices designed to increase students' chances of success, more students like Amy will come home announcing, "I got an 80 today. Not only is that a good score, but it's also a good grade."

1. Harold L. Hodgkinson, "The Changing Face of Tomorrow's Student," *Change*, May/June 1985, pp. 38-39.
2. The critics who have recently expressed concern about what students don't know include E. D. Hirsch, Jr., *Cultural Literacy: What Every American Needs to Know* (Boston: Houghton Mifflin, 1987); Chester E. Finn, Jr., Diane Ravitch, and Robert T. Fancher, eds., *Against Mediocrity: The Humanities in America's High Schools* (New York: Holmes & Meier, 1984); and Allan D. Bloom, *The Closing of the American Mind* (New York: Simon & Schuster, 1987).

Classroom Standard Setting and Grading Practices

James S. Terwilliger
University of Minnesota

James S. Terwilliger is Professor, University of Minnesota, Department of Educational Psychology, 319 Burton Hall, 178 Pillsbury Drive, SE, Minneapolis, MN 55455. He specializes in measurement and evaluation of educational achievement.

Assigning grades to students is undoubtedly one of the most distasteful aspects of teaching. If pushed, most teachers will state that the assignment of grades is, at best, a necessary evil that has little to do with the task of teaching. This point of view is also expressed in proposals for abolishing grading systems that appear in a cyclical fashion in professional journals aimed at teachers as well as in the popular press. Ebel (1974) summarizes the major arguments over grading and presents a strong case in favor of grades.

Interestingly, the process of grading has received relatively little attention in standard references on educational measurement. Textbooks on classroom measurement typically devote one chapter to issues related to grading, at least half of which deals with grading systems rather than the process of grade assignment.[1] Debates over

This is a revision of a paper presented as part of a symposium on classroom assessment research and training at the annual meetings of AERA and NCME, New Orleans, April, 1988.

grading systems have little to do with *grading as a judgmental process*. Therefore, this article presents an analysis of the grading process and recommends a specific approach to grading that can be employed regardless of the grading system in effect.

Assumptions Concerning Grading

I will start by stating six propositions concerning the grading process which I accept as self-evident truths.

1. Grading should be directly linked to an explicitly defined set of instructional goals that takes into account both the content of instruction and the cognitive complexity of outcomes. In principle, grades should reflect the *level* of the outcomes achieved by students with the highest grades being assigned to those who achieve the most advanced outcomes.

2. All data collected for purposes of judging student achievement should be expressed in *quantitative* form. This implies that (a) results on quizzes, tests, exams, and so forth, should be reported as scores or points earned based upon an explicit

scoring scheme; (b) homework, assigned projects, term papers, and so forth, should be scored using a clearly defined quantitative rating system; and (c) classroom performances, demonstrations, exhibitions, and so forth, should be evaluated using a well-defined system of numeric ratings or check lists.

3. The process of judging the quality of student performance (evaluation) should be distinguished from the process of collecting data about student performance (measurement). In particular, a valid judgment typically requires that (a) data be collected over a period of time, and (b) an explicit frame of reference be formulated as the basis for the judgment (evaluation).

4. From an educational viewpoint the assignment of a grade of failure, unsatisfactory, no credit, and so forth, has a special significance to students in terms of their future educational options. A failing grade should reflect a categorical judgment that the student does not possess a *minimal* level of competence independent of the student's performance relative to other students.

5. An evaluation plan should be

From *Educational Measurement: Issues and Practices*, Vol. 8, No. 2, Summer 1989, pp. 15-19. Copyright © 1989 by the National Council on Measurement in Education. Reprinted by permission of the publisher.

prepared for distribution to students. This plan should be explicit about (a) timing for data collection (e.g., dates for quizzes, exams, class presentations, etc.; due dates for assignments, projects, etc.), (b) conditions under which data collection takes place (e.g., format of items/ questions in quizzes and exams, time limits for quizzes and exams, availability of reference materials, computational aids, etc., during quizzes and exams, penalties for late assignments, etc.), and (c) how the data are to be employed in making summative judgments about students (e.g., the relative weight to be given to each item of data in arriving at evaluations).

6. Teachers need time to establish an approach to grading that is both practical and consistent with the particular classroom setting in which they work. Realistic expectations concerning student performance can best be arrived at through trial and error.

A Recommended Grading Process

Over the past 15 years I have developed and employed an approach to grading which utilizes both criterion-referenced and norm-referenced concepts. I currently use some variation of the procedure in every class I teach. This approach has been adopted by several colleagues (both at my institution and elsewhere) and a significant number of public school teachers who have taken courses with me.

Two Classes of Objectives

A general overview of the procedure is shown in Figure 1. The first step is to distinguish what Gronlund (1973) has called *minimal objectives* from what he terms *developmental objectives*.

Minimal objectives represent essential course outcomes that all students are expected to achieve, whereas developmental objectives represent more complex goals of instruction toward which students strive but which few, if any, fully achieve. Gronlund (1973) argues that the mastery approach to learning and testing (Bloom, 1968) is clearly appropriate for minimal objectives but is of less value in reference to developmental objectives.

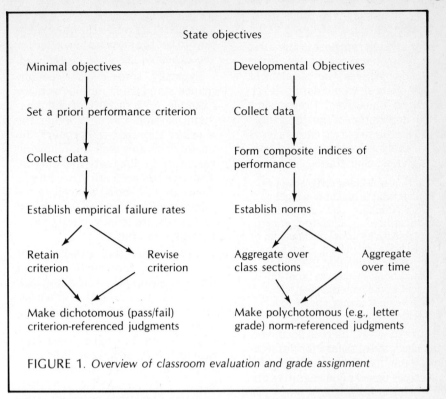

FIGURE 1. *Overview of classroom evaluation and grade assignment*

The distinction between objectives that are identified as minimal and those identified as developmental is somewhat arbitrary. Gronlund (1973) suggests a series of questions to help define minimal objectives that all students are expected to master. His questions include the following:

1. What minimum knowledge and skills are prerequisite to further learning in the same area (e.g., knowledge of terms, measurement skills)?

2. What basic skills are prerequisite to learning in other areas (e.g., reading skills, computational skills, language skills)? and

3. What minimum knowledge and skills are needed to function in everyday, out-of-school, situations (e.g., reading, writing, speaking)?

Obviously, the answers to questions such as these will vary from one teacher to the next. To identify objectives that are agreed upon by different instructors, it would be helpful if two or more teachers could share their judgments concerning what constitutes a set of minimal objectives in a given setting.

A rationale for the distinction between minimal and developmental objectives can also be based upon a cognitive analysis of instructional objectives. Minimal objectives typically correspond to lower level cognitive outcomes defined in terms of the acquisition of knowledge and basic skills. In contrast, developmental objectives are more clearly identified with higher level outcomes defined in terms of more complex cognitive processes.

For example, Presseisen (1986) has described *thinking skills* as falling into four categories:

Essential cognitive processes— the basic thinking skills that are the building blocks of thought development;

Higher-order cognitive processes —the more complex thinking skills, which may be harder to define but which are based on the essential cognitive processes;

Metacognitive processes—the learning to learn skills aimed at making thinking more conscious and the student more aware of the ways one can go about problem solving or decision making; and

Epistemic cognitive processes— the kinds of thinking related to particular bodies of knowledge or subject matters and the particular problems addressed by these knowledge areas as well as the interdisciplinary relationships among content areas. (p. 9)

For present purposes, the first category could serve as a basis for minimal objectives whereas a mix of the other three would define developmental objectives. Presseisen's (1986) description of the differences between the first two categories is remarkably consistent with Gronlund's view. She states,

There is a decided difference between what is meant as a higher-order thinking and the exact, standardized, minimal competency objectives often included in basic skills instruction. Simplistic, rote information that fits limited instructional sequences is not sufficient as the material upon which to develop students' higher-order thinking. (p. 11)

Unfortunately, there is no universally accepted standard for differentiating minimal from developmental objectives based upon cognitive criteria. One concept that I employ is *novelty*. I believe that outcomes that are defined as minimal objectives are those that test students' ability to deal with familiar concepts and rehearsed skills. By definition, such outcomes have a low level of novelty. In contrast, developmental objectives test students' ability to apply learning to new material or situations. Others may argue for a broader definition of minimal outcomes. They prefer to include certain higher order outcomes (e.g., problem-solving skills) within the category of minimal objectives. This certainly is justified if sufficient numbers of students are able to achieve these objectives. The performance expectations for minimal objectives is the next issue to be addressed.

Minimal Objectives and Pass/Fail Decisions

Once the domain of minimal objectives has been defined, a series of special quizzes or exercises can be designed to measure student achievement with respect *to these objectives only*. For practical purposes, the minimal objectives quizzes and exercises function just like mastery tests. That is, a performance standard for passing is specified a priori with the expectation that at least 90% of the students

will perform at or above the a priori standard. This raises the question of how to set the standard in order for the expected result to be realized.

Typically, some a priori performance standard is initially set, for example, 75% or 80% of the maximum possible score. Whether the a priori standard is "proper" depends upon how well the following assumptions are satisfied: (a) instruction has been effective, (b) students are motivated to achieve the minimal objectives, and (c) minimal objectives are achievable by most, if not all, students.

It is assumed that a teacher will do everything possible to meet the first two assumptions. But how can one know if an objective is within the reach of students? The only answer is an empirical one—test students and determine the success rate (difficulty level) for individual objectives and for the test as a whole. If the teacher has identified minimal objectives carefully, the success rate on each item will be high and the average performance on the total test will be well above the a priori standard. Few students will fail to reach the standard under these circumstances.

On the other hand, it may be that the success rate on certain items is extremely low. In such cases, the teacher needs to determine the cause of the problem. Perhaps the objective is one that is inherently difficult and should be removed from the domain of minimal objectives, or there may be a defect in the structure of the test question. In either event, items with low success rates obviously decrease the average score on the total test. Unless these items are omitted altogether, it may be necessary to alter the initial performance standard. After a couple of administrations of an instrument, a realistic and stable standard can be set.

This is one of the reasons I previously stated why a certain amount of trial and error is inevitable when designing a grading system. Performance standards must be calibrated to the difficulty level of the minimal objective measures in order to obtain results that are in line with expected (and acceptable) fail rates. Data from previous administrations

of a measure are frequently essential to setting future standards.

Decisions to Fail Students

Decisions to fail students should be made strictly upon their performance on minimal objectives type measures (quizzes, exercises, etc.). The reason for this is simply that the Pass/Fail decision is a dichotomous one and criterion-referenced tests are well suited for that purpose.

Students should be given specific advance information concerning the minimal objectives. Therefore, the items and exercises should tap only familiar knowledge and well-rehearsed skills. Assuming that students are motivated to do well and are given proper instruction, it is quite reasonable to expect very small fail rates on such tests. Failure to reach the specified standard under such circumstances reflects a serious deficiency.

Developmental Objectives and Grade Assignment

Assessment of the more cognitively complex outcomes of instruction is undoubtedly the most difficult measurement job faced by a teacher. Analyses of teacher-made tests such as those reported by Fleming and Chambers (1983) reveal that the great preponderance of questions sample factual knowledge—knowledge of terms and rules. Such learning constitutes the lowest level outcomes and more properly belongs under the heading of minimal objectives. By asking teachers to differentiate minimal objectives from developmental objectives at the outset, I hope to create a greater curiosity among teachers concerning the entire range of possible learning outcomes. With luck, that may lead to more attention to complex outcomes than is currently the case.

Measuring Developmental Outcomes

Teachers who seek proficiency in designing measures of the more complex learning outcomes must (a) become generally familiar with cognitively based systems for classifying higher order outcomes, (b) study techniques for developing questions that tap such outcomes, and (c) practice constructing questions that are designed to measure complex thinking and reasoning skills. This is one area in which teachers can frequently help one another by working cooperatively on item construction and reacting to each other's efforts.

As previously noted, a basic criterion I employ in measuring higher order outcomes is the degree and type of novelty in the questions. One cannot claim to have engaged a student in any higher level cognitive process without presenting in the question a situation that is different in important respects from situations the student has previously encountered during learning. So-called *context dependent* items that make use of graphs, diagrams, tables, maps, and so forth, are excellent vehicles for tapping higher order outcomes. Teachers need to be encouraged to write questions that use such materials more frequently.

Score Distributions for Developmental Objectives Measures

By definition, higher order objectives are designed to "stretch" every student to their highest possible level of achievement. Gronlund (1973) notes that such objectives are open ended in the sense that each student can continue to progress toward greater expertise. Under these conditions it is impossible to set realistic a priori standards because of the great variation in student performances. Also, different types of data (written tests, classroom presentations, major projects, etc.) should be collected on each student to reflect the variety and complexity of higher level outcomes. These data are typically combined into a composite performance index[2] for each student as indicated in Figure 1. It is the composite score for developmental outcomes that becomes the basis for all grade assignments except for fail decisions previously made on the basis of minimal objectives scores.

Assuming that truly higher order outcomes have been tapped, the developmental composite score distribution will differ from score distributions yielded by the minimal objectives measures in three ways as summarized in Table 1. The dif-

TABLE 1

Expected Characteristics of Score Distributions Resulting From Minimal Objectives and Developmental Objectives Measures

Distribution characteristic	Minimal objectives	Developmental objectives
Shape	Definite negative skew	Approximately unimodal symmetric
Central tendency (difficulty level)	Mean score well above a priori standard (say .05 to .10) when divided by maximum possible score	Mean score divided by maximum possible score in interval between .50 and .70
Variability	Can be small or large; depends primarily upon degree of skew in distribution	Should be quite large

ferences in shape, central tendency, and variability are closely linked to the purposes that each serves. The unimodal symmetry (approximate), lower central tendency, and greater variability that characterizes the ideal composite distribution makes it much better suited to multiple category grading reflecting reliable differences in levels of achievement of higher order outcomes. It should be noted that the assumption of unimodality is not as important as the need for lower central tendency and greater variability.

In my experience, teachers have a built-in resistance to constructing instruments in which the difficulty level is in the .50 to .70 range. There are several reasons for this. As previously noted, one reason is that teachers simply are not in the habit of writing questions at levels beyond minimal objectives. Historically, difficulty levels on teacher-made tests are in the .80 to .90 range. A second reason is the prevailing belief that the average score is a direct reflection on the quality of the instruction. The lower the average score, the poorer the instructor. A third reason is that many teachers consider it to be unfair to ask questions that go beyond the specific material studied by students. For such teachers, the practice of asking students to respond to novel problem settings is strictly unthinkable. Obviously, these are beliefs that need to be dealt with before teachers will be receptive

to the grading system which I am advocating.

Grade Assignment

Assuming that the composite score distribution approximates the desired result, grades can be assigned on a norm-referenced basis within constraints, if any, imposed by school district guidelines concerning grade distributions. This is a trial and error process similar to that of standard setting in the case of minimal objectives outcomes. Initial grade assignments necessarily reflect the novice teacher's preconceptions concerning what quality performances are deserving of A's, B's, and so forth. With some experience, a set of implicit norms are formulated. With still more experience, the norms can become quite explicit.

It is important to note that I am *not* recommending grading on the curve. That would imply that a student's grade depends upon her/his performance in relation to others in the same class. Instead, I am suggesting that a more inclusive reference group be the basis for norms. This group might include (a) all students in various sections of the same general course for whom common performance data are available, or (b) all students who have taken a particular course under the same instructor over a specified period of time. If class sizes are reasonable (say 25 or more), fairly stable norms can be constructed in a relatively short amount of time.

One dilemma that arises in establishing norms by pooling data over time is the problem of *security* versus *comparability*. In order to make sure that the data base for grading remains constant over time, it is necessary to use the same (or psychometrically parallel) instruments year after year. Obviously, a teacher who decides to use the same assessment instruments year after year must take precautions to assure that the tests, quizzes, and so forth, are not in the public domain. Otherwise, there is likely to be a noticeable rise in the average performance level due to advance knowledge enjoyed by students in each successive year. A teacher who makes public the instruments employed as a basis for grading avoids the security problem only to sacrifice comparability in the data base employed.

I favor the practice of keeping assessment instruments as secure as possible. There are several reasons (besides comparability of data) for taking this position. First, the construction of measures of developmental outcomes is a time-consuming job. Teachers should be encouraged to think of this as an ongoing process in which instruments change incrementally based upon analysis of responses to specific assignments, questions, items, and so forth. It is a waste of valuable time and data to start from scratch every year. Second, by analyzing responses to classroom instruments and building an item bank from which instruments are constructed, it is possible to design high quality measures that assure substantial (if not strict) comparability of results. For example, quizzes or tests given in successive years can have 70% to 80% of their items in common with 20% to 30% new items added. If there is reason to suspect group differences, the performance on the common items can be employed as a check of the differences, if any, between students in the 2 years. Also, the general difficulty level of the common items can be compared with that of the new items added to a test. Third, it is not necessary to treat all assignments as secure. Major out-of-class term papers, projects, and so forth, can be designed and scored in a

fashion such that it is of no great advantage for students to know in advance precisely what is expected of them. For such assignments there is no guarantee of strict comparability in the first place.

It should be noted that employing secure instruments does not deny students the benefit of valuable feedback from classroom assessments. I make it a practice of distributing and reviewing the results of quizzes, tests, and so forth, in class as soon as possible after each assessment. After students have reviewed their results, the instruments are returned to me and are available in my office for the balance of the term. At the end of the term all materials are destroyed.

Teachers have often asked me, "What is the ideal distribution of grades?" Of course, there is no generally acceptable answer. I do believe that it would be helpful if more school systems (and colleges) developed general guidelines suggesting reasonable grade distributions (10%–20% A's, 20%–30% B's, etc.). This could provide individual teachers with a framework within which to work. Teachers who wish to assign grades that are in conflict with the guidelines should be allowed to do so only if they can provide data to justify their action.

Some Concluding Remarks

The grading system outlined here can be adapted to a variety of settings. It is probably best suited to secondary school and undergraduate college classrooms where there is a need to use five or more grade categories. In settings where only a two-category Pass/Fail (or equivalent) system is used, the criterion-referenced approach using only minimal objectives would be sufficient. In classes where some students are enrolled on the Pass/Fail system and others are enrolled on a regular grading basis, the Pass/Fail students are required only to demonstrate achievement of the minimal objectives. Other students must complete both minimal and developmental objectives measures.

Of course, this flexibility is only possible if the two types of measures are constructed and administered as separate instruments. The minimal objectives measures

should be treated as Bloom (1968) and others have described mastery tests, that is, each measure should be relatively brief, measures should be given fairly frequently, parallel forms should be designed to provide second trials for students who do not perform at the standard on the first administration, and so forth.

Finally, although I believe that measures of mastery and measures of minimal objectives are functionally equivalent, I think Gronlund's (1973) terminology has the advantage that it more honestly describes outcomes that the great majority of the students are expected to attain. As defined by standard dictionaries, the term *mastery* should be reserved for describing exceptional (i.e., high level) accomplishment or skill. Obviously, such level of achievement is much more consistent with developmental objectives than with minimal objectives.

Notes

[1] A notable exception is Hills (1981). This text contains several chapters dealing with a variety of issues associated with grades and grading.

[2] Technical issues associated with differences between the desired weights and effective weights for individual performances in composites will not be addressed here. These are discussed in Oosterhof (1987).

References

Bloom, B. S. (1968). Learning for mastery. *Evaluation Comment, 1*(2).

Ebel, R. L. (1974). Shall we get rid of grades? *Measurement in Education*, National Council on Measurement in Education, Fall.

Fleming, M., & Chambers, B. (1983). Teacher-made tests: Windows on the classroom. In M. E. Hathaway (Ed.), *Testing in the schools*. San Francisco: Jossey-Bass.

Gronlund, N. E. (1973). *Preparing criterion-referenced tests for classroom instruction*. New York: Macmillan.

Hills, J. R. (1981). Measurement and evaluation in the classroom (2nd ed.). Columbus, OH: Merrill.

Oosterhof, A. C. (1987). Obtaining intended weights when combining students' scores. *Educational Measurement: Issues and Practice, 6*(4), 29–37.

Presseisen, B. Z. (1986). *Thinking skills: Research and practice*. Washington, DC: National Education Association.

Teaching to the (Authentic) Test

Testing can once again serve teaching and learning if tests clarify and set intellectual standards.

GRANT WIGGINS

Grant Wiggins is a special consultant to the National Center on Education and the Economy in Rochester, New York, and the Coalition of Essential Schools on issues of assessment and curriculum. He may be reached through the National Center.

Practical alternatives and sound arguments now exist to make testing once again serve teaching and learning. Ironically, we *should* "teach to the test." The catch is to design and then teach to *standard-setting* tests so that practicing for and taking the tests actually enhances rather than impedes education, and so that a criterion-referenced diploma makes externally mandated tests unobtrusive—even unnecessary.

Setting Standards
If tests determine what teachers actually teach and what students will study for—and they do—then the road to reform is a straight but steep one: test those capacities and habits we think are essential, and test them in context. Make them replicate, within reason, the challenges at the heart of each academic discipline. Let them be—authentic.

What are the actual performances that we want students to be good at, that represent model challenges? Design them by department, by school, and by district—and worry about a

fair, efficient, and objective method of grading them as a *secondary* problem. Do we judge our students to be deficient in writing, speaking, listening, artistic creation, research, thoughtful analysis, problem posing, and problem solving? Let the tests ask them to write, speak, listen, create, do original research, analyze, pose and solve problems.

Rather than seeing tests as after-the-fact devices for checking up on what students have learned, we should see them as instructional: the central vehicle for clarifying and setting intellectual standards. The recital, debate, play, or game (and the criteria by which they are judged)—the "performance"—is not a checkup, it is the heart of the matter; all coaches *happily* teach to it. We should design academic tests to be similarly standard setting, not merely standardized.

Reform of testing depends, however, on teachers' recognizing that standardized testing evolved and proliferated because the school transcript became untrustworthy. An "A" in "English" means only that some adult thought the student's work was excellent. Compared to what or whom? As determined by what criteria? In reference to what specific subject matter? The high school diploma, by remaining tied to no standard other than credit accrual and seat time, provides

no useful information about what students have studied or what they can actually do with what was studied.

To regain control over both testing and instruction, schools need to rethink their diploma requirements and grades. They need a clear set of appropriate and objective criteria, enabling both students *and outsiders* to know what counts, what is essential—what a school's standards really are. Until we specify what students must directly demonstrate to earn a diploma, they will continue to pass by meeting the de facto "standard" of being dutiful and persistent—irrespective of the quality of their work. And standardized testmakers will continue to succeed in hawking simplistic norm-referenced tests to districts and states resigned to using them for lack of a better accountability scheme.

Exhibitions of Mastery

The diploma should be awarded upon a successful final demonstration of mastery for graduation—an "Exhibition" .... As the diploma is awarded when earned, the school's program proceeds with no strict age grading and with no system of "credits earned" by time spent in class. The emphasis is on the students' demonstration that they can do important things.

—From the Prospectus of the Coalition of Essential Schools

The "exhibition of mastery," proposed by Ted Sizer in *Horace's Compromise*

The Rite of Passage Experience (R.O.P.E.) at Walden III, Racine, Wisconsin

All seniors must complete a portfolio, a study project on U.S. history, and 15 oral and written presentations before a R.O.P.E committee composed of staff, students, and an outside adult. Nine of the presentations are based on the materials in the portfolio and the project; the remaining six are developed for presentation before the committee. All seniors must enroll in a yearlong course designed to help them meet these requirements.

The eight-part *portfolio*, developed in the first semester, is intended to be "a reflection and analysis of the senior's own life and times." The requirements include:
- a written autobiography,
- a reflection on work (including a resume),
- an essay on ethics,
- a written summary of coursework in science,
- an artistic product or a written report on art (including an essay on artistic standards used in judging artwork).

The *project* is a research paper on a topic of the student's choosing in American history. The student is orally questioned on the paper in the presentations before the committee during the second semester.

The *presentations* include oral tests on the previous work, as well as six additional presentations on the essential subject areas and "personal proficiency" (life skills, setting and realizing personal goals, etc.). The presentations before the committee usually last an hour, with most students averaging about 6 separate appearances to complete all 15.

A diploma is awarded to those students passing 12 of the 15 presentations and meeting district requirements in math, government, reading, and English.

Note: This summary is paraphrased from both the R.O.P.E. Student Handbook and an earlier draft of Archbald and Newmann's (1988) *Beyond Standardized Testing*.

Fig. 1. An Example of a Final Exhibition

(1984) and a cornerstone of the "Essential School," is one attempt to grapple with these issues. The intent of the exhibitions project is to help schools and districts design more authentic, engaging, revealing, and trustworthy "tests" of a student's intellectual ability.

The reference to engagement is not incidental. The exhibition of mastery was initially proposed as an antidote to student passivity and boredom, not merely as a more valid form of assessment. The idea is to capture the interest value of an authentic test of one's ability, such as is often provided in schools by literary magazines, portfolios, recitals, games, or debates. Thus, "any exhibition of mastery should be the students' opportunity to show off what they know and are able to do rather than a trial by question . . ."[1]

The exhibition of mastery, as the name implies, is meant to be more than a better test. Like the thesis and oral exam in graduate school, it indicates whether a student has *earned* a diploma, is ready to leave high school.[2] The school is designed "backwards" around these standard-setting

tests to ensure that teachers and students alike understand their obligations and how their own efforts fit in a larger context. Teachers "teach to the test" because the test is essential—and teacher designed.

But why institute a radically new form of assessment? Why not just improve conventional teaching and course-related tests? As the "Study of High Schools" documented, a major cause of the high school's inadequacies is the absence of direct teaching of the essential skills of inquiry and expression. Even in "demanding" schools, students often fail to learn how to learn. The culprit is discipline-based curriculums that lead to content-based teaching and testing: the essential (cross-disciplinary) habits and skills of reading, writing, questioning, speaking, and listening fall through the cracks of typical content-focused syllabi and course credits; as indicated, for example, when teachers say "I teach English, not reading."

A required final public exhibition of know-how ensures that those essentials are taught and learned. The final

exit-level exhibition reveals whether a would-be graduate can demonstrate control over the skills of inquiry and expression and control over an intellectual topic that approximates the expert's ability to use knowledge effectively and imaginatively. A final exhibition provides students with an occasion to make clear, if only perhaps symbolically, that they are ready to graduate.

An exhibition challenges students to show off not merely their knowledge but their initiative; not merely their problem solving but their problem posing; not just their learning on cue, but their ability to judge and learn how to learn on an open-ended problem, often of their own design. The experience thus typically focuses on the essential skills of "inquiry and expression"—a synthesis that requires questioning, problem posing, problem solving, independent research, the creation of a product or performance, and a *public* demonstration of mastery. Significantly, there is often a component calling for self-reflection and analysis of what one has undergone and learned.

Thus, a *final exhibition* is a misnomer in an important sense. Many Coalition schools provide a semester- or yearlong course, an adult adviser, and a committee to ensure that a student has adequate guidance, evaluation, and incentive (see fig. 1 for an example of a final exhibition from a Coalition school). The exhibition of mastery is as much a process as a final product, if not more so. The process of choosing topics, advisers, and committees and refining one's ideas and skills is a yearlong exercise in understanding and internalizing standards.

A similar approach to a diploma at the college level has been used successfully at Alverno College, Milwaukee, Wisconsin, for over a decade.[3] Assessment is a central experience, with coursework a means to a set of known ends: students must achieve mastery in the following eight general areas, with their progress in each area being charted on a multistaged scale:

1. effective communication ability,
2. analytic capability,
3. problem-solving ability,
4. valuing in a decision-making context,
5. effective social interaction,

6. taking responsibility for the global environment,
7. effective citizenship,
8. aesthetic responsiveness.

Performances: Better Classroom Tests

Course-specific tests also have glaring weaknesses, not only because they are often too low level and content heavy. They are rarely designed to be authentic tests of intellectual ability; as with standardized tests, teacher-designed finals are usually intended to be quickly read and scored.

It seems wise, then, to talk about a move toward more intellectual performances in course-bound testing as a way of stressing the need to make tests more central, authentic, and engaging—as in the arts and athletics. (The term *exhibitions* would be reserved for those culminating graduation-level exercises designed to assess ability in the essentials underlying all course-work required for graduation.)

Designing performances implies a very different approach to standard setting than is implied by typical criterion-referenced tests or outcome-based views of mastery, though the instincts behind the designs are similar. Performances would ideally *embody* and *evoke* desired outcomes in authentic contexts. Too often, specifying only outcomes leads to tests that atomize and decontextualize knowledge: the testmaker designs a set of isolated pat exercises designed to elicit each desired outcome. Genuine tests of ability rarely provide such blatant cues and simple recall; they require us to have a repertoire, the judgment and skill to "put it all together" in one central challenge, repeatedly tried. (Imagine the assessment of music ability in a series of little exercises tried once, rather than through practice and performance of a complete piece in recitals.)

In sum, the goals behind the exhibition of mastery and the performance are to design standard-setting tests that provide more direct evidence of a student's intellectual ability; design tests that are thus able to stand by themselves as objective results; design more authentic intellectual challenges at the heart of a discipline; and design tests that are more likely to engage students and motivate them to raise their own intellectual standards to do well on

---

An Oral History Project for 9th Graders

To the student:
 You must complete an oral history based on interviews and written sources and then present your findings orally in class. The choice of subject matter is up to you. Some examples of possible topics include: your family, running a small business, substance abuse, a labor union, teenage parents, and recent immigrants.
 Create three workable hypotheses based on your preliminary investigations and four questions you will ask to test out each hypothesis.

Criteria for Evaluation of Oral History Project

To the teacher:
 Did student investigate three hypotheses?
 Did student describe at least one change over time?
 Did student demonstrate that he or she had done background research?
 Were the four people selected for the interviews appropriate sources?
 Did student prepare at least four questions in advance, related to each hypothesis?
 Were those questions leading or biased?
 Were follow-up questions asked where possible, based on answers?
 Did student note important differences between "fact" and "opinion" in answers?
 Did student use evidence to prove the ultimate best hypothesis?
 Did student exhibit organization in writing and presentation to class?

Note: This example is courtesy of Albin Moser, Hope High School, Providence, Rhode Island. To obtain a thorough account of a performance-based history course, including the lessons used and pitfalls encountered, write to Dave Kobrin, Brown University, Education Department, Providence, RI 02912.

Fig. 2. An Example of a Test of Performance

---

them. (See fig. 2 for an example of a performance that illustrates and illuminates these design standards.)

Toward More Authentic Tests

Exhibitions and performances sound fine on a schoolwide basis, you say, but districtwide or statewide? Isn't that too costly and cumbersome? I contend that the supposed impracticality and/or expense of designing such tests on a wide scale is a habit of thinking, not a fact. The United States is the only major country that relies so heavily on norm-referenced, short-answer tests instead of performance- and/or classroom-based assessment on a national level. In addition, a national committee on assessment in Great Britain has called for an exemplary system requiring flexible, criterion-referenced, and performance-based tests.[4] Many of the tests would be created by classroom teachers, who would be part of the standardizing process through "moderating" meetings to compare and balance results on their own and national tests.

In the U.S., more authentic skill assessment can now be found in various districts and states due, in part, to the

work in writing assessment by the National Writing Project and its state off-shoots (such as the California CAP writing test), and the American Council on the Teaching of Foreign Languages in the assessment of foreign language proficiency. Some states, such as Connecticut, have already designed and piloted performance-based assessment using ACTFL tests and criteria. In addition, they have piloted hands-on tests in graphics, small engines, and science. Vermont has proposed a statewide assessment system in writing and mathematics that would be portfolio based and teacher assessed.

We already have a national example in science: the 1987 NAEP pilot "Higher-Order Thinking Science Test," which includes some (though too few) hands-on experiments. One example:

Students are given a sample of three different materials and an open box. The samples differ in size, shape, and weight. The students are asked to determine whether the box would weigh the most (and least) if it were completely filled with material A, B, or C. There are a variety of possible approaches . . . NAEP administrators used detailed checklists to record each student's procedures and strategies.[5]

A. Structure and Logistics

1. Are more appropriately public; involve an audience, a panel, and so on.
2. Do not rely on unrealistic and arbitrary time constraints.
3. Offer known, not secret, questions or tasks.
4. Are more like portfolios or a *season* of games (not one-shot).
5. Require some collaboration with others.
6. Recur—and are *worth* practicing for, rehearsing, and retaking.
7. Make assessment and feedback to students so central that school schedules, structures, and policies are modified to support them.

B. Intellectual Design Features

1. Are "essential"—not needlessly intrusive, arbitrary, or contrived to "shake out" a grade.
2. Are "enabling"—constructed to point the student toward more sophisticated use of the skills or knowledge.
3. Are contextualized, complex intellectual challenges, not "atomized" tasks, corresponding to isolated "outcomes."
4. Involve the student's own research or use of knowledge, for which "content" is a means.
5. Assess student habits and repertoires, not mere recall or plug-in skills.
6. Are *representative* challenges—designed to emphasize *depth* more than breadth.
7. Are engaging and educational.
8. Involve somewhat ambiguous ("ill-structured") tasks or problems.

C. Grading and Scoring Standards

1. Involve criteria that assess essentials, not easily counted (but relatively unimportant) errors.
2. Are not graded on a "curve" but in reference to performance standards (criterion-referenced, not norm-referenced).
3. Involve demystified criteria of success that appear to *students* as inherent in successful activity.
4. Make self-assessment a part of the assessment.
5. Use a multifaceted scoring system instead of one aggregate grade.
6. Exhibit harmony with shared schoolwide aims—a *standard*.

D. Fairness and Equity

1. Ferret out and identify (perhaps hidden) strengths.
2. Strike a *constantly* examined balance between honoring achievement and native skill or fortunate prior training.
3. Minimize needless, unfair, and demoralizing comparisons.
4. Allow appropriate room for student learning styles, aptitudes, and interests.
5. Can be—should be—attempted by *all* students, with the test "scaffolded up," not "dumbed down," as necessary.
6. Reverse typical test-design procedures: they make "accountability" serve student learning (Attention is primarily paid to "face" and "ecological" validity of tests).[1]

1. Thanks to Ted Sizer, Art Powell, Fred Newmann, and Doug Archbald; and the work of Peter Elbow and Robert Glaser for some of these criteria. A more thorough account of them will appear in an upcoming issue of *Phi Delta Kappan* (in press).

Fig. 3. Characteristics of Authentic Tests

NAEP borrowed most of its experiments from the British Assessment of Performance Unit tasks, which have been used (and reliably scored) in Great Britain for a decade in reading, speaking, listening, math, and science.

Genuine tests *can* be widely implemented if we can overcome inertia and fatalism about current forms of standardized testing. Authentic, performance-based testing is a reality, not a romantic vision. There is also ample room for more intelligent design and use of conventional norm-referenced standardized tests.[6]

The state of Connecticut has developed a "Common Core of Learning," which lists objectives and criteria in all essential domains. Performance-based tests, built around criteria specified by experts in each field and involving tests administered by trained observers, are to be designed to honor those aims.

There are even standardized tests worth noting. ACT has developed a wide-ranging multimedia test of "general education knowledge and skills" called COMP, designed for colleges but easily adaptable to the high school level. The test uses art reproductions and audiotapes of news programs, for example, in testing writing and listening skills. On other items, students draft letters on different topics. There is even allowance for the student to respond orally on tape to a few test questions. The test takes six hours to administer, covers all the essential skills of inquiry and expression, and includes a 54-question self-assessment about one's patterns of activity related to each competency.

In sum, authentic tests have four basic characteristics in common. First, they are designed to be truly representative of performance in the field; only then are the problems of scoring reliability and logistics of testing considered. Second, far greater attention is paid to the teaching and learning of the *criteria* to be used in the assessment. Third, self-assessment plays a much greater role than in conventional testing.[7] And, fourth, the students are often expected to present their work and defend themselves publicly and orally to ensure that their apparent mastery is genuine. (See fig. 3 for a more thorough list of characteristics of authentic tests.)

Toward a Performance-Based Diploma

The diploma by exhibition implies radically different standards for graduation. Instead of seat time or the mere accrual of Carnegie units, the diploma is performance based and criterion referenced. We may not be ready for the demise of age grading and social promotion; but if the harm done by standardized testing is to be undone, we need to redesign schools "backwards" around graduation-level standards of performance.

The performances and exhibitions should be designed prior to instruction, thus setting the school's standards in functional, not merely abstract and idealized, terms. Seeing them as add-ons to the traditional curriculum is to miss the point. How must the school be redesigned to support exhibitions or any form of exit-level standards? This should be the question behind "restructuring" and the source of vigorous debate among faculties and school board members. Designing and institutionalizing exhibitions would better ensure, in other words, that the school had clear, coherent, and effective standards. Knowing the desired student abilities and work standards, as embodied in culminating performances and scoring criteria, would force key issues of policy: how will time, space, personnel, and other resources be best spent to ensure that diploma standards are met?

To talk with disdain of "teaching to the test" is to misunderstand how we learn. The test is the point of leverage—for learning and for reform. The issue is the integrity of the test: the genuineness, effectiveness, and aptness of the challenge. The finals (and the criteria by which they are graded) set the standards of acceptable work in a course and a school—irrespective of noble language in school district reports or teacher intentions as reflected in syllabi. Legitimate and effective assessment is as simple(!) as ensuring that tests, grades, diploma requirements, and the structures and policies of the schools practice what we preach as essential. If we so honor our professed aims, the problems associated with standardized testing will take care of themselves.

1. From *Horace's Compromise* (Sizer 1984), p. 68.

2. This (final) exhibition is patterned after the 18th century model of a public display of one's ability to engage in disputation: ". . . candidates for degrees expected to be academically tested at Commencement itself. Bachelor of Arts candidates prepared theses or topics on which they could be quizzed, and candidates for the Master of Arts submitted questions they were ready to defend. Titles of theses and questions were printed in advance and handed out at Commencement, and visitors often took the opportunity of challenging the candidates on their knowledge" (from the Harvard University Commencement program).

3. See the booklet *Assessment at Alverno College*, available from the college. For a history and an analysis of Alverno's program (as well as a general discussion of

competency-based higher education), see *On Competency* (Grant, Elbow et al. 1979).

4. *National Curriculum: Task Group on Assessment and Testing: A Report*. Available from the Department of Education and Science (1988). This is a landmark document, outlining in readable prose a plan for intelligent and humane assessment.

5. From *Learning By Doing* (Educational Testing Service 1987).

6. See the excellent article by Dan Koretz of the RAND Corporation in the Summer 1988 issue of *American Educator*, which sums up the current controversy about norm-referenced state testing (the "Lake Wobegon effect" of each state being above average) and provides a useful set of guidelines for assessing assessment.

7. At Alverno, self-assessment is often the first level of proficiency. Thus, in the speaking requirement, students must give a five-minute videotaped talk—with the first evaluations given on the student's self-assessment after watching the videotape.

References

Alverno College Faculty. (1979/1985). *Assessment at Alverno College*. Rev. ed. Milwaukee, Wis.: Alverno College.

Archbald, D., and F. Newmann. (1988). *Beyond Standardized Testing: Authentic Academic Achievement in the Secondary School*. Reston, Va.: NASSP Publications.

Department of Education and Science and the Welsh Office. (1988). *National Curriculum: Task Group on Assessment and Testing: A Report*. London: Her Majesty's Stationery Office, Department of Education and Science, England and Wales. A brief "Digest for Schools" is also available.

Educational Testing Service. (1987). *Learning By Doing: A Manual for Teaching and Assessing Higher-Order Thinking in Science and Mathematics*. A report on the NAEP pilot of performance-based assessment. A summary of the NAEP pilot of performance-based assessment. Princeton, N.J.: ETS. The full report: *A Pilot Study of Higher-Order Thinking Skills Assessment Techniques in Science and Mathematics*. ETS Report #17-HOS-80.

Grant, G., P. Elbow, et al. (1979). *On Competence: A Critical Analysis of Competence-Based Reforms in Higher Education*. San Francisco: Jossey-Bass.

Koretz, D. (Summer 1988). "Arriving in Lake Wobegon: Are Standardized Tests Exaggerating Achievement and Distorting Instruction?" *American Educator* 12, 2.

Sizer, T. (1984). *Horace's Compromise: The Dilemma of the American High School*. Updated ed. Boston: Houghton-Mifflin.

Wiggins, G. (In press). "A True Test: Toward Authentic and Equitable Forms of Assessment." *Phi Delta Kappan*.

Recommended Readings

Alverno College Faculty. (1984). *Analysis and Communication at Alverno: An Approach to Critical Thinking*. Milwaukee, Wis.: Alverno College.

Berk, R. A., ed. (1986). *Performance Assessment: Methods and Applications*. Baltimore, Md.: Johns Hopkins University Press.

Bloom, B., G. Madaus, and J. T. Hastings. (1981). *Evaluation to Improve Learning*. New York: McGraw-Hill.

Brooks, G. (1987). *Speaking and Listening: Assessment at Age 15*. Great Britain: The Assessment of Performance Unit (APU), Department of Education and Science. APU material exists on the results of performance-based assessment in language, history, math, science, and history in primary and secondary schools.

Elbow, P. (1986). "Trying to Teach While Thinking About the End" and "Evaluating Students More Accurately." In *Embracing Contraries: Explorations in Teaching and Learning*. New York: Oxford University Press. The former chapter originally published in Grant, Elbow, et al. (1979).

Higgs, T., ed. (1984). *Teaching for Proficiency, the Organizing Principle*. Lincolnwood, Ill.: National Textbook Company and ACTFL.

Sizer, T. (1986). "Changing Schools and Testing: An Uneasy Proposal." In *The Redesign of Testing for the 21st Century*. 1985 ETS Invitational Conference Proceedings. Princeton, N.J.: ETS.

Slavin, R., et al. (1986). *Using Student Team Learning*. 3rd ed. Baltimore: The Johns Hopkins Team Learning Project Press.

Snow, R. (1988). "Progress in Measurement, Cognitive Science, and Technology That Can Change the Relation Between Instruction and Assessment." In *Assessment in the Service of Learning*. 1987 ETS Invitational Conference Proceedings. Princeton, N.J.: ETS.

Spandel, V. (1981). *Classroom Applications of Writing Assessment: A Teacher's Handbook*. Portland, Oreg.: Northwest Regional Educational Laboratory.

Stiggins, R. (1987). "Design and Development of Performance Assessments." *Educational Measurement: Issues and Practices* 6, 3: 33-42. An Instructional Model (ITEMS), published by National Council on Measurement in Education (NCME). Comes with an Instructor's Guide.

Stiggins, R. (January 1988). "Revitalizing Classroom Assessment." *Phi Delta Kappan* 69: 5.

Wiggins, G. (Winter 1987). "Creating a Thought-Provoking Curriculum." *American Educator* 11, 4.

Wiggins, G. (Winter 1988). "Rational Numbers: Scoring and Grading That Helps Rather than Hurts Learning." *American Educator* 12, 4.

THE TYRANNY OF TESTING

A leading researcher on intelligence tells why all those tests you give don't measure what many of your students really know.

ROBERT J. STERNBERG

Robert J. Sternberg is IBM Professor of Psychology and Education in the psychology department at Yale University. He is actively involved in the thinking-skills movement. His latest book is *The Triarchic Mind: A New Theory of Human Intelligence* (Viking, 1988). For more information on the Sternberg Triarchic Abilities Test write its publisher, the Psychological Corporation, 555 Academic Court, San Antonio, TX 78204.

 hen Laura's father showed me her latest report card, I was surprised. The grades didn't represent the Laura I knew: a vibrant 7-year-old who writes poems, draws imaginatively, creates workbooks for younger children, and has prepared a booklet comparing several religions. And she's done all this on her own—no prodding.

Yet, on the report card, all the checks were in the middle column—the one labeled "satisfactory." In other words, Laura was doing okay, but nothing special.

The *written* comments Laura's teacher put on her report card did reflect this child's extraordinary abilities. "Laura shows interest in learning," she wrote, "always seeks additional information, gathers data and draws independent conclusions." Further, the teacher said, "Laura sees relationships, is insightful, and searches for the unique. She has an excellent oral vocabulary that she transfers easily to her highly creative written work."

When I analyzed Laura's report card carefully, I realized that the problem of the grades not fitting the child was neither with Laura nor with her teacher. The problem was with the report card itself. My research on intelligence, done over the past 13 years at Yale University, helped me see why. The standard report card—and, on a broader scale, the usual school environment—is dictated by the conventional standardized tests, which value certain aspects of human intelligence at the expense of others. They *don't* value Laura's strengths or the strengths of other kids like her.

Why the problem?

I've identified three kinds of intelligence: analytical, creative, and practical. Tests (and report cards) do a great job of measuring the first, a terrible job of measuring the second, and a limited job of measuring the third. Let me explain.

Analytical abilities—all the skills involved with acquiring and memorizing information—are the ones that most standardized and class tests measure. Consequently they are the ones our report cards primarily assess. (Half the boxes on Laura's re-

Another form of tyranny: test anxiety

When Adam was 9 years old he moved to a new school in another district. In his old school he'd been in the top reading group. In his new school, he was put in the bottom group. Why? Not because of a difference in the schools. In fact, both schools were quite similar in socio-economic makeup and in their expectations of students. No, Adam was misplaced because he did poorly on the reading test administered by the new school. And why did he do poorly? Test anxiety.

Even so, it was soon evident that Adam could read better than the other students in the bottom group. Was he put into a higher group? No. Nothing that simple. Instead, he was retested. This time he wasn't so anxious, so he did a little better. That got him transferred into the middle group.

After a while, because he was doing extremely well in the middle reading group, Adam was tested yet again. By now he felt quite comfortable at school and taking the test didn't make him anxious at all. As a result his test scores showed what had been true all along: He should be in the top reading group. Was he put in that group? No. Nothing as logical as that. Instead, noting that the children in the top group were a full book ahead of him by now, Adam's teacher said he was too far behind to join them. —R.S.

port card related to these abilities, and she didn't excel in them.) That's why schools place such high value on analytical abilities and reward students who excel in them. Those are the students in the top reading and math groups, the ones admitted to gifted programs, the ones being groomed for advanced tracks in high school and for prestigious colleges thereafter.

Creative children, on the other hand, don't always do particularly well on class assignments, tests—or report cards. (*None* of the boxes on Laura's report card assessed creative abilities. No wonder the checks labelled her average). So even if the teacher recognizes these abilities in

a child, there's no way to incorporate that recognition into traditional grading structures.

Furthermore, *none* of the conventional intelligence and achievement tests measure creative abilities. And sad to say, what's not quantified is often not valued. Creative students very quickly get the message that what they *do* have to offer just doesn't count. And they're likely to give up, or try to fit a mold that doesn't suit them.

The third aspect of intelligence, practical abilities, is frequently undervalued, too. Standardized tests generally don't measure practicality at all. Report cards do. (Roughly half the boxes on Laura's report card as-

> **Since *none* of the conventional or standardized tests measure creativity, creative students get a damaging message: What I'm good at doesn't count.**

sessed aspects of personal and social development and work habits.) But the bad news is that those boxes assess how well a child plays the *school's* game of following class rules, cooperating, and so on—not how well the child plays *his own* game of getting along in the world. And the two don't necessarily coincide. (See the insert on this page for more about the three aspects of intelligence.)

Who's to blame?
It would be tempting to point a finger at the teachers or the principal, but I can't. Laura is in one of the best public schools in my state. Many of the teachers are outstanding, and, if anything, what goes on in her school is a lot better than what goes on in many other schools. The blame isn't with the test publishers either. They're just responding to what they think the schools want.

Rather the blame lies with a self-perpetuating system of teaching and testing. As long as teachers must be held accountable, we're going to have tests; and as long as those tests measure a narrow span of intelligence, that's the span of intelligence teachers must emphasize. We need tests that measure not just the analytical aspects, but the creative and practical ones as well. Once we can evaluate these aspects, we can begin incorporating them into our teaching.

What's to be done
As a beginning, I've been developing a test that assesses all three aspects of intelligence. It's called the Sternberg Triarchic Abilities Test (STAT), and it will be published in 1991. The STAT is now being pilot tested around the country. Since it's a multiple-choice, paper-and-pencil test, it's suitable for group administration. But a sophisticated scoring procedure helps ensure that each student's abilities are recognized. The test not only provides separate scores for analyt-

---

Alice, Barbara, and Celia: three reasons to change testing and teaching

Our research at Yale University has produced the "triarchic theory"—which holds that intelligence has three basic aspects: analytical, creative, and practical. Alice, Barbara, and Celia typify students strong in each of the three. Their stories show how damaging the present analytical emphasis—in testing and in teaching—can be. I taught these students at the graduate level, but you may recognize their budding counterparts in your own classroom.

• *Alice was the analytical one.* She did wonderfully on tests and assignments, and was considered brilliant by virtually everyone. For years, she garnered praise—and top grades—by memorizing and analyzing the ideas of others. But that approach didn't work when she had to come up with ideas of her own. She seemed to have lost touch with whatever creativity she may once have had. Gradually, it became clear that Alice, like so many others of our schools' finest, was not going to be the stunning success everyone had expected her to be.

• *Barbara was the creative one.* She had truly rotten test scores and never did as well as Alice in school. Though she encountered myriad rejections and disappointments over the years, she persisted. Ultimately, she outshone Alice in her work because she proved to be a veritable fountain

of creative ideas. She succeeded *despite* the way the tests and the schools had assessed her.

• *Celia was the practical one.* She had neither Alice's memory and analytical skills nor Barbara's creativity. Her grades were usually average. Yet when it came to getting, and doing, a job, she was the real ace. Why? Because she had the practical skills that enabled her to figure out what she needed to do to succeed, and she used those skills to her best advantage. In short, she knew her strengths and weaknesses, and she made the most of the former while compensating for the latter.

Our research has shown that skills such as those of Barbara and Celia are more important in later life than they are in school. Just look at all the highly creative artists, writers, musicians, and scientists, the successful entrepreneurs and financiers. Many of them didn't do particularly well in school. In fact, they had to persevere despite the school's agenda of memory and analysis.

But how many others became discouraged and just marked time or even dropped out? A new breed of tests could identify strengths in each of the three areas of intelligence, then encourage the schools to value and nurture all three as students grow and develop.

—R.S

ical, creative, and practical abilities, it provides another set of scores for three kinds of content—verbal, quantitative, and figural.

Here are some ways the STAT fulfills its purpose.

• To measure creative abilities examinees are given problems that require them to think in novel ways. For example, a statement such as "Suppose balloons were evil," might set up an analogy question. Or in the quantitative problem area, examinees are introduced to new symbols for numbers and have to think with these new symbols.

• To measure practical abilities examinees might be shown an advertisement and asked how the reasoning in it is false. Some questions assess practical mathematical skills such as those used in shopping or understanding a train schedule. Others test the kinds of skills needed to plan an automobile trip or execute a series of errands efficiently.

• The STAT measures the ability to learn new words as they are presented in sentence contexts rather than testing for knowledge of vocabulary. Therefore children who don't have large vocabularies won't be penalized for lack of prior knowledge.

The STAT also represents a radical departure from conventional intelligence tests in another important—perhaps *the* most important—way. It does not assume that intelligence is stable, fixed throughout life; instead it assumes that intelligence is malleable and can be increased by appropriate teaching and learning. That's why the test includes nine separate levels and is designed to be given over the years from kindergarten to adulthood.

With tests that are based on a broader definition of intelligence, we'll be able to identify and value the strengths on which students such as Laura can capitalize. As a result, they'll have more positive feelings about themselves, and we'll be in a better position to help them improve in their weaker areas. That way *all* our students will be getting the educational evaluation *and* the education they deserve.

ability grouping: 122, 162; and gifted youth, 203–204, 205; hazards of, 143

acceleration: 121–122; and gifted youth, 202–203, 205

achievement: impact of cooperative learning on, 113–116; and teacher expectations, 101–109; motivation, 150

active learning, as learning strategy of gifted youth, 209, 211

adaptive instruction, 121

adaptive speed training, 122

adolescents: changing conditions for, 65–67; effect of divorce on, 46; and drug use, 43; meeting needs for, 68–73; and pregnancy, 43; and television, 74–75; variations in, 33

adultification, of children, hazards of, 45

advertising, effect of television, on children, 46

advisory groups, and adolescents, 68–69

affective models, and prosocial behavior, 62–63

analytical abilities, as aspect of intelligence, and testing, 238–239

anxiety, and testing, 238

appreciation, and art of teaching, 14

art of teaching: 12–14; vs. craft of teaching, 6–11

ARTS PROPEL, and theory of multiple intelligences, 85

Assertive Discipline, 173–176, 177–181

assessment, as barrier to creative environment, 144, 145

at-risk students: guidelines for teachers with, 159–163; motivation for, 155–158

attributions: of at-risk students, 154, 157; and motivation, 150

authentic tests, 235–237

autonomy, and motivation, 165

behavior modification: and discouraged learners, 162–163; ten management techniques for, 97–100; see also, discipline

behaviorists, and teaching, 118, 119

blacks: education for, 217, 218; unequal schooling for, 27; see also, minority students

bodily-kinesthetic intelligence, 84

body language, and teaching, 12–13, 183–184

Brophy-Good model, and teacher expectations, 102

calendar energy, 29

Canter, Lee, and Assertive Discipline, 173–176, 177–181

Center for Research on Elementary and Middle Schools (CREMS), and needs of adolescents, 68–69

character development, in children, and role of elementary schools, 56–60

child development, and early childhood education, 26–31

children: character development of elementary school, 56–60; effect of divorce on, 42, 43, 45, 46; formalized early education for, 26–31; moral development of, 58–60; social needs of, 45–51; variability of, 32–33

civil rights movement, and education, 27

class discussion, and discovery learning, 89

classroom control: as factor in fostering creativity, 142–143; see also, classroom management; discipline

classroom management: non-verbal techniques for, 182–187; use of research concerning, 18–21; see also, classroom control; discipline

clock energy, 29

cognitive models, and prosocial behavior, 62

communication, and art of teaching, 13

competent infant, 27, 28, 45

computer-assisted instruction, 121

concentration skills, and learning strategies, 209–210

concurrence-seeking, 127, 128

content, and educating minority students, 219, 220

context, and educating minority students, 215, 219, 220

controversy, critical thinking through structured, 126–130

cooperation, and art of teaching, 13–14

Cooperative Integrated Reading and Composition (CIRC), 113, 115

cooperative learning: 111–116; cooperative school, description of, 114; as effective for discouraged learners, 162; and mainstreamed students, 197–200; social environment of, 122

corrective feedback, and learning, 118, 119

craft of teaching, vs. art of teaching, 6–11

creative abilities, as aspect of intelligence, and testing, 239

creative problem solving, and discovery learning, 90

creativity, barriers to, in classroom, 142–145

critical thinking, and structured controversy, 126–130

criticism, and Native American students, 217–218

cues, and learning, 118–119, 120

cultural meanings, and non-verbal messages, 184–185

cultural norms, and prosocial behavior, 61–62

Darling-Hammond, Linda, and Assertive Discipline, 177–178, 179–180, 181

debate, 127, 128

decision-making, participatory, and character development in children, 56

depression, and adolescents, 74–75

developmental objectives, and grading process, 229–231

developmentally appropriate education, for 4-year-olds, 32–36

discipline: Assertive, 173–176, 177–181; and behavior modification, 97–100; and effective teaching, 169–172; and non-verbal language, 184, 185–187; prosocial, 63; see also, classroom control; classroom management

discouraged learners, 159–163

discovery learning, 88–91

divorce: effect of, on adolescents, 65–66; effect of, on children, 42, 43, 47, 48

drug use, and adolescents, 43, 66

early childhood education, questions of formalized, 26–31

early education, effect of societal changes on, 48

education, history of American, 6–8

Education for All Handicapped Children Act, see Public Law 94-142

educational experimentation, 7, 11

efficacy: and motivation of at-risk students, 155–156; perceptions, 150

elementary schools, and character development in children, 56–60

Elkind, David, 26, 45, 78

engagement, and learning, 118, 119

Erikson, Erik, 30

expectancy x value theory, 149

expectations, effect of teacher, on student performance, 101–109, 155–158, 226

experimentation, and developmentally appropriate curricula for science, 34

family: changes in, and adolescents, 65–66; and social pressures affecting children's needs, 45–47, 48, 49; values, and minority students, 215, 216

feedback: corrective, and learning, 118, 119; and motivation, 165–166

field independence, and learning strategies of gifted youth, 209, 210

field-dependent style, of teaching, and Native American students, 217–218

final exhibition, 234–235

formal education, for young children, 26–31

forms of representation, and thinking, 79, 80, 81

Freudian psychology, and early childhood education, 27

"gambler's fallacy," 28

gender differences, in prosocial behavior, 52

generic teaching, 20, 21

gifted children: education for, 201–208; learning strategies of, 209–212; and SAT scores, 82

goal setting, and motivating at-risk students, 156

government, and funding of early childhood education programs, 27

grading, 224–232

group advisory periods, and adolescents, 68–69

group norms, and prosocial behavior, 61–62

habitual behavior, as barrier to creativity, 143, 144

handicapped students: 124, 194–196; and cooperative learning, 197–200

Head Start, 27

hemispheric specialization, and learning style, 135–136

Hispanic students: education of, 216–217; see also, minority students

human rights, and moral development of children, 58–60

"hurried child," 45, 78

individualism, of minority students, 216, 217

Individualized Educational Programs (IEPs), 207

infants, early childhood education for, 27, 28

innovative environment, benefits of, and creativity, 144–145
inquiry approach, and staff development, 21, 22
inservice training, 124
instruction: dangers of prescribed, 7, 8, 9; strategies for, 117–125; *see also,* teaching
intelligence: aspects of, 238–239; dissatisfaction with present measurement of, 82–86; theory of multiple, 84–86; types of, 83
intelligence quotient (IQ), 82
interactive teaching, 35–36
interdisciplinary teaching teams, and adolescents, 69–71
internal locus of control, and learning strategies of gifted children, 209, 210–211
interpersonal intelligence, 84
intrapersonal intelligence, 84
intuitive psychology, and early childhood education, 28, 29

journals, and teacher research, 16

knowledge, and thinking, 78–81

labeling: effect of, on gifted children, 207, 208; and mainstreaming, 194–196
language, and thinking, 78–81
language-minority children, *see* minority students
"latchkey" children, 47, 48
learning disabled: masking behaviors of, 190–193; and mainstreaming, 194–200
learning strategies: of gifted children, 209–212; and motivating at-risk students, 156–157; *see also,* metacognition
learning styles: 134–140; and discipline, 171–172; importance of, to achievement, 162
linear programs, 121
linguistic intelligence, 83
Links-To-Success model, 156–158
locus of control, and learning strategies of gifted children, 209, 210–211
logical-mathematical intelligence, 83
love-oriented discipline, and prosocial behavior, 63

mainstreaming: 124, 194–196; and cooperative learning strategies, 197–200
manipulative materials, and teaching math, 123
masking behavior, of learning disabled, 190–193
mastery learning: 108, 121; and discouraged learners, 160–161
mathematical problem solving, and discovery learning, 90
mathematics, teaching techniques for, 123
mature learners, and metacognition, 94–95
means-ends contingencies, and erosion of motivation, 165
metcognition, 92–95
microteaching, 124
middle level schools, and adolescents, 67
minimal objectives, and grading, 229–230
minority students: education for, 213–221; unequal education for, 27

mobility, of families, and adolescents, 67
mode, and educating minority students, 219, 220
models: and prosocial behavior, 53, 54, 62–63; teachers as behavior models, 98
moral education, and elementary school children, 56–60
moral reflection, and character development in children, 56
motivation: of at-risk students, 155–158; and discipline, 171; strategies for, 148–154; and success probability, 164–165
multi-age grouping, 33–34
multiple intelligences, theory of, 84–86
musical intelligence, 84

National Institute of Child Health and Human Development, 42
Native Americans: education for, 217–218; *see also,* minority students
new math, 123
nongraded curricular materials, and developmentally appropriate education, 35
non-response, and discipline, 186
nonverbal cues, and art of teaching, 13
non-verbal language: and art of teaching, 12–13; techniques for classroom management and discipline, 182–187
non-verbal reinforcement, 98–99
norms, and prosocial behavior, 61–62

objectives, and grading process, 229–231
oral tradition, and education of black students, 217, 218
organizational pictures, and reading, 122–123

paralinguistics, and teaching, 13
parents: and Assertive Discipline, 180; and needs of adolescents, 72; role of, in cooperative school, 114
participatory decision-making, and character development in children, 56
partnership, between teachers and universities, and teacher research, 17
pass/fail decisions, 230
patient education, 124
peer coaching: and cooperative learning, 115; and teacher research, 16
perception, and art of teaching, 13
perceptual preferences, and learning styles, 136–137
persistence, and learning strategies of gifted children, 209, 211
person-centered approach, vs. object-centered approach, and black students, 217
phonics approaches, to reading, 122
Piaget, Jean, 26, 30, 31, 83
PL 94-142, *see* Public Law 94-142
positive discipline, and Assertive Discipline, 174–175
positive reinforcement: ten techniques for, 97–100
power-assertive discipline, and prosocial behavior, 63
practical abilities, as aspect of intelligence, and testing, 239
praise, and positive reinforcement, 98
pregnancy, teenage, 43, 66

problem solving: and discovery learning, 89–90; and teaching mathematics, 123
programmed instruction, 120–121
"Project SPECTRUM," and theory of multiple intelligences, 84
prosocial behavior, 52–63
prosocial discipline, 63
proxemics: and classroom management, 184; and art of teaching, 13
proximal goals, and motivating at-risk students, 156
psychological training, 124
Public Law 94-142, 191, 194, 206
punitive models, and prosocial discipline, 63

questioning, as teaching method, 131–133

reaction time, and intelligence, 82
reading, teaching techniques for, 122–123
reasoning, and prosocial behavior, 53, 62
reflection, as learning strategy of gifted children, 209, 210
reflective abstraction, and early childhood education, 30
rehearsal, and metacognition, 94
reinforcement: and discipline, 171; and motivation, 118, 119, 151; positive, 97–100
remembering, and thinking, 79
rewards, 165
risk taking, 166–167, 226–227
Rite of Passage Experience (R.O.P.E.), 230
Roncker v. Walter, 195–196

scales, for grading, 224–225
Scholastic Aptitude Test (SAT), 82
school transition programs, and needs of adolescents, 71–72
school-community broker, 85
schools: cooperative, 114; elementary, and character development in children, 56–60; of future and theory of multiple intelligence, 84–86; and moral development of children, 58–60; effect of societal changes on, 47, 50
science: developmentally appropriate curricula for, 34–35; learner autonomy in, 120; teaching techniques for, 123
science of education: 7; hazards of, 8
scientific management, and school administrators, 7
scientific problem solving, and discovery learning, 90
scientific technology, of teaching, 7
self-directed learning, 30
self-image, strategies for improving children's, 38–41
self-interrogation, and developing metacognition skills, 93–94
self-testing, and metacognition, 94
sense of self, and social needs of children, 45
sensual child, effect of concept of, on early childhood education, 27
set induction, and discovery learning, 89
sex, and adolescents, 66–67
silence, and classroom management, 185–186
sinful child, and early childhood education, 27
single parents, effect of, on children, 43, 45, 47, 48, 65

social needs, effect of social pressures on, of children, 45–50

social pressures, effect of, on children's social needs, 45–50

socialization, effect of peer groups on, 47, 48

sociological preferences, and learning style, 137–138

spatial intelligence, 84

special education: and cooperative learning, 115; and mainstreaming, 194–196

staff development, 19–22

standard setting, 233

Sternberg Triarchic Abilities Test (STAT), 239–240

stress, and formalized education for young children, 29, 45

structured controversy, and critical thinking, 126–130

student questions, 132

Student Teams-Achievement Division (STAD), 112, 113–114, 116

student-community broker, 85

students: challenge for, 164–167; as discouraged learners, 159–163; role of, and questions, 133; teacher expectations and, 101–109, 155–158, 226

suicide, and adolescents, 67

superintendents, 11

Sustained Silent Reading (SSR), 185

syntax, and thinking, 80

Taylor, Francis, 7

teacher expectations, and performance of students, 101–109, 155–158, 226

teacher research, 15–17

teachers: and needs of adolescents, 68–73; and discouraged learners, 159–163; effect of, expectations, on students, 101–109, 155–158, 226; and moral development of children, 58–60; and prosocial behavior, 53–55; and research, 15–17; role of, and questioning, 132–133; and staff development, 19–22

teaching: art of, 6–14; questioning as method of, 131–133; research for effective, 18–22; and staff development, 19–22; see also, instruction

Team Accelerated Instruction (TAI), 113–115

technology, and early childhood education, 28, 29

teenage pregnancy, 43, 66

television: effect of, on adolescents, 74–75; effect of, on children, 29, 45, 49, 50

test anxiety, 238

testing: authentic, 233–237; matching, to teaching, 225–226; as poor measure of intelligence, 238–240

thinking, nature of, 78–81

Thorndike, Edward L., 6, 7

time, as barrier to creativity, 143–145

time-of-day preferences, and learning style, 138–139

turtle geometry, 29

tutoring, 122

uniform school, and IQ, 83

university partnership, and teacher research, 17

value-laden problem solving, and discovery learning, 90

variability, of young children, 32–33

victim-centered discipline, and prosocial behavior, 63

videotape, and teacher research, 16

whole-group instruction, 122

"whole-word" approach, to reading, 122

women, working, effect of, on children, 43, 45, 66

"word-attack" approach, to reading, 122

writing, teaching techniques for, 123

"zone of proximal development," 120

Credits/ Acknowledgments

Cover design by Charles Vitelli

1. Overview
Facing overview—EPA Documerica.

2. Development
Facing overview—United Nations photo by Shelley Rotner. 26—Illustration by Barbara Roman. 75—Table: Marcia Scott.

3. Learning
Facing overview—EPA Documerica. 111—Photo by Barbara Bennett. 117—Illustration by Marcus Hamilton.

4. Motivation and Classroom Management
Facing overview—United Nations photo by O. Mosen.

5. Exceptional Children
Facing overview—United Nations photo by Yutaka Nagata. 214—Illustration by Kay Salem.

6. Measurement and Evaluation
Facing overview—United Nations photo by Marta Pinter.

ANNUAL EDITIONS ARTICLE REVIEW FORM

■ NAME: _____ DATE: _____

■ TITLE AND NUMBER OF ARTICLE: _____

■ BRIEFLY STATE THE MAIN IDEA OF THIS ARTICLE: _____

_____

_____

_____

_____

■ LIST THREE IMPORTANT FACTS THAT THE AUTHOR USES TO SUPPORT THE MAIN IDEA:

_____

_____

_____

_____

_____

■ WHAT INFORMATION OR IDEAS DISCUSSED IN THIS ARTICLE ARE ALSO DISCUSSED IN YOUR
TEXTBOOK OR OTHER READING YOU HAVE DONE? LIST THE TEXTBOOK CHAPTERS AND PAGE
NUMBERS:

_____

_____

_____

_____

_____

■ LIST ANY EXAMPLES OF BIAS OR FAULTY REASONING THAT YOU FOUND IN THE ARTICLE:

_____

_____

_____

_____

■ LIST ANY NEW TERMS/CONCEPTS THAT WERE DISCUSSED IN THE ARTICLE AND WRITE A
SHORT DEFINITION:

_____

_____

_____

_____

We Want Your Advice

ANNUAL EDITIONS:
EDUCATIONAL PSYCHOLOGY 91/92
Article Rating Form

Here is an opportunity for you to have direct input into the next revision of this volume. We would like you to rate each of the 46 articles listed below, using the following scale:

1. **Excellent: should definitely be retained**
2. **Above average: should probably be retained**
3. **Below average: should probably be deleted**
4. **Poor: should definitely be deleted**

Your ratings will play a vital part in the next revision. So please mail this prepaid form to us just as soon as you complete it.
Thanks for your help!

Annual Editions revisions depend on two major opinion sources: one is our Advisory Board, listed in the front of this volume, which works with us in scanning the thousands of articles published in the public press each year; the other is you—the person actually using the book. Please help us and the users of the next edition by completing the prepaid article rating form on this page and returning it to us. Thank you.

Rating	Article	Rating	Article
	1. Of Robins' Eggs, Teachers, and Education Reform		23. Critical Thinking Through Structured Controversy
	2. Does the "Art of Teaching" Have a Future?		24. Questioning: An Effective Teaching Method
	3. Tap Into Teacher Research		25. Survey of Research on Learning Styles
	4. Creating Conditions for Learning: From Research to Practice		26. Fostering Creativity: The Innovative Classroom Environment
	5. Formal Education and Early Childhood Education: An Essential Difference		27. Synthesis of Research on Strategies for Motivating Students to Learn
	6. Developmentally Appropriate Education for 4-Year-Olds		28. Motivation for At-Risk Students
	7. Societal Influences on Children		29. Teetering . . . on the Edge of Failure
	8. The Development of Self-Concept		30. Students Need Challenge, Not Easy Success
	9. Encouraging Prosocial Behavior in Young Children		31. Good Teachers Don't Worry About Discipline
	10. Four Strategies for Fostering Character Development in Children		32. Assertive Discipline—More Than Names on the Board and Marbles in a Jar
	11. Prosocial Influences in the Classroom		33. Order in the Classroom
	12. Changing Conditions for Young Adolescents: Reminiscences and Realities		34. Non-verbal Language Techniques for Better Classroom Management and Discipline
	13. Meeting the Needs of Young Adolescents: Advisory Groups, Interdisciplinary Teaching Teams, and School Transition Programs		35. The Masks Students Wear
			36. Educating the Handicapped in the Regular Classroom
	14. Respectful, Dutiful Teenagers		37. Facilitating Mainstreaming Through Cooperative Learning
	15. The Celebration of Thinking		38. Synthesis of Research on Gifted Youth
	16. Putting Learning Strategies to Work		39. Gifted Child Education
	17. Rediscovering Discovery Learning		40. Learning Strategies Can Help
	18. Linking Metacognition to Classroom Success		41. Educating Language-Minority Children: Challenges and Opportunities
	19. Practicing Positive Reinforcement		42. Teaching to the Distinctive Traits of Minority Students
	20. Teacher Expectations: A Model for School Improvement		43. It's a Good Score! Just a Bad Grade
	21. Cooperative Learning and the Cooperative School		44. Classroom Standard Setting and Grading Practices
	22. Productive Teaching and Instruction: Assessing the Knowledge Base		45. Teaching to the (Authentic) Test
			46. The Tyranny of Testing

(Continued on next page)

ABOUT YOU

Name_____ Date_____

Are you a teacher? ☐ Or student? ☐

Your School Name _____

Department _____

Address _____

City _____ State _____ Zip _____

School Telephone # _____

YOUR COMMENTS ARE IMPORTANT TO US!

Please fill in the following information:

For which course did you use this book? _____

Did you use a text with this Annual Edition? ☐ yes ☐ no

The title of the text? _____

What are your general reactions to the Annual Editions concept?

Have you read any particular articles recently that you think should be included in the next edition?

Are there any articles you feel should be replaced in the next edition? Why?

Are there other areas that you feel would utilize an Annual Edition?

May we contact you for editorial input?

May we quote you from above?

ANNUAL EDITIONS: EDUCATIONAL PSYCHOLOGY 91/92